JEROME S. BURSTEIN

School of Business, San José State University

COMPUTERS AND INFORMATION SYSTEMS

HOLT, RINEHART & WINSTON

NEW YORK   CHICAGO   SAN FRANCISCO
PHILADELPHIA   MONTREAL   TORONTO   LONDON
SYDNEY   TOKYO   MEXICO CITY   RIO DE JANEIRO   MADRID

To Michael and Lynne

Publisher: Paul Becker

Associate Editor: David Chodoff

Editorial Assistance: Jerry Ralya

Production Manager: Paul Nardi

Production Coordinator: Rachel Hockett, Cobb/Dunlop Publisher Services, Inc.

Interior Design and Art Direction: Gayle Jaeger

Cover Design: Paul Nardi

Cover Illustration: Albert D'Agostino

Photo Research: Teri Stratford

Illustrations: Scientific Illustrators

Composition: Science Press

Printing and Binding: R. R. Donnelley & Sons

Library of Congress Cataloging in Publication Data
Burstein, Jerome S.
 Computers and information systems.
 Includes index.
 1. Electronic digital computers. 2. Computer
software. 3. Information storage and retrieval systems.
QA76.5.B852 1986   658.4'038   85-16367
ISBN 0-03-070519-3

Printed in the United States of America
Published simultaneously in Canada
6 7 8 9 039 9 8 7 6 5 4 3 2 1

CBS COLLEGE PUBLISHING

Holt, Rinehart & Winston

The Dryden Press

Saunders College Publishing

BRIEF CONTENTS

DETAILED CONTENTS

PREFACE

Information systems exist to serve people, not the other way around. If a system doesn't help the people within an organization help their clients, then it shouldn't be there. This has been said so often recently that it seems commonplace, but those of us who work with information systems and who teach about them know how hard this principle is to carry out in practice. It's all too easy to slip into familiar patterns that leave users and clients on the sidelines.

The same is true of most textbooks on information systems. All of them at some point stress the importance of people—users and clients. But when they get into the meat of the subject matter, they slip into familiar patterns. The result is usually a laundry list approach—the authors draw up a list of topics and tick them off as they cover each one. Along the way they lose sight of the "systems" aspect of information systems.

When I set out to write this book, I was determined to avoid this trap. I wanted, of course, to be current and thorough. But more important, I wanted to keep the systems perspective and the importance of people always at the forefront. I wanted students to see how computers affected their lives personally and in the context of the kinds of organizations in which they are likely to work.

FEATURES OF THE TEXT

The key features of *Computers and Information Systems* were all developed with these goals in mind. They include readability, a systems approach, currency, and a flexible organization.

Readability

The first and most important feature of this text is clear, direct, and lively writing. Without good writing, even the simplest concepts can seem obscure. I use numerous examples to illustrate key points. The primary source for examples comes from the world of business, although many business problems, say, in accounting, are applicable in any area.

Systems approach

I have adopted a five-part model as an information system for this book. The parts in this model are people, rules and procedures, data, software, and hardware. The parts are not equal, however—people are more important than the other four. In every chapter I relate the subject matter to this model.

I have developed four fictional organizations, complete with a cast of characters, as a way of showing how the elements of an information system actually work in an organizational setting. Most chapters start with a story that draws on one of these organizations or the people in them. The story usually presents the people in the organization with a problem that relates to the subject matter of the chapter. A wrap-up at the end of the chapter then shows how the problem is resolved.

Currency

In a fast-changing field like that of information systems, currency is important. I have endeavored throughout to include material that is as up-to-date as possible.

Flexibility

Computers and Information Systems is divided into five parts: Introduction, Hardware, Software, Information Systems, and Social Issues. Hardware and Software were written to be independent modules—depending on your preference you can go from the introductory chapters directly to software before covering hardware, or you can cover the material in the sequence in which it appears.

Other features

In addition to these key features, the book includes many other learning aids. These include:

- *A **chapter outline** for each chapter.*
- *__Learning objectives__ for each chapter.*
- *An opening **vignette** or **story** and a closing **wrap-up** for each chapter. These are usually taken from one of the four fictional organizations introduced in Chapter 1 and present the subject matter of the chapter in a realistic setting.*
- ***Key terms** set in boldface type and defined when they are introduced.*
- ***Case in point boxes** that present real cases related to the chapter material.*
- ***Career boxes** that focus on a career related to the subject matter of the chapter.*
- ***Enrichment boxes** with interesting supplementary material.*
- *A concise **summary** at the end of each chapter.*
- *A **key terms list** at the end of each chapter that lists the boldface terms in that chapter and the page on which they appear.*
- *A comprehensive set of **review questions,** including true-false, multiple-choice, fill-in, short-answer, and essay questions. Answers to all except the short-answer and essay questions are listed in the back of the book. The short-answer and essay question answers are found in the Instructor's Manual.*
- *An **appendix on programming in BASIC** that provides a comprehensive introduction to the BASIC programming language.*
- *An **appendix on number systems and binary arithmetic**.*
- *A **glossary of key terms** that contains concise definitions of all the key terms in the book.*

Computers and Information Systems is designed for an introductory class in computers and information systems and meets or exceeds the curriculum for the first course in the Data Processing Management Association (DPMA) curriculum (CIS-1, Introduction to Computer-Based Systems). It presents a firm foundation for information system majors, for business students with other majors who must be familiar with information systems, and for students in other disciplines who need a general introduction to computers. Most students who take the course for which this book is written are business majors, but I do not intend the book to be limited to business students. It can also serve students of diverse majors in a general service course. In fact at San Jose State my classes have many nonbusiness majors from the social sciences, the humanities, aeronautics, engineering, and health science areas.

THE INSTRUCTIONAL PACKAGE

Computers and Information Systems comes with a complete package of ancillary materials for both student and instructor. The package includes a student *Study Guide*, an *Instructor's Manual*, *Transparency Acetates*, a *Test Bank*, and a *Tutorial Disk* to accompany the appendix on BASIC.

THE STUDY GUIDE

The student *Study Guide*, written by Jerry Ralya, uses self-testing to help students master the material in the textbook. For every chapter in the textbook the *Study Guide* provides an outline, a list of objectives, a pretest, a detailed summary, and extensive review questions (with the answers provided in an answer key). Each chapter also includes a new boxed extract and an expanded discussion of the vignette/wrap-up sections of the text (called "Information Systems at Work"), to stimulate student interest in the material further.

THE INSTRUCTOR'S MANUAL

The *Instructor's Manual* is a critical element in the instructional package. It contains material to help instructors organize lectures and class discussions and suggestions for using other elements in the package—including the *Transparency Acetates*, the *Test Bank*, and the *Study Guide*. In preparing it I tried to provide material useful to the full range of people who teach about information systems: both full-time and part-time instructors, veterans and first-timers.

For each chapter of the textbook the *Instructor's Manual* contains:

- *A brief summary of the chapter that stresses its major instructional objectives.*
- *Annotated learning objectives.*
- *A glossary with definitions of the key terms in the chapter.*
- *A lecture outline that reviews the key points of the chapter. This outline is keyed to the transparency acetates, indicating when they should be shown.*
- *Teaching suggestions with ideas for enlivening lectures and discussions and pointers on how to make the most of the textbook and the other elements in the package.*
- *Case studies related to the material in the chapter.*
- *Answers to the end-of-chapter short-answer and essay questions.*

TRANSPARENCY ACETATES

Computers and Information Systems comes with a set of ready-to-show *Transparency Acetates* for use with an overhead projector. All the diagrams have been rendered especially for projection. They include both completely original diagrams and important figures from the book.

THE TEST BANK

The *Test Bank* contains 3000 test items, including true-false, fill-in, multiple-choice, matching, and short-answer questions. The items were prepared with the help of my colleague, Curt Stafford, a specialist in testing and evaluation for the School of Education at San Jose State University.

The *Test Bank* is available in printed form and on disk for the Apple II family, the IBM PC, and the TRS-80 Model III.

BASIC TUTORIAL SOFTWARE

A tutorial disk is available to accompany the BASIC programming appendix in the text. The disk, for the Apple II family and the IBM PC, lets students work with the model programs in the appendix.

ACKNOWLEDGMENTS

A textbook like this could never be created in a vacuum. My goal, after all, is to serve the instructors and students who will use the book. Thus I owe a special word of thanks to the people who reviewed this book in all its many drafts and kept me in touch with the user perspective: Richard J. Batt, St. Louis Community College; George J. Brabb, Illinois State University; Frank E. Cable, Pennsylvania State University; J. Patrick Fenton, West Valley College, California; Richard Fleming, North Lake College, Texas; George Fowler, Texas A & M University; Carol C. Grimm, Palm Beach Junior College; Thomas M. Harris, Ball State University, Indiana; Rodney J. Heisterberg, Austin Community College; Lorinda Hite, Owens Technical College, Ohio; Prof. Peter L. Irwin, Richland College of the Dallas County Community College District; Cynthia E. Johnson, Bryant College, Rhode Island; Dee Joseph, San Antonio College; E. R. Lannon, University of Maryland; Ida W. Mason, California State Polytechnic University; Leonard Schwab, California State University at Hayward; Douglas A. Waechter, Sheridan College of Applied Arts and Technology, Ontario, Canada; Charles M. Williams, Georgia State University; A. James Wynne, Virginia Commonwealth University; and Fatemeh Zahedi, University of Massachusetts.

Special thanks are due also to a number of my colleagues at San Jose State for their advice and suggestions: Susan Ashley, Crossman J. Clark, Larry Gerston, Larry Lapin, Edward Laurie, John Lehane, Sheila Pickett, and Carrie Scott.

Many people helped me in creating and evaluating the text and in putting together the elements of the package. My wife Lynne Burstein created the glossary and index. She also served as my constant advisor and confidante for the entire project.

Curt Stafford wrote the 3000 questions in the *Test Bank*, and is responsible for their high quality. Jay Barta collaborated with me on writing and testing the computer programs in the text and the appendix. Paul Ross helped me with the Case Studies in the *Instructor's Manual*. Shelly Langman provided a rigorous and extremely helpful review of the appendix on programming in BASIC.

One person—Jerry Ralya—I cannot begin to thank enough. Jerry's work is evident on every page of this book. He edited the text and put together the material for most of the boxes, including the career and case in point boxes. He also wrote the *Study Guide*.

Rachel Hockett of Cobb/Dunlop Publisher Services saw the book through production under an incredibly tight schedule. With her efficiency, intelligence, and tireless good humor, she is as responsible as anyone for the handsome text you're reading.

I would also like to thank Gayle Jaeger for the extremely attractive design of the text, and Teri Stratford for her work as photo researcher.

Many people at Holt, Rinehart and Winston helped make this book possible. Tom Hogan, my Holt sales representative first discussed with me the prospect of writing this text. David Chodoff, Associate Editor at Holt, survived my thousands of questions, my lengthy telephone calls, and reams of manuscript to help organize what sometimes seemed a shapeless mass into a real textbook. Paul Nardi, Production Manager, is responsible for the overall appearance of the book. Also to be thanked at Holt are Paul Becker, Tom Gornick, Howard Weiner, John Tugman, Greg Kahn, and Mary Pickert.

Joan Meyer, a student in the Information Resource Management program at San Jose State University, read the entire manuscript from the student's perspective. Pam Read and Doris Elliot also read substantial portions of the manuscript.

Finally, I have to thank the students from my classes at San Jose State who used this book in all of its many drafts over the last several years. Their comments—both critical and encouraging—helped make this book what it is.

Jerome Burstein
San Jose, California

COMPUTERS AND
INFORMATION SYSTEMS

PART ONE

Welcome to this book on computers and
information systems. Part One introduces you
to basic concepts concerning the uses of
computers found all around us.
We begin in Chapter 1 with an
introduction to information systems and
computers as tools for business. In Chapter
2 we see what makes information systems
tick—the people, rules and procedures,
data, software, and hardware. Chapter 3
presents a series of examples
demonstrating information systems in the
workplace. Finally Chapter 4 discusses
the historical evolution of computers
and information systems.

CHAPTER 1

INFORMATION SYSTEMS AND COMPUTERS: TOOLS FOR BUSINESS

After studying this chapter you should understand the following:
■ *The importance of the computer in business.*
■ *How computers affect your life.*
■ *The difference between data and information.*
■ *How information systems convert data into information.*
■ *The four kinds of computers used today by individuals as well as companies, governments, and other organizations.*

Janis Roberts turned the key in the door of her travel agency office, closing it for the day. She then walked past its window displays, which beckoned to vacation as well as business travelers, toward her car. Janis had a lot on her mind. After locating her car she got in, started it, and set off toward home.

In a few minutes she stopped at a light near another Freddy Johnson's Travel Agency office which sported the same window displays as hers. There were actually four of the Johnson offices scattered across Oakriver. Less than a month had passed since Janis had been promoted from an agent at the downtown office to the manager of the new branch. New as her job was, the owner, Freddy Johnson, had asked her to lead the group that would select small computers for the four offices.

Janis parked her car, scooped the day's mail from the box, and entered her house while glancing at the envelopes. She held a letter from her mother, a mail-order catalog, a brochure from a local university, a telephone bill, and an unexpected letter from the Internal Revenue Service. She was already tired from a hard day and worried about the computer assignment her boss had given her. This stack of mail did not look like it was going to ease her mind.

Her mother's letter was the most important. Janis read that first. Her mother wrote that she had received the results of the hospital tests. One test employed a computerized body scan. Her mother assured her that there was no need to worry, since the doctor said the tests revealed no serious problems.

Janis next opened the phone bill. It seemed larger than usual. And what about those three long-distance calls to Anchorage? She didn't know anyone in Alaska! She decided to call her long-distance phone company tomorrow and give them a piece of her mind.

The mail-order catalog, a new one, caught her eye. She wondered why she kept receiving catalogs she hadn't requested. Placing the catalog aside, she saw the envelope from the IRS. Well, after dinner would be more than soon enough to open that one.

Any moment her family would arrive home. Her husband George, a quality control supervisor, had taken the day off from work, and said he would pick up their daughter Meagan from school. George intended to treat Meagan to a science-fiction movie filled with special visual effects. George and his co-workers used computers every day at the appliance factory. As quality control inspectors and supervisors, they relied on computers to check that goods were up to standard during all stages of production.

Meagan, nine years old, loved to play video games at home with her friends, and she was learning how to program computers at school.

"Perhaps we should buy Meagan a home computer," Janis

thought. In fact, it seemed to Janis that her life was becoming increasingly surrounded by computers. Still reflecting on her new assignment at the travel agency, she scanned the Oakriver University catalog and decided to sign up for the introductory computer course.

COMPUTERS IN THE 1980s

A LARGE PART OF OUR LIVES

1-1b.
Quality control.

1-1c.
Computerized switching.

In a single day Janis Roberts came into contact with computers used in office work, customer service, health care, education, government, and entertainment. Like her we have all felt the impact of computers on our personal and work lives. Let's briefly review the uses of computers that Janis encountered.

■ *Office work.* The travel agents whom Janis managed already used a link to a computer to make reservations and help issue tickets (Figure 1-1a). Janis was faced with the challenge of leading a team to select the new small computers that would smooth work at all four offices. Her husband George used computers at the factory to assure that materials, parts, and finished products were checked for quality (Figure 1-1b).

■ *Customer service.* The telephone company used computers to route calls (Figure 1-1c), as well as to create the bill from records of calls made by the Roberts family during the billing period. Janis wondered why she received so many mail-order catalogs. They were addressed from computerized mailing lists. Direct-mail companies and nonprofit organizations, such as churches and universities, often trade lists among themselves. Insurance companies, banks, brokerage houses, credit card companies, and many other businesses also trade or buy lists.

1-1a.
Making reservations.

FIGURE 1-1.
Some ways that computers affect our lives.

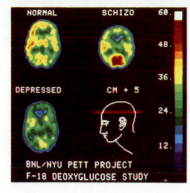

1-1d.
Diagnostic procedures.

1-1e.
In school.

- *Health care.* The good news from the body scan—which allowed a physician to look inside the body of Janis's mother without surgery—was made possible by computers (Figure 1-1d). Such scans are only one example of many applications of computers in medicine. Among other uses, computers routinely monitor the heart and other vital signs, help in diagnostic work in the laboratory, and keep tabs on the condition of both mother and infant during childbirth.

- *Education.* The computer age has affected all levels of education, from Meagan's elementary school classes all the way through to continuing education at colleges and universities for people like Janis (Figure 1-1e). As computers have become increasingly common in the workplace, more and more people have had to learn to use them. And computers are themselves used as teaching tools in a variety of subjects, from writing to mathematics.

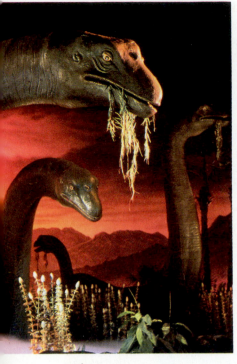

1-1f.
Entertainment.

- *Government.* Although Janis hasn't opened the envelope yet, the Internal Revenue Service relies extensively on computers to process tax returns. Among other tasks, computers help verify that figures on a return add up and that formulas are correctly applied. Of course the IRS is not the only computer user in government, but merely the tip of the iceberg.
- *Entertainment.* The special effects in the movie George and Meagan saw were produced by computers that create and manipulate animated images (Figure 1-1f). The video games Meagan loves to play with her friends also owe much of their rapid-paced entertainment value to the electronic speed of computers.

THE COMPUTER: WHAT IT IS AND WHAT IT DOES

A **COMPUTER** is a very-high-speed electronic device that can accept data and instructions, use the instructions to perform logical and mathematical operations, and report the results of the processing. Although a computer is only a machine, it can free us from laborious calculations, giving us time for more important creative tasks. Businesses use computers in thousands of ways. To businesspeople, the computer is a tool. With it business managers can provide themselves with the information they need to manage their companies' resources.

To know how to use a computer well, you must know what it can do in the office or home, how it operates, and how it might affect your life. Often we hear computer terms bandied about as if they were magic cures for every problem. In fact computers must be used very thoughtfully. They are only as smart as their users, and they must always be directed toward specific goals If garbage goes in, garbage comes out.

How much you need to know about computers depends on the tasks you want them to perform. For example, a marketing manager may only need to know how to request certain reports from the staff who run the company's computer system. On the other hand, a manager of computer operations will need to know in some detail how the computer works. Similarly, if you own a small computer, you will probably want to find out more about it than would a person who simply uses one.

Getting to know how a computer works is much like learning any other skill, from reading to algebra. Your own experience has certainly shown you that no magical formula can present you with these skills. It takes a certain period of time and a reasonable amount of organized study.

FOUR MODEL ORGANIZATIONS

To help you understand computers, we will explore their roles in three private businesses and one nonprofit institution. Throughout this text we will draw on these four organizations to illustrate many points about computer capabilities. Though these fictional organizations reside only in the invented city of Oakriver, they represent thousands of real-life workplaces across the country. We can start by revisiting Janis Roberts' agency.

- *Freddy Johnson's Travel Agency is a service-oriented retail company. Medium sized, it has four offices in Oakriver, with the main one downtown and the other three in major shopping centers.*
- *Global Electrical Equipment is a large multinational manufacturing company with plants in 25 countries and sales offices in over 80. Global Electrical's home appliance design and manufacturing facility in Oakriver employs several thousand people.*
- *Paul's House of Electronic Wonders is a wholesale distributor of electronic parts to retailers, wholesalers, and manufacturers. With customers across the country, the company faces many challenges in this ever-changing market.*
- *Oakriver University, a nonprofit institution, offers undergraduate, graduate, and professional degree programs. With 22,000 full-time students, OU also offers its surrounding community programs for job enrichment and continuing education.*

Each of these organizations must acquire and manage information to function. To do so more efficiently, they have turned increasingly to the computer.

THE NEED FOR INFORMATION

Earlier we learned that Freddy Johnson wants to use computers to extract useful information that his managers can use to make better decisions. If they cannot get this information, Johnson's travel business could suffer from incorrect or poorly timed decisions.

DATA AND INFORMATION

The information that Johnson seeks is drawn from data, and DATA are essentially facts. For a travel agent preparing a client's itinerary, relevant data would be such facts as the client's name, account number, credit status, departure and return dates, and desired airlines. These facts must be accurate and timely. Incorrect data or data acquired too late can be damaging. For example, if Freddy Johnson and his agents relied on outdated airline schedules, they would soon have a lot of disgruntled customers.

To a manufacturing company like Global Electrical Equipment, data are product types, their specifications, compatible subcomponents, the current number of units being produced, and suppliers by type. If the supplier of a switch can supply Global for only 30 or more days, where else can Global buy the part? If the data on suppliers by type are up to date, Global should find its answer there.

INFORMATION is knowledge communicated in a timely, accurate, and understandable fashion. Information is extracted, or distilled, from data. As a manager at Johnson's Travel Agency, Janis Roberts might need a monthly report on her agents' performance. The report, extracted from data on each agent's transactions, would help her determine which agents were performing well and which needed help. At Oakriver University the financial aid director uses reports extracted from data on student financial status and academic performance to allocate on-campus scholarships. These people need information to do their jobs effectively. And they need information that is accurate, prompt, and in a form they can readily understand.

At times data and information can seem identical, and often one person's information may be another's data. Penny Helmsley is a sales representative at Paul's House of Electronic Wonders. Susan Paul is vice-president for sales and marketing. Every week Penny prepares a report derived from sales records or data for the previous week. Penny considers the report information. Vice-president Paul treats these weekly reports as data for quarterly and annual sales reports. To her the reports covering a longer period are information.

THE VALUE OF INFORMATION

Information is valuable. It is a resource to be managed and protected. Information's value declines over time (Figure 1-2), which means that speed in gathering and communicating information is essential.

Freddy Johnson's agency managers need to know how to adjust their agent's schedules to fit peak travel periods. So managers must have information about expected demand soon enough to help shape their agents' schedules. Many customers pay for their tickets using credit cards or

FIGURE 1-2.
The value of information declines over time.

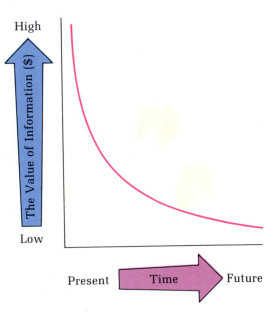

personal checks. Credit card records must be adjusted for each transaction and checked against the customer's credit limit. If a credit card is stolen but the owner does not report the theft immediately, the computer credit card verification system may not have this information on hand. As a result the card company risks losses because of illegal transactions. Personal checks are verified by similar methods.

A wholesaler needs to know the products that retail stores, manufacturers, and other wholesalers require. The type and volume of inventory needed are monitored so the wholesaler knows how much to order and when. Like the retail travel operation, wholesalers need up-to-date information to determine their customers' credit-worthiness.

Late or garbled information can cost time, money, and some times even lives. Minimizing these costs and maximizing the flow of information to the people who need it is the role of the information system.

CONVERTING DATA INTO INFORMATION

An **INFORMATION SYSTEM** converts data into information. Information systems are known by many names: data-processing systems, business-computer systems, electronic data-processing systems, information-processing systems. To avoid confusion, we will use only the term information system in this book.

A **SYSTEM** is a set of interrelated elements working together toward a goal. An *information* system is a set of interrelated elements working together to produce information. The elements in such a system must obtain data, process or convert the data into information, and then communicate the information to decision makers.

This process involves three stages: input, processing, and output. Figure 1-3 illustrates how the three stages in such a typical information-system interact. Arrows show the flow from input to processing and output. Ideally, if current, correct, and complete data are input to a system, processed data exit the system as timely, accurate, and useful information.

FIGURE 1-3.
The input, processing, and output stages for converting data into information.

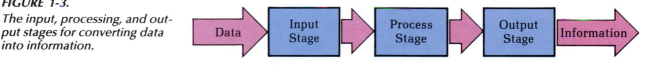

MEET THE COMPUTER

At the heart of today's information system lies the computer (Figure 1-4). It has tremendous capacity to accept, process, and retain data and information. It can perform calculations in billionths of a second and consistently produce accurate results. But it needs to be told exactly what to do.

This is where software comes into play. **SOFTWARE** is a general name for the **PROGRAMS**—lists of precise instructions written in a language the computer can interpret. These programs tell computers how to proceed step by step on particular processing jobs.

Computers cannot operate alone. They need additional hardware to function. Input, output, storage, and communication devices are called **PERIPHERAL EQUIPMENT** because they are attachments to the computer. Input devices present them with data and programs in a form they can under-

FIGURE 1-4.
A computer and its peripherals.

stand, and output devices transmit processed information in a form people can understand. Probably the most common input device today is the typewriter-like keyboard. Common output devices include printers (producing, for example, a book manuscript or ballgame tickets) and television-like display screens. Keyboards and screens are usually linked together in a device called a display terminal that is used for both input and output.

The computer itself has a memory where it stores data and programs during processing. Although this memory may be large, it cannot permanently hold all of an organization's programs and data. Thus in addition to input and output devices, computers also need a way to store data and programs in a machine-readable form. Secondary storage devices, such as magnetic tape readers and disk drives, serve this purpose. Finally, peripherals may be located some distance from the computer, linked to it or even to each other by communications devices.

FIVE ELEMENTS MAKE AN INFORMATION SYSTEM

Many people think an information system is simply a computer and its associated equipment. It is much more. In fact an information system does not really require a computer. Long before computers were invented, organizations devised systems to assure the flow of information to those who needed it. Today computers greatly increase the speed and efficiency of that flow.

At each stage—input, processing, and output—a modern information system has five major elements:

■ The *people* who run or depend upon the system
■ The organization's *rules and procedures*
■ *Data*, or facts from which information is drawn
■ *Software*, or *programs*, that execute the organization's rules and procedures
■ *Hardware*, including a computer and peripheral equipment, that physically handles and processes the data

This extract—from an article on the role of the information system at Marriott Corporation, owner of one of the nation's largest hotel chains—illustrates a crucial point: computers must serve users, not the other way around.

A CEO'S RECIPE FOR MIXING MANAGEMENT AND MACHINES

J.W. "Bill" Marriott, Jr., admits he occasionally wishes he could trade the slew of electronic time clocks that keep track of employees' hours at his hotels for one simple time machine. Then he could go back to the 1920s when his mother—whom his father affectionately refers to as "my Univac"—used to keep the books on a yellow legal pad. "I do sometimes wish we could bring back that yellow paper and get rid of all these computers," he confesses.

Looking back, however, is not something that Bill Marriott spends a lot of time doing. Though he admits that "most of us in my age group are scared of computers," he readily praises the computer's problem-solving prowess.

Knowing how much to spend on those computers, however, is "probably the most difficult management issue to deal with," he says. He recalls a payroll program "we did a year or two ago. The budget was a million and a half. It ended up costing three or four million dollars. You worry when things like that happen."

Something else that doesn't sit well with him is the way vendors talk to users. "I think the computer industry made a grievous error with all the language they have developed. You almost have to have a glossary to understand what they are talking about." He also wonders if vendors will "ever come up with a really super system" for his business.

Marriott feels that executives aren't always attuned to what computers can do for their companies either. The biggest mistakes an executive can make are "overdoing it, going too fast, and not clarifying objectives," he says. "You have to put in front-end homework and up-front analysis." The computer department, he adds, "has to realize that the user is his client." And if the executive doesn't force systems people to listen to the users, they are likely to "sail off into the stratosphere and design the perfect system that nobody is ever going to use."

The only way to ensure that doesn't happen is to put someone "in charge of technology who is first and foremost a businessman. He has to share your values of tight cost control and doing things that are practical and not overly complex. Of course, he needs to know systems, but he also needs to understand people, how to manage them and their productivity."

To make sure everyone is speaking the same language, Marriott "spends a great deal of time talking about computers. I personally have lots of meetings with our senior computer people to find out what they're working on. . . . I remind them to 'Put it in simple English so I can understand it. Tell me what the end result is going to be. Explain how it is going to reduce the hassle.' "

He expects computers to reduce his own hassles as well. "I've cut down on computer programming and questioned a lot of it. There's a tendency to generate too much information. We continually need to pare that down to a manageable level."

Marriott recalls the day when "I asked for some information on a specific problem, and in response they brought in a computer runout several inches high. I threw them out of the office. I said, 'You're not running a business when you bring in something like that. You're not contributing.' "

Although the computer is the system's most glamorous part, it is by no means the most important. People are. They use, run, and depend upon today's information systems. In Chapter 2 we will explore systems in general and information systems in particular. But let's look a little more closely right now at input, processing, and output.

FIGURE 1-5.

An example of a source document for use by Paul's House of Electronic Wonders. A salesperson would record the order on the form. The data on the form would then be transferred to a machine-readable form for input.

SALES ORDER

Paul's House of Electronic Wonders
1500 Commerce Way, Oakriver, California 90617-0012
Telephone (223)555-2112

Customer: _____   Ship to: _____

_____   _____

_____   _____

Account Number _____

Contact Person: _____   Bill to: _____

                                                            _____

                                                            _____

Item	Description	Unit Price	Quantity	Price

Terms [   ]

Salesperson: _____

Subtotal
Discount _____
Post Discount Total
Tax
GRAND TOTAL _____

INPUT   In the INPUT stage data (and programs) enter the information system. With computerized information systems, this means recording data in a machine-readable form. In most business settings data are first recorded on a SOURCE DOCUMENT—a sales order form, for example—and then transferred to some machine-readable format like magnetic tape or disk. Figure 1-5 shows a typical source document for Paul's House of Electronic Wonders.

Data aren't always transferred from a source document, however. Often they are recorded directly in machine-readable form. Whenever you use an electronic teller machine at a bank, for example, you enter data directly into the bank's information system.

The most important requirement of the input stage is accurate, timely, and useful data. If incorrect data enter the system, the resulting information will be misleading or wrong.

PROCESSING   In the PROCESSING stage data are transformed into information. Processing can be performed either manually or by computer. When performed by a computer, processing usually takes one of three forms: batch, time-sharing, or real time. With BATCH PROCESSING data are collected over a period of time and processed as a group. The data accumulation period for a batch run may be an hour, a day, a week, or longer. A common example of batch processing is the creation of payroll checks for a company's employees.

TIME-SHARING PROCESSING allows several users to run programs at the same time, giving all users the impression that they have the computer to themselves. Most time-sharing systems are terminal based and interactive, with the requests that a user makes, and the responses that the computer gives, taking place as a dialog or "conversation" between the user and the computer.

With REAL-TIME PROCESSING the computer processes data rapidly enough that the results can be used to influence a process that is still taking place. Credit-card verification systems often use real-time processing, as does space navigation. Like time-sharing, real-time processing is generally interactive, and usually involves more than one user of a computer. The principal difference is speed: with a real-time system the response must be immediate. With time-sharing the loss of a few seconds is not so crucial.

There is some overlap between these processing categories. For example, one of the users of a time-sharing system might run a program that performs batch processing; the person would be unaware that his or her program shared the machine with people using interactive programs. The type of processing that a computer performs is regulated by its operating system, a topic we will cover in detail in Chapter 13.

Processing, whether batch, time-sharing, or real-time, can consist of different types of actions. These include:

- *Calculating*
- *Comparing*
- *Communicating*
- *Sorting*
- *Summarizing*
- *Selecting*
- *Storing*
- *Recalling*

CALCULATING involves performing mathematical functions on data. These include addition, subtraction, multiplication, division, and higher functions such as exponentiation. Figure 1-6 shows an example of calculating on a real-time computer system. A salesperson at Paul's House of Electronic Wonders has just closed a sale for 1500 microprocessors at $6.85 each, with a 15 percent discount (85 percent of the list price). The salesperson, following prompts from the computer system that appear on the display terminal, enters data about the sale on the terminal (input). The computer calculates the total cost (processing), and a printer produces the invoice (output).

FIGURE 1-6.

Calculate. A salesperson enters data about a sale on a display terminal. The computer calculates the total and a printer produces the printout.

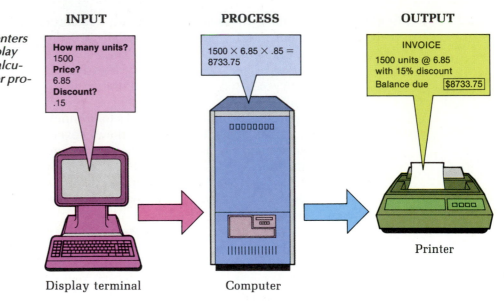

INPUT

How many units?
1500
Price?
6.85
Discount?
.15

Display terminal

PROCESS

$1500 \times 6.85 \times .85 = 8733.75$

Computer

OUTPUT

INVOICE
1500 units @ 6.85
with 15% discount
Balance due $8733.75

Printer

COMPARING involves determining whether two items of data are the same or different. **COMMUNICATING** involves transmitting data and information from one place to another. Figure 1-7 shows how a credit verification system uses comparing and communicating to let a retailer know whether or not to allow a credit sale to a customer. The retailer enters data about the customer's credit card and the sale on a display terminal in the store. These data are transmitted (*communicated*) over the phone lines to the credit card company's computer system. The system then retrieves data about the customer's account balance and credit limit from a storage device, *compares* these with the data about the current sale to determine whether the customer has exceeded the credit limit, and finally *communicates* the results back to the retailer's display terminal.

SORTING involves ordering data in some desired fashion, say alphabetically, as in Figure 1-8, or numerically from lowest to highest.

FIGURE 1-7.

Communicate and Compare. A retailer enters data about a sale and the customer's credit card on a display terminal. These data are communicated to the credit card company's computer system. The system compares the sale amount to the customer's balance and credit limit (stored on disk) and communicates credit approval back to the retailer's display terminal.

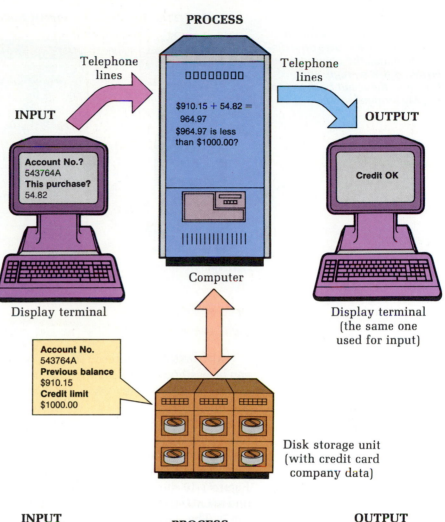

PROCESS

Telephone lines

Telephone lines

INPUT

OUTPUT

Account No.?
543764A
This purchase?
54.82

$910.15 + 54.82 = 964.97
$964.97 is less than $1000.00?

Credit OK

Computer

Display terminal

Display terminal (the same one used for input)

Account No.
543764A
Previous balance
$910.15
Credit limit
$1000.00

Disk storage unit (with credit card company data)

FIGURE 1-8.

Sort. A list of names is entered on a display terminal, the computer sorts the list alphabetically, and transmits the sorted list as output to the printer.

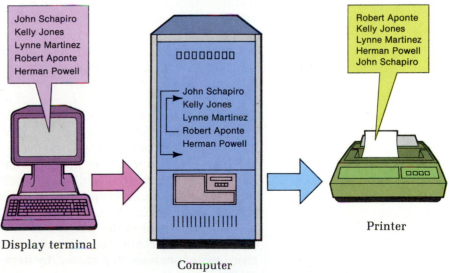

INPUT

PROCESS

OUTPUT

John Schapiro
Kelly Jones
Lynne Martinez
Robert Aponte
Herman Powell

John Schapiro
Kelly Jones
Lynne Martinez
Robert Aponte
Herman Powell

Robert Aponte
Kelly Jones
Lynne Martinez
Herman Powell
John Schapiro

Display terminal

Computer

Printer

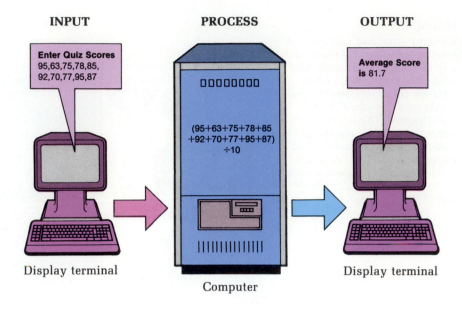

FIGURE 1-9.
Summarize. An instructor enters a list of test scores on a display terminal, the computer determines the average, and transmits the result back to the display terminal.

INPUT   PROCESS   OUTPUT

Enter Quiz Scores
95,63,75,78,85,
92,70,77,95,87

(95+63+75+78+85
+92+70+77+95+87)
÷10

Average Score
is 81.7

Display terminal

Computer

Display terminal

SUMMARIZING involves reducing a mass of detailed data to a form that can be easily grasped. Calculating the average of a group of numbers, say the scores of all students on a final exam (Figure 1-9), is an example of summarizing.

SELECTING involves extracting from a collection of data those items that have certain characteristics. If, for example, the administration at Oakriver University wanted to identify all the "A" students in a particular course, they would *select* those students from a list of all the students in the class. Figure 1-10 shows how this selection might occur. It also illustrates **STORING** and **RECALLING** by placing the data into secondary storage and later retrieving it. The names and grades of all students in a course are entered on a display terminal. The computer then takes this list and stores it in machine-readable form on a disk system. When the data in the list are needed again for processing, in this case to select the names of the "A" students, they are recalled from the disk system. The computer selects the appropriate names, and the resulting list appears as output on a printer.

OUTPUT   The **OUTPUT** stage conveys the results of processing. As the examples in Figure 1-11 show, output is often in a form people can understand. As we saw in our discussion of processing, however, output can also be in machine-readable form for storage. Output can be "permanent," as on paper, or temporary, as on a display terminal. Paper output may be printed on blank pages or on preprinted forms such as purchase orders, airline tickets, customer invoices, or grade reports. Output reports range from simple listings—all of the students at Oakriver University in alphabetical order—to highly condensed or summarized responses—a special report for the dean of students that shows, by department, the students who make OU's honor roll.

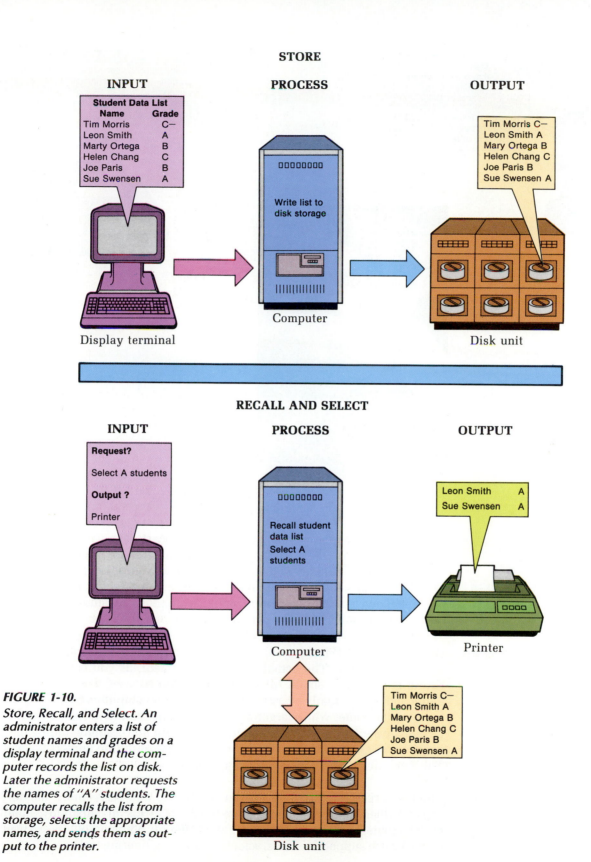

STORE

INPUT   **PROCESS**   **OUTPUT**

Student Data List	
Name	**Grade**
Tim Morris	C—
Leon Smith	A
Marty Ortega	B
Helen Chang	C
Joe Paris	B
Sue Swensen	A

Write list to disk storage

Tim Morris C—
Leon Smith A
Mary Ortega B
Helen Chang C
Joe Paris B
Sue Swensen A

Display terminal

Computer

Disk unit

RECALL AND SELECT

INPUT   **PROCESS**   **OUTPUT**

Request?

Select A students

Output ?

Printer

Recall student data list
Select A students

Leon Smith   A
Sue Swensen   A

Computer

Printer

FIGURE 1-10.

Store, Recall, and Select. An administrator enters a list of student names and grades on a display terminal and the computer records the list on disk. Later the administrator requests the names of "A" students. The computer recalls the list from storage, selects the appropriate names, and sends them as output to the printer.

Tim Morris C—
Leon Smith A
Mary Ortega B
Helen Chang C
Joe Paris B
Sue Swensen A

Disk unit

(a)

(b)

(c)

FIGURE 1-11.

Some examples of output readable to people. (a) A quality control report summary on a display terminal. (b) A printed sales report. (c) An airline ticket printed on a specialized printer.

TYPES OF COMPUTERS

Computers are ranked by how fast they can process data and by how much they can store in their memories. From smallest to largest, they are microcomputers, minicomputers, mainframe computers, and supercomputers. These four categories are not exclusive. Some larger microcomputers are more powerful than small minicomputers, and mainframes overlap with both minicomputers and supercomputers.

MICROCOMPUTERS

MICROCOMPUTERS (Figure 1-12), the smallest type, are frequently found in homes and offices. The actual processing element, as you can see in the figure, is extremely small. Microcomputers can be used for thousands of applications in virtually every field. Smaller microcomputers frequently are used in the home, while larger systems are more likely to be assigned to business-oriented tasks. Microcomputers are also increasingly finding their way into the classroom, from elementary school through the university level. This book was written on a microcomputer.

MINICOMPUTERS

MINICOMPUTERS (Figure 1-13) are larger, faster, and have more memory capacity than the typical microcomputer. In terms of capability, small minicomputers and large microcomputers overlap. Minicomputers are used frequently to support business, scientific, and engineering tasks.

(a)

(b)

(c)

(d)

FIGURE 1-12.
(a) A microcomputer. (b) The same microcomputer with the cabinet open. (c) A chip before it is mounted in its protective housing. (d) The processing element in its housing.

FIGURE 1-13.
A minicomputer.

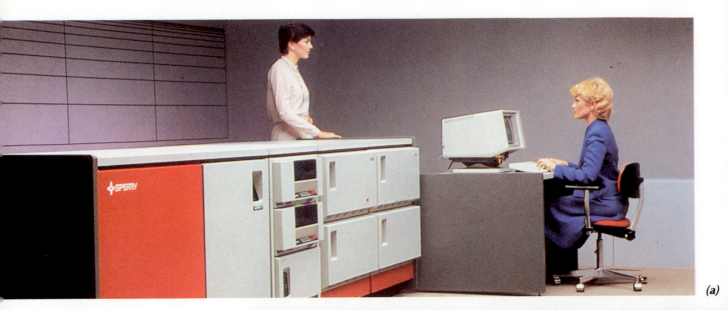

(a)

FIGURE 1-14.
(a) A mainframe computer. (b) The processing unit of a similar computer with the cabinet open.

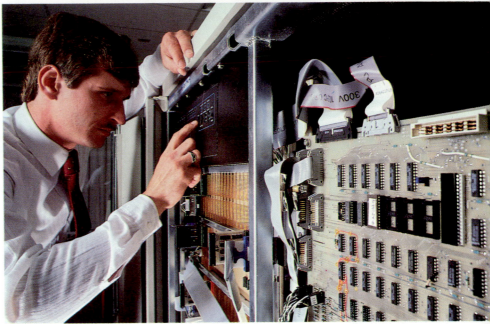

(b)

MAINFRAME COMPUTERS

MAINFRAME COMPUTERS (Figure 1-14) range over a wide spectrum of processing speeds and other capabilities. Used in a great variety of applications in business, government, science, engineering, and education, these systems are the basis of the popular image of the computer. Mainframe computers are used by wholesale and retail stores to manage inventories, check customer credit levels, handle accounting, personnel, and payroll tasks, and perform forecasting calculations. Manufacturers have access to mainframe systems which process thousands of production inquiries each day. Universities use such systems for research, student record keeping, and business-related procedures.

FIGURE 1-15.
A supercomputer.

SUPERCOMPUTERS

SUPERCOMPUTERS (Figure 1-15) are the biggest and the fastest machines in the computer world. These machines can execute hundreds of millions of calculations a second and can model extremely complex activities, such as the weather or the in-flight behavior of aircraft and rocket prototypes.

WRAP-UP | BUYING AN AIRPLANE TICKET

To illustrate the workings of an information system, let's see what happened when a customer phoned the travel agency that Janis Roberts ran. William Branscomb wanted to fly his parents from San Francisco to Hong Kong to see his new business venture and enjoy a relaxing vacation. William called Freddy Johnson's Travel Agency, where he had an account.

Janis herself took the call. Figure 1-16 shows what happened.

Mr. Branscomb's request for the San Francisco to Hong Kong tickets comprised the raw data shown in step 1 of Figure 1-16. Janis entered his request on a keyboard (step 2). A communications link then transmitted the data to an airline reservation system computer (step 3). The computer compared Mr. Branscomb's request with available flights from San Francisco to Hong Kong (step 4).

A flight was available with three seats open, and the computer sent a message stating this back to the travel agency. There the message appeared on Janis's screen (step 5). If the flight had been full,

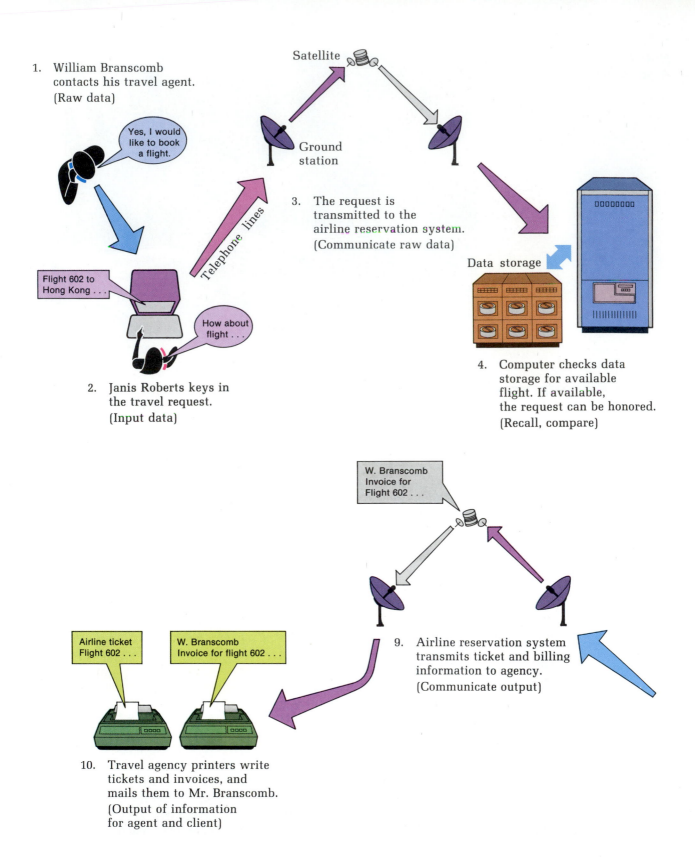

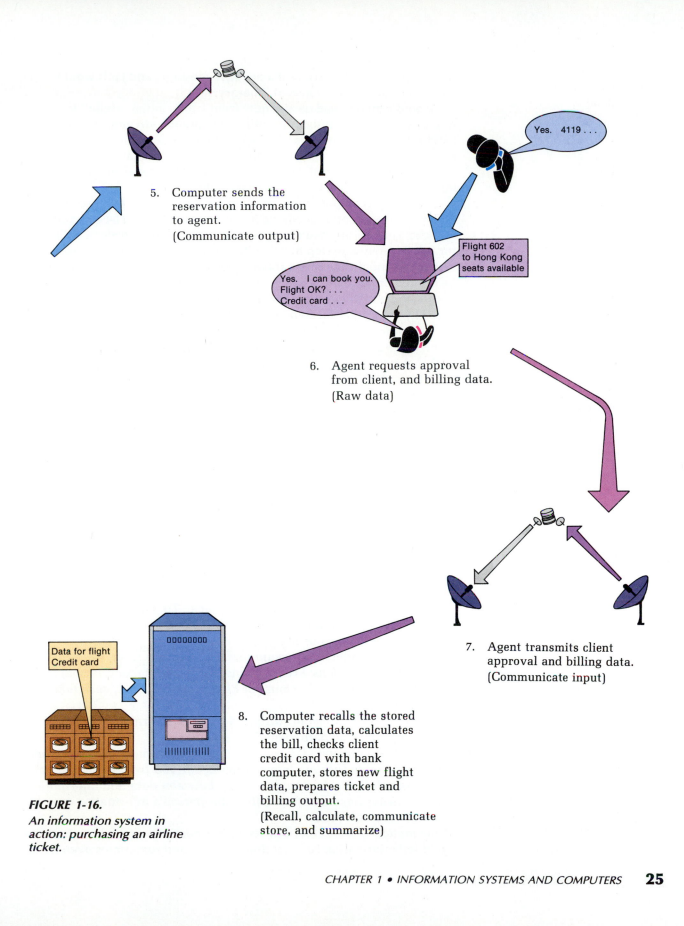

5. Computer sends the reservation information to agent.
(Communicate output)

Yes. 4119 . . .

Flight 602 to Hong Kong seats available

Yes. I can book you. Flight OK? . . . Credit card . . .

6. Agent requests approval from client, and billing data.
(Raw data)

7. Agent transmits client approval and billing data.
(Communicate input)

Data for flight Credit card

8. Computer recalls the stored reservation data, calculates the bill, checks client credit card with bank computer, stores new flight data, prepares ticket and billing output.
(Recall, calculate, communicate store, and summarize)

FIGURE 1-16.
An information system in action: purchasing an airline ticket.

the computer would have sent a negative message, and Janis would then have had to try a different itinerary.

About a minute had passed now from Janis's initial "Hello" to step 6, asking Mr. Branscomb—still on the phone—to approve the flight reserved. Mr. Branscomb gave his O.K., along with praise for Freddy Johnson's Travel Agency. Mr. Branscomb told Janis he would like to pay by credit card. Janis transmitted his approval, and the billing data, to the airline reservation computer (step 7).

The airline computer next recalled the data on the reservation that it had stored, and calculated Mr. Branscomb's bill. The computer also checked Mr. Branscomb's credit, and stored the traveler's data for future reference (step 8). Next the airline information-processing system communicated to the travel agency (step 9) the information to be printed on the actual tickets, as well as on the invoices for Mr. Branscomb and the agency. The tickets and invoices were then prepared by the printer located in Janis's office (step 10).

Janis informed the delighted Mr. Branscomb that he could pick up his three San Francisco to Hong Kong tickets whenever he liked, or that she could drop them in the mail.

Although this transaction was now complete, quite a bit of information could still be extracted concerning it that would be useful to Freddy Johnson, owner of the travel agency. Freddy and his branch managers needed information from all such transactions to help them operate the business in a more efficient and profitable manner. That is why Freddy wanted to see if it made sense to install a small computer information system in his agency.

SUMMARY

- A computer is a very high-speed electronic device that can accept data and instructions to perform logical and mathematical operations and report the results of the processing.
- Computers have assumed a growing role in almost all aspects of our lives, from the home to the workplace. To know how to use a computer well, you must know what it can do, how it operates, and how it might affect your life.
- To help you understand computers, we explore their roles in four fictional organizations: Freddy Johnson's Travel Agency, Global Electrical Equipment, Paul's House of Electronic Wonders, and Oakriver University.
- All organizations must acquire and manage information to function, and computers can help them do so efficiently.
- Information is knowledge communicated in a timely, accurate, and understandable fashion. Information is derived from data, and data are, essentially, facts. The distinction between data and information is not always hard and fast. Often one person's information may be another person's facts.
- Information is valuable, but its value declines over time. Late or garbled information can cost time, money, and sometimes even lives.

The role of an information system is to minimize these costs and maximize the flow of information to the people who need it.

- *A system is a set of interrelated elements working together toward a goal. An information system is a system that converts data into information. This process involves three stages: input, processing, and output.*

- *The most prominent item in a computerized information system is the computer itself. Software, or programs, are detailed instructions that tell the computer exactly what to do. Input devices make programs and data available to the computer. Output devices transmit processed information. Secondary storage devices store data and programs in a machine-readable form. Communications devices link the other parts of the hardware. Input, output, storage, and communications devices are called peripheral equipment.*

- *An information system does not require a computer, although computers can greatly increase the speed and efficiency of the flow of information.*

- *A modern information system has five major elements: people, rules and procedures, data, software, and hardware. The most important element is people.*

- *Data (and programs) enter an information system during input. Often data are first recorded on a source document such as a sales order form and then transferred to some machine-readable form. In other cases data can be input directly into a machine-readable form.*

- *Processing can be batch, time-sharing, or real-time. Processing tasks include calculating, comparing, communicating, sorting, summarizing, selecting, storing, and recalling.*

- *Output conveys the results of processing. Output may take many forms, some readable, others decipherable only by machine.*

- *Computers are ranked by how fast they can process data and by how much they can store in their memories. Microcomputers are small computers used in homes and offices. Minicomputers are larger machines, often used for business, scientific, and engineering tasks. Mainframes are large computers commonly used in businesses that require considerable information processing. Supercomputers, the most powerful units, are used for complex scientific problem solving.*

KEY TERMS

These are the key terms in the order in which they appear in the chapter.

Computer (8)	Source document (15)	Summarizing (18)
Data (9)	Processing (15)	Selecting (18)
Information (10)	Batch processing (15)	Storing (18)
Information system (11)	Time-sharing processing (15)	Recalling (18)
System (11)	Real-time processing (15)	Output (18)
Software (11)	Calculating (16)	Microcomputer (20)
Program (11)	Comparing (16)	Minicomputer (20)
Peripheral equipment (11)	Communicating (16)	Mainframe computer (22)
Input (15)	Sorting (16)	Supercomputer (23)

OBJECTIVE QUESTIONS

_____ 1.
_____ 2.
_____ 3.
_____ 4.

_____ 5.

_____ 6.
_____ 7.
_____ 8.
_____ 9.

_____ 10.

TRUE/FALSE: *Put the letter T or F on the line before the question.*
1. A system is a set of interrelated elements.
2. Source documents contain information to be converted into data.
3. Data refer to the output from an information system.
4. Real-time processing systems have faster reponse times than batch processing systems.
5. Considerable human effort is required to make computers perform various processing operations.
6. Large computers are often called microcomputers.
7. A sales report is an example of a source document.
8. Minicomputers generally have larger processing capacities than microcomputers.
9. Whatever comes out of the output end of an information system must be considered information.
10. Selection refers to extracting from a collection of data those items that meet certain characteristics.

_____ 1.

_____ 2.

_____ 3.

_____ 4.

_____ 5.

MULTIPLE CHOICE: *Put the letter of the correct answer on the line before the question.*
1. To be considered information, output from an information system must be
   (a) Timely.   **(c)** Understandable to the user.
   (b) Accurate.   **(d)** All of the above.
2. An information system
   (a) Focuses primarily on the best way to use new technology and equipment.
   (b) Emphasizes the processing.
   (c) Guarantees the user will make correct decisions in the future.
   (d) Takes five elements into account—people, rules and procedures, data, software, and hardware.
3. In an information system the three basic operations for converting data into information are performed in the following order:
   (a) Processing, input, output.   **(c)** Output, processing, input.
   (b) Input, processing, output.   **(d)** Input, output, processing.
4. Which of the following processing operations would be used to determine the sales tax a customer owes?
   (a) Summarizing.   **(c)** Sorting.
   (b) Calculating.   **(d)** Storing and recalling.
5. Hook-the-Resident, a mail-order company, sends out hundreds of thousands of advertising mailers every day. The lists are probably created using
   (a) Real-time processing.   **(c)** Batch processing.
   (b) Time-sharing processing.   **(d)** Either a or b.

_____ 1.

_____ 2.

_____ 3.
_____ 4.

FILL IN THE BLANK: *Write the correct word or words in the blank to complete the sentence.*
1. Knowledge communicated in a timely, accurate, and understandable fashion is _____.
2. A _____ is a set of interrelated elements working together toward a _____.
3. A _____ gives step-by-step directions to the computer.
4. During the _____ stage _____ are transformed into information.

5. Using _____ processing several users can run programs at the same time under the illusion that each has exclusive access to the computer.
6. Arranging by city a list of customers with overdue payments for a complete list of customers involves both _____ and _____ processing steps.
7. The processing step, _____, permits the reduction of data to a form that can easily be grasped.
8. The _____ of _____ declines over time.
9. The _____ is the largest and fastest type of computer.
10. An airline ticket is an example of a(n) _____ form.

SHORT ANSWER QUESTIONS

When answering these questions think of concrete examples to illustrate your points.

1. What is a computer?
2. What is the difference between data and information?
3. What is a source document?
4. What is meant by the value of information?
5. Contrast mainframes and microcomputers in terms of the applications for which they are used.
6. Describe the input and output stages in relation to an information system.
7. What are the differences between real-time and time-sharing processing systems?
8. What are the operations involved in processing?
9. What types of tasks do mini- and supercomputers perform?
10. What purpose does an information system serve?

ESSAY QUESTIONS

1. It has been said, "One person's data are another's information." How can this statement be true? What is the difference between data and information? Provide examples from the chapter.
2. Consider how you might use data from source documents, input the data, perform processing steps, and then communicate the results for the following situations:
   (a) Studying for an examination.
   (b) Looking for an apartment to rent.
   (c) Shopping for groceries.
3. How are computers used in your major field?
4. If you are working, describe the ways in which computers are used where you work.

CHAPTER 2

WHAT MAKES INFORMATION SYSTEMS TICK: FROM PEOPLE TO HARDWARE

After studying this chapter you should understand the following:
■ The parts of a simple system.
■ Which people are involved with an information system.
■ How an information system incorporates rules and procedures.
■ The hierarchy of data elements.
■ How software fits into an information system.
■ The general types of hardware used by information systems.
■ The steps in the system development process.

Janis Roberts greeted each of the travel agents in the downtown office as she walked past their desks toward the conference room in back. There she took her place at the conference table with the other managers.

Freddy Johnson entered the room a few minutes later. "Good morning, everyone," Freddy Johnson said. "Sorry to keep you waiting. I was up till three in the morning trying to pull some business records together. And then I overslept."

With everyone present they could start. "The reason Freddy and I called this meeting," Janis began, "was to define just what we want our computer system to do. We need to know that before we buy the hardware and set up the software that will run on it."

"You see, we just hired a systems analyst," Freddy said. "A consultant who specializes in the travel industry."

"What's a systems analyst?" Steve Garber asked.

Janis was glad she'd been to several sessions of her new computer class at Oakriver University—she could answer questions that would have mystified her before.

"A systems analyst helps set up computer systems," Janis said. "He's like an architect who builds, say, a house. He finds out what is needed—a house of a certain kind. Then he designs it in detail. Then, if his clients approve the design, he builds it—or rather hires people to build it."

"Right," Freddy said. "The house in this case is the computer system that's going to make life easier for us."

"The systems analyst will spend time watching how we work, and trying to figure out what we need a computer for," Janis said. "Then he'll recommend the type of system we need. This meeting is probably the last one we will have without him. Now I'm going to listen to your ideas and take notes. What do *you* want a computer to do? Who first?"

Cynthia Brown spoke. "Obviously we will all want it to do some of our work for us—or at any rate make our work easier for us to do. Besides that, though, my main concern right now is to give more service to our corporate accounts."

"In what way?" Janis asked.

"Corporate clients have been asking me for reports on how effectively their funds are being spent. We provide extensive travel services to them, and they are extremely cost conscious. They need to know, for instance, if they are wasting money by booking too many flights on short notice."

"Good point," Janis said. "We need summaries and perhaps other extra services for corporate clients."

"You see how far we are from being able to do that now,"

Freddy said. "We can't even prepare summaries for ourselves! That's what I was up late last night trying to do—and I did not succeed."

"O.K., Freddy," Janis said. "Why don't you tell us what the boss expects the system to do?"

Freddy leaned back and thought. "First," he began, "I want a method of linking the four offices electronically. I spend a a lot of time driving back and forth now, and when we phone each other, half the time we don't get who we want. Second, We need to service our clients more efficiently, as Cynthia said."

"Another need is special information for people sitting in this room," Freddy said. "We need reports that give us market share, do sales analyses, and show the quality of our travel agents. And all the general accounting and billing should be done by computer, so it can be done faster and more efficiently." Freddy paused for a moment. "That's all I can think of," he said.

Janis smiled. "Well it fills two pages," she said. "Can anyone else add something Freddy missed?"

Tom Rivera spoke up. "My office doesn't have many corporate accounts. Cynthia has them sewn up downtown. My agents cater to individuals, and individuals don't want analytical reports at all, they want tips. You know, not just a four-star hotel in Tokyo, but a four-star hotel that's worth all of those stars, that's in a neighborhood they'll like, and that fits their individual personalities. Now Janis, with electronics running everything, how are we going to give people those little nuances that make a big vacation or honeymoon worthwhile?"

Janis thought for a moment. "Tom, I don't know enough about computers to say if one can help with individual tips. At the least a computer shouldn't *interfere* with catering to individual preferences. I'll write down your point as 'give individualized service to travelers taking advantage of recommendations, complaints, and other comments.' Will that do it?"

"Sure will," Tom said.

"Steve, do you have any additional points?"

"Yes," Steve said. "We're all experienced travel agents, so we know that there are rules and procedures that have to be followed— for instance, we have to account strictly for what we do with every blank airline ticket."

"That's true," Tom said.

"But as I understand it," Steve went on, "data about all kinds of things are going to pop up on a screen at us, at the touch of a button. How can we keep control of our work—of who is supposed to know what, of where those blank tickets go, things like that—with some machine rather than ourselves in charge?"

"Excellent point," Janis said. "One thing I've learned in the computer course I'm taking is that computers are approached differently today than in the past as a result of some problems that have come up in the past, including the kinds of problems you mentioned, Steve."

WHAT IS A SYSTEM?

In Chapter 1 we defined a system as a set of interrelated elements working together toward a goal. Systems surround us. A factory assembly line is a system, as is a refinery, a subway network, or an automobile. Within a business, the accounting department, personnel department, and sales department are systems—and at a higher level so is the business itself.

A **SUPERSYSTEM** consists of two or more smaller systems, which are, in turn, frequently composed of **SUBSYSTEMS**. Your body can be thought of as a supersystem, made up of circulatory, nervous, digestive, and other subsystems. In a business setting the company itself is the supersystem, made up of such subsystems as manufacturing, accounting, marketing, and other divisions. Each subsystem can often be broken down into its own subsystems—manufacturing, for example, can be broken down into assembly stations.

PARTS OF A SIMPLE SYSTEM

Systems do not exist in isolation, but within an **ENVIRONMENT**, which consists of those external factors that affect the system. The environment is shown by the cloud-shaped line in Figure 2-1. The environment for a business system includes government regulations such as tax laws, competitors' sales prices, and the state of the economy.

Environmental factors from another part of a company can also affect a business subsystem. Suppose you are developing a salesperson compensation package for your sales force. The personnel department may have certain companywide rules on such packages. These rules are an environmental factor you must consider in your plans.

As Figure 2-1 shows, there are three stages in a system's operation: input, processing, and output. **INPUT** brings data into a system from the environment. Input can include business receipts, sales orders, data about personnel, or data about competitors. The emergency services system of a large city receives a flood of input daily from citizens calling for ambulances and reporting accidents, crimes, and fires; from police officers investigating traffic or criminal offenses; and from other sources.

In the **PROCESSING** stage data are manipulated to produce the desired information. Processing creates order out of all the incoming data, which includes determining which data are important and which are not. In your body the nervous system must screen out unneeded facts and focus first on the most important incoming signals, for basic survival. These signals are analyzed, organized, and the correct course of action determined.

OUTPUT is the result of the processing stage, and the end product of a system. Output communicates the results of processing.

In Figure 2-1 you will see that following output, some of the flow continues through a box called feedback back to input. **FEEDBACK** allows a system to regulate itself by treating the effect of its output on the environment as new input. Suppose, for example, that our electronics wholesale company, Paul's House of Electronic Wonders, after analyzing costs and expected demand, decides to sell superduper chips at $87.95 each. After a few weeks, they find the chips aren't selling well and they're losing money on them. Using this information as *feedback*, they lower the price to stimulate sales. If sales pick up, they will stick to the new lower price. If the chip sales start weak, they might reduce the price further, or tell their supplier that they're not interested in stocking the item any more.

FIGURE 2-1.
A simple system.

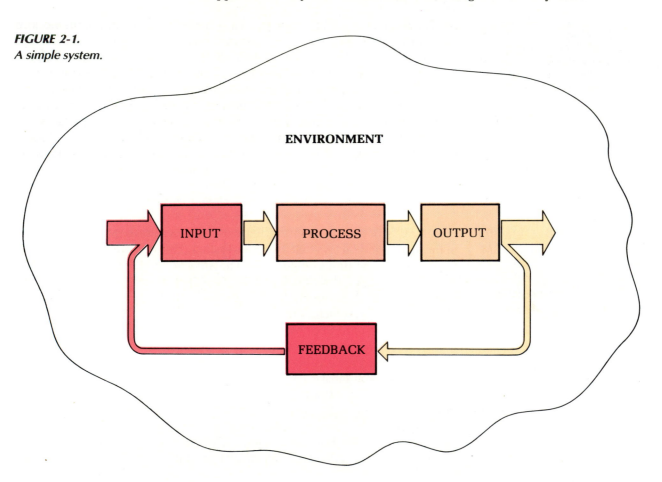

An **INFORMATION SYSTEM** provides users with timely, accurate, understandable, and relevant information. Viewed from the perspective of an organization—itself a supersystem—an information system is a subsystem.

Information systems do not themselves make decisions; nor do they guarantee that managers will make the right decisions every time. Instead, a well-run information system assists people in determining what choices or actions are available. Figure 2-2 shows how an information system fits into a business organization.

Five elements make up an information system: people, rules and procedures, data, software, and hardware. Note that in terms of the input-processing-output model, the five elements of an information system are found throughout each of these stages (see Figure 2-3). For instance, in the input stage people gather data following various rules and procedures. Software helps carry out these rules, and hardware physically transmits the data. All five elements need to work together if an information system is to be effective.

Let's look at some of the points touched upon in the example at the start of this chapter in terms of the elements of an information system. In his little speech that concluded the meeting, Freddy Johnson stressed the importance of *people*. Steve Garber was worried about how the *rules and procedures* that the agency followed would be retained and implemented under the new system. Janis also observed that one of the jobs of the systems analyst would be to watch how people worked, to learn how a computer could help them—again, relating to rules and procedures.

Data were the focus of Cynthia Brown and Freddy Johnson, and also of Tom Rivera, who was concerned about how a computerized system would deal with specific tips for individual travelers. *Software*, although no one specifically mentioned it, will be intimately involved in handling all of the data and producing information. *Hardware* involves capital expense to the travel agency, as well as setting limits on how much the system can do and how fast it can do it. These will be items of most concern to Freddy Johnson

FIGURE 2-2.

Relating the information system to a business organization. Data enter the information system from other parts of the organization. The information system produces useful information for the rest of the organization. Some of the information returns as feedback.

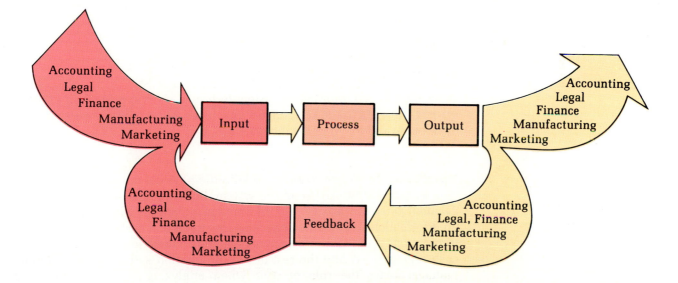

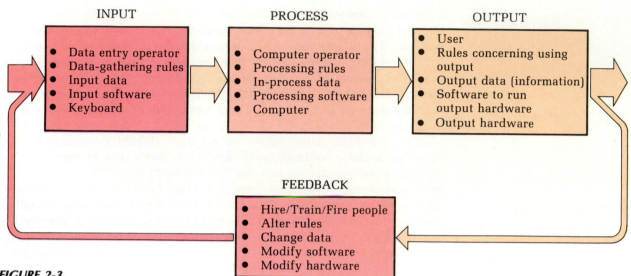

FIGURE 2-3.

Relating the information system elements to the model of a simple system.

and Janis Roberts. Although Freddy will not want to go broke financing the new system, he will also want hardware sophisticated enough so that the firm can stay competitive within a rapidly changing industry.

Now let's take a more detailed look at each of the five elements of an information system.

PEOPLE   People are the most important part of an information system. How people relate to the other elements directly affects the success or failure of the system. Obvious as this may seem, in the history of information systems the lesson has been learned the hard way. It is recognized today that people's needs must be paramount in any information system from its inception.

Three main categories of people are involved in any information system:

- *Users*
- *Clients or clientele*
- *Information system staff*

USERS employ the information system to provide services for their **CLIENTS**. **INFORMATION SYSTEM STAFF** support the users by providing assistance in developing and maintaining the system.

Users

Users generally are not concerned with the physical operations of the system. Rather they make use of the system. Both management and nonmanagement personnel are users of information systems. A wholesale clerk uses an information system when checking the credit of a customer, and records transactions using a point-of-activity machine (which looks like a very large cash register) tied into the rest of the information system. The wholesale manager plays the role of user when analyzing the performance of employees, examining sales patterns, or evaluating future buying decisions.

Clients

Clients are those people for whom the users provide a service. The service may be either voluntary or involuntary. Note that a user and a client can sometimes be the same person. If you have ever used an automatic teller machine at a bank, you have been both a user of the bank's information system (the teller machine is tied in directly to the bank's computer) and a client of the bank. At Freddy Johnson's Travel Agency the clients are the customers who seek to make various travel arrangements. The travel agency also takes on the role of client when negotiating with the managers of the airline's reservation system, individual hotels, and tour operators.

Information system staff

The information system staff support the users by developing, operating, and maintaining an effective information system. We can classify the information system staff by the element of the information system they most interact with. Figure 2-4 shows some typical job categories in an information system.

In a small information system many of these tasks may be performed by one or two people. For instance, many hardware and software tasks fall on your shoulders when you use a small personal computer. At the other extreme, large corporate and governmental information systems sometimes have thousands of employees.

One common job category is the computer programmer. This person designs, codes, and fixes some of the software that controls what a computer does. Another important job, at least in large information systems, is that of computer operator, who keeps the machine physically running, punching buttons on the devices that require it.

FIGURE 2-4.

Some of the occupations found in an information system. Note that some occupations may overlap among categories.

PEOPLE-ORIENTED
    User Representative
    Systems Analyst
    Information Resource Manager
RULES-AND-PROCEDURES-ORIENTED
    User Representative
    Systems Analyst
    Decision-Support Analyst
DATA-ORIENTED
    Data Entry Operator
    Data Administrator
    Database Manager
    Information Resource Manager
SOFTWARE-ORIENTED
    Computer Programmer
    Software Designer
    Systems Analyst
HARDWARE-ORIENTED
    Computer Operator
    Operations Administrator

On the nation's list of top direct-mail companies, L.L. Bean ranks only thirteenth. But to the readers of the 60 million catalogs it mails out each year, Bean is every bit as American as motherhood and apple pie. Bean's marketing is a brilliantly conceived combination of down-home prose, old-fashioned satisfaction guarantees, durable products, and high-tech tracking. Its sensible tweeds, corduroys, and leathers are *de rigeur* for hard-core preppies, urban jocks, and aging alumni. . . .

The Maine hunting shoe, Leon Leonwood Bean's rubber-bottomed, leather-topped answer to damp feet during deer-hunting season, is now seen splashing its way to high-rise offices around the world. . . .

Success, however, hasn't spoiled L.L. Bean. . . . Although it has not forgotten things like integrity and quality that make it so synonomous with its home state, Bean has quietly developed a series of computer systems and an up-to-date marketing strategy that can make the best use of them.

Thanks to those systems—which Leon A. Gorman, L.L.'s grandson and president of the company since 1967, began introducing in the mid-1970s—Bean management knows exactly who its dyed-in-the-Hudson-Bay-wool preps are and how much they spend on what. . . .

Its new systems do the following:

- *Track customers. As it turned out, women were by far the fastest growing segment of Bean's market, a tidbit of information that's been worth millions in sales and has forever changed the look of the catalog.*
- *Sample mailing lists. According to Gorman, "Four-hundred thousand outside names were tested in 1975. By 1980 we were renting nearly 5 million names. This has been the key factor in our growth."*

- *Evaluate advertising. Bean can tell where advertising pays off, and where it doesn't. . . .*
- *Control inventory. The system makes sure that the stock turns over frequently throughout the year and pushes up delivery times for items that are turning over faster than expected.*

These essential systems control picking, packing, and movement of stock. It's a perfect example of how Bean refuses to put itself at the beck and call of technology. Instead, it combines sophisticated computer systems with hand-checking of orders. . . .

People play just as big a role as the machines designed to make them more efficient. In peak season, for example, 200 telephone operators sit at IBM 3178 terminals, which are linked to one of two IBM 4321 mainframes. When someone calls to place an order, the operators can access the item on the screen and tell the customer immediately whether it's in stock, and when and how it can be delivered. Once the operator has written the order, it is optically scanned, put onto tape, and fed into the computer. If the order comes in through the mail, it is keyed onto a disk and immediately fed into the computer.

In a perfect example of how Bean trusts computers—almost— the information is brought back out of the computer, printed out, and checked for accuracy in an edit and postedit procedure. Editors make a visual comparison between the original documentation and the computerized order form. Should anything be wrong with the order, it's Bean's policy to phone the customer up to rectify problems. Then, in a postedit, which is online, final corrections are made and the order is released.

The final order is automatically printed out, including a mailing label and the amount of postage required.

The computer prepares a shipping manifest for the most appropriate means of transportation—United Parcel Service or the U.S. Mail— automatically calculating the dimensions and the construction of the package the items will have to be mailed in, the weight of all items in the shipment, and the destination of the order. . . .

As Gorman and his management team decide what markets to tackle next from down home in the woods of Maine, one thing is for sure: Bean's walls may be covered in barn siding, but that's a bit like sheep's clothing. Inside the place is humming with big plans and a lot of hefty computers to help weigh all the alternatives. . . .

RULES AND PROCEDURES

All organizations have **RULES AND PROCEDURES** to govern their operations. These rules may be formal and clearly written out, or they may be informal and perhaps quite vague. Understanding these rules is critical in examining an information system. The "generally accepted accounting principles" (GAAP) provide an example of formal rules used in setting up, working with, and auditing any business organization. Tom Rivera, in contrast, is applying an informal rule when he tries to reserve accommodations in Bangkok for his customers only in hotels that he has stayed at himself and enjoyed.

Whether formal or informal, rules and procedures fall into two categories: (1) those for normal conditions and (2) those for exceptions. In normal situations decisions are usually made using **STANDARD OPERATING PROCEDURES** (SOP). In some cases, for example when a manufacturer tests a product for electrical malfunctions, there can be no exceptions to standard procedure. In other situations **EXCEPTION PROCEDURES** may be permitted. In a retail store the normal check-approval procedures might not be followed if the customer is known to the clerk or store owner, or if the check is for a small amount.

Under certain conditions exceptions may even be built into the rules. For example, if on vacation you become ill, you can often rearrange your airline tickets without paying a penalty. A good information system should be able to handle exceptional conditions as well as standard operating procedures.

DATA

In an information system, data must be organized and protected. The **DATA HIERARCHY** is a classification of data from the lowest or most basic level to the highest or most inclusive level. Moving from the lowest level to the highest, there are four main categories:

- *Field*
- *Record*
- *File*
- *Database*

The levels of the hierarchy are shown in Figure 2-5.

FIGURE 2-5.

The data hierarchy. Fly-By-Night's database consists of a collection of related files, including flight files, crew schedule files, and aircraft maintenance files. Each file consists of a collection of related records. A flight file contains records for all passengers on the flight. Each record consists of related fields; in the flight file records contain fields with information on each passenger. A field is a single data element and is made up of one or more characters.

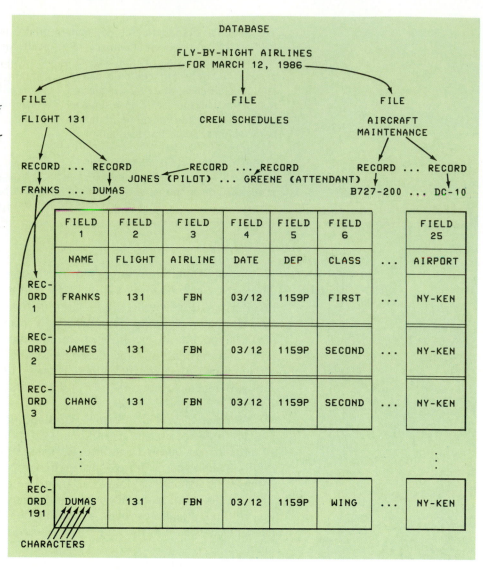

A **FIELD** is a single data element, such as name, age, or social security number. Fields are made up of one or more **CHARACTERS** (individual letters, numbers, or other symbols like "t", "5", or "+"). In Figure 2-5 Fly-By-Night Airlines uses 25 fields to record data about each reservation. The fields contain data consisting of passenger name, flight number, airline code, date, and so on.

A **RECORD** is a set of related fields. Each record contains the field information for a single case. In Figure 2-5 all the fields for a single customer's reservation make up a record.

A **FILE** is a set of related records. In Figure 2-5 the records for all of the passengers on Fly-By-Night Airlines flight 131 make up a file. That is, the entire grid shown represents the file; the horizontal rows are the records, and the vertical columns are the fields.

The **DATABASE**, a set of interrelated files, is at the top of the data hierarchy. As Figure 2-5 shows, Fly-By-Night's database includes a file with data on passengers for each of its flights (including flight 131), a file on crew schedules, and a file on aircraft maintenance. Databases will be covered in detail in Chapter 16.

SOFTWARE

System and application software

SOFTWARE, or **PROGRAMS**, provides the detailed instructions that direct hardware. These instructions tell the physical equipment what actions to perform and when to perform them. Software converts the rules and procedures of the organization into a form that computers can understand. **PROGRAMMING** refers to the process of designing and writing programs. The two major categories of software are application software and system software.

APPLICATION SOFTWARE directs the actual input, processing, and output activities for users. The program that allows Freddy Johnson's agents to make airplane reservations for their clients is an example of application software. Application programs can be written by the user, developed within another part of the company, or purchased as a prewritten software package from an outside supplier. Common business application packages can be purchased that meet a wide range of business needs, including accounting packages, electronic spreadsheets (used for forecasting and managerial analysis), and word processing programs (used for writing reports, letters, and other printed output). In later chapters we will learn more about how to write application programs and how to select prewritten software packages.

SYSTEM SOFTWARE links the application software to the computer hardware (Figure 2-6). The most important system software component, the **OPERATING SYSTEM**, supervises and directs all of the other software components. Other system software manages databases and translates application software into a form the computer can understand. System software is the subject of Chapter 13.

FIGURE 2-6.

The relationship among hardware, system software, application software, and the users of an information system.

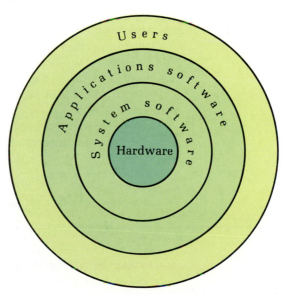

PROGRAMMING AND PROBLEM-SOLVING

We all solve problems every day, often without being aware that we are doing so. When we want a computer to solve a problem for us, however, we have to tell it exactly, step by step, how to do so. We do this in a program.

Because it forces you to analyze problems rigorously, learning to program—even if you have no plans to become a programmer—can teach you a great deal about how to solve problems.

Let's look at a simple example to see what designing and writing a program involves. Many business problems require comparisons. To do a comparison we must perform a test. The result of the test will determine our action. Take, for example, checking a person's credit card limit. Suppose George and Janis Roberts wanted to use their bank credit card to buy a new television from an appliance store. Their current credit status with the National Bank of Oakriver was as follows:

    Roberts' credit limit   = $1500.00
    Roberts' current balance   = $ 567.53
    Charge for a new television = $ 535.95

Should the appliance merchant approve their credit? Knowing the Roberts' credit status, you would probably answer yes. How would you go about writing a program that would allow the merchant to get the same information from the bank's information system?

The first step is to visualize what the solution should look like. Special diagrams called flowcharts aid in communicating the steps needed to write a program. Over the years, people have come to agree upon which flowchart symbols should represent particular functions. Figure A illustrates the most commonly used symbols. Figure B shows how these symbols can be used to diagram the logic of the credit approval process.

Once we have worked out the logic of a problem in a flowchart, we can write and test a program to solve it. The program (Figure C) is written in a language called BASIC (*B*eginner's *A*ll-Purpose *S*ymbolic *I*nstruction *C*ode). Entering the program into the computer, and typing the system command RUN, lets us execute the program.

The actual results appear at the bottom of the figure. Note that the numbers in the flowchart correspond to line numbers in the program. These have been put there to make it easier for you to follow both the flowchart and the program (a flowchart doesn't normally include line numbers).

For a detailed look at programming turn to Part 3, especially Chapters 9, 10, and 11.

FIGURE A.
Common flowcharting symbols used for progrmming.

Symbol	Name	Meaning of the Symbol
	System interrupt (start, stop)	Indicates the beginning and end of the program.
	Comment or remark	Remarks do not affect running the program. They allow the programmer to annotate the program.
	Input or output	Represents any input or output operation.
	Process	Represents calculations and other processing functions.
	Decision	Indicates decisions or comparisons.
On-page Off-page	Connectors	Connect the parts of a flowchart.
	Lines and arrows	Connect the boxes and show the solution flow.

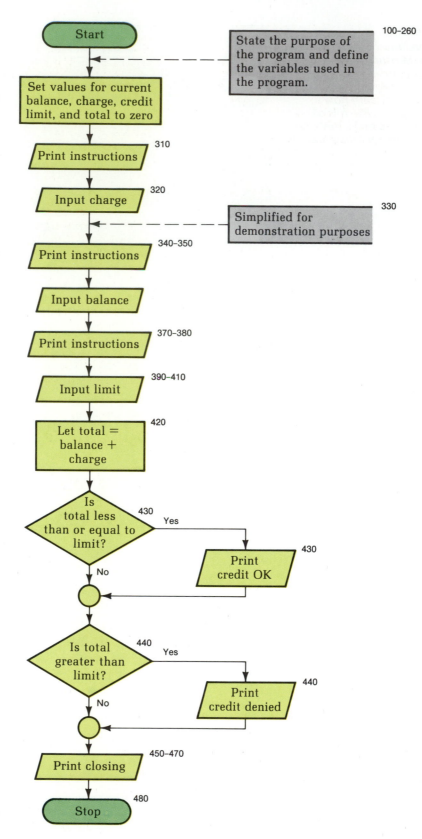

FIGURE B.
The flowchart used to help write the program shown on the right. Numbers shown at the upper corner of symbols refer to the line numbers of the program.

Start

State the purpose of the program and define the variables used in the program. 100–260

Set values for current balance, charge, credit limit, and total to zero

Print instructions 310

Input charge 320

Simplified for demonstration purposes 330

Print instructions 340–350

Input balance

Print instructions 370–380

Input limit 390–410

Let total = balance + charge 420

Is total less than or equal to limit? 430

Yes → Print credit OK 430

No

Is total greater than limit? 440

Yes → Print credit denied 440

No

Print closing 450–470

Stop 480

FIGURE C.

A program to check a customer's credit balance. Entering the system command RUN executes the program. Later in this book you will learn how to write programs like this one— in fact, how to make this a better and more realistic program.

```
100 REM This program checks a customer's credit balance.
110 REM The program was written by Benjamin Levin.
120 REM This programs adds the amount to be charged to the
130 REM customers's current balance and indicates whether
140 REM the combined charges exceed the customer's limit.
150 REM The program is written in the BASIC programming
160 REM language.
170 REM ****************************************
180 REM The variables used are:
190 REM          B = Current balance
200 REM          C = Amount to be charged
210 REM          L = Credit limit
220 REM          N = The total of the current balance and
230 REM              the amount to be charged. N must be
240 REM              less than or equal to the credit limit
250 REM              for the credit sale to be approved.
260 REM ******THE FOLLOWING LINES EXECUTE THE PROGRAM
270 LET B = 0
280 LET C = 0
290 LET L = 0
300 LET N = 0
310 PRINT "Please enter the amount to be charged";
320 INPUT C
330 REM FOR SIMPLICITY WE WILL ENTER THE VALUES FOR B AND L
340 PRINT
350 PRINT "Please enter the current balance";
360 INPUT B
370 PRINT
380 PRINT "Please enter the customer's credit limit";
390 INPUT L
400 PRINT
410 PRINT
420 LET N = B + C
430 IF N <= L THEN PRINT "Customer's credit is approved."
440 IF N > L THEN PRINT "Customer's credit is not approved !!!"
450 PRINT
460 PRINT
470 PRINT "End of program—Have a nice Day!"
480 END

RUN
```

> Note: This is a system software command.

```
Please enter the amount to be charged? 535.95

Please enter the current balance? 567.53

Please enter the customer's credit limit? 1500


Customer's credit is approved.


End of program—Have a nice day!
```

> Note: The underlined values are what you key in when the program is run.

HARDWARE   The term **HARDWARE** refers to the physical equipment used in an information system—the computer (the central processing unit) and the peripheral devices that support it. Peripheral devices include:

- *Input and ouput devices*
- *Secondary storage devices*
- *Communications equipment*

Figure 2-7 shows the hardware components in a typical small computer system associated with a microcomputer; Figure 2-8 shows those commonly associated with much larger mainframe systems.

Later in this book (Part 2) we will take a detailed look at hardware. Right now we'll confine ourselves to a brief overview.

Central processing unit

The central piece of hardware in an information system is the computer itself, also known as the **CENTRAL PROCESSING UNIT (CPU)**. This is the machine that, under software control, does the actual processing of input data. As we mentioned in Chapter 1, computers come in a variety of sizes, ranging from microcomputers that fit on a desktop to huge supercomputers in which the CPU occupies an entire room. In Chapter 5 we will discuss the way the CPU

FIGURE 2-7.

Hardware components of a typical microcomputer system.

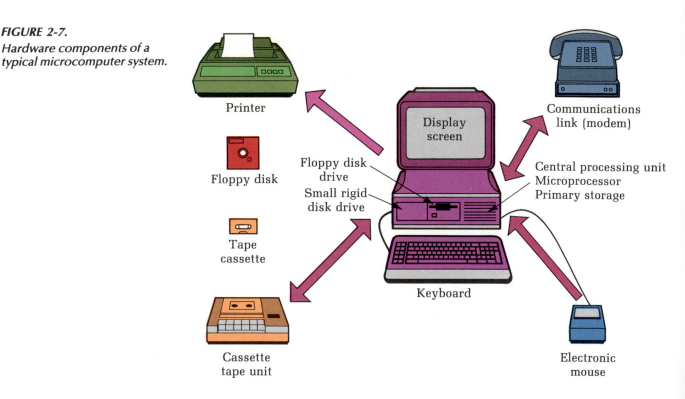

Printer

Floppy disk

Tape cassette

Cassette tape unit

Floppy disk drive

Small rigid disk drive

Display screen

Keyboard

Communications link (modem)

Central processing unit
Microprocessor
Primary storage

Electronic mouse

FIGURE 2-8.
*Hardware components of a
typical mainframe computer
system.*

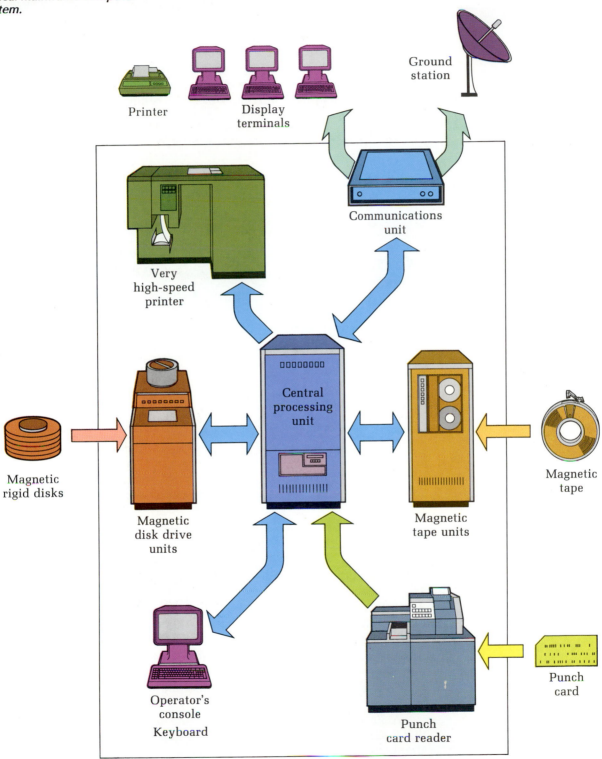

Printer

Display
terminals

Ground
station

Communications
unit

Very
high-speed
printer

Central
processing
unit

Magnetic
rigid disks

Magnetic
disk drive
units

Magnetic
tape units

Magnetic
tape

Operator's
console
Keyboard

Punch
card reader

Punch
card

works in some detail. For now, however, let us cautiously pry the lid off the "black box" and peer inside. Figure 2-9 shows what we see.

- *The **CONTROL UNIT** serves as the "brain" of the computer. Working under the direction of a stored program, the control unit directs the input, processing, and output of data.*
- *The **ARITHMETIC/LOGIC UNIT** performs calculations and logical operations with the data, as directed by the control unit.*
- ***MAIN MEMORY** stores data and instructions that have been input and are waiting to be processed, and stores the results of processing until they are released to output devices.*

FIGURE 2-9.
Parts of the central processing unit.

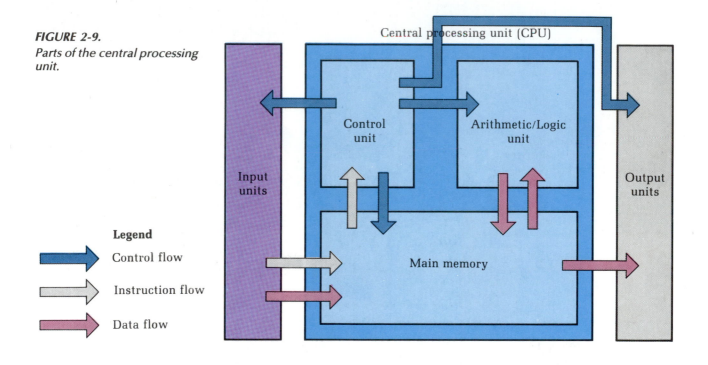

Legend

Control flow

Instruction flow

Data flow

Input and output devices

To get your data and software into the central processing unit, you need **INPUT DEVICES**; and to make use of the processed information, you need **OUTPUT DEVICES**. Input devices (Figure 2-10) transmit data and instructions to a computer for processing. Output devices (Figure 2-11) reverse the process, producing information in a form that people can read or recording it in machine readable form in secondary storage. Some machines, such as magnetic disk units, combine input, output, and secondary storage functions.

At Freddy Johnson's Travel Agency the agents use a **KEYBOARD** for input that is similar to an electric typewriter with a few special keys added. They simply "key in" (or "type" or "input") the data concerning travel arrange-

FIGURE 2-10.
Some input devices. (a) A keyboard. (b) A card reader. (c) An optical scanner.

(a)

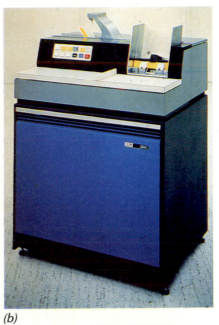
(b)

(c)

FIGURE 2-11.
Some output devices. (a) Graphic output on display terminal screen. (b) A slow-speed printer. (c) A very high speed printer.

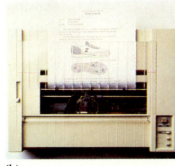
(b)

(a)

ments. Janis may key in data concerning her travel agents' efficiency. These data can be output for external storage on a magnetized surface such as that of a magnetic tape or magnetic disk. A **MAGNETIC TAPE UNIT** or a **MAGNETIC DISK UNIT** can read and write magnetic codes onto the storage surface. Magnetic devices send input data and receive output at high rates of speed and are suitable for handling large amounts of data.

Some other input devices include card readers, cassette tape devices, and optical scanners. **CARD READERS**, which sense the holes punched into a paper card, were once the predominant input device and are still in use. **CASSETTE TAPE DEVICES** are used for reading from and storing data onto cassette-style magnetic tapes. **OPTICAL SCANNERS** read marks written on packages or paper forms. A common type of scanner uses laser beams to read the product codes on grocery items.

Output can appear on a television-like screen of a **DISPLAY TERMINAL** or it can be produced by a **PRINTER** on blank paper or preprinted forms (such as invoices or airline tickets). Output on a display terminal is not permanent, whereas printed output is. Permanent output from printers is often called **HARD COPY**, and nonpermanent displays, **SOFT COPY**. Output for storage is commonly recorded on a magnetic surface such as a tape or disk, usually by the same device that will later read the data again for input.

Chapter 6 will examine input and output devices in greater detail.

Secondary storage devices

SECONDARY, or **EXTERNAL**, **STORAGE DEVICES** (Figure 2-12) record data and programs on a machine-readable medium for later use. Figure 2-13 shows some of the most important storage media. Magnetic disk units and magnetic tape units are the most common secondary storage devices. **HARD DISK**

FIGURE 2-12.
Secondary storage devices. (a) A reel-to-reel magnetic tape drive. (b) A Cassette-tape drive (c) A hard-disk drive. (d) A floppy disk drive.

(b)

(a)

(d)

(c)

FIGURE 2-13.

Storage media. (a) A variety of magnetic media: tape reels, floppy disks, cassette tapes, and 3 1/2-inch diskettes. (b) A hard disk pack. Each pack contains several disks. (c) Punched cards store data as holes in designated rows and columns.

(b)

(a)

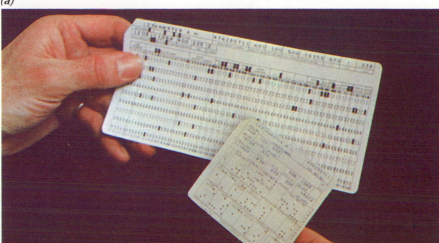

(c)

systems record data on rigid metal disks; **FLOPPY DISK** or **DISKETTE** systems, common on microcomputers, record data on flexible plastic disks. Large **REEL-TO-REEL TAPE** systems have long been used in conjunction with mainframe computers. **CASSETTE TAPE** systems were once popular with microcomputers, but they are much slower and less efficient than floppy disk systems and no longer have a significant price advantage.

Secondary storage may be classified by its accessibility to the computer. The computer has direct control over **ONLINE STORAGE** and can access data and software stored there without human intervention. Online storage systems generally use magnetic disk or magnetic tape as the storage medium. **OFFLINE STORAGE** is not under the direct control of the computer; as soon as an online device is turned off, it becomes offline. Similarly, when a reel of magnetic tape, or a removable disk, is taken out of the unit that reads and writes upon it, perhaps for storage in a library, the data on the tape or disk are offline as far as the computer is concerned. For real-time processing online storage is required, generally on magnetic disk devices. The same is generally true for time sharing. In Chapter 7 we will take a more thorough look at secondary storage devices.

Communications devices

COMMUNICATIONS DEVICES link the information system together. It can be as simple as a series of wires or cables connecting the central processing unit to the various input, output, and secondary storage devices located but a few feet away. Computers of all sizes can be linked together into **NETWORKS**. A large network can include special communications processors, transmission lines, and space satellite switching systems to link widely dispersed components.

For the information system shown in Figure 2-14, communication links include transmission lines—in this case telephone lines linked to the computer through a special device called a modem—from a one-computer center to a satellite ground station, to a communications satellite, to a receiving ground station, and then to a large computer center.

Multinational firms use communications networks to tie farflung offices and factories into their information systems. At a college students, faculty, and staff use a network of terminals in dormitories, offices, and labs to tie into the computer system. In Chapter 8 we will describe the techniques and hardware used for communications.

FIGURE 2-14.
Hardware links in a communications network. A user at a computer (a), linked to the telephone system through a special device called a modem (b), can send data to a satellite ground station (c), which bounces microwave signals off a satellite (d) to another ground station (e) that could be thousands of miles away, which in turn transmits the data over phone lines to a large computer center (f).

(a)

(b)

(c)

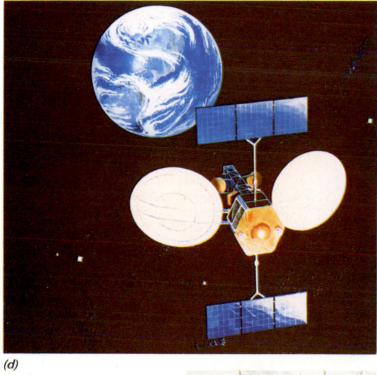

(d)

(e)

(f)

THE SYSTEM DEVELOPMENT PROCESS

All systems, including information systems, go through a cycle of birth, growth, maturity, and decline. The owners of a rapidly expanding business, for example, may find that the informal information system that served them well when they were operating out of their own home and had no employees is inadequate now that they have a staff of fifty and are approaching sales of $20 million. Information systems must adapt to the changing needs of the organizations of which they are a part. The **SYSTEM DEVELOPMENT PROCESS** provides a method for studying and changing systems.

The structured approach to the system development process, which Janis touched on in our opening example, will be explained in more detail in Chapters 9, 10, and 15. In general this approach stresses that the more careful we are in the early stages of a system's life, the easier the growth, maturity, and even the decline will be to manage.

The system development process can be broken down into six stages (summarized in Figure 2-15). These are:

- *Problem recognition*
- *Systems analysis*
- *System design*
- *System development*
- *System implementation*
- *System maintenance*

FIGURE 2-15.

Steps in the system development process.

Problem Recognition	Users and/or managers become aware of a problem.
Systems Analysis	Systems analyst or team performs preliminary investigation of problem. If warranted, systems analyst prepares detailed feasibility report and suggests alternative solution approaches.
System Design	Systems analyst or team creates designs for the new system's elements such as software and hardware and develops test plan.
System Development	Systems analyst or team creates the new system based on the design. This includes acquiring hardware and writing programs.
System Implementation	Systems analyst or team handles conversion from old system to new, training, and acceptance test.
System Maintenance	Information system staff operates, maintains, and modifies the system.

At each stage the different parts of the information system (people, rules and procedures, data, software, and hardware) must be contended with. People called systems analysts assist users through the steps of the system development process. **SYSTEMS ANALYSTS** are often responsible for studying and developing systems that meet the needs of users and clients. We will give an overview of the stages now; Chapter 15 will cover them in detail.

The system development process begins with **PROBLEM RECOGNITION**— that is, when someone realizes that something isn't working right. For instance, the managers of a clothing store chain might notice that losses from bad checks have been increasing at an alarming rate. Their problem is how to screen out bad checks without turning away—and losing sales to— credit-worthy customers.

SYSTEMS ANALYSIS is a method for examining how an existing system works in order to determine the cause of the problem that prompted the initial concern. The goal of the analysis is to suggest ways to solve the problem. All five elements of the information system must be considered. At our retail store, for example, we would need to know the rules and procedures for approving checks, what kind of data approval was based on, who wrote the checks, who approved them, and what hardware and software, if any, were used in the process.

The suggested solutions might range from relatively simple changes in the existing system to developing a completely new system. Analysis of the retail chain's bad check problem, for example, may show that checkout clerks have been too lax in applying the company's rules for check approval and all that's needed is tighter supervision and stricter enforcement of the rules. Or it might show that the company would benefit from investing in equipment and software that would allow them to tie into a nationwide credit checking service.

During the **SYSTEM DESIGN** stage general and then more detailed plans for the new system or for changes in the old system are drawn up. Again all five elements come into play. Must anybody be retrained, hired, or laid off? How will rules and procedures change? What new data must be collected? What new hardware and software are needed?

SYSTEM DEVELOPMENT refers to the actual creation of the new system designed in the preceding stage. Looking at software, for example, development means designing, writing, and testing programs for the new system. Sometimes it means purchasing prepackaged programs.

SYSTEM IMPLEMENTATION refers to the changeover from the old system to the new one. **SYSTEM MAINTENANCE** refers to the continuing process of keeping a system in good working order. Maintenance is an ongoing process. People need continual retraining. Rules and procedures must change to keep up with new legal and competitive requirements. The kinds of data collected for the system may change. Software must be adjusted to account for these changes in data and procedures. And hardware may need to be reconfigured as the ways people use the equipment change.

The systems analyst plays a critical role in any information system. More than anyone else, the systems analyst deals with the problems in an organization that most need solving—and provides the solutions, generally with a computer system.

Effective systems analysts are generalists in that they must possess strong analytical skills suitable to a wide range of problems. They must be equally comfortable talking to top management about productivity and costs, to technical specialists about hardware and software specifications, and to low-level employees about the details of their day-to-day problems.

Systems analysts work singly or in teams, depending on the size of the organization and the problem. Small businesses with no systems analyst on the staff can hire a consultant for the purpose. Larger firms employ a number of systems analysts, generally within their information system department. In terms of pecking order the bottom of the pyramid of data-processing jobs is occupied by computer operators; above them, in varying gradations, come programmers; above them the systems analysts; and above them the managers. Movement up this pyramid is not only possible but encouraged by many organizations.

A good systems analyst needs above all to be familiar with the user's needs. The systems analyst is responsible for analyzing the existing system to determine those needs, which are not always the same as what users say they are.

The systems analyst must be very skilled in handling interpersonal relationships—his or her mere presence may send some users uneager to greet computerization scurrying for cover. Other users will fear that the system will eliminate their jobs. A systems analyst has to avoid alarming people, to explain that some jobs may change but not disappear, and through interviews, questionnaires, and direct observation to find out exactly how work is presently being done.

Once the analyst knows what the problem is, the job is to design an alternative information system that solves the problem. When a plausible design for a solution is at hand, the analyst must oversee its implementation, which means guiding programmers who will produce the system (or evaluating and purchasing appropriate packaged software), arranging for the purchase and installation of necessary hardware, vigorously testing the system, training people who will use the system, writing documentation, and arranging for the task of conversion from the old system to the new. Even once the system is running well the job isn't done, as the system will require tuning, correction of errors that crop up, and modification to fit emerging needs. Like a good doctor who has performed major surgery, a systems analyst does not merely shake his or her user's hand and say goodbye—follow-up visits are in order.

All of these tasks are done in steady communication with users and management, which means that a good systems analyst must know how to write effectively and make convincing presentations, as well as how to listen to others who have different ideas, and to use these ideas when they are good. Yet despite the need for strong interpersonal and communications skills, a systems analyst needs to be able to work independently with little supervision. The systems analyst is the only person involved with the problem who is in possession of all the relevant facts and all of the knowledge necessary to solve it. Managers can judge only whether or not a proposed solution sounds as if it will work, and then whether it in fact does work; and managers will not fail to determine the latter.

Systems analysts need training in the areas of information and data processing, general management and business practices, general programming techniques, statistics and research methods, and communications skills. Detailed knowledge of the user's requirements is an absolute necessity, but is often picked up as the first phase of a systems analysis assignment.

One can become a systems analyst in either of two principal ways. The first is to advance up the operator-program-mer-analyst-manager hierarchy within the information-processing structure. The second is to cross over from the ranks of users of the information system to become a systems analyst. People who do this have the advantage of knowing user needs thoroughly; their training then consists of picking up computer skills. Corporations often follow this latter route of career development for selected employees.

DEVELOPING THE NEW INFORMATION SYSTEM

With Janis Roberts working hard as liaison, Ron Sloan—the systems analyst Freddy had hired as a consultant—was able to perform the systems analysis, system design, and system implementation for the new information system at Freddy Johnson's Travel Agency.

Ron studied people's work methods and needs, and then proceeded to create a design for the new information system. At prearranged key points Ron asked Freddy and the other managers for approval for what had been done so far and permission to continue. Eventually he and Janis developed the final specifications and testing requirements for the equipment and software. Among the alternatives offered Freddy Johnson chose a type of computer that had proved reliable in use in other agencies, rather than a brand-new machine potentially more exciting but also potentially more full of headaches.

At the insistence of both Freddy and Janis, Ron stressed proper training of the travel agents during the implementation stage. Apart from Ron, Janis was the most knowledgeable person about computers. Her branch was therefore the first to try the system.

Ron and Janis successfully installed the system at her office, ironed out the kinks, trained the other managers how to use it, and convinced doubters of the system's worth. Once Freddy gave his permission, the system was then installed at all of the other branches, too.

Let's take a look at how the system sized up after three months of operation.

People. The managers were adjusting to the new system, and were happy with the new reports and analyses that the system produced for them "automatically."

Together with Ron Sloan and Janis, the managers trained the agents in how to use the system. Some caught on rapidly and some did not. Two agents moved to different—less automated— agencies. After three months the average working speed of a travel agent had about caught up to what it was before the new system was installed.

Once the slower agents became fully accustomed to the new system, work efficiency would presumably increase.

Clients saw evidence that a new system was in use only through the new information offered them. Cynthia Brown's corporate clients responded so well to the reports on travel costs that now the same reports were being provided to individuals who did a lot of traveling.

Three people were hired to operate and manage the new equipment at the main office. Janis transferred to the main office, to head that team and continue helping Freddy and the other managers to exploit the new system. The systems analyst and Janis still met occasionally to iron out problems that accompanied the new system. With her second promotion within a year, Janis now found herself fully within the computer mainstream. To help catch up in terms of background knowledge, she was taking additional courses at Oakriver University.

Rules and Procedures. With the new system these actually stayed about the same. One major change was that managers were expected to use an electronic message system as much as possible to communicate from branch to branch. The other major change was the standardization of comments and complaints about travel arrangements. A traveler's advice file informed both travel agents and customers about the "best" places to stay and the ones to avoid. Agents were required to enter data of this sort as soon as they received and evaluated it. Tom Rivera was no longer concerned about sacrificing the tips he gave to customers because of having to use computers; on the contrary he saw his tips being passed on to more people than ever.

Some managerial information—such as statistics on how well travel agents performed—was private, and the new system protected it in a way such that only managers could see it. This eased the mind of Steve Garber, as did a computerized tracking system for blank airline tickets that proved even tighter than the manual one had been.

Data. The data for the travel agency were stored in a database, to allow fast access to clients' records by the travel agents. In addition managers alone could inspect the personnel file and other sensitive data concerning their workers. Freddy Johnson and one assistant were permitted access to data concerning the managers. The new office information system was tied into the existing airline, hotel, and automobile reservation systems.

Messages also constituted a form of data. These were sent from one manager to another between offices, or sent from clients to the agency when the offices were closed, for retrieval when the offices opened again.

Software. System software supported the companywide database system and the office-to-office message communication system. The application software design stressed programs that required as little keying as possible. ("By that I mean, when feasible, one keystroke," analyst Ron Sloan said.) Application software included programs to perform sales analysis, create reports of travel usage, perform financial planning, and handle accounting. The software supported the traveler's advice file, useful in selecting services with which an agent was not entirely familiar.

Hardware. A minicomputer was installed at the main office. To minimize equipment expenses the terminals already in use in each office were retained and modified to communicate with the minicomputer. In addition to the minicomputer several inexpensive microcomputers were purchased for the four offices, for use by the managers and people concerned with marketing and accounting.

The database was stored in secondary storage at the main office. Three printers were purchased for each office, one just to produce airline tickets, and two to produce invoices, reports, and letters. Communications hardware was installed to allow for the peripheral devices to communicate with the minicomputer, and to permit expansion should more devices be added later.

SUMMARY

- *A system is a set of interrelated elements working together toward a goal. A supersystem consists of two or more smaller systems, which are, in turn, frequently composed of smaller subsystems.*
- *Systems exist within an environment. Input enters the system from the environment, the system processes it and communicates the results to the environment as output. Feedback allows a system to regulate itself by treating the effect of its output as new input.*
- *An information system provides users with timely, accurate, understandable, and relevant information. The five components of an information system are people, rules and procedures, data, software, and hardware.*
- *People are the most important part of an information system. The people involved in an information system include the users of the system, their clients, and the information system staff.*
- *Rules and procedures fall into two categories: standard operating procedures (SOP) for normal situations, and exception procedures for unusual conditions.*
- *The data hierarchy is a classification of data from the lowest, most particular level to the most inclusive. The categories are field, record, file, and database. A field is a single data element made up of one or more characters. A record is a set of related fields, a file a set of related records, and a database a set of related files.*
- *Software, or programs, falls into two general categories: application software and system software. Application software performs the actual input, processing, and output activities for users. System software helps the application software use the computer. The most important type of system software is the operating system, which supervises and directs all of the other software components.*
- *Flowcharts are special diagrams that help communicate the steps needed to write a program. Programming is the process of writing software.*
- *Hardware consists of the physical equipment used in an information system. The central piece of hardware is the computer itself, or*

central processing unit (CPU), which, under software control, does the actual processing of data. The three parts of the CPU are the control unit, the arithmetic/logic unit, and main memory.

- *Input devices make data and software available to the CPU, output devices communicate the results of processing, and secondary, or external, storage devices record data and programs in a machine-readable form for later use. Communications devices link the hardware together. Some machines, such as tape and disk units, combine input, output, and storage functions.*

- *Common input devices include keyboards, optical scanners, and card readers. Common output devices include display screens and printers. Printers produce hard copy; display screens produce impermanent soft copy. Common storage devices include magnetic tape units and magnetic disk units. Tape units can be reel-to-reel (for large computer systems) or cassette tape devices (once popular with microcomputer systems). Disk units can be either hard disk systems or floppy disk (diskette) systems.*

- *If the computer has direct control over a storage device, it is online; otherwise it is offline.*

- *Communications hardware links the parts of an information system, making it possible to join widely dispersed elements into networks.*

- *All systems go through a system development process, which has six steps: problem recognition, systems analysis, system design, system development, system implementation, and system maintenance. Problem recognition means simply realizing that something is wrong. Systems analysis involves studying the existing system to pinpoint the problem. During system design details of the new system are worked out. System development refers to the actual creation of the new system. During system implementation the new system is started up. System maintenance refers to the process of adjusting the system to changes in the environment as well as to performing routine upkeep.*

- *Systems analysts are actively involved in systems development. Their job is to study systems, pinpoint problems, suggest solutions, and help guide the organization through design, development, and implementation.*

These are the key terms in the order in which they appear in the chapter.

Supersystem (33)	Input device (48)
Subsystem (33)	Output device (48)
Environment (33)	Keyboard (48)
Input (33)	Magnetic tape unit (50)
Processing (34)	Magnetic disk unit (50)
Output (34)	Card reader (50)
Feedback (34)	Cassette tape device (50)
Information system (35)	Optical scanner (50)
User (36)	Display terminal (50)
Client (36)	Printer (50)
Information system staff (36)	Hard copy (50)
Rules and procedures (39)	Soft copy (50)
Standard operating procedures (39)	Secondary, or external, storage device
Exception procedures (39)	(50)
Data hierarchy (39)	Hard disk (50)
Field (40)	Floppy disk or diskette (52)
Character (40)	Reel-to-reel tape (52)
Record (40)	Cassette tape (52)
File (40)	Online storage (52)
Database (41)	Offline storage (52)
Software (41)	Communications device (52)
Program (41)	Network (52)
Programming (41)	System development process (54)
Application software (41)	Systems analyst (55)
System software (41)	Problem recognition (55)
Operating system (41)	Systems analysis (55)
Hardware (46)	System design (55)
Central processing unit (CPU) (46)	System development (55)
Control unit (48)	System implementation (55)
Arithmetic/logic unit (48)	System maintenance (55)
Main memory (48)	

REVIEW QUESTIONS

OBJECTIVE QUESTIONS

TRUE/FALSE: *Put the letter T or F on the line before the question.*

_____ 1. The database is the least inclusive part of the data hierarchy.

_____ 2. Clients are the people who operate the information system.

_____ 3. Input units include keyboards and optical scanners.

_____ 4. The operating system is a type of hardware.

_____ 5. The first stage in the system development process is problem recognition.

_____ 6. The most important part of the information system is the computer.

_____ 7. The roles of user and client can be combined in such areas as the use of automatic teller machines for making deposits and withdrawals.

_____ 8. Rules and procedures should not permit exception conditions.

_____ 9. The system design phase occurs after the system development phase in the system development process.

_____ 10. Today people must adapt their behavior to the other parts of the information system.

Put the letter of the correct answer on the line before the question.

_____ 1. In an information system the person who receives a service, such as a customer buying an airline ticket from a travel agent, is a
(a) User.
(b) Client.
(c) Programmer.
(d) Systems analyst.

_____ 2. The data hierarchy in order from broadest to narrowest is:
(a) Database, field, record, file.
(b) Database, file, record, field.
(c) File, record, field, database.
(d) Field, record, file, database.

_____ 3. The rules and procedures of an organization are
(a) Not affected by the environment in which a system exists.
(b) Developed by the information system staff.
(c) Developed by the users of the information system.
(d) Developed to apply only to standard operating conditions.

_____ 4. Software or programs
(a) Should only contain instructions to handle standard operations.
(b) Consist of two major categories: application and user programs.
(c) Should be developed or purchased by the information system staff without consulting the users of the system.
(d) Consist of two major categories: application and system software.

_____ 5. Hardware
(a) Consists only of the computer
(b) Must be purchased first in any information system.
(c) Usually includes input, processing, output, secondary storage, and communications equipment.
(d) Is so complex that only information system staff should be involved in decisions to purchase equipment.

_____ 6. The system development process steps from beginning to end are:
(a) System maintenance, system design, systems analysis, problem recognition, system development, and system implementation.
(b) Systems analysis, problem recognition, system development, system design, system maintenance, and system implementation.
(c) Problem recognition, systems analysis, system design, system development, system implementation, and system maintenance.
(d) Problem recognition, systems analysis, system development, system design, system implementation, and system maintenance.

_____ 7. Users of an information system should
(a) Passively accept the system selected for them by the analyst.
(b) Take an active role in assisting the analyst in performing the system study.
(c) Attempt to block the efforts of the systems analyst in learning how the existing system behaves.
(d) Only become involved at the system implementation stage.

_____ 8. An information system
(a) Consists primarily of technology and equipment.
(b) Is concerned primarily with processing.
(c) Guarantees users will make correct decisions in the future.
(d) Consists of five elements—people, rules and procedures, data, software, and hardware.

_____ 9. Which of the following allows a system to regulate itself?
(a) Input.
(b) Environment.
(c) Process.
(d) Feedback.

FILL IN THE BLANK: *Write the correct word or words in the blank to complete the sentence.*

1. Rules and procedures must account for both _____ and _____ conditions.
2. The people associated with creating and then operating the information system are called the _____.
3. The _____ is used to link application programs to the hardware used in the information system.
4. _____ storage is directly accessible to the computer.
5. The three parts of the CPU are the _____, _____, and _____ units.
6. The smallest or narrowest usable element of the data hierarchy is the _____.
7. The _____ is often responsible for studying and developing systems that meet the needs of users and clients.
8. Secondary storage not directly accessible to the computer is called _____.
9. The five components of an information system are _____, _____, _____, _____, and _____.
10. From the perspective of this chapter the most important component consists of _____.

SHORT ANSWER QUESTIONS

When answering these questions think of concrete examples to illustrate your points.

1. Describe the five elements of an information system.
2. Describe the interrelationship between the users of an information system and their clients.
3. Which information system staff members would primarily work with the data element of the information system?
4. Refering to Figure 2-5: Why would field 6 be included for the flight data?
5. What are the functions of system software?
6. What are some examples of application software that may be used by an airline?
7. For a microcomputer-based information system what are the equipment requirements?
8. Why are communication units useful in an information system?
9. What is another name for the central processing unit?
10. What is the difference between "hard copy" and "soft copy" output?
11. What is the difference between online and offline external storage?
12. What input hardware would Janis Roberts use in her role as office manager?
13. What are the steps of the system development process?
14. What occurs in system design?

ESSAY QUESTIONS

1. Consider how information systems might be used in your area of training or at your job.
2. Do you think government agencies should share information systems and databases with each other? Take a position pro or con.
3. It has often been stated that many purchasers of computers buy these machines without really knowing what to do with them. Comment on this statement.
4. How would this chapter help a decision maker, or you in your own job?

CHAPTER 3

INFORMATION SYSTEMS IN THE WORKPLACE: COMPUTERS IN BUSINESS

■ SALES WITH A DIFFERENCE
INFORMATION SYSTEMS IN BUSINESS
Business functions at the office / Office systems /
CAREER BOX: The Office Manager
Toward the virtual office / Working at home
■ CASE IN POINT: At J.C. Penney, It's Home Sweet Home Work
FROM RAW MATERIALS TO THE FINAL USER
Design and manufacturing / Agriculture / Resource
extraction / Transportation / Communications / Wholesaling and
warehousing / Retailing / Finance, insurance, and real estate
■ WRAP-UP: The Orders Must Go Out

After studying this chapter you should understand the following:
■ Those functions common to any business.
■ How preindustrial, industrial, and information-age offices are
organized.
■ Trends for the future in offices.
■ The pervasiveness of information-system use beyond office and
traditional business functions.

Penny Helmsley put down the phone. That had been a good sale. She made a last few notes on her pad. Penny really liked her sales job at Paul's House of Electronic Wonders. With locations in four cities in North America, and customers across the world, Paul's House of Electronic Wonders faced many opportunities and challenges. The electronics market was changing rapidly and unpredictably, and was rife with competition. Paul's distributed electronic parts to retailers, other wholesalers, and manufacturers.

Penny enjoyed the sales game immensely. As in the call just completed she had learned how to negotiate over the phone in terms of prices and delivery dates, and to make sure that the staff at Paul's gave her clients the speedy and attentive service they demanded. One thing she had learned was to follow up on every sale, making sure the customer was satisfied with the service and the product. This paid off in repeat sales and larger reorders.

Penny turned to her terminal and invoked the sales analysis software package she used. From the database the program displayed some information about the customer she had just sold to. This customer accepted gifts—that was what she wanted to find out. Some companies did not allow their buyers to accept gifts, no matter how small, while with other companies gift giving and receiving was common. Penny switched off the terminal and got out her catalog, as a reminder to send an appropriate gift later in the day.

The information system at Paul's was quite handy for Penny. She used it to maintain the data just mentioned, and also to keep track of who her sales rivals were and how best to counter their tactics. In fact there were so many uses for the information system that Penny almost forgot that she used it to place orders, too. She switched the terminal back on, and keyed in the complete order for the sale she had just made. Penny spent a minute proofreading all of the data on the screen, and then transmitted the order.

"Does everything happen that fast around here?" Bonnie Meyer asked from over Penny's shoulder. Bonnie was a new member of the sales staff.

"Well it usually starts that way," Penny said. "Placing the order from our end is fast. But now the accounting department gets it and has to approve credit and create a bill. And then shipping gets the data too, and has to act on them."

"That's our first training area, right?" Gene Tomaselli asked. Gene was the other trainee Penny was responsible for instructing. Their training program called for them to spend brief periods in accounting, marketing, finance, and warehouse operations. "Yes, the shipping department's your next stop," Penny said. "And to answer your original question, Bonnie, people do work hard here, but an order has to go through a lot of steps. For instance, take shipping. If the

INFORMATION SYSTEMS IN BUSINESS

BUSINESS FUNCTIONS AT THE OFFICE

Our opening example illustrates several important points about the use of information systems in offices. Stated briefly:

- *People.* The users of an information system depend upon it to help them perform their jobs properly. Penny Helmsley works with an information system to track her sales prospects.
- *Rules and procedures.* The rules of an organization help determine the nature of its information system. The accounting department's rules at Paul's House of Electronic Wonders are used to evaluate the credit-worthiness of a client.
- *Data.* Even after orders have been shipped the data gathered by Penny and others should be retained and converted into useful information. The higher management people at Paul's, in particular the owner Philip Paul, Jr., require information based on the sales data.
- *Software.* The programs at Paul's serve to process the data gathered, given the rules of the organization. It is possible that a credit sale negotiated by Penny would be disallowed, because the procedures within the credit-approval software package found the client to be a poor risk.
- *Hardware.* The physical equipment used by Penny allows her to transmit the order details electronically from one part of the office to another. The computer and its peripherals process and print the sales order.

All five information system elements must fit together well, and work in concert, for a business to gain full benefit from its information system.

Let's turn now to look at the main applications that an organization's information system can handle. Our example with Penny Helmsley touched on some but not all of them. No matter how big or small, any business deals in some way with the areas of accounting, marketing, finance, and personnel. Computer-based information systems can assist in carrying out each of these functions (Figure 3-1). Let's briefly review the ways computers can help.

Accounting

ACCOUNTING involves maintaining organized business and financial records. These records are used to support a variety of business-related functions. When a business computerizes its information system, accounting is one of the first areas to be automated. The accounting operations listed in Figure 3-1 typically occupy about 30 percent of the computer's time in a business information system.

ACCOUNTS RECEIVABLE records keep track of money that is owed to a company. An accounts receivable report produced by the information

FIGURE 3-1.

The most important information system business applications.

Application	Brief Description
Accounting	Maintain financial records
Accounts Receivable	Money owed the company
Accounts Payable	Money the company owes
General Ledger	Summary of business accounts used to prepare balance sheets and income statements
Billing	Prepares statements for customers (part of accounts receivable)
Inventory	Manages items in stock either finished or unfinished
Payroll	Manages payroll records and issues paychecks
Marketing	Moving goods and services from producers to consumers
Order Processing	Order entry, processing, status
Sales Analysis	Sales call analysis, market share analysis
Finance	Use and management of funds
Financial Analysis	Long- and short-term financial planning and budgeting
Credit Analysis	Client credit status
Personnel	Management of human resources
Hiring	Testing new personnel
Training	Training and evaluating personnel
Management	Handling personnel records and creating reports

system at Paul's House of Electronic Wonders is given in Figure 3-2. It lists the amounts that the business is owed by various customers for goods purchased.

ACCOUNTS PAYABLE records show money that a company owes others. When a wholesaler purchases goods from a manufacturer, the wholesaler treats money owed on the purchase as an accounts payable item until it pays the bill. An accounts payable report for Paul's House of Electronic Wonders is shown in Figure 3-3.

The GENERAL LEDGER contains a summary of all of the accounts of a business. It is used in preparing (1) balance sheets, statements of the financial position of a business at a particular time; and (2) income statements, summaries of the financial position of a business over a period of time. Paul's has the general ledger on its information system as well; Figure 3-4 shows an income statement.

FIGURE 3-2.
Accounts receivable report showing the aging of various accounts.

Paul's House of Electronic Wonders

Accounts Receivable Report

September 1, 1986

Customer Number	Customer Name	Current Balance	Balance Over 60 Days Past Due	Balance Over 90 Days Past Due	Total Balance
19244	Bits and Bytes	$2535.34	$35.42	$0.00	$2570.76
24411	World of Computers	355.22	24.53	0.00	379.75
26331	Terminal Connection	3441.35	244.34	424.32	4110.01
29353	Consolidated Storage	1100.00	600.00	452.00	2152.00

FIGURE 3-3.
Accounts payable report.

Paul's House of Electronic Wonders

Accounts Payable Report

October 15, 1986

Vendor Number	Vendor Name	Current Balance	Discount Balance	Discount Terms	Nondiscount Balance	Date Due
13343	Quick Chips	$13457.15	$9033.81	2/10	$4423.34	10-20-86
25241	Octopus Cable	13500.00	13500.00	1.5/10	0.00	11-10-86
24532	Global Elec	4547.55	2535.56	2/10	2011.99	11-15-86
27465	Big Sky Comp	35660.00	34500.00	2/10	1160.00	10-30-86

BILLING, another accounting function, involves the preparation of statements of money owed by customers. Technically billing is part of the accounts receivable process. **INVENTORY MANAGEMENT SYSTEMS** are used to minimize the total cost of ordering and stocking various items sold or used by a company. We will discuss them more later in the chapter. **PAYROLL** systems—computerized by virtually any business of at least medium size—

FIGURE 3-4.
Income statement.

```
          Paul's House of Electronic Wonders Corporation
                 Consolidated Statement of Earnings
                    Year Ended December 31, 1986

                                              Current Earnings
                                              (in thousands of
                                                  dollars)

Gross Sales                                          $41,700

Returns and Discounts             $ 2,140

Net Sales                                             39,560

Cost of Goods Sold                 29,276

Gross Profit                                          10,284

Selling and Administrative          6,172
  Expenses

Operating Income                                       4,112

Other Income                                             340

Other Expenses                        428

Earnings Before Income Taxes                           4,024

Income Taxes                        2,052

Net Income                                           $ 1,972
```

keep track of employee wages, deductions, and benefits, and issue pay-checks.

Marketing

The second major application for a business information system is marketing. **MARKETING** refers to the movement of goods and services from producers to consumers. To accomplish this transfer the consumer must be made aware of the product through promotion. Additionally the product's price and place of distribution must be acceptable to the consumer. Penny Helmsley, through her sales efforts, promotes the product, offers it for a competitive price, and sets the distribution effort in motion.

Two areas where computer information systems are used in marketing are order processing and sales analysis. **ORDER PROCESSING** entails entering orders, processing these orders, and monitoring the status of the orders. **MARKET ANALYSIS** focuses on such matters as sales strategies, market share of competitors, and sales-call strategies.

Finance

FINANCE refers to the acquisition and use of funds. Computerized information systems offer the thoroughness and speed to monitor the whereabouts and use of funds more efficiently than manual systems. **FINANCIAL ANALYSIS** involves examining and attempting to predict the best way to obtain funds for long- and short-term corporate financial needs. Two aspects of financial analysis are corporate planning and budgeting. Computerized information systems, with their rapid ability to manipulate and summarize great quantities of data, give corporate planners the flexibility to explore the financial

FIGURE 3-5.
Corporate budget report.

Estimated Income Statement for
Paul's House of Electronic Wonders Corporation
Fiscal Year 1989

	Estimated Earnings (in thousands of dollars)	
Gross Sales		$66,000
Returns and Discounts	$ 3,400	
Net Sales		62,600
Cost of Goods Sold	47,600	
Gross Profit		15,000
Selling and Administrative Expenses	9,000	
Operating Income		6,000
Other Income		400
Other Expenses	520	
Earnings Before Income Taxes		5,880
Income Taxes	2,660	
Net Income		$ 3,220

implications of alternate strategies. Figure 3-5 shows an example of a corporate budget report.

CREDIT ANALYSIS refers to methods for determining the credit status of clients. Advancing credit is a classic method of stimulating sales, although at the risk that some clients may default. Information systems are used extensively today to analyze speedily how great the risk is for particular customers.

Personnel

PERSONNEL systems are concerned with managing employees. Information systems can aid in finding individuals to fill specific jobs, such as by searching the records of present personnel to locate individuals with the requisite skills. Reports concerning compensation, affirmative action, and security clearances can be created from data stored in the information system database.

OFFICE SYSTEMS The functions discussed above, whether performed with a computerized information system or by hand, are performed in an office. The office is the place where many of you will work. Offices are places where people meet and perform transactions, exchange money, provide services, and plan and manage business operations as well as engage in social activity. Offices may be small, such as a one- or two-person law or medical office; medium-sized, like a bank branch or the regional office of a wholesaler; or large, such as the headquarters of a major manufacturer, bank, or government agency.

The office of the present and future—the information-age office—bristles with computerized equipment: word processing systems, electronic mail/message systems, intelligent copiers, facilities for teleconferencing, and more. The core of this or any office remains people, and the office manager who is effective in managing people and in coordinating high-tech equipment is a new breed.

Computers are having ever more impact in office automation. The technologically proficient office manager can therefore be expected to have rich and varied career opportunities.

Office managers come at different levels. The individual on top, the administrative office manager, is responsible for seeing that offices meet the needs of the organization. This means planning and controlling the people, financial resources, materials, and relevant automated systems. The systems include word processing facilities, records management, telecommunications, and teleconferencing. Sometimes the administrative office manager is charged with acquiring and disseminating information in the broadest sense, including not only the systems just mentioned but the tranditional computer functions of systems analysis, programming, and computer operations.

At the next lower level, the middle-level office manager assists top management in planning policy, and plays a more active role in carrying it out. The supervisory-level office manager, the lowest in the hierarchy, carries out plans that middle management develops, and typically supervises a particular area, such as word processing, control of interoffice communications, or purchase of materials. More managers are required at the supervisory level than at the middle level, and the fewest openings exist at the top.

How do you become an office manager? As a fairly new career, in an area undergoing fast-paced change, there is no sure route. The ability to interact with people effectively is one prerequisite. A business administration background wouldn't hurt. Above all, though, today's office manager must demonstrate technical comprehension of automated equipment. Knowledge of information systems figures heavily, and hands-on experience in word processing, telecommunications, or other relevant areas, in today's job market, can separate you from the pack.

The ways in which offices go about doing their work have changed considerably over the years. Vincent E. Giuliano (in "The Mechanization of Office Work," *Scientific American*, Sept. 1982) suggests that there are three different types of office organization:

- *Preindustrial*
- *Industrial*
- *Information age*

As their names imply these types have a historical dimension: preindustrial offices appeared before industrial offices, which appeared before information-age offices. They are not mutually exclusive, however—a company today may have any one or more of the three types of office organization. Let's take a look at each, starting with the earliest.

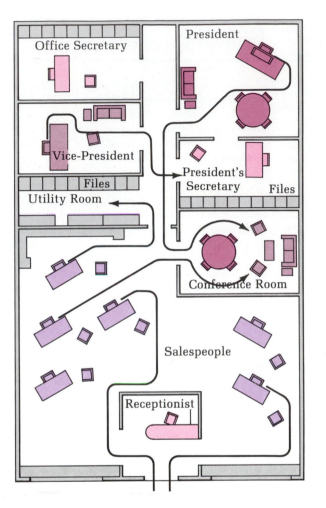

Figure 3-6 shows the organization of a typical preindustrial office, in this case a real estate office. As the arrows show, the people who work in the office can move about as need be to assist clients, search files, and gather for meetings. This type of office was (and is) geared to providing personalized service to the customer or client. Many offices today, such as those of some physicians, attorneys, and corporate executives (as well as real estate brokers), still follow the preindustrial pattern, which encourages a more individual working style and offers greater human interaction than the other types of office.

Industrial-style offices marked a step forward, at least in terms of efficiency, from the preindustrial office. Industrial-style offices make use of assembly-line methods to organize tasks (Figure 3-7). The work is broken down into small, repetitive steps, performed at a series of work stations. A batch of paperwork is received from the previous desk or work station, processed as required, and then passed on to the next station. The business functions that are most easily placed into this format are accounting and sales processing. This method of moving paperwork was ideal for early batch-oriented computer systems. Many large businesses still work this way.

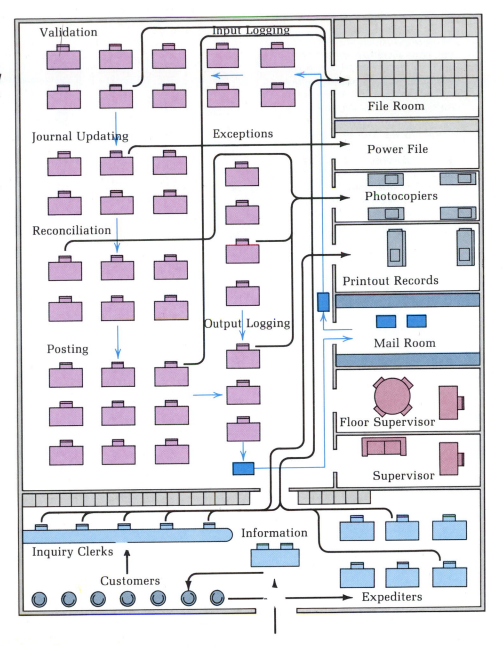

Historically such rigid, batch-oriented systems broke down for at least two reasons. First, new techniques such as word processing were introduced, and terminals and small computers started to appear right in the office, linked to larger computers via teleprocessing. These developments reduced the need for large, centralized offices. Second, in response to worker discontent caused by the impersonal environment of the assembly-line office, management permitted offices to move away from the factory-like approach.

What followed was the information-age office, which, as Figure 3-8 suggests, more closely resembles the organization of the preindustrial office

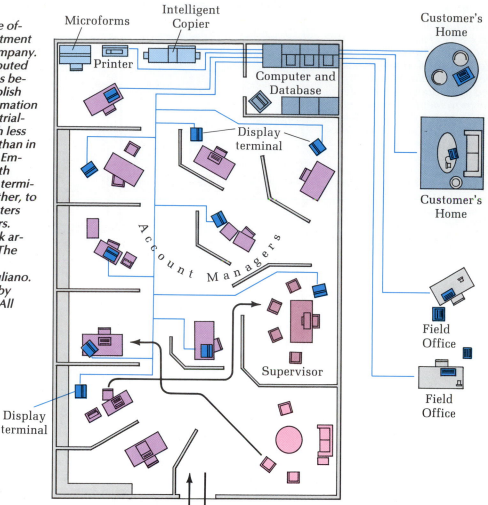

FIGURE 3-8.
The information-age style office: again a claims-adjustment office of an insurance company. With the spread of distributed information systems it has become possible to accomplish the same volume of information processing as in an industrial-style office, but in a much less rigidly organized setting than in an industrial-style office. Employees work at desks with computer terminals. The terminals are linked to each other, to field offices, and to adjusters making calls on customers. Physical movement (black arrow) is reduced. (From "The Mechanization of Office Work," by Vincent E. Giuliano. Copyright © Sept. 1982 by Scientific American, Inc. All rights reserved.)

Microforms

Intelligent Copier

Customer's Home

Printer

Computer and Database

Display terminal

Customer's Home

Account Managers

Supervisor

Field Office

Display terminal

Field Office

than the industrial office. The power of computerized information systems makes it possible to handle the same volume of information as in an industrial office, but in a much less rigid environment.

The information-age office utilizes computerized information systems wherever possible, and takes advantage of new technologies. Three of these new technologies are electronic mail/message systems, word processing systems, and teleconferencing systems.

ELECTRONIC MAIL/MESSAGE SYSTEMS (EMMS) allow people to send memos, messages, facsimiles or illustrations and photographs, and other materials electronically. Also called electronic mail, messages may be routed locally within an office, between branch locations, or across the world through satellite-based telecommunications.

WORD PROCESSING SYSTEMS allow people to compose, edit, and store text using a computer. The text can be recalled, modified, printed, or transmitted electronically at a later date. Input or keying speeds on machines that perform word processing are faster than with many electric typewriters, corrections are simpler to make, and blocks of text can be moved around with ease for editing.

TELECONFERENCING uses a computer network to link people who are remote from each other in a meeting. Participants can talk to one another and can often see one another as well. Teleconferencing can save a lot of time and travel costs.

What effect the new technologies will have on the people who work in information-age offices is not yet clear. The challenge remains to make the work in the information age interesting and rewarding. It is true already that people who understand how to use the new systems are at an advantage. This has, however, always been true of office work. Clerks may find themselves with a greater number of responsibilities than in the past. The trend toward automation may continue to the point that offices become "paperless," with all records and documents created, stored, and retrieved electronically.

TOWARD THE VIRTUAL OFFICE

Today it is possible to take your office anywhere (Figure 3-9). Portable personal computers can be linked up to regular or mobile telephone communications systems. In this way you can transmit vital data to your central office, and receive responses, without actually being there. You can truly have a "virtual" office, one that can follow you anywhere, unlike a regular "physical" office, which, of course, can't.

Electronic mail/message systems can reach you almost anywhere. A sales representative can use such a system to call up records on a client while on route to the sales call. At the sales call the representative can use the system to transmit questions and receive responses to customer inquiries, and to send in sales orders and other messages. These messages can go to a variety of destinations at the salesperson's office. One message might be sent to the word processing center, requesting that a letter of thanks be sent to the customer for placing an order with the company.

FIGURE 3-9.
You can take your office anywhere.

Teleconferencing can also be arranged between a customer and the home office to help answer questions. In such ways an information system can help increase sales-call productivity. Similar applications abound in other fields where quick responses are crucial to completing transactions. In the area of health care such systems can be utilized to transmit diagnostic results to specialists for quick response to medical difficulties.

WORKING AT HOME

A new "cottage industry"

With distributed information systems and the availability of personal computers it is possible to perform many office functions at home (see Figure 3-10). Working for a distant employer at a home terminal or computer has come to be known as **TELECOMMUTING**. A microcomputer or terminal attached to a telephone line can communicate with the office computer. Electronic mail/message systems can be used to communicate between the home work station and the office. Most tasks can be done at home—writing memos, analyzing data, preparing reports, updating database information, and other operations—and the results or data can be transmitted to co-workers or to other computers. Teleconferencing even makes it possible to "attend" meetings without leaving the house. Such in-home systems allow people greater flexibility over their personal schedules and, potentially, the opportunity to work with greater concentration than many office environments permit. From the employer's point of view, telecommuting can also offer a welcome flexibility (see Case in Point box).

But having your work station at home is not without its problems. In an office people meet each other and establish social contacts; working at home precludes these contacts. Some people get a high-tech version of cabin fever. Another problem is setting some boundaries around the periods that one works—after all the office is right there nights and weekends, too. Nonprofessionals working at home may have problems confronting supervi-

FIGURE 3-10.
Information systems for your in-home office. The in-home work station has certain advantages, such as a short commute to work and flexibility over how you decorate your office.

When Carl Kirkpatrick wakes to another snowy Milwaukee day, he doesn't worry about having enough sales operators to take catalog orders at his J.C. Penney Telephone Sales Center. He knows his operators won't have any trouble getting to work, because they're already there: at home, telecommuting on computers linked to those at the Center.

Kirkpatrick, manager of staff development at Penney's Milwaukee Regional Center, needed a fast, efficient way to get enough operators to handle unexpected peak periods of incoming calls each day. The problem was that there was no way to predict when all these peaks would occur and Kirkpatrick needed immediate access to operators. Sales could be lost if customers called and were not able to reach an operator. Concurrently Penney was considering building another telephone sales center to create another geographic center. To solve Kirkpatrick's problem and possibly save on construction costs, Penney decided to test the idea of using sales operators at home.

Before the telecommuting program was implemented two years ago, it was inconvenient and chancy for Kirkpatrick to find a way to meet high-volume demand. He would call an unscheduled operator at her home and ask her to come into the Center. If that operator was unable to work, many operators might have to be called until Kirkpatrick found a willing one. In inclement weather—hardly uncommon in Milwaukee—the time lag would be even greater. By the time the operator arrived the peak period might have passed with calls lost, and a slow period begun, making the operator's presence unnecessary. Penney would have to pay for the operator's time. Telecommuting seemed to fit Kirkpatrick's and his operators' needs for a smoother, faster way to answer phones.

Now Kirkpatrick just calls a telecommuter at home and asks her to come online even if she's not scheduled. Says Kirkpatrick: "With telecommuting I'm able to react more quickly to changes in incoming calls. I use telecommuters as a buffer for unexpected peaks. The telecommuter team is used as a crisis team. I request peak-load assistance and reaction time has been shortened."

The first step in implementing the program was to conduct a survey among sales operators to learn if anyone was interested. Of the 165 operators polled 120 replied that they would like to telecommute. From this pool of volunteers Kirkpatrick chose seven women who had been at the Center for at least one year.

Kirkpatrick says that experience has shown that to be effective, telecommuters must be "self-starters, work well without supervision, have strong customer awareness and selling capabilities, have good communication skills and problem-solving capabilities, be of pleasant disposition, and remain cool under pressure." Finally, he adds, they must be able to respond to a variety of scheduling requests. . . .

The physical removal of the operator does not change her status as an employee, and she is entitled to the same considerations and rights as those in the Center. "The telecommuter is still considered to be a part-time employee of the Center, paid the same rate, and given the same benefits with the same promotional opportunities," reports Kirkpatrick. . . .

Kirkpatrick has the security of knowing there is a group of qualified operators that he can depend upon. As he sees it, "Penney has insured a stable and reliable workforce and at the same time made a part-time position more appealing."

sors with questions concerning working conditions and other economic questions. Where is your bargaining position when you and your colleagues are scattered far from the office and you want to negotiate better wages?

For some the new type of cottage industry may mean a return to the era of preindustrial social relationships. Such areas of concern have been little explored, although they may have profound effects upon our society.

FROM RAW MATERIALS TO THE FINAL USER

The office functions summarized earlier are used in every industry. But the use of information systems does not stop when you move out of the office. **PRODUCTION** and **OPERATIONS MANAGEMENT** refers to the process of organizing people and machinery for converting resources into finished products and services. Let's explore how information systems are used in various fields. Some of these production and operation applications may surprise you. Many people are not aware of how extensively computers are used today.

DESIGN AND MANUFACTURING

Computer information systems are intimately involved in the design, testing, and manufacture of many products. When designers have ideas for new or improved products, they can use **COMPUTER-AIDED DESIGN (CAD)** systems to create detailed designs in a fraction of the time it would take with conventional methods. By reducing the time it takes to produce blueprints, write parts specification lists, and build models of the product, CAD systems allow designers time for greater creativity.

A CAD system is shown in Figure 3-11. The designer works at a terminal and draws on a special pad that transfers the information in the drawing to the computer, which simultaneously displays the plans on the computer terminal. Some systems allow the designer to "draw" directly on the display screen with a tool called a light-pen. When the design is complete, it can be stored for later use, such as to combine with other components or to guide the manufacturing process. In addition graphical output devices can create permanent copies of the design for visual reference.

FIGURE 3-11.
Computer-aided design (CAD) system. The designer can create an initial design, modify it, look at it from different perspectives, and store it for later retrieval for production.

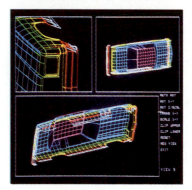

Once a component or a product has been designed, it can be tested using computer simulation. **COMPUTER SIMULATION** programs model real-world events and attempt to predict the possible consequences of those events. Airplane pilots, for example, train to fly on computer-directed simulators that mimic the behavior of airplanes without ever leaving the ground. In the same way simulation programs can test the design of a product for weaknesses before a prototype is even built.

If the decision is made to start manufacturing a product, computers can help here, too. Using simulation programs engineers and managers can determine the optimal way to design the production process or assembly line to minimize production costs. Once the line is designed and set up, **COMPUTER-AIDED MANUFACTURING (CAM)** can use a computer to direct the actual production or assembly process. For example, the machine tools—such as grinders, lathes, and drill presses—used to produce the product can be programmed with exact specifications, such as how deep to drill a hole. Figure 3-12 shows a CAM system in operation.

Robots perform various production tasks today, ranging from welding or painting to final assembly. Quality-control systems use computerized methods to detect errors. The trend in manufacturing is toward greater use of computers, information systems, and robots to reduce costs further. Some

FIGURE 3-12.
The computer-aided manufacturing (CAM) process—building an automobile. (a) The overall view of the assembly line. (b) Computer-directed machine tools. (c) Robots painting automobiles. (d) Final assembly.

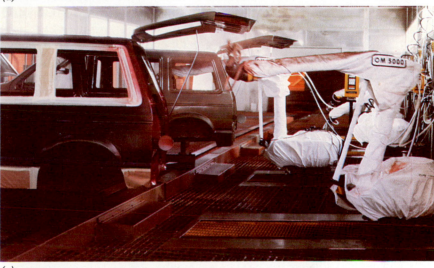

(a)

(b)

(c)

(d)

factories in Europe, Japan, and North America have introduced the **FLEXIBLE MANUFACTURING SYSTEM (FMS)** approach, which emphasizes the use of computer-directed machinery throughout the production process. With FMS robots are not only used to produce and assemble the product, but to move it from one work station to the next along the assembly line.

AGRICULTURE

Agriculture is one of the largest industries in the United States, Canada, and other countries, and is often a major source of export dollars. Information systems are available to the farmer of today to help determine the best way to manage the farm (see Figure 3-13). Computer programs can determine the right feed mix to give animals from chickens to cows. Microprocessors attached to sensing devices can determine how to adjust the level of fertilizer to be placed in the soil, and how deep the plow should cut into the earth.

Applications of computer technology are not limited to such futuristic arrangements or to large corporate farms. Even organic gardening and counterculture magazines carry advertisements showing back-to-nature enthusiasts how to use computers on the family homestead. Computer programs exist to help design a garden and select the best organic methods for pest control.

University and private researchers use information systems to analyze and develop new strains of plants and animals. Databases contain records about the genetic characteristics of thousands of plant and animal species and varieties.

Farmers have always been faced with questions about what to plant, when to plant, and when to harvest. Today's technologies, combined with information systems managed by both universities and private companies, assist farmers in making the best decisions in this age-old guessing game.

FIGURE 3-13.
Information systems in agriculture. A computer and a laser scanner built into a harvester select tomatoes for canning.

FIGURE 3-14.
A computer-enhanced satellite photograph of an oncoming storm.

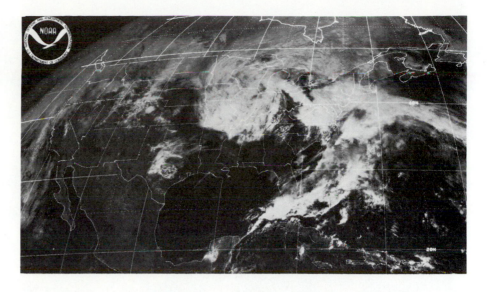

Soil conditions can be measured using probes monitored by microcomputers. Weather forecasts based on computer predictions (Figure 3-14) can help farmers determine when to plant, water, fertilize, and harvest. To give weather forecasters a better picture of the weather conditions, satellite photographs or radar images can be made clearer using computers. Computer-enhanced imagery visually emphasizes the contrasts between different parts of a picture. For example, high wind speeds can be assigned very dark colors; wind blowing in one direction can be displayed as shades of blue, in another direction as red, and so forth. Computers do not produce the original image, but they can make it far more readily intelligible.

By receiving up-to-the-minute information a farmer can determine the optimal time to sell animals, grain, and produce to wholesalers, slaughterhouses, and other merchants. Both before and after farmers deliver their goods to market, the use of information systems continues, as brokers and traders seek to buy and sell the commodities in the hopes of making a profit.

RESOURCE EXTRACTION

Forestry

Information systems aid foresters in selecting and breeding better trees for timber production. Researchers can analyze different species of trees in order to determine the best types for various soil, water, and temperature conditions. Information systems help in this job by keeping tabs on large amounts of data and automating many time-consuming calculations.

When trees are mature enough to cut selecting the right area to log depends in part on the environmental impact of logging. Computer simulation programs can draw upon information in databases to give a picture of the environmental effects logging may have on soil erosion, water purity, wildlife, and the esthetic appearance of the landscape.

Lumber companies can use computers to determine competitive bidding strategies for stands of timber. Even at the sawmill, computers are no stranger: they can be used to align the logs to minimize waste and maximize the usable timber obtained from the logs.

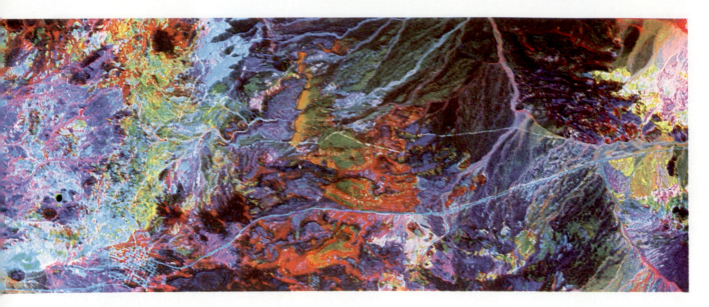

FIGURE 3-15.
Information systems in mining. Computers can interpret satellite images to identify resources and give an idea of their value.

Mining

Information systems help locate and extract mineral resources (Figure 3-15). Computers can interpret satellite images to identify resources and give an idea of their value. Computers can also be used to help evaluate the best method for mining the minerals, testing the quality of the ore, monitoring antipollution controls, and other functions. Computer-directed robot mining machines can detect coal seams and then extract the coal at the rate of almost 500 tons per day.

Energy resources

Information systems are used in all phases of energy resource management: exploration, extraction, and production. Petroleum exploration teams use computer-based information systems to analyze potential oil- or gas-bearing rock formations deep below the surface. Once wells are drilled the oil and gas quality is evaluated for future large-scale production. Another application of computer technology includes the use of submersible robots to repair offshore undersea oil drilling rigs or sites. The entire process of transporting, refining, and distributing oil and gas products is monitored by computer-based information systems.

Electrical utilities depend heavily on information systems (Figure 3-16). Electric companies use information systems to determine how much power should be generated to meet the demands of consumers. Almost all generating facilities use computers to monitor energy consumption and power output, as well as to design and maintain the plants themselves. Large power plants that burn conventional fuel are not the only users of such systems; wind farms, solar energy stations, geothermal installations, and hydroelectric projects also depend upon them. National power grids are protected from equipment failure by computers that will shut down or restructure portions of the electrical grid in order to protect the expensive power-generating equipment from possible damage and consumers from a resulting blackout.

FIGURE 3-16.

Information systems in electric power generation applications. (a) The control room of a large conventional power plant. (b) A wind farm in California. (c) (two photos) A solar energy system controlled by computers. (d) A computer-generated picture of a power grid.

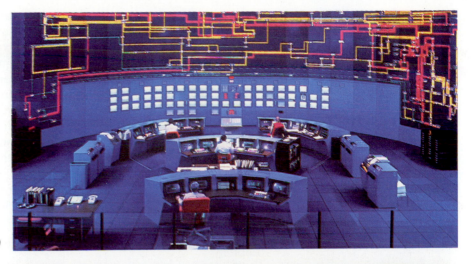

(a)

(b)

(c$_i$)

(c$_{ii}$)

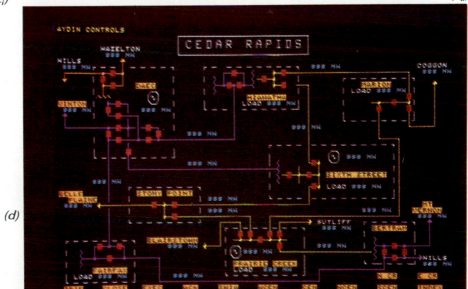

(d)

TRANSPORTATION

Railroads rely on computerized switching facilities to guarantee safe uncoupling and redirecting of railcars bound for various destinations (Figure 3-17). For most railroads trains on mainline tracks rely upon signals and switches set under the direction of traffic-management programs. Many railroad companies have attempted to use information systems to monitor operations by giving each railroad car a unique machine-readable identification code. At a switching yard this code is read by an optical scanner (similar to the ones found in supermarkets today), which provides data concerning the contents of the car, its destination, and other factors. Some railroads have abandoned this method, however, because the scanners were unable to read the codes reliably.

Some commuter railroads and rapid transit lines also use information systems. The Bay Area Rapid Transit District (BART) in the San Francisco region uses computers to run the trains; the onboard personnel only announce the stations, and do not touch the controls unless there is a problem.

Trucking companies use data-based information systems to determine schedules for drivers, the times for vehicle maintenance, and cargo shipping requirements. Even the cargo in a truck can be arranged so that the first items in are the last to be delivered, using load-scheduling software programs available to modern trucking companies. Once on route the truck or any other vehicle will encounter computerized traffic-light systems. Dispatchers of fleet vehicles, such as buses and taxis in large cities, often have access to computer-supplied information to aid them in their jobs.

At sea ships use signals from satellites to onboard navigational computers to determine their positions (see Figure 3-18). In areas of heavy shipping traffic the United States Coast Guard staffs special radar stations that use computer-enhanced images to aid in locating and directing ship traffic. Onboard computers also assist in monitoring the engines, propeller, fire-protection devices, and other equipment. Oceangoing freight is often shipped in containers the size of truck trailers. The movements and contents of each container can be tracked through use of an information system database.

FIGURE 3-17.

Information systems working on the railroad. (a) A computerized railroad switching yard. (b) The computer center for the Washington, D.C., subway system.

(a)

(b)

FIGURE 3-18.
Information systems afloat. (a) The Coast Guard Houston/Galveston vessel traffic service. (b) The monitor screen shows the location of shipping channels. (c) A container-handling facility run by the Port Authority of New York.

(a)

(b)

(c)

Figure 3-19.

Information systems for safe air travel. (a) Ground-based air traffic control systems depend heavily upon computers to maintain up-to-the-second track of airplanes in the air. (b) Onboard computers can literally fly the modern aircraft—in this case the space shuttle—to its destination.

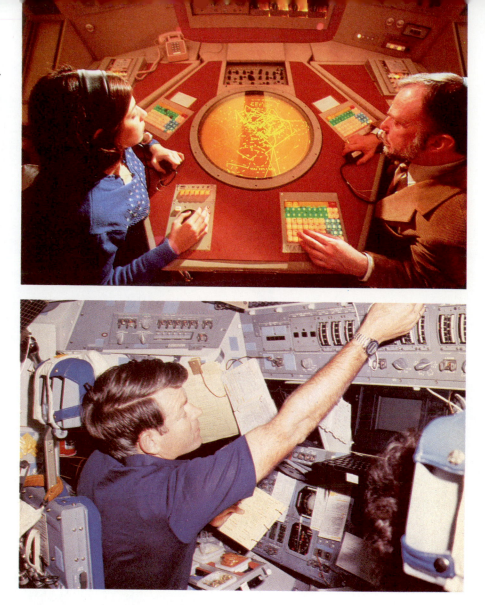

The airline industry was one of the earliest and remains one of the heaviest users of information systems (Figure 3-19). Airlines use these systems to schedule aircraft, flight crews, and aircraft maintenance, and to track passenger reservations and air freight packages. Air traffic control systems could not exist without computer-based information systems to monitor aircraft on the ground and in the air. Onboard computer systems on commercial aircraft, in concert with airport-based systems, can even land planes with minimal pilot assistance. These onboard computers can steer to a predirected course, operate the flight controls, monitor the engines, and perform other navigational functions. Weather reports to pilots have become more useful through the use of computer-enhanced radar imaging of storms, clear air turbulence, ground fog, unusual wind conditions, and other situations.

COMMUNICATIONS

The communications systems that we have come to expect today would be impossible to operate without the support of information systems. The switching of telephones, both local and long distance, is made possible by specialized computers used to select the proper transmission line. Many of the parts of our information systems depend upon fast communication of data within and between offices, factories, and other places of business. Chapter 8 will explore computers and communications in more depth.

WHOLESALING AND WAREHOUSING

Information systems allow wholesalers more precise means of controlling their levels of inventory. A wholesaler such as Paul's House of Electronic Wonders can deal directly with a manufacturer or with other wholesalers to obtain supplies for clients. Many wholesalers are tied together through modern telecommunications networks. For example, auto parts recyclers (formerly called junkyards) use communications links to help one another trace hard-to-find parts.

Many warehouses have undergone considerable change from the past. In a modern warehouse cargo rolls into the warehouse on computer-controlled pallets or platforms for holding cargo (see Figure 3-20). An optical scanner can read the product code on cartons. An inventory program assigns cartons to specific locations, which the system will remember. Cartons and containers do not have to be stored alphabetically or by product type any more. Computer-controlled machines can physically store and retrieve cartons. Manufacturers use similar systems to store parts and finished goods.

FIGURE 3-20.

Information systems in wholesaling and warehousing. An automated warehouse uses computerized storage methods.

FIGURE 3-21.
A laser scanner reads in sales data from a product code.

Information systems are used at all stages of a customer's transaction. A common input device is a **POINT-OF-SALE (POS) TERMINAL**, which combines a cash register with a computer terminal linked to an information system. When the salesperson rings up the sale, the following steps occur. First the employee number is entered by the clerk. After the information system checks the validity of the number, the transaction proceeds. The clerk uses a wand or a laser scanner to read the product code and other inventory information, such as size and color of the item being purchased (Figure 3-21).

For cash sales the machine calculates the correct change. On a credit card transaction the credit card company's database can be accessed to determine the customer's credit status. Check-approval systems use similar methods to allow merchants a chance to inquire about the customer's account. After the sale is approved, the point-of-sale terminal communicates data to the store computer for calculating commissions and changes in inventory level. Some point-of-sale terminals even keep a record of how quickly and accurately the clerk inputs the data.

Retailers frequently face problems in stocking the right amount of inventory for customers. Too much inventory involves costs such as interest and taxes. On the other hand, if merchandise levels are kept too low and shortages develop, customers may become dissatisfied and take their business elsewhere. Inventory-management systems help retailers determine when and how much of a product to order from a wholesaler or manufacturer. Of course, manufacturers and wholesalers also use various inventory-management packages.

FINANCE, INSURANCE, AND REAL ESTATE

The finance industry is concerned with managing money. Information systems allow these companies an opportunity to track clients' records. Banks and savings and loan companies use information systems for such purposes as reconciling deposits and withdrawals by customers, determining credit-worthiness of loan applicants, and analyzing the investment opportunities for trust departments. Banks also make extensive use of automated tellers, which accept deposits and give out cash, and of electronic funds transfers (EFT), which enable clients to transfer funds from one account to another without physically moving the funds or writing a check. Credit bureaus maintain extensive files on credit histories of millions of people. Investment brokerages need quick access to information to determine the optimal place to earn money.

Insurance companies are major users of information systems. Life insurance firms use mortality tables to determine suitable rates for the coverage they offer. Health, automobile, and other types of policies rely upon similar statistical methods, all rendered somewhat more painless by the use of computers. Detailed records concerning clients are compiled and maintained on databases.

The real estate industry uses information systems to track investments on the market and to handle paperwork for contracts. Real estate agents can access a database of available properties and extract a list of those properties that meet the requirements of a potential buyer.

A company like Paul's House of Electronic Wonders thrives by serving its customers. Once an order has been processed, people in the shipping and receiving department must see that the items are shipped out to the customer as quickly as possible. If an item is out of stock, a buyer in the purchasing department must order it from the manufacturer. If some of the required items are in stock and some aren't, Paul's often sends a partial shipment.

Incoming goods go through the receiving part of the warehouse. The items are checked for damage and then stored. Highly valuable items, and hazardous substances, are stored in special areas to minimize the risk of theft or fire.

Penny Helmsley introduced Bonnie Meyer and Gene Tomaselli, the two trainees, to Herman Lemming, manager in charge of shipping and receiving. Herman explained to the rookie employees why it was important to enter the sales data properly. If the data were inaccurate, the customer would receive the wrong parts, or in some cases, nothing at all. Additionally, the people in shipping and receiving used optical scanners to read some of the forms and labels on the stored items, to help minimize the possibility of confusing different items and shipping a customer the wrong thing.

Although goods were still stacked on pallets and moved around by employees driving fork-lift trucks, Herman envisioned a completely automated cargo-handling system for the not-too-distant future.

The computer-generated shipping forms showed the type of transportation the customer selected. Who would pay the transportation costs was an item of negotiation during the sales process. Bonnie and Gene made a mental note that it was important for salespeople to know about these costs. Herman Lemming was happy to elaborate. Usually items needed quickly were sent via an express courier service, while other items were shipped with a regular delivery truck. Shipper selection was based upon rules and procedures developed by both Paul's House of Electronic Wonders and its customers. Selecting the proper shipping method could save Paul's and its customers thousands of dollars a year. Because of the complexities of deregulated trucking and airfreight rates, managers in shipping and receiving used a database to help select the right company to carry the goods—yet another use of computers right out near the loading docks.

By the time Bonnie and Gene returned to Penny in the marketing department after several days spent in shipping and receiving, they had become aware of the link between shipping and sales in a way that they would never forget. Expecting merely a loading dock and a few trucks, they had found those—but also a specialized information system on shippers, sophisticated methods of handling shipping forms and labels on goods, and a concern that salespeople in the organization negotiate their sales and enter their orders in a realistic way that would cut costs for everyone.

SUMMARY

- No matter how large or small, any business deals with the areas of accounting, marketing, finance, and personnel. Computerized information systems assist with accounting functions such as monitoring accounts receivable, accounts payable, general ledger, inventory management systems, and billing and payroll systems. Information systems are used in marketing for order processing and market analysis. They are used in finance for financial analysis and credit analysis. And they are used in personnel departments to help find appropriate people to fill jobs.

- An office can be classified as one of three types depending on how it is organized: preindustrial, industrial, and information age. The information-age office places modern technology—particularly electronic mail/message systems (EMMS), word processing systems, and teleconferencing systems—into a service-oriented context.

- Portable personal computers that can link to communications systems make it possible in effect to take the office almost anywhere. Personal computers and communications links have also made it possible to perform many office functions at home, a form of work known as telecommuting.

- The use of information systems does not stop when you move away from the office. They are involved in a great variety of applications today.

- All phases of production and operations management use information systems to aid in creating finished goods and services.

- Engineers design products using computer-aided design (CAD) systems, and test the designs with computer simulation programs. Computer-aided manufacturing (CAM) can then produce the actual product. Flexible manufacturing systems (FMS) use computer-directed machinery throughout the production process.

- In agriculture information systems are used to help with farm operations, forecasting, and marketing.

- In forestry information systems assist in the genetic selection of trees, in assessing the environmental impact of various cutting strategies, and in determining optimal logging and milling strategies. Information systems are used in all phases of energy resource management: exploration, extraction, and production. Computerized information systems help the mining industry by aiding exploration and process control.

- Railroads and trucking companies use information systems to monitor and control operations. At sea onboard computers help navigate and perform other functions. The airline industry uses information systems to schedule overall operations, to direct planes at air traffic control centers, and onboard to aid in navigation.

- The communications systems that we have come to demand today would be impossible to operate without the support of information systems.

- Information systems offer wholesalers, warehouses, manufacturers, and retailers more precise means of controlling their levels of inventory. Sometimes the goods are physically moved about under computer control as well.

- *In retailing information systems are used at all stages of a customer's transaction. Clerks often use point-of-sale (POS) terminals to speed the transaction process.*
- *The finance, insurance, and real estate industries are also among the major users of information systems.*

x

KEY TERMS

These are the key terms in the order in which they appear in the chapter.

Accounting (66)
Accounts receivable (66)
Accounts payable (67)
General ledger (67)
Billing (68)
Inventory management system (68)
Payroll (68)
Marketing (69)
Order processing (69)
Market analysis (69)
Finance (69)
Financial analysis (69)
Credit analysis (70)

Electronic mail/message systems (EMMS) (74)
Word processing system (74)
Teleconferencing (75)
Telecommuting (76)
Production and operations management (78)
Computer-aided design (CAD) (78)
Computer simulation (78)
Computer-aided manufacturing (CAM) (78)
Flexible manufacturing system (FMS) (80)
Point-of-sale (POS) terminal (88)

REVIEW QUESTIONS

OBJECTIVE QUESTIONS

TRUE/FALSE: *Put the letter T or F on the line before the question.*

1. Accounts receivable systems keep track of the money a company owes to creditors.
2. About 30 percent of a company's computer resources are devoted to accounting operations.
3. Inventory management systems only have an impact on accounting operations.
4. Computer simulation is usually done after a physical prototype of a new product has been tested.
5. Electronic mail/message systems (EMMS) are used to create documents.
6. Teleconferencing systems allow managers to hold meetings without physically being in the same location.
7. Telecommuting and teleconferencing mean the same thing.
8. Point-of-sale (POS) terminals are used primarily in the wholesale business.
9. Using the computer to analyze photographic data is called computer-enhanced imaging.
10. Flexible manfacturing systems (FMS) use few CAM techniques.

MULTIPLE CHOICE: *Put the letter of the correct answer on the line before the question.*

1. The accounting operation associated with collecting debts owed a company is
   (a) Accounts payable.
   (b) Accounts receivable.
   (d) Credit analysis.
2. A method for communicating with people within an automated office is called
   (a) Telecommuting.
   (b) Electronic/mail message systems.
   (c) Word processing.
   (d) Teleconferencing.

3. The use of assembly-line methods within an office setting is typical of the _____ office.

(a) Preindustrial.
(b) Industrial.
(c) Information age.
(d) Telecommuting.

4. The use of computer-directed machinery throughout the production process is called

(a) Computer-aided manufacturing (CAM).
(b) Camputer-aided design (CAD).
(c) Flexible manufacturing systems (FMS).
(d) Robot manufacturing systems (RMS).

5. Point-of-sale (POS) terminals are most commonly used in the

(a) Transportation industry.
(b) Retail industry.
(c) Insurance industry.
(d) Wholesaling industry.

FILL IN THE BLANK: *Write the correct word or words in the blank to complete the sentence.*

1. A method for managing the process of converting resources into finished goods and services is _____.

2. The process of using the computer to model real-world situations is called _____.

3. Computer applications in the product design and manufacturing process include _____, _____, and _____.

4. The ability to edit documents quickly is a valuable feature of _____.

5. Order processing is usually considered a part of the _____ area of the company.

6. An _____ system is used to monitor the amount of items a company has in stock.

7. The rise of the computer terminals in the home permits _____ commuting between home and the office.

8. _____ makes it possible for people to participate in meetings without physically being in the same room.

9. Retail clerks use _____ terminals to speed ringing up customers' purchases.

10. An _____ allows users to transmit quickly correspondence and other messages to co-workers on a throughout an office- or company-wide computer network.

SHORT ANSWER QUESTIONS

1. What is the difference between the accounts receivable and accounts payable parts of an accounting office.

2. Describe two information system applications used by people involved in marketing.

3. Describe the likely information system applications used in the area of finance—focus on the banking industry.

4. What are the features of the information-age office?

5. What are the features of FMS factories?

6. Describe some information system applications in the area of operations management.

7. What is the difference between telecommuting and teleconferencing?

1. In what type of businesses have you worked? How were information systems used in the office? In other parts of the organization?

2. What does the phrase "the bills have to go out before the money comes in" mean in terms of an information system?

3. Go to your library and find and summarize three short articles on the use of information systems in any one of the following areas:

   Accounting
   Marketing
   Finance
   Personnel
   Production and operations management
   Computer-aided design (CAD)
   Computer-aided manufacturing (CAM)

CHAPTER 4

THE EVOLUTION OF DATA PROCESSING AND INFORMATION SYSTEMS: A BIT OF HISTORY

After studying this chapter you should understand the following:
■ The general historical trends in the development of information systems.
■ How the four generations of computers differ.
■ The manner in which present and potential users affect the development of an information system.
■ How software has evolved to meet new demands.
■ The challenges of future developments for you and your career.

Have you ever used a small computer? If so, it probably seemed able to do quite a bit for its size. Microcomputers are actually quite powerful machines. They have far more computing power than the earliest electronic computers, and at a fraction of the price. Forty years ago the first electronic computer was unveiled. Called the ENIAC—short for Electronic Numerical Integrator and Calculator—it was as large as a house, with over 18,000 vacuum tubes and thousands of other electrical parts. The electrical bill was $3000 a week.

Yet the ENIAC would be no computational match for the microcomputers we use today. In fact an experiment was carried out to prove this. In 1981 students at the University of Pennsylvania, where the ENIAC was built, tested a Radio Shack TRS-80 microcomputer against ENIAC. The students used parts of the old machine to perform the same test that the TRS-80 did. Each machine was to create a table of squares for the numbers from 1 to 10,000. The ENIAC completed this formidable job in six seconds; the TRS-80 did it in one-third of a second, or one-eighteenth as long.

A humiliating defeat? That depends on your point of view. Compared with present technology the venerable ENIAC is truly a museum piece, and now most of it resides in the Smithsonian Institution. For that matter the microcomputer that the students used in 1981 would also be substantially outpaced by newer microcomputers, to say nothing of today's mainframe computers.

In its time, though, ENIAC delivered a crushing defeat to a rival technology. It was over a thousand times faster than the MARK I, a computer developed just a couple of years earlier which used mechanical parts (absent in ENIAC) as well as electrical switches to perform calculations. The MARK I would have taken 6000 seconds (nearly two hours) to perform the task of squaring those numbers.

For a final comparison, what if you had to do these calculations by hand, without the aid of a computer or calculator? The work would be very tedious. The first few squares you could probably recall from memory. But what about bigger numbers? How fast can you find the square of 2426?

A century ago this work would have been done manually or by use of a simple mechanical calculator. When labor was plentiful and inexpensive and the answers were not needed immediately, such methods made economic sense. As the Industrial Revolution gained force the demand arose for mathematical tables and standardized calculation methods to speed the process. Labor was more expensive, and results were needed more rapidly. The search for ways to solve complex equations more quickly, or to sift through millions of pieces of data, spurred the search for machines to aid in the process. This led to the modern electronic computers of today and tomorrow.

THE EARLIEST CALCULATING MACHINES

People have recorded data, processed data, and transmitted the results for thousands of years. Cave paintings communicated information to young hunters concerning the best way to stalk and kill animals. Early civilizations used clay tablets to record business transactions and keep government and community records. Calculating for such records can be tedious work. Simple devices allowed people to reduce the labor and increase the accuracy of recording and processing information. We will make a rapid survey here of some of the most significant early devices.

The abacus

An early manual calculating device was the ABACUS. Still in everyday use in parts of the world today, such as Japan, China, and the Soviet Union, its origin dates back thousands of years. Shown in Figure 4-1, the abacus is based on a ten-digit number system. It offered a better way to perform the calculations that until its invention had been made by scratching symbols into clay tablets or on the bare ground, or by arranging pebbles in patterns. Extremely easy to manufacture, the abacus serves as an example of a product that has withstood the test of time.

FIGURE 4-1.
The abacus.

The Pascaline

In 1642 the French mathematician BLAISE PASCAL (1623-1662) invented the first mechanical calculator (Figure 4-2). Called the PASCALINE, the calculator could add and subtract. Pascal, 19, was the son of a tax collector, and meant the device to save the drudgery of manual tax calculations. But the Pascaline was not successful. The technology did not then exist to produce the parts needed for the Pascaline in quantity to a sufficient degree of exactness. Moreover, given the low wages paid clerks at the time, the drudgery of calculating by hand was cheaper.

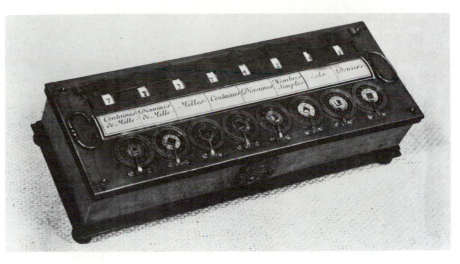

FIGURE 4-2.
Blaise Pascal and his calculator. The Pascaline was read from left to right and had two decimal places to the right of the decimal line (point).

FIGURE 4-3.
Jacquard's loom used punch cards to set the pattern for weaving.

FIGURE 4-4.
Charles Babbage and Lady Ada Lovelace.

Jacquard loom

Another invention that had an effect on the creation of computers had nothing to do with mathematics. **JOSEPH-MARIE JACQUARD** (1752-1834) invented a weaving loom in 1801 that used a **PUNCH CARD** reading system. The **JACQUARD LOOM**, illustrated in Figure 4-3, was controlled by punch cards which carried the codes to order the machine to weave in a certain pattern. Rods attached to the different colored threads were able to pass through the cards where there were holes, and were blocked where there were not. Forms of this machine are still in use today. More importantly for the development of computers, the means of controlling a machine by a variable program was born, and a now-venerable input-output medium, the punch card, was introduced.

The difference and analytic engines

The next major effort in developing machines to perform calculations was by the English mathematics and engineering professor and inventor, **CHARLES BABBAGE** (1792-1871). Professor Babbage (Figure 4-4) was concerned

FIGURE 4-5.
The difference engine used to calculate numerical tables.

about the accuracy of mathematical tables available at the time for astronomy, military gunnery, and various business functions. These tables were calculated by hand using polynomial formulas such as $3ab^2 + ab - b$. The calculation tasks were divided among teams of workers with various skill levels. The most mathematically adept would perform the initial calculations, and then solve the equations at periodic intervals to serve as checkpoints for the other workers. Less skilled people would do simple additions and subtractions.

Babbage persuaded the British government to grant him money to develop a machine to calculate these tables. He called his machine the **DIFFERENCE ENGINE** (Figure 4-5). The difference engine's switches could be preset to generate tables of squares, cubes, and other functions following various algorithms (rules that break down calculations into simple, repetitive operations), and the machine would then print the results. In theory using the machine would be much faster and less error-prone than finding the answer by hand. After a number of years of unsuccessfully attempting to build a full-scale model of the difference engine, however, Babbage lost interest in the project. His principal benefactor, the British government, was not amused.

But Babbage had bigger plans. He had an idea for a machine that could be applied to solving any mathematical problem, which he called the **ANALYTIC ENGINE**. The machine had two major parts: a "mill," which would perform various control and mathematical and logical comparisons, and a "store," which would hold the data until they were needed. The engine would be powered by the dominant energy source of his era, steam. Reputedly it would be as large as a football field.

Babbage had many design problems with his project. Finally one of his students came to his rescue. Her name was **LADY ADA AUGUSTA, THE COUNTESS OF LOVELACE** (1816-1852), daughter of the British poet Lord Byron. A brilliant mathematician, Lady Ada Lovelace translated an article concerning the analytic engine written by an Italian engineer. She added an extensive commentary concerning the input and output requirements and other features.

Lady Lovelace developed a series of instructions to tell the engine what steps to perform. She invented a programming technique called a loop, which directs a machine to perform a set of instructions repetitively. Lady Ada Lovelace became the world's first **PROGRAMMER**. Her portrait is shown in Figure 4-4.

When funding for the analytic engine was cut off by a disgruntled British government, Charles and Ada attempted to raise funds by applying the machine to pick winning horses at the racetrack. This too was unsuccessful.

Though the demand for the machine was present, the product failed. We know from Chapter 2 that the idea of having a control and calculation element (mill) and a primary storage element (Babbage's store) is exactly how computers are designed today, with their central processing unit and primary storage unit. What went wrong initially with Babbage's idea? The precision needed to machine the internal parts required for the analytic engine was lacking. Thus the analytic engine was a product failure.

Would his machine have worked if the parts could have been produced?

Yes. A group of IBM engineers working with Babbage's plans developed a working model of his machine in the 1950s—one hundred years later. More significantly, by the time of that experiment IBM and other firms were already selling computers which incorporated Babbage's basic concepts. Lady Ada, who died of cancer at the age of 36, is memorialized by a programming language (Ada) developed in her name for the U.S. Department of Defense.

Hollerith's tabulating machine

The idea of using punch cards to transmit coded data received further application in the work of HERMAN HOLLERITH (1860-1929), who is shown in Figure 4-6 with his invention. The United States Bureau of the Census took almost eight years to record and tabulate the data obtained from the 1880 census. Hollerith, a statistician with the Bureau, devised a paper punch card TABULATING MACHINE to speed up the process of summarizing the census records for the 1890 census. The tabulator, combined with card punching and sorting machines, reduced the time to process the data to two and one-half years, or one-third of the time it would have taken under the old system.

Hollerith went on to found the Tabulating Machine Company in order to market these devices all over the world. He made a fortune in after-market sales producing and selling the punch cards used in the operation of the tabulating machines. Billions of these cards are still being produced, punched, bent, spindled, and mutilated throughout the world. His company was later merged into the Computing-Tabulating-Recording Company, which was eventually renamed International Business Machines Corporation (IBM).

FIGURE 4-6.
Herman Hollerith and his tabulating machine.

One type of career evolved fairly early in the history of commercial computers and has remained in demand ever since: teaching others how to use a particular computer system, programming language, software package, or whatever. While this function is sometimes carried out by the personnel involved in developing or installing a particular system—who then try to explain to users and others what the system does—often such training is given by a training and education specialist.

Two prerequisites are very important in order to obtain and keep such a job: (1) the ability to teach, and (2) familiarity with the topic being taught.

Teaching ability is usually found in people who are interested in the idea of showing others how to do something, who are talented in communicating with others, and who have had the opportunity to try their hand at it during their own schooling or career. Familiarity with the training topic is acquired by careful study of the particular subject to supplement a general familiarity with computer concepts.

Well organized, larger information centers maintain a department that does nothing but train. Specialized courses are aimed at each of the three different types of people involved with computers: users, technical staff, and managers. Smaller computer centers may hire outside training specialists or simply ask those involved with a project to explain it to others.

Training and education specialists are responsible for more than conducting courses. Some firms pride themselves on the in-house training opportunities that they offer to help employees keep abreast of new technology and to expand their skills. The training department is then involved in selecting, designing, and coordinating the course offerings, and sometimes in establishing training schedules and goals for particular types of employees.

As for the courses themselves, there are many options used by smaller as well as larger training departments. Courses can be taught by videotape and accompanying written materials supplied by a training firm or a hardware or software vendor. Courses can also be taught right on the employee's microcomputer or terminal, through programs designed for the purpose. Regular classroom courses remain a mainstay of the training process.

Training and education specialists are employed by organizations that use computers, firms that sell support services, hardware vendors, software vendors, and educational institutions. Training and education specialists can move to other careers within an organization. Since technical expertise is required to teach courses, it is possible to switch (or return) to programming or systems analysis. Since administrative and managerial acumen are involved in designing courses and running the department, successful training and education specialists can pursue a career in management.

Electromechanical accounting machines

The next major breakthrough in automating information processing was the **ELECTROMECHANICAL ACCOUNTING MACHINE (EAM)**. An electromechanical machine (Figure 4-7) uses electrical pulses to activate mechanical elements. These machines employed punch card technology to process data. Source document data were keypunched, verified, interpreted with human-readable type, sorted, extracted, merged, reproduced, and printed in a noisy factory-like setting. Feeding large piles of cards to machines was a physically demanding task. Today many of these accounting operations can be done by accessing a database and invoking prewritten programs with a few simple strokes on a keyboard. The largest manufacturer of electromechanical machines was IBM.

FIGURE 4-7.

Electromechanical accounting machines (EAM).

The MARK I

The **MARK I**, or Automatic Sequence Controlled Calculator, developed from 1939 to 1944, was an electromechanical computer. A joint project by **DR. HOWARD AIKEN** of Harvard University and IBM Corporation, the MARK I (Figure 4-8) could perform a multiplication operation in three seconds. An electromechanical computer represented an advance over electromechanical accounting machines, because a computer controlled the processing steps without the frequent human intervention necessary with accounting machines. The MARK I was a massive machine, about the size of one wall of a house. After building the MARK I, Aiken discovered he had incorporated the key ideas of Babbage, with whose work Aiken had been unfamiliar. The MARK I was, in effect, a working model of the analytic engine.

FIGURE 4-8.

The MARK I, or Automatic Sequence Controlled Calculator, and its inventor, Dr. Howard Aiken. Input to the MARK I was in the form of paper tape, shown at the far right of the machine. Output consisted of punch cards.

FIGURE 4-9.
The Atanasoff-Berry computer
and its inventors.

John V. Atanasoff

Clifford E. Berry

The Atanasoff-Berry computer

Who invented the first electronic computer? Proper credit has been the subject of historical as well as legal disputes. An **ELECTRONIC COMPUTER** uses only electrical switches and circuitry to carry out processing or computing functions, instead of the slower mechanical relays of an electromechanical computer like the MARK I.

Based on a court decision, legal credit for the first electronic computer should be given to a machine designed and built by **DR. JOHN V. ATANASOFF**, a professor at Iowa State University, and his graduate assistant, **CLIFFORD E. BERRY**. The **ATANASOFF-BERRY COMPUTER (ABC)**, developed from 1937 to 1942, preceded its nearest competition by several years. This computer (shown in Figure 4-9) was designed to solve special types of linear equations, and was not a true general-purpose machine.

Unfortunately the university failed to patent the ABC, losing a potential $500 million in royalties. Ironically, when Dr. Atanasoff approached IBM for assistance in exploiting the project, he was turned down because IBM's president, **THOMAS WATSON, SR.**, could see no commercial future for electronic computers. The ABC was known, however, to the inventors of the ENIAC, a machine which rapidly led to the first commercially available computers.

ENIAC

The **ENIAC**—short for **ELECTRONIC NUMERICAL INTEGRATOR AND CALCULATOR**—was built between 1943 and 1946. Created by **DR. JOHN W. MAUCHLY** and **DR. J. PRESPER ECKERT** of the University of Pennsylvania, it was used for calculating ballistics tables for the U.S. Army. Illustrated in Figure 4-10, it was considered to be the first general-purpose completely electronic digital computer. The ENIAC used on-off digital pulses to solve a wide range of problems electronically. The ENIAC was one thousand times faster than the electromechanical MARK I. In bulk ENIAC was also enormous. It weighed 30 tons, was as big as a three-bedroom house, and employed over 18,000

FIGURE 4-10.

The ENIAC or Electronic Numerical Integrator and Calculator and its inventors, Drs. John W. Mauchly and J. Presper Eckert of the University of Pennsylvania.

John W. Mauchly

J. Presper Eckert

vacuum tubes to store and process data. The lights in parts of Philadelphia dimmed when ENIAC was on the job. The machine was used until 1955. ENIAC read in and stored its data, but not its programs. Whenever a new problem had to be run, operators had to reset switches and change around numerous wires on plugboards.

Following the completion and success of ENIAC, Eckert and Mauchly formed their own computer manufacturing company, called the Eckert-Mauchly Computer Corporation. Financial difficulties forced them to sell their firm to Remington-Rand, now a division of Sperry Corporation.

The stored program concept

The electronic machines discussed so far were cumbersome to program, with their switches and plugboards that had to be changed by hand. The mathematician JOHN VON NEUMANN (Figure 4-11) proposed a solution to this problem—the STORED PROGRAM CONCEPT. A stored program is one that is

FIGURE 4-11.

John von Neumann (right) proposed storing program instructions in the computer. He is shown here with J. Robert Oppenheimer, who directed the project that created the atomic bomb.

coded and stored the same way data are. Von Neumann suggested that instructions could be read into a computer on paper tape and then stored in the banks of vacuum tubes along with the data the program was to manipulate. Inside the computer's memory stored data and instructions would be indistinguishable from each other. The control unit of the computer would be directed as to where to find the program instructions. In this way the program that a computer followed could be changed much more easily and quickly than with ENIAC, which had to be wired anew for each job.

The **EDSAC**, or **ELECTRONIC DELAY STORAGE AUTOMATIC COMPUTER**, created at Cambridge University in England was the first stored program computer. EDSAC became operational in 1949. In effect the EDSAC became the first working prototype of the computers we use today. Now let's turn to these.

THE EVOLUTION OF COMMERCIAL COMPUTERS

Computers have been commercially available long enough that we divide them into "generations." The computer generations constitute different technological eras. The primary technological element is the central processing unit. Each generation of commercial computers differs considerably from other generations in terms of the technology employed in this unit.

What is important in our discussion here is not only when a machine or component was invented, however, but how the new technology was commercially applied and popularized. Technology does not exist in a vacuum. There has to be a demand for it. For a product based on technology to become a success, consumers from either the public or private sectors must find some beneficial use for it.

Each computer generation has seen the adoption of new types of software. These software breakthroughs will be discussed within the generation when they became commercially popular.

Dividing computer generations into these three categories— technology, demand, and software—is solely to help you learn the material. In reality these three categories interact and affect each other in complex ways. As we shall see, demand may push the technology and software to new frontiers; or changes in technology may give rise to whole new areas of demand.

FIRST-GENERATION COMPUTERS (1951-1958)

Technology
The major hardware characteristic of **FIRST-GENERATION COMPUTERS** is the use of **VACUUM TUBES** for internal computing operations as shown in Figure 4-12, these devices were considerably faster than electromechanical devices for processing data. Calculations could be performed in **MILLISECONDS** (thousandths of a second). The principal disadvantage of vacuum tubes is the amount of heat they generate. Special air-conditioning units were required to dissipate the heat. (Although heat problems became less severe in subsequent generations, mainframe computer rooms are still air-conditioned to this day.) Due both to the heat level and the nature of the available materials, vacuum tubes had a short life and "blew out" frequently. Another disadvantage is the amount of space that circuits using vacuum tubes occupy. Compared with systems of today first-generation computers were more subject to breakdowns.

Punch cards and punched **PAPER TAPE** were the principal media for the

FIGURE 4-12.

An example of the vacuum
tubes used in first- generation
computers.

input, output, and external storage of data and instructions, although on
some machines **MAGNETIC TAPE** was available. For internal storage most
first-generation computers used **MAGNETIC DRUMS**, large spinning cylinders
with programs and data recorded on them.

Demand

The main focus of demand for first-generation computers was to perform
scientific applications, particularly military contract work. For business
users applications were primarily limited to batch processing of accounting
and payroll operations, essentially an extension of the techniques used with
the electromechanical accounting machines (described above) of an earlier
era. Data were primarily read in sequentially, one record after another.
Rules and procedures focused on standard operating conditions, and
programs capable of handling exceptional situations were far more difficult
to write.

The first commercially produced computer was the **UNIVAC I**, or **UNIVER-
SAL AUTOMATIC COMPUTER**, which became available in 1951. The U.S. Bureau
of the Census purchased three of these machines (shown in Figure 4-13) to
aid in tabulating the 1950 census. The UNIVAC I was designed by Eckert

FIGURE 4-13.

The UNIVAC I, or Universal Automatic Computer, the first successful commercial computer.
This picture shows Walter
Cronkite, right, with J. Presper
Eckert and an unidentified
operator. In 1952 the UNIVAC I
was the first computer to tabulate early returns in a presidential election successfully and
predict the winner—Dwight D.
Eisenhower.

It must be every inventor's dream to stumble on some device that creates a new field of endeavor and ensures success and fame. The International Business Machines Corporation, the world's largest maker of computers, fits this picture only to a degree. Herman Hollerith created the firm, first as the Tabulating Machine Company (in 1896), and eventually, after mergers, as the Computer-Tabulating-Recording Company (in 1911). The firm changed its name to IBM in 1924. The object of the firm was to sell Hollerith's punch-card tabulating machines that had proven so successful with the 1890 census. For years "the IBM machine" was what people called devices that handled punch cards, though as the decades passed these machines diversified into many different devices made by various manufacturers. Electromechanical technology reached its high point with the MARK I computer, built in part by IBM.

However, when the inventor of the first electronic computer, John V. Atanasoff, suggested that IBM help market his ABC computer, the firm declined. Then IBM President Thomas J. Watson stated that he did not believe electronic computers had a future.

With such a beginning, how did the computer giant get to be the computer giant?

IBM did enter the computer arena, following UNIVAC by two years, with the IBM 701, introduced in 1953. IBM started making the 650 in 1954, which proved the most popular commercial computer for some years. Through the subsequent march of computer generations, IBM has sold more computers than all of the world's other computer makers combined. Today, the firm employs 395,000 people and has annual sales of $46 billion (1984). Its business plans call for quadrupling that sales figure, to $185 billion, by 1994.

At many points in its life IBM has not had the latest, the fastest, or the most sophisticated computer to sell. For example, microcomputers had been selling like hotcakes for the better part of a decade before IBM decided to produce one. How, then, does the behemoth attract the lion's share of the computer market?

A large part of the answer is the people. Remember the five-part model of an information system? People, rules and procedures, data, software, and hardware? Along with its hardware (and later, software), IBM has always stressed the people element, encouraging loyalty among its employees, and offering the services of these employees to customers right along with the hardware or software purchased.

IBM, of course, is not unique in stressing people: it would be hard to make your way through a recruiting brochure from almost any company without reading about the value of people to the organization. What many companies did not do, especially in the early years of computing, was to offer people along with the hardware, and to offer people who spoke the user's non-specialized language. But when you bought an IBM computer, the services of a team of professionals—who would do their best to see that the machine did exactly what you wanted, and kept doing it—were thrown in.

Indeed, the "throwing in" was a point of contention in a lengthy suit brought by other computer manufacturers against IBM in the 1960s; the Justice Department ordered IBM to start charging for these people services. "Unbundling" then became the rule of the industry, and hardware, software, and people services began to be priced separately. No longer could you buy an IBM machine and get for "free" (in reality, of course, the costs were included in the price of the hardware) a phalanx of experts as well as the software you needed.

A reputation remains a reputation,

however. Do a bit of field research to-day by visiting installations with IBM computers, and ask why IBM was chosen over many other makers of excellent machines. The odds are excellent that you will hear the "people" argument, often referred to as "support." Good support inspires confidence, and the word gets around. Though purchasers must pay for it, everyone wants it.

Today IBM is not unique in providing it, but there was a time when it almost was.

No matter what end of the computer industry you examine, people remain the most important of the five elements. Many factors make for successful computer hardware, but the world's largest computer manufacturer got that way by putting people first.

and Mauchly, the builders of the ENIAC, and completed while they were at Remington-Rand. The machines remained in use for over a decade at the Census Bureau. The UNIVAC I gained a reputation as an electronic "brain" when, with only about 5 percent of the votes counted, it correctly predicted for CBS television that Dwight D. Eisenhower would win over Adlai E. Stevenson in the 1952 presidential election.

In 1953 IBM introduced its first commercial computer, the **IBM 701**. A year later IBM introduced the **IBM 650** (shown in Figure 4-14), a machine that established the firm's dominance in the computer industry, which has continued (through many subsequent types of computers) to the present day. IBM initially expected to sell 20 of its 650s; instead it sold or leased over 1800. A major factor in IBM's success was that their machines were designed to work compatibly with existing electromechanical accounting machines, using the same punch card codes, and designed to emulate and supplement the older generation of machines in solving business problems. As a result users felt more comfortable with the IBM 650 machines than with computers made by rival companies. The 650 was viewed by purchasers as a less risky investment, and one which complemented existing ways of doing business.

FIGURE 4-14.
The IBM 650 computer, the most popular first-generation computer.

Software

Programs on some first-generation computers were entered by wiring plugboards, as with electromechanical accounting machines and the ENIAC. On other first-generation machines programs were written in **MACHINE LANGUAGE**, and read into the computer's memory as a stored program. The computer reads the code as a series of 1s and 0s—the numbers used in the **BINARY NUMBER SYSTEM** that correspond to the actual circuitry of the machine. Number systems are discussed in greater detail in Chapter 5. Coding in machine language is a tedious process. To speed up the programming effort symbolic languages called **ASSEMBLY LANGUAGES** were created, using symbols easier for people to work with and remember than strings of binary or octal code. A program written in the symbolic assembly language was then translated into the numeric machine codes. To compare machine and assembly languages, Figure 4-15 shows the codes for an assignment function that adds the values in one field (B) to another (A). The general formula is A = A + B, which might be used to accumulate a running total for a customer's bill. Computer languages are discussed in Chapter 11.

FIGURE 4-15.

Examples of machine language code and assembly language code to add the value of B to A (A = A + B).

Machine code:

```
11111010010100101001000000000000100100000001100
```

Assembly code:

```
AP TOTALA, VALUEB
```

SECOND-GENERATION COMPUTERS (1958–1964)

Technology

Two major hardware features of **SECOND-GENERATION COMPUTERS** were the use of transistors to replace the fragile vacuum tubes of the previous generation, and the use of magnetic cores to replace the first generation's magnetic drums for internal storage. The transistor was invented in 1948 at Bell Telephone Laboratories by **WILLIAM SHOCKLEY**, **JOHN BARDEEN** (the only person to receive two Nobel prizes in the same field, physics), and **WALTER H. BRATTAIN**. Shown in Figure 4-16, a **TRANSISTOR** is a solid-state semiconducting device. A **SEMICONDUCTOR** is a compound which has electrical properties between those of a conductor (like copper wire) and an insulator (like rubber). Transistors were much smaller, more reliable, less fragile, and cheaper than vacuum tubes, and produced far less heat.

Another feature of second-generation computers was the use of **MAGNETIC CORE MEMORY** for main memory rather than a magnetic drum. The "core," as it was called, consisted of tiny iron doughnuts wired together (Figure 4-17). The computer could store and access data and instructions by magnetizing and demagnetizing these tiny cores much more rapidly than reading and writing from a magnetic drum. With these improvements second-generation computers could perform arithmetic and logical operations in **MICROSECONDS** (millionths of a second).

Magnetic tape units also came into more frequent use for peripheral operations such as input, output, and secondary storage. Punch card and paper tape systems were also still used for these operations.

In the second generation computer manufacturers began to organize their computers into product lines or series. An example of a highly

FIGURE 4-16.

The transistor, a breakthrough in solid-state technology. The developers of the transistor— William Shockley, John Bardeen, and Walter H. Brattain— received the Nobel prize in physics for their work on semi-conductors.

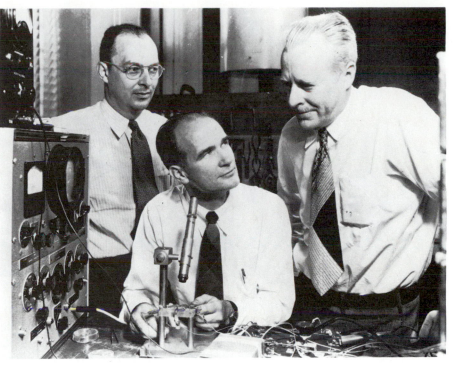

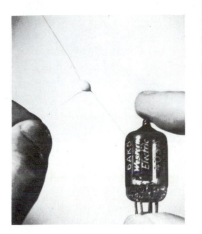

FIGURE 4-17.

Magnetic core storage of the type used in second- generation computers.

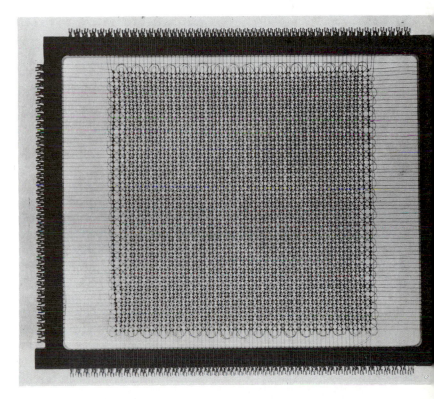

successful product line was the IBM 1400 series, shown in Figure 4-18. A manufacturer's machines were compatible with one another but not with those made by rival companies; this encouraged staying with the same company when upgrading from one computer to another. Competitors of IBM in the second generation included Burroughs, Sperry-Univac, National Cash Register, Control Data, and Honeywell (collectively known as the BUNCH), as well as General Electric and RCA.

Demand

The major demand for second-generation computers was from users in government agencies and both large- and medium-scale businesses. Smaller businesses and individuals could not afford computers. The main business uses included accounting, payroll, marketing, and manufacturing applications, where data could be processed in batches. Universities used computers to process research projects as well as for their regular accounting operations. As with the previous generation, systems focused on standard operating procedures.

Software

The second generation saw the popularization of two major programming languages, FORTRAN and COBOL. Examples of these languages are given in Figure 4-19. Even today these remain extremely popular languages.

A scientific-oriented language, **FORTRAN** (short for FORmula TRANslator) was developed at IBM Corporation by **JOHN BACKUS,** and was introduced into the market in 1957. A standardized version was not available until the mid-1960s. A very powerful language for mathematical problems, it is useful in many scientific and engineering application areas. Business applications include market research and production control.

COBOL (short for COmmon Business Oriented Language) was released in 1959, largely through the efforts of **DR. GRACE HOPPER**. Programs written in

FIGURE 4-19.

FORTRAN and COBOL, two second-generation languages. Dr. Grace Hopper worked on the development of the COBOL compiler. Compare the FORTRAN and COBOL statements with the examples shown in Figure 4-15. Note how much more readable the FORTRAN and COBOL statements are.

The FORTRAN statement for adding the value of B to the total value A:

```
A = A + B
```

The COBOL statement looks like these examples:

```
004100      ADD B to TOTAL.
```

or, another way:

```
004100      COMPUTE TOTALA = TOTALA + VALUEB.
```

languages such as FORTRAN and COBOL use a language translation program called a compiler to convert the program into the computer's own machine language.

Considered by many to be the world's second programmer (with Lady Ada Lovelace the first), Dr. Hopper began her work on programming languages with the MARK I project described earlier in the chapter. She wrote the machine codes for the project, and was credited with taming Aiken's beast of a machine. She moved on to developing programs for the UNIVAC I computer. For her distinguished efforts in developing programming languages, she was named "Man of the Year" in 1969 by the Data Processing Management Association.

COBOL is a language that simplifies and to some degree standardizes business applications. Not as powerful as FORTRAN for mathematics, COBOL can be much more readily used for tasks common in commercial programs such as processing large files and producing reports. The multibillion-dollar inventory of programs used today by businesses and government is for the most part written in COBOL.

Other languages were also developed during the second generation. In addition simple operating systems were introduced.

THIRD-GENERATION COMPUTERS (1964–1971)

Technology

The major technological breakthrough to **THIRD-GENERATION COMPUTERS** was the development of the integrated circuit. An **INTEGRATED CIRCUIT** combines transistors and related circuitry into one unit. Integrated circuits are etched onto small wafers of glass called **SILICON CHIPS**. An advantage silicon chips have over previous types of circuitry is their ability to operate under greater temperatures and vibration. A second-generation transistor would fail at about 120°F. In fact it was the demand for transistors capable of withstanding high temperatures that led to the development of integrated circuits. An advantage of integrated circuits is that the distance between the parts of a circuit is so small that electricity has a shorter distance to travel to carry out any given computer operation. Smaller, with computers, means faster.

Integrated circuits have gone on to revolutionize not just computers but many other areas, from automobiles to zoology. An example of a third-generation integrated circuit is shown in Figure 4-20. As computers continued their steady march forward in speed, processing operations were eventually measured in *microseconds* and eventually **NANOSECONDS** (billionths of a second).

FIGURE 4-20.
An early integrated circuit
(right) compared to a vacuum
tube and a transistor.

The **IBM 360** was the most significant computer of the third generation. Displayed in Figure 4-21, it was conceived as a general-purpose machine that would service a full circle of scientific and business users (the 360 model number represents the degrees in a circle). In previous generations computers tended to specialize as "scientific" or "business" computers.

Improvements in input, output, and external storage devices, and communications equipment, continued the trend toward faster processing. The most significant change was the increased popularity of the **MAGNETIC DISK**. Instead of using punch cards or magnetic tape systems, programmers tended increasingly to store software and data on magnetic disks. On a disk as opposed to tape or cards, a record to be read can be selected without reading the preceding ones, which greatly increases speed for some applications.

Demand

In the United States demand for third-generation computers was spurred by the competition with the Soviet Union in the race to the moon and the development of more sophisticated missiles and warheads. To assure reliable control of these sophisticated rockets and weapons, advances in computer circuitry and data communications were required.

To increase the reliability of electronic components, especially in outer space or under battle conditions, governments spent millions of dollars funding the development of integrated circuits. The development of advanced telecommunication systems allowed for data communications between computerized monitoring systems onboard spacecraft and land-based data-processing centers (Mission Control). There was no time to wait for data to be accumulated for a batch-processing run. Instead responses had to be made to events still in progress, in what is called **REAL-TIME PROCESSING**.

FIGURE 4-21.

The IBM 360, the mainframe
computer that signaled the start
of the third generation.

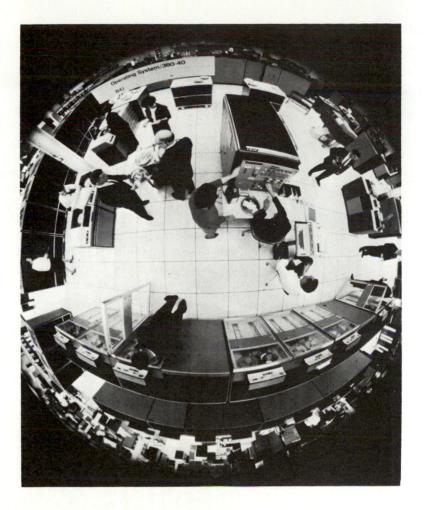

Software

Changes in software included the development of the first full-scale operating systems to manage all of a computer's hardware and software resources, and the introduction of system and application software to handle online processing of data.

The major new language developed in this era was BASIC (Beginner's All-Purpose Symbolic Instruction Code). Developed by JOHN G. KEMENY and THOMAS KURTZ, two mathematics professors at Dartmouth College, BASIC was designed with the novice programmer in mind (see Figure 4-22).

FOURTH-GENERATION COMPUTERS (1971-?)

Technology

The technological change that distinguishes the FOURTH-GENERATION COMPUTERS from the third is the development of the microprocessor. A MICROPROCESSOR contains the control and arithmetic/logic units of the central processor etched on a single silicon chip (see Figure 4-23). Many microprocessors also have storage elements etched into the chip. Microprocessors are produced by LARGE-SCALE INTEGRATION (LSI), which is the process of placing many integrated circuits on a chip. The first commercial microprocesor was produced by Texas Instruments Corporation in 1971. Since that time billions

Here is a line of BASIC for the equation A = A + B:

```
200 LET A = A + B
```

of microprocessors have found their way into everything from automobiles and computers to toasters and x-ray machines. The most notable product is the microcomputer or personal computer.

The first microcomputer was marketed in 1976. In 1977 Apple Computer Corporation, founded by **STEPHEN WOZNIAK** and **STEVEN JOBS**, released its first computer (see Figure 4-24), the **APPLE I**. In less than a decade Apple Computer Corporation rose into the Fortune 500. Many other companies joined the race to establish themselves in this new market, and a number of them failed. In 1981 IBM began selling its own microcomputer, called the Personal Computer. Which companies and products now on the market will survive into the 1990s is subject to great speculation, as prices continue to fall for this sophisticated equipment.

Although microcomputers are the golden children of the fourth generation, great strides in performances of other types of computers have occurred. Processing speeds for the fastest computers can now be measured

FIGURE 4-23.
An advanced microprocessor.

FIGURE 4-24.
Stephen Wozniak (left) and
Steven Jobs (right), the founders
of Apple Computer.

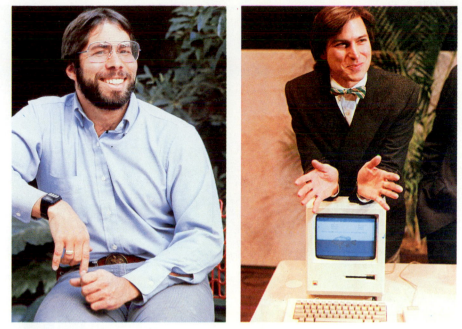

in *nanoseconds* and **PICOSECONDS** (trillionths of a second). Figure 4-25 shows some representative fourth-generation computers.

Other parts of the information processing industry have also undergone significant changes. Data input methods have become more highly automated; for example, laser scanners can read product codes far faster than people can key in the prices using an old-style cash register. In addition the scanner transmits the transaction data to external storage units to aid in controlling inventory levels. External storage units are now capable of retaining far greater amounts of data in smaller physical units, speeding data-handling while lowering its per-item cost. Magnetic disk systems have evolved into high-density hard disk models and inexpensive floppy disk systems. Output devices can create more personalized output than those of previous generations. Communications systems are using **FIBER OPTIC CABLES** made of ultrathin glass filaments to transmit more data at faster rates of speed.

The principal engineering trend in the fourth generation is toward further miniaturization of the components of computers. Currently it is possible to store over 256,000 binary digits on a single silicon chip. There are experimental storage chips capable of storing over one million binary digits of data on a chip. Such elements are examples of **VERY-LARGE-SCALE INTEGRATION (VLSI)**, which is the process of placing a great number of integrated circuits on a chip. In addition to offering rapid processing speeds due to their small size, these circuits are also more reliable, and use less power, than their predecessors.

One area of great technological interest is the application of information-processing elements to the field of **ROBOTICS**, or the study and application of robots. A **ROBOT** is a machine capable of coordinating its movements itself by reacting to changes in the system environment. The most common

FIGURE 4-25.
Fourth-generation computers.
(a) A mainframe system. (b) A
minicomputer system. (c) A
large microcomputer.

(a)

(c)

(b)

application of robots in the work world is carrying out routine assembly operations (Figure 4-26). We will learn of other robot-related applications in future chapters.

Demand

Demand for greater levels of integration, with more and more circuitry packed into a chip, was pushed by the need for developing "smart" weaponry as well as for cheaper and more sophisticated consumer products. The result has been that for the first time, the average individual can afford a computer. Further demand rose for **DISTRIBUTED DATA PROCESSING** systems. A distributed data processing system shares computing power among several different computers. For example, a company can link its computers into a communications network, and give different jobs to the different computers. Microcomputers or minicomputers can be linked into various network patterns either with other micros, minis, or mainframe computers to share in information processing.

FIGURE 4-26.
A robot moving paper products
from one point to another.

Since the late 1970s there has been an explosion in the popularity of microcomputers. Users are now able to purchase microcomputers and the software they need at a reasonable price to help solve their computational and other information system problems at work, school, or home.

Software

Distributed data processing evolved further in the fourth generation with the development of system software capable of managing many users at once. **DATABASE MANAGEMENT SYSTEMS (DBMS)** were developed first for large mainframe computers, and eventually database systems were created for use with microcomputers. Database management software allows users with different application needs access to a shared database.

In addition there has been a veritable explosion of prepackaged software programs, especially in the area of business applications (Figure 4-27). You can perform many information-processing operations without knowing how to write programs—all you need to know is how to invoke a program on your terminal or microcomputer with a few simple and easily used commands. Interpreting the results still does require you to be knowledgeable about the subject area. An example of a popular software package for business use is Lotus 1-2-3, a combination spreadsheet (visual calculator), file handler, and graphics package (see Figure 4-28).

During the fourth generation structured programming techniques have become more popular. Structured programming techniques substantially reduce the overall cost of writing, correcting, testing, and maintaining programs. The programmer is required to design solutions using special organizing rules. **PASCAL** is a programming language which requires the use

FIGURE 4-27.
Fourth-generation software. This program simulates airplane cockpit meters to help engineers test a digital fuel- indicating system.

of structured programming techniques. Developed by **NIKLAUS WIRTH,** Pascal is named after the inventor of the Pascaline calculator, discussed earlier in this chapter.

Another development in the fourth generation is of programs permanently recorded on integrated circuits. Programs of this sort are called **FIRMWARE,** a blend of hardware and software. In a way this harks back to ENIAC's plugboards, though on a microminiaturized level.

The fourth generation has also seen growing interest in **ARTIFICIAL INTELLIGENCE (AI),** which refers to efforts to capture the way humans think and learn in computer programs. Artificial intelligence has had an impact on areas as diverse as the psychology of human learning and memory and the design of robots capable of complex tasks. A distinguishing characteristic of AI software is its ability to learn from mistakes.

TOWARD FUTURE GENERATIONS— FIFTH AND BEYOND

Technology

Up to now, we have generally underestimated the impact of computers on our society. What might the future look like?

Some feel the technology of future generations will probably be based upon further improvements in the integration of circuitry. Greater reductions in the size of the circuits, and increases in density, have been predicted. Processing speeds will drop further into the picosecond range for faster computers. To maintain such levels of speed and density of circuits, the vital parts of the computer may be immersed in a solution of liquid helium or nitrogen.

Home and personal types of systems may continue to proliferate, providing more and easier-to-use computing power for your money. More sophisticated robots are already being created for use in the workplace. Researchers have begun experimentation on laser-optic computers, designs for biotechnological methods of storing information, and other ideas.

Demand

Demand for future generations of information systems is expected to come from the same institutions as before. Businesses will probably want faster computers to assist in reducing production and management costs. Also, information systems may be used increasingly for earning money as well as saving money; predicting, for example, future investment or market penetration possibilities.

Governments probably will continue to sponsor research in the area of new types of information systems in order to maintain competitive advantages for their strategic industries, and for the creation of more efficient weapons systems. Further use of robots is predicted, affecting the kinds and quality of work many of us may perform.

Software

The principal effort here will be in the area of artificial intelligence—attempts to develop software that more closely resembles how humans think. Researchers are already considering how to move from machines that respond to on or off conditions for single tasks, to ones that can perform many tasks simultaneously, as humans do. The biological circuits in human brains process data more slowly than computers can, but because people can deal with a number of data items simultaneously, they are able to think and reason. Computers, for all their speed, are incapable of thinking—so far.

A final note on trying to predict the future. Earlier in this chapter we mentioned that IBM Corporation predicted they would sell only 20 of their first-generation IBM 650 series computers. They wound up building over 1800. With a break- even point at about ten computers, imagine the return on investment. Given the transitions we have covered from movable beads and steam engines to pinhead-sized computers, think what possibilities, as yet unpredicted, may arise in the future for you.

WRAP-UP   **THE MARCH OF THE GENERATIONS**

From our discussion in this chapter it should be apparent that a lot of change has taken place from the earliest computing devices to the rapid computers of the present. Even from the time when we started counting computer generations—the arrival of the first commercially available computers—the nature of computers has changed enough to transform how society does business. A fourth-generation collection of circuits containing the equivalent of thousands of the first generation's vacuum tubes occupies no more space than would a fleck of dust on one of those vacuum tubes. Speed has changed as dramatically, and cost has plunged, making computing power avail-

FIGURE 4-28.
Selected features of four generations of commercial computers.

System Element	Generation			
	First	**Second**	**Third**	**Fourth**
Hardware				
(Computer)	Vacuum tubes Magnetic drums	Transistors Magnetic core	Integrated circuits	Large-scale integrated circuits
(Speed)	Milliseconds	Microseconds	Microseconds and nanoseconds	Nanoseconds and picoseconds
(Input, secondary storage output communication)	Paper tape Punch cards Magnetic tape Standard output	Punch cards Magnetic tape Standard output	Punch cards Online terminals Magnetic disk Standard output Telecommunications	Online terminals Magnetic disk Floppy disk Robotics Standard and personalized output Fiber optic cables
People (Business users only)	Accounting	Accounting Production Marketing	Data communications General business	Information systems General business
Rules	Standard procedures emphasized	Standard procedures emphasized	Exception and standard procedures	Exception and standard procedures
Data	File oriented	File oriented	File oriented	Databases for large and personal computers
Software	Machine and assembly languages	FORTRAN COBOL	BASIC	Easy-to-use business packages for personal computers Structured language: Pascal Artificial intelligence

able not only to government and big business, but to anyone reading this book.

In Figure 4-28 we summarize the characteristics discussed in this chapter of each of the four generations. These are divided into the five elements of an information system: people, rules and procedures, data, software, and hardware. In this case, however, we have put hardware first (before people), since hardware most clearly delineates one generation from the next. It is worth spending a few moments with this figure to grasp the magnitude of the changes that have taken place in less than four decades.

SUMMARY

- *A successful information systems product depends upon three factors: demand for the product, the technical ability to produce the product, and the software or instructions to make use of the product.*
- *The first devices used for calculating include the abacus and Pascal's mechanical calculator, the Pascaline. Early in the nineteenth century Joseph-Marie Jacquard invented an automated loom that used a punch card reading system.*
- *The nineteenth century also saw Charles Babbage's attempts to build first the difference engine, and then, with the assistance of Lady Ada Lovelace, the analytic engine. Although it never appeared as a succesful product, the analytic engine, as Babbage conceived it, contained all the basic elements of the modern computer.*
- *Herman Hollerith developed a paper punch card tabulating machine to speed the processing of the U.S. Census of 1890.*
- *Electromechanical accounting machines using punched card technology were developed to automate accounting procedures. Howard Aiken used this technology to build one of the first working computers, the MARK I.*
- *The first electronic computer, the Atanasoff-Berry Computer, was completed in 1942. At the time Thomas Watson, Sr., the head of the IBM Corporation, felt electronic computers were not a marketable product. John Mauchly and J. Eckert's giant ENIAC, successful in calculating ballistics tables, soon followed in 1946. The EDSAC and similar machines introduced John von Neumann's concept of stored programs to speed the processing of data.*
- *The age of commercially available computers began in earnest with the UNIVAC I in 1951. Since then, computers have been divided into "generations" based on the changes in hardware.*
- *First-generation computers used vacuum tubes for processing and magnetic drums to store data and instructions inside the computer. Processing operation speeds were measured in milliseconds. The primary input, output, and external storage media were punch cards, paper tape, and (on some machines) magnetic tape. Accounting programs with a focus on standard operating procedures were emphasized. IBM established its leadership in the computer industry with the introduction of the 701 and 650 computer models. Data were*

organized into files which were dependent on specific application programs. Machine languages (using the binary number system), and later assembler languages, were used to write programs.

- *In the second-generation senmiconducting transistors (developed by the team of Shockley, Bardeen, and Brattain) were used inside the computer for switching, and magnetic core elements for storage. Processing speeds increased into the microsecond range. Magnetic tape and punch card systems continued to dominate the input, output, and external storage elements of information-processing systems. Business applications expanded to include production and marketing. Data were still file oriented. Two higher-level languages were popularized: FORTRAN for engineering and scientific applications, developed by John Backus; and COBOL, designed by Grace Hopper, primarily for large businesses and government organizations. Simple operating systems were developed.*

- *Integrated circuits on silicon chips were incorporated into third-generation computers. The speed of processing rose into the nanosecond range. Magnetic disk systems served to handle data for external storage, although magnetic tape and punch cards were still used for input and output. Most areas of business need could be addressed in this generation. General-purpose computers, such as the IBM 360, were built to serve a wide variety of users. These computers were capable of real-time processing. Data communication systems were developed. BASIC, a programming language for novices, was created by Kemeny and Kurtz at Dartmouth College.*

- *Large-scale integration (LSI) characterizes the fourth and present generation, especially the development of the microprocessor or computer on a chip. Processing speed on the fastest systems reaches into the picosecond range. Magnetic disk systems have evolved into high-density hard disk models and inexpensive floppy disk systems. Microprocessors allow the creation of more sophisticated robots (through the study of robotics), personal computers, and fiber-optic-cable-based communications systems. Stephen Wozniak and Steven Jobs created the Apple I computer, helping to fuel the microcomputer age. Mature information systems are available for virtually any business-related problem. Systems can handle both standard and exceptional operating conditions as well as distributed data processing. Online databases handled by database management systems (DBMS) were initiated for large computer systems and are now available for personal computers. Niklaus Wirth devised Pascal, a structured programming language. Easy-to-use business-oriented software packages are available for personal computers. The software packages can even be incorporated onto chips in the form of firmware. The quest to create computers that can "think" like humans has been pushed along by the development of artificial intelligence programming languages and very-large-scale integrated (VLSI) circuits.*

- *Future generations may see the continuation of present trends or follow some breakthrough that cannot be predicted. How the future will affect us remains, of course, to be seen.*

These are the names of people in the order in which they appear in the chapter.

Blaise Pascal (96)
Joseph-Marie Jacquard (97)
Charles Babbage (97)
Lady Ada Augusta, the Countess of
    Lovelace (98)
Herman Hollerith (99)
Howard Aiken (101)
John V. Atanasoff
    and Clifford E. Berry (102)
Thomas Watson, Sr. (102)

John W. Mauchly and J. Presper Eckert
    (102)
John von Neumann (103)
William Shockley, John Bardeen,
    Walter H. Brattain (108)
John Backus (110)
Grace Hopper (110)
John G. Kemeny and Thomas Kurtz
    (113)
Stephen Wozniak and Steven Jobs (114)
Niklaus Wirth (118)

These are the key terms in the order in which they appear in the chapter.

Abacus (96)
Pascaline (96)
Punch card (97)
Jacquard loom (97)
Difference engine (98)
Analytic engine (98)
Programmer (98)
Tabulating machine (99)
Electromechanical accounting machine
    (EAM) (101)
MARK I (101)
Electronic computer (102)
Atanasoff-Berry Computer (ABC) (102)
ENIAC (Electronic Numerical Integra-
    tor and Calculator) (102)
Stored program concept (103)
EDSAC (Electronic Delay Storage Auto-
    matic Computer) (104)
First-generation computers (104)
Vacuum tube (104)
Millisecond (104)
Paper tape (104)
Magnetic tape (105)
Magnetic drum (105)
UNIVAC I (Universal Automatic Com-
    puter) (105)
IBM 701 (107)
IBM 650 (107)
Machine language (108)
Binary number system (108)
Assembly language (108)

Second-generation computers (108)
Transistor (108)
Semiconductor (108)
Magnetic core memory (108)
Microsecond (108)
FORTRAN (110)
COBOL (110)
Third-generation computers (111)
Integrated circuit (111)
Silicon chip (111)
Nanosecond (111)
IBM 360 (112)
Magnetic disk (112)
Real-time processing (112)
BASIC (113)
Fourth-generation computers (113)
Microprocessor (113)
Large-scale integration (LSI) (113)
Apple I (114)
Picosecond (115)
Fiber-optic cables (115)
Very-large-scale integration (VLSI) (115)
Robotics (115)
Robot (115)
Distributed data processing (116)
Database management systems
    (DBMS) (117)
Pascal (117)
Firmware (118)
Artificial intelligence (AI) (118)

OBJECTIVE QUESTIONS

TRUE/FALSE: *Put the letter T or F on the line before the question.*

_____ 1. Pascal is an example of a second-generation programming language.

_____ 2. Vacuum tubes were used for processing in first-generation computers.

_____ 3. Grace Hopper was instrumental in developing the programming language BASIC.

_____ 4. The ENIAC could perform computations over one thousand times faster than the MARK I.

_____ 5. The analytic engine was a product failure because the technology did not exist to machine the needed parts.

_____ 6. IBM delivered the world's first commercial computer.

_____ 7. Magnetic core memory is a feature of fourth-generation computers.

_____ 8. Howard Aiken developed the punch card tabulating machine to help compile the results of the United States Census of 1890.

_____ 9. The analytic engine was developed by the team of Charles Babbage and Lady Ada Lovelace.

_____ 10. Robotics is the study of creating hardware and software capable of thinking like humans.

MULTIPLE CHOICE: *Put the letter of the correct answer on the line before the question.*

_____ 1. The programming language COBOL was developed by
(a) John Backus.   (c) John Kemeny and Thomas Kurtz.
(b) Grace Hopper.   (d) Niklaus Wirth.

_____ 2. The reason the analytic engine was a product failure was
(a) Because of a lack of demand by government and industry for the machine.
(b) The difficulty in machining the parts required to operate the machine.
(c) The inability of the designers to work out the logical processes to be used by the machine.
(d) All of the above.

_____ 3. Which development team successfully designed the ENIAC?
(a) John W. Mauchly and J. Presper Eckert.
(b) Stephen Wozniak and Steven Jobs.
(c) Charles Babbage and Lady Ada Lovelace.
(d) John V. Atanasoff and Clifford E. Berry.

_____ 4. The transistor was developed by the team of
(a) John V. Atanasoff and Clifford E. Berry.
(b) Thomas Watson, Sr., and John von Neumann.
(c) John W. Mauchly and J. Presper Eckert.
(d) William Shockley, John Bardeen, and Walter H. Brattain.

_____ 5. Which is *not* a feature of the fourth-generation of computer?
(a) Microprocessor.   (c) Firmware.
(b) Large-scale integration (LSI).   (d) Magnetic drum.

FILL IN-THE BLANK

_____ 1. The team of _____ and _____ developed the Apple Computer.

_____ 2. The two major programming languages developed during the second generation were _____ for scientific applications and _____ for business applications.

_____ 3. Online terminals and databases are primarily features of _____-generation computers.

4. The field of _____ refers to efforts to design programs that reflect the way people think and learn.

5. The "race to the moon" was an important stimulus for the development of _____-generation computers.

6. The _____ made it possible for computers to accept instructions as well as data into memory.

7. _____ an interactive programming language for novice users was developed by the team of _____ and _____ .

8. _____ developed a punch card coded weaving process.

9. The earliest form of calculating instrument was the _____ .

10. _____ is a fourth-generation programming language that stresses structured methods.

SHORT ANSWER QUESTIONS

1. Compare Charles Babbage's design for the analytic engine with today's computers.

2. What are major features of first-generation computers?

3. What are the major features of third-generation computers?

4. Match the software languages with the computer generation in which they first became popular.

5. How did the "race for the moon" affect the development of real-time processing?

6. Which computer generations favored the development of computers and software capable of easily handling exception procedures?

7. What is the study of robotics?

8. What was the principal means of secondary storage for each generation?

ESSAY QUESTIONS

1. Describe how demand for computers has affected the development of the four generations of computers.

2. Compare the features of the information system elements found in first- and fourth-generation computers.

3. What are the features expected to be found in fifth-generation computers? A trip to the library will help uncover some sources on this topic.

PART TWO

Part One introduced information systems, briefly explaining what they are, the steps in their evolution, and the jobs they perform today. In Part Two, we focus on a key element of information systems– hardware.

CHAPTER 5

THE CENTRAL PROCESSING UNIT: SMALLER AND QUICKER

After studying this chapter you should understand the
following:
■ The difference between analog and digital computers.
■ What the parts of the central processing unit are, and how
they work together.
■ How data are represented and stored inside the computer.
■ The types of silicon chips the central processing unit uses for
processing and storage.
■ How microcomputers, minicomputers, mainframe computers,
and supercomputers differ in terms of performance and
price.

Nat Bergstein and David Cunningham drove into the main parking lot at Global Electrical Equipment's appliance design and manufacturing facility in Oakriver.

"At least the smokestacks are still putting out smoke," David said.

"Manufacturing is controlled by the minicomputer," Nat said. "That's still all right. It's the mainframe that's down." Nat pulled the car right up to the visitor parking area in front of the main entrance. "Besides, they don't call it smoke here, they call it steam."

Nat and David gathered together their manuals and disk pack, left the car, and signed in at the front desk. A minute later they reached the computer center, where the atmosphere was one of crisis. Clayton Johns, the computer center manager, spotted them.

"Mr. Johns," Nat said, "let me introduce my colleague, David Cunningham." David and Clayton shook hands.

"Welcome, Gentlemen," Clayton said. "The whole system's down, and everybody's on my back. If you can't get it running again by lunch, I might as well enlist in the French Foreign Legion!"

"I hear the food's good in the legion," Nat said, leading the way to the computer console. "But we have to get your system up again. Otherwise I'll be in the legion with you." Nat twirled the fastener on the lid of the cake-tray-like disk pack he was carrying, and removed the pack. "Before we run the test program, tell me what's wrong," he said.

"The computer power's up all right," Clayton said, "but the operating system won't run. Instead it hangs up and displays the strangest system errors."

"And you think it's hardware?" Nat asked.

"Definitely," Clayton said. "You see, the trouble began when the computer started terminating programs for illegal operations."

"Production programs?" David asked.

"Yes. Programs that have run fine for years."

"And now even the operating system itself won't run," Nat said. "O.K., this should tell us what's wrong." He took the disk pack and mounted it on a disk reader, returned to the console, entered a few commands, and got the machine to start running the test program. Several magnetic tape drives started twirling and the laser printer began spewing out pages.

"What is it testing now?" Clayton asked.

"Main memory," Nat said. "Let me just look at the printout." Nat and David crossed the room to the printer. "Good news. Memory's all right. All 32 million bytes of it. This program diagnoses faster than we can with our meters. The problem might not be hardware at all. It could be in the operating system. But we'll see. Right now the pro-

TYPES OF COMPUTERS

A **COMPUTER** is a very-high-speed electronic device that can accept data and instructions, use the instructions to perform logical and mathematical operations on the data, and report the results of its processing. This chapter will describe the inner workings of the computer. First, however, we need to differentiate among three different types of computer.

ANALOG, DIGITAL, AND HYBRID COMPUTERS

An **ANALOG COMPUTER** operates on data values that it represents by using an analogy to the data (hence the name). Usually data are represented by using varying levels of energy. For example, an equation might be expressed by using different voltage levels for its different values. Analog computers treat data as continuous rather than breaking them up into separate values. Changes in voltage level would correspond to different values in an equation much the way a dimmer switch gradually varies the intensity of lighting. Analog computers are used for a small number of engineering and scientific applications, but not for business applications.

DIGITAL COMPUTERS are the main type of computer in use today. They are used for all types of applications. A digital computer represents data as discrete (meaning "separate and unconnected") values. This is the opposite of the continuous way in which analog computers handle data. Data in digital computers are expressed by the "on" or "off" state of electrical components. Like a light switch on a wall, a component must be either on or off. As we will see later in the chapter, all numbers, as well as special symbols, can be reduced to an "on/off" representation.

A **HYBRID COMPUTER** combines features of both digital and analog computers. In a hybrid computer some switches respond to on/off conditions as with a digital computer, and other components respond to variable charges as with an analog computer. This type of machine sees use in a small number of engineering and scientific applications.

GENERAL- AND SPECIAL-PURPOSE DIGITAL COMPUTERS

As you can see from our definitions above, our only concern will be with digital computers. These can, however, be subdivided into two categories. **GENERAL-PURPOSE COMPUTERS**, by far the most common, can be used for a variety of large and small business, engineering, and scientific applications. Indeed a single general-purpose computer can tackle all of these applications (even simultaneously), a situation common on college campuses.

SPECIAL-PURPOSE COMPUTERS are designed to perform a specific function, and lack the flexibility of general-purpose machines. For example, special-purpose computers are sometimes used for navigational control, regulating heating and lighting in a large building, or, on a smaller scale, running a video game.

Our focus in this text will be on general-purpose digital computers—the kind used in information systems.

THE COMPUTER AND THE INFORMATION SYSTEM

It is easy to lose sight of the fact that computers are just a small part of an information system. The most important part, as we have said before, is the people who work with and depend on the system. The needs of the *people* working in or affected by the system must determine the particular *hardware* configuration (mixture of computers and peripherals—input/output, storage, and communications units) of the system. The other elements are also important. The *rules* and *procedures* developed by management and carried out by other users will help determine the equipment requirements. The types of *data* and how they are most economically captured for processing will also affect the hardware mix. Finally the *software* will affect the specific hardware we might select.

As users of information systems, however, you need to be familiar with the characteristics of computer hardware, including the computer itself.

THE CPU: WHAT IT IS AND HOW IT WORKS

The hardware of a computer system is made up of four parts: (1) the central processing unit (CPU), (2) input and output devices, (3) secondary storage devices, and (4) communications equipment. Figure 5-1 shows how the four components relate. This chapter deals with the central processing unit; input and output devices, secondary storage devices, and communications equipment will be the topics of the next three chapters respectively.

THE PARTS OF THE CPU

The **CPU (CENTRAL PROCESSING UNIT)** is the computer itself. It carries out the instructions given it by software to process the input data and produce the output information.

Figure 5-2 shows the different functional units of the computer. These are the control unit, main storage, and the arithmetic/logic unit. Each is described below.

- *The* **CONTROL UNIT** *is the "brain" of the computer. It interprets program instructions and directs the other parts of the CPU, and also communicates with external input/output devices and secondary storage devices.*

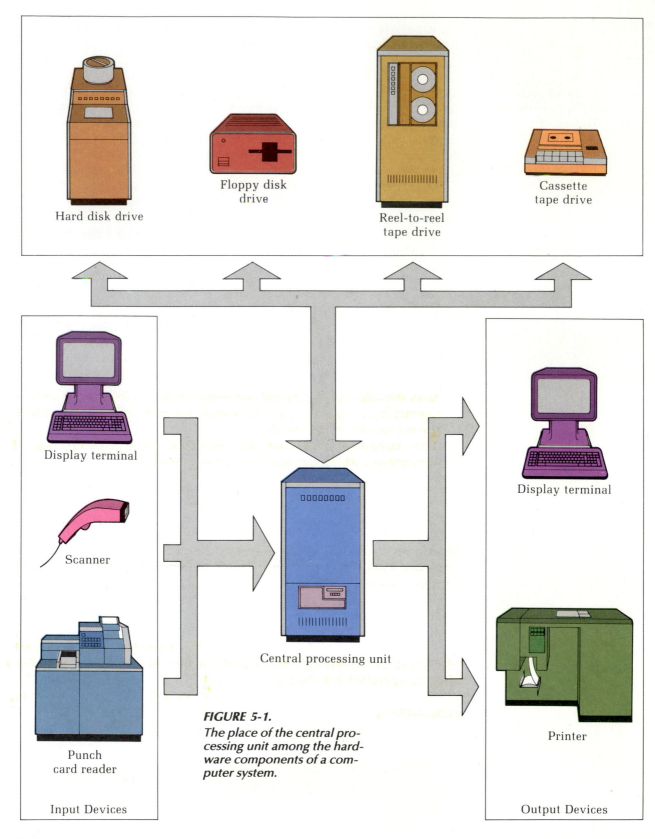

Hard disk drive

Floppy disk drive

Reel-to-reel tape drive

Cassette tape drive

Display terminal

Scanner

Punch card reader

Input Devices

Central processing unit

FIGURE 5-1.
The place of the central processing unit among the hardware components of a computer system.

Display terminal

Printer

Output Devices

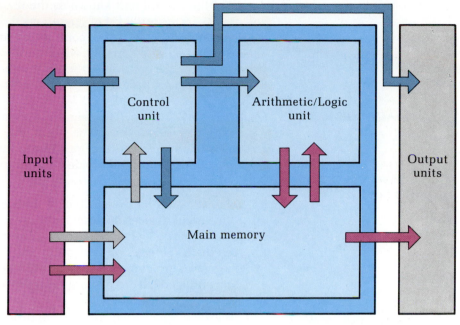

FIGURE 5-2.
The central processing unit. The three functional units are the control unit, the arithmetic/ logic unit, and main memory. Arrows indicate the general flow of instructions, control, and data.

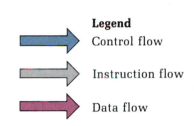

Legend

Control flow

Instruction flow

Data flow

- **MAIN MEMORY** *stores data and instructions that have been input and are waiting to be processed, and stores the results of processing until they are released to output devices.*
- The **ARITHMETIC/LOGIC UNIT (ALU)** *performs calculations and logical operations with data, as directed by the control unit.*

In the following sections we will examine each of these functional units in turn.

CONTROL UNIT

The job of the CPU's control unit is to direct all hardware operations. The control unit interprets the instructions of the application or system program that is being run, one instruction at a time, and issues the necessary orders to the other parts of the system to carry out the instructions. The control unit also communicates with the input/output devices and secondary storage devices.

The machine instructions supplied to the control unit consist of an operation code and one or more operands. The **OPERATION CODE** or **OP CODE** tells the computer what operation to perform. An **OPERAND** tells the computer what the operation is to be carried out on. Usually the operand gives the address of data that are to be operated on. An **ADDRESS** is a unique location in main memory.

Here is an example of a machine-level instruction (written in assembly language) to subtract the value found in location B from the value found in location A:

Op code	Operand 1	Operand 2
SUB	A	B

A part of the control unit known as the **DECODER** reads the operation code and matches it against a list of operations the computer can perform. When the decoder finds a match, the control unit sets the correct circuitry to carry out the operation. For example, when the decoder encounters the command for subtraction, the control unit sends messages to the arithmetic/logic unit to set the electronic switches to perform subtraction.

MAIN MEMORY

Main memory—also called primary storage and internal storage—holds data and instructions that have been input for processing, intermediate results, and the final results of processing until they are released to output devices. Main memory is divided into four functional areas (see Figure 5-3):

- **INPUT STORAGE** holds data that have been read from an input device. Since input devices operate at slower speeds than the central processing unit, part of the input storage area serves as a buffer. BUFFERS help free the CPU to get on with other work while the slower input/output operations are completing. Input storage acts as a buffer, accumulating data until enough are present to justify processing them.
- **PROGRAM STORAGE** holds instructions from both system and application programs, which enter the central processor from an input device.
- **WORKING STORAGE** holds the results of work in progress, such as intermediate answers to mathematical computations the CPU is carrying out.
- **OUTPUT STORAGE** holds information that has been processed and is ready to output. Like input storage this area too can serve as a buffer. Output storage receives a quantity of output information from processing, and then retains the data so that they can be sent gradually out of the CPU at a speed appropriate to the slower output devices.

FIGURE 5-3.
Main memory and its four functional subcomponents.

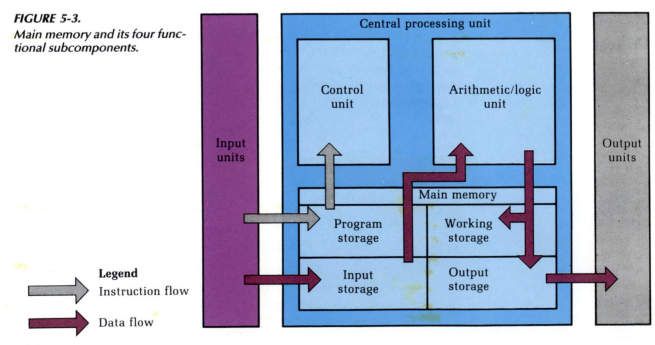

Legend

Instruction flow

Data flow

As with a number of the CPU concepts we will describe, these four types of storage are handled differently from one machine to the next. Even within a particular machine, as the computer processes its programs, it may increase or decrease the amount of main storage that it allocates for program storage, output storage, or whatever, depending on program needs. The point is that all four types of storage needs must be met by any CPU.

Every location within main storage has a unique address. The address identifies one, and only one, particular point in the computer hardware. For an analogy we can think of addresses as referencing mailboxes that can, however, only hold one letter (data item) at a time. If another letter (data item) is placed in a mailbox, it destroys whatever was there first. This process of writing new material into a storage location and erasing the old material in the process is called **DESTRUCTIVE WRITE**. Examining or copying data from a storage location, in contrast, does not destroy it. **NONDESTRUCTIVE READ** refers to the ability to look at or copy the data in a storage address without destroying them.

ARITHMETIC/LOGIC UNIT

The arithmetic/logic unit (ALU) performs calculations and logical operations on data. The ALU circuitry works under the direction of the control unit. Given an instruction by the control unit— such as to compare two numbers to find out which is larger—the ALU performs the comparison.

There are three main components of the ALU: mathematical gates, logic gates, and registers. A **GATE** is an electronic switch with several entrances but only one exit. Data come in through the entrances and the answer comes out via the exit. **MATH GATES** perform basic calculations, such as addition, subtraction, multiplication, and division. **LOGIC GATES** perform comparisons (see box). Depending on the results of a comparison, the control unit tells the computer to do one of two things, as the program directs.

REGISTERS

Among its various types of switches the CPU relies extensively on registers. A **REGISTER** is a high-speed temporary storage unit for data or a program instruction. Registers are used in several parts of the CPU. The circuitry of a register is designed such that data can be placed into a register, or removed from it, faster than from a location in main storage.

To illustrate some of the specialized functions registers perform, let's look at how the decoder uses them. The decoder (described in the "Control Unit" section earlier in the chapter) matches instruction codes against a list of permissible codes, and when a match is found, sets the correct circuitry to carry out the operation the code specifies. No fewer than four types of registers are used in the process. These are:

- *The sequence control register, which keeps track of the steps in the processing sequence.*
- *The instruction register, which holds the operation code to be decoded and the operand.*
- *The address register, which also holds the address specified in the instruction's operand.*
- *The instruction address register, which holds the address of the next instruction to be fetched from main memory.*

Logic functions are crucial to the way a computer works. Yet understanding how logic switches operate can cause the beginner trouble. Engineering diagrams that show the correct way to symbolize logic circuits tend to confuse rather than enlighten nonengineers. So let's use an offbeat example to explain the concept just as well. In fact let's use a dog.

There are two main types of logic functions that a computer uses, the logical AND and the logical OR. The logical AND tests to see if two or more conditions are true. If they all are, the result of the test is "true." If at least one of the conditions is false, the result of the test is "false." In terms of gates only true values can enter the gate in order for a true value to exit the gate.

The logical OR tests to see if any of two or more conditions is true. If at least one is, the result of the test is "true." If all of the conditions are false, then the result of the test is "false." In terms of gates at least one true value must enter the gate in order for a true value to exit the gate.

Now back to the dog, whose name is Myrtle. Imagine Myrtle in a fenced yard. The yard is divided into two parts, and Myrtle is not much of a jumper or digger. In (a), for her to get out of the inner yard both gates must be open. This corresponds to a logical AND, which requires that all conditions be met before something can be done. In this case both gates must be open in order for Myrtle to take herself for a walk.

In (b) we see the logical OR situation. Here Myrtle is in a different yard. She can get out if either one or both of the gates are open. As you can see, the requirements to meet a logical OR are less stringent than those to meet a logical AND.

Businesses use such logical tests to perform a variety of tasks. For example, mailing lists can be sorted using logical AND statements. Freddy Johnson's Travel Agency might want to send out mail advertising a round-the-world tour package to everyone who could conceivably afford it. Based on a general list of Oakriver residents supplied by a mailing-list firm, a computer could single out families that live in certain high-income areas *and* own two cars. Those who pass this logical AND test would get the mailer—and a few might take the trip.

Logic gates—an example using a household pet. (a) Logical AND gate. (b) Logical OR gate.

Logical AND gate.

(a)

Logical OR gate.

(b)

Well-designed registers permit the most efficient use of the most expensive parts of the CPU, the decoder and the math and logic gates. Registers reduce the distance signals must travel to and from these parts, and thus reduce idle time, much the way an airline reduces the amount of time an airplane is idle on the ground by collecting everything needed to service and fill the plane—fuel, luggage handlers, flight crews, passengers—near the plane at the right time.

THE MACHINE CYCLE

The term MACHINE CYCLE refers to the interaction of the components of the CPU for the time required to carry out one machine operation. It can be compared to a heartbeat. An electronic clock within the computer gives out pulses at regular intervals, which fix the machine cycle. Machine cycles are short: today's computers squeeze as many as hundreds of millions of machine cycles into a single second. A single program may require millions of machine cycles to run.

The machine cycle has two substages, the instruction cycle and the execution cycle. During the INSTRUCTION CYCLE, the CPU fetches an instruction, figures out which operation to perform by decoding it, and then interprets the operand to find the data to perform the operation upon. During the EXECUTION CYCLE, the CPU performs the operation. Then the CPU moves on to the next cycle.

Let's follow one machine cycle through, to illustrate how the components of the CPU interact. We will assume that a program and the data it will use are already in main memory, and that the operating system has instructed the CPU to start running the program.

During the machine cycle the control unit fetches the first instruction from main memory. Within the control unit the decoder matches the instruction code against the machine's repertoire of possibilities (called the instruction set). Upon finding a match the decoder sends messages to the arithmetic/logic unit to set the necessary gates to carry out the operation. The arithmetic/logic unit performs the operation. If the operation generates output (or intermediate results, which will be used by another operation), the output or result is stored in main memory. The machine cycle is complete—a tiny fraction of a second has gone by—and the machine begins the next cycle.

When the program directs the computer to produce output, it is transferred from main memory to the appropriate output unit, under the control of system software. When the program finishes running, the CPU is sure to find work with another application program, or with running instructions of the operating system itself.

DATA REPRESENTATION

Computers—fast as they are—need numbers, characters, and symbols presented to them in a very simple fashion. Digital computers respond only to yes or no, on or off signals. Therefore our rich and diverse number systems, alphabets, and symbolic codes must be translated into a two-state, on or off, pattern.

To represent this two-state condition, only two numbers are used. The numeral 1 represents the "on" state of an electrical component, and the numeral 0 represents the "off" state. No other numbers are allowed.

POWERS OF TWO: NUMBER SYSTEMS AND THE COMPUTER

The number system we are all familiar with is the DECIMAL (base 10) NUMBER SYSTEM. "Decimal" is derived from the Latin word for "ten." By base is meant the number of available numerals in the system. The decimal system has ten available numerals, consisting of 0 through 9. As you recognize that all the numbers we know can be made up of the numerals 0 through 9, then you have come part of the way to understanding it can be done with only the numerals 0 and 1.

There are three other number systems used in connection with computers: the binary, octal, and hexadecimal number systems. Binary is the number system that the computer itself uses. Octal and hexadecimal are used for the convenience of people because they compress binary numbers, which tend to be long and hard to understand, into many fewer digits. These number systems have the following features:

- The BINARY (base 2) NUMBER SYSTEM is central to digital computers—computers understand nothing other than binary. It utilizes only the numerals 1, corresponding to the *on* state of an electrical component, and 0, corresponding to the *off* state. "Binary" is derived from the Latin word for "two." A single binary digit (a 1 or 0) is known as a BIT, a word derived from "binary digit."

- The OCTAL (base 8) NUMBER SYSTEM. This system uses only the numerals 0 through 7. "Octal" is derived from the Greek term for "eight." Octal is useful in connection with computers because its base, 8, is a power of 2 (2^3), making it a cousin of binary. The octal number system compresses binary numbers—which tend to be lengthy—into a more compact form easier for people to read.

- The HEXADECIMAL (base 16) NUMBER SYSTEM. This system uses not only the numerals 0 through 9, but also the *letters* A through F, in order to add another six possibilities beyond 0 through 9. If you believe this is a difficult concept, don't worry, that's exactly how programmers found it when it was introduced in the 1960s; it has continued to be a test of their skills ever since. The virtue of hexadecimal is that, like octal, it is also a cousin of binary, and a more powerful one. That is, the base of hexadecimal (16) is a power of 2 (2^4). Hexadecimal can compress binary numbers even more tightly than octal can.

Figure 5-4 compares the first 16 integters as represented in the decimal, binary, octal, and hexadecimal number systems. The decimal number 7, for instance, comes out exactly the same in octal and in hexadecimal; in binary, however, it is 111. By the time we reach the decimal number 16, the equivalent binary number (10000) occupies five digits. You can see how bulky binary numbers become, and how octal and hexadecimal numbers reduce the space required for human-readable output of machine instructions or stored data. Hexadecimal compresses numbers the most (it is even tighter than the decimal system we are used to), but has the drawback that it includes letters as numbers. For people this reduces the readability, since we are not accustomed to reading letters mixed with our numbers. For more on number systems turn to Appendix B on number systems at the end of this book.

FIGURE 5-4.

The first 16 integers in the decimal, binary, octal, and hexadecimal systems.

Decimal	Binary				Octal		Hexadecimal
0				0		0	0
1				1		1	1
2			1	0		2	2
3			1	1		3	3
4		1	0	0		4	4
5		1	0	1		5	5
6		1	1	0		6	6
7		1	1	1		7	7
8	1	0	0	0	1	0	8
9	1	0	0	1	1	1	9
1 0	1	0	1	0	1	2	A
1 1	1	0	1	1	1	3	B
1 2	1	1	0	0	1	4	C
1 3	1	1	0	1	1	5	D
1 4	1	1	1	0	1	6	E
1 5	1	1	1	1	1	7	F
1 6	1 0	0	0	0	2	0	1 0

BITS, BYTES, AND CHARACTERS

A bit, as we saw earlier, is a single binary digit. For convenience computers work with a larger unit than the bit, called a byte. A **BYTE** is a string of adjacent bits that the computer processes as a unit. Although other sizes have been and are used on some of today's computers, the usual number of bits per byte is eight.

Another term you will sometimes encounter is a **NIBBLE** or **NYBBLE**. This is simply half a byte, which is usually four bits.

In Figure 5-4 we saw how numbers could be represented in binary. If a computer could only read numbers, however, its usefulness would be limited. We would not be able to use the computer for many practical business problems such as alphabetic sorting and word processing. Some coding conventions have been developed to solve this problem.

EBCDIC AND ASCII

Besides representing numbers, a byte can also represent letters, punctuation, and other symbols. This is done by following agreed-upon conventions used in designing hardware and software. The conventions say that certain patterns of bits in a byte will be taken not for binary numbers at all, but for a particular letter or symbol.

One such set of conventions, widely used, is known as EBCDIC. The acronym EBCDIC is short for EXTENDED BINARY CODED DECIMAL INTERCHANGE CODE. Taking the eight bits of a byte, EBCDIC assigns a bit pattern to each of the decimal numbers 0 through 9, lowercase and uppercase alphabet, and commonly used special symbols (such as plus signs and dollar signs). Some input/output devices need specialized control characters, and EBCDIC even has values that stand for these.

In all, eight bits can represent 256 (2^8) characters, enough to account for our entire repertoire of numerals, letters, special characters, and control characters, and still leave space open for future use or customized meanings on particular systems. Figure 5-5 shows the EBCDIC system.

FIGURE 5-5.
How EBCDIC represents numbers, letters, and special symbols.

Character	8-Bit EBCDIC 8421 8421 (place values)	Character	8-Bit EBCDIC 8421 8421 (place values)
0	1111 0000	K	1101 0010
1	1111 0001	L	1101 0011
2	1111 0010	M	1101 0100
3	1111 0011	N	1101 0101
4	1111 0100	O	1101 0110
5	1111 0101	P	1101 0111
6	1111 0110	Q	1101 1000
7	1111 0111	R	1101 1001
8	1111 1000	S	1110 0010
9	1111 1001	T	1110 0011
A	1100 0001	U	1110 0100
B	1100 0010	V	1110 0101
C	1100 0011	W	1110 0110
D	1100 0100	X	1110 0111
E	1100 0101	Y	1110 1000
F	1100 0110	Z	1110 1001
G	1100 0111	+	0100 1110
H	1100 1000	$	0101 1011
I	1100 1001	.	0100 1011
J	1101 0001	<	0100 1100

Character	8-Bit ASCII 8421 8421 (place values)	Character	8-Bit ASCII 8421 8421 (place values)
0	1011 0000	K	1100 1011
1	1011 0001	L	1100 1100
2	1011 0010	M	1100 1101
3	1011 0011	N	1100 1110
4	1011 0100	O	1100 1111
5	1011 0101	P	1101 0000
6	1011 0110	Q	1101 0001
7	1011 0111	R	1101 0010
8	1011 1000	S	1101 0011
9	1011 1001	T	1101 0100
A	1100 0001	U	1101 0101
B	1100 0010	V	1101 0110
C	1100 0011	W	1101 0111
D	1100 0100	X	1101 1000
E	1100 0101	Y	1101 1001
F	1100 0110	Z	1101 1010
G	1100 0111	+	1010 1011
H	1100 1000	$	1010 0100
I	1100 1001	.	1010 1110
J	1100 1010	<	1011 1100

The other set of conventions that is also widely used today is known as ASCII. This acronym stands for AMERICAN STANDARD CODE FOR INFORMATION INTERCHANGE. Like EBCDIC, ASCII has a specific bit pattern assigned to every number, letter, symbol, and control code in common use. Unlike EBCDIC, which uses eight bits, ASCII has a version that uses only seven bits, and another—known as ASCII-8—that uses eight bits. Figure 5-6 shows the ASCII-8 system.

Developed by IBM, EBCDIC is used on mainframes produced by IBM, as well as on mainframes produced by some other manufacturers. ASCII is commonly used by microcomputers and data-communication systems.

PARITY BITS

When data are communicated between a computer and its peripherals, or from computer to computer over a communications link, they may sometimes be garbled. Often this garbling is caused by binary digits accidentally flipping from 1 to 0, or from 0 to 1, leaving the computer with a pattern it cannot understand. A **PARITY BIT**, or **CHECK BIT**, is used to detect the presence of such possible garbling. A parity bit is simply an additional bit appended to a byte. Thus an EBCDIC or eight-bit byte will have a ninth parity bit and a seven-bit ASCII byte will have an eighth parity bit.

Here is how the parity bit works. The ASCII-8 code for the letter G is 11000111. There are five 1s in that code. We can place another 1 in the parity bit, giving a total of six 1s. Six is an even number. We can follow the convention that all bytes in our computer system must contain an even number of 1s, counting the parity bit. Thus whenever the data value contains an odd number of 1s, as in the example, we simply set the parity bit to 1, to give an even total. If the data value already contains an even number of 1s, we set the parity bit to 0. This system is known as "even parity."

The opposite approach, "odd parity," requires that the total number of 1s in a byte plus its parity bit be odd. For example, the ASCII-8 code for a dollar sign is 10100110. There are four 1s in the code. If we need an odd number of 1s, we would set the parity bit to 1, giving a total of five 1s. This is simply the opposite procedure to that with even parity.

Figure 5-7 shows the parity-bit settings for each of the characters that spell out "GREETINGS," using the even parity system. Parity bits can be used with EBCDIC, ASCII, or any other binary-based convention.

The parity bit does not change the data value contained in the byte itself. It is merely a protective measure to help spot many cases of garbled bytes. If,

FIGURE 5-7.

Using a parity or check bit. In this example the "even parity" system is used. The letter G contains an error—a 1 where there should be a 0—and the total number of 1s in that byte, including the parity bit, adds up to 7, an odd number.

Letter	Parity bit	ASCII-8 Code
G	1	1 1 0 0 [1] 1 1 1
R	0	1 1 0 1 0 0 1 0
E	0	1 1 0 0 0 1 0 1
E	0	1 1 0 0 0 1 0 1
T	0	1 1 0 1 0 1 0 0
I	0	1 1 0 0 1 0 0 1
N	1	1 1 0 0 1 1 1 0
G	1	1 1 0 0 0 1 1 1
S	1	1 1 0 1 0 0 1 1

for example, our computer uses even parity, every single byte of data will be checked at key points to assure that the number of 1s in the byte plus the byte's parity bit is even. When an odd total turns up, something is amiss. In this situation the computer generally prints an error message stating that there is a parity error, and outputs the suspect data (or instruction) byte as well.

COMPUTER WORDS A **COMPUTER WORD** is made up of one or more consecutive bytes. The length of a computer word is a design feature of the particular computer, closely tied to the way that the CPU interprets and executes instructions (which themselves must be placed into bytes or words). Typical word sizes are one byte (8 bits), two bytes (16 bits), four bytes (32 bits), and eight bytes (64 bits). Word sizes for microcomputers range from 8 bits in older machines to 32 bits in newer machines. Mainframe computers have word sizes ranging from 32 to 64 bits. Depending on how they treat words, computers may be classified as either fixed-length-word or variable-length-word machines.

Fixed-length systems

A computer with **FIXED-LENGTH WORDS** is designed to handle words that contain a specific number of bytes.

By placing several bytes together in one word, and working with words as a unit instead of bytes, the size of the numbers that can be handled is increased, as is the speed of the computer. What makes it possible for the computer to work faster is that data and instructions can be obtained an entire word at a time, and worked on a word at a time. Performing an operation on all of a word at once, so that calculations can be performed on all the digits of a number simultaneously, is known as **PARALLEL ARITHMETIC**. Parallel arithmetic is the opposite of slower **SERIAL ARITHMETIC** in which operations occur on a byte-by-byte basis.

Fixed-length computers are most often used for scientific and engineering applications, which require high processing speeds to perform complex calculations.

The drawback of the fixed-length system is that it tends to waste storage space. When data do not fill a word, the unused bytes of the word are left empty.

Variable-length systems

Computers with a **VARIABLE-LENGTH WORD** handle each byte or character individually. Many microcomputers and other smaller computers are of this type. With each byte having its own address, we can minimize wasted space in main storage. This is the advantage. The drawback is that performing operations on the data is slower because serial arithmetic must be employed.

Some larger computers, such as the IBM 4300 series, are capable of performing either fixed- or variable-word-length operations. Thus when eliminating wasted storage space is the focus of an application, the variable-length system can be used; when calculation speed is the prime factor, the fixed-length approach can be taken.

Packed into the central processing unit of today's computers are miniature electronic circuits etched onto small wafers of glass called **SILICON CHIPS**. The chips are so tiny that a lot of circuits can be squeezed into a small space. We find them popping up in many places today, controlling appliances, automotive systems, watches, and much more. They are the brainchild of the computer industry, however, and are used throughout the CPU. Today's silicon chips work faster than earlier silicon chips and transistors, because they are so small that electricity must travel only a short distance from one circuit path to the next. Chips are also tougher and more reliable than earlier components. Figure 5-8 shows how chips are made.

Today's mainframe computers and minicomputers use semiconductor silicon chips throughout the central processing unit. Chips are used in the control unit to monitor processing, decode instructions, and serve as registers. The arithmetic/logic unit uses chips to perform mathematical and logical operations.

FIGURE 5-8.

How chips are made. (a) Computer chips are made from wafers of silicon. The creation of a chip starts with an enlarged circuit design created with the help of computer-aided design methods. This design is scanned and stored in digitized form. (b) The silicon wafers are sliced from a pure silicon ingot. (c) The wafers are polished.

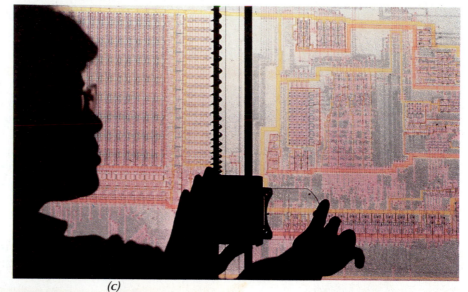
(a)

(b)

(c)
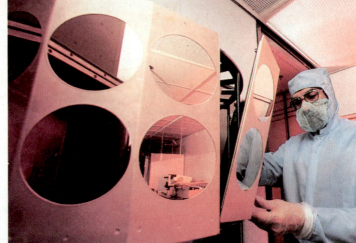

(d)

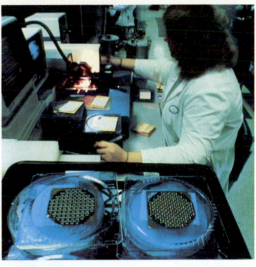

(e)

FIGURE 5-8 (cont.)

(d) The circuit pattern from the original enlarged design is reduced to microscopic size and printed onto a photomask. Each of the little squares in the mask contains a copy of one layer of the design; each square represents a layer of a single chip. The mask is placed over a wafer, which is then exposed to ultraviolet light. The wafer has been previously treated with a light-sensitive "doping" compound. Where the mask blocks the ultraviolet light, the compound remains soft; the places exposed to light harden. The wafer is then placed in an acid bath and the soft, unexposed areas wash away. (e) The fabrication process takes place in "clean rooms" ten thousand times cleaner than a hospital operating room. (f) (g) Inspectors monitor the fabrication process. (h) A needlelike probe tests the contacts on each chip on the wafer. After this stage the chips are separated and the failed chips discarded.

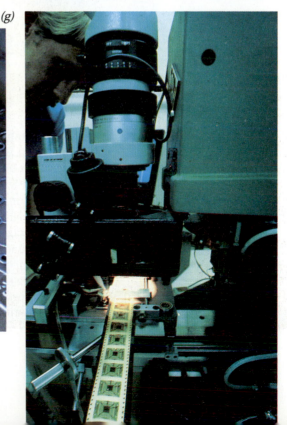

(f)

(g)

(h)

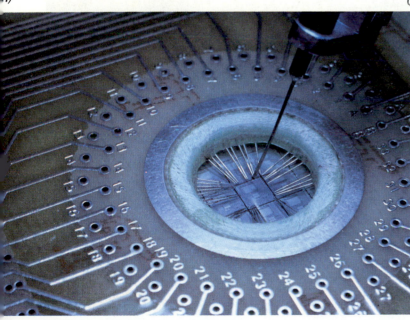

(i)

(j)

FIGURE 5-8 (cont.)
(i) The chips are soldered onto frames. (j) The chip and frame are placed in a protective jacket, which has connector pins to fit onto circuit boards. (k) Circuit boards containing chips are then assembled into a wide variety of products.

(k)

MICROPROCESSORS

In microcomputers the entire CPU is contained on a single silicon chip known as a **MICROPROCESSOR**. A microprocessor can contain the control unit, the arithmetic/logic unit, and some of the main memory. An example is shown in Figure 5-9.

Microprocessors are often categorized by word size, or the number of bits the processor can operate on. The earliest microprocessors could only handle 8-bit-sized words. Then 16-bit microprocessors were developed. Today 32-bit microprocessors allow a substantial increase in processing speeds, since more data and instructions can be processed in a given time interval than with 8- or 16-bit systems. In addition the larger word size makes it possible to build more main storage into the machines. The number of each memory location must be able to fit into a word; with larger words more main storage can be used and referred to.

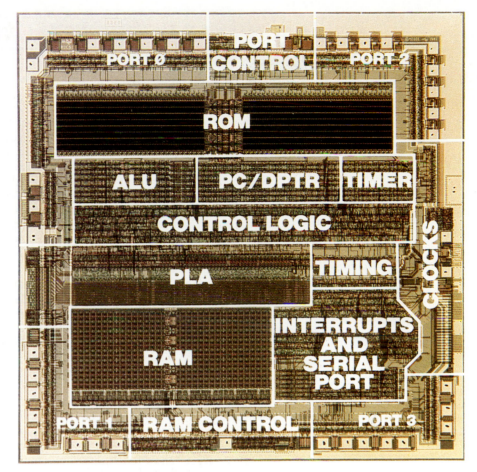

Further increases in processing speed can be obtained by combining microprocessors. In large microcomputers, minicomputers, and mainframes the CPU may contain a number of microprocessors linked together.

RANDOM ACCESS MEMORY (RAM) CHIPS

It is in their role as main memory that silicon chips serve their most visible purpose: fast storage. Chips used for main memory have a variety of different names that reflect their various functions.

The mainstay of main memory is the highly price-competitive RANDOM ACCESS MEMORY (RAM) chip. It is called "random access" because the address of any memory location can be reached ("accessed") without the necessity for checking or referring to any adjacent locations.

On some computers a special storage area of high-speed RAM chips sits between the rest of main memory and the other parts of the central processor. Called CACHE STORAGE (cache is a French word meaning a place for storing provisions, pronounced *cash*), this area holds data and instructions likely to be transferred to the registers for processing. The aim is to save time fetching the instructions once the program needs them.

RAM chips are volatile—that is, they immediately lose their data when the power is turned off. To avoid costly losses of instructions or data,

Neil Lincoln, a senior engineer at Control Data Corporation, defines a supercomputer as "a computer that is only one generation behind the user's needs." Since it takes considerable time to design and build the world's fastest, most sophisticated, and most expensive computers (they start at $4 million and often cost as much as $20 million)—used at such places as Los Alamos and Lawrence Livermore Scientific Laboratories, the National Center for Atmospheric Research, and the Department of Defense—there just aren't too many around. Seymour Cray used to work with Neil Lincoln and was CDC's top designer. A complete recluse and workaholic, Cray demanded in 1962—during the Cuban missile crisis—that CDC, headquartered in Minneapolis, allow him to move his lab to his hometown of Chippewa Falls, Wisconsin, far from any possible nuclear hubbub. CDC acceded, but in 1972 Cray resigned and formed his own supercomputer company, Cray Research, Inc., and went into head-on competition with CDC.

It took Cray four years to deliver his first computer, the Cray-1, but it was the fastest computer on earth. Installing a Cray-1 is no simple task. A Cray team goes to the site months in advance to install a false floor strong enough to support the computer; several thousand dollars' worth of special Freon plumbing, to cool the thousands of circuits,

must be installed underneath. The Cray-1 is tested for months, then mounted on a platform and moved by truck to the site. In the case of certain Defense Department installations, the truck stops in a deserted location, the drivers lock it up and leave, and military drivers take the Cray to its secret location. Otherwise, Cray delivers the machine complete with two engineers to maintain and upgrade it—forever.

By the summer of 1982, about forty Cray-1's had been installed, and it was still the fastest computer. Yet for the past two years there were two projects under way to develop a computer ten times faster. One project was in Mendota Heights, a suburb of Minneapolis and Cray Research headquarters, and was conducted by a group of bright young engineers; the other was in Chippewa Falls and was Seymour's very own. Both projects were completed at about the same time; the first was an improvement over the Cray-1 and was dubbed the X-MP. The other was an entirely new computer that achieves its speed by supercooling—in this case the entire computer is immersed in a tank of subzero fluorocarbon fluid; the computer was called the Cray-2.

Source: Jack B. Rochester and John Gantz, *The Naked Computer*, 1983, pp. 38–39. Copyright © 1983 by Jack B. Rochester and John Gantz. By permission of William Morrow and Co.

uninterruptible backup power supplies such as batteries should be provided.

A memory chip can be thought of as a large grid with many rows and columns. At the intersection of a row and column a bit can be stored. To find what is stored at any intersection, only the row and column numbers need to be known. With a RAM storage unit you can store data at storage locations, read them later, and then erase the data by writing over them.

Storage capacity on a chip is expressed in multiples of 2^{10} or 1024 bits, often called 1K (where K means one thousand). A common RAM storage chip has 256×2^{10}—or 262,144 or 256K—bits. Many newer systems for home and personal applications use 256K RAM chips. If each byte in your computer is eight bits in size, it takes eight of these 256K-bit chips to give you 256K *bytes* of primary storage. Currently some RAM chips can hold just over 1 million bits, and 4-million-bit RAM chips are on the drawing boards.

READ-ONLY MEMORY (ROM) CHIPS

READ-ONLY MEMORY (ROM) chips are chips on which programs (or data) have been permanently encoded. A ROM can be read but cannot be written onto by the user. ROMs are used for a variety of purposes. In many microcomputers, for example, part of the system software is stored on ROM, as is the program that allows the computer to run application software written in the BASIC programming language. ROM is also used to store machine-level instructions for frequently used procedures—such as how to calculate square roots. ROM can also be used to store entire applications programs. Some portable microcomputers, for example, come with word processing and spreadsheet programs built in on ROM.

Software encoded on ROM chips is often called FIRMWARE, because, strictly speaking, it is neither "hard" nor "soft."

Sometimes users of an information system want to program and protect their own procedures on a read-only memory chip. PROGRAMMABLE READ-ONLY MEMORY (PROM) chips serve this purpose. Some PROMs are erasable under special circumstances so that they can be reprogrammed. These are called ERASABLE PROGRAMMABLE READ-ONLY MEMORY (EPROM) chips. The erasure process might involve exposing the EPROM to ultraviolet light or to an electrical charge—in which case the chip is known as electrically erasable programmable read-only memory (EEPROM). PROMs and EPROMs give users greater flexibility in designing systems that meet their needs.

OLD MEMORIES, NEW MEMORIES

In this section we will look at the dominant type of memory used in the past, at an emerging memory technology, and at one that holds promise for the future.

Magnetic cores

A common type of main memory in older computers, MAGNETIC CORE MEMORY consists of tiny iron doughnuts wired together in a fine grid of wires. Each doughnut can store one bit of data. These doughnuts serve as tiny magnetic storage elements. An electrical charge aligns the magnetic properties of the core. Depending on the direction of the charge, the core is set as a 1 or 0. As with semiconductor memory chips, any point in the grid can be reached using random access methods.

Magnetic core memory is nonvolatile; that is, it retains its charge if there is a power failure. Magnetic core memory has lost its popularity due to its high manufacturing cost and the large amount of space it consumes compared with RAM chips.

Bubble memory

Another type of primary storage is BUBBLE MEMORY, which provides nonvolatile storage using tiny, movable magnetic bubbles implanted in thin film on a garnet wafer. The presence of a bubble in a given location stands for a binary 1, and the absence of a bubble for a 0. While costlier than silicon chips, bubble memory has found a marketplace in such areas as the

With its computer rooms constructed like a triple-decker sandwich, the Online Computer Library Center (OCLC), Dublin, Ohio, has stacked up considerable savings in cabling costs and improved communications between computers.

Conventional computer rooms are large, one-level, and require very long cable runs between computers. OCLC avoided this inconvenience by building three smaller computer rooms, each taking up a full floor. The computer equipment is connected floor to floor with short vertical cables. "Vertical cables are less expensive than the long horizontal cables used in large computer rooms," says Donald Trotier, vice president and project manager of the center during the time it was being built. "Also, there are usually fewer communication problems between computers with short cable because the data don't have to travel as far."

OCLC is a nonprofit library service and research organization that provides centralized and local turnkey systems to libraries. Its computer rooms occupy OCLC's second, third, and fourth floors, although the first and basement levels are also working floors. The second-floor computer room houses the administrative and production equipment.

The third floor houses the online database, containing 11.5 million bibliographic records. This database, the Online Union Catalog, was created and assembled by nearly 3,800 libraries that participate in the OCLC network.

OCLC's fourth-floor computer room contains the telecommunications system, where nearly 6,000 OCLC-modified terminals from the various worldwide libraries are online. OCLC's online system is a unique setup of several different computers, including 30 Digital Computer Controls Model D-116 minicomputers; a Tandem Computers TNSI and TNSII 16-processor system;

an IBM 4341; two Data General MV10000s; Data General MV6000 and MV4000 systems; and 13 Xerox Sigma 9 computers.

OCLC is also a value-added dealer for the IBM Personal Computer, buying personal computers from IBM and then enhancing and modifying them in its basement terminal-assembly room to act as terminals on the OCLC system. OCLC sells the modified version, the OCLC M300 workstation, to its member libraries for $3,590.

OCLC has abandoned the traditional concept of the library as a facility that primary stores and preserves information. In an average week, libraries equipped with OCLC's modified terminals use this database to catalog over 50,000 items, lend more than 35,000 items from library to library, and order over 20,000 items from publishers and vendors.

Through the OCLC online system, institutions catalog books, serials, and other library materials; order custom-printed catalog cards; create machine-readable data files; maintain location information on library materials; and place and control acquisitions orders.

All OCLC's computer rooms are fully equipped with security-access systems supplied by Kidde Automated Systems. With this system, OCLC can control access to any computer room at any time. All three computer rooms are also safeguarded by a micro-based Halon fire-extinguishing system supplied by Pyrotronics.

OCLC employs 700 data processors. The center was built by Gilbane Building Co. (Providence, RI) and occupied in February 1981. The center's designers were Brubaker/Brandt, Inc., Columbus, Ohio.

Source: Theresa Conlon in Computer Decisions, The Management Magazine of Computing, A Hayden Publication, vol. 17, no. 7, April 9, 1985, pp. 67–72.

FIGURE 5-10.

A bubble memory chip. This type of memory offers nonvolatile storage.

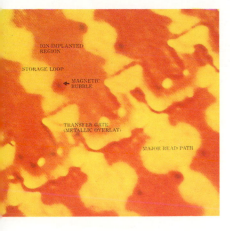

machine-tool industry, where electric power surges could erase or alter volatile chips. It is also finding increasing use in portable microcomputers. Bubble memory chips operate at a slower speed than RAM. Figure 5-10 shows a bubble memory chip.

Josephson junctions

JOSEPHSON JUNCTIONS (named after Brian Josephson, the inventor) offer extremely fast memory access because they exploit electrical properties of switches in a supercooled environment only a few degrees above absolute zero. The circuits are made of thin film strips separated by a thin barrier. Supercooling lowers resistance of the materials to the point that electrons can penetrate the barrier. Guided by a magnetic field, the electrons can move much faster than under normal (not supercooled) conditions. Figure 5-11 shows a Josephson junction.

If future computers are built that employ Josephson junctions, switching speeds might be up to 100 times what they are today. The circuitry would also require very little power, generate little heat, and could be packed more closely together, further increasing speed. The computer might occupy a few cubic inches. The liquid helium refrigeration unit would be about the size of a small household refrigerator.

FIGURE 5-11.

A Josephson junction circuit. In the future this technology may greatly increase computer speeds.

THE CPU AND COMPUTING POWER

The CPU in today's computers is an impressive device, as we have seen. This is true regardless of whether the CPU is a single-chip microprocessor in a microcomputer or a multichip version in a minicomputer or mainframe.

Figure 5-12 compares performance and price of the four main categories of computer—microcomputers, minicomputers, mainframes, and supercomputers. As you can see, the four categories overlap.

Figure 5-13 summarizes the characteristics of each type of computer. Note that the general trend has been for computers in all four categories to offer better (lower) cost-to-performance ratios over the past years. A continuation of such trends will lead to even greater processing speeds, more internal storage, and lower prices in the future.

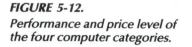

FIGURE 5-12.
Performance and price level of the four computer categories.

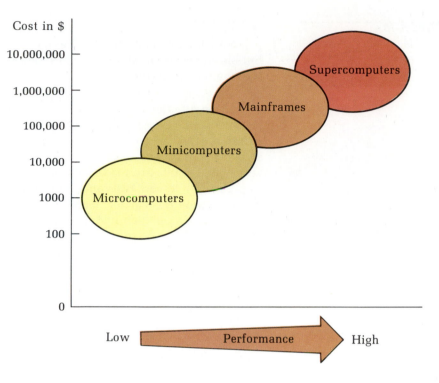

FIGURE 5-13.
Comparing the different types of computers.

Computer Type	Characteristics					
	Size	**Memory**	**Speed**	**Peripherals**	**Cost**	**Environment**
Microcomputers	Desktop or smaller; some are portable	64 K to 1000 K bytes	Microseconds	Keyboard, printer, and disk units	$500 – $20,000 for the CPU	No special requirements
Minicomputers	About the size of a file cabinet	500 K to 4000 K bytes	80–100 nano-seconds	Several dozen different devices	$10,000 – $250,000	Air-conditioning, security recommended
Mainframe computers	A large office desk or file cabinet	1000 K to 96,000 K bytes	50–70 nano-seconds	Hundreds of devices	$100,000 – several million dollars	Special cooling, fire protection, security
Supercomputers	Several large file cabinets	32 M to 256 M bytes	5–15 nano-seconds	Special high performance devices	$10,000,000 +	Special protection required

"Well, that's it," Nat Bergstein said, looking at the last page of output from the diagnostic program.

"Have you found the problem?" asked Clayton Johns, Global Electrical Equipment's computer center manager.

"I believe so," Nat said. "It's in the control unit of the CPU."

"Does that program actually tell you what chip?" Clayton asked.

"No," David said. "It indicates functional components. The control unit of the CPU has a part known as the decoder. It figures out what the program instructions are and rigs up the circuits to carry them out. Some portion of the decoder hardware isn't working."

"Can you install a new one?" Clayton asked.

"Yes," Nat said. He picked up the phone on the computer console and called his office.

"We'll be back on the air in ten minutes," Nat said as he hung up the phone. "The new decoder is coming by taxi."

Nat leaned back in the console chair. "The funny thing is, the decoder was working right 99 percent of the time. A failure on the order of 1 percent—maybe a blown register or something— was enough to confound your operating system and as good as shut down the mainframe.

"Why would a register just burn out?" Clayton asked.

"Everyone assumes hardware is perfect," Nat said. "It *is* amazing in terms of its power and how tiny it is. But it isn't magic, and it still breaks."

"Or starts out with flaws to begin with," David said.

A messenger placed a package with the decoder on the console. Nat unwrapped the circuit board with its chips already in place and walked to the CPU. He opened a panel, clicked off the power switch inside, and following a diagram in the book David held open, found the right board. Nat detached the old board and set the new one in place.

"O.K., Clayton," Nat said, closing the panel. "Fire 'er up!"

Clayton summoned a computer operator to sit at the console. "Bring up the real-time jobs first," Clayton said. "We can catch up on the batch runs later."

The operator nodded, and then made a number of entries at the console terminal. In a few moments the computer was up and running.

"So far, so good," the operator said. "We've got 40 users on line and the system hasn't croaked."

"Never underestimate the power of a CPU," Clayton said.

"That's for sure," Nat said. "Without it, where would we be?"

"In the Fren . . ." Clayton began.

"I know, I know," Nat said, packing up.

SUMMARY

- A computer is a very-high-speed electronic device that can accept data and instructions, use the instructions to perform logical and mathematical operations on the data, and report the results of its processing.

- Analog computers represent data as energy levels, and treat data as continuous. Digital computers, in contrast, represent data by the "on" and "off" states of electrical components and treat data as discrete.

- Hybrid computers combine the features of analog and digital machines. General-purpose computers can be used for a variety of applications. Special-purpose computers are designed to perform a specific function. The focus of this textbook is on general-purpose digital computers.

- The central processing unit (CPU) is the computer itself, the core of an information system. The CPU carries out the instructions given it by software to process the input data and produce the output information.

- There are three functional units in the CPU: the control unit, main memory, and the arithmetic/logic unit (ALU).

- The control unit is the "brain" of the computer. It interprets program instructions, directs the other parts of the CPU, and communicates with external input/output devices and secondary storage devices. The machine instructions supplied to the CPU consist of an operation code (op code) that tells the computer what operation to perform, and one or more operands that tell what the operations are to be performed on. The decoder interprets the op code. An address is a unique location in main memory.

- Main memory (or internal memory or primary memory) stores data and instructions that have been input and are waiting to be processed. It also stores the results of processing until they are released to output devices. Incoming data are placed in input storage; program instructions into program storage; intermediate results in working storage; and output in output storage. When data are stored in an address in main memory, they destroy any data that were there before (destructive write). Reading data from an address leaves them unaffected (nondestructive read).

- The arithmetic/logic unit (ALU) performs calculations and logical operations with the data, as directed by the control unit. Math and logic gates are the electronic switches in the ALU that perform these operations.

- Registers are high-speed temporary storage units.

- The machine cycle has two phases—the instruction cycle and the execution cycle. During the instruction cycle instructions are fetched, decoded, and the appropriate parts of the CPU made ready. During the execution cycle the CPU performs the operation.

- With a computer all numbers, letters, and symbolic codes must be translated to a two-state, on or off, pattern. Our everyday decimal numbers, in other words, must be converted to binary. Each binary number inside a computer is known as a bit. Two numbering systems, octal (with a base of 8) and hexadecimal (with a base of 16), are used to represent binary numbers to the user in a compact form.

- A byte is a string of adjacent bits that the computer processes as a unit. The usual number of bits per byte is eight. A nibble (or nybble) is half a byte, usually four bits.

- Letters, punctuation, and other symbols are represented by following conventions that designate certain binary patterns as their equivalents. EBCDIC (Extended Binary Coded Decimal Interchange Code) is one such set of conventions. ASCII (American Standard Code for Information Interchange) is another.

- A parity or check bit is an extra bit added to an EBCDIC or ASCII byte to make it possible to detect communication errors.

- A computer word is made up of one or more consecutive bytes. Fixed-length-word machines handle words that contain a fixed number of bytes. Variable-length-word machines handle each byte individually. Some machines can use either system. Fixed-length-word machines can perform parallel arithmetic. Variable-length-word machines use serial arithmetic.

- Today's mainframe computers and minicomputers use silicon chips throughout the CPU. On microcomputers the entire CPU is etched onto a single chip known as a microprocessor. Main memory today is contained on random access memory (RAM) chips. On some computers a special storage area of high-speed RAM chips called cache storage sits between the rest of main memory and other parts of the CPU. Storage capacity is usually expressed in terms of K. One K equals 1024 bytes of characters or 1024 bits on a chip.

- Read-only memory (ROM) can be read from but cannot be written onto. ROM is often used on microcomputers to store parts of the system software and to store machine-level instructions for frequently used procedures. ROM can also be used to store entire application programs. Software encoded on ROM is often called firmware. Variants on ROM are programmable read-only memory (PROM), and erasable programmable read-only memory (EPROM).

- In the past magnetic cores were used for main memory. Bubble memory provides nonvolatile storage using magnetic bubbles implanted in a thin film on a garnet wafer. Josephson junctions, which exploit the electrical properties of a supercooled environment, offer the promise of computers with switching speeds up to 100 times faster than what they are today.

- The four categories of computers—microcomputers, minicomputers, mainframe computers, and supercomputers—differ in terms of a number of variables. Two of the most important are price and performance.

These are the key terms in the order in which they appear in the chapter.

Computer (130)
Analog computer (130)
Digital computer (130)
Hybrid computer (130)
General-purpose computer (131)
Special-purpose computer (131)
Central processing unit (CPU) (131)
Control unit (131)
Main memory (133)
Arithmetic/logic unit (ALU) (133)
Operation code (Op code) (133)
Operand (133)
Address (133)
Decoder (134)
Input storage (134)
Program storage (134)
Working storage (134)
Output storage (134)
Destructive write (135)
Nondestructive read (135)
Gate (135)
Math gate (135)
Logic gate (135)
Register (135)
Machine cycle (137)
Instruction cycle (137)
Execution cycle (137)
Decimal number system (138)
Binary number system (138)

Bit (138)
Octal number system (138)
Hexadecimal number system (138)
Byte (139)
Nibble or nybble (139)
EBCDIC (Extended Binary Coded
    Decimal Interchange Code) (140)
ASCII (American Standard Code for
    Information Interchange) (141)
Parity bit or check bit (142)
Computer word (143)
Fixed-length word (143)
Parallel arithmetic (143)
Serial arithmetic (143)
Variable-length word (143)
Silicon chip (144)
Microprocessor (146)
Random access memory (RAM) (147)
Cache storage (147)
K (148)
Read-only memory (ROM) (149)
Firmware (149)
Programmable read-only memory
    (PROM) (149)
Erasable programmable read-only
    memory (EPROM) (149)
Magnetic core memory (149)
Bubble memory (149)
Josephson junction (151)

REVIEW QUESTIONS

OBJECTIVE QUESTIONS:

1.
2.
3.
4.

5.

6.
7.
8.
9.

1.

TRUE/FALSE: *Put the letter T or F on the line before the question.*

1. Assuming even parity, the parity bit for the eight-bit byte 11011010 is 0.
2. The decoder is a key feature of the control unit of the CPU.
3. Registers are high-speed temporary storage areas.
4. Fixed-word computers are slower at mathematical computations than variable-word computers.
5. Intermediate processing results are stored in the working storage area of main memory.
6. Mainframe computers do not have microprocessors inside the CPU.
7. Random access chips are nonvolatile memory.
8. Logical tests are performed in the control unit.
9. Small minicomputers cost considerably more than large microcomputers.

MULTIPLE CHOICE: *Put the letter of the correct answer on the line before the question.*

1. Assuming even parity, which of these values is incorrect?
   (a) 1 11011010.
   (b) 0 11010010.
   (c) 0 11001000.
   (d) 1 00000010.

2. The parts of the central processor include:
(a) The input unit, the arithmetic/logic unit, the primary main memory unit, and the output unit.
(b) The control unit, the arithmetic/logic unit, and the output unit.
(c) The arithmetic/logic unit, the control unit, and the main memory unit.
(d) The arithmetic/logic unit, the control unit, and the input unit.

3. The number 676.4 is being moved from the accumulator register to primary storage for use later in the program. What part of main memory will it be stored in?
(a) Input storage.   (c) Working storage.
(b) Output storage.   (d) None of the above.

4. The op code:
(a) Tells the decoder where to find whatever is to be operated on.
(b) Tells the decoder what instruction is to be carried out.
(c) Is located in working storage.
(d) Is an abbreviation for the term optional code.

5. A logical gate has two switches, A and B. An "on" setting will let the current pass through the switch. If we were to use these switches to test for logical AND, what configuration would test true?
(a) Switch A "on," B "off."   (c) Switch A "on," B "on."
(b) Switch A "off," B "on."   (d) All of the above would work.

FILL IN THE BLANK: *Write the correct word or words on the blank to complete the sentence.*

1. The _____ unit is reponsible for interpreting instructions.
2. The four parts of main memory are _____, _____, _____, and _____ storage.
3. A _____ chip cannot be altered by a programmer.
4. The _____ number system is the only kind understood by digital computers.
5. Continuous electrical voltages are a feature of _____ computers.
6. A _____ computer is used to perform only a specific function.
7. In the control and arithmetic/logic units _____ serve as very fast temporary storage.
8. Almost all computers in business today are _____ computers.
9. The _____ tells the control unit where to find whatever is to be operated on.

SHORT ANSWER QUESTIONS

When answering these questions think of concrete examples to illustrate your points.

1. What are the differences among digital, analog, and hybrid computers?
2. What function do the parts of the control unit perform?
3. Describe the differences between the instruction and execution cycle.
4. What is the function of a gate?
5. What are the differences among ROM and RAM chips?
6. Describe the functions minicomputers may perform in business environments.
7. What is a magnetic core?
8. What is a bubble memory chip?
9. What are the differences among ROMs, PROMs, and EPROMs?
10. What is cache storage?

ESSAY QUESTIONS

1. Compare and contrast the features of microcomputers, minicomputers, mainframes, and supercomputers.
2. Describe the three parts of the CPU and how they interact.

CHAPTER 6

INPUT AND OUTPUT DEVICES: FASTER AND FRIENDLIER

After studying this chapter you should understand the following:
■ Some concepts and trends that apply to input and output generally, such as the steps in data entry and the meaning of user-friendly output.
■ How terminals are used in information systems.
■ Which types of input devices are used for source data automation.
■ How impact and nonimpact printers differ, and some of the printing techniques that each type uses.
■ The role of voice, graphics, and microfilm for input and output.

It was Saturday afternoon, and the Roberts family—Janis, George, and nine-year-old Meagan—drove off to run errands.

At a hardware store they picked up some fertilizer, seeds, and a shovel. The clerk at the checkstand rang up the sale on a large register linked by cables to the store's computer. Janis paid with a credit card, which the clerk placed in a small machine next to the register. The machine read the magnetic strip on the back of the card, and a few seconds later a message appeared on the register that the card was valid and that the credit limit had not been exceeded.

After stopping for a soda at a fast-food restaurant—where the cashier rang up the sale on a keyboard that had symbols for burgers, drinks, and fries on it—the Roberts family headed for the supermarket. While Meagan and George started pushing the cart down the aisles, Janis stopped at the check-approval machine. She inserted her check and check-approval card and keyed in some code numbers. After a few seconds the machine printed an approval message on the back of the check.

Janis caught up with her family at the dairy department, and they proceeded through the store to the checkout counter. The clerk passed the items they bought over a scanning device that read their labels. Janis paid for the purchase using the check already approved by the other machine.

Both Janis and George worked with computers at their jobs. George drove away from the supermarket thinking of the number of different computer input devices they'd seen on their shopping trip, and how clever such devices were becoming these days. Also, he stopped to realize that the family's cash supply was low.

He swung the car off in a new direction and headed for the bank. He inserted a card in the automatic-teller machine and typed some codes. In return the machine gave him a packet of much-needed cash.

"Now it's time to head home before the ice cream melts," George said. He enjoyed gardening and was looking forward to doing some this afternoon. After some digging he would have a chance to press some seeds into the earth—which, he reflected, was not yet computerized.

INPUT AND OUTPUT: OUR CONTACT WITH COMPUTERS

In this chapter we will look at the machines that enable us to interact with the computer—the input devices that read our data, programs, and queries, and the output devices that provide us with the results of processing. Before we get to the actual devices, however, let's review some concepts and trends that apply to input/output generally. ("Input/output," incidentally, means "input and output.") These concepts and trends apply regardless of the size of computer involved—micro, mini, mainframe, or supercomputer.

INPUT AND OUTPUT CONCEPTS

INPUT brings data, and instructions on how to process the data, into an information system. The most important requirement of the input stage is to capture accurate, timely, and useful data. First-class processing and timely output cannot possibly overcome the effects of negligent input.

Data entry

DATA ENTRY refers to the process of getting the facts into a form that the computer can understand. Data entry can be broken down into four steps:

1 *Obtaining the source document with the data.*
2 *Preparing the source document for entry.*
3 *Entering the data from the document.*
4 *Verifying the data (checking that they were correctly entered).*

These steps can be performed one stage at a time by people. For example, you can obtain a sheet of data values (step 1), round off all the numbers to three decimal places (step 2), key in the numbers at a terminal (step 3), and check the numbers displayed on your terminal screen against the sheet of data values before transmitting the data (step 4).

Alternately machines can do part of the job on their own. When the Roberts family went to the supermarket checkout counter, the bar-code reader there did steps 3 and 4 by itself, with a little help from the computer it was hooked up to.

Two major expenses incurred in running an information system are the labor and material costs for the input process. To reduce these two expenses, there has been a push to design documents that can be read and checked by machine. Later in this chapter we will see plenty of devices that enter data on their own. Chapter 17 will discuss some problems involved with checking data by machines.

Types of output

Let's skip for a moment to the other end of the process. When a program has received its input and processed it into meaningful information, output occurs. **OUTPUT** from an information system conveys the results of processing. There are three categories of output:

- *Permanent, human-readable output.* The most common medium here is printed reports or forms. By "permanent" we do not mean that the output will outlast the Parthenon, but that it will not disappear when you turn your display screen off.
- *Temporary, human-readable output.* The most common medium here is the display screen.
- *Permanent, machine-readable output.* This is output produced in a format that only machines can understand, and is meant to serve later as input to the same or another machine. The most common machine-readable media are magnetic disk and magnetic tape.

Our focus in this chapter will be on the first two kinds of output. The third, machine-readable output, we will cover in Chapter 7.

Medium and device

In looking at both output and input, it is useful to distinguish between the

Why not aim for the top? As director of information systems, you would be in charge of the entire computer operation. In smaller companies, or in firms with a more traditional management structure, this position will be the highest that relates to information systems. In larger organizations, or in firms with a more modern management structure, the director of information systems will report to the information resources manager or vice-president (this position is described in the Chapter 14 career box).

What would you manage? All five elements of an information system. Directors of information systems are sometimes in charge of hundreds or even thousands or *people*, including intermediary tiers of managers. In many organizations the director of information systems takes part in working out *rules and procedures* affecting information systems, together with other high-level managers. This includes identifying the need for new information systems. The director of information systems must ensure that *data* flow smoothly into the computer center, and that timely and useful information flows out of it.

As far as *hardware* goes, the director of information systems is responsible for acquiring it in the first place, seeing that it is used sensibly, and insuring that it is up and running. A single computer, or dozens of them, may be involved. *Software,* too, is acquired or developed under the supervision of the director of information systems. Like all the elements in the picture, it must function well, or the director's job is on the line.

In smaller shops the director of information systems will be involved in day-to-day operations. In larger firms, he or she will be in charge of other executives who manage the major areas, such as database administration, telecommunications, and computer operations.

Directors of information systems are well paid and are in great demand. Prerequisites are proven technical competence and managerial ability. The best way to become a director of information systems is to work your way up through the information systems ranks, demonstrating your technical proficiency and leadership skills. It's not unreasonable to expect to spend a decade or more in doing so. In a smaller shop this time might be shortened.

medium and the device that works with it. Media include printed forms, visual displays, magnetic tape, magnetic disk, sound, microfilm, and punch cards. The corresponding devices are printers, display terminals, magnetic tape units, magnetic disk units, speech recognition and voice output devices, microfilm units, and card readers and punches.

Input devices take the data contained on the medium and convey them to the computer's main storage. Output devices take information contained in main storage and convey it or record it on a medium. Some of the same media (such as magnetic disk) are used for both input and output, and some devices (such as a magnetic disk unit) are capable both of accepting input and of producing output.

INPUT, OUTPUT, AND THE INFORMATION SYSTEM

As with all the other elements of an information system, the mix of input and output equipment an organization acquires must be considered in the context of the whole system. First to consider are the needs of the *people* using the system and how these needs translate into the *rules and procedures* by which they operate. If an organization needs *data* available quickly and accurately, it might consider using automated input methods. If time is not so important, data could be input from written forms by someone working at a terminal. A need for high-volume, attractive printed output calls for a sophisticated printer; a need for only a "quick and dirty" listing calls for a much simpler device. Within a single organization a variety of different input and output equipment may be required. Finally appropriate *software* and *hardware* (computers and peripherals) must be obtained to permit the organization to use whatever input/output devices it selects.

INPUT AND OUTPUT TRENDS

We have observed a number of trends in this book. In Chapter 5 we saw how CPU hardware has become steadily smaller, and the CPU steadily faster. Input/output also has its trends.

One of these is toward source data automation. **SOURCE DATA AUTOMATION** refers to the use of machine-readable source documents for data entry,

Automated System

 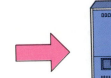 

George places object on counter.

Clerk passes optical wand over coded price information.

Computer retrieves price from data base, adds tax. Mistakes are rare. Computer updates inventory, since now there is one item fewer.

Terminal at checkstand prints receipts.

George pays and exits with item.

Manual System

George places object on counter.

Clerk fills out sales slip as service document.

From sales slip clerk keys in sales price, tax, and code of item sold on cash register. Mistakes happen.

Cash register prints receipt.

George pays and exits with item.

Cash register totals are matched against sales slip totals at end of day, to catch some discrepancies (though the damage has already been done).

Inventory will be updated eventually by separate system. Meanwhile, the item may go out of stock, resulting in a possible loss of sales. Sales slips may serve as source documents for inventory-updating system (itself a lengthy process).

and offers faster and more accurate input than manual data entry. Over the past decade source data automation in real-time environments has developed at an explosive rate. It reduces the steps between acquiring data and entering them into the information system for processing. This means that more timely data can enter the system, and more timely information can exit it. As for accuracy, machines do make mistakes; enough checks are built into source-data-automation procedures, however, to ensure that the process is less error-prone than manual data entry.

A second major trend evident today concerns output. Advances in output technology have increased the variety of output possibilities and made output easier to understand and use. Whether displayed on a screen, printed, or produced in some other medium, today's output can be presented in a variety of ways. Take reports. These can be produced on a printer that produces "letter-quality" output, or on a printer geared to volume output that produces legible but lower-quality output, or on a printer or plotter that creates professional-looking multicolor graphics. Output which is uncomputerlike and instead geared to people's expectations—a letter that looks as though it rolled off a typewriter for example—is known as **USER-FRIENDLY OUTPUT**.

Working with data to create information—today known as input and output—has come a long way since the manual systems in use before computers arrived on the scene. At the start of the chapter we saw the Roberts family make a number of purchases. Figure 6-1 contrasts the way that would have been handled with a manual system, and the faster, cheaper, and more thorough way that a computerized information system took care of it.

TERMINALS: THE LONG ARM OF THE COMPUTER

A **TERMINAL** is a computer input/output device that can send data to, and receive information from, a computer through a telecommunications link. An early type of terminal, which still has many applications, was the **TELEPRINTER**. These have a keyboard for input and a small printer for output (Figure 6-2).

FIGURE 6-1.

Processing a department store purchase on an automated and a manual system.

FIGURE 6-2.
A teleprinter.

DISPLAY TERMINALS

DISPLAY TERMINALS consist of an input unit, a display screen, and a screen control unit that links the two. Today the most common type of terminal is the display terminal, and a variant of the display terminal, the point-of-activity terminal. There are several different types of input units (Figure 6-3). These include the following:

- *KEYBOARDS, typewriter-like sets of keys set in tiers, used for entering numeric and alphabetic data. Keyboards are the most common type of input unit on terminals.*
- *ELECTRONIC MICE, palm-sized devices that can be rolled on wheels or ball bearings over a surface in order to move a pointer on the display screen, or to input graphical data such as a diagram that the mouse is passed over.*
- *GRAPHICS TABLETS or DIGITIZERS, electrically wired surfaces upon which a user can draw diagrams for entry as data.*
- *LIGHT PENS, pencil-like light-sensitive rods that can be pointed at a display screen to perform functions indicated there or to draw diagrams.*

Display terminals often use more than one of these input methods. For example, a user might enter data with a keyboard, and use an electronic mouse to move a pointer quickly about the screen.

FIGURE 6-3.

Four ways to enter data at a display terminal. (a) Using a keyboard and a mouse on a microcomputer. (b) Using a digitizing tablet. (c) Using a light pen.

Terminal intelligence

On the basis of whether or not a display terminal can perform certain functions on its own, it is classified as "intelligent" or "dumb." An **INTELLIGENT TERMINAL,** or **SMART TERMINAL,** can do some processing on its own, such as perform some preliminary editing and formatting of data being entered, without the help of the computer it is hooked up to. Such terminals have a small microprocessor and a built-in memory, and can be programmed. The degree of "intelligence" varies, from a simple terminal with a few keys that can be programmed to do certain jobs, to a complex terminal with its own operating system and a great deal of internal storage.

A word is in order about the difference between a microcomputer and a display terminal. Like any other computer a microcomputer consists of a central processing unit, one or more input devices, one or more output devices, and the cables necessary to hook all the parts together. The fact that most microcomputers have a keyboard for input and a display screen for output does not make microcomputers terminals, even if the keyboard and display screen are built right into the same unit as the CPU. Only when a microcomputer is linked in a telecommunications network to a mainframe or minicomputer, does it sometimes function as an intelligent terminal.

There is no ambiguity surrounding the definition of **DUMB TERMINALS.** These have no information-processing capabilities, but rather serve passively to channel data to a computer. Any editing and formatting of data which must be done cannot be handled by the terminal, but must be performed by the computer receiving the data, although the editing operations appear on the display screen.

Screen technologies

Various technologies are used today for display screens (Figure 6-4). Three common types include:

- *Cathode-ray tubes (CRTs), which are like television picture tubes.*
- *Light-emitting diodes (LEDs), which produce green or red letters of the type found in many calculators and clocks.*
- *Liquid crystal displays (LCDs), which produce a dark gray display against a light background, often seen in calculators and watches.*

FIGURE 6-4.

Display terminals. (a) A cathode-ray tube (CRT). (b) A portable microcomputer with a liquid crystal display (LCD) screen.

Cathode-ray tubes are still the most common type of screen in use. CRT screens tend to be bulky. LED and LCD screens, in contrast, are very thin, making them ideal for lightweight portable microcomputers.

We should add that the initials CRT, LED, LCD, and also VDT (which stands for "video display terminal") are often used synonymously with "display terminal," merely to indicate a terminal with a screen rather than to single out any specific technology.

Display terminals currently available have a wide range of color and graphical display capabilities. The "resolution" or crispness (as opposed to blurriness) of the image varies, ranging from only slightly better than a television set for a low-priced terminal to extremely good for sophisticated graphics terminals. Most data entry personnel work at terminals with monochrome screens. These display text in a single color such as green or orange against a background color that is supposedly easy on the eyes (such as black or dark green).

The **CURSOR** on a display screen is a moveable and sometimes blinking symbol that tells you where you are. Generally it shows where the next character that is typed at the keyboard will be displayed.

A **WINDOW** is that part of the data being worked with that can be seen on the screen at a given time. Displays can be created that are much bigger than what a screen can hold; users can then examine these displays one screen (window) at a time. Electronic spreadsheets, discussed in Chapter 12, are often large enough that they must be viewed a window at a time. Some programs split a screen up into parts, each of which can display a window, so that several windows can be seen at once (though each will be small) (see Figure 6-5).

A cousin to using windows is the process of **SCROLLING**, which refers to moving the data shown on the screen forward or backward. For example, if you are entering text with a word-processing program, but want to peek back to something entered earlier that no longer fits on the screen, activating the program's scrolling feature can move the lines displayed slowly backward until you reach the point you want. By scrolling forward—moving ahead—you can look in the opposite direction (assuming something is there).

ICONS are pictorial representations of an operation the computer can carry out. Displayed on a screen—say at the margins—icons can be pointed to by the cursor. When a user selects an icon, the program then carries out the function shown. For example, the icons in a word-processing program for moving text from one place to another might be a scissors and a glue brush (for cutting and pasting).

Display screens can do a lot of other things. For example, they can be programmed to reverse the colors of the text and background for designated words or portions of the display to gain attention; or they can flash part of the display on and off for the same purpose. In addition many display terminals include a small yet impressive repertoire of sound output possibilities that can also be programmed as attention-getters.

Keyboards

Like display screens today's keyboards come in different types (Figure 6-6). Typewriter-style keys are found on most high-quality display terminals

FIGURE 6-5.

Windows allow you to see portions of several documents on the screen at the same time.

where heavy usage is expected. These keys are sturdy little individual boxes, like those found on electronic typewriters, and will take a lot of pounding. Calculator-style keys are smaller and lack the same solid feeling. These are found on simpler terminals, and are often used for entering numeric data rather than text. Diaphragm-style "keys" are areas on a flat plastic membrane that are treated electronically as keys. In other words, diaphragm-style keys do not stick up. This type of keyboard often sees use in environments where the keyboard may get wet or dirty, such as outdoors or in fast-food restaurants.

Of mice and pens

As we saw at the start of our look at terminals, keyboards are not the only possible input device. An electronic mouse can be moved to shift the position of the cursor on the display screen quickly. The mouse's relative motion is converted into electronic signals, transmitted to the screen control unit, and then displayed on the screen. Transparent pressure-sensitive tablets can be placed against the screen to allow a person to "draw" the diagram or "push" the menu command shown on the screen.

Light pens can read a small part of the display screen at a time. The data a light pen reads are conveyed to the computer, which can then identify the exact position on the screen being read. For example, pointing the light pen at an icon can cause the program to carry out the function that the icon stands for. With a graphics package pointing the light pen to a portion of an

FIGURE 6-7.

Using a touch screen. The user can call up a function simply by touching the appropriate box and interrupting the light beams.

image can cause the computer to rotate the image so that a part of interest faces the viewer directly. On some systems one can draw diagrams by moving the light pen across the screen.

Still other display screens have a grid of infrared beams that is broken when someone touches the screen. The point in the grid where the break occurs indicates what the computer should do. Figure 6-7 shows an example.

(a)

FIGURE 6-8.

Point-of-activity (POA) terminals. (a) Banking—tellers entering transaction data directly into the computer. (b) Maintenance—A service engineer transfers data from computer memory in a railroad locomotive to his portable computer. (c) Warehousing—keeping track of inventory.

(b)

(c)

POINT-OF-ACTIVITY TERMINALS

Years ago data entry was routinely done at locations far removed from where the actual activity occurred. For example, data generated by credit card sales would be collected for entry and processing in a batch at a centralized computer center.

Today input units are often located at the point where a specific activity occurs, to capture data at their source. We call these machines **POINT-OF-ACTIVITY (POA) TERMINALS**. Figure 6-8 shows some sample applications.

The most common type of POA terminal is known as a **POINT-OF-SALE (POS) TERMINAL.** These units may receive their input via a keyboard or from a scanning device. (Scanning devices will be discussed later in the chapter.) POS terminals see frequent use in department stores, supermarkets, and fast-food restaurants.

Point-of-activity terminals, in effect, go to the data in order to gather data in a timely and efficient manner and cut costs. The productivity of people using POA terminals can be boosted still more by source data automation.

SOURCE DATA AUTOMATION

With source data automation the input medium and the source document are one and the same. There is no need to convert source documents into machine-readable form, because they are already machine-readable. The effect is to reduce the amount of manual labor involved in entering data. With fewer steps there are fewer opportunities for error, and the data can be input much more quickly.

In this section we will first look at the use of scanners for source data automation. Scanners read data directly from source documents and accumulate data far faster than the speediest typist could manage. In some instances, as we will see, data could not be gathered at all without scanners. In addition we will show how human speech can be used for source data automation.

OPTICAL SCANNERS

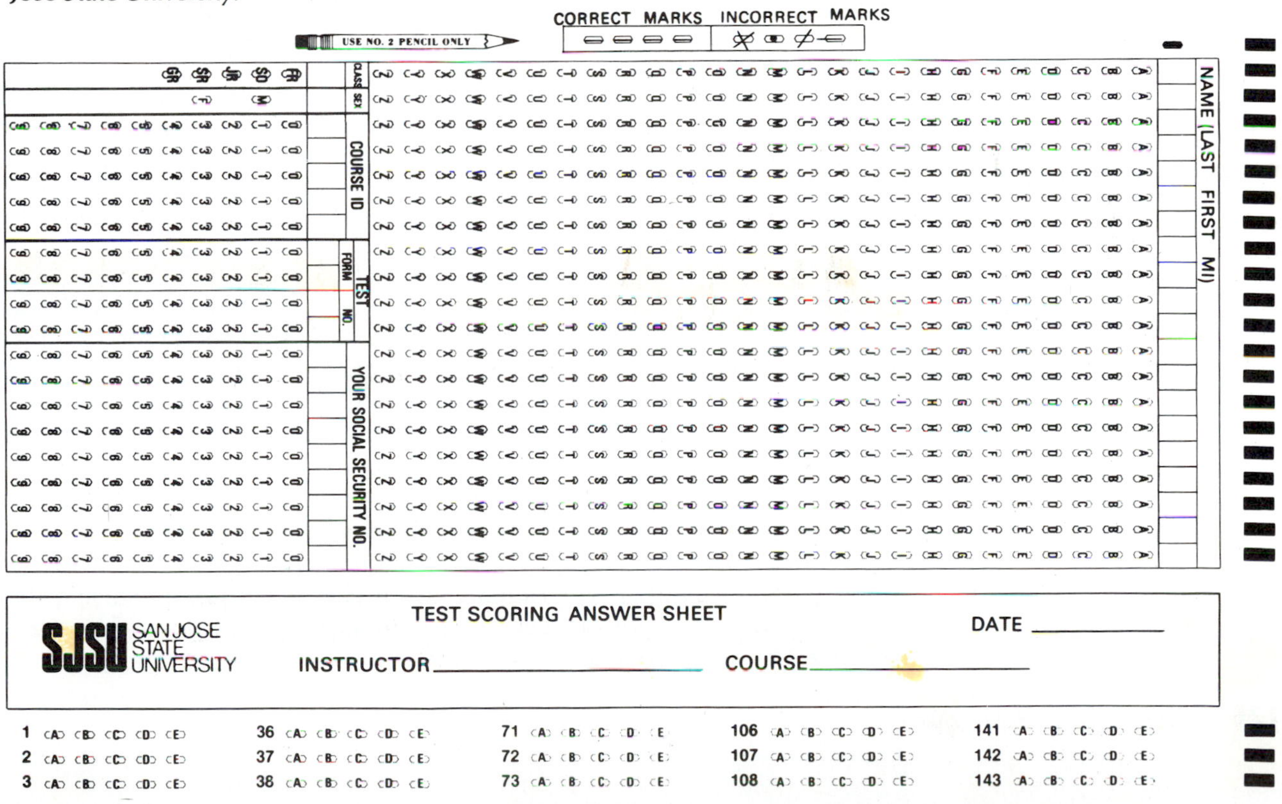

FIGURE 6-9.

An optical mark reader (OMR) senses special marks on forms like this test answer form. Reprinted by permission of San José State University.

OPTICAL SCANNERS use visible light to read characters, numbers, or patterns. The three types we will look at are optical mark readers, optical character readers, and bar code readers.

An **OPTICAL MARK READER** (OMR) senses marks on special paper forms. The scanner converts the marks into binary code, and the results are transferred to tape or disk for further processing (see Figure 6-9). There is no

TEST SCORING ANSWER SHEET

SJSU SAN JOSE STATE UNIVERSITY

INSTRUCTOR _____   COURSE _____   DATE _____

need for a data entry operator to key in data. You may have taken tests using optical scanning forms. Your answers were compared against an answer key form prepared by the instructor or testing service. Some systems require the use of special marking pencils. The U.S. Bureau of the Census, market research companies, and testing agencies make extensive use of optical mark readers.

Another type of scanner, the **OPTICAL CHARACTER READER (OCR)**, can detect printed letters and numbers as well as marks. Figure 6-10 shows an optical character reader and a form that it can read. Characters must be carefully printed to ensure accurate recording of the data. Some OCRs can recognize a variety of fonts (type faces), while others can only recognize special fonts. OCRs are available to read paper rolls such as cash register tapes, documents smaller than page size, and full-page documents. Applications include mail-order catalog forms, accounting forms, tax forms, and billing by utilities.

FIGURE 6-10.

(a) An optical character reader (OCR), and (b) an insurance bill printed with an optical character font.

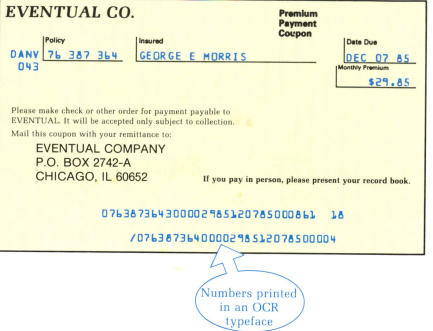

Numbers printed in an OCR typeface

A **BAR CODE READER**, shown in Figure 6-11, is a scanner that reads data coded as lines (bars) of varying length. Bar code technology is used in a wide number of applications—including manufacturing and wholesaling. Initially introduced into high-volume supermarkets, their use has spread to smaller and more specialized stores. Almost all boxed, canned, or prepackaged goods bear a **UNIVERSAL PRODUCT CODE (UPC)** on the label. At the checkstand, a low-intensity laser reads the coded data and sends them to the checkstand microprocessor, where the code is checked for accuracy. Then the code is transmitted to the store's main computer, where the price and product data for each code are kept in the database. The main computer retransmits the product information to the checkstand for preparing the sales slip. In addition the main computer can update the inventory level. We will see in the wrap-up example at the end of the chapter that products

FIGURE 6-11.

Using bar code readers. A low-intensity laser reads the bar code patterns. The 12-digit Universal Product Code (UPC) has 11 human-readable digits plus a check digit. The checkstand's microprocessor will display the item purchased on a small screen and print out a detailed receipt.

```
         ACME MARKET #1851
       SO. 4TH ST, ALLENTOWN
      05/05 12:52PM STORE  1851
      CUST 274 REG 9 OPR    131

         TOTAL    $     .00
 OS JCE CRANGRAPE      1.89*
 PRD FM FAM WHEAT      1.69*
 SCOTT TOWEL FLWR      1.19
 HANDY PUFF SPG         .99 TX
 MIRROR HOLDERS       1.19 TX
 MIRROR HOLDERS       1.19 TX
     GEN MDSE          .59 TX
         TOTAL    $   8.97
      CASH TEND       9.00

       SUBTOTAL       8.73
       TAX PAID        .24

        03 CHANGE
```

unique to a store can also be tagged with UPC labels. Hand-held bar code readers can also help stores keep track of shelf and stockroom inventory.

The use of UPC codes has sparked considerable debate over consumer rights. The major point of contention is whether or not items should be labeled with prices people can read. Store managers prefer to mark the price only on the shelf, sticking to bar codes on the individual items, which call forth the right price from the database at the checkstand. Many consumers want prices they can read on the individual items. Legislation in a number of states supports consumers.

MAGNETIC SCANNERS

In a process known as **MAGNETIC-INK CHARACTER RECOGNITION (MICR)**, letters, numbers, and symbols written using an iron-oxide ink can be read magnetically (Figure 6-12). This type of input occupies an important niche in the business environment, the processing of checks through our banking system. The stylized numbers at the bottom of your checks are magnetic-ink characters.

FIGURE 6-12.

An MICR reader. MICR machines write, read, and sort checks throughout the banking system. The machine shown here can read both MICR and OCR codes and operate alone or in conjunction with a host computer (continued on p. 172).

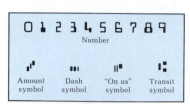

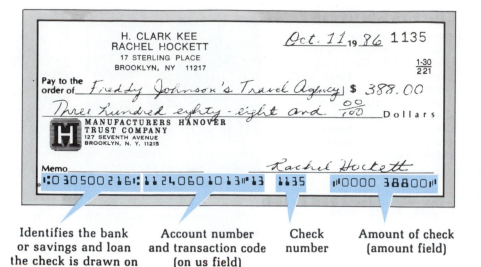

FIGURE 6-12 (cont.)
The 14-character e-13B MICR font; and a check with MICR characters. The check has four fields displaying data concerning the bank or savings and loan and Federal Reserve district, the payer's account number, the check number, and the amount of the check.

Identifies the bank or savings and loan the check is drawn on (transit or FRABA field)

Account number and transaction code (on us field)

Check number

Amount of check (amount field)

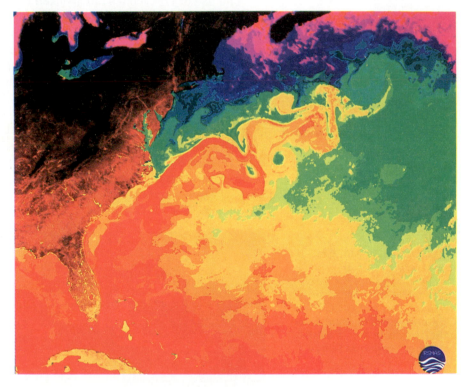

FIGURE 6-13.
Three-dimensional scanners are used to gather data for many applications. This computer-enhanced image—which shows seawater temperature zones off the east coast of the United States—was derived from satellite data.

THREE-DIMENSIONAL SCANNERS

A **THREE-DIMENSIONAL SCANNER** can look at objects in terms of their width, length, and depth. Different types of these scanners react to electromagnetic wavelengths and patterns ranging from X rays, through the visible light range, and on up to infrared and beyond. Applications include creating three-dimensional maps of underground geologic deposits, satellite mapping of large-scale climatic conditions (Figure 6-13), and the diagnosis of disease.

The use of scanners in medicine has aided in the diagnosis of diseases that are difficult to spot. Scanners have the advantage of providing detailed data without the need to intrude physically into the body via probing devices or exploratory surgery. The first machines in this field used X rays in a scanning technique known as **COMPUTERIZED AXIAL TOMOGRAPHY (CAT)**. X rays enter the body from three different directions, and as they hit bones and tissues, they are selectively absorbed. The computer sorts out these absorption patterns using triangulation techniques to create a picture of a thin "slice" of the body.

A new device uses the same general approach but detects the vibrations emitted by atomic nuclei rather than X rays. Scanners that employ this technology, known as **NUCLEAR MAGNETIC RESONANCE (NMR)**, are used to detect and analyze cancer growth rates (Figure 6-14).

FIGURE 6-14.
Computerized nuclear magnetic resonance (NMR) scanners are used to view inside the body for diagnosis of disease.

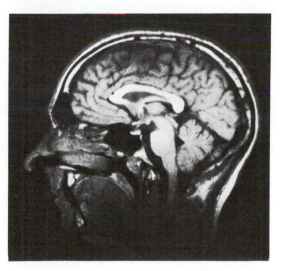

SPEECH RECOGNITION SYSTEMS

Computers that listen when we talk, and that talk back, are not reserved for science fiction but are present reality—though they do not yet have the versatility of the HAL-9000 machine shown in the movies *2001* and *2010*. Having computers listen when we talk (Figure 6-15) is known as **SPEECH RECOGNITION** (and also as "voice input" or "speech input"). Voices are received by a microphone and translated by the input device and its associated software into the binary code that the computer's own software can translate and work with.

FIGURE 6-15.
Speech recognition systems— no-hands computing.

Voice-dependent speech recognition systems work with a particular speaker or speakers, who have to prepare the system for use by speaking into it so that it can record their voices to match input against. Once this is done, voice-dependent systems can have quite large vocabularies, up to thousands of words and numbers. In effect the input device takes dictation and feeds it to the computer.

Voice-independent systems are intended to work with any speaker. These systems require much more software for analysis of sounds and the vocabulary is usually far more limited than those of voice-dependent systems. Such systems tend to be used for production or warehouse activities where hands are not readily available for keyboard input; by following a small vocabulary workers can input commands to the computer to direct machines. Credit-card-approval systems also use speech recognition devices to accept and translate for the computer a credit card number, amount of purchase, and merchant's identification number, spoken through the telephone.

Speech recognition systems free the hands and have a futuristic quality about them. They are prone to errors, however (many detect possible error situations themselves and request further information), expensive, and easily the most limited type of input device in terms of the range of data they will accept. One area where they are already in use and perform an invaluable service is in accepting data input from the blind and vision-impaired, and from people whose physical handicaps prevent them from using a keyboard.

PUNCH CARD INPUT AND OUTPUT

In Chapter 4 we saw how punch cards were originally used by Joseph-Marie Jacquard in the early 19th century to control a loom, and by Herman Hollerith for the U.S. Census of 1890. After Hollerith, punch cards became the established medium for tabulating machines and for **PUNCH CARD DEVICES** used for input and output on the earliest computers.

Punch cards are made of paper, and contain data in the form of punched-out holes in designated positions. Punch cards were the dominant input medium, and also an output medium, until magnetic tape, magnetic disk, and terminals rose in prominence due mainly to their much greater

FIGURE 6-16.

An 80-column punch card. (From Understanding Computers and Data Processing: Today and Tomorrow, *by Charles S. Parker. Copyright © 1984 by CBS College Publishing. Reprinted by permission of CBS College Publishing.)*

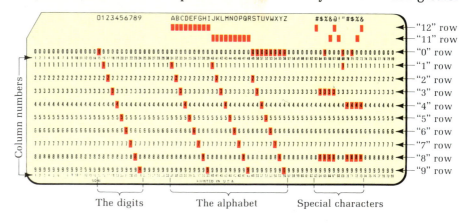

speed and convenience. Today punch cards are no longer predominant, but are still used.

Figure 6-16 shows an 80-column punch card. The cards come in different sizes in addition to the one shown. Data are entered into punch cards via an offline keypunch machine. Other, separate offline machines verify or check the data punched into the cards, and make copies of the cards. A card reader inputs data from the punch cards into the computer. If punch card output is desired, a card punch device under control of the computer can create it.

TOWARD FRIENDLIER OUTPUT

The display terminals that we studied earlier in the chapter as input devices are also output devices. Information systems often rely on data output to terminal screens for quick answers to queries.

In many cases, however, people need to be able to retain output in order to use the information that it contains to make effective decisions. Printed computer output has always served this purpose.

Output destined for managers or users used to mean bulky printouts of oversized paper full of blurry, all-caps letters and equally blurry numbers. The nearer one came to a computer center, the higher were the piles of forgotten printouts. Many ended up in the trash bin, which, given the quality, did not seem inappropriate.

Today the quality of print on the paper is better (it need not be all caps), paper comes in different sizes and colors, color graphics can be mixed with text or produced separately, and other media besides print are not only available but in common use. The trend generally in output devices today is to make output destined for users or managers more attractive, less "computerlike" in appearance (or sound), and—as always—faster and cheaper wherever possible.

IMPACT PRINTERS

IMPACT PRINTERS have printing mechanisms that physically contact the paper. Impact printers can be categorized by print quality and printer speed. Print quality can be either "letter quality," which means that the output looks good enough to have been typed, or nonletter quality, which means that the output looks clearly as though it were produced by a computer printer.

Printer speeds vary as well, from comparatively slow **CHARACTER PRINTERS** (or **SERIAL PRINTERS**), which print only one character at a time, to more rapid **LINE PRINTERS**, which print an entire line at once. Some character printers can print in either direction across the page, which speeds their operation. Multiple copies of output can easily be created with impact printers, by printing on multi-ply paper.

A common type of character printer is the **DOT-MATRIX PRINTER**. The printing element of a dot-matrix printer consists of a series of tiny pins arranged in a cluster. To print a particular character—say the letter "G"—a hammer mechanism in the printer strikes those pins from the cluster that will form the letter. The pins in turn strike a ribbon which prints the character on the page. Dot-matrix line printers have a complete pin cluster positioned at each possible print position of a line. Figure 6-17 shows a dot-matrix printer and illustrates how it forms characters. Dot-matrix printers are available that print an entire line at a time.

FIGURE 6-17.

(a) A dot-matrix printer and (b) a diagram of a dot-matrix printing mechanism. These printers form characters when selected pins are hammered against a ribbon.

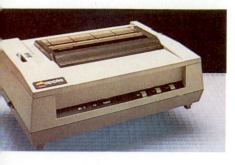

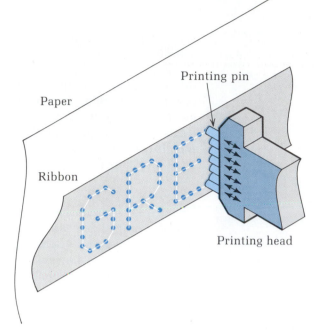

Paper

Printing pin

Ribbon

Printing head

The quality of a dot-matrix printer depends on the density of the pins in the cluster. In general the more pins, the higher is the print quality and the more expensive the printer. Better dot-matrix printers approach letter quality. Most dot-matrix printers can also strike the same location more than once to darken the character and make it look more complete, though this slows the printing process.

DAISY-WHEEL PRINTERS are character printers that produce letter-quality output. Daisy-wheel printers are much slower than dot-matrix printers. Figure 6-18 shows a daisy-wheel printer and its print element. The print element is called a daisy wheel because its spokes with the letters at the end can be thought to resemble a daisy's petals. To print, a daisy wheel spins until the appropriate character is in position. A hammer then strikes the character against a ribbon, leaving an impression on the paper. It is easy to change the daisy wheel in such a printer, thus changing the printer's type style. Daisy wheels are also widely used in electronic typewriters.

The great advantage of line printers over character printers is that they produce a whole line of print at once. This makes them much faster than character printers. We have already seen that dot-matrix printers can be line printers. Other types of line printers are chain printers, band printers, and drum printers.

FIGURE 6-18.

(a) A daisy-wheel print element and (b) a daisy-wheel printer.

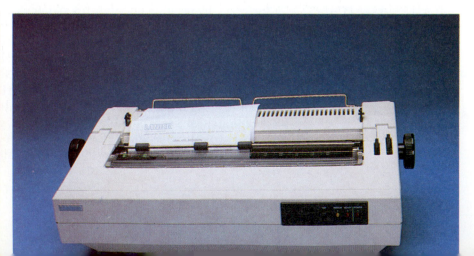

For some time I had sensed the ideal computer out there—a computer that would let me manipulate the universe with a wink and a nod. It lay just beyond the edge of my mind, and it demanded my attention. I began talking to experts, and they fed my enthusiasm. My search intensified, became a quest of almost medieval nature, as though I were looking for the Holy Grail without even knowing what it was.

I ultimately found my dream machine. It is a two-part model. It has a workstation form, and a detachable, portable form, which can be carried anywhere. I'll begin with the most general features. It has low cost; 100 gigabytes of nonvolatile RAM, so mass storage is unnecessary; lightning speed, derived from gallium arsenide chips; and a display with zoom, pan, and color screen resolution so minute that you can't detect the pixels.

The portable version would have a screen of 8½ by 11 inches, an adjacent trim keyboard, a light pen, a cellular modem, and a laser printer-copier-scanner, all weighing about five pounds. It wouldn't have to fit into a briefcase—it would replace the briefcase.

The workstation version would have several page-sized screens that display pages of my document, which I could call up instantly by topic; a large keyboard with programmable functions I could invent myself; a mouse and a touch pad; a modem that could adjust automatically to the other side's settings; a laser printer-copier-scanner; an accurate speech recognition device; the ability to store, edit, and play back any video or audio data, including voice-mail, hi-fi music, television, and photographs; compatibility with every program written; the capacity to regulate household activities, particularly to control the robots that will be doing the dishes, polishing my clarinet, and performing other routine chores; and an independent power source, in case of blackouts.

The software for my vision of an ideal computer would exploit all of the above. It would have a very friendly interface; mutability and the capacity to anticipate my needs; true integration that lets me draw directly on a word processing document or spreadsheet; and plenty of expert systems, so I can choose among experts I know something about.

My dream machine is not a modest machine—after all, it's ideal. But it brought me to the end of the line, and yet my main feeling was that I had not reached the end. I had the sensation of travelers who reach such exotic outposts as Patagonia or Lhasa and find that there is still a horizon beyond which they cannot see. In 10 or 15 years, I might look back on this vision of an ideal computer as quaint. But that's a small enough price to pay for a dream.

Source: From *Popular Computing*, April 1985. Copyright © 1985 by McGraw-Hill, Inc. Reprinted by permission.

CHAIN PRINTERS (Figure 6-19) use a chain made up of several (usually five) print "slugs" connected in a loop. Each slug is engraved with the entire character set that can be printed—that is, all the letters, numbers, and symbols. The chain spins at a rapid speed past a row of print hammers (usually 132), one for each possible print position on a line. When the right character passes, the hammer strikes.

BAND PRINTERS use the same technique, but employ a rapidly rotating scalloped steel band that is engraved with the multiple character sets (Figure

FIGURE 6-19.
A chain printer mechanism.

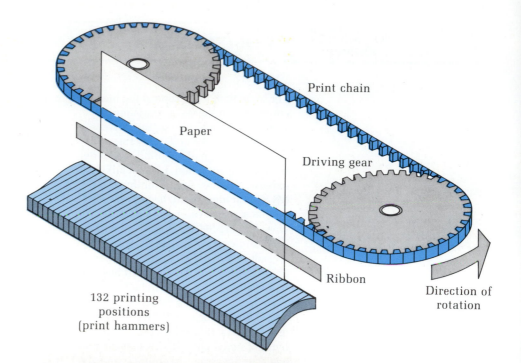

Print chain

Paper

Driving gear

Ribbon

132 printing
positions
(print hammers)

Direction of
rotation

FIGURE 6-20.
The print band from a band printer.

6-20). Band printers allow for greater flexibility, since bands can be changed more easily than chains, giving the printer a different type style.

DRUM PRINTERS use a rapidly rotating cylinder as a printing mechanism. Each possible print position on a line has a complete character set spread in a band around the drum for that position. When the right character passes, the hammer for the position strikes.

Line printers can print up to about 3000 lines per minute. This is a maximum speed, attained for long print jobs. In practice printers often work for short bursts of a few seconds, pause, and then go on to the next job.

NONIMPACT PRINTERS

NONIMPACT PRINTERS are so called because their printing mechanism does not touch the paper. Nonimpact character printers, illustrated in Figure 6-21, include both inexpensive thermal printers and extremely versatile ink-jet printers.

THERMAL PRINTERS are used to provide "quick and dirty" output. They are very popular among scientists and engineers for recording intermediate results where the quality of the output is not important. One type of thermal printer uses heated dot-matrix pins to "burn" the dots onto specially coated paper.

INK-JET PRINTERS use electrically charged ink droplets to form letter-quality images on the paper. The droplets are sprayed between two electrically charged deflection plates. As the ink droplets pass between, they are deflected to form the appropriate characters. The type style of ink-jet printer can be changed electronically, and some models can print simultaneously with different colored inks, and can produce graphical output.

FIGURE 6-21.

Nonimpact character printers. Thermal printers (a) provide quick, inexpensive permanent copies. Ink-jet printers (b) can provide great versatility, including the ability to create color output.

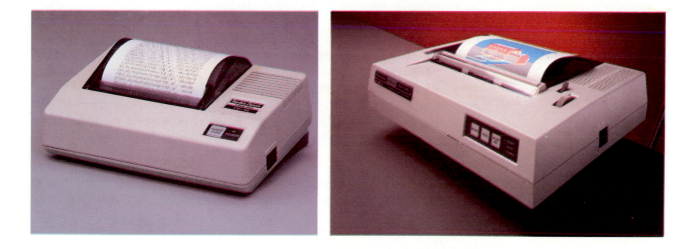

HIGH-SPEED PAGE PRINTERS (Figure 6-22), primarily using laser-xerographic technology, produce an entire output page at one time. High-speed printers can produce over 45,000 lines of output per minute. They can print on both sides of a sheet, and can reduce a 12-page report to a still readable format on one double-sided 8 1/2- by 11-inch sheet of paper. Moreover, since no impact is involved, these printers are quiet.

The **LASER-XEROGRAPHIC PRINTER** prints an entire page at once using a low-intensity laser to lay a dense matrix of dots. Characters can be printed with high resolution, giving the appearance of typeset letters even at high operational speeds.

Costs for high-speed printers can rise into the hundreds of thousands of dollars. Recently, however, laser printers that cost as little as a few thousand dollars have appeared. With this type of printer forms can be printed onto the paper along with the data that fill in the forms. The formats for forms can be stored on magnetic disk and called as needed by the processor directing the printer. In addition to forms, graphical output of many other types can be produced.

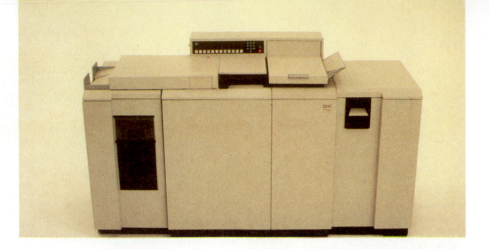

Nonimpact printers cannot print multi-ply forms, since the printing mechanism does not contact the top page at all, which would be necessary to make an impression on pages below. However, some of the faster nonimpact printers can produce multiple copies of the same report faster than impact line printers can do a single run with multi-ply paper.

Such capable printing equipment has led to the rise of a business-support area known as reprographics. REPROGRAPHICS refers to the computerized production of graphical and textual output in a variety of media. A reprographics center has a range of printing hardware available, and can print original output from the computer as well as duplicate existing output, produce slides and illustrations, or transmit output to intelligent copiers located elsewhere.

GRAPHICAL OUTPUT DEVICES

The more sophisticated printers, particularly the high-speed page printers, are capable of producing high-quality illustrations and other graphical material. Many simpler printers also can produce graphics.

Display terminals have varying degrees of graphics capability, ranging from those that can do charts and graphs for business presentations to those that can handle extremely complicated technical illustrations and high-quality computer art. Once created at a display terminal, a graphical design can be stored for future reference or output on a printer or plotter. Figure 6-23 shows some examples of computer-generated art.

PLOTTERS are devices that output computer graphics. They are available for all sizes of computer, including microcomputers. Figure 6-24 shows the two main types of plotters, flat-bed and drum. Flat-bed plotters work with paper that lies flat in a frame. A pen directed by the device's control unit moves rapidly over the paper, drawing output from the computer. These devices come in a variety of sizes, work at an impressive speed, can use different colors and create three-dimensional effects, and produce professional-looking output.

The other type of plotter, the drum plotter, draws upon paper that is wound around a cylinder. The machine rotates the paper, and the pen moves back and forth, to reach the right positions in a diagram. Changes in pen and paper speeds can produce the desired curves and angles.

Not all plotters use pens; some use a dot-matrix printing technique like the dot-matrix printers described earlier in the chapter.

FIGURE 6-23.
Some examples of computer-generated art.

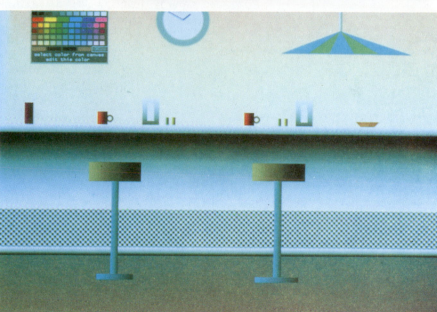

FIGURE 6-24.
The two main types of plotters, (a) the flat-bed plotter, and (b) the drum plotter.

(a)

(b)

AUDIO OUTPUT DEVICES

AUDIO OUTPUT DEVICES (Figure 6-25) allow the user to listen to the computer. Audio output devices exist that will speak any word, letter, or number given to them by the computer to output, just as a printer would print the same thing or a terminal display it. The quality of the spoken speech remains somewhat artificial, but is improving.

Audio output devices often work in concert with the speech recognition systems described earlier in the chapter. Application areas for audio output include credit-card verification systems, onboard computers for military aircraft, and "talking books" or other computer output for the blind or vision-impaired. Some systems aid in musical composition and instrument testing.

FIGURE 6-25.
This audio-output device enables people who otherwise cannot speak to communicate short verbal messages.

MICROFILM OUTPUT DEVICES

Many documents and records need to be retained for a number of years because of various rules and procedures. Tax records, student data, and accounting records are examples. **MICROFILM**, which provides highly reduced photographs of documents, thereby saving space, is a popular medium for compactly storing large quantities of documents. Microfilm is stored on reels. **MICROFICHE** places frames of microfilm on a flat card (up to around 1000 pages of a document per card), which can then be stored as cards.

In the past every page of a document to be recorded on microfilm had to be photographed by hand. Today **COMPUTER-OUTPUT MICROFILM (COM)** systems can produce up to 50,000 lines per minute of output on microfilm, using a high-speed camera. Figure 6-26 shows a COM system. When a document on microfilm needs to be retrieved for later use, a computer-assisted retrieval system can search for the correct microfilm reel (or microfiche card); the microfilm can then be read using a special reader, and photocopied onto paper if desired.

FIGURE 6-26.
A computer-output microfilm
(COM) system.

COSENTINO'S VEGETABLE HAVEN

Japanese tourists taking photographs in an American food store! Seem unusual? Not in this case. Amid the click and whir of Nikons and Canons, we find ourselves not just in any grocery store, but in one that can justify being a stop for tour buses. Welcome to Cosentino's Vegetable Haven, in San Jose, California.

Founded in 1947 by four brothers as a fruit and vegetable stand, Cosentino's has since grown into a $12-million-per-year grocery business with a work force of 100 full- and part-time employees. Cosentino's is a single-store business, not a chain, and has less floor space (about 32,000 square feet) than most chain supermarket stores. Computers barely existed when Cosentino's was founded; since then Silicon Valley has grown up around the store, and Cosentino's management did not fail to note the trend.

When bar codes and optical scanning devices were first introduced to retailing, many people predicted that this would lead to an even more sterile, artificial shopping experience for the consumer. This may often be the case, but it need not be. The strengths of Cosentino's are its vegetable and meat departments, where greengrocers and butchers have the same personal contact with customers that they have always had. For example, meat is not prepackaged, but the butcher personally cuts and wraps it, based on your request. How can this be the case in a highly automated store with laser readers at the checkstands?

The butcher weighs the meat on an electronic scale, and keys in a short code number for the particular meat. The weight, product code, and price are electronically communicated to a bar-code-generating machine that prints a label for the meat. The label contains a machine-readable bar code as well as words and numbers that the customer can read. When the customer takes the meat package to the checkstand at the front of the store, the laser scanner there will handle it exactly as it does all of the store's prepackaged items. The same type of procedure is followed in the bakery, produce, and deli departments.

The laser scanner system at the checkstands was designed and installed by TEC Corporation of Japan. The prices for 22,000 items stocked in the store are stored on floppy disks. Laser scanners read the Universal Product Codes or the store-produced labels.

The store's computer communicates ordering information to the wholesalers' computers. The wholesalers retain extra copies of the price information in case the floppy disks develop problems. In addition wholesalers provide the store with reports on how fast products are moving. Cosentino's managers can change prices of items either at a terminal near the computer or by inserting a special key into a checkout register. The price changes are then communicated to the wholesaler, who prints new shelf labels and ships them to the store. As for the customer, he or she receives top-quality food, personalized service, and a receipt that describes each item and its price.

The equipment cost about $115,000. Sal Cosentino, president and co-owner, feels both the customers and employees have benefited from the use of scanners. "The scanners are more accurate, faster, and reduce the amount of theft," Sal says.

SUMMARY

- *Input brings data, and instructions concerning how to process the data, into an information system. Data entry refers to the process of getting facts into a form that the computer can understand. Output conveys the results of processing.*

- *As with all the other elements of an information system, the mix of input and output equipment an organization acquires must be considered in the context of the whole system.*

- *Trends in input and output include the use of source data automation and the production of user-friendly output.*

- *A terminal can send data to and receive data from a computer. Teleprinters are terminals with a keyboard and a printer.*

- *Display terminals are the most common type of input device. They consist of an input unit, a display screen, and a screen control unit that links the two. Input units include keyboards, electronic mice, graphics tablets or digitizers, and light pens. An intelligent or smart terminal can do processing locally, whereas a dumb terminal cannot. A variety of different screen technologies and features are employed by terminals, as well as different kinds of keyboards. Some common features of display terminal technology include cursors, windows, scrolling and the ability to use icons.*

- *Point-of-activity (POA) terminals are located at the point where a specific activity occurs to capture data at their source. The most common type of point-of-activity terminal is the point-of-sale (POS) terminal seen in stores.*

- *With source data automation, the input medium and the source document are one and the same. The effect is to reduce the amount of manual labor involved in entering data. Source data automation uses optical scanners, magnetic scanners, three-dimensional scanners, and speech recognition systems. Optical scanning methods include optical mark readers (OMR), optical character readers (OCR), magnetic-ink character readers (MICR), and bar code readers such as those that read Universal Product Codes (UPC). In medicine computerized axial tomography (CAT) and nuclear magnetic resonance (NMR) assist in diagnosis and research.*

- *Punch card devices enable the computer to use punch cards for input and output.*

- *Output devices include display terminals, impact printers, nonimpact printers, graphical output devices, audio output devices, and microfilm output devices. Printers are the most frequently used device for permanent output. Impact printers can print a character at a time or a line at a time. Character or serial printers are available that use dot-matrix or daisy-wheel printing mechanisms. Line printers use the dot-matrix system or chains, bands, and drums to attain greater speeds.*

- *Nonimpact printers are the most sophisticated of all, particularly the high-speed page printers which may employ laser-xerographic technology. Such machines are capable of producing graphical and textual output quietly at great speeds. Nonimpact character printers use thermal and ink-jet technologies. The availability of such capable printing equipment has led to the rise of a business support area known as reprographics.*

- *Additional output devices include plotters, audio output devices, and computer-output microfilm (COM) systems that produce microfilm and microfiche output.*

KEY TERMS

These are the key terms in the order in which they appear in the chapter.

Input (160)
Data entry (160)
Output (160)
Source data automation (162)
User-friendly output (163)
Terminal (163)
Teleprinter (163)
Display terminal (164)
Keyboard (164)
Electronic mouse (164)
Graphics tablet or digitizer (164)
Light pen (164)
Intelligent terminal
  or smart terminal (165)
Dumb terminal (165)

Cursor (166)
Window (166)
Scrolling (166)
Icon (166)
Point-of-activity (POA) terminal (168)
Point-of-sale (POS) terminal (169)
Optical scanner (169)
Optical mark reader (OMR) (169)
Optical character reader (OCR) (170)
Bar code reader (170)
Universal Product Code (UPC) (170)
Magnetic-ink character recognition
  (MICR) (171)
Three-dimensional scanner (172)
Computerized axial tomography (CAT) (173)

Nuclear magnetic resonance (NMR) (173)
Speech recognition (173)
Punch card device (174)
Impact printer (175)
Character printer or serial printer (175)
Line printer (175)
Dot-matrix printer (175)
Daisy-wheel printer (176)
Chain printer (177)
Band printer (177)

Drum printer (178)
Nonimpact printer (179)
Thermal printer (179)
Ink-jet printer (179)
High-speed printer (179)
Laser-xerographic printer (179)
Reprographics (180)
Plotter (180)
Audio output device (182)
Microfilm (182)
Microfiche (182)
Computer-output microfilm (COM) (182)

REVIEW QUESTIONS

OBJECTIVE QUESTIONS

TRUE/FALSE: *Put the letter T or F on the line before the question.*

1. Impact printers can produce multi-ply copies.
2. Optical scanners are often used to detect brain tumors.
3. Source data automation refers to machines automatically punching cards for data entry.
4. Laser printers generally are slower than ink-jet printers.
5. A daisy-wheel printer produces "dotlike" characters.
6. A drum printer is a type of nonimpact line printer.
7. Users in information systems should work with the most technically advanced input and output devices regardless of the cost.
8. Obtaining, preparing, entering, and verifying data are steps in the data entry process.
9. A display terminal consists of an input unit, a display screen, and a screen control unit.
10. Punch card media and devices are strictly museum pieces today.

MULTIPLE CHOICE: *Put the letter of the correct answer on the line before the question.*

1. A common type of scanner used in the banking industry is the
   (a) OCR.
   (b) CAT.
   (c) OMR.
   (d) MICR.
2. Which of the following is *not* an example of an impact printer?
   (a) Thermal printer.
   (b) Daisy-wheel printer.
   (c) Dot-matrix printer.
   (d) Band printer.
3. Special symbols used on display terminals to illustrate particular functions are called:
   (a) Mice.
   (b) Cursors.
   (c) Windows.
   (d) None of the above.
4. The most important factor in determining the variety of input and output devices used in an information system is:
   (a) The hardware available.
   (b) The rules and procedures concerning the proper mixture.
   (c) The information needs of the users.
   (d) The data capture needs of the organization.
5. Bar codes are commonly used in:
   (a) The banking industry.
   (b) Medical laboratories.
   (c) Supermarkets.
   (d) College examinations.

FILL IN THE BLANK: *Write the correct word or words in the blank to complete the sentence.*

1. A terminal that only channels data to the CPU is known as a(n) _____.
2. A _____ printer uses metal pins which selectively strike a ribbon against the paper.
3. Using _____ and the _____ features allow a person to view different parts of the data not yet on the display terminal screen.
4. The capture of data when and where a transaction occurs is a fundamental feature of _____.
5. Daisy wheels are _____-at-a-time _____ printers capable of "_____-quality" output.
6. The creation of high-quality computer-generated output for printing, slide presentations, and other visual media is called _____.
7. Generally _____ printers are faster, quieter, and offer more diverse type styles than _____ printers.
8. COM is an acronym for _____.
9. Both _____ and _____ are scanners used for medical diagnosis and research.
10. A _____ is an example of a page printer.

SHORT ANSWER QUESTIONS

When answering these questions, think of concrete examples to illustrate your points.

1. What are the four parts of the data entry process?
2. What are the three types of output? Do they overlap?
3. What is meant by the term source data automation?
4. What do the initials COM, OMR, OCR, UPC, and MICR mean?
5. Describe the different types and uses of optical scanners.
6. Discuss some applications for magnetic and three-dimensional scanners.
7. What are different types of character printers?
8. Compare the different types of line impact printers.
9. What are the advantages of page printers?
10. What is meant by the term reprographics?
11. What types of businesses would use COM?
12. What types of businesses would use voice input and output?

ESSAY QUESTIONS

1. Discuss the effect of source data automation in business. Focus on an industry of your choice for this problem.
2. Compare and contrast impact printers with nonimpact printers.
3. Find up to ten ways in which source data automation affects your life today.
4. What is meant by the term user-friendly output? Discuss examples where such output may make your life easier.

SECONDARY STORAGE: DISKS, TAPES, AND MORE

After studying this chapter you should understand the following:
■ The place of secondary storage in the storage hierarchy.
■ How online and offline storage differ.
■ The main characteristics of magnetic disk storage and magnetic tape storage.
■ Some typical uses for magnetic disk storage and magnetic tape storage.
■ Which technologies offer mass storage capability.

George Roberts wished he were still home gardening. Instead he sat at his desk at Global Electrical Equipment. This Monday he had to prepare a difficult report. As quality control supervisor he had to evaluate how well his subordinates carried out their inspections of appliances manufactured at the Oakriver plant. Based mainly on his report, higher management would determine which promotions and pay increases were in order.

For an inspector performing well meant rejecting bad appliances and approving good ones. Each particular type of appliance had a numerical goal that George's employees had to meet. For toasters an inspector had to test at least 30 per hour, and had to classify at least 29 of the 30 correctly. Pushing that 29 figure nearer to 30 was what the best inspectors did.

George got up from his desk and walked toward his assistant's office down the hall. The assistant would retrieve the data from Global's computer this morning while George worked on other administrative tasks. Then this afternoon George—using the data—could write the report.

Before turning into his assistant's office, George glanced over his shoulder through the windows of Global's computer room. The data George needed were kept there. According to an article in the company newsletter, Global had billions of items of data in that room and in the data library adjacent to it. Most of the data were kept on magnetic disk packs. The wall of the computer center opposite the windows was entirely occupied by a long row of disk storage units that read the data from the packs and also wrote new data onto them.

George paused to watch an operator place a disk pack in the device that read it. The system worked, George had to admit. George's assistant would be able to obtain the right data from his office terminal, and rapidly enough so that George could write his report today. Unauthorized people could not view the data, following the same logic that kept George and his assistant from studying the data maintained by other departments. The operating system kept it all straight. Data that the computer didn't need to work with at any given time were not stored in it at that time. Instead they were stored on the disks or tapes. The most-used disks and tapes were right in the computer room in contact with the computer, and the others were stored in the data library next door.

George entered the office his assistant shared with several other people.

"Ward," George said, "I have to prepare my favorite report again. So I need performance data on everyone this morning."

"Which report?" Ward asked.

THE ROLE OF SECONDARY STORAGE

SECONDARY STORAGE, also known as **EXTERNAL STORAGE** and **AUXILIARY STORAGE**, supplements main memory by holding data and instructions in machine-readable form outside of the central processing unit but under the central processing unit's control.

THE STORAGE HIERARCHY

Before turning to specific devices, let's place secondary storage in context with other types of storage in an information system. We can think of computer storage as being arranged in a **STORAGE HIERARCHY**, as shown in Figure 7-1. Speed and cost—as we have often seen in this book—are key concerns. Storage shown at the top of the hierarchy is both the fastest and the most expensive per unit of data stored. As we move down the hierarchy, speed slows, and cost drops.

The top two levels of the hierarchy in Figure 7-1 are occupied by components of the CPU. Registers, used in the CPU's control unit and arithmetic/logic unit, provide extremely fast access to data. In the level below registers are the different types of main memory, running from the fastest and most expensive at the top, down to slightly slower and cheaper main memory. The types of main memory were described in Chapter 5.

The bottom level of the hierarchy is occupied by secondary storage. Here too there is a hierarchy, ranging from the high-speed and more expensive hard disks down to the slowest and cheapest tape cassettes.

As speed and price decrease as we go down the hierarchy, capacity increases. Registers contain a very small quantity of data, such as a single instruction. Main memory, on the other hand, can hold up to millions of bytes. Within secondary storage hard disks have the greatest capacities of the media shown in Figure 7-1—some can accommodate several billion bytes.

FIGURE 7-1.
The storage hierarchy.

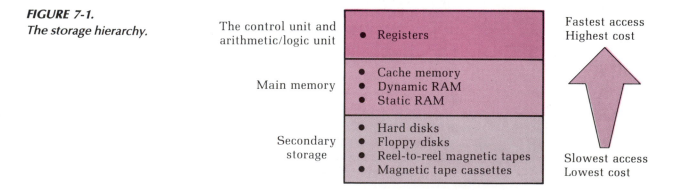

The control unit and arithmetic/logic unit	• Registers	Fastest access Highest cost
Main memory	• Cache memory • Dynamic RAM • Static RAM	
Secondary storage	• Hard disks • Floppy disks • Reel-to-reel magnetic tapes • Magnetic tape cassettes	Slowest access Lowest cost

INFORMATION SYSTEMS AND SECONDARY STORAGE

As with other hardware, the role secondary storage plays in an information system depends on the needs of management and other users. *People* have to evaluate which storage media will give them a cost-effective mixture. The next section will show how costs are calculated.

The characteristics of the *data* to be processed also strongly determine storage requirements. As you will recall from Chapter 2, the smallest usable unit of data is the field. Records are a collection of related fields, files a collection of related records, and a database a collection of interrelated files. The storage requirements of an information system with a vast, complex online database are clearly different from those of a system with a few files that need to be updated once a month.

To enforce management decisions, *rules and procedures* for storing and securing data on various media must be developed and implemented. Secondary storage devices are controlled by system *software*. The software in turn determines how the *hardware*—the central processing unit and the secondary storage devices themselves—interacts.

SELECTING THE SECONDARY STORAGE MIX

When discussing the storage hierarchy, we mentioned that cost and speed were key points that differentiated the media. Both are considerations in choosing the right secondary storage mix for an organization. A third important consideration is security.

Storing data in any form incurs *costs*. One goal in determining the best storage mix for an information system is to minimize the total cost of data storage. Costs go beyond the purchase price of the particular device used, such as a magnetic tape unit. Specifically costs comprise:

- *Storage cost*, *which includes the cost of purchasing the secondary storage device and the media it uses, the cost of making extra copies of the stored material, the security costs necessary to protect the material, and the holding costs of keeping the media and extra copies when not in use.*
- *Access cost*, *which is the price of reading data from a secondary storage device, or of writing data to a secondary storage device. The faster the device, the higher is the access cost for retrieving a given data item.*
- *Handling cost*, *which refers to the labor and other expenses necessary to place the secondary storage medium on the secondary storage device, and to remove the medium from the device.*

The second factor to consider in choosing a storage mix for an information system is *speed*. Specifically this refers to the access time. ACCESS TIME is the amount of time necessary to retrieve a data item from secondary storage and place it into main memory. Note that access time is not the same as RESPONSE TIME, which is the amount of time between making an inquiry or request and the start of the response. For example, if George Roberts types in a request at his terminal, the total time that elapses until the terminal starts displaying his answer is the response time. Buried within this time is the access time necessary for the CPU to read the data George asked about.

Among the media most often used for information systems, the fastest access times are obtained with hard disk devices. Access times for any device increases if it is necessary first to place the secondary storage medium on the device. This is especially true of magnetic tape.

The third important factor in choosing a secondary storage mix is *security*. Both programs and data must be kept safe and secure. They must be protected against accidental or deliberate destruction or alteration. Generally speaking, security measures increase costs and slow down speed, but are justified in the long run by both the money and time saved for the organization by not leaking vital information or having to regenerate original data.

Chapter 17 will discuss data security in greater detail.

ONLINE AND OFFLINE STORAGE

Secondary storage can be either online or offline. The computer has direct control over **ONLINE STORAGE** and can access data and software stored there without human intervention. Online storage systems generally use magnetic disk as the storage medium, but can also use magnetic tape and other media. Online storage is required for real-time processing, and is generally used for time-sharing as well.

OFFLINE STORAGE is not under the direct control of the computer. As soon as an online device is turned off, it becomes offline. In the same way, when a reel of magnetic tape or removable disk is taken out of the device that reads and writes upon it, the tape or disk is offline. Some offline storage is archival in nature, retaining information in a machine-readable form in case an organization needs it again at some future time. Offline storage is most often associated with batch processing.

MAGNETIC DISK STORAGE

MAGNETIC DISKS provide very fast, high-capacity secondary storage. Disk units come in a variety of forms, each designed to read from and write on a different style of disk.

Disk is generally the medium of choice for applications that need ready availability of large amounts of data. For example, law-enforcement agencies store data about stolen vehicles on magnetic disk systems because disk storage has enough capacity to hold all the relevant data about license plate numbers and vehicle type, and can deliver the data fast enough for officers to act upon them. Other applications include storing credit- and check-verification data, maintaining current levels of inventory in a warehouse, storing financial quotations, and recording patient laboratory test results at hospitals.

In addition magnetic disk storage is used for many routine day-to-day business processing tasks. Databases are usually stored on disk, as are operating systems and other frequently used programs. In an information system that includes both magnetic disk and magnetic tape for secondary storage, disk is typically used for programs with a higher priority or greater importance, and for programs that work with a large quantity of data.

It is important to keep in mind that disk storage devices, or, for that matter, any type of secondary storage device, including tape drives, are also input/output devices. Data stored on disk are input to the computer; processed information is output to disk for storage.

Data can be output to disk by a program, and the output used as input for subsequent processing. For example, an accounts receivable program might create an output file of all accounts more than 60 days outstanding. Later

An important specialist in today's large and diversified centers is the media librarian.

The media librarian is responsible for controlling the storage and use of removable magnetic storage media—magnetic disks and magnetic tapes.

In early computer centers, the computer operators took care of cataloging the tapes on an impromptu basis by different personnel. Imagine a conventional library with no catalog for the books, with no particular organization on the shelves—or with a catalog and organization begun by one person in a certain way, taken up again in an altogether different way by another, and forgotten by a third. Before the assignment of a media librarian to the job, this type of library existed in many otherwise sophisticated computer centers. The result was lost time hunting for the tape or disk sought and needless duplication of materials.

The media librarian is an orderly person who pays attention to details, yet is not overwhelmed by rush requests or by the sheer volume of materials handled (it is not uncommon for thousands of labeled and numbered tapes to hang on their storage racks). The librarian will be responsible for either devising a classification system for labeling and storing the media, or for following the system already in effect. Disks and tapes are usually checked in and out of the library with an accompanying form filled out by the responsible party. The aim is to keep unauthorized material out of the hands of people who have no legitimate need for it or permission to use it. The skills of classification, efficient storage logistics, and smooth check-in/check-out control, are those of a librarian. Accordingly, media librarians often have degrees in library science, like their book-like counterparts. Some familiarity with computers will be acquired today when pursuing a library science degree, since that field is highly automated. It is not necessary to have computer experience beyond this to become a media librarian. Library or other detail-oriented administrative experience would be a plus.

People and managerial skills are important. The media librarian interacts with people, some of whom must be diplomatically told no. The librarian may also help plan the efficient use of media together with the director of information systems or the database administrator.

The media librarian may also work with the information system security specialist and manager of computer operations to see that check-in/check-out procedures effectively hinder improper use of data, yet do not unduly impede the organization's work.

another program might use this file as input, and create an updated file that eliminates customers who paid since the original file was created and adds newly delinquent customers.

New data can be entered onto disk from source documents through a device that operates offline from the computer. Such key-to-disk or key-to-diskette systems (Figure 7-2) consist of a keyboard, display screen, and a unit to enter the data onto the disk. These devices allow for a certain amount of editing and checking of the data. Once the data are entered, the disk or diskette can then be removed for use as input to a computer.

FIGURE 7-2.
Entering data on a key-to-disk system.

TYPES OF MAGNETIC DISKS

All types of magnetic disks share the ability to store data so that programs can have direct access to the data. **DIRECT ACCESS** refers to the ability to retrieve or write a given record without first having to process all of the records leading up to it. Direct access offers a fast way to retrieve or write data. Certain techniques of organizing and referring to data on disk make direct access possible; we will examine these in Chapter 16.

Magnetic disks are slower in their operation than main memory, but can hold considerably more data. Main memory can contain from tens of thousands to millions of bytes, whereas magnetic disks can hold a number of bytes ranging from hundreds of thousands into the billions.

All magnetic disks are circular like phonograph records and coated with a magnetic surface. In the surface, particles can be aligned into bit patterns to record data. **MAGNETIC DISK UNITS** read data from, and write data upon, magnetic disks. Such units contain the read/write mechanism, the drive motors, and support circuitry. A magnetic disk unit is often called a **DASD**—short for **DIRECT-ACCESS STORAGE DEVICE**. Magnetic disks are divided into two categories, hard disks and floppy disks.

Hard disks

HARD DISKS, or **RIGID DISKS**, are made of metal and, as their name indicates, are rigid. This type of disk has a greater storage capacity than floppy disks. Hard

FIGURE 7-3.
A "Winchester" hard disk system used for microcomputers. This system stores over 10 million bytes.

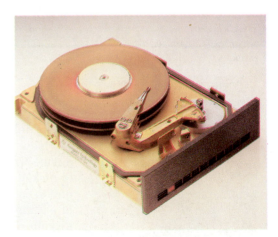

FIGURE 7-4.
A large multiple-disk storage
system.

FIGURE 7-5.
A removable disk cartridge.

FIGURE 7-6.
Mounting a removable disk
pack.

disk systems are available for any size of computer. Figure 7-3 shows a common type of hard disk system used for microcomputers. Figure 7-4 shows a large system commonly used with mainframe computers.

One or two hard disks can be placed into a sealed **DISK CARTRIDGE** (Figure 7-5). A number of disk platters can also be stacked vertically into a **DISK PACK** (Figure 7-6). Disk cartridges and disk packs may be permanently installed in the DASD or removable. In addition large units exist that combine multiple disk units to hold billions of bytes.

Access arms within a DASD hold the read/write mechanism. When the disk reaches an operating speed of about 3000 to 4500 revolutions per minute, the access arm can move the read/write head over the disk. Figure 7-7 shows a read/write head. The arm holds two read/write heads, one for each side of the disk. The head does not touch the surface of the disk at all, but rather its aerodynamic qualities allow it to float just above the surface.

Floppy disks

The other category of disk, **FLOPPY DISKS** or **DISKETTES**, are made from flexible plastic. They remind most people of small phonograph records. Shown in Figure 7-8, floppy disks come in three main diameters: 8 inches, 5 1/4 inches, and 3 1/2 inches. Floppy disks in the 8-inch and 5 1/4-inch sizes remain permanently in a special square envelope made of light cardboard. The envelope protects the disk, and has small openings to allow the read/write mechanism access to the disk surface. Floppy disks in the 3 1/2-inch size are encased in plastic and have a protective metal flap over the openings for the read/write mechanism.

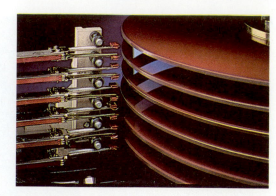

FIGURE 7-7.
The read/write mechanism of a disk system. It floats over the disk surface.

(a)

FIGURE 7-8.
Examples of floppy disks. There are three major sizes—(a) 8-inches, 5 1/4 inches, and (b) 3 1/2 inches. The 3 1/2-inch size has a protective shield over the actual disk.

(b)

A floppy disk is placed in a floppy disk drive (Figure 7-9). Floppy disk drives are available for any size of computer, though they are most commonly associated with microcomputers. In contrast to hard disk systems, the read/write mechanism physically touches the floppy disk surface. Floppy disks store only about a twentieth the amount that a comparable hard disk platter can hold, though floppy disk capacities range from about 120,000 bytes to over 1 million bytes.

RETRIEVING DATA FROM MAGNETIC DISK

We have already seen how access arms and read/write heads handle reading and writing data from disk. Since some programs require data records to be read and written many thousands of times, speed is an important consideration. "Speed" in this case means access time, the amount of time necessary to retrieve a data item from secondary storage and place it into main memory, or, in reverse, the amount of time necessary to locate an appropriate secondary storage location and transfer data from main memory to the location.

Access time is made up of three stages: (1) seek time, (2) search time, and (3) data-transfer time. SEEK TIME is the time required to position the read/write head over the right part of the disk. SEARCH TIME is the time it takes for the data to spin under the head (or, for writing, for the appropriate locations

FIGURE 7-9.

to spin under the head to receive the data). Once the data (or write locations) have been found, the data must be transferred to the CPU (for a read) or to the disk (for a write). The speed for the transfer is the **DATA-TRANSFER TIME**.

Hard disk systems take from about 10 to 100 milliseconds (thousandths of a second) for the seek and search time together, and have a data-transfer rate somewhere between 2 and 16 million bits per second. Floppy disks take from 75 to 600 milliseconds for the seek and search time together, and have a data-transfer rate of about 250,000 bits per second. These rates may seem fast—they are—but most CPUs operate in the millionth to billionth of a second range. In other words, a CPU with a 60-nanosecond cycle time can perform a million operations during the same time that a hard disk with a seek and search time of 60 milliseconds finds one data item.

Data arrangement on hard disks

Now let's see how data are organized on a hard disk. Each side of a hard disk in a disk pack or stack of disks is called a surface. Permanently installed disks make use of all the surfaces, while removable disk packs use all but the top surface of the top disk and the bottom surface of the bottom disk, which are the surfaces most likely to be contaminated.

Let's view the disk surface from above. If we could see the magnetized bits, they would appear to be arranged along concentric rings. Each ring is known as a **TRACK**. The number of tracks a disk can hold varies from about 300 to 1000. Traveling along a single track, we can store around 10,000 bits per inch. Figure 7-10 is a schematic drawing of a disk pack showing the relationship of disks, surfaces, tracks, and the access mechanism.

CYLINDERS are a conceptual "slice" of a disk made up of vertical stacks of tracks. The first cylinder on a disk is made up of all the first tracks; the second one of all the second tracks; and so on. Thus if a disk platter has 600 tracks, the disk pack has 600 cylinders. Some systems place the data for a file onto one cylinder at a time, while other systems fill the disk on a track-by-track basis. Working with a cylinder at a time shortens seek time, since for most operations the read/write heads will already be over the right cylinder.

SECTORS are pie-shaped sections radiating out from the center of the disk (Figure 7-11). Usually each of the tracks within a sector holds the same

FIGURE 7-10.

The relationship of disks, surfaces, tracks, and the access
mechanism in a disk pack.

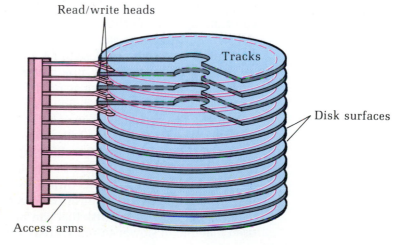

Read/write heads

Tracks

Disk surfaces

Access arms

FIGURE 7-11.

Tracks and sectors on a floppy disk. Usually the disk surface is divided into eight to twenty sectors. This disk has nine sectors.

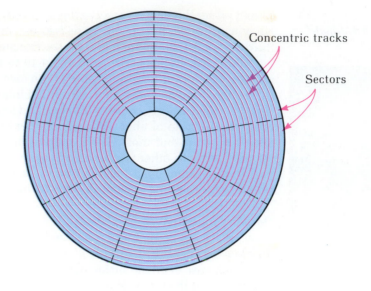

Concentric tracks

Sectors

number of bytes. This means that the larger-diameter outer tracks are written less densely than the shorter-diameter inner tracks.

FORMATTING refers to the way a particular computer and operating system order the disk drive to position the magnetic signals for the tracks, cylinders, sectors, and byte locations on the surface. The number of bytes that can be stored on a disk depends on its format.

There are other techniques to reduce seek and search times. Some DASDs have multiple read/write heads for each surface. Others totally eliminate seek time by substituting fixed heads over every track. These types of systems are faster, but more expensive.

Data arrangement on floppy disks

Floppy disks arrange data a bit differently. Some floppy disks only use a single surface; we call these single-sided disks. Other floppy disks—double-sided disks—use both surfaces. Like hard disks, floppies have tracks. The tracks for floppy disks are not as densely packed as for hard disks. Floppy disks contain between 40 and 100 tracks per inch, and along a track can store up to about 6000 bits per inch. The trend has been to ever greater density. Early systems stored about 120,000 bytes on a 5 1/4-inch diskette. Recent systems can store close to 1.5 million bytes in the same space.

Floppy disks generally use sectors for organizing data on the disk surface. Disks with the sectors predefined on them are said to be hard-sectored; disks without predefined sectors are called soft-sectored. Most floppy disk drives sold today use soft-sectored disks. Soft-sectored disks can be read and written upon by different machines; so can hard-sectored disks, provided both machines follow the same formatting conventions.

With either hard or floppy disks, special disk-management software and circuitry built into the DASD direct the storage and retrieval of data and instructions. These disk-control packages can even place frequently used materials in parts of the disk that can be reached more quickly and rarely used material in slower-to-reach areas, thus minimizing arm travel.

ADVANTAGES AND DRAWBACKS OF MAGNETIC DISK STORAGE

The main advantage of using magnetic disks for secondary storage is that they can maintain a lot of data online. The time delays due to frequent mounting and removing of media common with tape are reduced for disk. Another key advantage is that disks permit direct access, which is fast and efficient.

There are drawbacks as well. Disks are sensitive to environmental hazards. Even tiny particles of dirt, bacteria, or hair can cause major complications if they come into contact with the surface of a disk (Figure 7-12), although most hard disk systems are sealed against these environmental hazards. Too much handling of a disk can distort it, causing the read/write head to crash on the surface and damage data, and possibly the DASD as well. Electromagnetic radiation can also damage data—special shielding can reduce this risk. Creating extra backup copies of disk files is a must, and backup copies of vital files should be stored far enough from the computer that originals and backups could not possibly be destroyed by the same disaster.

Another drawback is vulnerability to unauthorized access. A disk can hold a lot of data from a variety of sources. A small number of disks—even one—sometimes contains all of an organization's data. If these disks are online, the chance exists that someone could deliberately or accidentally read, change, or destroy your data without your even being aware of it. Software packages are available to help reduce these risks. One solution is to use removable disk packs; when data are not required, the pack can be taken out of the disk unit and stored in a safe area.

FIGURE 7-12.

The read/write mechanism of a disk drive is very sensitive to environmental damage. Even dust or smoke particles can cause a crash.

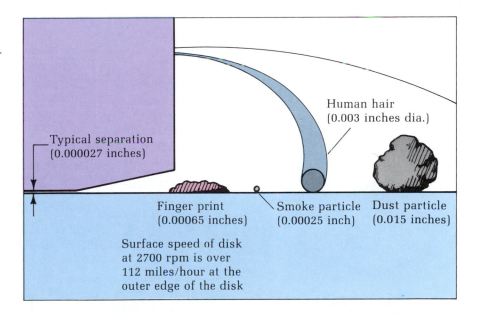

Human hair
(0.003 inches dia.)

Typical separation
(0.000027 inches)

Finger print
(0.00065 inches)

Smoke particle
(0.00025 inch)

Dust particle
(0.015 inches)

Surface speed of disk
at 2700 rpm is over
112 miles/hour at the
outer edge of the disk

MAGNETIC TAPE STORAGE

MAGNETIC TAPES provide rapid, high-capacity secondary storage. In both of these particulars magnetic tape cannot compete with magnetic disk, which is much faster and holds a lot more. But tape is substantially cheaper.

Like disk, magnetic tape is an input/output medium as well as a storage medium. As with disk files, tape files may be created as program output, and used as input to another program or to the same program at a later time. In addition offline key-to-tape devices can be used to enter data. Magnetic tape is generally the medium of choice for offline and archival storage of data. Tapes are frequently used to make backup copies of files stored on disk. Reels of tape are inexpensive, compact, and easy to move and store. Batch processing programs often use magnetic tape for data input and output.

TYPES OF MAGNETIC TAPE

Magnetic tape, regardless of its type, can provide only sequential access to data records. SEQUENTIAL ACCESS refers to the necessity of reading every record leading up to a sought-after record. The direct access that disks make possible cannot be done with tape. If we have a file containing 40,000 records, and we want to read record number 40,000, we have to read the other 39,999 records first to get there. In practice programs that work with magnetic tape generally sort data in sequence to minimize this type of situation, and use smaller files. We will examine concepts concerning sequential access in Chapter 16.

Magnetic tape is made of plastic and coated with a magnetic surface. Particles in the surface can be aligned into bit patterns to record data. Magnetic tape comes in the reel-to-reel style and in cassettes. Both types are shown in Figure 7-13, together with the MAGNETIC TAPE UNITS that read them. Magnetic tape units are sometimes referred to as TAPE DRIVES.

REEL-TO-REEL TAPE records data one byte at a time, spreading the bits that make up the byte across the width of the tape. Figure 7-14 shows an example of how the message "GREETINGS" is represented in EBCDIC on a tape containing nine tracks. For tape, a track runs along the length of the tape, and records a certain bit of each byte (the first track records the first bit of all the bytes, the second track records the second bit, and so on). Each of the 8-bit EBCDIC bytes has a ninth bit for parity, which is why the tape has nine rather than eight tracks. (For a refresher on parity bits, the EBCDIC coding system, or even bits and bytes, turn to the "Data Representation" section of Chapter 5 and to Appendix B on number systems.)

CASSETTE TAPES are used primarily with microcomputers that do not have magnetic disk units. Cassettes handle data differently: the bits for a character follow one another in a single track. When all of the bits for one character are finished, then the bits for the next character begin.

FIGURE 7-13.

Magnetic tapes and the tape drives that read them. (a) Two sizes of reel-to-reel tape. (b) Reel-to-reel tape drives. (c) A cassette tape and drive.

(a)

(c)

(b)

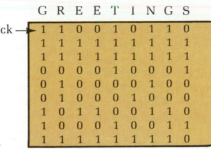

G R E E T I N G S

Parity track →

1	1	0	0	1	0	1	1	0
1	1	1	1	1	1	1	1	1
1	1	1	1	1	1	1	1	1
0	0	0	0	1	0	0	0	1
0	1	0	0	0	0	1	0	0
0	1	0	0	0	1	0	0	0
1	0	1	1	0	0	1	1	0
1	0	0	0	1	0	0	1	1
1	1	1	1	1	1	1	1	0

FIGURE 7-14.

Data representation on magnetic tape. The bit pattern is shown for "GREETINGS" in EBCDIC. The topmost track is used for parity, and here the even parity system is followed.

RETRIEVING DATA FROM MAGNETIC TAPE

Once a magnetic tape is mounted in a magnetic tape unit, the unit will read or write upon the tape as directed by the CPU. Reading or writing is done as the tape passes a fixed read/write head. Reel-to-reel tapes move at speeds up to 200 inches per second, and they hold data at a density ranging from 800 to 6250 bytes per inch. Reel-to-reel tapes are usually 2400 feet long, and wound on a reel 10 1/2 inches in diameter. The data-transfer rate for these tapes can approach 1.3 million bytes per second. In practice transfer rates are usually much lower, however, because of the frequent stops and starts the tape drive makes.

To allow for these starts and stops, magnetic tapes must contain either interrecord gaps or interblock gaps. These gaps are simply a sufficient amount of space between data records to allow the tape to reach operational speed before reading or writing data, and to allow the tape to slow down after reading or writing is finished. **INTERRECORD GAPS** are placed between each record. This can take up a prohibitive amount of space; as much as 90 percent of a tape, for instance, might consist of interrecord gaps rather than data.

To economize on space, records may be written adjacent to each other in blocks. An **INTERBLOCK GAP** then provides the start-up/slow-down time the tape drive needs, and interrecord gaps are eliminated. A single read then transfers a block, consisting of a number of records, to the computer, where the block is placed in a buffer. A **BUFFER** is a temporary storage area used to accumulate data from the relatively slow input device until enough data are present to justify processing by the more rapid CPU; or in the case of writing data, a buffer receives a burst of output data from the CPU when it is ready, and parcels the data out at the appropriate speed to the slower output device. Besides helping out with this speed disparity between the CPU and the input/output devices, buffers are handy for receiving blocks. If blocks rather than records are being read or written, then the block size must be kept small enough to fit into the buffer. Buffers are located in the main memory part of the CPU and in the tape unit.

Gaps notwithstanding, an enormous amount of data can be stored on a single magnetic tape. Assuming a 2400-foot tape, and allowing for interblock gaps, approximately 140 million bytes—the equivalent of more than 50 copies of this book—can easily be stored on the tape. To store the same amount of data on punch cards would require more than 1.7 million cards. The tape would weigh three pounds, and the cards over a ton!

With its plain exterior, National Safe Depository looks like any of hundreds of anonymous businesses that stand amid the commercial clutter of Stevens Creek Boulevard in San Jose.

But in this case appearances are deceiving. Little short of a commando attack could pierce National Safe's bullet-resistant glass. It would take a barn-burner of a fire to melt inch-thick steel walls, and video cameras silently record all comings and goings.

National Safe is using its fortress-like setting to blend the traditionally staid safe deposit box business with high-technology records storage. Already, the company has been successful enough to buy out two competitors . . . and it is preparing to acquire a third. . . .

Experts say National Safe is one of a number of companies cashing in on a boom in "off-site data storage."

Records "have got to be protected from earthquake, fire, flood and natural diaster," said Robert Austin, who heads a Colorado records management consulting company as well as the standards committee of the Association of Records Managers and Administrators. "Off-site storage is increasing at a very rapid rate."

In Silicon Valley, vital records often means high tech. Some samples in the vaults at National Safe include computer tapes and packs of computer disks storing information about payrolls, personnel lists, customer accounts, computer chips, engineering drawings for new computers and other products, and results of research and development work.

Not everything stored at National Safe is as exotic, but some of it is unusual. Travel agents, for instance, store blank ticket stock that potentially can be worth thousands of dollars.

For a typical account, National Safe charges $100 to $300 per month, including courier service, Weller said. After making pitches to more than 2,000 companies, National Safe now has "hundreds" of customers, said president Reginald H. Weller, although he won't say how many.

National Safe is filling an important business need, say some of its customers.

"The earthquake we had back in April and a lot of casualties around the country have reawakened people to the fact that you should have some off-site storage," said John L. Buckley, industrial security manager for United Technologies' chemical systems division in San Jose.

United stores some 900 to 1,000 computer tapes at National Safe. The tapes contain engineering, contractual, legal, and financial information—"things you would need to restart your business if you had a casualty," said Buckley.

The ordinance division of FMC Corp. in San Jose stores cases of microfiche as well as several hundred reels of tape. Because the company receives government contracts, it must keep records and documents on file for potential audits. The division also stores disaster recovery materials, including operating systems for a number of computers, said data processing Security Manager Edward J. McFadden.

"When you get it condensed down like that, you need a little more security than leaving it around an office," he said.

Source: From "San Jose Firm Aims to Help Clients Play It Safe," by Christopher H. Schmitt. *San Jose Mercury News,* October 1, 1985.

ADVANTAGES AND DRAWBACKS OF MAGNETIC TAPE STORAGE

The main advantages of using magnetic tape for secondary storage are that tape is inexpensive, compact, and provides fairly fast retrieval of data. Tapes cost about $20 each, and the price per byte stored on a tape is negligible. The cost of storing an individual tape in a tape library is fairly low as well. Often copies of important records are stored in underground fireproof vaults far from the computer center where the tape was originally made. Corporations maintain vital proprietary information, stockholder data, and customer and personnel records in such vaults, as insurance against a disaster at the main computer center.

The main drawback of tape is that data can only be retrieved and written sequentially, as discussed earlier in the chapter. In addition there are environmental hazards, as with disks. Environmental dangers include exposure of a tape to a magnetic field, dust from a tape drive or elsewhere sticking to a tape, and extreme temperatures. Any of these can distort or destroy data.

MASS STORAGE

Imagine storing all of the accounts of millions of insurance customers, or the ticket information for people who fly on commercial airlines, or—bigger yet—the files for the U.S. Social Security Administration. Files of this size would overwhelm the resources of a simple magnetic disk or tape system. For such large and massive files, storage of comparable scope is needed: **MASS STORAGE**.

There are several different types of mass storage devices of interest to us: magnetic strip cartridge systems, multiple-disk systems, optical disk devices, and videotape units. Let's briefly examine each of these.

MAGNETIC STRIP CARTRIDGE SYSTEMS

The **MAGNETIC STRIP CARTRIDGE SYSTEM**, or **DATA CELL**, is one of the most common types of mass storage (Figure 7-15). This device stores data on short strips of magnetic tape. The strips are wound up and placed in cartridges that serve as containers, and the cartridges are stored in individual cells of a giant honeycomb-like structure.

FIGURE 7-15.
A mass storage system using magnetic strip cartridges.

To retrieve or write data, a mechanism scoots to the storage location of the appropriate cartridge, pulls the cartridge from the honeycomb, removes the tape from the cartridge, and reads the data from it or writes the data upon it.

Slower than disk systems, these devices offer a compromise between offline and online storage. That is, all of the data are in fact online—the data do not have to be fetched by a human being from a library somewhere, but only by a mechanism from within the system itself. It does, however, take a little while actually to get at any of the online data. Seconds can easily be tallied while waiting. Like disks, the devices offer direct access to data. Enormous quantities of data can be held: IBM's 3850 Mass Storage System stores up to 472 gigabytes (billion bytes) of data.

MULTIPLE-DISK-DRIVE SYSTEMS

Another type of mass storage teams up magnetic disk units into **MULTIPLE-DISK-DRIVE SYSTEMS**. Such systems can coordinate dozens of DASDs and occupy several large rooms. These are frequently used for large-scale real-time applications that handle vast amounts of data, such as travel reservation systems and credit-card validation systems.

OPTICAL DISK SYSTEMS

An **OPTICAL DISK SYSTEM** (Figure 7-16), also known as a laser disk system, can store and retrieve billions of bytes of data. Some optical disk systems are available for microcomputers. The same technology has made possible the compact digital audio disk that has revolutionized sound recording.

An optical disk system works by using the intense light of a laser to melt tiny bubbles into the surface of a disk. These bubbles change the optical qualities of the surface. A lower-power laser can then read the pattern and transfer the bits to the CPU. Optical disk systems operate on the same principles as video disks used to record and show movies in the home.

Compared with a magnetic disk, an optical disk has a much greater capacity, about 20 times as much. Optical disks provide direct access to data.

FIGURE 7-16.
Optical storage systems use laser technology for storing archival data. Such systems can hold billions of bytes of data. This one optical disk can store as much information as an encyclopedia.

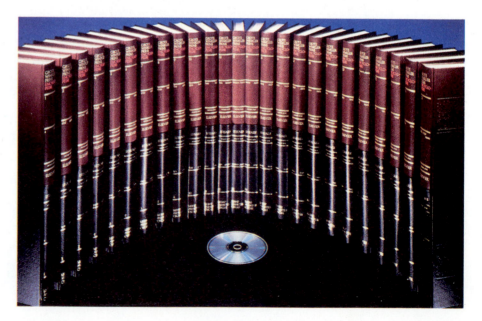

To date the drawback of optical disk systems is that the little bubbles that record that data are, alas, permanent. This means that the data on optical disks cannot be erased so that the disks, which are expensive, can be reused for other data. Attempts are being made to produce erasable disks by using either a combination of magnetics and lasers or by developing surfaces that can be optically altered back to the original state. The main application of optical disks today is to provide archival storage of documents that are needed for reference but that will not require any changes. The fact that the documents cannot be changed is a useful feature for auditors. Such documents include accounting, banking, insurance, and payroll records.

VIDEOTAPE SYSTEMS

Again relying upon technology first put to commercial use in the home-entertainment industry, VIDEOTAPE SYSTEMS can store vast amount of data, providing sequential (not direct) access to the data. Instead of recording a picture for later playback, a video cassette recorder can register bit patterns and, when needed, play these values back. In fact the same types of recorders used in the home to record television shows can be, and often are, used to provide backup storage for microcomputer disk files. Videotape systems can be programmed to perform automatically such backup operations just as you would program them to tape a favorite television show. A 30-minute tape can hold 100 million bytes.

OTHER TYPES OF SECONDARY STORAGE

Although we have covered quite a few different types of secondary storage systems, we have not yet exhausted the possibilities. In this final section we will look at two more: charge-coupled devices and bubble memory.

CHARGE-COUPLED DEVICES (Figure 7-17) are a form of semiconductor storage. A very fast storage medium, these devices use tiny storage cells to hold charges that represent desired bit patterns. The data bits are transferred to and from the device in small "pipelines" when required. Direct access is not possible, but only sequential access to one *bit* at a time. Unfortunately when the power is turned off, charge-coupled devices lose the data being stored there. Another rapid type of storage, though not quite as fast as charge-coupled devices, is BUBBLE MEMORY. What long-term role charge-coupled devices and bubble memories will play in the area of secondary storage remains to be seen. As we noted in Chapter 5, bubble memory chips are already used for main memory in some devices, especially those requiring ruggedness and nonvolatility, such as portable computers.

FIGURE 7-17.
A charge-coupled device, slightly longer than 1/4 inch.

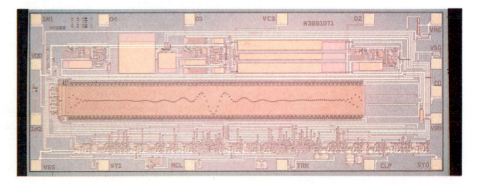

At Global Electrical Equipment, as we saw at the beginning of the chapter, George Roberts sought data on how well his employees were doing, in order to prepare a report the same day for his own manager, who would use it to determine salary increases and promotions. The data George needed were contained in secondary storage. Let's look more closely at what that means.

The data on inspector performance were maintained online on a multiple-disk-drive system. The purpose of keeping the data online was to allow ready access for just such uses as George had in mind, and to permit frequent updating of data and the addition of new data. Keeping the data on disk made possible direct access to sought-after items by query programs such as that which George's assistant would use from his terminal.

Besides the online data, a second copy existed offline on magnetic tape. This was strictly a backup copy, for use only if something happened to the originals.

Ward sat at his terminal and requested the data George needed. The computer system permitted both Ward and George to view these particular data. They could not, however, look at data kept by the marketing, engineering, or accounting departments.

Just before lunch, Ward handed George a one-page report containing the sought-after information.

"Thanks Ward," George said, taking the page. "And now . . ." George began.

Ward finished it for him, making a slicing motion with his finger at his neck.

George placed the report on his desk and skimmed the figures. For each inspector he could see the average number of inspections per hour and the average number of incorrect choices per hour. Much of it was as he had guessed—yet there were a few surprises.

For example, Irma Halpern turned out to be even better than he'd thought. She had inspected an average of 38 machines an hour—eight more than the standard—yet she averaged only one incorrect choice per hour. George was always glad to go to bat for his people, and get them promotions, when they were merited. For Irma it certainly was. George scanned the figures for the other inspectors. This was the kind of information he could get enthusiastic about. His manager would sense that and probably grant most of George's requests for his employees.

Soon George would have his report finished, could feel proud of himself, and would go home early and get in a bit of gardening before dinner. He deserved it, he decided. Looking up briefly from his work, he noticed that heavy rain had begun.

- *A computer's central processing unit lacks the main memory capacity to store all of the data and programs at once that an information system needs. Secondary storage (or external storage or auxiliary storage) fills the need for additional memory, holding data and instructions in machine-readable form outside of the CPU.*

- *Within an information system storage can be thought of in terms of a storage hierarchy. Main memory, at the top of the hierarchy, is the fastest, most expensive, and most limited in capacity. Secondary storage, at the bottom of the hierarchy, has great capacity and is slower and less expensive. Of the technologies commonly used for secondary storage, hard disk systems are the fastest, have the greatest capacity, and are the most expensive.*

- *Considerations that go into selecting a storage mix are cost, speed, and security. Speed is generally measured in terms of access time—the time needed to transfer data from storage to main memory. Users, however, are usually most interested in response time—the time between making an inquiry and receiving a response.*

- *Secondary storage can be either online (under computer control) or offline (not under computer control).*

- *Magnetic disks provide very fast, high-capacity secondary storage, and offer direct access to data. Disk units (often called DASDs for direct-access storage device) read from and write on magnetic disks. Disks come in two types—hard (rigid) metal or flexible (floppy) plastic. Hard disks may be permanently installed in the DASD or placed in removable disk packs or small disk cartridges. With disk units, access time includes seek, search, and data-transfer times.*

- *Data on disks are arranged in concentric rings, called tracks, on the surface of the disk. With multiple surfaced disk packs, the sets of tracks above and below each other make up a cylinder. Disks can also be broken up into pie-shaped segments called sectors. The process of formatting determines the exact location of tracks, cylinders, and sectors on the disk surface.*

- *Magnetic disks are sensitive to environmental hazards and vulnerable to unauthorized access.*

- *Magnetic tapes provide secondary storage that is neither as fast nor as high in capacity as disk, but is cheaper. With magnetic tape only sequential access to data is possible. Magnetic tape units or drives read reel-to-reel tapes; cassette readers read cassette tape. To allow the drive mechanism room to start and stop, interrecord or interblock gaps are placed between data records. When data are grouped into blocks, they are transferred a block at a time from tape to a buffer in the CPU. Like disks, tapes are sensitive to environmental dangers.*

- *Mass storage refers to devices and media that can store very large quantities of data online. Four mass storage systems are magnetic strip cartridge systems, multiple disk systems, optical disk devices, and videotape units.*

- *Looking ahead, charge-coupled devices and bubble memory are among the technologies that might conceivably transform the future of secondary storage.*

KEY TERMS

These are the key terms in the order in which they appear in the chapter.

Secondary storage (or external storage or auxiliary storage) (190)
Storage hierarchy (190)
Access time (191)
Response time (191)
Online storage (192)
Offline storage (192)
Magnetic disk (192)
Direct access (194)
Magnetic disk unit (194)
DASD (direct-access storage device) (194)
Hard disk or rigid disk (194)
Disk cartridge (195)
Disk pack (195)
Floppy disk or diskette (195)
Seek time (196)
Search time (196)
Data-transfer time (197)

Track (197)
Cylinder (197)
Sector (197)
Formatting (198)
Magnetic tape (199)
Sequential access (200)
Magnetic tape unit or tape drive (200)
Reel-to-reel tape (200)
Cassette tape (200)
Interrecord gap (201)
Interblock gap (201)
Buffer (201)
Mass storage (203)
Magnetic strip cartridge system, or data cell (203)
Multiple-disk-drive system (204)
Optical disk system (204)
Videotape system (205)
Charge-coupled device (205)
Bubble memory (205)

REVIEW QUESTIONS

OBJECTIVE QUESTIONS

TRUE/FALSE: *Put the letter T or F on the line before the question.*

1. Primary storage is generally cheaper than secondary storage.
2. Magnetic disks are used to store data for direct access systems.
3. Optical disk storage systems offer less storage than comparably sized magnetic disk systems.
4. Magnetic tapes are used for direct access systems.
5. Because of the reliability of today's storage devices there is no need to back up your files.
6. The most expensive type of secondary storage is magnetic tape.
7. Online storage is less vulnerable to security breaches than offline storage.
8. Sequential storage is useful when processing requires most of the records to be accessed.
9. Floppy disks can hold about 20 times more data than comparably sized hard disks.
10. The total cost for secondary storage is only concerned with the cost of accessing the data.

MULTIPLE CHOICE: *Put the letter of the correct answer on the line before the question.*

1. A removable disk pack with 12 platters has _____ recording surfaces.
   (a) 10.   **(c)** 22.
   (b) 12.   **(d)** 24.

2. A removable disk pack with with 450 tracks on eight platters has _____ cylinders.
   (a) 450.   **(c)** 6300.
   (b) 3600.   **(d)** 7200.

3. Records on magnetic tape are often grouped into _____ in order to speed read/write operations.

(a) Sectors.
(b) Blocks.
(c) Tracks.
(d) Files.

4. The secondary storage mixture selected for an information system depends upon:

(a) The cost of the total secondary storage mix.
(b) The security level desired for the data.
(c) The response required by the users of the information system.
(d) All of the above factors must be considered in selecting the secondary storage mixture.

5. Fly-By-Night Airlines uses its information system to service the reservation requests of passengers as well as traditional business operations such as payroll. What type of secondary storage mixture would be best for the airline?

(a) Direct access storage systems.
(b) Sequential access storage systems
(c) Mass storage systems.
(d) A combination of all three types.

FILL IN THE BLANK: *Write the correct word or words in the blank to complete the sentence.*

1. Microcomputers most commonly use _____ access secondary storage.

2. The acronym DASD means _____.

3. A _____ storage system is used for the optical recording of sequential data.

4. An _____ uses a laser to store data for direct access retrieval.

5. The _____ time refers to the interval required to retrieve data from secondary storage and place the data into main memory.

6. The _____ allows us to visualize differences in storage in terms of cost and speed.

7. The _____ time is the amount of the time between the start of an inquiry and receiving the response.

8. The process of preparing a disk or diskette for data storage is known as _____.

9. Data on disks are often written onto tracks contained within pie-shaped areas called _____.

10. Access time consists of three subparts: _____, _____, and _____.

SHORT ANSWER QUESTIONS

When answering these questions, think of concrete examples to illustrate your points.

1. What are the differences between primary and secondary storage?
2. What are the differences between offline and online storage?
3. What is the difference between an interrecord gap and an interblock gap? Why are these gaps used?
4. What are the differences between hard and floppy disks?
5. What are some examples of mass storage devices?

ESSAY QUESTIONS

1. What are the advantages and disadvantages of magnetic disk storage?
2. What are the advantages and disadvantages of magnetic tape storage?
3. Recalling the vignette and the wrap-up example, defend the position of not allowing George Roberts the right to alter the original data in the database.
4. Referring to the previous question: Should Mr. Roberts be able to alter these figures? If so, why? Should the reasons for the alterations be recorded? Why?

TELEPROCESSING: LINKING THE WORLD

After studying this chapter you should understand the following:

■ What types of applications lend themselves to teleprocessing.
■ How distributed data processing differs from centralized data processing.
■ Which five network forms are in common use.
■ What types of media are available for telecommunications.
■ In a general way, some of the characteristics of message or data transmission.

Something George Roberts saw in the Global Electrical Equipment newsletter startled him. The computer across the hall—the same computer that had given him the performance data on his inspectors—was in constant touch with Paris, Hong Kong, and Madrid. Several space satellites were used in the link-up. The only weak part of the system, the article concluded, was that data took a few seconds to go halfway around the world.

George already knew something about teleprocessing. After all he was an engineer. He knew teleprocessing involved hooking up computers and peripherals over distance, generally using the telephone system, in order to get work done. If he'd stopped and thought about it, he guessed he already knew that you could send and receive data globally by satellite. But he hadn't been aware that it happened across the hall from him, every day, in silence. He was impressed.

A voice cut into his thoughts. It was Sylvia Fischer, standing in the entrance to his office.

"George, my micro is down," Sylvia said. "Can I use yours?"

"Sure," George said. "Ward's got it in his office."

"Will it read my disks?"

"That's a good question," George said. "Let's go see."

George got an idea as he and Sylvia walked down the hall. "Sylvia, how many micros do we have around here anyway?"

"In this plant? I don't know—several dozen, I think."

"Do you know what we should do?" George asked. "We should link them together. Because now we're working in the dark ages, everybody using different programs and different microcomputers as if we were reinventing the wheel. We should be able to share data and even get in touch with the mainframe."

George paused and pointed to the computer room. "Do you know where the machines are that the mainframe is hooked up to? Madrid, Hong Kong, Paris. If that machine can bounce signals off satellites," he said, "shouldn't we be able to run a few cables under the floor here in the plant to let our micros communicate?"

"Let's pursue it," Sylvia said.

TELEPROCESSING TODAY

Before looking at how computers and peripherals are joined today into powerful systems, let's define three important terms. TELEPROCESSING refers to processing performed by a computer system at a distance from the user. The distance may be great, such as from the West Coast to the East Coast, or small, such as between two floors of the same building.

Teleprocessing is made possible by TELECOMMUNICATIONS, the transmission of data over distances. Teleprocessing and telecommunications are not

difference

the same thing. Teleprocessing is what happens, and telecommunications is part of what makes it possible.

The third important term is **NETWORK.** A network is a combination of devices linked together for teleprocessing. The devices can be both computers and peripherals.

As with all hardware, the specific configuration of teleprocessing equipment in an information system is determined by the other elements in the system, most important, the needs of *people*—users, clients, and staff—who depend on it. People determine the *rules and procedures* for teleprocessing and define the *data* to be processed. And, of course, the hardware requires appropriate communications *software* if it is to work at all.

Teleprocessing systems can be simple or complex, big or small. The idea behind any teleprocessing system, however, is simple: the different *hardware* elements of an information system are linked together by some medium such as cables. Data travel over the system from one point to another, and are processed. There is nothing profound in the idea: components of a stereo system are linked together in much the same manner.

Teleprocessing systems become impressive when many computers and peripherals are linked together, or when the distances between them are great. But the concept remains straightforward. Even a microcomputer that has its keyboard, disk drives, and display screen built into a single cabinet with the CPU links the different components through an internal telecommunications medium, although the microcomputer could not be said to be performing teleprocessing since it is all right there in one spot.

APPLICATIONS OF TELEPROCESSING

FIGURE 8-1.
Some uses of teleprocessing. (a) Over-the-counter stock prices are maintained in a single, coast-to-coast network by NASDAQ (National Association of Securities Dealers Data Acquisition). (b) Without telecommunications there would be no space program. (c) Commercial teleprocessing companies make a variety of services—electronic mail, conferencing, news wires, travel information, and business data—available to both home and business subscribers.

Teleprocessing systems serve many types of applications. A computer in a police squad car can be linked to the police department's central dispatch computer. A commodities trader in Chicago can use a teleprocessing network to obtain financial data from around the world on everything from gold to pork bellies without leaving the terminal. And really to stress the "tele" in teleprocessing, spaceships and their ground stations are linked in teleprocessing systems responsible for bringing back human beings and equipment intact. Figure 8-1 shows some representative teleprocessing applications. Microcomputers are capable of teleprocessing. In fact many users converse with each other across the nation via electronic bulletin boards. An **ELECTRONIC BULLETIN BOARD** is a computer-maintained list of messages that can be posted and read by different computers, often concerning a topic of common interest. Users exchange tips on software; write essays, poems, or tirades on matters that interest them and "post" them on the bulletin board for all the world to see; and carry on late-night private dialogs with strangers in distant cities. Their link to the modern world of teleprocessing is a plain old telephone, found in just about every home.

(a)

(b)

(c)

TELEPROCESSING AND THE INFORMATION SYSTEM

If businesses used to get along just fine without teleprocessing, you may wonder, why can't they now? Some can get along without it. Many others, however, have found that as their business has changed, they are much better off with it. Organizations use teleprocessing for three reasons: organizational, economic, and geographic.

Organizational structure—the way responsibilities are distributed within the organization—affects the way that a business does its teleprocessing. A tightly controlled, centralized organization usually constructs a teleprocessing network to match, with headquarters in command of the network. At the other extreme, a loosely organized company may prefer a decentralized teleprocessing structure.

Economic considerations involve economies of scale. In general the more a computer is used, the cheaper each transaction becomes. Also, opening up a computer system means that more users can retrieve data from databases and use hardware to which they would not otherwise have access. The organization benefits from reduction in the time between the capture of data and the availability of information derived from them. For example, stock market activity in London can be instantly transmitted to brokers all over the world, allowing analysts to make informed decisions on whether to buy or sell a particular security.

The compelling geographic reason is that businesses today often carry out their functions over large territories. A firm like Global Electrical Equipment must hook together its many offices and manufacturing facilities in its own self-interest. The more the scattered facilities communicate, the better the firm operates.

Given these three considerations—organizational, economic, and geographic—it is easy to see why no "perfect" teleprocessing system exists that can meet the needs of every organization. Instead information systems that perform teleprocessing must balance the same five elements that other information systems do: people, rules and procedures, data, software, and hardware.

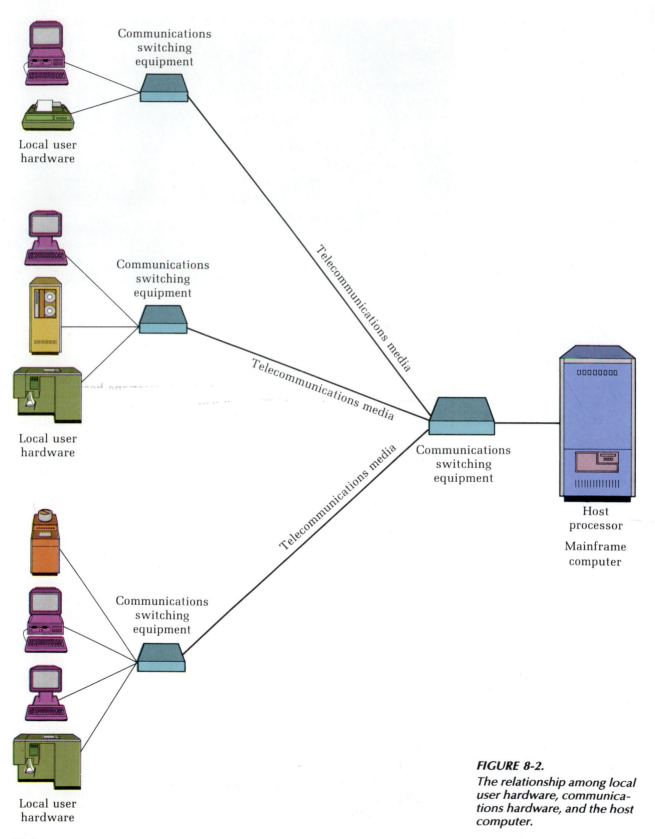

Communications
switching
equipment

Local user
hardware

Communications
switching
equipment

Telecommunications media

Local user
hardware

Telecommunications media

Communications
switching
equipment

Telecommunications media

Communications
switching
equipment

Host
processor

Mainframe
computer

Local user
hardware

FIGURE 8-2.
The relationship among local user hardware, communications hardware, and the host computer.

Information system personnel concerned with teleprocessing combine their knowledge of telecommunications with that of methods of processing data. *Users,* who determine the organizational structure, and their *clients* have come to expect fast results of teleprocessing systems.

Rules and procedures determine who has authority to use the teleprocessing system and what these people can do to the data— examining, recording, changing, or transmitting. Standard rules help ensure that proper procedures are followed. Exception rules permit selected users to circumvent normal procedures when necessary.

Data not only include the material being transmitted, but also the logs of communications to and from the various locations. The latter data provide records for billing and for monitoring the security of the communications network.

The communications *software* consists of system software designed to make possible rapid communication and information processing. Communications software is based upon the rules and procedures of the organization(s) using it and government regulations. For example, some communications software is designed to scramble and then unscramble coded messages. This procedure helps prevent unauthorized "listening in" to sensitive messages.

Hardware

The fifth information system element, hardware, can be divided into local user hardware, the host processor, and communications hardware. These hardware types are shown in Figure 8-2 and discussed below.

LOCAL USER HARDWARE can consist of one or more peripheral devices, such as display terminals, printers, and secondary storage units. Local user hardware can also consist of a computer of any size. The function of local user hardware is to transmit data to a computer elsewhere in the teleprocessing network for processing, or to receive data from this other computer. If local user hardware is itself a computer—or a computerized device such as an intelligent terminal—it can also be used to perform local information processing independently of the teleprocessing network.

The HOST PROCESSOR is the other computer to which the local user hardware is connected, and which does the actual processing of data. In some networks a computer can serve simultaneously as a host processor for distant users and as a local processor for nearby users. Some networks have more than one host processor, and others do without the host processor altogether, as we will see when we discuss networks later in the chapter.

The COMMUNICATIONS DEVICES link the local user hardware with the host processor. There are two types of communications devices. First, communications switching equipment serves as intermediary between local user hardware and telecommunications media, and between the host processor and telecommunications media. Second, telecommunications media handle the actual transmission of data between local user hardware and the host processor.

The "processing" in "teleprocessing"

Teleprocessing systems can be used for time-sharing, for real-time processing, for batch processing, or for a combination of these different methods. In other words all of the types of computing that you have studied thus far in this book can be done with teleprocessing systems. A host processor can maintain an electronic bulletin board for microcomputer users. Global Electrical Equipment links together its powerful computers. At the same time that one computer is answering inquiries from local user hardware on a time-sharing basis, another might be guiding a batch application program or two on the side while it waits for queries to come in, and a third might be giving top priority to a real-time test it is monitoring but still be communicating with the other computers when free.

The price of teleprocessing

For all its utility there are some drawbacks associated with teleprocessing. Data are vulnerable to loss during transmission over telecommunications media. The cost of using telecommunications media can be quite high, and must be balanced against the benefits gained by teleprocessing. In addition teleprocessing involves more equipment than a locally contained information system; the more equipment one uses, the more possibility there is of equipment failure and the consequent disruption of an organization that has to limp along with a weakened information system.

The drawback that has received the most press is unauthorized snooping and tampering with data. When a lot of data are placed online in a teleprocessing system, sensitive data can sometimes be viewed, and even changed, by people who have no right to do so. In 1984, for example, one of the largest consumer credit bureaus in the United States had its files illegally broken into via telecommunications media. The breach occurred because the credit bureau ignored one of the cardinal rules of teleprocessing security: change the "password," which must be given to gain access to the system, often. Running along comfortably on the old password, the company did not discover the breach until months later.

In another highly publicized incident, several young people from Milwaukee—nicknamed "the 414s" after their telephone area code—used their home computers to attempt to break into information systems at Los Alamos National Laboratory, a government facility in New Mexico that develops nuclear weapons, and at the Sloan-Kettering Memorial Cancer Institute in New York City. The FBI caused quite a sensation by arresting the 414s and seizing their computers in the middle of the night. Chapter 17 will discuss security considerations and preventative measures at greater length.

NETWORK ORGANIZATION

CENTRALIZED VERSUS DISTRIBUTED DATA PROCESSING

Early in the history of computers, an organization had a computer, and that was that. Anybody who wanted to use the computer would bring their data to the computer center, and some time later would go back to pick up their output. There were no other options. This is known as CENTRALIZED DATA PROCESSING.

As computers became cheaper and more popular—and as users became frustrated with the bottlenecks at the centralized computer —some organizations began to add more computers. These functioned completely independently of the first. This is known as DECENTRALIZED DATA PROCESSING. Organizations which themselves operated in a decentralized way tended to adopt this approach. Each computer was part of its own information system, with the local managers in control over the hardware, software, data, and rules and procedures. Despite the hands-on computer power, communication within an organization was stifled, as was control of resources.

DISTRIBUTED DATA PROCESSING (DDP) seeks a middle way between the other two, somewhat extreme, approaches. Distributed data processing spreads information-processing capabilities throughout an organization. Computers, perhaps of various sizes, are used at different points in the organization, and are linked together for teleprocessing. This makes it possible to centralize control of computer resources, to share important data companywide, and to provide backup in case a particular computer fails. With this approach, users in local areas also have access to their own computers to get work done, and do not have to rely on a centralized system.

None of the approaches is perfect. Centralized data processing's advantage is that it makes efficient use of the computer rather than letting it sit idle. This efficiency is obtained at the cost of reducing user flexibility, however. A modified form of centralized data processing—quite common today —places terminals in the hands of users, and links the terminals to the centralized computer in a hierarchy. This is not distributed data processing, however, unless the terminals are so intelligent (or are in fact microcomputers) that they are doing substantial processing on their own.

With decentralized data processing it is often difficult to maintain and share data on an organization-wide basis because the procedures, hardware, software, and database at each location may not be compatible with those at other locations. Thus an organization with a decentralized system should try to use compatible hardware and software to ease the exchange of data, and many do.

Distributed data processing efforts may face resistance from supporters of centralized or decentralized data processing supporters.

Downward-spiraling computer costs, coupled with software that is growing steadily easier to use, suggest that the current trend to place computers at many points within an organization will continue. Linking a number of these computers together through teleprocessing, for true distributed data processing rather than merely decentralized data processing, can help ease the problems of compatibility and control.

As you can see, the most sophisticated businesses and organizations do use teleprocessing—either connecting computers together in a network for distributed data processing, or at the least linking terminals to a centralized computer.

NETWORK FORMS

Teleprocessing networks come in a variety of forms. The particular form an organization uses will reflect the structure and size of the organization, the applications for which it requires teleprocessing, and the telecommunications technology available to it.

Star network

With a **STAR NETWORK** (Figure 8-3) a central computer is connected to remote peripherals or other computers, which are not connected to each other. If terminals form the points of the star, then we have a "liberated" form of centralized data processing—one computer does everything but users at

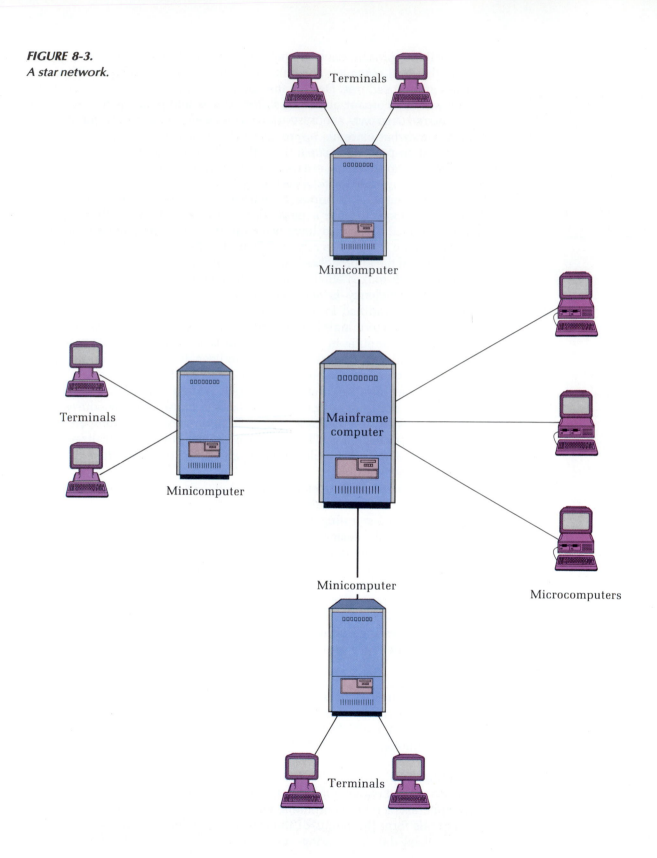

FIGURE 8-3.
A star network.

Terminals

Minicomputer

Terminals

Minicomputer

Mainframe
computer

Minicomputer

Terminals

Microcomputers

least get terminals. If microcomputers or other computers are used as points of the star then we have a form of distributed data processing in which the central computer clearly remains in command.

An example of a star network with computers at the points would be a department store with several branches. The main department store has the central computer—a mainframe—at the center of the star pattern. The central computer performs most processing for all the stores, such as keeping personnel records up to date, writing paychecks, verifying credit card purchases, and analyzing sales trends. Each branch has a minicomputer of its own to keep track of sales data, which are communicated to the central computer and processed there. The local computers keep track of local matters, such as scheduling personnel for their particular branch, without the involvement of the main computer.

Hierarchical network

The **HIERARCHICAL NETWORK** (see Figure 8-4) has a main computer at its top, the most important level in terms of control. Communication links spread downward and outward, much like the roots of a tree. At each branching point is a computer; the further down the hierarchy, the smaller is the

FIGURE 8-4.
A hierarchical network.

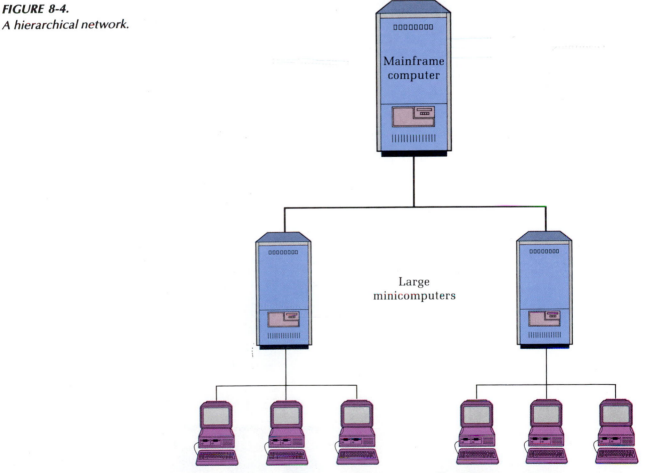

Mainframe computer

Large minicomputers

Microcomputers or small minicomputers

computer. The main computer at the top of the hierarchy is in command of everything, with successively subordinate tasks performed at each lower level.

This type of structure might be used by a large organization that must retain central control of the information system and yet needs to delegate substantial computing power to individual departments or offices within the organization. Corporate headquarters would have the computer at the top, with the manufacturing, marketing, and research divisions receiving the subordinate yet substantial computers at the next level down. Within each corporate division a further distribution of computer power could be made. In the manufacturing division, for example, the computer could assist and co-ordinate the computers at the next lower level that handle control of the production line, process quality control test results, and update the inventory.

FIGURE 8-5.
A ring network.

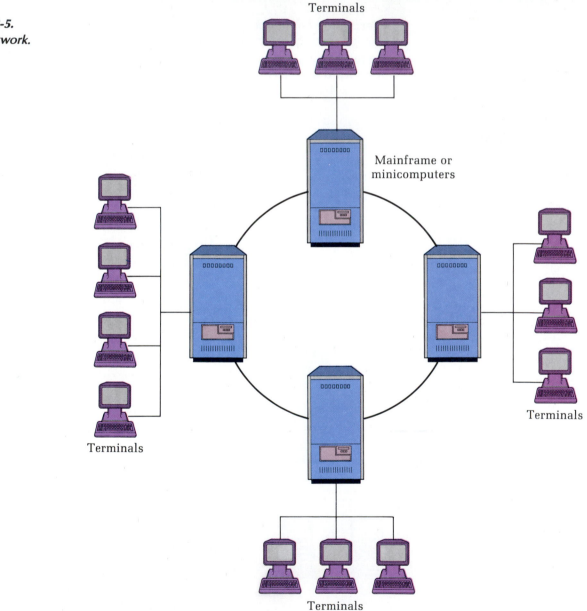

Ring network

A **RING NETWORK** links computers into a loop, as shown in Figure 8-5. The loop has no central computer; instead all of the computers are equal and communicate with one another. As an example, several mainframes might be hooked together in a loop for a large insurance firm. Users could perform the processing they needed at a particular computer, and could also communicate through that computer with any of the others in the loop when necessary. One mainframe might handle administrative details, another life insurance, another health insurance, and another automobile insurance. If the computer at the life insurance processing center turned out to have free time while the computer processing health insurance forms was overburdened, the computer with the extra time could share the other's load.

Multiply connected network

MULTIPLY CONNECTED NETWORKS (Figure 8-6) allow computers to communicate along two or more possible paths. Here not only can one computer share another's job, as in the ring network, but alternate telecommunications media are available between any two computers should one link fail.

FIGURE 8-6.
A multiply connected network.

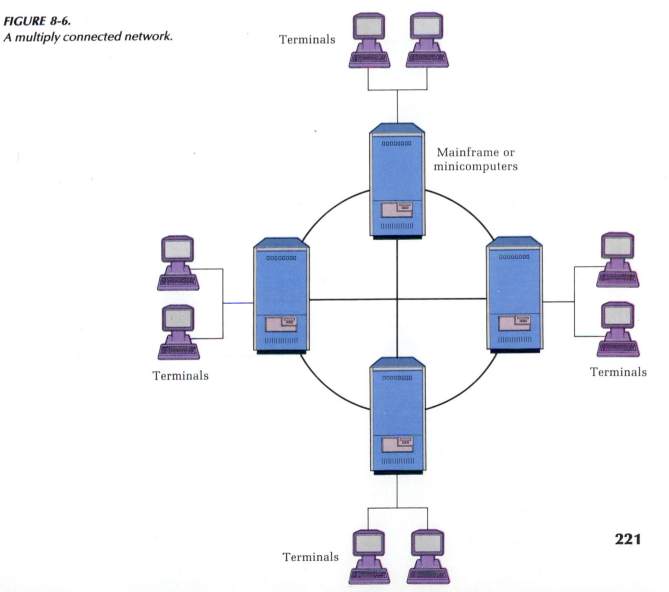

Terminals

Mainframe or minicomputers

Terminals

Terminals

Terminals

221

Mixed network

Some telecommunications systems have a **MIXED NETWORK**, also known as an unconstrained network, which uses a combination of the four approaches covered above. In the example shown in Figure 8-7 the network has a combination of the star (left), multiply connected (middle), and hierarchical (right) configurations. Other combinations are, of course, possible. Often several ring networks are joined together, with each serving as the point of a star network, or as a level in a hierarchical network.

FIGURE 8-7.
A mixed network.

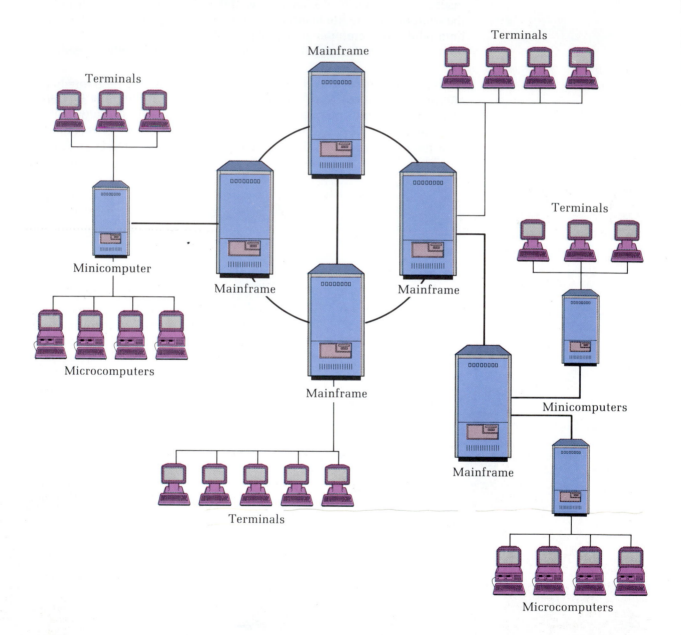

Teleprocessing is made possible by the transmission of data via telecommunications media. In this section we will describe the different types of media, and then look at media capacity and at the directions that data travel.

TYPES OF MEDIA

A **TELECOMMUNICATIONS MEDIUM** is the physical link by means of which data are transmitted from one part of the teleprocessing system to another. The particular medium chosen for a given connection depends upon such factors as distance, volume of data, and security needs. The main types of media available are wire pairs, coaxial cables, fiber-optic cables, and microwave systems. Figure 8-8 shows the different media.

FIGURE 8-8.

Telecommunications media. (a) Wire pairs—a telephone switching center. (b) Cross section of a coaxial cable. (c) Fiber-optic cable. (d) A transportable microwave station.

Wire pairs

WIRE PAIRS consist of two copper wires twisted around one another. The oldest type of medium, the advantage of wire pairs is that they still form the backbone of the telephone system, and are thus readily available.

Wire pairs have only a limited capacity for transmitting data, however, as we will see later. When wire pairs are bound together into heavier cables that make up the telephone lines visible above the ground in most parts of the country, they are subject to "crosstalk," in which messages cross from one wire pair to another. This occurs when you are talking on the phone and hear another conversation faintly in addition to your own. Crosstalk is a nuisance during phone conversations, but worse for data communications, where it can garble data.

Coaxial cables

Overcoming some of the limitations of wire pairs, **COAXIAL CABLES** consist of one conducting wire surrounded by an insulator, which is in turn encased in a second conductor. A group of coaxial cables is bound together into cables. Transmission capacity is considerably greater than for wire pairs, and crosstalk is minimized. The major drawback of coaxial cables is that they are more expensive than wire pairs and are not as extensively used. Coaxial cables are often employed to link high-speed peripherals to nearby computers, to link telephone switching centers together, and for other high-volume applications.

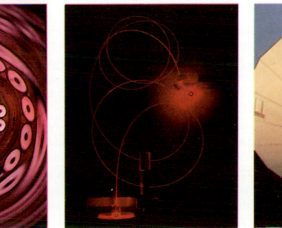

Fiber-optic cables

FIBER-OPTIC CABLES involve a completely different technology. Here tiny fibers of glass can transmit data as light-beam signals generated by lasers. Fiber-optic cables are so tiny that far greater numbers can be bound together into a cable than with twisted wire or coaxial cables. Fiber-optic cables have the greatest transmission capacity of any telecommunications medium. Stepping out of the laboratory only in recent years, fiber-optic cables have begun to replace coaxial cables for data transmission as well as for transmitting voice and television signals.

Microwave systems

MICROWAVE SYSTEMS use high-frequency electromagnetic waves to send messages through space to microwave receiving stations. Microwave systems have a greater transmission capacity than coaxial cables or wire pairs. No cables are involved here. Earthbound or terrestrial microwave systems send signals through the atmosphere between repeater stations. The stations must be within "line of sight" of each other, and hence are placed close enough together—no more than 30 miles apart—that the curve of the earth does not interrupt this line of sight. The terrain in between must also be free of intervening tall buildings and hills; in fact the microwave stations themselves are often placed on top of such features. Dust and humidity can also interfere with data transmission.

Microwave systems using communications satellites overcome the distance limits of the terrestrial systems. Communications satellites are placed in a geosynchronous orbit in space, which means that the satellite remains in place over a given geographic area of the earth, since its speed allows it to match exactly the earth's rotation. Microwaves are then transmitted from an earth station to the satellite, and from the satellite to another earth station that may be thousands of miles away. To reach farther points, the signal can be bounced between additional satellite and earth stations. Terrestrial and satellite-based microwave systems are widely used for long-distance telephone calls.

MEDIA CAPACITY AND MODE

Telecommunications media are not evaluated only in terms of their physical nature, but (as we have already touched upon) in terms of their capacity, and also in terms of the directions that the transmission can travel.

Medium capacity: bandwidth

A given communications medium has a bandwidth associated with it. **BANDWIDTH,** or width of the frequency band, refers to the capacity of a medium. The bandwidth determines how much data can be sent over it within a given amount of time. The more data that can be transmitted per second, the faster is the medium.

The three bandwidths commonly associated with telecommunications media are narrowband, voice grade, and wideband. Figure 8-9 shows which apply to the media we discussed above.

NARROWBAND, or **SUB-VOICE-GRADE, MEDIA** transmit data at from 40 to 300 bits per second (bps). These media are used to transmit to and from low-speed data terminals. Teletypewriter and telegraph systems use narrowband systems.

Type	Capacity	Application
Wire pairs	Narrowband to voice grade	User to teleprocessing system
Coaxial cables	Voice grade to wideband	Linking high-speed devices
Microwave systems	Wideband	Long-distance links
Fiber-optic cables	Wideband	Long-distance links

VOICE-GRADE MEDIA, characteristic of the telephone system, transmit data at rates ranging from 300 to 9600 bps. Specially conditioned lines that boost the signal power at specific intervals are necessary to obtain the higher speeds. Applications include connections between terminals and the central processing unit for data entry and inquiry systems.

WIDEBAND MEDIA transmit data at the greatest speeds of all, ranging from 19,200 up to more than 500,000 bps. Applications here are links from one computer to another.

The greater the bandwidth, the faster a single message can be sent over the medium. If we can settle for less than maximum speed, however, greater bandwidths then translate to sending *more* messages at the same time. For example, a number of transmissions at the voice-grade rate can be made simultaneously with a wideband medium.

Medium mode: direction of transmission

Now that we have seen the different types of media, and classified the speeds at which data may be transmitted over them, one more consideration remains: which way? Data can be sent in one direction only; in both directions, but only one way at a time; or in both directions simultaneously. Figure 8-10 illustrates simplex, half-duplex, and full-duplex transmission between a terminal and a computer.

SIMPLEX TRANSMISSION, like a one-way street, allows for transmission in only one direction. The direction might be, for example, from a computer to a peripheral device, with no response possible or desired back to the computer. Commercial radio and television use simplex transmission—signals go out from a transmitter to receivers, but not the other way.

HALF-DUPLEX TRANSMISSION allows transmission in one direction at a time. Once a message has been received and the line cleared, then a message can go back the other way. Telegraph and two-way radio comunications follow this mode. Half-duplex transmission is frequently adequate for links between terminals and a computer.

FULL-DUPLEX TRANSMISSION (also known as **DUPLEX TRANSMISSION**) allows for simultaneous, bidirectional traffic. The most powerful mode, full-duplex transmission is used by most computer-to-computer links and some terminal-to-computer links. Telephone communication, in which both parties can talk at the same time, is an example of full-duplex transmission.

FIGURE 8-10.
Simplex, half-duplex, and full-duplex transmission.

Simplex lines allow only one-way travel.

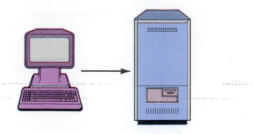

Half-duplex lines allow two-way communication, but only one way at a time.

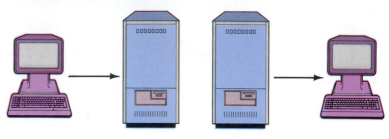

Full-duplex lines permit simultaneous two-way communication.

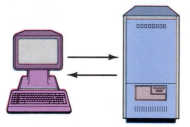

TELE-COMMUNICATIONS CONVENTIONS

Although the concept of teleprocessing is not difficult, an examination of the field quickly gets into technicalities that are difficult, or at least specialized. This section deals with several such technicalities.

Teleprocessing follows certain telecommunications conventions that make life easier. The ones we will cover here are the conversion of digital to analog signals, transmission codes used, asynchronous versus synchronous transmission, and certain rules of the house known as protocols.

DIGITAL TO ANALOG AND BACK

Digital computers generate digital signals, which show an abrupt on and off pattern (Figure 8-11). In contrast many telecommunications media—most notably a fair percentage of telephone lines—accept only analog signals, which show rounded wave patterns. To transmit digital signals over analog telecommunications media requires that the original signal be translated from digital to analog patterns. This process is called modulation. **MODULATION** converts the digital signal into a form that can be carried over analog

Managing the often extensive telecommunications activities of today's organizations is an important and demanding job. Unknown in the early days of computing, the position of telecommunications manager has become vital to the life of modern corporations, government agencies, and larger nonprofit institutions. People who can fill this slot are in great demand.

Telecommunications is a field that is evolving so rapidly that no one can predict where it will go with certainty. Ever more telecommunications is taking place, however, and people are required who are capable of taking charge of it. The telecommunications manager reports to an organization's information resources manager or director of information systems (these positions are described in the career boxes of Chapters 14 and 6, respectively). In turn, the telecommunications manager is responsible for coordinating specialists in telecommunications. In a larger organization, these will include telecommunications analysts and telecommunications programmers, who develop the systems, and the hardware-oriented telecommunications technicians who install and repair the electronic equipment.

Smaller organizations will consolidate some of these positions.

The telecommunications manager is responsible for managing all telecommunications activities within an organization. This includes planning the systems, implementing them, and seeing that they work day-to-day, with the help of the appropriate specialists. The networks involved can be far-flung multinational arrangements, local area networks, or both.

In an area as new as this, entry is best made by being able to demonstrate expertise. That is, if you know a lot about telecommunications, and are able to pick up some hands-on experience as an analyst, programmer, or technician, you are on your way. In an area where there is a strong need for personnel, and few people available with appropriate experience, it is possible to rise quickly to become an "expert." As in any information system job, people skills are important, since you will have to keep your own technical team humming, as well as to effectively interact with other managers in the organization in order to determine and meet their telecommunications needs.

lines. Likewise, the signal must be converted back to digital form at the receiving end, a process called DEMODULATION.

FIGURE 8-11.
Digital and analog signals.

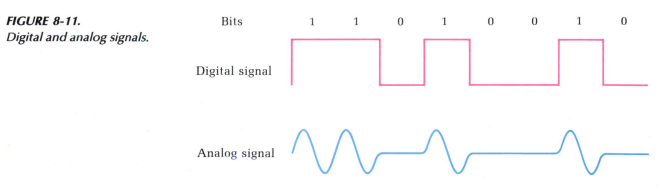

FIGURE 8-12.
A modem.

A MODEM (Figure 8-12) performs the tasks of modulation and demodulation. The term "modem" is derived from "modulation-demodulation." Many modems are "hard-wired" into the device that uses them. In contrast another type of modem, an ACOUSTIC COUPLER, can use any telephone receiver on a temporary basis. The acoustic coupler then handles the conversion from the digital "talk" of the device to the telephone line's analog, or from the telephone line's analog to the device's digital. This type of device permits people on the road to link portable terminals to their central information system, even from a phone booth, automobile telephone, or payphone aboard a commercial flight.

Some telecommunications media, including many telephone lines, can transmit digital signals. In these situations a modem is unnecessary. Instead a line interface unit links a device or computer to a teleprocessing network.

Regardless of whether they are analog or digital, signals are subject to noise and distortion. To counter the loss of signal integrity because of a weakening signal over distance, analog telecommunications media use amplifiers to regenerate the signal. Digital systems use repeaters for the same purpose.

TRANSMISSION CODES

In Chapter 5 (in the "EBCDIC and ASCII" section) we introduced the two main systems used to represent bytes within a computer. These are ASCII (short for American Standard Code for Information Interchange) and EBCDIC (Extended Binary Coded Decimal Interchange Code). These same codes are also used for data transmission. ASCII was actually designed to try to standardize data transmission in the first place, and is the code most often used today for data transmission.

EBCDIC, however, is widely used by computers themselves. When a computer or device receives a transmission in a code (such as ASCII) other than the one it works with (such as EBCDIC), translation is required. Communications software performs this function.

ASYNCHRONOUS AND SYNCHRONOUS TRANSMISSION

Devices can send and receive data at different speeds. Peripherals are much slower than CPUs, and peripherals also vary widely from one another in speed. In addition devices with a keyboard, such as a display terminal, do not send data steadily but in spurts that correspond to the person's thought processes as he or she keys in the data.

To assure that devices can send and receive data despite these kinds of speed differences, the sending and receiving devices need to agree completely on what constitutes one byte. They will then know when a byte ends and the next starts.

There are two conventions followed for doing this. ASYNCHRONOUS TRANSMISSION sends a byte at a time. So that the receiving device will recognize the series of bits as a byte, a start bit precedes the byte, and a stop bit follows it. In other words the sending device in effect shouts "Ready!" before sending a data byte, then sends the byte, and then shouts "That's all for this one!" Bytes thus do not need to be sent at regular intervals, since the receiving device can always tell what it's dealing with.

SYNCHRONOUS TRANSMISSION uses another approach to solve the same problem. Here bytes are sent in blocks, or groups of bytes, between devices that are "in synch"—that is, timed to match one another precisely. Clock

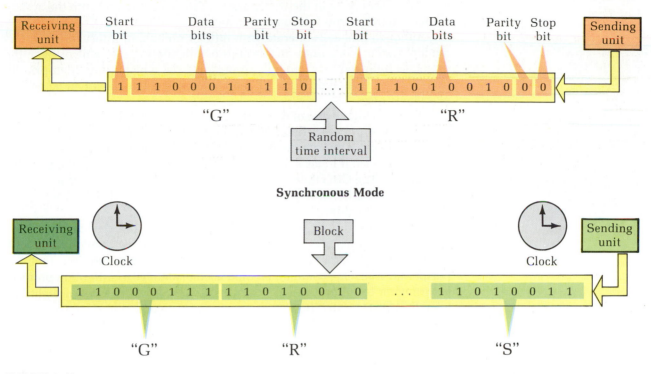

Asynchronous Mode

Receiving unit

Start bit Data bits Parity bit Stop bit   Start bit Data bits Parity bit Stop bit

Sending unit

1 1 1 0 0 0 1 1 1 1 0   1 1 1 0 1 0 0 1 0 0 0

"G"   "R"

Random time interval

Synchronous Mode

Receiving unit   Clock   Block   Clock   Sending unit

1 1 0 0 0 1 1 1 1 1 1 0 1 0 0 1 0   . . .   1 1 0 1 0 0 1 1

"G"   "R"   "S"

FIGURE 8-13.

Asynchronous and synchronous transmission. In asynchronous transmission data are transmitted a byte at a time. Each byte is preceded by a start bit and followed by a stop bit. The amount of time between bytes is random. In synchronous transmission groups of bytes are transmitted in a block. The receiving and sending devices are synchronized so each can recognize where one byte ends and another begins. Here we see how the word "GREETINGS" would be transmitted in both modes using ASCII-8.

mechanisms at both the sending and receiving end coordinate the signal timing. Special signals flag the start and end of the transmission, much like start and stop bits; but within the transmission, the receiving device itself separates one byte from another through the timing coordinated with the sender.

Synchronous transmission is often used to link high-speed peripherals such as magnetic disk units to computers, or one computer to another. Because of the necessary timing mechanisms, synchronous transmission systems cost more initially, but will save money in high-volume applications. Figure 8-13 illustrates asynchronous and synchronous transmission.

PROTOCOLS   Imagine driving on a busy highway where there were no traffic regulations. It would be a scary and dangerous experience. The fact that almost everyone follows traffic regulations makes orderly transportation possible. The same is true with teleprocessing. We can follow all of the conventions described so far and still have chaos. We would not know where data were coming from and going to. We would have head-on collisions, traffic jams, and little chance to perform teleprocessing of meaningful data.

PROTOCOLS are rules and procedures governing the use of telecommunications media. Specifically, protocols govern how to choose among users competing for system resources, coordinate the transmission of messages, and check for errors in the transmission. Protocols are built into the system software that controls telecommunications.

Although protocols operate with little or no human intervention, information system personnel and users do ultimately have control over the protocols followed. For example, protocols exist which allow high-priority users not to wait their turn to send a message but to cut in ahead of everybody else.

Protocols follow one of two methods to determine which device to allow to transmit at a given time. These methods are known as polling and contention. With POLLING the central processing unit in charge periodically asks each device if it has a message to send. If the device does, the message is then sent. The CPU then goes on to ask the next device if it has a message to send. Eventually, in round-robin fashion, the CPU will come back to ask the first device again.

CONTENTION takes the opposite approach, with the device asking the CPU if the medium is free for transmission. If it is free, the message is sent. If another device is using the medium, the protocol requires that the peripheral wait. One common method used to manage a contention protocol is through a technique called TOKEN PASSING. A token is a set of eight bits (usually 11111111) that permits access to the network. When a terminal has received the token, it can transmit its message to the appropriate receiving device. The token then passes to the next terminal, and so on, granting each, in turn, access to the network. Polling usually works best when terminals are in frequent use, and contention when they are infrequently used.

Another protocol, used in multiply connected networks, is called PACKET SWITCHING. Messages are broken into standard-sized units called packets. Each packet can then be transmitted from the sending to the receiving device along a different communications path and the whole message reassembled at the receiving station. The advantage of packet switching is that it makes possible the most efficient use possible of the network—if one line is too crowded, the message, or part of it, can be sent along another.

Protocols also check the parity bits appended to transmitted bytes for errors. When an error is detected, the protocol dictates that the byte (for asynchronous transmission) or block (for synchronous transmission) containing the error be sent again, in the hope that it will come through error-free. If the error is still present, the protocol follows predetermined procedures.

Telecommunications and computer equipment manufacturers, software designers, and users are still debating over protocols. At this point no standard protocol exists that allows all devices to communicate with one another.

COMMUNICATIONS PROCESSORS

In a teleprocessing network there is a trade-off between access to a computer and the economics of providing that access. At one extreme every user should have his or her own direct line to the computer. At the other extreme all users would have to share one line.

As an example of how remote sites are differentiated by application and equipment, consider the network established with the ARCO Petroleum Products Co. It serves the network needs of corporate staff and of eight other ARCO operating companies. It consists of remote sites ranging from Philadelphia to Los Angeles, from Houston to Prudhoe Bay, Alaska, and many points in between. Only the major regional sites connect to a microwave network, which will soon be converted to a satellite link: Prudhoe Bay and Anchorage, Los Angeles, Denver, Chicago, Dallas, and Philadelphia. The other sites within each region link up via microwave and/or leased telephone lines to the nearest satellite center, using that regional site as a network gateway.

The network is available from 4 AM until midnight each day for interactive data transmissions and for remote batch job entry any time of day or night. All of the equipment at each site is standard-ized for use in either an on-line or remote batch mode. It includes a mix of IBM 4331 and 4341, 3790, Series/1, 8140, remote batch terminals and Four-phase computers. All link to 3705 front-end processors in Los Angeles.

Sophisticated automated network control and management systems permit managers to test new equipment and monitor effectiveness of new applications or system modifications in an on-line mode. Management decisions can be made realistically because user satisfaction can be compared specifically to the costs of system upgrades. Also, network standards can be established and enforced.

In effect, the network itself has become as important to the companies as the DP equipment it links. This requires that network management be as sophisticated and disciplined as possible.

Source: Reprinted from *Infosystems,* March 1983, vol. 30, no. 3, pp. 30–34. Copyright © Hitchcock Publishing Co.

With the each-one's-own extreme the telecommunications links would be expensive to provide, and so many users would want to use the computer at once that they would not all be able to do so anyway, since the computer would become overloaded. For the stand-in-line extreme long waiting times are guaranteed.

Compromises are the order of the day in this area. Historically the first compromise was the multidrop line. Later came communications processors. Let's look at each alternative.

MULTIDROP LINES link devices together like the beads on a chain, and allow them to contend for use of the shared line to a computer (see Figure 8-14). This was an early technique used to link terminals and printers to a CPU. The main drawback is that while one user is on the line, the others have to sit back and wait.

To develop more efficient ways of serving multiple users, **COMMUNICATIONS PROCESSORS** were created. These handle the switching and coordination of messages and data. The four major types of communications processors are multiplexers, concentrators, front-end processors, and message switchers.

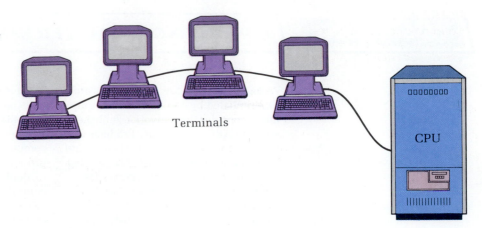

FIGURE 8-14.
Multidrop lines string terminals together onto a shared line.

Terminals

CPU

MULTIPLEXERS

FIGURE 8-15.
Multiplexers allow several users to share a line.

MULTIPLEXERS (sometimes spelled "multiplexors") allow multiple users simultaneously to share a common telecommunications medium. Figure 8-15 shows an example. The earliest and least sophisticated of communications processors, a multiplexer interleaves, or layers together, simultaneous messages and data for users of the transmission line. This type of transmission method allows a number of users to communicate with the computer at the same time. Two multiplexers are required: one at the transmitting end combines the messages, and one at the receiving end separates them.

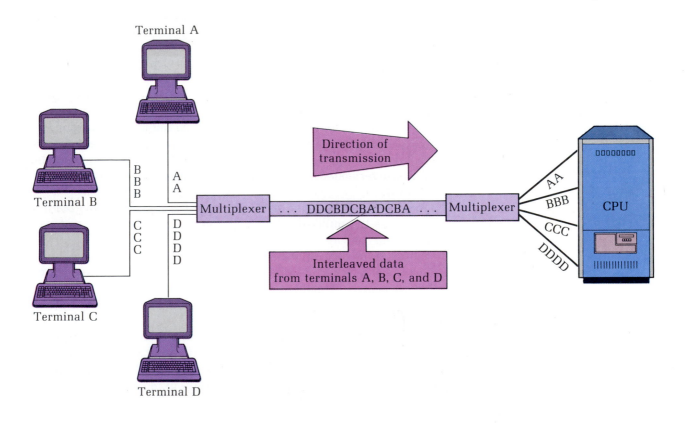

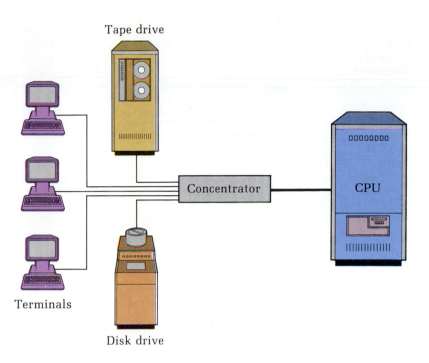

FIGURE 8-16.
Concentrators adjust for remote devices with different speeds and coding methods.

Tape drive

Concentrator

CPU

Terminals

Disk drive

CONCENTRATORS Like multiplexers, **CONCENTRATORS** combine incoming and outgoing messages into a more compact unit. Concentrators are more complex devices, however, and can be programmed to edit data, compress data, convert between ASCII and EBCDIC, and check for errors, for both incoming and outgoing data. Figure 8-16 illustrates a concentrator's operation.

FRONT-END PROCESSORS **FRONT-END PROCESSORS** (Figure 8-17) are usually located near a computer that receives data from peripheral devices or from other computers. Front-end processors are generally minicomputers that relieve the larger computer of overseeing input and output. Besides doing everything that a concentrator can, a front-end processor can be programmed to do more, such as checking for reasonableness of incoming data values and message switching.

A close relative, the back-end processor, is a small computer used to link the larger computer to a database stored on a direct-access storage device. A back-end processor relieves the front-end processor of this task.

MESSAGE-SWITCHERS While multiplexers, concentrators, and front-end processors are capable of coordinating messages from different sources, some systems demand the power of a dedicated message switcher. A **MESSAGE SWITCHER** helps route messages from many incoming telecommunications media into the front-end processor, and may even reroute transmissions that can't be handled right away to less heavily used front-end processors. Modern information systems often make use of a variety of combinations of multiplexers, concentrators, front-end processors, and message switchers.

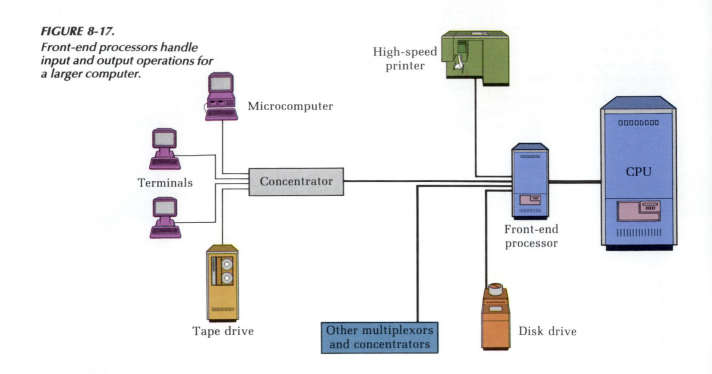

FIGURE 8-17.
Front-end processors handle input and output operations for a larger computer.

High-speed printer

Microcomputer

Terminals

Concentrator

Tape drive

Other multiplexors and concentrators

Front-end processor

Disk drive

CPU

OWNERSHIP AND CONTROL

As with other information system resources, money changes hands when telecommunications media are used. Media can be purchased outright for an information system, or leased. Some leased media are accompanied by extra services. We will describe each of these possibilities, and close the section with a description of very-short-distance teleprocessing networks.

PRIVATE AND COMMON CARRIER NETWORKS

Teleprocessing networks can use private telecommunications media, which are purchased by the information system for its exclusive use. This is expensive and generally limited to larger teleprocessing systems. Alternatively, teleprocessing networks can lease telecommunications media provided by a common carrier. A **COMMON CARRIER** furnishes communication services for the public, abiding by published regulations and rates. Telephone and telegraph companies are examples of common carriers. A teleprocessing system may use a combination of services provided privately and by common carriers. In the United States common carriers are regulated by the FCC (Federal Communications Commission) and state public utility commissions.

VALUE-ADDED NETWORKS

Information systems can lease telecommunications media through a **VALUE-ADDED NETWORK (VAN)**. Value-added networks provide not only the media that an information system needs, but offer extra services (hence the "value-added" in the name) and charge higher rates. VANs offer communications processors, the use of large databases, and even sophisticated computers that one can tap into. You pay only for the services used (see box on p. 235). The VAN operators generally do not own the telecommunications media that they lease out, but lease them in turn from common carriers. Some VANs offer so many services that they are called super-VANs.

COMPUTING POWER FOR SALE

A veritable alphabet soup of VANs (value-added networks) offer their services to the public these days. Indeed, for a price, no one with a computer and a modem need be without the ability to telecommunicate. Moreover, everyone can hook into powerful minis and mainframes to perform teleprocessing if they so desire.

Tymnet, placed in operation by Tymeshare Inc. in the 1970s, offers a nationwide common carrier network. As a Tymnet user you can send messages or data to points of your choice in the network, or send your data to host processors offered by Tymeshare or other companies to be processed for a fee.

Telenet, a subsidiary of General Telephone and Electronics, is another major provider of telecommunications services, but to businesses rather than the general public. Telenet offers access to hundreds of host computers. Many other firms supply telecommunications media and/or teleprocessing ability to businesses or the general public. These include McAuto, offered by the McDonald-Douglas Automation Corporation (which acquired Tymeshare); Boeing Computer Services; The Source; and CompuServe.

The last two networks are specially designed for microcomputer users. They offer the ability to send messages and data throughout the network, to read and post items on electronic bulletin boards, to retrieve data from large databases, and to perform processing using the host computers. Networks such as these, which offer consumer services to micro users, are known as *videotex systems.* More are springing into life all the time, offering banking, shopping, reservations, research, and other services from the home.

Computer manufacturers are not absent from the VAN scene. Burroughs, Digital Equipment Corporation, IBM, Sperry-Univac, National Cash Register, Hewlett-Packard, and Prime Computer all supply network services in addition to the machines able to use them. The standard for the industry is set by IBM's Systems Network Architecture (SNA), which uses a hierarchical network. Markets for an SNA VAN include general commercial customers as well as specialized industries such as banking and retailing.

Regardless of whether you are a hacker or a corporation, you and your computer can still be alone if you want to—but not for lack of opportunities to telecommunicate with other people and machines.

LOCAL AREA NETWORKS

LOCAL AREA NETWORKS (LANs)—sometimes simply called local networks—provide offices with the capability of teleprocessing in a smaller setting. Remember we said at the start of the chapter that teleprocessing does not need to span a great distance. LANs don't. Usually a LAN includes a single office, or a set of offices. The telecommunications media are owned rather than leased. Generally fiber-optic cables or coaxial cables are used. As with any other information system, a LAN can also be connected to outside teleprocessing facilities. Figure 8-18 shows an example of a LAN.

LANs are being increasingly used today to hook together microcomputers. The same thought that occurred to George Roberts at the beginning of the chapter has occurred to many other microcomputer users: Why are many machines in close proximity unable to communicate with one another? The price tag on interface hardware offered by microcomputer manufacturers to permit attachment to a network has dropped steadily, at the same time as the equipment has improved in reliability.

Microcomputers linked together in a LAN can share peripheral devices such as sophisticated printers and secondary storage systems, making it possible to justify devices that a single microcomputer user might not be able

FIGURE 8-18.

An example of a local area network (LAN). Here all the computing equipment in a branch office is linked together in a LAN, which in turn is linked to other offices through communications equipment.

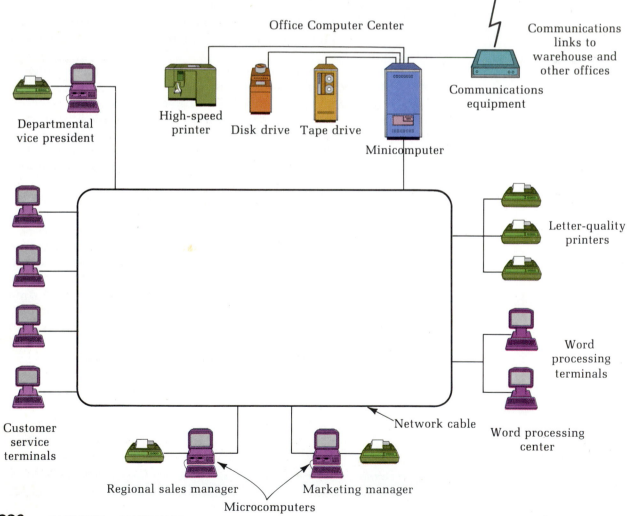

to afford. Another advantage of a LAN is that microcomputer users can share data that are kept up to date on one of the machines. For example, if the current database is contained on a single hard disk, to which all of the microcomputers in a LAN have access, the problem of each microcomputer maintaining its own copy—some of which are sure to be out of date—is resolved. Microcomputer users in a LAN can also communicate with one another by means of electronic mail and message systems, saving flurries of telephone calls and "while you were out" messages.

Creating a LAN has proved more complex for some microcomputer users than they initially expected. For example, some hardware can only be connected in a LAN if the computers and peripheral devices are made by a single manufacturer. In other cases machines of different makes can be joined. In a rapidly evolving field the promises of microcomputer makers about how easy their machines are to interconnect have not always corresponded to reality. Nevertheless, growing pains aside, this is a burgeoning area of activity that seems certain to have a major impact on the future of microcomputers, just as LANs used for larger machines are also increasing in popularity.

WRAP-UP

GLOBAL GO HOME

The new teleprocessing network that George Roberts and Sylvia Fischer persuaded Global Electrical Equipment to install had been in place now for a full month.

There were 43 micros in the plant. Of these 26 were in the local area network (LAN). The network form that George, Sylvia, and the other managers had arrived at was part ring and part star. That is, all the micros were linked in a ring; in addition each was linked to the mainframe in a star.

Seventeen microcomputers weren't part of the LAN because of equipment compatibility problems in some cases, and because of people who simply did not want to share data in other cases. As an engineer George had enjoyed finding out about cables, transmission methods, and the like. Fiber-optic cabling now ran under the floor, joining the 26 microcomputers and the mainframe. Full-duplex transmission was used. The cables handled digital signals, so there was no need for modems.

The mainframe turned out already to have several front-end processors in use. Global's computer center staff reprogrammed one of the front-end processors so that the new microcomputer network could use it to gain access to the mainframe.

Global owned the LAN—no leased media or telephone lines were involved. George and his quality control inspectors out on the line communicated constantly using their micros. For example, the inspectors recorded the serial number of every device inspected and the findings and relayed these to George's machine, where a program processed the data, did some totaling, stored the data on George's hard disk, and produced a report.

George also *enjoyed* teleprocessing. He looked at his watch. It was 3:30 p.m., and a Friday. The data his employees had sent in today showed that everyone had done a full day's quota of inspections already: the whole week had been well above quota. George swirled in his chair, turned on the micro, and typed in the codes that signaled to the teleprocessing system that whatever he typed *next* would be displayed on the microcomputers out on the line.

GO HOME, GANG, IT'S BEEN A SWELL WEEK, George typed.

The first response came. YOU SERIOUS, BOSS? flashed on the screen of George's microcomputer.

WOULD I LIE TO YOU? he typed back.

Deciding he did not want to wait around for the answers to that, he shut off his computer, locked his desk, put on his jacket, and left for the week.

SUMMARY

- *Teleprocessing refers to processing performed by a computer system at a distance from the user. The distance may be great, but need not be. To allow for teleprocessing, telecommunications transmits data over distances. A network is a combination of devices linked together for teleprocessing; the devices can be both computers and peripherals.*

- *Teleprocessing has many applications, most of them motivated by organizational, economic, and geographic considerations. In short teleprocessing helps firms—particularly those that cover or deal with a wide area—to operate more efficiently and to save money. Any type of computing can be done with teleprocessing systems.*

- *Electronic bulletin boards permit users to post and read messages covering a wide variety of interests.*

- *Information systems that perform teleprocessing must balance the same five elements involved in any information system: people, rules and procedures, data, software, and hardware.*

- *In teleprocessing the host processor performs the actual computing. Local user hardware hooks into the host processor through the use of communications hardware.*

- *Besides advantages of teleprocessing, there are some drawbacks: cost, more equipment to fail, and the possibility of others tampering with your data.*

- *Early in the history of computers an organization had a computer and that was that. People came to it and used it. This is known as centralized data processing. Decentralized data processing, in which computing facilities are scattered throughout an organization, often without any plan, arose partly in response. Distributed data processing (DDP) seeks to place computers of various sizes throughout an organization with a plan, and to link them together for teleprocessing.*

- *Teleprocessing network forms used include the star, hierarchical, ring, multiply connected, and mixed networks.*
- *The main types of telecommunications media available are wire pairs, coaxial cable, fiber-optic cable, and microwave systems.*
- *Bandwidth refers to the capacity of a medium—how much data can be sent over it in a given amount of time. The three bandwidths commonly associated with telecommunications media are narrowband or sub-voice grade, voice grade, and wideband.*
- *Simplex transmission permits data to be sent in only one direction; half-duplex, both directions but not at the same time; and duplex or full-duplex in both directions simultaneously.*
- *Digital signals used by computers must be transformed to analog signals to be transmitted over ordinary phone lines. Modulation converts digital signals to analog signals; demodulation reverses the process. The devices that accomplish this process are called modems. Acoustic couplers are portable modems that can be used with most telephones.*
- *ASCII is the code most often used today for data transmission; EBCDIC is widely used within computers. When two communicating devices use different codes, translation is necessary.*
- *In asynchronous transmission one byte is sent at a time. In synchronous transmission bytes are sent in blocks synchronized by a clock mechanism.*
- *Protocols are rules and procedures governing the use of telecommunications media. These include polling, contention, token passing, and packet switching.*
- *The multidrop line was an early hardware technique for letting more than one user do teleprocessing at once. Communications processors followed; these are more sophisticated, and include multiplexers, concentrators, front-end processors, and message switchers.*
- *Telecommunications media can be purchased outright or leased from a common carrier. Some firms offer value-added networks (VANs), which provide extra services in addition to the media. For teleprocessing within a very limited area—such as the same office—local area networks can fill the bill.*

KEY TERMS

These are the key terms in the order in which they appear in the chapter.

Wideband medium (225)
Simplex transmission (225)
Half-duplex transmission (225)
Full-duplex, or duplex, transmission (225)
Modulation (226)
Demodulation (227)
Modem (228)
Acoustic coupler (228)
Asynchronous transmission (228)
Synchronous transmission (228)
Protocols (229)
Polling (230)

Contention (230)
Token passing (230)
Packet switching (230)
Multidrop line (231)
Communications processors (231)
Multiplexer (or multiplexor) (232)
Concentrator (233)
Front-end processor (233)
Message switcher (233)
Common carrier (234)
Value-added network (VAN) (234)
Local area network (LAN) (236)

REVIEW QUESTIONS

OBJECTIVE QUESTIONS

TRUE/FALSE: *Put the letter T or F on the line before the question.*

1. Wire pairs are affected by "crosstalk."
2. A star network is usually associated with centralized teleprocessing systems.
3. Time-sharing networks allow users to gain access to more computing power than they could otherwise afford.
4. Telecommunications has the same meaning as teleprocessing.
5. A telecommunications link which requires you to use a modem to link your terminal into the system does not require a modem for the host processor.
6. A multiplexer is used to link high-speed disk drives to the host computer.
7. A LAN cannot be linked into a VAN.
8. A VAN provides communications processing to network users.
9. Mixed networks are the most common type of network.
10. One of the major disadvantages of teleprocessing is its vulnerability to unauthorized use.

MULTIPLE CHOICE: *Put the letter of the correct answer on the line before the question.*

1. A company where computing power and data are shared among the various user departments would most likely have a _____ teleprocessing network.
   (a) Decentralized.
   (b) Distributed.
   (c) Centralized.
   (d) None of the above.
2. Some contention protocols use _____ to manage which sending unit should have access to the network.
   (a) Polling.
   (b) Token passing.
   (c) Packet switching.
   (d) Multiplexing.
3. A _____ transmission line permits only unidirectional sending of data or messages.
   (a) Duplex.
   (b) Half-duplex.
   (c) Simplex.
   (d) Half-simplex.
4. The most powerful type of communications processor is the
   (a) Message switcher.
   (b) Multiplexor.
   (c) Concentrator.
   (d) Front-end processor.
5. The transmission of randomly spaced bytes is a feature of
   (a) Synchronous transmission.
   (b) Packet switching.
   (c) Analog signals.
   (d) None of the above.

Write the correct word or words in the blank to complete the sentence.

1. A _____ is used to convert data from a digital to an analog form and back again.
2. An organization where managers in the headquarters office desire a great deal of control over outlying operating divisions would want to impose a _____ teleprocessing network.
3. A _____ network can serve to link several equal host processors.
4. A _____, made up of tiny glass fibers, can be used for _____ band transmissions.
5. _____ provide telecommunications facilities to any paying customer.
6. A _____ usually links several users in the same office.
7. The acronym VAN stands for _____.
8. _____ transmission requires that sending and receiving units be coordinated.
9. Simultaneous two-way transmissions are permitted with _____ links.
10. The breaking and later recombining of messages into easily transmitted units is called _____.

SHORT ANSWER QUESTIONS

When answering these questions, think of concrete examples to illustrate your points.

1. What is the diffence between teleprocessing and telecommunications?
2. What are the advantages and disadvantages of wire pair and microwave transmission lines?
3. What is meant by the term bandwidth? Describe the three major types.
4. What are the types of communications processors? How do they differ in functions performed?
5. What is the difference between asynchronous and synchronous transmission?
6. How do centralized and distributed networks differ?
7. Describe the different network forms.
8. What is a common carrier?
9. Describe the function of a value-added network.
10. What is a LAN?
11. What are two disadvantages of teleprocessing networks?

ESSAY QUESTIONS

1. How does organizational structure affect a teleprocessing network used in an information system.
2. What kinds of modems and communications processors would Global Electrical Equipment and Oakriver University make use of?
3. What are the advantages and disadvantages of teleprocessing?

PART THREE

Part One introduced information systems, briefly explaining what they are, the steps in their evolution, and the jobs they perform today. In Part Two, we looked at the hardware that goes into a modern computerized information system. Now we shift our focus to software, the instructions that tell the machines what to do and how to do it.

Chapter 9 takes a look at programming and how the concepts of structured design are applied to create today's programs. In Chapter 10 we explore specific methods of defining, writing, and testing programs. Chapter 11 describes the programming languages in which software is written, and Chapter 12 discusses software that can be purchased ready-made. Finally, Chapter 13 deals with system software, the master programs that enable the others to work.

CHAPTER 9

DESIGNING SOFTWARE: PROGRAMS TO PROVIDE SOLUTIONS

After studying this chapter you should understand the following:

■ *The importance of software to all five elements of an information system.*

■ *The steps in the program development cycle.*

■ *How programming fits into the system development process.*

■ *Why information system users, programmers, and managers favor structured programming methods.*

■ *Several approaches to managing the development of structured programs.*

■ *The main features of the HIPO program design technique.*

As at other schools, keeping student records up to date at Oakriver University is a challenge. Students, faculty members, and deans need timely and accurate records. Some factors, however, work against this.

Fully aware of the difficulties of student record-keeping, Alice Smith, a systems analyst, greeted the two other meeting participants and sat down at the conference table.

"I guess we all know what we're up against," Alice said.

"Basically, yes," Frank Barnes said. "Your boss and mine decided that yesterday. We have to solve the honor roll problem." Frank worked in the university's Student Records Office.

"And solve it by the end of the early part of next semester," said Tom Lee. "That will be a tall order!" Tom was a programmer. Both he and Alice worked for the university's Information Processing Center.

"Frank, why don't you summarize the problem in terms of the Student Records Office," Alice said. "Exactly what is it that you need?"

"All right," Frank said. "At present one program does everything concerning grades. We run it at the end of each semester. It gives grade reports for each student, and prepares all sorts of summaries for different groups of students, such as the honor roll."

"That's all from one program?" Tom asked.

"I guess so," Frank said. "At least we run it all at once."

"That's the problem, as my boss explained it," Alice broke in. "He said I should form a team to separate the honor-roll program from the program that generates grades."

Frank said, "You see, we get so many incompletes, that some students eventually qualify for the honor roll—but we don't find that out until weeks after the honor roll has been prepared."

Alice got up, walked to the blackboard, and wrote: "Problems," and under it, "Incompletes."

"Any other problems with the present system?" Alice asked.

"Yes, grades get changed occasionally, too," Frank said. "Either the professor made a mistake in the first place, or reconsiders it after talking with the student. Sometimes, too, the optical readers that take the grades from the professors' forms just plain get it wrong."

"O.K.," Alice said. "Let's lump all that together as 'Corrections.'" She wrote "Corrections" on the board. "Anything else?"

"No," Frank said. "Those are the problems. That's why we can't produce the honor roll at the same time as the grade reports. So that it will be accurate, we want to do it several weeks later, after most of the incompletes are in, and after we key in all the corrections. But we have to do it in time to send out the invitations to the awards ceremony!"

On the board Alice drew a big box and labeled it "Grade Reports." Then she lopped off an end of it with the eraser, and labeled the end "Honor Roll."

Tom Lee chuckled. "That won't be done as easily as cutting off a slice of salami."

"True," Alice said. "Tom, you've worked on parts of the grade report program before, haven't you? Is it a structured program?"

"Yes, as I remember," Tom said. "It has over 20 modules."

"Modules," Alice said to Frank, "are small units of a program that do just one thing, and that follow certain conventions that make changing them easier."

"It's a batch system, runs on the mainframe," Tom said. "People with the right passwords can also make inquiries online with their terminals."

"I didn't quite understand that jargon," Frank said. "But it is a very complicated program. I'll vouch for that."

"Then we will have to be careful changing it," Alice said. "We'll have to follow a conservative, structured programming approach. Frank, thank you for telling us what the Student Records Office needs. Now Tom and I have got to get busy on the details. I'll design the solution, and Tom will code and test it. We'll have to ask you more questions at certain points as we go along, to make sure we stay on target."

PROGRAMS AND THE INFORMATION SYSTEM

The focus of the present chapter is software. Although software is only one element of an information system, it has a vital relationship with all of the others, as we shall now see.

SOFTWARE AND RULES AND PROCEDURES

Computer PROGRAMS, or SOFTWARE, consist of detailed step-by-step instructions written by PROGRAMMERS that a computer can interpret and act upon. These instructions in effect codify, or explicitly state, some of the *rules and procedures* of an organization, by placing them in a form that a computer can carry out. The rules state under what conditions people can gain access to information. Still more rules, translated into programs, influence the data gathering, data storage, and information distribution process. Software determines how you can use the hardware—both the central processor and the peripherals. Some software also serves to screen user access to other software.

SOFTWARE AND PEOPLE

Consider the situation at Oakriver University described at the beginning of the chapter. Software affects how the *people*—the students, faculty, and staff—interact with the information system. The software puts into effect rules and procedures that are part of university policy. For instance, students gain access to grades only at prespecified times, and then are not allowed to change them. Faculty members use class rosters maintained at the Records Office to determine who is enrolled in their classes. These rosters are prepared according to rules governing student registration prerequisites, class sizes, class schedules, and faculty work load. While it is true that faculty members have a say in formulating these rules, once the rules are implemented in a successful system (one that works as intended), faculty members must also abide by them.

Deans use the records data to know how many students they have and what their majors are. The Oakriver University staff also utilize the data, and indeed it was the staff's inability to use the data at the right time that brought about a clash between what the software actually did, and the rules and procedures it was *supposed* to be implementing. That is, students who qualified for the honor roll, on the basis of their grade-point averages, were not being placed on it because their grades, although they were posted accurately, were posted too late for processing.

SOFTWARE AND DATA

Since grades are a matter that can affect people in a very strong and possibly permanent way, the Oakriver University program should be dealing with correct grades rather than false ones. A maze of rules and security regulations determines who can submit grades to the program, alter grades, or even just examine the grades. Many of these rules and regulations are built into the software itself. This is an example of how software affects *data.*

In addition to controlling the entry, examination, and changing of the data, software also governs data storage and recall. The programmers must follow rules codified in software effectively to store and recall data with their modules. This type of control has nothing to do with whether the data are timely or are being handled ethically or legally, but governs their efficient movement and processing through the components of a computer system.

SOFTWARE AND HARDWARE

Software also implements rules stating how to use certain *hardware*. For instance, the university's Information Processing Center has a printer in its computer room, to print the various reports created by the grades program, as well as other programs. There is an enormous gap, however, between the desire to have the information printed and inducing that physical object—the printer to move its mechanical parts and spew out the printed information: this gap is bridged by software.

SOFTWARE AND OTHER SOFTWARE

Even the *software* itself is affected by rules embodied in software. Tom Lee has been asked to change the grades program to produce the honor roll in a new way. He will have to follow the rules of other programs governing such matters as the type and meaning of the programming language in which he works. In a nutshell, no matter which of the five information system elements we look at, software plays a crucial role.

PROGRAMMING AND PROBLEM SOLVING

EVERYBODY SOLVES PROBLEMS

Every day of your life you must solve problems. Some require almost automatic solutions—for example, reacting to an oncoming automobile that has just crossed over to your side of the road. Other problems need careful thought, such as deciding which college to attend or what career to pursue.

Each time you face a new challenge—purchasing a personal computer, say, or scheduling study time for finals—you need to plan a solution to the problem. You may plan well or you may plan poorly, but you have to plan. You can't create a successful complex program, however, without disciplined planning. In this section we will look at a general model for program development that can also apply to any complex problem.

THE PROGRAM DEVELOPMENT CYCLE

The process of **PROGRAMMING** involves creating or altering a computer program. If it is at all complex (as is Oakriver's honor-roll program), it requires a systematic problem-solving approach. We can identify eight steps required to solve a programming problem. These are:

1 *Problem recognition*
2 *Problem definition*
3 *Program design*
4 *Program coding*
5 *Program testing*
6 *Program implementation*
7 *Program maintenance*
8 *Beginning again*

These steps comprise the **PROGRAM DEVELOPMENT CYCLE**, shown as a loop in Figure 9-1. The eight large arrows represent steps in the solution cycle. The first step—recognizing the problem—is at the top. Other steps follow in sequence, until we begin the program development cycle again.

As we move through the cycle we need **CHECKPOINTS** where we ask whether we have successfully completed a step. At each checkpoint a decision must be made whether to continue the process or to return and redo the previous step. These checkpoints are shown in Figure 9-1 by the five smaller arrows. Now let's take a closer look at each of the program development steps.

Problem recognition

PROBLEM RECOGNITION is the first step in solving a problem. You can't solve a problem, after all, if you don't know you have one. Of course the problem must be one that can be solved with a new computer program or modifications to an existing one.

Problem definition

PROBLEM DEFINITION involves focusing on the problem to identify exactly what it is and how best to solve it.

Program design

PROGRAM DESIGN involves specifying the structure of the program in detail. Later in this chapter and in Chapter 10, we discuss some important techniques of program design.

The solution to a programming problem is often expressed as an **ALGORITHM**, or set of rules that break down the solution into a simple, repetitive procedure. Everyone uses algorithms, even if unconsciously, all the time. When doing household chores you follow some sort of routine. When balancing your checkbook you follow another set of rules. Programming languages are designed to express algorithms efficiently, so that a computer can carry out the steps.

FIGURE 9-1.

*The program development cy-
cle. Note that the eight large arrows represent the main flow of
the cycle. The five smaller arrows show feedback or verification loops within the cycle at
the checkpoints.*

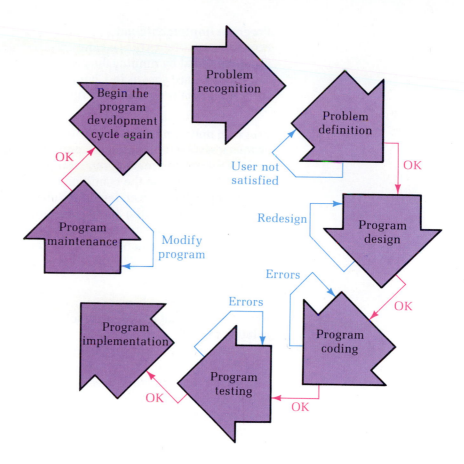

Sometimes previously developed algorithms may be used for different purposes than those for which they were originally intended. For example, the algorithm for baking a lemon sponge cake can be used with only minor changes for an orange sponge cake. In the same way some algorithms, or even complete programs, designed to solve one problem can also be used to solve another.

Program coding

PROGRAM CODING means translating the design into a programming language that will run on the computer. At this stage you would write the detailed step-by-step instructions necessary to tell the computer what to do. We shall see some examples of program code in Chapter 11.

Program testing

PROGRAM TESTING involves checking the program for errors and rewriting parts of the program to correct the mistakes. This process of finding and correcting errors in programs is called DEBUGGING.

This phase of the program development cycle can be very time consuming. In the latter part of Chapter 10, we explore some methods to ease frustrations often associated with testing and debugging.

Program implementation

PROGRAM IMPLEMENTATION means using the program. A programmed solution is implemented by running the program. Sample program runs for the honor roll problem are shown in Chapter 11. If the results are satisfactory, all is well. If not, the program needs further testing.

Program maintenance

PROGRAM MAINTENANCE involves correcting any previously undetected errors in the program and making any other needed changes. Often programs must be modified because the conditions affecting the original problem change. For example, if Oakriver decided to change the honor roll cutoff to a GPA of 3.75 instead of 3.5, the honor-roll program would have to be changed accordingly. If the program is designed flexibly enough to handle the possibility of future changes, modifications will be much easier to make.

Beginning again

The solution process begins again, to complete the cycle. We may move on to new problems that require new solutions, or we may improve on an existing solution to an old problem.

If we look back at our opening vignette, we can see how Oakriver's honor-roll program fits into this cycle. The people in charge of the Student Records Office first *recognized* the problem of an inaccurate honor roll. When Alice, Frank, and Tom met, they *defined* the problem. Alice will now *design* a program to solve the problem and Tom will *code* and *test* it. The program will then be *implemented* and the staff of Oakriver's Information Processing Center will *maintain* it.

BUYING SOFTWARE

Just because you have a programming problem doesn't mean you need to create your own program. Many small- and medium-sized organizations, and of course many individuals who use microcomputers, don't have the resources to write their own programs. Instead they buy the programs from software vendors. When you buy software you shift responsibility for program design, coding, and implementation from yourself or your organization to the vendor. You must still, however, have a clear sense of the problem you expect the software to solve, be sure you have the correct software to solve it, and be sure that it is implemented properly for your system.

In Chapter 12 we discuss packaged software at length.

PROGRAMMING AND THE SYSTEM DEVELOPMENT PROCESS

In Chapter 2 we briefly introduced the system development process. There we noted that all systems go through a process of birth, growth, maturity, and decline. The system development process will be the main topic of Chapter 15. For now it is enough to observe that the system development process has an integral relationship with the programming development cycle—program development is part of system development. In Chapter 15 we shall see how the program development cycle fits into the system development process.

STRUCTURED PROGRAMMING

THE NEED FOR STRUCTURED PROGRAMS

Cast yourself in the role of a manager. You have decided to implement changes in your company's inventory control procedures. You contact the information-processing manager and arrange to discuss the changes. At the meeting you are shocked to hear that the changes will take twice as long to reprogram as you expected. One reason for the delay is that the programmers who originally worked on the inventory control problem have left for other jobs, and the new programmers are having difficulties tracking the complex logic of the program. In addition the existing program can handle only 4000 different types of parts used in the production process, and your future needs require a system capable of tracking twice as many types. If the existing program had been written using a structured approach, maintaining and modifying the program would be greatly simplified.

STRUCTURED PROGRAMMING refers to a set of techniques for organizing and writing programs to make them simple, easy for the person who wrote them as well as for others to understand, and easy to change. A program written following the techniques of structured programming is known as a STRUCTURED PROGRAM. Structured programming was developed to control the haphazard programming methods once common in the industry. In the 1970s people came to recognize the value of structured methods in reducing the overall costs of a program throughout its useful life.

The two main goals of structured programming are detecting errors as early as possible in the program development cycle and simplifying the maintenance or modification of programs. In both cases costs are reduced in comparison with the earlier, nonstructured methods.

In a narrow sense a structured program is one that employs only certain specific logical constructs, which will be discussed in detail in Chapter 10. "Structured," however, has come to be applied in a broader sense to a collection of techniques for creating structured programs.

For programmers, creating a structured program means dividing it into MODULES, which are self-contained subparts of a program. Each module performs a single function that is well-defined and simple, such as "read a grade" or "write a line of the honor roll." A module can be taken out, modified, or replaced without substantially affecting other modules of the program, just as a worn-out part of a television set can be replaced or upgraded. We can think of modules as building blocks. It is easier to correct errors in a program made up of modules than one that is not, because only one module may be involved and hence only one may need to be changed. The same applies to modifying a program or expanding what it does—the changes can be isolated to certain modules, and the rest of the program remains unaffected.

In structured programming programmers relate their modules to one another following a TOP-DOWN APPROACH. That is, a solution is planned starting with the overall design at the general level, and then progresses to details of the solution. This means that modules at the top of the hierarchy give orders to other modules further down, which do the actual work. The modules at the top are designed and coded first. Use of this standard approach to the relationship among modules makes it easier to create as well as to understand and modify the logic of a structured program at a later time.

As the cost of computer hardware continues to drop, larger and more complex computer systems become economically feasible; hence our ability to design large, complex software systems of high quality becomes more important. So it is not surprising that the demand for software and competent software designers has increased dramatically over the last two decades, to the extent that today we are outstripping our supply of trained talent and our current development methodologies.

These shortfalls are particularly apparent in large software development efforts (those requiring more than 100K source lines or 50 staff years). In such projects, complexity seems to increase in nonlinear fashion both within the software itself and the structure of the organization charged with its development.

Nowhere is this complexity more intensely felt than in the debugging phase. Indeed, it is here that software developers have come to realize that we can no longer afford to rely on debugging as a means of assuring software quality. Rather, quality must be built into the software throughout the design and implementation process.

In our work at AT&T Bell Laboratories, we participated in the development of the computer-controlled 5ESS switching system. Early in the project, we realized that the challenge of large-scale software development could only be met by creating increasingly sophisticated procedures. Although our own software needs were more extensive than those of many others, we feel our experience is applicable to most projects. . . .

To improve quality and productivity and reduce development time, the management team established a project structure wherein work assignments and staff responsibilities logically reflected one another. Clear and effective lines of communications were estab-

lished with well-understood goals, responsibilities, and expectations. Management also fostered a team spirit requiring strong, positive work attitudes and firm commitments toward our goals by the entire organization. A formal, rigorous development methodology was implemented to provide a uniform structure to the development process and to assure a high level of designed-in quality. . . .

The software of the 5ESS switching system was developed using the phased validation technique. This approach was essential to uncover problems early and to build in the desired quality during all phases of development. A critical attribute of a good methodology is to maximize the number of problems found and corrected in the same development phase as they occur. Thus requirements problems were to be discovered and resolved during the requirements phase, design problems in the design phase, etc. . . .

The most important aspect of quality is the performance of the system as perceived by the user. For switching systems this means the capacity to switch phone calls, the reliability of the system to provide continuing service, the percentage of calls completed, the frequency and duration of recovery actions due to software or hardware faults, the response time to the commands input by the telephone company craft personnel, etc. . . .

During the early stages of development a large percentage of the calls were not properly completed due to either hardware or software problems. As development progressed and the system approached field quality, the completion rate improved to over 99.99 percent.

Source: Adapted from "Building Quality and Productivity into a Large Software System," by Edward M. Prell and Alan P. Sheng, *IEEE Software.* Copyright © 1984 IEEE.

A note on packaged programs

One of the issues addressed in program development is whether to write your own software or to buy prepackaged software. Structured programming methods are applicable to both situations. They provide design standards for developing your own programs or for evaluating the quality of the programs developed by outside vendors. In general software developed using structured design techniques, whether created by your own organization or purchased from an outside vendor, will provide you with a better performing and more cost-effective program.

HOW STRUCTURED PROGRAMMING AIDS PROGRAMMERS AND MANAGERS

Structured methods apply not only to the way we design and write programs, but also to the ways programmers do their work. These methods are applicable to both individual programmers and programming teams.

For managers of programming projects, structured methods provide useful management control techniques in the following areas:

- *Assigning reasonably sized tasks to programmers.*
- *Assuring that programmers use standard methods.*
- *Determining task accountability and responsibility.*
- *Helping limit problems caused by employee turnover.*

Programmers as well as managers prefer a structured programming approach. For programmers structured programming defines job tasks and accountability clearly and offers support services where required. The structured programs that result are easier for programmers to modify and maintain.

CRITICISMS OF THE STRUCTURED APPROACH

One weakness of structured techniques perceived by some people is the amount of time spent initially designing a project. Why not just get on with the project and worry about maintenance problems when they occur? For two decades after computers became commercially available, that is exactly what was done. Studies have proved, however, that the cost of correcting an error is higher in the implementation stage of a problem solution than during earlier design stages. Figure 9-2 shows how the cost of correcting an error increases at a geometric rate over the course of program development.

For example, a payroll program that does not allow for modification when the tax laws change would probably need to be extensively rewritten, or even scrapped, after only one year. Otherwise a company using it could face legal penalties and fines for improperly withholding taxes. A well-planned and well-designed program does not guarantee perfection, but a poorly planned and designed program most likely will lead to unsatisfactory results.

Another complaint is that with the separation of tasks encouraged by structured techniques, it is difficult to see how a person's work fits into the overall picture. Interested employees can, however, take the trouble to figure this out; structured walkthroughs, described later in the chapter, provide an excellent opportunity. There are also cases where separation of tasks is an important plus, as with money-related or sensitive corporate work. Consider a project for creating a payroll program. One person may work on a small module that checks for invalid employee numbers, while another person works on the employee name and address verification

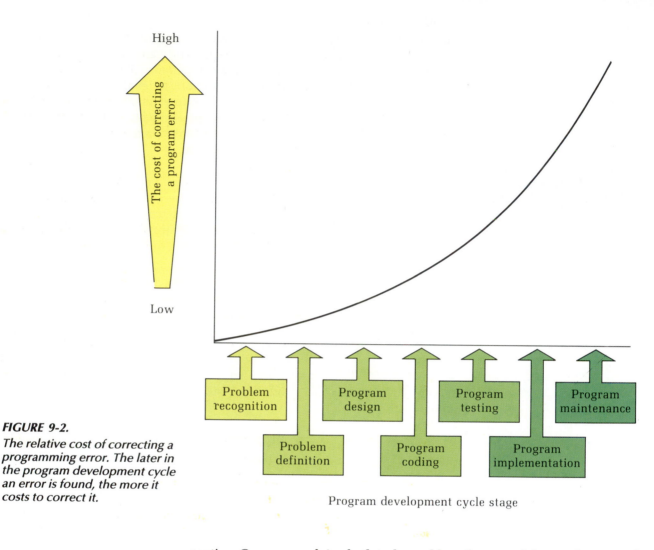

FIGURE 9-2.

The relative cost of correcting a programming error. The later in the program development cycle an error is found, the more it costs to correct it.

High

The cost of correcting a program error

Low

Problem recognition

Problem definition

Program design

Program coding

Program testing

Program implementation

Program maintenance

Program development cycle stage

routine. One person doing both tasks could easily create fake employees and addresses.

MANAGING FOR STRUCTURED PROGRAMMING

There are three major approaches to managing the programming effort. In historical order of appearance, they are the early programming approach, the chief programmer team, and "egoless" programming. Organizations may use one method exclusively or some combination of the three. The structured walkthrough is a method of programmer peer review that has emerged in conjunction with the chief programmer team and egoless programming.

THE EARLY PROGRAMMING APPROACH

The **EARLY PROGRAMMING APPROACH** stressed getting the initial program for the user done as quickly as possible. A programmer was assigned a software project by the data processing manager. The programmer then proceeded to design and write the program using whatever techniques were necessary to get the initial program finished. Upon completion the manager would probably reassign the programmer to a different project in need of one. The manager and the programmer were not directly concerned with long-range problems of program maintenance—that was someone else's headache.

The major problem with the early approach was that the people initially involved with a program lacked long-term responsibility for it. Another weakness was that the programmer was not bound by any rules about coding practices, and the program could thus be coded in a very unconventional and confusing manner. The program might work well for the initial problem, but alterations could prove time consuming, or even impossible.

THE CHIEF PROGRAMMER TEAM APPROACH

The second approach, the CHIEF PROGRAMMER TEAM, grew out of an effort to reduce software errors through teamwork. The chief programmer team could be compared to a highly skilled surgical team. The first major application of the chief programmer team concept was developed by the IBM Corporation in the early 1970s for the *New York Times* . The project involved automating the newspaper's extensive "clippings" file to allow fast retrieval of subject materials based on an index consisting of key words and dates. Over 83,000 lines of program instructions or code were written, which took almost two years and required the equivalent of approximately 11 person-years of time (equal to one person working 11 years). The project was completed ahead of schedule, with few errors, and below budget estimates.

A chief programmer team is made up of the following people:

- The CHIEF, or LEAD, PROGRAMMER, *who manages, plans, organizes, and reviews the overall activities of the project. This person may also design the overall control part of the program, and assign more routine programming tasks to subordinate programmers.*
- The SENIOR, or BACKUP, PROGRAMMERS, *who carry out assignments under the direction of the lead programmer. These assignments include the development of subparts of the program.*
- JUNIOR PROGRAMMERS, *present on larger projects to perform the most routine programming tasks.*
- PROGRAMMING SPECIALISTS, *who are brought into the team to offer support services. Support services speed and ease a programmer's job by carrying out certain separable parts of it. For instance, the specialists might devise test data to challenge every element of the program package in order to detect errors, or might create problem-solving algorithms. Administrative and clerical personnel are available to the programmer, as well as access to a PROGRAM LIBRARY of prewritten algorithms or routines.*
- A TECHNICAL WRITER, *a person familiar with programming concepts and able to describe them clearly, is part of some teams. Technical writers help programmers create good DOCUMENTATION, consisting of manuals, easy-to-understand screen displays, and possible audiovisual material telling users how to use the program, operators how to run it, and programmers how to change it.*

A good chief programmer must know how to manage people, maintain high team morale, and delegate tasks to others. The goal of the chief programmer is to ensure a unified design that follows structured programming methods. A drawback of the chief programmer team approach is the possible clash of egos among the team members.

EGOLESS PROGRAMMING

Average people can be trained to accept their humanity—their inability to function like a machine—and to value it and work with others so as to keep it under the kind of control needed if programming is to be successful. Consider the case of Bill G. who was working in one of the early space tracking systems. His job was to write a simulator which would simulate the entire network of tracking stations and other real-time inputs. His system had to check out the rest of the system in real-time without having to have the worldwide network on-line. The heart of the simulator was to be a very small and very tight loop, consisting, in fact, of just thirteen machine instructions. Bill had worked for some time on this loop and when he finally reached the point of some confidence in it, he began looking for a critic—the standard practice in this programming group.

Bill found Marilyn B. willing to peruse his code in exchange for his returning the favor. This was nothing unusual in this group; indeed, nobody would have thought of going on the machine without such scrutiny by a second party. Whenever possible an exchange was made, so nobody would feel in the position of being criticized by someone else. But for Bill, who was well schooled in this method, the protection of an exchange was not necessary. His value system, when it came to programming, dictated that secretive, possessive programming was bad and that open, shared programming was good. Errors that might be found in code he had written—not "his" code, for that terminology was not used here—were simply facts to be exposed to investigation with an eye to future improvement, not attacks on his person.

In this particular instance, Bill had been having one of his "bad programming days." As Marilyn worked and worked over the code—as she found one error after another—he became more and more amused, rather than more and more defensive as he might have done had he been trained as so many of our programmers are. Finally, he emerged from their conference announcing to the world the startling fact that Marilyn had been able to find *seventeen* bugs in only thirteen statements. He insisted on showing everyone who would listen how this had been possible. In fact, since the very exercise had proved to him that this was not his day for coding, he simply spent the rest of the day telling and retelling the episode in all its hilarious details.

Source: Selection from "The Psychology of Computer Programming," by Gerald M. Weinberg. Copyright © 1971 by Van Nostrand Reinhold Company, Inc. Reprinted by permission of the publisher.

THE "EGOLESS" PROGRAMMING TEAM APPROACH

The most recent approach is the "EGOLESS" PROGRAMMING TEAM. With the other programming approaches, a programmer has a personal stake in how a program is written and is apt to take personally any criticism—even constructive criticism—of the quality of the program. The "egoless" programming approach seeks to avoid this kind of negative personal involvement. An egoless programming team consists of a closely-knit group of people of equal rank working on a project, often with additional help from support people and services. Team members make decisions in a democratic fashion that avoids personal conflict.

STRUCTURED WALKTHROUGHS

One method of detecting errors in a program is to seek assistance from your programming peers. A STRUCTURED WALKTHROUGH is the name associated with a programmer peer review meeting. Structured walkthroughs are used with both the chief programmer team approach and the egoless programming team approach, and may be held at any point in a project from design through coding.

The purpose of a structured walkthrough is to provide a nonthreatening environment in which to evaluate a programmer's work for errors. The best meetings of this type involve the programmer working on the program, a moderator (a programmer trained for this task), other programmers to "walk through" the steps of the program and record potential errors for later correction, and a representative from the user group that originally requested the program. *Managers are not present* at these meetings, to help ensure that the emphasis will be on solving problems rather than on the performance of a particular employee. The programming materials should be distributed to the peer group before the meeting to allow people an opportunity to review them before the session. Walkthrough sessions may last about an hour.

Criticism and suggestions should focus on programming errors, not on programming style. Avoiding a focus on style prevents the meeting from getting stalled over personal issues. In addition all notes and suggestions should be recorded anonymously to avoid suspicions of potential misuse of the meeting report. Although such meetings can slow down the initial phases of a project, the payoff in timely error reduction far outweighs the disadvantages.

STRUCTURED PROGRAMMING: THE HIPO METHOD

There are many different methods used to design structured programs. We will focus here on one technique, called HIERARCHY PLUS INPUT, PROCESS, OUTPUT (HIPO). The HIPO method follows the top-down approach to structured programming described earlier in the chapter.

There are four major steps in the actual development process:

1 Creation of the VISUAL TABLE OF CONTENTS (VTOC), which shows the overall structure of the program and identifies the HIPO diagrams for each module.

2 Development of the OVERVIEW HIPO DIAGRAMS, which contain the general input, process, and output requirements for each module.

3 Design of DETAILED HIPO DIAGRAMS, which show in whatever detail required the input, processing, and output steps necessary to execute the module.

FIGURE 9-3.

Hierarchy plus Input Process Output (HIPO) tools used in structured programming: The visual table of contents (VTOC) shows the top-down approach. Control modules are placed in the upper levels and processing ones in the lower levels. The dashed box encloses unused (dummy) modules for future expansion.

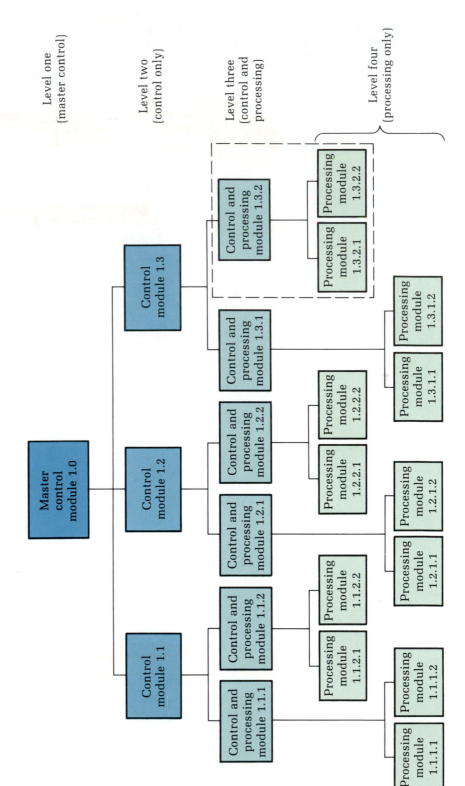

Level one (master control)

Level two (control only)

Level three (control and processing)

Level four (processing only)

4 *Writing detailed flowcharts and/or pseudocode statements. A* **FLOW-CHART** *uses special symbols to show the logical flow of the steps in the program solution.* **PSEUDOCODE** *is an English-like code to help the programmer understand the steps needed to execute the program. Flowcharts and pseudocode are then translated into the actual programming language.*

We will now look at only the first three elements on our list. Chapter 10 will explore flowcharts and pseudocode.

VISUAL TABLE OF CONTENTS

Program design begins with the visual table of contents (VTOC). The visual table of contents is a special type of top-down structure chart. A *structure chart* shows the hierarchal relationships between modules of a program. A VTOC (Figure 9-3) is called a top-down structure chart because the design of the program starts at the top of the chart and moves down to the more specialized areas, following the top-down approach described earlier in the chapter.

Each module in the VTOC has an identification number for the appropriate HIPO overview diagram for the module. These reference numbers for each module direct the programmer to the overview and detailed HIPO diagrams, shown later in Figure 9-6. As we move deeper into the table, the numbers become more complex. In addition to the numbering system, the visual table of contents should include any other references concerning the proper flow of control and data through the program. Note that the general flow of the VTOC is from left to right and from top to bottom.

CONTROL MODULES at the top give orders to the other modules below. **CONTROL-AND-PROCESSING MODULES** perform both control operations over lower level modules and carry out processing functions. **PROCESSING MODULES** are at the lowest level, and enact the orders required by the higher modules. Dummy modules (at the bottom right of Figure 9-3) simply allow room for expansion.

MORE ON MODULES

Let's spend a moment to explore some of the features that make modules so helpful in the program design process. These desired features include:

- *Independence from other modules. For example, a processing module concerned with calculating a grade-point average should have all the formulas for multiplication, addition, and division in the module, and should not need to call another module to do the work.*
- *One entrance and one exit (see Figure 9-4). There should be only one way of accessing the module from other modules and of leaving to go to other modules. With multiple entrances and exits, correcting or modifying the program becomes more difficult. In addition results might be passed to the wrong module.*
- *One function. A module should perform only a single task that can be described in two to three words, such as "read grade."*
- *Automatic return to the superior module. Upon task completion control returns to the calling (higher up) module that ordered the execution of the task. Lower level modules are not allowed to call higher level modules. For example, module 1.3.2 in Figure 9-4 can call module*

FIGURE 9-4.

Modules have only one entrance and one exit. To get from one low-level module to another always requires passing through a higher level module. Thus module 1.3.1.2 cannot itself invoke module 1.3.2.1. Instead, when module 1.3.1.2 has finished its task, control automatically returns through 1.3.1 to 1.3. Module 1.3 can then call module 1.3.2, which can in turn call 1.3.2.1.

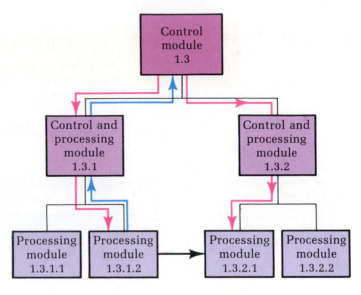

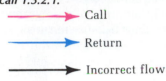

Call

Return

Incorrect flow

FIGURE 9-5.

How a main program and its subroutines interact.

Main program

Subroutines

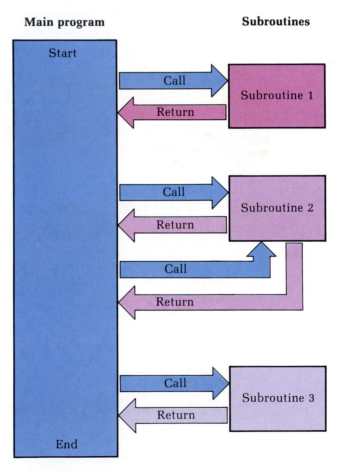

FIGURE 9-6.
Overview and detailed HIPO diagrams.

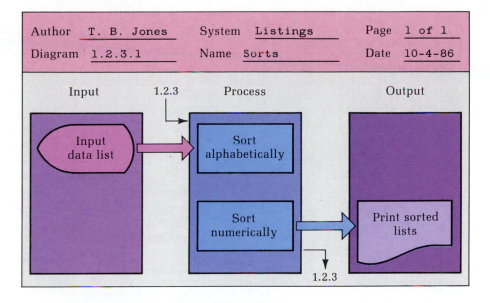

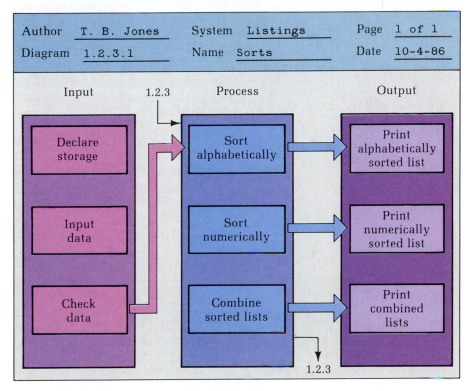

Computer programmers design, code, test, document, and install software of two kinds: (1) application software and (2) system software. Application programmers and programmer analysts handle application software. Systems programmers handle system software. These three types of programming jobs are described in the career boxes for Chapters 10, 11, and 13 respectively.

Although each of these three types of programming has different requirements (described in the career boxes), they also have a lot in common. First, they all deal with the same basic concepts; differences lie in the levels of responsibility and the degree of involvement with the machine. A certain orderliness in terms of mental habits, and perhaps work habits, seems to be required to program well, along with the ability to be creative. To some extent these two personality characteristics are opposites; the good programmer unites them.

Programmers come from every conceivable background, age group, and walk of life. If one characteristic could be found that a great many share, it would be that they are "loners." This does not mean that they are inept at social relationships or unwilling to take an active part in a programming team, but that they enjoy puzzling out intricate matters themselves. For all the team-oriented, "egoless" emphasis of contemporary structured programming, there is still plenty of opportunity to work alone. At some point being a programmer boils down to that lonely moment of truth when you either get the machine to do what it has to, or you fail.

To break into programming these days usually requires some post-high school training—preferably an AA or BS degree in a computer-related field. Some experience with computers will help to make you more likely to be hired compared to the mass of inexperienced people looking for programming jobs. It is sometimes possible for a person presently working for a company to become involved with programming as an outgrowth of a present job, and then to make a career switch.

Programming is a well-paid field with excellent career prospects. For the forseeable future neither business nor government will be able to function without programmers. Each of the three types of programmer is broken down into different levels, with appropriate gradations of salary and responsibility. Most programmers join organizations as regular employees; some work as consultants. Consultants are described in Chapter 19 and in the career box of Chapter 15. The career path out of programming is most often into systems analysis, sometimes into management, and also into such other information systems careers as training and education specialist, technical writer, database administrator, and information systems auditor.

If a programmer has a particular area of expertise that is sought after, this makes it easier to find that first job, change jobs, and advance up the career ladder. Such areas include telecommunications, distributed data processing, the use of databases, and online as opposed to batch applications.

1.3.2.1, but not vice versa. The term "call" refers to a programming technique of transferring control to a subroutine when a main program requests it. A **SUBROUTINE** is a subpart of a program which can be called by another part of a program. A **MAIN PROGRAM** is the overall program that directs subroutines. Figure 9-5 shows an example of a main program and its subroutines.

A common size limit for a module is 24 lines, the maximum number that can be displayed on most display terminal screens. Modules of greater size present greater challenges in terms of debugging and testing.

Module coding and testing can proceed in three possible ways: (1) hierarchally, (2) in order of execution, or (3) using a combined approach. With the hierarchal method individual coding and testing begin with the highest level (the master control module) and proceed to the lowest level modules. The order-of-execution method starts with the first module to be used—most likely an input module—and then proceeds to the next to be executed. The final module is the output or termination module. The combined approach borrows from both methods. For example, a set of modules for input that come early in a program (in order of execution) might be coded from the top down (hierarchally). Modules concerned with performing calculations (which follow in order of execution) would be coded next, and finally, output and termination modules would be coded.

OVERVIEW AND DETAILED HIPO DIAGRAMS

Each module in the VTOC is expanded into an overview HIPO diagram, which shows the broad input requirements, basic processing steps, and overall output needs for the module. An overview HIPO diagram is shown in the top part of Figure 9-6. First the input requirements are listed in order of appearance. Arrows show the flow from the input column into the process steps and then into the output column. Special symbols and short, written labels indicate the steps being followed. A section for an extended description (not shown in Figure 9-6) provides a place in which to refer to special routines, labels, and references. Such notes provide helpful guides to programmers, especially when a number of people are working with a module over a period of several years.

Detailed HIPO diagrams (bottom of Figure 9-6) are similar to the overview diagrams, but contain much more information. The input descriptions are expanded, the processing steps show greater complexity, and the output details are clearer. Here again, both symbols and written descriptions are used. Even with a detailed HIPO diagram, not every step in a module will be laid out. Those very detailed steps come in the flowcharting or pseudocode-writing stages of the programming process.

WRAP-UP **DEFINING OAKRIVER UNIVERSITY'S SOLUTION**

Recall the problem that began this chapter. The Student Records Office at Oakriver University wanted to produce the honor roll after all other grade calculations were done. This would allow corrected grades, and grades replacing incompletes, to be considered in calculating eligibility for the honor roll.

Alice Smith, the systems analyst assigned to lead the project, and Tom Lee, the programmer, first obtained documentation for the ex-

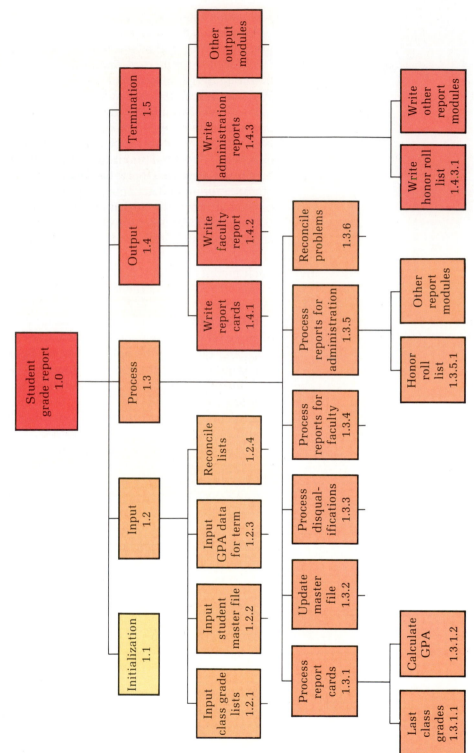

FIGURE 9-7.
Visual table of contents for the student-grade-report package. The honor roll list module is 1.3.5.1.

isting grades program. They found that it was a structured program containing over 25 modules, designed using the top-down method. The only problem was that some of the modules were too large (containing several hundred statements) and did more than one thing. The module that created the honor roll also produced other reports. So with the aim of changing this module —but as few others as possible—Alice approached the problem afresh.

Two basic steps were necessary to create the honor roll. First, a data file had to be created. The file would contain student names and grade-point averages. Second, the file had to be read and the names of those students with grade-point averages of 3.5 or more separated from the others and placed on the honor roll.

Alice used the HIPO method to develop her understanding of how the new grades program (that is, the old grades program with a small number of the modules changed) must work, and graphically to communicate program organization and function to others, principally Tom. The visual table of contents is shown in Figure 9-7.

The main control module for the student grade report is labeled 1.0, and the subordinate control modules for initialization (start-up procedures), input, process, output, and termination are labeled 1.1, 1.2, 1.3, 1.4, and 1.5 respectively. Before the honor-roll module (1.3.5.1) can be processed, the input module must be completed. Control commands (modules 1.0, 1.3, and 1.3.5) direct the activation of the honor-roll-selection program to create a file containing the list of the honor-roll students. To produce the written report using the selected data, control is first returned to the main control module (1.0); then control is transferred to module 1.4.3.1 (through modules 1.4 and 1.4.3).

In other words, with this arrangement the honor-roll program can now be run whenever the Student Records Office specifies, not as a by-product of the entire package but "on its own."

The overview HIPO diagram for module 1.2.3 and module 1.3.5.1 is shown in Figure 9-8. The detailed HIPO diagram (Figure 9-9) displays the steps needed for data entry in module 1.2.3 and 1.3.5.1. In all of these diagrams steps that relate to input are shown in the far left column. The middle column shows the processing steps required. The column on the right displays the output commands. Alice and Tom can both tell by looking at them what the program design should be, and that it will solve the problem of the Student Records Office. Now they can move on to more specific design of the required modules, and programming them, as we will see in the next two chapters.

FIGURE 9-8.
The general or overview HIPO diagram for the grade point average listing and honor roll modules.

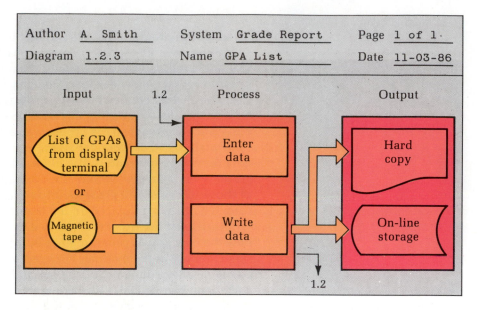

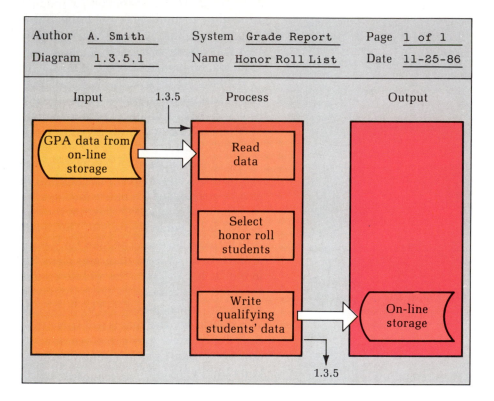

FIGURE 9-9.

The detailed HIPO diagram for the student honor roll calculations. The incoming solid arrow shows which control module directs or calls the module procedures. The exiting solid arrow directs the flow of the program back to the calling module.

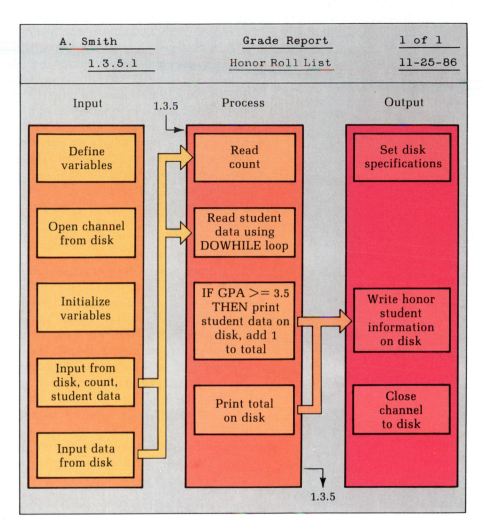

A. Smith	Grade Report	1 of 1
1.3.5.1	Honor Roll List	11-25-86

Input   1.3.5   **Process**   **Output**

Input:
- Define variables
- Open channel from disk
- Initialize variables
- Input from disk, count, student data
- Input data from disk

Process:
- Read count
- Read student data using DOWHILE loop
- IF GPA >= 3.5 THEN print student data on disk, add 1 to total
- Print total on disk

Output:
- Set disk specifications
- Write honor student information on disk
- Close channel to disk

1.3.5

SUMMARY

- Five elements need to work in harmony in an effective information system: people, rules and procedures, data, software, and hardware. Programs, or software, codify some of the rules and procedures of an organization placing them in a form that a computer can carry out. Software affects how people interact with the information system, how data are manipulated and used, and how the hardware of a computer system functions. In addition, software itself is affected by rules embodied in other software.

- Programmers write software as part of the programming effort.

- People as well as computers solve problems. Solving problems can be made much easier with an organized problem-solving approach. In the program development cycle, problem solving follows a series of steps. These steps include problem recognition, problem definition, program design, program coding, program testing or debugging, program implementation, and program maintenance. Checkpoints within the cycle provide an opportunity to ask whether we have successfully completed a step. Algorithms or routines are developed or adapted to solve parts of the program. Program development also has an integral relationship with the system development cycle.

- *Structured programming refers to a set of techniques for organizing and writing programs. The two main goals of structured programming are to detect errors as early as possible in the program development cycle, and to simplify the maintenance or modification of programs. In both cases costs are reduced in comparison with earlier, nonstructured methods.*

- *In a narrow sense a structured program is one that employs only certain specific logical constructs. "Structured," however, has come to be applied in a broader sense to a collection of techniques for creating structured programs.*

- *For programmers creating a structured program means dividing it into modules or self-contained subparts, and relating modules to one another following a top-down approach. For managers structured methods provide useful control techniques in assigning reasonably sized tasks to programmers, assuring that programmers use standard methods, determining task accountability and responsibility, and helping limit problems caused by employee turnover.*

- *The early programming approach stressed getting the initial program for the user done as quickly as possible. Long-range problems of program maintenance and modification were someone else's headache.*

- *A second method, the chief programmer team, grew out of an effort to reduce software errors through teamwork. A chief programmer team usually consists of a lead (the chief programmer), backup (senior), and junior programmers. Programming specialists help provide support services. Prewritten algorithms are kept in the program library. Technical writers assist the team by developing documentation as the project progresses through the program development cycle.*

- *The most recent approach, the "egoless" programming team, attempts to increase productive teamwork on a project by reducing any one programmer's personal stake in it. Egoless programming teams consist of people of equal rank who make decisions in a democratic manner.*

- *Peer review meetings, known as structured walkthroughs, are used with both the chief programmer team approach and the egoless programming team approach. Structured walkthroughs provide a nonthreatening environment for evaluating a programmer's work; managers are not present.*

- *HIPO (Hierarchy plus Input, Process, Output) is one technique for designing structured programs. This technique has four steps: (1) creation of a visual table of contents (VTOC), (2) development of overview HIPO diagrams, (3) design of detailed HIPO diagrams, and (4) creation of the more detailed flowcharts or pseudocode from which programs can be prepared.*

■ *Modules should be independent from other modules, have only one entrance and one exit per module, perform only a single task that can be described in two to three words, and return automatically to the superior module upon task completion. Control modules at the top direct the lower level control-and-processing modules and processing modules. When the program is finally created, the main program steps will control the various processing modules found in the subroutines.*

KEY TERMS

These are the key terms in the order in which they appear in the chapter.

Programs (246)
Software (246)
Programmer (246)
Programming (248)
Program development cycle (248)
Checkpoints (248)
Problem recognition (248)
Problem definition (248)
Program design (248)
Algorithm (248)
Program coding (249)
Program testing (249)
Debugging (249)
Program implementation (250)
Program maintenance (250)
Structured programming (251)
Structured program (251)
Module (251)
Top-down approach (251)
Early programming approach (254)
Chief programmer team (255)

Chief, or lead, programmer (255)
Senior, or backup, programmer (255)
Junior programmer (255)
Programming specialist (255)
Program library (255)
Technical writer (255)
Documentation (255)
"Egoless" programming team (257)
Structured walkthrough (257)
Hierarchy plus Input, Process, Output (HIPO) (257)
Visual table of contents (VTOC) (257)
Overview HIPO diagram (257)
Detailed HIPO diagram (257)
Flowchart (259)
Pseudocode (259)
Control module (259)
Control-and-processing module (259)
Processing module (259)
Subroutine (262)
Main program (262)

REVIEW QUESTIONS

OBJECTIVE QUESTIONS

TRUE/FALSE: *Put the letter T or F on the line before the question.*

1. Early programming approaches did not use structured programming techniques.
2. Structured programming provides little benefit to the managers of programmers.
3. Modules should have only one entrance and one exit.
4. The HIPO method uses a top-down approach.
5. The VTOC is contained within the HIPO overview diagram.
6. Checkpoints serve to aid managers and programmers in determining progress within the program development cycle.
7. Process modules cannot call control modules.
8. The first step in the program development cycle is program design.
9. Program maintenance is not an important consideration in the program development cycle.
10. Modules should be as independent of each other as possible.

1. _____ The first stage in the program development cycle is
(a) the creation of the program design.
(b) testing the program.
(c) implementing the program.
(d) recognizing a problem exists.

2. _____ In creating modules one goal is to
(a) make the modules as interdependent on one another as possible.
(b) allow subordinate modules to call superior ones.
(c) provide one entrance and several exits from each module.
(d) make the modules as independent of one another as possible.

3. _____ The overall structure of the HIPO solution is shown in the
(a) overview diagram.
(b) detail diagram.
(c) visual table of contents.
(d) none of the above.

4. _____ The latest structured programming team approach is the
(a) "egotistical" programming team.
(b) "egoless" programming team.
(c) chief programmer team.
(d) lead programmer team.

5. _____ Generally, structured programs compared to unstructured programs
(a) are cheaper to design.
(b) are cheaper over the useful life of the program.
(c) cost more in the program maintenance stage.
(d) permit a less disciplined approach to problem solving.

FILL IN THE BLANK: *Write the correct word or words in the blank to complete the sentence.*

1. The _____ program "calls" subordinate modules called _____ .

2. The _____ programming team method puts a premium on cooperative problem solving.

3. A _____ provides a nonthreatening environment for peer reviews.

4. The writing of the actual program is part of the _____ phase of the program development cycle.

5. To codify the organizations rules and procedures into a form understandable to the hardware, _____ are used.

6. The cost of correcting a programming error is highest in the _____ stage.

7. The term _____ refers to a set of programming techniques used to create easier to debug and maintain software.

8. A _____ team is organized like a surgical team.

9. Writing _____ or _____ represents the final stage in the HIPO method.

10. Programmers relate modules to each other through the _____ approach.

SHORT ANSWERS QUESTIONS

When answering these questions, think of concrete examples to illustrate your points.

1. What is a structured program?
2. What are the advantages of structured programming?
3. Who are the members of the chief programmer team?

4. What are the steps in the program development cycle?
5. What is an algorithm?
6. How does an "egoless" programming team differ from a chief programmer team?
7. What is the purpose of a structured walkthrough?
8. What are the steps in the HIPO method?
9. What are the criticisms of structured programming?

1. What benefits does structured programming provide managers and programmers?
2. Compare and contrast early programming methods with the "egoless" programming approach.
3. Discuss the steps in the program development cycle.
4. Discuss the steps in the Hierarchy plus Input Process Output (HIPO) method.

CHAPTER 10

STRUCTURED PROGRAMMING: TOOLS FOR PROGRAMMERS

After studying this chapter you should understand the following:
■ How program steps can be outlined using flowcharts and pseudocode.
■ The three basic logic patterns of structured programming.
■ The main techniques used to debug programs, and checkpoints employed in the debugging process.
■ Why and for whom programs are documented.
■ Some shortcuts to take in constructing the flowchart or pseudocode for, and the coding and running of, that very first program.

"Whoever wrote this program should be fired!" Tom Lee said. Tom stood before Alice Smith's desk waving the program listing.

"Hang on, Tom," Alice said. "What's wrong?" Alice was the systems analyst, and Tom the programmer, responsible for changing the Oakriver University grades program so that the honor roll would be produced at the right time (the problem described in Chapter 9).

"You see, I hoped to use some of the original code, to save time. But when I got into the code, it turned out to have so many unconditional branches that it looks like a plate of tangled spaghetti." Tom spread out the listing on Alice's desk. "See!" Tom said. "There, and there, and there—everywhere—GO TO statements!"

"But the documentation said this was a structured program," Alice said.

"Sure it's structured," Tom said. "Twenty-some modules, organized using top-down design. So far so good. But some of the modules are way too big, and the module that does the grades is one of them. A module is supposed to fit on a screen. This one won't fit in a book!"

Alice saw what Tom meant. She glanced at her calendar—there wasn't a whole lot of time left on this project, either. "O.K.," she said. "Let's see where we stand. I did all the HIPO diagrams showing the way the new grades program should be set up."

"Yes," Tom said. "And from the HIPO diagrams I drew flow-charts for each of the modules we need to change to produce the honor roll. It is really just a matter of breaking up this one big module. I thought I could use some of the old code, but no way!"

"I'm trying to remember the documentation," Alice said. "What was it like?"

"Brief!" Tom said. "No flowcharts. And for the problem module, only a one-paragraph description of what the module does. Everyone knows what it does, but I can't figure out *how* it does it!"

"It looks like we'll have to throw it out and start over," Alice said.

"I agree," Tom said. "But are we going to extend my deadline now that I'm coding from scratch?"

"No," Alice said. She paused. "But I have confidence in you, Tom."

Tom returned to his desk with the useless listing. It was good that he retained a certain gallows humor about the matter. Working from his flowchart, he started to code—to write the program. He would do it the structured way to the letter. No GO TOs for him. No over-stuffed modules. And he would be sure to create suitable documentation. When some future programmer had to alter the thing some day, at least the programmer wouldn't be in Tom's shoes.

*PROGRAMMING AS A
RITE OF PASSAGE*

Learning to write a computer program can be thought of as a modern-day rite of passage. A rite of passage separates one group of people (the initiated) from another (the uninitiated), often on the basis of some skill, clan ritual, or religious experience. In the distant past the rite may have been a test of endurance or hunting skills. Today's rites of passage are more subtle. Writing programs is a test of mental endurance. After you write your first successful computer program, the way you view the computer will change. Most people feel a sense of euphoria and accomplishment. The computer will seem less magical and forbidding and more like a mere tool—a tool to serve your needs.

Most of you taking this class will not write programs at your job or at home after successfully completing the course. There will be no need to. Instead you will rely upon the services of others. Nonetheless the materials presented in this chapter will help you understand the effort required to produce the software that you will use, and will help you to evaluate it.

*DETAILING THE
PROGRAM LOGIC*

Logic tools

In Chapter 9 we described the program development cycle. One of the steps in that cycle is program design. In this chapter we will take a closer look at that process.

We already know that a cornerstone of structured programming is dividing a program into modules. To trace the internal steps of each module, two major methods are used: the flowchart and pseudocode. A **FLOWCHART** is a diagram that shows how a program works in terms of sequence, movement of data, and logic. **PSEUDOCODE** is an English-like code that helps the programmer understand the steps needed to execute the program. Once the pseudocode steps, or the flowchart steps, necessary to solve the problem have been formulated, they can be converted into the actual programming language code for the computer. We will describe this conversion or coding process in the next chapter; our focus here is on creating the flowchart or pseudocode steps that define the problem solution.

Flowchart symbols and pseudocode phrases

Flowcharts consist of symbols connected by lines. The symbols are drawn using a plastic **FLOWCHART TEMPLATE**. Each symbol has a different meaning. Figure 10-1 shows the meaning of the flowchart symbols, and gives the corresponding pseudocode phrase.

An example of a whimsical problem to illustrate flowcharting is shown in Figure 10-2. Here we are preparing supper for some friends. Let's define each of the flowcharting symbols given in Figure 10-1, and see how they're used in Figure 10-2.

The **SYSTEM START/TERMINATION SYMBOL** indicates the beginning or end of a program or a subroutine within a program. The commands (usually not part of your actual program) send messages to the computer to get its attention and say that you want to start or stop.

FLOWLINES are used to guide the reader to different parts of the flowchart. Arrows should be drawn on the lines to help the reader follow the flow. Flowlines link the flowchart symbols. Generally flowcharts start in the upper left part of the page, and then move down the page and to the right. The circular **CONNECTORS** link parts of the flowchart on the same page, while the five-sided connectors are used to link parts on different pages. Any connectors leading the reader up the paper or to the left must use arrows to point the way.

The **ANNOTATION SYMBOL** represents comments or remarks that do not affect the actual operation of the program. Annotations explain the meaning of various programming steps (such as how a complicated formula works). Comments aid future programmers in following the program in case revisions need to be made.

FIGURE 10-1.
Flowchart symbols and pseudocode phrases.

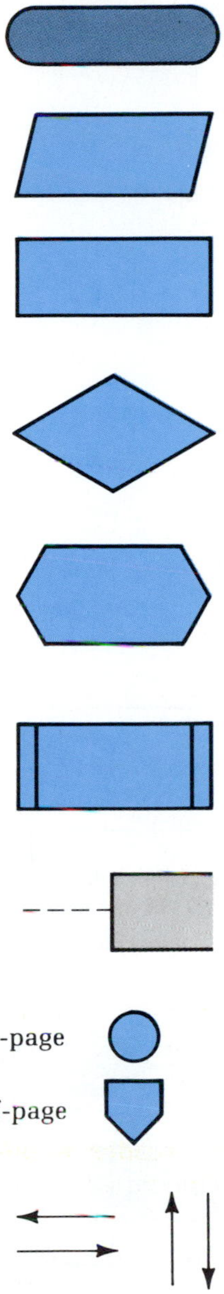

Operation	Flowchart Symbol	Pseudocode Phrase	Meaning
System interrupt (Start, Stop)		START STOP	Notes the beginning or end of a program or subroutine
Input, output		Input, get, read, print, write	All input/output operations
Process		Process, compute, calculate, initialize to a value	Process functions for arithmetic and data manipulation
Decision		IF ... THEN, or IF ... THEN ... ELSE : ENDIF	Decision operations for logic tests and comparisons
Preparation		Prepare, initialize	Prepare the program for later stages, set variables to a starting value (used at the beginning of FOR/NEXT loops in BASIC)
Predefined process		CALL, subroutine	Use of a predefined function: usually a subroutine or library routine
Annotation		Comment, note, remark, annotate	These comments provide guidance to the reader of the program, but do not affect its operation
Connector	on-page off-page	Not used in pseudocode	Connector to other parts of the flowchart on the same or different pages
Flowlines		Not used in pseudocode	Shows the direction of the flow, usual flow is from top to bottom and from left to right

FIGURE 10-2.

The dinner party—flowchart and pseudocode outlining the steps for entertaining your friends.

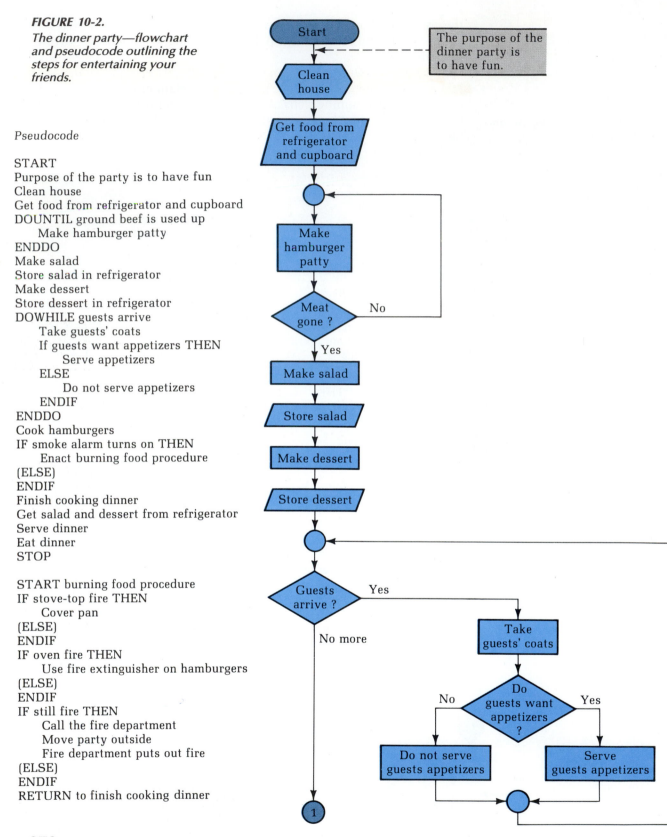

Pseudocode

START
Purpose of the party is to have fun
Clean house
Get food from refrigerator and cupboard
DOUNTIL ground beef is used up
    Make hamburger patty
ENDDO
Make salad
Store salad in refrigerator
Make dessert
Store dessert in refrigerator
DOWHILE guests arrive
    Take guests' coats
    If guests want appetizers THEN
        Serve appetizers
    ELSE
        Do not serve appetizers
    ENDIF
ENDDO
Cook hamburgers
IF smoke alarm turns on THEN
    Enact burning food procedure
(ELSE)
ENDIF
Finish cooking dinner
Get salad and dessert from refrigerator
Serve dinner
Eat dinner
STOP

START burning food procedure
IF stove-top fire THEN
    Cover pan
(ELSE)
ENDIF
IF oven fire THEN
    Use fire extinguisher on hamburgers
(ELSE)
ENDIF
IF still fire THEN
    Call the fire department
    Move party outside
    Fire department puts out fire
(ELSE)
ENDIF
RETURN to finish cooking dinner

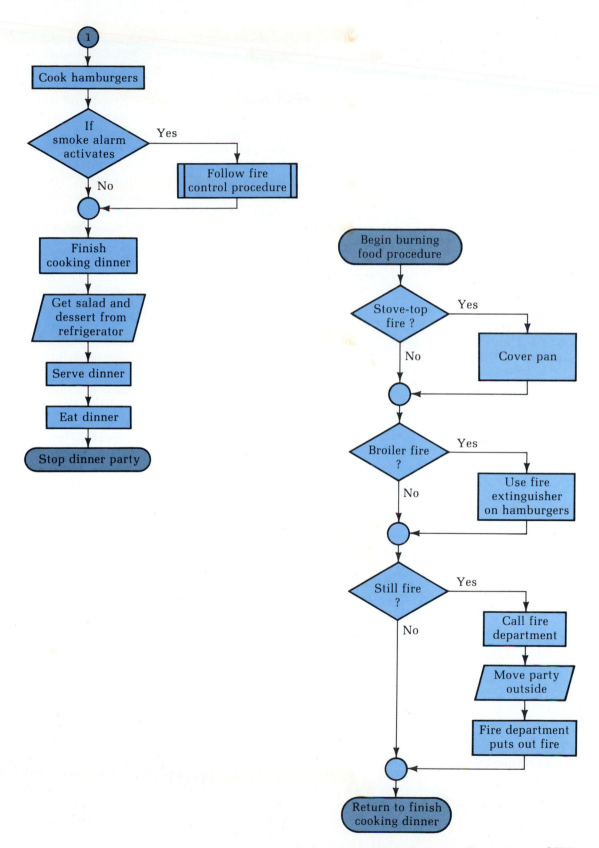

The **PREPARATION SYMBOL** denotes any steps that involve preliminary or preparatory functions. Examples are initializing a variable (setting it equal to zero or some other number), or reserving for the program's use a number of data storage locations in main memory.

The **INPUT/OUTPUT SYMBOL** refers to any input and output operation, such as reading in data from a card reader, keyboard, or magnetic medium. Output can be to a printer, display terminal, magnetic tape or disk system, or some other device. Usually the writing inside the input/output symbol labels the function and piece of equipment involved.

The **PROCESS SYMBOL** represents mathematical computations and data manipulation such as calculations and summarizations. This symbol is also used when constants or variables are assigned specific values.

The **DECISION SYMBOL** denotes choices based upon comparisons. While the process symbol and input/output symbol have only one flowline entering and exiting them, at least two flowlines must exit from a decision symbol. An example of a choice might concern whether to grant credit to a client. The favorable choice would be to grant credit, and the unfavorable choice to deny credit. At some point later in the program module the two exiting lines must converge.

A **PREDEFINED FUNCTION SYMBOL** refers to a prewritten subprogram or subroutine, which is called upon request. The predefined function might be a short series of mathematical formulas, such as calculating interest paid on a loan using different rules (simple versus compound interest). In Figure 10-2's dinner-party example, the predefined function is a fire-control routine to be followed if things get out of hand.

Flowcharts have been used to advantage since the very earliest days of computing. They serve to show what a program that has not yet been written will do, so that a programmer can write code from them. They also make it possible for others to understand a program once it has been written without having to study the code in great depth.

Flowcharts, however, have certain disadvantages. For some people a visual approach to problem solving may be confusing. The display of boxes and lines can be cluttered and difficult to trace, especially if critical steps overlap from one page to the next. Also, when changes are made in a flowchart, the entire chart may need to be redrawn. Software packages that help generate and update flowchart graphics are available, but they can be expensive. Without the appropriate software and hardware, all the work has to be done by hand.

Another problem is a lack of standardization for some flowchart symbols. The process of initialization, such as setting a counter equal to zero, could be flowcharted using two different symbols:

Which symbol you use at work or school basically depends upon the choice of your supervisor or instructor.

Pseudocode was developed to overcome some of the visual clutter associated with flowcharting. Pseudocode is not the same as programming language code (hence the "pseudo" in its name), but rather serves as a general English-like guide to solving the problem. That is its main advantage—it can be written much like one talks, without any complications of templates or graphics. In many working environments, pseudocode is used to the exclusion of flowcharts. If you were literally to key in pseudocode, the resulting "program" would not work on your computer. Pseudocode, like a flowchart, must be converted into real programming-language code for the computer to understand.

The first word in a line of pseudocode is usually an action verb written as an imperative—get, read, print, calculate, and so on. The verb is then followed by a short description of what it is acting upon—for instance, "get" might be followed by "manufacturing parts list."

As with flowcharts questions also arise about the correct way to write pseudocode. The lack of standardization revolves around which words in a line should be capitalized. The command to read a data file might be written "read data file," or "READ DATA FILE." Once a style—for either flow-charting or writing pseudocode—has been selected, stay with that format throughout the entire problem.

Regardless of whether you use flowcharts, pseudocode, or some other design tool, the basic goals of program design are *clarity* and *simplicity*. The purpose of both flowchart and pseudocode is to help you or someone else code a program correctly.

STRUCTURED PROGRAM LOGIC PATTERNS

In structured programming there are three types of logic patterns: sequence, selection, and loop. Any processing that a computer program has to do can be performed with one or more of these patterns. Figure 10-3 shows a flowchart and pseudocode for each of the three patterns.

Sequence

A **SEQUENCE** (Figure 10-3a) is a set of linear steps, to be carried out in the order of their appearance. If you look back at the dinner party example (Figure 10-2), you will see many examples of sequence. The commands for a sequence are always action verbs—read, add, print (or for the dinner party, finish, get, serve, eat).

Selection

SELECTION logic patterns (Figure 10-3b) use comparisons based on decisions or choices to split a program into different paths. Usually the choice is a comparison phrased in the form of a logical test. If the test proves true, then one course of action is followed; if false, another. Such selection patterns are often called **IFTHENELSE** logic steps. The diamond-shaped decision symbol must be labeled showing the direction for both the true (yes) result of the logical test and the false (no) result.

As you can see in the figure, pseudocode indents components of the IFTHENELSE procedure to show their subordinate role. When the choice in a selection is between doing an action and doing nothing, ELSE is placed in parentheses. This convention indicates that no action is intended so the reader will not suspect a line of code has been forgotten. The ENDIF line indicates the end of the IFTHENELSE structure.

Several selection operations are shown in the dinner party example in Figure 10-2. One, for example, involves deciding whether or not to serve the guests appetizers.

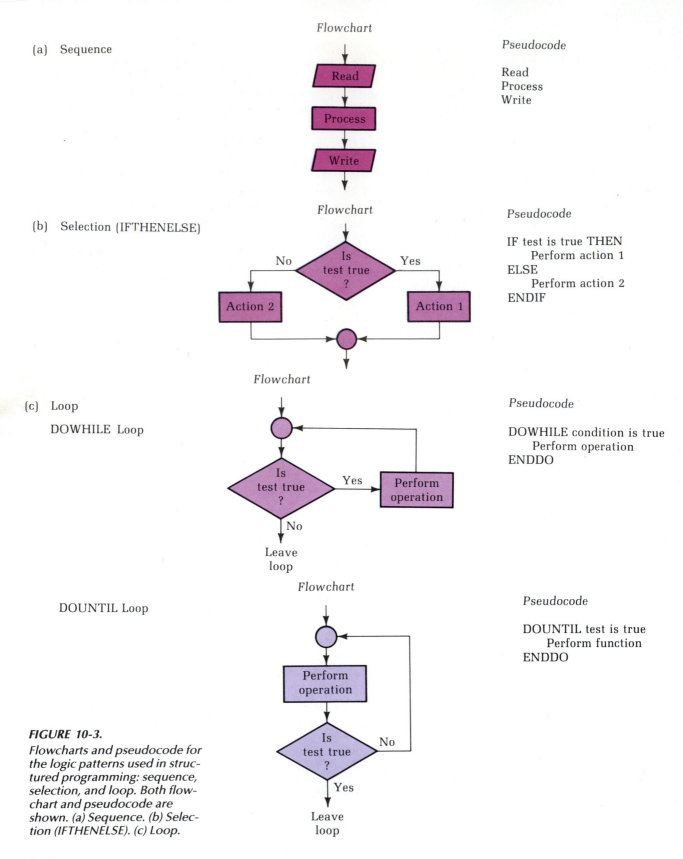

(a) Sequence

Flowchart

Read

Process

Write

Pseudocode

Read
Process
Write

(b) Selection (IFTHENELSE)

Flowchart

No ← Is test true ? → Yes

Action 2   Action 1

Pseudocode

IF test is true THEN
    Perform action 1
ELSE
    Perform action 2
ENDIF

(c) Loop

DOWHILE Loop

Flowchart

Is test true ? — Yes → Perform operation

No

Leave loop

Pseudocode

DOWHILE condition is true
    Perform operation
ENDDO

DOUNTIL Loop

Flowchart

Perform operation

Is test true ? — No

Yes

Leave loop

Pseudocode

DOUNTIL test is true
    Perform function
ENDDO

FIGURE 10-3.
Flowcharts and pseudocode for the logic patterns used in structured programming: sequence, selection, and loop. Both flowchart and pseudocode are shown. (a) Sequence. (b) Selection (IFTHENELSE). (c) Loop.

Loop

A **LOOP** (Figure 10-3c) allows the program repetitively to execute one or a series of steps. Each pass through the loop is called an iteration. There are two major types of loops: DOWHILE and DOUNTIL. A **DOWHILE LOOP** continues as long as a condition is true. In the dinner-party problem a DOWHILE exists while the guests are arriving, where you take the guests' coats and offer appetizers. A **DOUNTIL LOOP** keeps working until the specified condition is met, as shown in the dinner party example for making hamburger patties. In this case you make patties until you run out of meat. As with selection operations, notice how the pseudocode indents the processes performed inside the loop, and closes the loop with an ENDDO statement.

MORE EXAMPLES OF DETAILED DESIGN

Let's spend a few moments longer studying the three structured program logic patterns. Here we work through one example each for sequence, selection, nested selection, and the various kinds of loops.

Sequence—creating an airline ticket

Consider the problem of calculating the total bill for an airline ticket for one customer—a problem that occurs many times each day at Freddy Johnson's Travel Agency. Such a bill calculation demonstrates the sequence control structure. The flowchart pattern and pseudocode are shown in Figure 10-4. Each represents a simple sequence of steps to calculate the bill. The steps are starting, reading the ticket price, performing multiplication operations to calculate the taxes, summing the values, printing the sum, and ending the program.

FIGURE 10-4.

Sequence—creating an airline ticket.

Flowchart

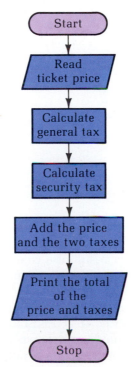

Pseudocode

START
Read the airline ticket price
Calculate the general tax
Calculate the security tax
Add the price and the two taxes
Print the total
STOP

In later examples we will show several commands within the same symbol or on the same line. The two tax calculations in Figure 10-4 could, for instance, be combined into one, "Calculate taxes."

Selection—inspecting the inspectors

The program displayed in Figure 10-5 compares the quality control inspection percentages for the different inspectors who work at Global Electrical Equipment (our multinational manufacturer model organization). Inspectors are supposed to take the correct action no less than 97 percent of the time. Correct actions include approving an appliance that is good and rejecting a defective appliance. An incorrect action would be to approve a bad or defective appliance, or to reject a good appliance.

For this problem we read in the inspector's percentage of correct actions (let's call this value PERCENTAGE). After PERCENTAGE is read in, a test is made. If PERCENTAGE is equal to or greater than 97, then we print a favorable statement (such as "Inspector X is meeting the standard"). If PERCENTAGE is less than 97, then we print an unfavorable comment (such as "Inspector X is not meeting the standard—take action").

FIGURE 10-5.
Selection—inspecting the inspectors.

Flowchart

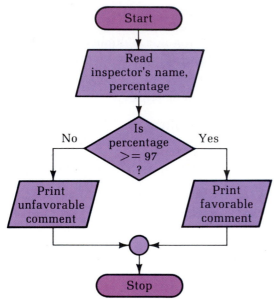

Pseudocode

```
START
Read the inspector's NAME and PERCENTAGE
IF PERCENTAGE >= 97 THEN
        Print favorable comment
ELSE
        Print unfavorable comment
ENDIF
STOP
```

Nested selections—accounts receivable

In many situations multiple selection steps are required to solve a problem. When either result of a comparison leads directly to another comparison, then we have such a situation, known as nested selections.

Let's look at an example. Choosing among several options in the accounts receivable procedures at Paul's House of Electronic Wonders involves nested IFTHENELSE statements. The flowchart and pseudocode for this example are shown in Figure 10-6. The first selection routes the program to a predefined routine (note the use of the predefined process

FIGURE 10-6.
Nested selection—accounts receivable.

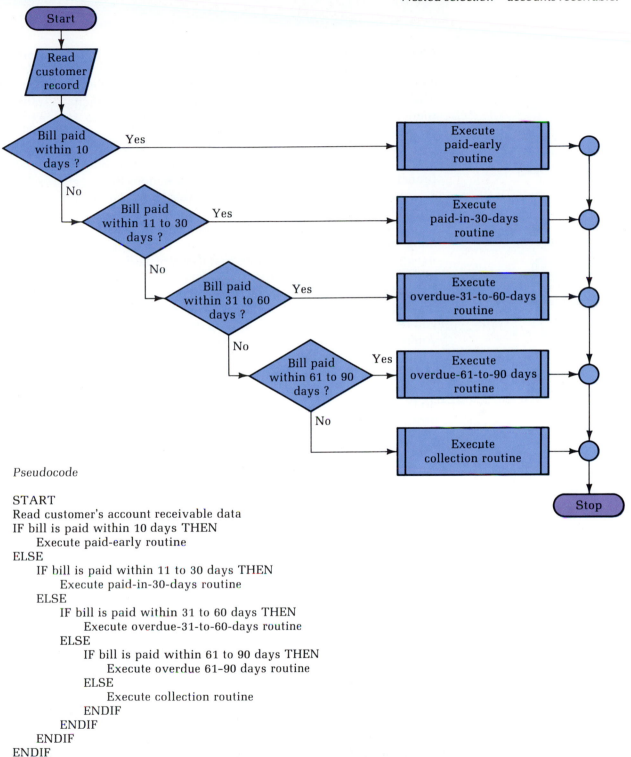

Pseudocode

```
START
Read customer's account receivable data
IF bill is paid within 10 days THEN
    Execute paid-early routine
ELSE
    IF bill is paid within 11 to 30 days THEN
        Execute paid-in-30-days routine
    ELSE
        IF bill is paid within 31 to 60 days THEN
            Execute overdue-31-to-60-days routine
        ELSE
            IF bill is paid within 61 to 90 days THEN
                Execute overdue 61-90 days routine
            ELSE
                Execute collection routine
            ENDIF
        ENDIF
    ENDIF
ENDIF
STOP
```

WHAT'S WRONG WITH GO TO?

One type of logic structure that was once very commonly used is forbidden in structured programming. This structure is the *unconditional branch*, which directs a program to go from one part of itself to another. The mechanism for accomplishing an unconditional branch is a statement telling the program to *go to* some other line of code. Hence the term GO TO.

A branch splits a program into parts. The selection structure, for example, is a type of branch. Selection, however, involves a *conditional* branch—a test determines which of two directions the program will take. An unconditional branch does not involve a test. It simply splits a program abruptly into parts using GO TO statements.

GO TO statements violate three principles of structured programming: modularity, linear program flow, and ease of program maintenance. The problem with them is that they are easily misused to patch together a poorly designed program.

Imagine yourself faced with the problem of designing a program to read a file, process the records, and write the results. It's late at night, you're tired and don't feel like writing the program correctly. Besides, you're changing jobs and won't have to worry about this program when it's time to make program maintenance changes. You've written the flowchart for the first and second process of the records when suddenly you remember that you have to write an intermediate result before you can do the second process. All you do is insert a GO TO statement into the processing step, splitting the process operation. After printing the intermediate step, you need another GO TO to return to the processing operation. One more GO TO branch is required to avoid repeating the intermediate step, and reach the end of the program. The flowlines blur together. The result, as the figure shows, is a tangled mess, like a plate of spaghetti. And in fact programs with an overabundance of GO TOs are often called spaghetti code.

Flowchart

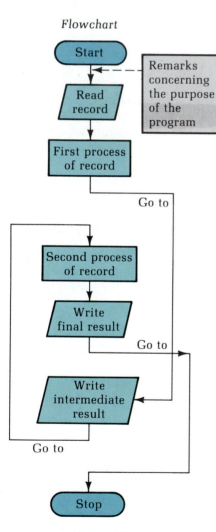

Pseudocode

```
START
Read record
First process of record
GOTO write intermediate record
Second process of record
Write final result
GOTO stop
Write intermediate result
GOTO second process of record
STOP
```

symbol) if the customer paid in ten days or less. If the customer did not pay within ten days, the program goes on to another test. In all the program contains four nested levels of selection steps or tests.

The flowchart for this example is, as you can see, quite cumbersome to design and read. Some people will find that the pseudocode more clearly expresses the nest structure.

DOWHILE loop—reading student records

The example in Figure 10-7 shows in flowchart and pseudocode form a DOWHILE loop for reading a file of student records at Oakriver University and printing the students' addresses. The DOWHILE loop requires that iterations continue *while*, or as long as, a condition tests true. In this case the condition being tested is whether or not the record just read is the last record in the file. When the condition tests false, the loop operation ends.

Before the loop is entered the first student's record is read—an operation often called a "priming" read. The first step within the loop is a test to determine if the record just read is *not* the last one in the file ("end of file" or EOF). If it isn't (the test condition is true), the student's address is printed out and the next record is read for testing. When the test condition is false (the record just read *is* the last one in the file), the program leaves the loop.

Keeping track of loops: counters, trailer values, and flags

A major problem in designing loops is to keep track of them and find a way out. In Figure 10-7, for example, if we didn't know what constituted the end of the file, we would be trapped in the loop.

FIGURE 10-7.
DOWHILE loop—reading student records.

Flowchart

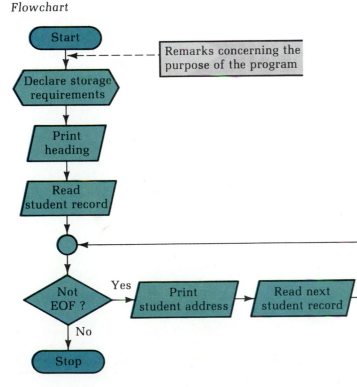

Pseudocode

```
START
Remarks concerning the purpose of the program
Declare storage requirements
Print heading
Read first student record
DOWHILE student record <> End of File (EOF)
    Print student address
    Read the next student record
ENDDO
STOP
```

FIGURE 10-8.
Nested loops—reading test
scores.

Pseudocode

START
Remarks concerning the purpose of this program
Declare storage requirements
Print headings
Initialize row counter to 1
DOUNTIL row counter equals 31
    Read name
    Print name
    Initialize column counter to 1
    DOUNTIL column counter equals 5
        Read the test score
        Print the test score
        Increment column counter by 1
    ENDDO
    Increment row counter by 1
ENDDO
STOP

Flowchart

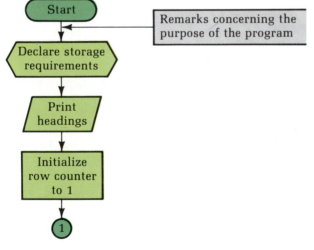

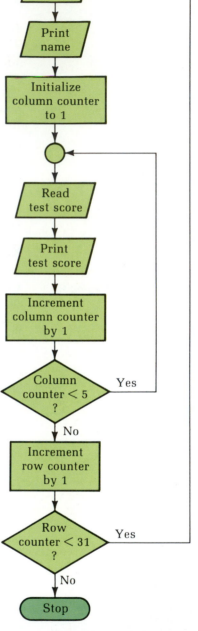

Three devices for keeping track of loop operations are counters, trailer values, and flags. A **COUNTER** keeps track of the number of times a program has met a certain condition. Just before a program enters a loop, the value of the counter is set to a specific value—usually zero or one—by the process of **INITIALIZATION**. Every time the program enters the loop and satisfies the condition the counter is keeping track of—the number of records in the file—for example, the value of the counter increases.

A **TRAILER VALUE** is a nonsense value placed at the end of a data file specifically to mark the end of the file. The program in Figure 10-7, for example, might be instructed to leave the loop when it encountered "NONAME" in the student name field, or "9999999" in the student ID field.

A flag is another way to mark the end of a file. The **END-OF-FILE FLAG** (or **EOF FLAG**) is a kind of switch set at one value—say "0" or "no" for a DOWHILE loop—before the loop starts. When the program encounters the end of the file, the switch changes value—to "1" or "yes"—and the program leaves the loop.

DOUNTIL loops—student test grades

A DOUNTIL loop continues repeating some operation *until* a test is true. When the test is true, we exit from the loop. There are certain times when this technique is quite handy.

Figure 10-8 shows a nested DOUNTIL loop controlled by counters to read four test scores for each of 30 Oakriver University students. The program would go on to average each student's four test scores to give a grade, but for simplicity's sake we omit that part of the program. For each student we use a "row" of data with four columns, one for each test. For 30 students we therefore have a 30-row, four-column set of data. On paper we would record the data as a rows-and-columns chart. Computer languages can follow some conventions to make data stored in a computer's memory seem like such a chart—do not worry about the details.

The point of Figure 10-8 is the nested loop structure. The inner loop reads the scores for one student into the columns of one row, and then the outer loop advances to the next student when one student's row is full. The inner loop is shown on the flowchart by the shorter flowline on the right, and the pseudocode that is indented. For simplicity, in the flowcharting diagram looping operations are listed down the page.

Nested loop operations are used in many business applications. One notable example is their use on electronic spreadsheets (popular with microcomputer users) where rows and columns of financial figures can be quickly manipulated to show the results in company profits or other areas of interest.

PUTTING THE DETAILED PLAN INTO ACTION

Once we have defined the logic patterns or combination of patterns we will need in our program, and described them in a flowchart or pseudocode, we have a detailed plan of what the program should be. So far as we can tell, the resulting program will solve the problem that we set out to solve.

Now we are ready to put the detailed plan into action. Putting the plan into action involves three steps: (1) coding the program, (2) correcting errors, (3) documenting the program.

If you decide to enter a career in information systems and look for a job, this is probably the first job you will look for. More people work as application programmers than at any other position in the computer field. It is a stepping-stone to many career opportunities in the field.

The position of application programmer, however, is by no means at the bottom of the pyramid. To become an application programmer, you need to demonstrate technical aptitude (often determined in a test or technical interview) and almost always must have a two-year or four-year college degree or post-high school technical training involving computers. What companies seek in addition is experience (often so that new hirees can help them out of whatever jam they're in right away). If you have programming experience—even in the summer, even unpaid, even for a brief period—that can help separate you from the pack.

It may come as a surprise that interpersonal skills are also sought by organizations hiring application programmers. Sure, application programmers spend most of their time designing and coding programs to run on a machine, but these days they are generally organized into teams that stress cooperation, and the application programmer who shows potential can move quickly up the organizational pyramid. Typical next rungs on the ladder are programmer analyst and systems analyst—with an ever-increasing proportion of management responsibility at each level.

What would you do as an application programmer? As an entry-level person, you probably would help someone else with minor programming tasks until you got to know the particular system. You might be asked, for instance, to modify a simple working program that is in need of updating to meet new user needs. Eventually, perhaps after a few months, you would be asked to write a program from scratch. Since your program would have to relate to others in existence or preparation, and since you were new, in all likelihood a senior-level application programmer, programmer analyst, or systems analyst would design the program for you. From the HIPO diagram or other overview that this person provides, you would design and code the program, test it, write the documentation, and get it working perfectly.

To follow our first-job scenario, once this simple program works, you would be asked to work on a larger, more important one. Soon you would take a hand in the design yourself, perhaps proposing a design for review at programming team meetings. Certainly by this time—about a year after joining the firm—you would notice that you are no longer a newcomer, since you know the system. In this dynamic, ever-changing environment—where the quantity of work to be done probably exceeds the personnel on hand to do it, and the stakes for the organization are high, as is job turnover—you have every opportunity for advancement. Technical ability, strength in working on a team and communicating with others, a general businesslike attitude, and commitment to the organization—none of this would be overlooked by a competent superior. You would receive ever more responsibility. For instance, in large organizations it is typical for newcomers to be placed on teams involving batch-processing programs. It is considered something of a plum, after you have shown your competence with the batch system, to get moved to a project designing on-line programs.

However a particular scenario may vary from our generalized story, one thing is certain: application programmers rarely gather cobwebs. They are rewarded with high salaries, promotion, new responsibilities, and every chance to move upward.

To code the program you translate the flowchart or pseudocode instructions into specific computer programming language statements. The codes used depend upon the programming language. Chapter 11 will explore how to write code in various languages. For now we'll focus on correcting errors—known as debugging—and on documenting the program.

DEBUGGING PROCEDURES

Basic techniques

Debugging programs can take as long as the rest of the program design stages put together. There are three major debugging methods: desk-checking, tracing, and dumping.

DESK-CHECKING can be done both before and after a program is run on the computer. Typically the programmer sits down with a copy of the failed program and its output, and attempts to correct any errors that may have occurred. Generated with the failed program is an error report, which will tell on what line, and sometimes even in what column, an error was detected. The programmer makes repeated passes trying to correct the mistakes. Sometimes after several tries the programmer cannot find the error. In this case another programmer can take a look at the program. It is astounding sometimes how easy it is for someone else to look at your program and quickly spot that troublesome error. Desk-checking is a bit like writing a second draft of a term paper: you correct major and minor errors from the first draft, and might discuss it with a friend to gain valuable criticism.

Today most people write programs in an interactive environment. Much of your desk-checking in an interactive environment will not be done at a desk at all, but at a terminal, with the aid of the computer itself. Some call this "screen-checking." A more formal type of desk-checking also occurs in the structured walkthrough (discussed in Chapter 9).

TRACING, another aid to debugging, uses a special system program to trace the flow of your application program from step to step. Normally when a program is executed, only output is printed. Tracing lets you know what's happening in your program as each line of output is generated. The term for running a program in the tracing mode is often abbreviated as TRON, for "trace on." TRON, you may recall, was the title of a popular movie in which a programmer was physically placed into the program to trace an error in the main operating system.

Another debugging aid is the **DUMP**, which prints the storage contents of the central processing unit. With a dump a programmer can see what was actually stored in various locations, and thereby puzzle out what may have gone wrong with the program. Reading a dump is much more difficult than reading a trace.

Checkpoints to guide the debugging process

As an aid to debugging, programming checkpoints along the way can help guide our progress. Four checkpoints will serve our needs: order, content, syntax, and logic. Let's use a nonprogramming example and apply these steps to writing a term paper.

An **ORDER CHECK** determines whether the problem-solving steps are arranged in the right sequence. In writing a term paper you begin with an introduction, and then move linearly to the main body of the paper, and

THE KISS THEORY OF PROGRAMMING

Assume that your programming assignment is coming due next week. How can you get it finished and keep your wits? Some irreverent hints are in order.

We can observe in the management of many organizations the maxim, "Keep It Simple, Stupid," or KISS for short. Structured programming methods help us in attaining this goal of simplicity. Let's review some helpful hints:

- *Allow yourself plenty of time. Even a small program may take several hours to complete. Most computer center terminal rooms get very crowded and noisy when hordes of people rush to complete projects.*

- *Do not code or flowchart in ink. You're going to change your program and flowchart several times before the project is done. Do not consider a flowchart as cast in stone. There is a two-way feedback process, where changes in the program will lead to changes in the flowchart; and changes in the flowcharts, to changes in the program.*

- *Use variable names that make sense. If using names with a single letter, use the first letter of the particular variable, such as "G" for "gross tax." Another technique is to use letters consecutively for variables— A, B, C, and so on. If you use words for variable names, limit them to about six characters and make them memory-jogging. Don't forget to spell them right as well as to use discretion, as a potential employer may want to see your program someday.*

- *Break the problem into small pieces: initialization, input, process, output, and termination. Any program can be reduced to those five parts. Each part can be flowcharted, or expressed in pseudocode, on a separate sheet of paper to give you enough room. Then in your final draft, you can combine the segments. When coding your program you can follow the same process. Do not worry about fancy style at the beginning—just get the program to work, and then make it pretty.*

- *Write out your program before you sit down at the keyboard. The input process will go easier, and others in the computer center waiting to use the terminal won't glare at you as you slowly and painfully compose the first draft of your program one character at a time.*

- *Most problems assigned to you use test data with easy-to-find answers. You can use a hand calculator to check the results.*

- *Pretend that you are a piece of data yourself and walk your way through each step of the flowchart or pseudocode and program.*

- *Add extra print lines in various parts of your program to display the intermediate steps of the processing. This will aid in detecting errors. Once your program runs successfully, you can drop these extra lines. For example, when taking an average of some numbers, you should print a running total of the values as well as the final average. The printed running totals can be deleted from the final program run.*

■ *Take some time to learn the keyboard. Keyboards are similar to, yet different from, traditional typewriters in a number of ways. Many people—even good typists—feel nervous when using a keyboard rather than a typewriter for the first few times. Keyboards are easier to use than typewriters. So don't worry if you are not a perfect typist because corrections are easier to make.*

finally proceed to the summary. With a computer program a linear sequence is also followed: input, processing, and ouput. And within each of these areas, tasks should be executed in order, to avoid unnecessary skipping around. For example, the calculation of a subtotal should appear earlier in the program than the calculation of the total.

A **CONTENT CHECK** determines if the program solves all the parts of the problem it is supposed to solve. This is comparable to making sure you covered all the relevant points in your term paper. The content of the program should match whatever was asked for in the initial request.

A **SYNTAX CHECK** determines if the grammatical style and spelling in the program are correct. Syntax refers to the rules of proper grammar for any language. When writing your term paper it is improper to use double negatives. In computer languages similar rules exist, and programs will not run unless these rules are followed to the letter.

A **LOGIC CHECK** determines whether or not the program produces reasonable results. In writing a term paper you also need to check for logical consistencies in your arguments. Building effective logic checks is a skill that can begin early in the programming process. Logic errors occur when grammatically correct program steps are misused; they might, for example, be executed out of their proper order. Test data are created and the program run with them, in an attempt to show up any logical errors in the program.

In the course of developing a successful program, the four checkpoints can be repeated as needed, and need not be done in the order presented above. For instance, we might begin with a content check to see if we have addressed all parts of a problem, proceed with an order check to make sure the program itself is arranged in the right sequence, and then do a careful statement-by-statement syntax check. Then we could run the program, which would probably reveal more syntax errors and necessitate another syntax check. Once we got the program running, we might perform a logic test by running the program with extreme data values to attempt to make it fail. After all our goal is not a program that works right sometimes, but one that works right all the time.

PROGRAM DOCUMENTATION

PROGRAM DOCUMENTATION consists of manuals, display screens, and perhaps audiovisual materials that tell users how to use the program, operators how to run it, and programmers how to change it. Explanatory material present in the program itself, and on screens that the program displays, is considered part of the documentation.

Documentation should be written in a clear, simple style understandable to the average user, operator, or programmer. It should contain as little jargon as possible; the best documentation contains none whatsoever. Documentation should be written while the program is being developed. When changes are made in a program, the documentation for the program should be reviewed, and updated where necessary.

Effective writing is always done with the audience in mind. Program documentation also must consider its audience. Users, operators, and programmers need to know different things about a program, and separate documentation must be prepared for each group. This can mean three separate manuals; three different parts of the same manual; or other combinations, such as screen displays for users, a run manual for operators, and HIPO diagrams and pseudocode for programmers.

User-oriented documentation

In the distant past of electronic computing, documentation was oriented toward aiding programmers and other members of an information system staff, and users were left to fend for themselves. Users have since come to demand good documentation, a demand reinforced by management practices.

USER-ORIENTED DOCUMENTATION includes those written documents, and screen displays, that assist the user in exploiting the benefits of the program. Written materials are contained in a manual to that effect. Screen displays are built into the program itself. What the user needs to know is how to run or interact with the program, what the program can do, and what steps to take if something goes wrong.

The description of how to run the program concerns hardware requirements, system software needed to support the program, and instructions showing how to get the program started. Showing what the program will do focuses on leading the user through the series of steps for initiating the program, using it for processing, and ending the processing session. Narratives or descriptive stories of these steps, as well as examples, are helpful. As we will see in Chapter 12, packaged software for such areas as spreadsheets and word processing often includes interactive tutorials to teach you how to use the software package. In fact successful sales of packaged software depend upon clearly written documents for the user.

Clear explanations of what to do if you have a problem is another critical feature of good documentation. For example, what happens if you accidentally hit the wrong key when typing in data? How can you correct the error? The documentation should help you with these problems.

Operator-oriented documentation

Programs that run on mainframes and minicomputers require documentation for the people who will operate the programs. The operator is distinct from the user, who may sit at a terminal thousands of miles away from the computer. OPERATOR-ORIENTED DOCUMENTATION is generally in the form of a run manual kept near the computer console. It should tell how to run the program—the magnetic tapes or removable disks that must be mounted, the peripherals that need to be online, the type of paper for the printer, and similar considerations.

Time moves forward, and corporations grow. And to handle this growth, management turns to increasingly sophisticated technology. Networks are expanded, batch systems go online. Yet as the corporate engine is revved for the surge ahead, its power is restrained by application programs that are obsolete.

Obsolescence occurs when programs written for outmoded equipment or for old applications begin to drag on the organization, rather than pull it forward. According to Roger Martin, computer scientist at National Bureau of Standards (NBS), Washington, your systems could be losing punch if they're more than five years old, if their failure rate is growing, and if it takes longer than ever to repair failures. Users will voice complaints more loudly, and the system will grow overly complex as patches are made to code. Also, programmers will have more and more trouble maintaining the system.

Software can grow old overnight, but it doesn't have to become obsolete. Planning for obsolescence—recognizing each application's limited life cycle and budgeting for its replacement, just as you do for office equipment—prevents aged systems from crippling operations.

Carol Houtz, software branch chief of the General Services Administration's Software Management Center, is vitally interested in preventing application obsolescence. Her branch manages over $100 million a year in contracts to modernize software paid for by tax dollars.

For example, the Social Security Administration is modernizing 4,000 to 6,000 programs totaling over 5 million lines of Cobol code, says Houtz. First, the code will be made uniform. Next it will be upgraded to Cobol 74 and restructured.

At first, Houtz says, users wanted to throw out the old code, which they said was confusing. But as soon as it was realigned, "50 percent of the users understood it. Simple data standardizations and minimal improvements gain increasing user acceptance for the software, until finally the end user can make functional decisions for minor design modifications."

Houtz suggests these steps to deal with obsolete applications:

- *Develop improvement recommendations.*
- *Take inventory of existing programs.*
- *Catalog user problems.*
- *Solicit recommended solutions.*
- *Match organization goals and objectives to application functionality.*

Houtz also recommends a "software improvement plan" that includes these major elements:

- *Plan the evolution of your system to build on its investment.*
- *Provide planned, incremental enhancements to decrease risk and management exposure.*
- *Include the highest possible management levels in planning with progress feedback originating at the lowest levels of the user and programmer organizations.*
- *Develop a pilot project using the "software-improvement plan."*
- *Publish the specifications of the improvement.*
- *Incorporate a software-engineering methodology in your maintenance efforts.*

Source: Reprinted from *Computer Decisions*, "Software: Slowing Time's March," by Don Shafer, vol. 17, #2, January 29, 1985, pp. 108–115. Copyright © 1985 Hayden Publishing Company.

The operator also needs to know what to do if the program is obviously running incorrectly. Operators usually have no way of telling if the program is giving incorrect information as output, but if they see a batch program taking ten times as long as usual to run, or printing one character on each page of output, they know something is amiss and need to be told how to handle it. In large information-processing centers, the run manual often includes the work and home telephone numbers of the programmer who will be on call to handle problems 24 hours a day.

The run manual should also tell the operator to whom to distribute the output, and give security and other information that the operator needs to know concerning the program and its output. With microcomputers the user and operator are almost always the same person, and hence one combined set of documentation for using and running the program is prepared.

Programmer-oriented documentation

PROGRAMMER-ORIENTED DOCUMENTATION focuses on how to maintain and modify the program. Today most programs that users work with are protected against unauthorized people changing the actual program. Users normally do not even see the computer code in which the program was written. For example, the actual program that operates a check-writing procedure at a corporation would not be available to the people using the program to write the checks. To access the actual program the programmer must know the security codes. In some cases a programmer would only have access to a specific module being modified.

Documentation for programmers responsible for maintaining and changing a program consists of the results of the structured design and programming effort: visual table of contents, HIPO diagrams, flowcharts, and pseudocode. Also included may be complete sample runs, program run times, and program listings. In addition programmers have access to user and operator documentation.

WRAP-UP

THE HONOR ROLL FLOWCHART AND PSEUDOCODE

At the start of the chapter we left Tom Lee in the act of coding the honor roll portion of the grades program afresh, from a flowchart of his own design. The flowchart had in turn been prepared using the HIPO diagram that Alice Smith had drawn.

Figure 10-9 shows the flowchart that Tom drew for the program. The second part of Figure 10-9 shows the equivalent pseudocode. The presentation here is something of a simplification, since in reality the modules involved in honor roll creation are part of the much larger grades program. Here we show them on their own, in order to focus on the logic for the actual honor roll creation.

All three of the logic structures permitted by structured programming are illustrated. In this case the structures appear as fol-

Pseudocode

START
Remarks concerning the purpose of this program
Declare the storage requirements
Initialize the total to 0
Print headings
Read the first student record
DOWHILE student record <> EOF
    IF grade point average > = 3.50 THEN
        Print student name, and GPA
        Add 1 to total
    (ELSE)
    ENDIF
    Read next student grade record
ENDDO
Print total number of honor roll students
STOP

FIGURE 10-9.

Flowchart and pseudocode for the Oakriver honor-roll program.

Flowchart

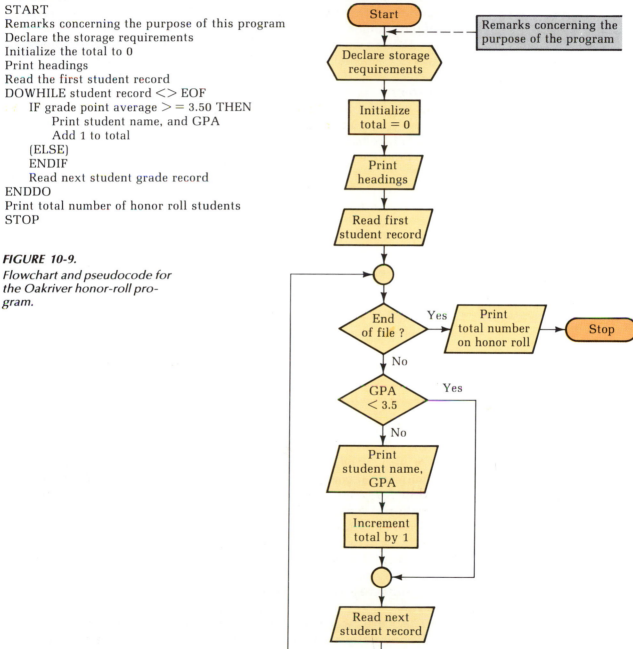

Sometimes we do not know the exact amount of storage required, but we can estimate it. Next we print the heading for the report and initialize the counter that will keep track of the total number of students on the honor roll to 0.

The DOWHILE loop follows. It contains the major input, processing, and ouput steps of the program. The processing steps use an IFTHENELSE structure. If a student's grade-point average is greater than or equal to 3.5 on a scale of 0 to 4, then the student's name and grade-point average are printed. In addition the counter keeps track of the total number of students who made the honor roll.

When a student's grade-point average is below the required level (the "ELSE" case), nothing is printed, and the counter is not incremented. The DOWHILE loop ends after the last student record is processed.

After the program leaves the loop, a short sequence prints the closing part of the report, and the program ends. In the next chapter we will see how Tom handles the actual computer code for the honor roll program.

SUMMARY

- Flowcharts and pseudocode are tools for defining the internal logic of a program or program module.
- Flowcharts consist of symbols joined by flowlines and connectors. Standard flowchart symbols (available on flowchart templates) include system start/termination, annotation, preparation, input/output, process, decision, and predefined function.
- Pseudocode expresses program steps with English-like expressions. The first word in a line of pseudocode is usually an action verb such as get, read, or print. This is followed by a short description of what the verb is to act upon.
- Whether you use flowcharts, pseudocode, or some other design tool, the goals of program design are clarity and simplicity.
- In structured programming there are only three types of logic patterns: sequence, selection, and loop. Any processing that a computer program has to do can be performed with one or more of these patterns. A sequence is a set of linear steps that are carried out in the order of their appearance. Selection, or IFTHENELSE, uses comparisons based on decisions or choices to split a program into different paths. A loop allows a program repetitively to execute one or more steps. Loops come in two varieties: DOWHILE, which iterate while a condition is true; and DOUNTIL, which iterate until a condition is true.
- There are three devices for keeping track of the operations within a loop: counters, trailer values, and end-of-file (EOF) flags. Initialization of counters and flags must be done before a loop begins.

- *Once we have defined the logic patterns or combination of patterns we will need in a program, and described them in a flowchart or pseudocode, we have a detail plan of the program that can be put into action. Putting the detail plan into action involves coding the program (the topic of Chapter 11), correcting errors, and documenting the program.*

- *Debugging can take as long as the rest of the program design stages put together. Three major debugging methods are desk-checking, tracing, and dumps. In desk-checking the programmer sits down with a copy of a failed program and its output, and attempts to correct any errors. Tracing uses a special system program to trace the flow of an application program in detail. A dump prints the storage contents of the central processing unit, showing what has been stored in any locations of interest.*

- *Four checkpoints can help smooth the task of debugging. An order check determines if the steps in the program are arranged in the right sequence. A content check determines if the program solves all the parts of the problem that it was meant to. A syntax check determines if the grammatical style and spelling in the program are correct. Finally, a logic check determines whether or not the program produces reasonable results. The four checkpoints can be repeated as needed, and need not be met in any particular order.*

- *Program documentation consists of manuals, screen displays, and perhaps audiovisual materials telling users how to use the program, operators how to run it, and programmers how to change it. Documentation must be written with the audience in mind, and in a clear and simple writing style. Documentation is created while the program is being developed. When the program is changed, documentation must also be reviewed, and changed where necessary.*

KEY TERMS

These are the key terms in the order in which they appear in the chapter.

OBJECTIVE QUESTIONS

TRUE/FALSE: *Put the letter T or F on the line before the question.*

_____ 1. Pseudocode is a method for outlining program logic in a visual form with flowlines and a variety of visual symbols.

_____ 2. The selection logic structure is often called IFTHENELSE.

_____ 3. A DOWHILE loop continues as long as a condition is false.

_____ 4. The ENDIF statement in pseudocode is used to close a loop.

_____ 5. The (ELSE) statement in pseudocode means nothing is to be performed during the ELSE part of an IFTHENELSE operation.

_____ 6. A DOUNTIL loop continues as long as the test condition is false.

_____ 7. A counter used for loop control accumulates the number of the record containing the trailer value.

_____ 8. Desk-checking is the least common type of debugging.

_____ 9. A syntax check is used to detect logical errors in a program.

MULTIPLE CHOICE: *Put the letter of the correct answer on the line before the question.*

_____ 1. Which of the following would not be represented by a decision symbol in a flowchart?
(a) Selection.   (c) DOWHILE loop.
(b) Sequence.   (d) DOUNTIL loop.

_____ 2. What symbol is used to represent program termination?

(a)   (c)

(b) 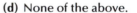   (d) None of the above.

_____ 3. With a DOWHILE loop
(a) the loop operation continues while a condition is false.
(b) it is possible never to enter the loop if the first test result is false.
(c) a trailer value rather than a counter must be used as a loop control method.
(d) all of the above.

_____ 4. A check writing program incorrectly writes a check for $ 0.00 instead of $4,500.00. This type of error would be detected during a(n):
(a) order check.   (c) syntax check.
(b) content check.   (d) logic check.

_____ 5. The KISS theory of programming
(a) argues for complex solutions whenever possible.
(b) argues for simple solutions whenever possible.
(c) requires the use of DOUNTIL rather than DOWHILE loops.
(d) both (b) and (c) are correct.

FILL IN THE BLANK: *Write the correct word or words in the blank to complete the sentence.*

_____ 1. A DOUNTIL loop continues as long as a condition is _____.

_____ 2. In a nested loop the inner loop iterates _____ than the outer loop.

_____ 3. Three methods: _____, _____, and _____, are used for loop control.

_____ 4. A _____ is a listing of a program in main memory.

_____ 5. The _____ symbol is used for predefined functions.

6. A _____ check would show if a square root operation was performed instead of a squaring function.

7. The _____ is not used in structured programming.

8. A decision symbol requires at least _____ flowlines exiting from it.

9. The _____ line in pseudocode shows the end of a loop.

10. During execution a _____ for a BASIC program lists the line numbers and the normal output.

SHORT ANSWER QUESTIONS

When answering these questions think of concrete examples to illustrate your points.

1. Describe the three types of logic operations.
2. What purpose do nesting operations serve?
3. How do DOWHILE and DOUNTIL loops differ?
4. What four checks are used in debugging?
5. What is the KISS theory of programming?
6. Why are GOTOs (unconditional branches) not recommended?
7. What is the difference between a dump and a trace?
8. How does a trailer value work?

PROGRAM DESIGN EXERCISES

Write a flowchart and pseudocode to solve the following programming problems:

1. Oakriver University's president M. C. Laude needs to calculate the percentage of students who are registered as business majors. Design a program to solve his problem. There are 22,000 students, and 4000 of them are business majors.

2. Susan Paul needs to know the total of the commissions earned by her salespeople for the past month. Design a program to solve her problem and use the data below to test your design.

Tom Alberts	$2234
Harry Jones	$3716
Leon Klaus	$2452
Milt Weiss	$2345
Joe Topaz	$1901

3. Dr. Clara Chips wants to give an award to those students who earned "A"s (90 percent) in her introductory information systems class. Design a program to determine who receives an award and use the data below to test your design.

Student name	Numeric grade	Letter grade
Eugene Alton	89	B
John Burton	78	C
Lynne Davis	70	C
Mike Franks	90	A
Cindy Smith	91	A

4. Myrtle, owner of Myrtle's Burgers, needs a program to calculate a 6 percent sales tax on items purchased at her restaurant. Each item and its cost, the subtotal, tax, and grand total must be printed out. Design a program to solve her problem and test the solution using the following order of one of each item:

1 Super Burger @ $ 1.79
2 Large Fries @ $0.79
3 Small Shake @ $0.89

CHAPTER 11

PROGRAMMING LANGUAGES: A COMPARISON

- **CHOOSING APPROPRIATE LANGUAGES**
  SPEAKING THE COMPUTER'S LANGUAGE
  All those languages: a programmer's Tower of Babel /
  Information-system elements and language selection / How computer
  languages differ
  - **CAREER BOX: Programmer Analyst**
  LOW-LEVEL LANGUAGES FOR HARDY PROGRAMMERS
  Machine language / Assembly language
  HIGH-LEVEL LANGUAGES
  BASIC / Pascal / COBOL / FORTRAN / Additional high-level
  languages
  VERY-HIGH-LEVEL LANGUAGES
  RPG / Simulation languages / List-processing languages / Toward
  natural languages /
  - **CASE IN POINT: Branches of the AI Tree**
  - **WRAP-UP: Oakriver University Picks Some Languages**

After studying this chapter you should understand the
following:
- The differences among low-level, high-level, and very-high-level
  programming languages.
- Some of the main characteristics that can be used to describe
  and compare programming languages.
- The key features of the four main high-level languages: BASIC,
  Pascal, COBOL, and FORTRAN.
- Why very-high-level languages point the way toward the
  future.

The Oakriver University campus was flooded with sun this crisp October day. Jasper Thomas, a physicist, crossed the campus toward the information-processing center. It was a Wednesday afternoon, when Thomas and most other people did not have scheduled lectures. He spotted Ralph Grosse on an adjacent path and joined him. Grosse was a teacher in the foreign languages program.

"It's a shame to have to go indoors now," Ralph said. "I considered holding my last French class outside today."

"If the University Computer Users Committee met outside, nothing would get done," Jasper said.

"Is anything getting done?" Ralph asked.

The two teachers entered the information-processing center and found the vacant classroom where the University Computer Users Committee had assembled. In a few minutes the committee chairperson, Miguel Abreu, announced that this was the first of three meetings about software, and then introduced Marty Castillo, an information-processing staff member.

Marty stood up and turned to the first of some flip charts at the front of the room. "Today's topic is language," Marty said. "Computer language. As you can see from this simplified diagram, a computer language stands between you and the machine." The chart showed a drawing of a person, a drawing of a computer, and a box labeled "language" in between.

"The day will probably come quite soon when you can talk to the computer in your own language and it will do what you say," Marty said. "For now, though, we have to speak the computer's language."

In the back of the room, Jasper whispered to Ralph: "Languages—that's your area."

"These languages have nothing to do with mine," Ralph said. "I teach French and Rumanian—computer languages are gobbledygook. Binary and hexadecimal and all sorts of dreadful stuff."

"Let me apologize for restating the familiar to those of you who already know a lot about computer languages," Marty said. "It'll be new to some." Marty smiled. "Like me. I've been programming for ten years and only know a handful of languages. And new ones are being invented all the time."

"How many computer languages are there?" Jasper asked.

"There are dozens of major computer languages," Marty said.

"Why do we have to go through a selection process?" Ralph asked. "Can't we just have them all?"

Several people around the room laughed. "That's a good question," Marty said. "But if we had all the languages, that would be like placing our new computer in the General Assembly at the United Nations. Everyone in the room could speak a different language to the computer—but they could not speak to one another."

Alice Smith—the systems analyst in charge of the honor-roll problem—cut in. "There are some practical constraints, too," she said. "Certain languages are good for solving scientific problems, and some are pretty useless at it. Several languages are specially designed for doing things like moving data around and printing reports, which the administration needs plenty of. Using a language unsuited to a particular application ends up costing a fortune in the time it takes to write the program as well as the time it takes to run it over and over again."

"Alice has given several of the main reasons for choosing one particular computer language over another," Marty said. "Another consideration is training—it is not practical to teach students 30 different languages. Nor can experienced programmers be found to handle certain languages. In fact some languages are widely used by colleges and other organizations, while others are as rare as aardvarks."

"So how many can we choose?" Ralph asked.

"The committee can choose as many as necessary to meet the diverse needs of the people in this room," Marty said. "That might be six languages, say, or it might be more."

"Some of us have had fairly limited exposure to computers," Jasper said. "How on earth should we know which languages to pick?"

"Ah!" Marty said. "That is what I will tell you. By considering these points." Marty flipped to a chart that ranked languages with respect to ten different attributes. He went on to explain each. This chapter will do the same.

SPEAKING THE COMPUTER'S LANGUAGE

ALL THOSE LANGUAGES: A PROGRAMMER'S TOWER OF BABEL

Like the builders of the biblical Tower of Babel, we seem stricken by a multitude of different programming languages. There are dozens of computer languages and dialects. Certainly we cannot review them all here. Instead we will focus on just a few, and approach them from several perspectives that can be used for any language.

Proximity to the machine

One useful way to categorize a computer language is by how much attention you must pay to the workings of the computer when you program in the language. With a low-level language you pay the most attention. With high- and very-high-level languages you pay less.

LOW-LEVEL LANGUAGES are so-named because they are very close to the computer itself. Each instruction of a low-level language corresponds to an instruction for a particular computer. The programmer has to be familiar with the inner workings of the computer, as well as with the procedures or algorithms used to solve the problem. The term "low level" is actually somewhat misleading, since programming in these languages requires a *high level of skill.*

HIGH-LEVEL LANGUAGES use English-like statements and mathematical symbols. Each instruction of a high-level language is converted by software into sequences of actual computer instructions. Using a high-level language is easier than using a low-level language; the programmer is less concerned about the inner workings of the computer, and can spend more time developing the actual problem solution. We will concentrate on four high-level languages: BASIC, Pascal, COBOL, and FORTRAN. In addition the languages APL, Ada, C, and PL/1 will be discussed briefly.

VERY-HIGH-LEVEL LANGUAGES move even further away than high-level languages away from the inner workings of the computer. Very-high-level languages are the easiest of all to learn. With both low-level and high-level languages, the concern of a programmer is describing *how* the computer is to solve the problem. With a very-high-level language, in contrast, we tell the computer *what* it should do, and let the software responsible for interpreting the very-high-level language worry about how the computer will do it. The key drawback of very-high-level languages is that they are aimed at a fairly narrow range of applications—such as generating reports—and are limited beyond that range. High-level languages have a far wider range of applications, and low-level languages can do anything at all that the computer can.

Several very-high-level languages are of interest to us in this chapter: report generators, simulation languages, and list-processing languages.

Which came first

Historically the first computer languages to be developed were low-level languages. Next came high-level languages oriented toward batch processing. Later came the rise of high-level languages used for interactive processing, and of very-high-level languages used for batch or interactive processing. Today all three levels of languages are still in use. Interactive programs can be written in any level of language. In general the higher the language level, the easier the language is for the problem-solver to use.

Language translation

Languages are translated into machine instructions by system programs known as compilers or interpreters. That is, if you write a program in COBOL, a system program designed for the purpose translates the COBOL language statements in your program into the machine instructions the computer demands. Chapter 13 will describe such system software.

The main thing to grasp now is that the rules of a language are built into the system program that translates it. For instance, the programmers who wrote the system programs that translate the high-level language FORTRAN, decided that ".GE." had to be used to state the condition of greater than or equal to. Thus a programmer using FORTRAN must use ".GE." to express this condition or the program won't work.

INFORMATION-SYSTEM ELEMENTS AND LANGUAGE SELECTION

Software selection does not occur in a vacuum. The selection of the programming languages that an information system will use depends upon the existing hardware, people, rules, programs, and data in an information system. Usually the individual programmer has little say about what languages are picked. However, managers in businesses and other organizations need to know something about assessing and comparing languages in order to make informed selections.

All five information system elements must be taken into account to ensure the selection of languages to suit an organization's needs best. In terms of *people* the types of reports or output desired by users may lead to selecting one language over another. The programming languages that the programmers on the information-system staff already know also can be a factor.

The types of *data*, the frequency of their usage, and their arrangement need close consideration in choosing a language. For instance, numeric data subjected to complex calculations need different treatment than large files of customer data.

Rules and procedures affect the programming language selected. For example, the need for graphics for management presentations might lead to selecting a language capable of creating good visual displays.

The *hardware* available to the user has an impact as well. Some languages are particularly suited to a particular category of computer, such as mainframes. The *system software* available to translate the language is also a factor. Programs are not available to translate some languages on some computers, or may be available only in a form that exhibits dubious efficiency.

HOW COMPUTER LANGUAGES DIFFER

Choosing the right programming language for an information system is not an easy task. As we saw in the example concerning Oakriver University at the start of the chapter, many people in an organization have a say in language selection, management in particular.

Programmers may also have a measure of choice in selecting among an organization's existing languages when writing a particular program. A bank may decide that its main programming language is COBOL, but allow PL/1 for certain applications, and find that a few tricky operations can be done in only assembly language. Programmers within a given organization thus may have the chance to try different languages, and should be well aware of their characteristics. The ten factors presented here can help managers as well as programmers to understand and—when appropriate—select languages better, as well as to evaluate new computer languages as they are developed.

Many of us will not be programmers, but will use programs written by others for us. As informed users we also need to know how languages differ, the better to evaluate the software we use. Also we may well find ourselves buying a microcomputer and therefore be interested in the languages it can handle, or we may find our employers polling us—as at Oakriver University—to determine our language needs.

As a guide to helping us evaluate a language, we need to look closely at the following factors:

- *Application area*
- *File-handling ability*
- *Mathematical computing ability*
- *Machine independence*
- *Availability on microcomputers*
- *Level of self-documentation*
- *Quality of interactive form available*
- *Allowance for structured programming*
- *Relative cost for a few runs*
- *Relative cost for many runs*

CAREER BOX — PROGRAMMER ANALYST

The position of programmer analyst generally represents a promotion from that of application programmer (described in the Chapter 10 career box). The programmer analyst not only designs and codes application programs, but performs some or all of the systems analysis of the user applications that require the programs. Although not a full-fledged systems analyst—and occupying a lower rung of the career ladder than the systems analyst—the programmer analyst has more responsibility than the application programmer.

We should note that titles are confusing, and sometimes the title "programmer analyst" is used merely to mean "application programmer." Some companies, for example, start people as "programmer trainee" and then promote them to "programmer analyst" after a probation period, even though the job is that of application programmer.

Semantics aside, working as a programmer analyst offers more nitty-gritty hands-on participation with the computer than the systems analyst has in his or her loftier, more administrative, sphere; and more opportunity to think through concepts, and interact with users, than the application programmer has. The programmer analyst can follow a project all the way from its earliest inception through to successful implementation, carrying out all the work rather than delegating it. This may offer the best of both worlds.

To become a programmer analyst, you must first become an application programmer (Chapter 7 career box), and then prove your mettle. Since programmer analyst has traditionally been seen as a kind of way station en route to systems analyst, a difficulty with the position, if you like it, is to keep it rather than being promoted out of it. Some information centers today approach system development projects with a team that does both the programming and the systems analysis. The programmer analyst is a natural member of such a team.

As with other programming positions, any specialization enriches career opportunities. Specialized areas include online applications, teleprocessing, distributed data processing, and database handling.

These factors are shown on the left-hand side of Figure 11-1. The languages evaluated in the figure will be discussed later in the chapter. For now let's take a closer look at what the evaluation factors mean.

APPLICATION AREA refers to the general types of uses to which a computer can be put. We can identify four broad application areas: business, government, engineering, and science. Business and government information systems usually require computer programs capable of handling large files. "Large" can mean thousands, or even millions, of records. Processing large files strains or binds the input and output capacity of an information system. Such programs are said to be **INPUT/OUTPUT BOUND**. In general, business and government applications need languages with strong file-handling abilities.

Engineers and scientists need software with the capacity to manipulate complex mathematical algorithms. With these problems the information system can become **PROCESS BOUND**, where mathematical processing efforts

| Feature | Programming Language | | | | |
	BASIC	Pascal	COBOL	FORTRAN	RPG
Application Area	Business Engineering Government Science	Business Engineering Government Science	Business Government	Engineering Science	Business
File-Handling Ability	Medium	Medium	High	Medium	High
Mathematical Ability	High	High	Medium	High	Low
Machine Independence	Low	Medium	Very high	High	Medium
Available on Microcomputers	Almost all	Most	Some	Most	Few
Level of Self-Documentation	Low	Medium	High	Low	Low
Quality of Interactive Form Available	Good	Good	Fair	Fair	Fair
Allowances for Structured Programming	Low	Very high	High	Medium	Medium
Relative Cost for a Few Runs	Low	Low	High	Low	High
Relative Cost for Many Runs	High	High	Medium	High	Very high

rather than input/output are the point of constraint. Science and engineering applications therefore demand languages with strong mathematical computing abilities.

Of course, some application overlap exists—businesses or government agencies sometimes have to work with complex mathematical algorithms, and engineers and scientists sometimes have to process large files.

The second factor, **FILE-HANDLING ABILITY**, refers to the facility with which a language can manipulate large input and output data files. Data manipulation includes sorting, summarizing, listing, and other operations. Examples of large files include the employment and earnings records kept by the Social Security Administration, which involve over 200 million records. Within the topic of files and file handling we can also look at data structures and declarations. Some languages require that variables be carefully predefined by how the data are named (declared) and organized (structured) before the program is run. Other languages allow the programmer to define variables within the program as needed. In Chapter 16 we will learn more about specific file-handling methods.

MATHEMATICAL COMPUTING ABILITY refers to the strengths of a language in expressing calculations and in carrying them out efficiently. Languages strong in this area best allow a researcher or programmer to exploit algorithms to aid in solving problems. Mathematical computing ability and file-handling ability are the factors that generally define the application areas for which a language is suitable.

Computer languages also differ in how tied they are to a given computer. **MACHINE INDEPENDENCE** refers to how easily a program written to run using one particular make and model of computer can be run on another. A program written in a machine-independent language could, with just a few changes, be run successfully on a different computer. On the other hand, *machine dependence* refers to programs that will work only on one make or model of computer; to run the program on another would require conversion, or possibly a complete rewrite. Organizations with a variety of different computers strongly prefer the use of machine-independent languages to reduce the cost of converting and rewriting programs. Even organizations with a single computer are well-served by machine independence, because when their computer becomes obsolete they will undoubtedly change to another but wish to continue using as many of the same programs as possible.

The availability on microcomputers of a programming language has become important, since millions of people have access to them. Today most of the major programming languages are available in some version for microcomputers.

The concept of **SELF-DOCUMENTATION** refers to how easily a program can be read and understood. Languages that allow descriptive variables or names—GROSSINCOME, for example, instead of G or GRI—make reading a program easier. Some languages even force the programmer to be much more descriptive. Programs lacking in self-documentation are usually harder for a maintenance programmer to understand or modify.

The quality of the interactive form of the language is also a consideration. **INTERACTIVE PROCESSING** allows you to converse with the computer when using the program. The short time between entering commands and getting the program's response gives a feeling of immediacy to your solution. Programs that a user can *run* interactively can be written in any computer language. With many languages programs can also be *written* on an interactive basis, with the computer helping. The quality of this interactive form is the evaluation factor mentioned in Figure 11-1. Some languages are better than others for writing programs interactively, since they were designed for it. These are called **INTERACTIVE PROGRAMMING LANGUAGES**, and include BASIC and APL. Indeed with a language such as APL the distinction between writing and using a program fades altogether, and the computer becomes in effect a powerful calculator.

STRUCTURED PROGRAMMING methods are encouraged by some computer languages, and thwarted by others. The structured programming technique of most interest is the use of modular design in the development and execution of programs. In addition some languages discourage the use of unconditional branches or GO TO statements, which cannot be used in structured programs.

The **TOTAL PROGRAM COST** is the sum of the cost to write (a fixed cost) and the costs accumulated for each time the program is run (a variable cost). Factors that go into determining total cost are the time it takes programmers to create programs in a language, the ease with which the programs can be maintained and modified, the cost and speed of the system software that translates them, and CPU processing speeds.

When performing the same functions, languages may differ greatly in both their fixed and variable costs. The goal is to minimize total program costs. With some languages it takes a long time to write programs, but they execute very quickly and are easy to maintain. These programming languages are cost effective when used for operations that are performed thousands and sometimes millions of times over many years—they have a low relative cost for many runs, and a high relative cost for few runs. In other languages programs can be written quickly but take a long time to run—they have a low relative cost for a few runs, and a high relative cost for many.

Interestingly, in the early years of computers, the cost of programming was cheap compared with the cost of running the program on the computer. Today the situation has been reversed: while the cost of programming has increased, the cost of computing has declined markedly. This has altered the total cost picture for the various languages.

LOW-LEVEL
LANGUAGES FOR
HARDY PROGRAMMERS

MACHINE LANGUAGE

MACHINE LANGUAGE is the true language of the computer. It is the only one the central processing unit understands. Machine language is written in binary code, consisting solely of combinations of the numbers 1 and 0. This code is suited to computers because it corresponds to the bipolar or on/off state of electrical components (where "on" equals 1 and "off" equals 0).

The specific machine language depends upon the central processing unit's design. Most mainframe computer manufacturers design a "family" of machines that use the same machine language. The language will differ, however, from one manufacturer's family to another manufacturer's family. Microcomputer manufacturers, on the other hand, often use the same microprocessors; therefore several different brands of microcomputer may have the same machine language.

When you write a program in machine language, no translation process is necessary for the machine to use it. With all of the other languages, translation is needed.

The main features of machine language are these:

- *Each line of machine language refers to one operation represented by a series of 1s and 0s.*
- *The first few binary digits give the operation code (or op code), which instructs the computer what operation to perform.*
- *Following the op code comes one or more operands. An operand tells the computer on what the instruction is to be carried out. Usually the operand shows the address of data to be operated on. An address is a unique location in the computer's memory.*

FIGURE 11-2.

Machine-language instruction. The instruction adds the value of B to A, as in the equation A = A + B. The op code says to add the second value to the first value and store the answer in the first value's address. The first value, or operand A, is the variable A; the second, operand B, is variable B.

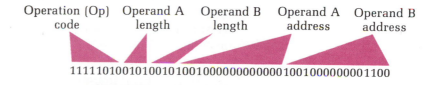

Figure 11-2 shows a machine-language instruction, with the parts of the instruction identified. For more on operation codes, operands, and addresses, see Chapter 5.

Machine-language programs can be applied to any application area. If you have the patience and skill, anything written in a higher-level language—and more—can be accomplished in machine language. The file-handling ability and mathematical computational ability of machine language are as great as those of the computer itself. After all, the other languages have to be converted into machine language to work.

Machine-language manuals are available if you want to learn how to write this type of code on a microcomputer. The level of self-documentation is obviously very poor (we do not speak binary), and it may take hours to write and debug the simplest program. It is possible to create interactive programs with machine language. Structured programming methods are not required when using machine language, but program design can benefit from the modular approach. The major cost of using machine language is the expense of writing and debugging the program code. Unless the program will be used many times, machine language is not cost effective. This is one reason why early programming applications for business and government focused on large, repetitive batch operations such as payroll processing. Few other operations could justify the programming expense. Today the main use of machine language is to create system software, which allows us to work with higher level programming languages.

ASSEMBLY LANGUAGE

ASSEMBLY LANGUAGE is one step removed from the machine language of the computer. Assembly language uses symbols easier for people to work with and remember than strings of 1s and 0s. System software translates each assembly-language instruction into one or more machine-language instructions.

Like machine language, assembly language is machine dependent. In addition assembly-language programs are similar to those written in machine language in terms of applications, file-handling ability, mathematical computing ability, availability on microcomputers, the level of self-documentation, the capability of writing interactive programs, allowance for structured programming, and the cost of writing, maintaining, and running programs.

Assembly language has the following features:

- *The use of mnemonics to represent machine operation codes and operands. MNEMONICS are symbolic codes that people can remember, such as SUB for subtraction.*
- *In the first assembly languages each instruction usually represented one line of machine language. Later assembly languages used MACRO INSTRUCTIONS to generate a sequence of several machine-language instructions from a single assembly-language instruction.*

FIGURE 11-3.
Example of assembly-language code for the equation A = A + B.

Figure 11-3 shows an example of a line of assembly language. The op code AP means add the contents of the second storage location (VALUEB) to the contents of the first (TOTALA) and place it into the first storage location. If you compare Figure 11-3 with Figure 11-2, you can see the great leap forward for programmers that assembly language represented over machine language.

HIGH-LEVEL LANGUAGES

The same trend that assembly language represented when compared with machine language—moving away from the way the machine runs and toward the way that people think—was carried further with high-level languages. High-level languages allow the programmer to focus on the procedures for problem solution, giving less attention to how the machine runs.

Consider, for example, a line of code in BASIC

```
200 LET A = A + B
```

This statement does exactly what the machine-language and assembly language codes in Figures 11-2 and 11-3 do. Clearly high-level language code is less cumbersome and easier to use.

In this section we will review four of the most frequently used high-level languages: BASIC, Pascal, COBOL, and FORTRAN. We will evaluate each based on the ten factors given in Figure 11-1.

In addition we will compare the way each of the four languages handles the same program and expresses the logical structures of sequence, looping, and selection (IFTHENELSE). The program is derived from the one Tom

Lee wrote for Oakriver University.* It reads a list of students and their grade-point averages (on a scale of 0 to 4). From the list the program selects those students with a grade-point average of 3.5 or more, and prints their names and grade-point averages for the honor roll.

Figure 11-4 shows the input data for the programs. The programs read the data from this file.

BASIC

BASIC or **BEGINNER'S ALL-PURPOSE SYMBOLIC INSTRUCTION CODE,** is an interactive programming language. BASIC is one of the first languages that many people learn. Developed by John G. Kemeny and Thomas Kurtz while they were mathematics professors at Dartmouth College, BASIC was designed with the novice programmer in mind.

BASIC is suited for all four application areas: business, government, engineering, and science. It has modest file-handling ability and loose data-structure rules, but is strong when used for numerical manipulation, including graphics and other visual displays.

Machine independence for BASIC is fairly low, because there are a variety of "dialects" of the language. The core of the language is consistent from one version to another, but there is a lack of standardization in two areas: the commands for working with data files, and those for creating sophisticated output displays.

BASIC was one of the first languages available on microcomputers. Its level of self-documentation is low. Although structured programming methods may be used with BASIC, this language also permits you to use less structure than most of the major languages. BASIC is one of the fastest languages in which to code and debug programs because you can do so on a thoroughly interactive basis. When few runs of the resulting program are made, the total cost is relatively lower than for many other languages. However, operations requiring the manipulation of large data files—such as processing thousands of payroll checks—are not cost effective in BASIC.

Figure 11-5 shows the honor-roll program in BASIC. As you can see, each line in BASIC begins with a line number. Just after the line number is a key word, such as PRINT. Following the key word is the value that word acts upon, such as the data to be printed. The REM ("Remark") lines do not affect the actual execution of the program. If used generously, these comments serve as a form of self-documentation.

PASCAL

PASCAL was developed by Niklaus Wirth and is named after the famous French inventor and mathematician Blaise Pascal. As Wirth intended it to be, Pascal is a truly structured programming language.

Pascal is useful in all four application areas. It has moderate file-handling ability and good mathematical computing ability. Three major versions of Pascal are available on the market: standard Pascal, UCSD (University of California at San Diego) Pascal®, and TURBO Pascal®. Because of the differences among these three versions, Pascal has only a medium level of machine independence.

Pascal has a medium level of self-documentation and is available in an interactive form. Unique among the major languages, Pascal was designed

FIGURE 11-4.

The data for the honor-roll problem.

Student	GPA
Mary Smith	3.75
Robert Lopez	2.95
Christine Jones	2.85
Tom Toshiba	3.95
Janis Roberts	3.49
Ralph Brown	3.20
Ronald Chang	3.00
Susan O'Malley	3.50
Cathy Schwartz	3.00
Michael Ramirez	3.65

*All the versions of the program that follow were written for a Control Data Corporation Cyber 174 system.

FIGURE 11-5.

The honor-roll problem in BA-SIC. In this example, as in the rest of the examples in this chapter, the data are read in from a separate data file.

```
110 REM This program extracts the names of those students who
120 REM have a grade-point average (GPA) greater than or equal
130 REM to 3.50.    The name and GPA of each qualifying student, and
140 REM the total number of the qualifying students is printed out.
150 REM The variables are:
160 REM        N$ = Student name
170 REM        G  = The grade point average
180 REM        S  = The total number of honor roll students
190 REM        I  = The array count value (not used for loop control)
```

```
200 **** The main program ****
210 DIM N$(10), G(10)
220 LET S = 0
230 LET I = 0
240 FILE #1 = "SCOREB"
250 PRINT TAB (6); "Oakriver University Honor Roll Report"
260 PRINT
270 PRINT TAB (11); "The Honor Roll Students"
280 PRINT
290 PRINT "     Student Name                    GPA"
300 PRINT
```
SEQUENCE (label for lines 200–300)

```
310 IF END #1 THEN 390
320 I = I + 1
330 INPUT #1, N$(I), G(I)
```

LOOP

```
340 IF G(I) < 3.5 THEN 380
350 PRINT USING E$; N$(I), G(I)
360 LET E$ = "     ###################         #.##"
370 LET S = S + 1
```
IFTHENELSE

```
380 GOTO 310
```

```
390 PRINT
400 PRINT
410 PRINT "     The number of honor roll students is: "; S
420 END
```
SEQUENCE (label for lines 390–420)

```
RUN
```

```
        Oakriver University Honor Roll Report

             The Honor Roll Students

        Student Name                    GPA

        Mary Smith                      3.75
        Tom Toshiba                     3.95         OUTPUT
        Susan O'Malley                  3.50
        Michael Ramirez                 3.65

        The number of honor roll students is: 4
```

with structured programming in mind. It forces programmers to use a modular approach, and makes it very difficult to write GO TO statements. Relative costs for both few and many runs is higher for Pascal programs than for BASIC programs. Pascal's modular approach, however, reduces the cost of modifying and maintaining a program.

A Pascal program to solve the honor-roll problem is shown in Figure 11-6. Pascal programs are divided into modules or blocks. The first block in a Pascal program concerns defining the variables and constants used in the program. These definitions are called declarations. The Pascal program is directed by the use of control statements. These statements assign values to variables, and direct the procedures that the program follows, such as testing for conditions and looping. The coding rules are more restrictive than for BASIC.

FIGURE 11-6.

The honor-roll problem in Pascal.

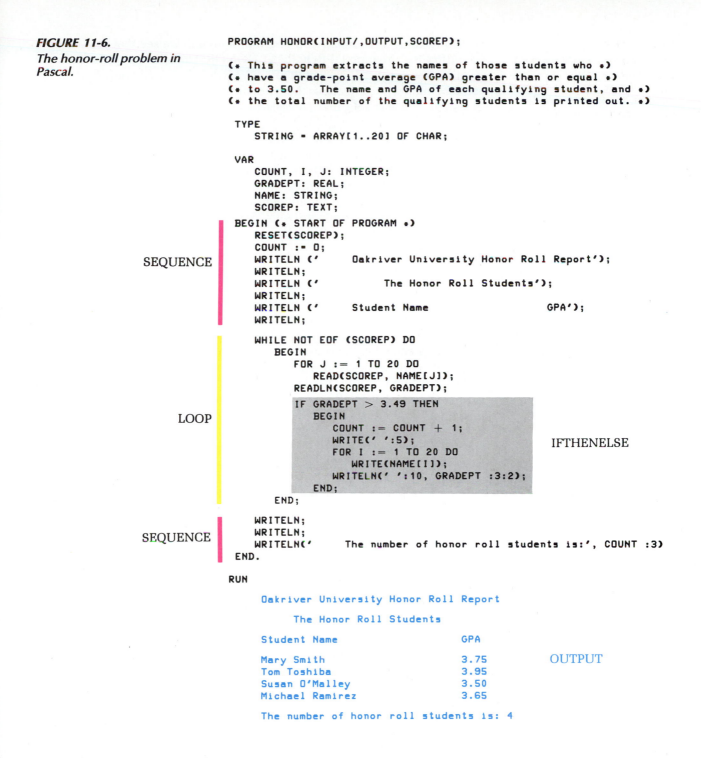

```
PROGRAM HONOR(INPUT/,OUTPUT,SCOREP);

(* This program extracts the names of those students who *)
(* have a grade-point average (GPA) greater than or equal *)
(* to 3.50.   The name and GPA of each qualifying student, and *)
(* the total number of the qualifying students is printed out. *)

  TYPE
      STRING = ARRAY[1..20] OF CHAR;

  VAR
      COUNT, I, J: INTEGER;
      GRADEPT: REAL;
      NAME: STRING;
      SCOREP: TEXT;
```

SEQUENCE
```
  BEGIN (* START OF PROGRAM *)
      RESET(SCOREP);
      COUNT := 0;
      WRITELN ('      Oakriver University Honor Roll Report');
      WRITELN;
      WRITELN ('            The Honor Roll Students');
      WRITELN;
      WRITELN ('      Student Name                      GPA');
      WRITELN;
```

LOOP
```
      WHILE NOT EOF (SCOREP) DO
         BEGIN
            FOR J := 1 TO 20 DO
                READ(SCOREP, NAME[J]);
            READLN(SCOREP, GRADEPT);
```
```
            IF GRADEPT > 3.49 THEN
               BEGIN
                  COUNT := COUNT + 1;
                  WRITE(' ':5);
                  FOR I := 1 TO 20 DO
                      WRITE(NAME[I]);
                  WRITELN(' ':10, GRADEPT :3:2);
               END;
```
IFTHENELSE
```
         END;
```

SEQUENCE
```
      WRITELN;
      WRITELN;
      WRITELN('      The number of honor roll students is:', COUNT :3)
  END.
```

```
RUN
```

        Oakriver University Honor Roll Report

            The Honor Roll Students

        Student Name   GPA

        Mary Smith   3.75   OUTPUT
        Tom Toshiba   3.95
        Susan O'Malley   3.50
        Michael Ramirez   3.65

        The number of honor roll students is: 4

In looking at the honor-roll program in detail, we see that the first line identifies the program ("PROGRAM HONOR") and indicates the data are coming from a file called "SCOREP." TYPE defines the storage array for the student names. VAR declares the types of variables being used—NAME, for instance, is a variable that consists of alphabetic characters (a character "string").

BEGIN starts the procedural part of the program. This section contains a series of steps to print the heading, read in the data, test to see if the student qualifies for the honor roll, and, if so, print the student's name. The statements also count the number of students who make the honor roll and print out the final count. Indentation helps to make clear the nested loop structure. The loops terminate with "END" followed by a semicolon. The "END" for the last line of the program is followed by a period rather than a semicolon.

COBOL

COBOL, or **COMMON BUSINESS-ORIENTED LANGUAGE** is used extensively by both businesses and government agencies. Its principal strength is file processing. Today COBOL can be used for both interactive processing and batch-oriented processing. Payroll problems, accounting, inventory, report writing—these are the areas in which COBOL excels. By far the greater part of the application programs used in American businesses today—representing an investment worth billions of dollars—are written in COBOL. For many major corporations it is the *only* language used for business applications.

COBOL was released in 1959. Dr. Grace Hopper (her contributions are also discussed in Chapter 4) developed a way to make COBOL run on any computer. Since its initial release COBOL has been revised to keep up with advances in machine performance as well as program design concepts. Today's version of COBOL has moderately strong mathematical features to support its powerful file-handling ability, helpful for such operations as calculating check amounts, tax withholding amounts, or inventory reorder points.

COBOL was designed to be machine independent, a feature of great importance to large users with many different brands of computers. The use of COBOL was originally encouraged by the United States government. All mainframe computers supplied to government agencies, such as the Department of Defense, were required to be able to run COBOL programs. The negotiating leverage here was immense, and the manufacturers complied. COBOL has international syntax standards, a great help in using the same program on different machines around the world. The American National Standards Institute released the first version of COBOL in 1958. A revised version was issued in 1974. The latest version, COBOL-80, has yet to be released.

COBOL is available on microcomputers. With the highest level of self-documentation of any of the major languages, COBOL allows the programmer to use phrases in English (or other native tongue) to define variables. Interactive COBOL programs can be run on microcomputers, minicomputers, and mainframes. Structured programming methods can be applied to COBOL. The actual implementation of structured techniques depends upon the programmer, and that person's working environment and training. COBOL programs can be quite unstructured if proper care is not taken by programmers and their managers.

COBOL takes longer to program than other major languages; thus its relative cost for a few runs is fairly high. For running a program thousands of times, however, COBOL is very cost effective, because COBOL executes a program much more efficiently than the other high-level languages. COBOL is most cost effective for programs that perform extensive input and output operations, a common trait of many business applications. And if the program is well structured, maintenance costs should be relatively low.

As Figure 11-7 indicates, there is a hierarchical arrangement to COBOL programs. From broadest to narrowest the hierarchy is as follows: program, division, section, paragraph, and sentence. Notice that each sentence of COBOL end with a period.

All COBOL programs are divided into four divisions— identification, environment, data, and procedure. The identification division identifies the program ("PROGRAM-SCORE"), the author, and where and when the program was written. The environment division has two parts, the configuration section and the input-output section. The configuration section identifies the source computer (where the program was originally written) and the object computer (the machine that will run the program). Usually the same machine is used, but not always. The input-output section defines certain input and ouput requirements.

The data division has two sections. The file section describes the input and output files. The working storage section defines the format and other storage needs of every variable in the program.

The procedure division details the steps used to solve the honor-roll problem. The division has four parts. The MAIN-PROGRAM section calls the other parts of the procedure division. START-PROCESS prints the headings. DECISION-FOR-HONOR-ROLL reads in the data, makes the comparisons, and prints out the names. The loop is controlled by an end-of-file (EOF) flag. WRAPITUP prints the number of students on the honor roll. STOP RUN (in MAIN-PROGRAM) ends the program.

Unlike BASIC and Pascal, COBOL requires programmers to follow very specific coding rules for each line. A line of code in COBOL uses up to 80 columns (because COBOL and most other programming languages were originally designed for 80-column punch cards). Each column is designated for certain types of information, and a programmer must follow these rules. For instance, columns 1 through 6 are used for sequence numbers, column 7 marks lines for special purposes such as comments or remarks, and columns 8 through 11 denote major parts of the program, such as divisions, sections, and paragraphs. The main body of the program is written in columns 12 through 72. Columns 73 to 80 are unused except for programmer comments.

FORTRAN   FORTRAN, or FORMULA TRANSLATION, is a programming language designed chiefly for applications in science and engineering. Created in the mid-1950s at IBM Corporation by a team headed by John Backus, FORTRAN has proven a real survivor. Many languages have sought to replace it, yet FORTRAN endures.

Moderately proficient for file handling, particularly for numerical files,

FIGURE 11-7.

The honor-roll problem in
COBOL.

```
IDENTIFICATION DIVISION.

PROGRAM-ID.            PROGRAM-SCORE.
AUTHOR.                TOM LEE.
INSTALLATION.          ORISC.
DATE-WRITTEN.          JANUARY-12, 1987.

ENVIRONMENT DIVISION.

CONFIGURATION SECTION.
SOURCE-COMPUTER.  CYBER-174.
OBJECT-COMPUTER.  CYBER-174.
INPUT-OUTPUT SECTION.
FILE-CONTROL.
     SELECT RECORDS-IN ASSIGN TO SCORES, USE "RT=Z".
     SELECT PRINT-OUT ASSIGN TO OUTPUT.

DATA DIVISION.

FILE SECTION.
FD  RECORDS-IN
     LABEL RECORDS ARE OMITTED.
01  IN-RECORD                PIC X(72).
FD  PRINT-OUT
     LABEL RECORDS ARE OMITTED.
01  PRINT-LINE              PIC X(72).
WORKING-STORAGE SECTION.
77  STUDENT-COUNT          PIC 9(3)       VALUE ZEROES.
01  FLAG.
     05  END-OF-FILE-FLAG PIC X          VALUE "N".
     05  NO-MORE-DATA     PIC X          VALUE "Y".
01  STUDENT-RECORD.
     05  NAME-RD          PIC X(20).
     05  GRADE-PT         PIC 9V99.
     05  FILLER           PIC X(49).
01  HDG.
     05  FILLER           PIC X(5)       VALUE SPACES.
     05  FILLER           PIC X(9)       VALUE "OAKRIVER ".
     05  FILLER           PIC X(11)      VALUE "UNIVERSITY ".
     05  FILLER           PIC X(17)      VALUE "HONOR ROLL REPORT".
     05  FILLER           PIC X(30)      VALUE SPACES.
01  HDG-1.
     05  FILLER           PIC X(10)      VALUE SPACES.
     05  FILLER           PIC X(15)      VALUE "THE HONOR ROLL ".
     05  FILLER           PIC X(8)       VALUE "STUDENTS".
     05  FILLER           PIC X(39)      VALUE SPACES.
01  HDG-2.
     05  FILLER           PIC X(5)       VALUE SPACES.
     05  FILLER           PIC X(12)      VALUE "STUDENT NAME".
     05  FILLER           PIC X(18)      VALUE SPACES.
     05  FILLER           PIC X(3)       VALUE "GPA".
     05  FILLER           PIC X(34)      VALUE SPACES.
01  HDG-3.
     05  FILLER           PIC X(72)      VALUE SPACES.
01  STUDENT-LINE.
     05  FILLER           PIC X(5)       VALUE SPACES.
     05  NAME-LN          PIC X(20).
     05  FILLER           PIC X(10)      VALUE SPACES.
     05  GRADE            PIC 9.99.
     05  FILLER           PIC X(33)      VALUE SPACES.
01  TOTAL-LINE.
     05  FILLER           PIC X(5)       VALUE SPACES.
     05  FILLER           PIC X(14)      VALUE "THE NUMBER OF ".
     05  FILLER           PIC X(11)      VALUE "HONOR ROLL ".
     05  FILLER           PIC X(12)      VALUE "STUDENTS IS:".
     05  STUDENT-NUMBER   PIC ZZ9.
     05  FILLER           PIC X(27)      VALUE SPACES.
```

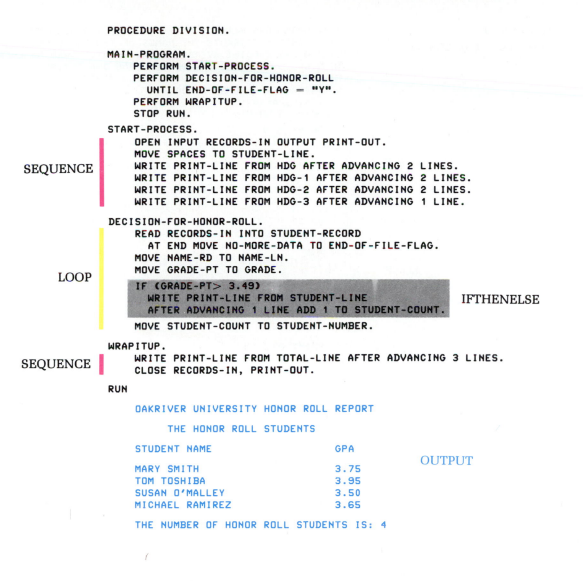

```
PROCEDURE DIVISION.

MAIN-PROGRAM.
    PERFORM START-PROCESS.
    PERFORM DECISION-FOR-HONOR-ROLL
      UNTIL END-OF-FILE-FLAG = "Y".
    PERFORM WRAPITUP.
    STOP RUN.
START-PROCESS.
    OPEN INPUT RECORDS-IN OUTPUT PRINT-OUT.
    MOVE SPACES TO STUDENT-LINE.
    WRITE PRINT-LINE FROM HDG AFTER ADVANCING 2 LINES.
    WRITE PRINT-LINE FROM HDG-1 AFTER ADVANCING 2 LINES.
    WRITE PRINT-LINE FROM HDG-2 AFTER ADVANCING 2 LINES.
    WRITE PRINT-LINE FROM HDG-3 AFTER ADVANCING 1 LINE.

DECISION-FOR-HONOR-ROLL.
    READ RECORDS-IN INTO STUDENT-RECORD
      AT END MOVE NO-MORE-DATA TO END-OF-FILE-FLAG.
    MOVE NAME-RD TO NAME-LN.
    MOVE GRADE-PT TO GRADE.
    IF (GRADE-PT> 3.49)
       WRITE PRINT-LINE FROM STUDENT-LINE
       AFTER ADVANCING 1 LINE ADD 1 TO STUDENT-COUNT.
    MOVE STUDENT-COUNT TO STUDENT-NUMBER.

WRAPITUP.
    WRITE PRINT-LINE FROM TOTAL-LINE AFTER ADVANCING 3 LINES.
    CLOSE RECORDS-IN, PRINT-OUT.

RUN
```

SEQUENCE

LOOP

IFTHENELSE

SEQUENCE

OAKRIVER UNIVERSITY HONOR ROLL REPORT

   THE HONOR ROLL STUDENTS

STUDENT NAME   GPA   OUTPUT

MARY SMITH   3.75
TOM TOSHIBA   3.95
SUSAN O'MALLEY   3.50
MICHAEL RAMIREZ   3.65

THE NUMBER OF HONOR ROLL STUDENTS IS: 4

FORTRAN's real strength is in "number crunching" of complex mathematical algorithms. FORTRAN is moderately machine independent, and is available on microcomputers. It has a low level of self-documentation, and is available in interactive forms. Early FORTRAN programmers were notorious in their use of GO TO statements, but the language can be used with structured programming methods. The relative cost for using FORTRAN is just slightly higher than for using BASIC. Like COBOL, FORTRAN has international syntax standards. And like COBOL, FORTRAN has been revised many times. The latest version, FORTRAN-77, incorporates attributes of structured programming and permits more efficient handling of files than earlier versions.

As in COBOL, every line of code in FORTRAN follows certain rules. Columns 1 to 5 are used for the statement number, column 6 to declare continuation of a line, columns 7 through 72 for the instruction itself, and columns 73 through 80 for comments.

FIGURE 11-8.

The honor-roll program in FORTRAN-77.

```
                    PROGRAM HONORF(INPUT,OUTPUT,SCOREF,TAPE60=INPUT,TAPE61=SCOREF)
        C   THIS PROGRAM EXTRACTS THE NAMES OF THOSE STUDENTS WHO
        C   HAVE A GRADE-POINT AVERAGE (GPA) GREATER THAN OR EQUAL
        C   TO 3.50.    THE NAME AND GPA OF EACH QUALIFYING STUDENT, AND
        C   THE TOTAL NUMBER OF THE QUALIFYING STUDENTS IS PRINTED OUT.
                    CHARACTER * 20 NAME(10)
                    REAL GPA(10)
                    INTEGER COUNT
                    COUNT = 0
                      PRINT *,'        OAKRIVER UNIVERSITY HONOR ROLL REPORT'
                      PRINT *,' '
                      PRINT *,' '           THE HONOR ROLL STUDENTS'
                      PRINT *,' '
                      PRINT *,'        STUDENT NAME                      GPA'
                      PRINT *,' '
                    DO 70 I  1, 10
                      READ(61,40) NAME(I), GPA(I)
         40         FORMAT(A20,F4.2)
                      IF (GPA(I) .GE. 3.5) THEN
                         PRINT 50, NAME(I), GPA(I)
         50            FORMAT(5X,A20,10X,F4.2)
                         COUNT = COUNT + 1
                      END IF
         70 CONTINUE
                    PRINT 80, COUNT
         80 FORMAT(//,5X,'THE NUMBER OF HONOR ROLL STUDENTS IS',I3)
                    END

        RUN
```

SEQUENCE

LOOP   IFTHENELSE

SEQUENCE

```
            OAKRIVER UNIVERSITY HONOR ROLL REPORT

                 THE HONOR ROLL STUDENTS

            STUDENT NAME                      GPA

            MARY SMITH                        3.75        OUTPUT
            TOM TOSHIBA                       3.95
            SUSAN O'MALLEY                    3.50
            MICHAEL RAMIREZ                   3.65

            THE NUMBER OF HONOR ROLL STUDENTS IS:   4
```

Figure 11-8 shows the honor-roll problem in FORTRAN. Notice how the statement numbers are used for input, output, and loop control.

ADDITIONAL HIGH-LEVEL LANGUAGES

There are a variety of other high-level languages available today. Here we will discuss four: Ada, APL, C, and PL/1.

Ada

ADA was developed for the U.S. Department of Defense and first released in 1980. It is named for Lady Ada Lovelace, the world's first programmer (see Chapter 4).

Efforts are under way to supplant both COBOL and FORTRAN with Ada. However, the acceptance of Ada has been hampered by three factors. First, interservice rivalry between the Air Force and the Navy (which helped develop COBOL) has slowed adoption of Ada as a standard. Second, the system software necessary to translate Ada has been developed very slowly. Third, there has been little support for Ada outside the Department of Defense.

In many respects Ada is similar to Pascal. The major difference is that Ada incorporates within itself SOFTWARE ENGINEERING, or program creation methods, developed over the last decade, especially modular program-building algorithms. Software engineering speeds up program design.

Proponents claim Ada successfully weds the file-handling powers of COBOL with the mathematical computing abilities of FORTRAN. Ada is designed to be machine independent. A version of Ada should soon be available on larger microcomputers. Ada has moderate self-documentation, and it can be used to write interactive programs. Like Pascal, Ada not only allows, but requires, the use of structured programming methods.

While Ada has not been subjected to the economic scrutiny of the other programming languages, the total cost picture should be about the same as for Pascal. Whether Ada will compete successfully against other languages such as COBOL remains to be seen. Relatively few programmers are familiar with Ada, and businesses and government agencies have invested billions of dollars in COBOL programs that would have to be rewritten if Ada became standard.

APL

APL, or A PROGRAMMING LANGUAGE, was developed in 1962 by Kenneth Iverson of Harvard University in cooperation with the IBM Corporation. Designed primarily for engineering and scientific applications, APL code looks quite different from the other programming languages. In fact APL requires a special keyboard. The symbols in APL are Greek letters and symbols borrowed from standard mathematical notation.

APL has weak file-handling abilities. Its real strength is in its mathematical power. APL is a good language for developing and testing mathematical models. APL is quite machine independent, and is available on many microcomputers. Since APL is a free-form interactive language, its level of self-documentation is low and it does not lend itself to structured programming. Typically APL programs can be understood only by the person who wrote them. When doing only a few runs (as is most often the case with applications that use APL), APL is a cost-effective language. However, its cost effectiveness drops if substantial program modifications are needed, or if programs are run many times.

C

One language is called simply C, so-named because it was developed from a language called B. C was developed at Bell Telephone Laboratories by Dennis Ritchie in 1972. C has features of both high- and low-level languages, and resembles Pascal in its structure. It is a modular language used primarily to write software packages for nonprogramming users. In fact C has begun to replace assembly language for this purpose because it is relatively machine independent. Available on microcomputers, this language has been used to create sophisticated business and word-processing packages. C shows promise of becoming a popular programming language.

PL/1

PL/1, or PROGRAMMING LANGUAGE 1, was developed by Bruce Rosenblatt and George Radin at IBM Corporation to combine the best features of COBOL and FORTRAN. First released in 1964, PL/1 can be used for a wide range of business as well as scientific problems. It has both good file-handling and mathematical capabilities. PL/1 was originally created for the IBM System/360 series of computers during the mid-1960s. Since then the language has been adapted for the machines of other mainframe manufacturers, increasing its machine independence. PL/1 is available on some microcomputers. It is used primarily for batch-oriented rather than interactive processing. PL/1 has a moderate level of self-documentation, and uses a modular approach that allows for structured programming methods.

PL/1 is more expensive to run than other high-level languages. It executes more slowly, and uses more storage space.

Its creators expected PL/1 to supplant FORTRAN and COBOL. This did not happen, largely because people were reluctant to give up languages they already knew and programs in which they had already invested. Furthermore there was no push by the government to impose PL/1 on its clients, such as defense contractors. Although PL/1 is used today and has its proponents, some observers have argued that PL/1 is becoming a "dead" language of historical interest only. It is still used at the IBM Corporation to support many applications.

VERY-HIGH-LEVEL LANGUAGES

The purpose of a very-high-level language is to do a particular type of work. The focus within an application area is much narrower than with a high-level language. For example, the high-level language FORTRAN can tackle almost any type of mathematical or engineering problem. A very-high-level simulation programming language, in contrast, can address only a narrow range of such problems—building and testing models. Within this range, however, the very-high-level language is very powerful, and is easier to learn. Very-high-level languages are part of the recent trend to develop USER-FRIENDLY SOFTWARE —programs that can be used easily, are documented clearly, describe problems in a user's own terms, and often actively assist a user to solve problems through an interactive dialogue. With some very-high-level languages, a programmer is not required at all, since the user can work with the language directly without extensive training.

We will describe three types of very-high-level languages here: report-generating language, simulation languages, and list-processing languages.

RPG RPG, or REPORT GENERATING LANGUAGE, was developed by the IBM Corporation primarily to service small-business users. RPG applications focus on batch-oriented accounting procedures, and are used mainly on small mainframe and minicomputers. RPG can handle moderately complex files. The language is not strong in mathematical computing ability, but can handle the calculations necessary to process payroll, accounts receivable, and other accounting applications. Although primarily available to users of IBM machines, versions of RPG are also available for hardware produced by other manufacturers, such as Digital Equipment Corporation and Wang, including some microcomputers. The latest version, RPG III, has the ability to work with databases.

RPG programs follow a rigid format. Special coding forms enhance the level of self-documentation. The forms are letter coded: F for file specifications, I for input, and so on. Although primarily a batch-oriented language, more recent versions have allowed for the interactive input of data for processing. As RPG allows only one type of program design, the programs do have an identifiable structure. In addition program maintenance is enhanced with this language—a great benefit to small businesses. The trade-off for the convenience of RPG is its high cost per run. Compared with high-level languages for comparable accounting programs, RPG takes longer to run.

RPG is not the only report-generating language available. Others include POWERHOUSE®, NOMAD2®, EASYTRIEVE®, GIS®, and MARK IV/REPORTER®

SIMULATION LANGUAGES

SIMULATION PROGRAMMING LANGUAGES use mathematical or logical formulas to model real-world events, and to predict the possible consequences of those events. For example, the behavior of a new airplane engine can be modeled and tested by a computer program before any version of the engine is actually built. If an engineer has some basic specifications for what seems a good engine design—maximum thrust generated, weight, fuel-consumption rate, and so on—he or she can "test" this would-be engine under thousands of computer-simulated environmental conditions. This is much easier and less expensive than building the engine, mounting it on a test plane, and after some months finding that it fails under certain conditions. With a program written in a simulation language, months of work can be condensed into minutes, and the model refined and tuned to ever-greater perfection. Then the physical prototype can be built and—once it passes tests in an actual laboratory—mounted on a plane and tried some more.

Business applications include modeling production and other management problems. The user of a simulation language describes the general constraints of the problem, such as the materials and other resources, wages, worker skills, and other factors in the business system. The simulation program then translates the general model into machine language the computer can understand. Once again, the advantage is that simulating something makes it possible to find out that it won't work—or will—before doing it. These languages are often taught and applied in management science courses.

Examples of simulation languages include DYNAMO, GPSS (General-Purpose System Simulator), and SIMSCRIPT. A few simulation programs allow interactive processing, are modular in nature, and have good self-documentation. Some are available on microcomputer systems. Total cost figures are hard to estimate, since most simulations are not repeated over and over again. The real cost benefit is in the savings gained by reducing the trial-and-error research and design costs of projects.

LIST-PROCESSING LANGUAGES

A LIST-PROCESSING LANGUAGE, as the name says, processes data in the form of lists. Generally the logical order of data in the list can be changed without physically moving the data. List-processing languages are valuable for research. An example of a list-processing language is LISP (short for LISt Processing), developed in 1958 by John McCarthy at the Massachusetts Institute of Technology. One of the most important applications of LISP is in the development of artificial intelligence programs—programs that attempt to mimic human thought. LISP is an unstructured, interactive language, and is available on some microcomputers.

LOGO (which means "word" in Greek) was derived from LISP during the 1960s. LOGO was meant to be so user-friendly that it would be fun to use. Relying upon simple words for commands, LOGO allows the programmer to communicate with the computer in a free-form, unstructured style. LOGO is a very popular language for children and adults alike. This interactive language is available on microcomputers, and is extensively used in schools from the lowest grades upward to familiarize children with computers.

TOWARD NATURAL LANGUAGES

The long-term trend in programming languages is toward those that are easier for the average person to use. This means that new very-high-level languages will be developed, and existing very-high-level languages will be refined. As computers continue to become cheaper, faster, more plentiful, and more accessible to the average person, the languages that make it possible to use the computer can be expected to impose ever-fewer demands.

Ideally people should be able to talk to the computer as they do to each other—in a NATURAL LANGUAGE such as Chinese, English, or Greek. Very-high-level languages will resemble ever more closely natural languages. Applications already exist where spoken commands activate a computer program and then provide the necessary input data. So far the repertoire of commands for such applications is fairly limited, much like the verbs in a computer program; but the systems can take into account individual variations in speech and get the right command much of the time. Is it far-fetched to speculate that these may be but the humble beginnings of a process that will end with the use of natural languages as computer languages?

Japan attracted the attention of many computer-industry watchers by announcing a "fifth generation" of computers for the 1990s. Part of the government plan for such a generation is to build the hardware in a manner that can come closer than anything yet to mimicking human thought, and to use software that moves further in the direction of natural languages. Perhaps someday Tom Lee could request the Oakriver University computer to handle the honor-roll problem for him, in writing or verbally, like this:

```
Please print a list of the names and grade-point
averages of all students who had a grade-point average
of 3.5 or more last term. Give me the number of such
students as well.
```

When this type of request becomes possible, we will have reached the end of our developmental odyssey that started with machine language. When computers can be "programmed" in a natural language, then computer languages will be a topic of interest only to software designers.

The development of artificial intelligence has been going on long enough—some 25 years at least—so that the computer-oriented discipline now breaks into several key branches. Their application in corporate and professional work varies considerably.

SYSTEMS WITH EXPERTISE

Expert systems handle business problems differently than traditional computer systems. The standard business system treats either large masses of data or specific cases by encoding programs with relatively fixed sets of rules. An expert system uses a somewhat generalized program called an inference engine. It establishes the relationships among rules and places them in a rule or knowledge base. . . .

Traditional data processing systems are usually programmed in languages such as COBOL and FORTRAN. Expert systems, by contrast, have generally been written in languages such as LISP or PROLOG, which are specially designed to handle symbolic content.

Despite AI language differences, expert systems of every ilk help solve problems in which information is partially missing or uncertain. That's in contrast to traditional data processing which would either fail or provide ambiguous responses under such conditions. . . .

ROBOTS IN ACTION

. . .Robots using AI techniques can recognize the shape, size, and position of objects, pick them up and correctly position them for work, or conduct a series of steps that assemble irregularly shaped and positioned objects into a predetermined pattern or product. . . .

GRASPING HUMAN LANGUAGE

Another area of AI research comes under the formidable heading of "computational linguistics," which copes with the problem of developing programs that understand human language. Among the main advances researchers have achieved so far:

- *Japanese computer manufacturers have recently made significant announcements about using computational linguistic methods to translate English into Japanese and Japanese into English. . . .*

- *Closely related to this is research into machine understanding of the human voice. While there are still many problems, such as separating words in continuous speech (people tend to run words together when speaking), IBM has successfully captured human speech and produced written text from voice output in recent experiments.*

- *Work is going on to interpret texts in such a way as to identify specific subject matter within a context that proves that the subject is of interest to the person seeking the information. A physician can search for references to, say, "lungs" or "diseases of lungs" within the context of specific types of patients (for example, members of a particular occupational group of people over 65) for certain symptoms. . . .*

- *Currently on the market are AI products that enable people to access and retrieve information from databases by using English-like "natural language" to enter instructions or ask questions. . . .*

Source: Louis Fried, "Expert Systems Enter the Corporate Domain," *Management Technology,* January 1985. Reprinted by permission of *Management Technology.* Copyright © International Thomson Technology Information, Inc., January 1985. All rights reserved.

OAKRIVER UNIVERSITY PICKS SOME LANGUAGES

Miguel Abreu, the committee chair, thanked Marty Castillo, Alice Smith, and the other information-processing center staff for their helpful presentation and their patience in answering the many questions posed by members of the University Computer Users Committee.

"Now it's your turn," Miguel said to the committee members. "What language needs do you see for your particular schools?"

Elizabeth Slater, who taught in the Information Resource Management Department of the School of Business, spoke first. "The Business School needs several different programming languages," Elizabeth said. "For our introductory computer courses, most instructors teach BASIC, although a few prefer Pascal. The main language for more advanced courses is COBOL. In addition, several instructors use report generating and simulation languages for classes in such areas as marketing and production management."

"Naturally our needs differ," Daniel Powers said. "In the School of Engineering we use C, FORTRAN and assembly language extensively, and would also like the new system to include APL. Besides, it turns out that many defense contractors are hiring our graduates and need engineers with experience in using Ada. So we have to teach Ada, too."

Ralph Grosse spoke up. "What you presented about those very-high-level natural languages was enlightening. I know my colleagues in the Foreign Languages Department would be interested in using some of them for research."

Bobby-Joe Peters, the representative from Administrative Services, joined the discussion. "We really don't have a language-selection problem," he said. "The administration will continue to use COBOL for virtually all of its large-scale programming needs. The cost of changing languages now would be simply too great."

After every interested committee member had spoken, Miguel Abreu asked the committee to rank the desired languages. As the "output" of today's meeting, the top eight languages would be chosen. More languages will be added later if funds permitted and interest was strong.

The top languages were COBOL, BASIC, FORTRAN, Pascal, C, Ada, APL, and assembly language.

"Now that we have resolved the language problem for the present," Miguel said, "our meeting next Wednesday will discuss prewritten software packages."

SUMMARY

■ One useful way to categorize the many different programming languages is by how much attention you must pay to the workings of the computer when you program in the language. With a low-level *language you have to pay the most attention. With a high-level language you pay less, and can therefore concentrate more on solving the problem at hand. Very-high-level languages are furthest from the workings of the machine and are designed to make it easy to solve a narrow range of problems. Historically languages developed in the same order, from low to high. Today all three levels are in use.*

- *The selection of a programming language within an information system depends upon the existing hardware, people, rules, existing programs, and data. Usually the individual programmer has little say about what languages are picked. It is useful for programmers to know the characteristics of the main languages anyway, as they may have a choice of which to use for a given application; and a knowledge of programming-language characteristics can make those of us who are not programmers more informed users and purchasers of software.*

- *Ten characteristics can be used both to describe a language and to compare one with another. These are application area, file-handling ability, mathematical computing ability, machine independence, availability on microcomputers, level of self-documentation, quality of interactive form available (both for interactive processing and interactive programming languages), allowance for structured programming, relative cost for a few runs, and relative cost for many runs.*

- *Large file-handling applications are said to be input/output bound, whereas applications involving complicated mathematical algorithms are said to be process bound. Total program cost includes the cost of writing the program, the costs accumulated for each time it is run, and the cost of maintaining it.*

- *Machine language is the true language of the computer. Programs written in any other language must be translated into machine language by system software to run. Machine language consists of strings of 1s and 0s. Assembly language, also a low-level language, is one step removed from machine language, using mnemonic symbols that are easier for people to work with and remember. Macro instructions combine several machine instructions into one line of code of nonmachine language.*

- *High-level languages use English-like statements and mathematical symbols, allowing the programmer to focus on problem-solving procedures rather than on the inner workings of the machine. Among the high-level languages, BASIC is one of the first languages that many people learn. Pascal is a language designed with structured programming in mind. COBOL must be ranked as the prime language of business, if only because at this point in history most programs for corporations are coded in it. FORTRAN is another venerable language, but with the essentially opposite characteristics that make it useful for technical applications.*

- *Other high-level languages include, among others, Ada, APL, C, and PL/1. A special characteristic of Ada is that it incorporates software engineering methods that speed program design.*

- *Within a fairly narrow application range, very-high-level languages are both powerful and easy to learn. These languages are part of the trend toward the development of increasingly user-friendly software. Included in this category are report generators such as RPG, simulation languages, and list-processing languages such as LISP. LISP has been used extensively in artificial intelligence research. LOGO, also a list-processing language, is extensively used in schools from the earliest grades on.*

- *Very-high-level languages point the way toward the future: the replacement of computer languages by the natural languages that we speak every day.*

KEY TERMS

These are the key terms in the order in which they appear in the chapter.

Low-level language (302)
High-level language (303)
Very-high-level language (303)
Application area (305)
Input/output bound (305)
Process bound (305)
File-handling ability (307)
Mathematical computing ability (307)
Machine independence (307)
Self-documentation (307)
Interactive processing (307)
Interactive programming language (308)
Structured programming (308)
Total program cost (308)
Machine language (308)
Assembly language (309)
Mnemonics (310)
Macro instruction (310)

BASIC (Beginner's All-Purpose Symbolic Instruction Code) (311)
Pascal (311)
COBOL (COmmon Business-Oriented Language) (314)
FORTRAN (FORmula TRANslation) (315)
Ada (318)
Software engineering (319)
APL (A Programming Language) (319)
C (319)
PL/1 (Programming Language 1) (319)
User-friendly software (320)
RPG (RePort-Generating language) (320)
Simulation programming language (321)
List-processing language (321)
LISP (322)
LOGO (322)
Natural language (322)

REVIEW QUESTIONS

OBJECTIVE QUESTIONS

TRUE/FALSE: *Put the letter T or F on the line before the question.*

1. COBOL has the ability to handle large files.
2. BASIC has a high level of machine independence.
3. The level of self-documentation for COBOL is low compared to other major languages.
4. The relative cost for many runs of a program is higher for FORTRAN than for COBOL.
5. The relative cost for a few runs of a program is higher for BASIC than for RPG.
6. The PROCEDURE division in COBOL is used to declare the working storage requirements of the program.
7. LISP is an example of a simulation language.
8. Pascal is noted for its requirements for structured programming techniques.
9. Assembly languages use mnemonics to aid programmers in writing program code.
10. RPG is primarily used for business-oriented applications.

Put the letter of the correct answer on the line before the question.

_____ 1. Which languages are available on microcomputers today, BASIC, Pascal, COBOL, FORTRAN, or RPG
(a) BASIC and Pascal.   (c) BASIC, FORTRAN and COBOL.
(b) BASIC and FORTRAN.   (d) All five languages are available.

_____ 2. Razor-Thin Lasers markets shaving devices. Their accounting department needs a new payroll program. The program must be well-documented, and usable on several different computers. Which language would you recommend?
(a) BASIC.   (b) COBOL.   (c) Pascal.   (d) FORTRAN.

_____ 3. Professor Genie Splitter needs a "quick and dirty" program to perform some calculations on the DNA configuration for a "new" animal. What language would she be unlikely to use?
(a) FORTRAN.   (b) C.   (c) APL.   (d) RPG.

_____ 4. Easy Money Loan shop often has to change locations on extremely short notice. They need a programming language capable of calculating simple (but extremely high) interest payments using a number of different computers. What language would you recommend?
(a) FORTRAN.   (b) RPG.   (c) BASIC.   (d) None of the above.

_____ 5. Two examples of low-level, highly machine-dependent languages are
(a) COBOL and FORTRAN.   (c) machine and assembly.
(b) BASIC and assembly.   (d) BASIC and machine.

FILL IN THE BLANK: *Write the correct word or words in the blank to complete the sentence.*

1. A _____ programming language is used to model real world events.
2. The programming language, _____, is a high-level structured language that makes extensive use of software engineering techniques.
3. The scientific-oriented programming language, _____, requires a special keyboard (including Greek letters and symbols).
4. Programs that require extensive I/O capacity are said to be _____.
5. A _____ program is one that overburdens the arithmetic/logic unit.
6. The term _____ refers to how "English-like" the program code reads to people.
7. The _____ tells the computer what operation to carry out.
8. Mnemonics are a common feature of _____ languages.
9. The _____ division in COBOL states the type of computer used to compile and run the program.

SHORT ANSWER QUESTIONS

When answering these questions think of concrete examples to illustrate your points.

1. What is the difference between machine and assembly languages?
2. What are the major weaknesses of BASIC?
3. What are the major distinguishing features of COBOL?
4. What languages are best for business applications?
5. What are the major strengths of Pascal?
6. What are the major strengths of FORTRAN?
7. What languages are used for science and engineering applications?
8. What is the purpose of each of the divisions in COBOL?
9. What is a natural language?

ESSAY QUESTIONS

1. Compare and contrast BASIC and Pascal.
2. Compare and contrast COBOL and FORTRAN.
3. In your business or in an area of interest at school which languages would be frequently used? Why?

SOFTWARE PACKAGES: PROGRAMS OFF THE SHELF

After studying this chapter you should understand the following:

■ *The chief advantages and disadvantages of using prewritten software.*
■ *Which general types of prewritten software have found wide application in both business and the home.*
■ *Some important business application areas—such as accounting, management, and marketing—for which specialized prewritten software is available.*
■ *The types of home-use software available for fun, education, and convenience.*
■ *How to evaluate prewritten software.*

The Oakriver University Information Processing Center was ablink with dazzling color graphics on display screens. People moved from one display to another as at a carnival, pausing here and there to make entries at a terminal, and then walking on as the spirit moved. Alice Smith—the systems analyst who arranged the hands-on demonstration—circulated among them. The aim today was to let everyone know what prewritten software was available. The idea seemed to be working.

"This is the most interesting meeting the University Computer User's Committee has ever had," Miguel Abreu, the committee chair, said to Alice.

"Thank you," Alice said.

"Did it take long to set all this up?" Miguel asked.

"No, we really just had to move in a few microcomputers to the terminal room. The software is all canned."

"Then what people say really does seem true," Miguel said. "You can just take programs off the shelf, plug them in, and they work?"

"If they're good, yes," Alice said. "But you have to do some careful evaluating too. Some of these packages are just fluff. As with buying something in a store, when you take the wrapping off and try it out you may be disappointed."

Elizabeth Slater, from the School of Business, looked up as Alice passed. Elizabeth was seated watching a tutorial program extoll the virtues of a new type of electronic spreadsheet. "Do you have written descriptions of all of these programs?" Elizabeth asked.

"Yes," Alice said, "on the tables in the middle of the room."

"Alice!" Jasper Thomas called from several terminals away. "I never saw graphics of this quality!" He gazed at a screen across which shapes were moving that looked like peach-colored giant ants. "The Physics Department will probably want to buy this package."

"What would you want to run the program on?" Alice asked.

"Well, I suppose on microcomputers," Jasper said. "We'll have quite a few of those."

"This particular package only runs on minicomputers, and requires very expensive special-purpose display terminals."

"Come on, Jasper, what does Physics need with that anyway?" Daniel Powers asked from the next terminal. "You scientists are happy with a blackboard and a piece of chalk. We *engineers*, however, use computer-aided design right and left." He motioned to the screen he stood before, which showed a cross section of a roadway with the different layers represented in varying colors and textures.

Miguel Abreu tapped Alice on the shoulder and pointed to the back of the room. "Is that a canned program too?" he asked.

Alice turned and saw one of the computer operators playing a fast-paced video game on her lunch break. Alice laughed. "Actually I

PREWRITTEN PROGRAMS READY TO RUN

SPEEDING UP THE PROGRAM DEVELOPMENT CYCLE

PREWRITTEN SOFTWARE refers to programs that were written and tested by someone else and are ready to run. The terms prewritten software, CANNED PROGRAMS, PACKAGED SOFTWARE, and OFF-THE-SHELF PROGRAMS, are used interchangeably. Such a program may have been created by someone else within the same organization, obtained free or on an exchange basis from a computer users' group, or purchased from an outside supplier. Most often prewritten software is purchased. A number of companies exist that write software for sale. Major hardware manufacturers also write and sell software. For-purchase software packages are the ones that have had a major impact on the world of business management over the last decade, and will be the main focus of this chapter. Although much of the chapter deals with software for microcomputers, vast amounts of prewritten software are available for minicomputers, mainframes, and supercomputers.

THE ADVANTAGES AND DISADVANTAGES OF PREWRITTEN SOFTWARE

An advantage of using prewritten software—assuming, of course, that software is available for your specific problem—is the almost immediate availability of the program for you to use. Ideally you can simply purchase the program, read the introductory instructions, work with a tutorial program that accompanies the one you bought, and begin to solve your problem. In contrast, developing software at your computer center can take months or years.

A second advantage is that good off-the-shelf programs have the major problems already ironed out of them. If high-quality user documentation is available, you can learn how to use the package quickly.

A final advantage is the lower cost of purchasing a program compared with the cost of developing it yourself. The development costs are passed on to the many purchasers of the product instead of being borne by you or your department alone.

There are also some disadvantages to using prewritten software. One is uncertainty as to whether the software will perform as promised. In some cases the virtues of a particular canned program are oversold. Another is that you may pay for more than you need. To make their software more marketable, suppliers often pack features into programs that you might not need but nonetheless must pay for. For example, many spreadsheet programs provide mathematical functions that you may never use. In comparison with the cost of custom programs, however, the cost of these extra features may be insignificant.

Should you want to change a canned program, you will discover a third drawback. To avoid "piracy" of their products, most sellers of software protect the programs so that users cannot have access to the actual code for the program. This is certainly a reasonable precaution for the vendors. Without it they stand to lose money to people who make illegal copies or modifications of their property. As a result, however, modifications in the software may be impossible, or illegal, or, in any case, quite tricky to make. Some programs circumvent this problem in part by allowing you to write your own special functions in a separate subprogram, which can then be called by the package.

If you're a programmer or a company with a programming staff, a final disadvantage of buying rather than writing software is the loss of potential income from selling the program yourself. Many business-oriented software packages were originally developed internally by a company to help solve a problem, and then sold to other companies with similar problems. The rights to a program can be assigned to a software supplier or marketed directly by the company itself. Large computer firms, such as National Cash Register Corporation, Hewlett-Packard, and IBM, have followed the self-marketing approach.

CANNED SOFTWARE AND YOUR INFORMATION SYSTEM

Like software produced in-house or custom-built, prewritten software has an effect on the other elements of the information system. The *people* in the system must be trained in the proper use and maintenance of these packages. Users need to know what the software package can do for them. They need to be trained individually or in groups on how to make best use of the software. Information-systems staff must be able to answer questions from users, as well as ensure that the prewritten package can make use of the other elements of the information system—that the package can, for instance, use existing data and run on existing hardware.

Rules and procedures need to take into account the tremendous rise in the variety of canned software available. For instance, if departments and individual users throughout a large organization are buying their own canned software right and left and tapping into the company's database, the security procedures that protect the data as well as prevent unauthorized access may have to be rethought.

Besides being accessible to those who need it, and inaccessible to those who don't, *data* must be in a form the prewritten software can use. Usually database management software—itself prewritten—can aid in linking a canned program to the data. Other *software* may need to be linked up with the canned programs to provide special operations. Proper *hardware*—such as color terminals for graphics packages—allows the user to exploit the software to its fullest. Mainframes generally allow you to run bigger and faster packages, whereas microcomputers give you greater control over what you do with the package.

Let's expand upon the software aspect of our information system and its relationship to canned programs. What makes canned software easy to use is the way it is designed for the nonprogrammer. Canned programs may be coded in assembly language or in a high-level language such as BASIC, C, FORTRAN, or Pascal. In addition system programs (the topic of Chapter 13) are used by the canned software. The beauty of a canned program is that in order to make use of its power, you do not need to know how to write in a programming language, or very much about how the canned program and system programs interact.

Much of the most popular canned software presents you with a series of choices concerning the use of the program that are known as a **MENU**. This is analogous to a restaurant's menu. You see what alternatives are available and select one that is appropriate. Depending on the software, the menu can be flexible (allows user-specified substitutions) or inflexible (no substitutions, please).

If you don't understand what an item is on a restaurant menu, you ask for help or clarification from the person taking your order. Similarly, canned software often allows you to ask for help. How helpful the response to your query is determines whether you will patronize the restaurant—or use the software— again (provided you have a choice).

Prewritten software is generally designed to execute in a modular fashion. The first module allows the user to enter the program. At this point the user can select from the menu what he or she wants to do. For example, the menu of a word-processing program would include such choices as creating a new document, recalling an old document for modifications, destroying an old document, or printing a document. Once you make a choice, the program then generally switches to a submenu for that choice. If you selected printing the document, the submenu choices might include printing all or part of the document, using special type-style and page-format options, and printing onto paper or writing onto a magnetic medium such as a diskette. Help modules aid in learning how to use the program. The final module allows you to exit the package easily.

Wrapping the package

Packaged software is often supplied to the purchaser on a magnetic input/output medium. For a microcomputer this usually means one or more floppy disks that contain the canned program (Figure 12-1). For larger computers the program is often supplied on one or more reels of magnetic tape; the computer then reads the program from the tape and stores it on disk

FIGURE 12-1.

Microcomputer software packaging. The package for Lotus® 1-2-3®, an integrated program that includes spreadsheet, database, and graphics capabilities, contains the software itself on a set of floppy disks, a manual, and a keyboard template. Most major microcomputer packages include similar elements.

for more rapid future reference. For information systems that use removable disk packs rather than nonremovable disks, the canned software can also be supplied on such a disk pack.

Another possibility increasingly used for some microcomputer systems is supplying the program right on a memory chip, generally a **READ-ONLY MEMORY CHIP (ROM)**, from which programs can be read into the computer system for use, but upon which no changes can be made. Software supplied this way is generally convenient and fast. It also provides excellent protection against piracy for the software developer.

Even the simplest canned program comes with documentation of some sort. Many packages are accompanied by tutorial programs. Very expensive mainframe packages may even be installed by personnel from the software company, who also iron out bugs and train users in getting the most out of the software.

MULTIPURPOSE PACKAGED SOFTWARE

In this section we will look at the most extensively used types of packaged software: word-processing software, electronic spreadsheets, database management systems, electronic mail and message systems, graphics packages, and combined packages. These are the software products that have set the pace for the software industry recently, particularly that portion of it devoted to microcomputers.

WORD-PROCESSING SOFTWARE

WORD-PROCESSING SOFTWARE is used to key in, modify, format, and print text material. The text material may include almost anything—accounting reports, business letters, lines of computer code, term papers, legal documents, recipes, novels, personal letters. Word processing can be done on any size of computer, although it is most often performed with microcomputers. A word-processing software package can be purchased for use on a general-purpose computer. For applications that do extensive word processing and nothing else, **DEDICATED WORD PROCESSORS** are available—minicomputers or microcomputers especially designed for, and limited to, word processing.

Popular among secretaries, managers, writers, and other people, word-processing software has one key attraction: the ability it gives users to make changes as often as necessary in a document without having to type the document over. Once you have entered the text, you can easily change it, and check it over again on the display screen, before printing it. If you have to make changes in a document that has already been printed, you do need to have the computer print it again; but you don't need to type it over again—you only have to enter the changes.

Other features of word-processing software include the ability to insert text into an existing document or to relocate blocks of text and have the software package reformat the new text. Wordwrap is a feature that automatically moves your type to the next line as you type so you don't have to hit the return key. Boldface, underline, subscript, and superscript operations can also be performed, and text can be right-justified. In addition some systems will check your spelling, and allow you to create text and addresses for mailing-list letters. Figure 12-2 shows an example of text entry and correction using word-processing software.

FIGURE 12-2.
Entering text, and correcting it, using word-processing software.

Original text
as entered

> If you are working on a typewriter and decide after you have typed something that you don't like the word order you have chosen, you usually have to start over on a new sheet of paper. With a word processing program, you can make the change electronically._
>
> Cursor

Marked text
to be moved

Cursor

The block to be moved
is highlighted and
the cursor moved to
the new location.

> If you are working on a typewriter and decide after you have typed something that you don't like the word order you have chosen, you usually have to start over on a new sheet of paper. With a word processing program, you can make the change electronically.

Corrected text after the
block has been moved
and the paragraph
reformatted.

> If you are working on a typewriter and decide that you don't like the word order you have chosen after you have typed something, you usually have to start over on a new sheet of paper. With a word processing program, you can make the change electronically._
>
> Cursor

Originally word processing could be done only in English, in part because the input process could move only from left to right across the page or screen (unsuitable for Arabic, for instance, which moves from right to left). Software now exists to allow you to do word processing in virtually any language (Figure 12-3).

FIGURE 12-3.
A keyboard for multilingual word processing.

SUBVERSIVE WORD PROCESSORS

A few of us who love writing on computers suspect that, in some dark way, machines have ruined our style. It's probably true. Most current word-processing programs simply outdistance our writing skills, and their promised ease turns out to be a deception. When programs are loaded with user-friendly, obsessively distracting features, an already difficult job can get out of control.

All writers face the same basic challenges of creating ideas, organizing information, and revising for a better effect. A computer could help them, but it really doesn't know how.

Simply trying to get started is a hard job for anyone, and any word processor that softened this block would be a help. It should encourage moving forward at top speed and saving corrections until later.

I like to think of this as separating creativity from analysis. Peter Elbow, a widely published teacher of writing, calls it "freewriting" and has shown that writers develop ideas more easily when they keep thinking of the subject and ignore trivial mistakes. Sophisticated word-processing programs don't understand this—they encourage instant revision.

. Simple programs like Bank Street Writer, on the other hand, make shifts to the revising mode so awkward that users forge ahead out of necessity, abandoning all hopes of a perfect first draft. The rigidity irritates some, but many writers find their ideas flow more smoothly and their sentences sound less stilted. Because it will just boot up and go with no housekeeping, Bank Street Writer is comfortable, an Underwood among Selectrics.

Average writers fall back on pet rituals to plan their attack. They plot connections with elaborate maps, trees, and other designs, or they catalog relationships by outlining, listing, and serious notetaking.

Can a computer handle this planning more effectively? Well, at least it can make it neater. An outlining program like Thinktank emulates most of these creative strategies and has real potential for the writer.

I use it every day, but I'm still not good enough for it. I have this habit of tinkering with formal structures and conceptual arrangements, never seeming to know when to get busy and write. And who would? Outlining on a computer is so much fun that it's seductive.

So there goes style again. When an outline gets too good, it gets tight in the seams, leaving no room for the spontaneous thoughts and loose rhythms that separate quick writing from the dead. We learned that by doing outlines in high school.

Then there is revising. If you still believe that computers make writing easier, you're probably thinking about the power of insert and delete. Besides, moving blocks of copy is almost as much fun as outlining.

But too many writers squander this power on surface corrections and minor rearrangements. We move one awkward paragraph ahead of another and call it an improvement.

Not that we're lazy. We might not have seen the real problem. When that happens, a computer can get downright subversive and respond in a literal-minded way, as if all our commands were purposeful and exact. When we get really involved, we begin to think that they are.

I recently asked my students to rewrite some essays that they had turned in, and I watched while they processed their texts into flabby, textureless mush. They just Cuisinarted everything because it was easy.

Source: John Strommer, *Popular Computing,* May 1985. Reprinted with permission. Copyright © 1985 by McGraw-Hill, Inc. All rights reserved.

ELECTRONIC SPREADSHEETS

An **ELECTRONIC SPREADSHEET** is a type of software that offers the user a simulated financial worksheet on a display screen and an easy way to change figures around within the worksheet. The term "spreadsheet" comes from the name given the paper printed with rows and columns used as worksheets by accountants. Electronic spreadsheets are used principally on microcomputers. Their strength and popularity rest on their ability to do projections: you can alter a figure or two on the spreadsheet and let the program update all of the related figures based on your change. This is very handy for doing financial plans and budgets.

A typical spreadsheet can be thought of as a large grid with several thousand cells. Since the cells are arranged in rows and columns (there may be hundreds of rows and columns), we can select any one cell by keying in its specific row and column number. Often each row is given a number and each column a letter. Thus the cell in the seventh column and 16th row is called cell G16 (G being the seventh letter of the alphabet). Each cell can be filled with either a label—such as "January" or "Gross Margin"—or a value. A value can be either a number or a mathematical formula.

We can use a simple example to show how spreadsheets can be developed, cells altered, and the effect of the alterations projected in related cells. Susan Paul, sales manager at Paul's House of Electronic Wonders, wants to project her company's operating income by month for the year 1987. Figure 12-4a shows the spreadsheet displayed on her screen. The work area at the top of the screen indicates which cell she is currently working on and what she has entered there. She has entered as a value a formula to subtract the contents of cell G15 from the contents of cell G14. The result, 30, the projected operating income for April, appears in the current cell, G17.

Because Susan is thinking about instituting a special sales incentive program in April, she wants to see what will happen to operating income if the cost of sales increases 20 percent in that month. The result is shown in Figure 12-4b. She enters the new value for selling expenses, 204, in cell G15. The change in operating income is calculated automatically and appears in cell G17.

From this simple example we can see what makes spreadsheets so powerful. The user can create a spreadsheet, alter it in certain cells as data change, and then observe how the altered data affect related cells. Such a tool allows users to ask a lot of "what if" questions and see the results with far less effort (and far more accuracy) than older paper-and-pencil and calculator methods.

Additionally the user can subdivide the spreadsheet into smaller grids (as small as one cell) and manipulate the data mathematically, or replace the data entirely by keying in new data. Data can also be transferred from a larger database, such as one maintained by a mainframe or minicomputer-oriented information system, to the microcomputer running the spreadsheet program. If appropriate, the results could be sent back to the larger system for storage. As with any method of making projections, however, the projections will only be as good as the data entered and formulas applied. Setting up spreadsheets inaccurately has cost some companies considerable sums of money (see Case in Point box on p. 340).

DATABASE MANAGERS

A database is made up of a set of interrelated files. **DATABASE MANAGEMENT SYSTEMS (DBMS)** are programs to create, access, and modify databases. They are used extensively on computers of all sizes. A database management system contains three different types of software:

1 *Data definition software. This provides users with a means of*

FIGURE 12-4.

Using an electronic spread-sheet. (a) Susan Paul enters a formula in cell G17 that gives her the company's projected operating income for April.

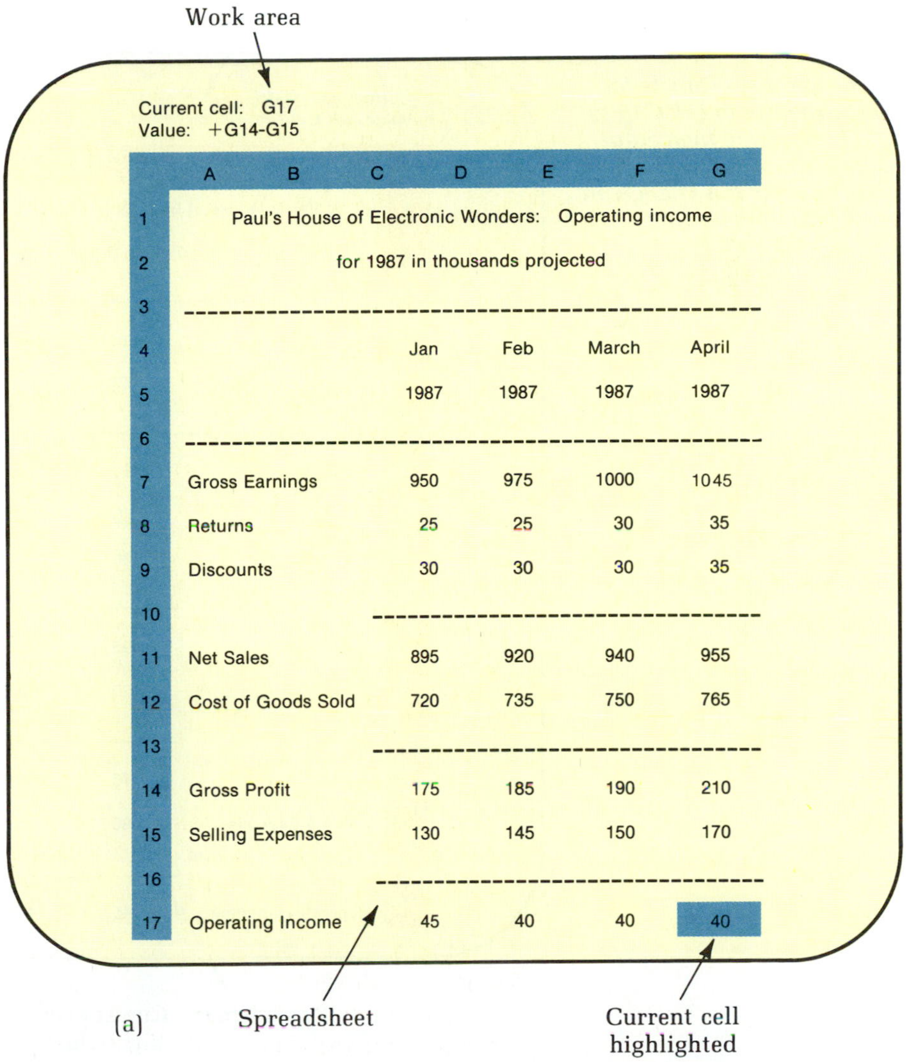

Work area

Current cell: G17
Value: +G14-G15

	A	B	C	D	E	F	G
1	Paul's House of Electronic Wonders: Operating income						
2	for 1987 in thousands projected						
3	---						
4			Jan	Feb	March	April	
5			1987	1987	1987	1987	
6	---						
7	Gross Earnings		950	975	1000	1045	
8	Returns		25	25	30	35	
9	Discounts		30	30	30	35	
10			-------------------------------				
11	Net Sales		895	920	940	955	
12	Cost of Goods Sold		720	735	750	765	
13			-------------------------------				
14	Gross Profit		175	185	190	210	
15	Selling Expenses		130	145	150	170	
16			-------------------------------				
17	Operating Income		45	40	40	40	

(a) Spreadsheet   Current cell highlighted

describing the characteristics of the data and the interrelationships among different data elements.

2   *Data manipulation software.* This allows users to enter, alter, and delete data from the database.

3   *Data inquiry software.* This enables users to extract data from the database in response to questions.

Oakriver University, for example, maintains a central database on faculty members. For a given faculty member the database contains the department, home address and telephone, degrees earned, courses taught, and publications. The "degree," "courses taught," and "publication" data items may be repeated as many times as necessary to record the faculty member's different degrees, courses taught, and publications. Figure 12-5 shows how a user might use the data inquiry software that is part of the database management system to gain information about a particular instructor. We will learn more about databases in Chapter 16.

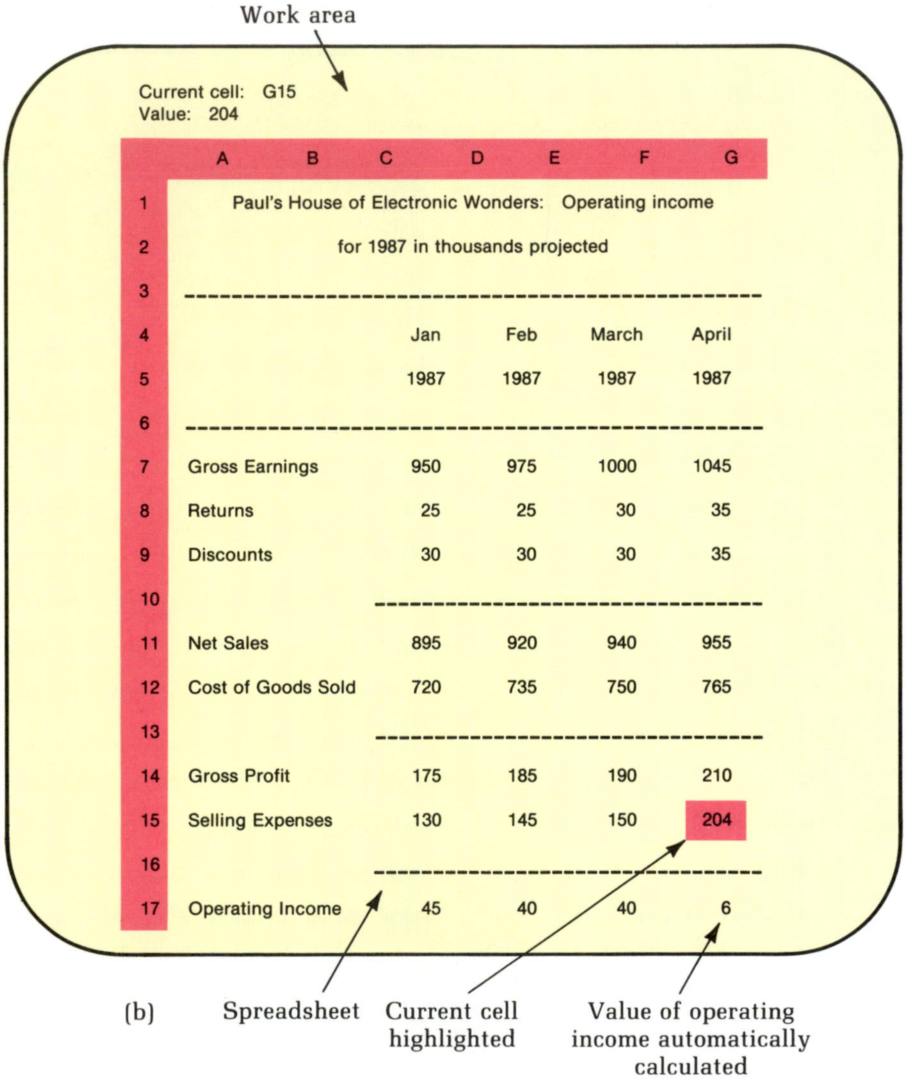

FIGURE 12-4b.

She changes her estimate for selling expenses in cell G15 to 204. The software then automatically calculates and adjusts for the effect of this change on April's operating income.

Work area

Current cell: G15
Value: 204

	A	B	C	D	E	F	G
1	Paul's House of Electronic Wonders: Operating income						
2	for 1987 in thousands projected						
3	---						
4			Jan	Feb	March		April
5			1987	1987	1987		1987
6	---						
7	Gross Earnings		950	975	1000		1045
8	Returns		25	25	30		35
9	Discounts		30	30	30		35
10			-----------------------------------				
11	Net Sales		895	920	940		955
12	Cost of Goods Sold		720	735	750		765
13			-----------------------------------				
14	Gross Profit		175	185	190		210
15	Selling Expenses		130	145	150		204
16			-----------------------------------				
17	Operating Income		45	40	40		6

(b)   Spreadsheet   Current cell highlighted   Value of operating income automatically calculated

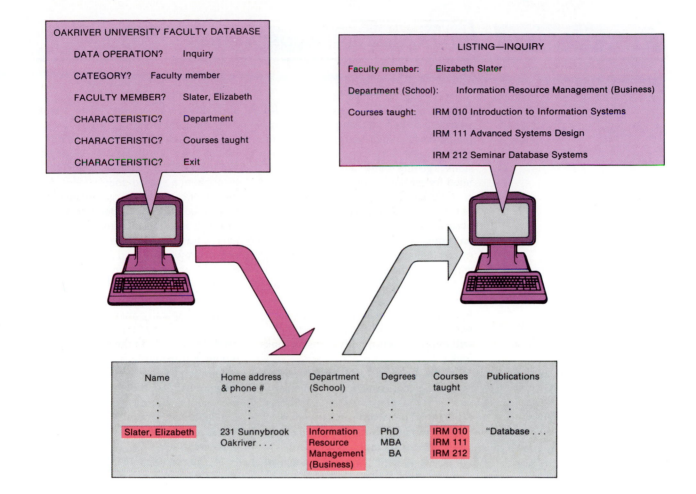

FIGURE 12-5.

Using a database management package. Here an administrator at Oakriver uses data inquiry software—part of the DBMS— to gain information about a particular instructor from Oakriver's faculty database.

ELECTRONIC MAIL/MESSAGE SYSTEMS

An **ELECTRONIC MAIL/MESSAGE SYSTEM**, or **EMMS**, allows people to send memos, messages, facsimiles of illustrations and photographs, and other materials electronically. The information or materials sent can be routed locally within an office, between branch locations, or across the world through satellite-based communications (see Chapter 8).

As we saw in Chapter 3, such systems are part of the information-age office. The flow of messages and paperwork can be speeded up using an EMMS. When messages are sent from one terminal to another, a paper copy may not be needed at all; indeed some companies claim to run a virtually "paperless" office.

An EMMS works as follows. When you want to send a memo or

If you're like most managers, the decisions you make based on personal computer spread sheets are already big and getting bigger. The scope of those decisions is getting wider. And, the likelihood for serious problems is growing.

A Dallas-based oil and gas company recently fired several executives for oversights costing millions of dollars in an acquisition deal. The errors were traced to faulty financial analysis in a spreadsheet model.

How can we avoid disasters such as the one in Dallas? What are the problems we should look out for? How can we improve spread sheets so that they will improve high-quality decision making?

The old computing dictum, "garbage in, garbage out," used to imply a clear answer to the question of spread sheets' reliability: They were just as good or bad as you made them. But the acclaim given personal computers and the wholesale adoption of spread sheets as planning tools seems to have turned the old adage on its ear. "Garbage in, garbage out" has become "garbage in, gospel out."

Managers and executives responsible for decisions based on personal computer spread sheets should look behind those reassuring printouts to the logic and makeup of the spread-sheet models themselves.

The following problems are accompanied by real examples taken from businesses I have analyzed or worked with:

(1) A model is logically inconsistent; rules applied to one part of the spread sheet should be applied to another part, but are not. In forecasting revenues, a California manufacturer applied price discounts to one part of a product line, but overlooked them when forecasting sales of complementary products. Actual sales for the complementary lines turned out to be higher than forecast,

and bottlenecks resulted when production could not keep up with delivery.

(2) A model, though logically consistent, is conceptually flawed. Here, bad formulas are faithfully reproduced throughout a spread-sheet model. A finance officer with a large savings and loan association submitted five-year forecasts for divisional profits. However, a mistake in a formula for compound growth resulted in the figures becoming progressively overstated for years two through five of the forecast.

(3) Data format is inconsistent or garbled. Typically, these problems occur when different types of data are used side by side in the same or parallel model. For example, a national retailer, accounting for manpower needs, discovered field reports stated in persons, man-hours, man-days and man-months. Consolidation proved impossible until an exhaustive rewrite of field reports was completed.

(4) The wrong tool is used for the task. This problem is common and growing. An international distributor of industrial goods based its plans for sales to a South American country on an analysis of that country's manufacturing capacity. But, the distributor's products were only used in secondary manufacturing, a small part of the country's total output. The distinction was not made in the spread sheet so that sales were far below forecasts; production and inventory costs ended up consuming thousands of extra dollars.

In all of these examples, gross inconsistencies or major problems will quickly stand out. Many times, though, subtle problems will not be readily detected.

Worse, problem detection becomes more and more difficult as data users are removed from the data's source. This frequently occurs when one department uses data generated by another department's spread sheets. Even if detected, problems may be nearly impossible to trace, not to mention correct.

Managers are not without tools to address this mushrooming problem. A carefully followed set of "spread-sheet audit" procedures combined with software for isolating mistakes can all but eliminate most common spread-sheet problems.

The steps to be followed are straightforward:

(1) Insist on an audit of all spread sheets used for important decision making. Recently available software, such as —DocuCalc for Apple computers or the Spreadsheet Auditor for IBM PCs, gives two-dimensional printouts with detailed listings of the spread-sheet formulas—thus making verification of the model's underpinnings routine.

(2) Create and enforce an audit trail. As data, printouts or diskettes move beyond their source, this becomes indispensable. In addition to the printout of the formulas mentioned above, an audit trail should include the name of the model's author, the date it was created, a unique name or number, what type of input and output are expected, and a brief narrative describing the purpose and operation of the model.

(3) Establish responsibility for the model. Do not let it wander. Changes to the model should be made by authorized personnel only. More importantly, managers using other departments' spread sheets should be responsible for them as if they were their own. Enforcement of this rule will bolster enforcement of rule No. 2 above. A manager responsible for a spread sheet's output will insist on an audit trail and will not just blindly "plug in his own numbers."

(4) Require a re-audit each time the model is modified. Document these changes in the audit trail. Spread sheets seem to take on a life of their own, growing in size and complexity as more and more variables are factored into the model. Even minor changes can have unintended effects on otherwise sound spread sheets.

In addition to these specific rules, a final suggestion may be useful: Raise the visibility of the issue. Find out who is using spread sheets for what sort of decision making. If the decisions are important, ensure that procedures similar to these are implemented and followed.

message, you enter it into the system. Most likely you would do this with a word-processing system to speed the creation of the message. You indicate the recipient or recipients of the information, and specify other details concerning the communication, such as whether or not a message is confidential and whether or not a response is required.

The message is then routed by the EMMS to the terminal(s) of the recipient(s) indicated. To read a confidential message, the user first would have to enter a password. Anyone who did not know the password would not be able just to sit down at a terminal and view the message. If the "message" sent were in the form of a photograph or facsimile, then it would be transmitted to equipment capable of reproducing it rather than a standard terminal.

Individual microcomputer users can also communicate with one another through messages without buying an EMMS. For a subscription and/or a service charge, microcomputer users can transmit messages over telephone lines to an information service such as The Source or CompuServe. The computers run by the service will "post" the message on an electronic bulletin board. An **ELECTRONIC BULLETIN BOARD** is a computer-maintained list of messages that can be posted and read by different computers, often concerning a topic of common interest. Curious "readers" can look at the messages the bulletin board contains, and read and respond to those they wish. Typical topics are science-fiction novels, good restaurants in the area, and microcomputers.

GRAPHICS PACKAGES   Although print is the dominant medium for computer output, it is by no means the only one. **GRAPHICS PACKAGES** allow you to construct and output pictorial information. The information can be displayed on a screen, plotted on a hard-copy pictorial output device known as a plotter, produced by a printer, or converted to transparencies for projection. Graphics packages are available for all sizes of computers—mainframes, minicomputers, and microcomputers.

Businesses use graphics packages to develop charts that summarize situations at a glance (Figure 12-6). The old saw that "one picture is worth a thousand words" still rings true, and a continual concern in designing output for management in any medium is presenting it in brief, summary fashion. Graphical output is well suited to this. A typical use is to show statistics in summary fashion to management. Corporate income might be displayed in a multicolored "pie chart," showing which slices of the pie came from which sources. Sales projections could be shown with a bar-chart display.

FIGURE 12-6.

A picture is worth a thousand words—some examples of the kinds of graphs and diagrams graphics packages can produce.

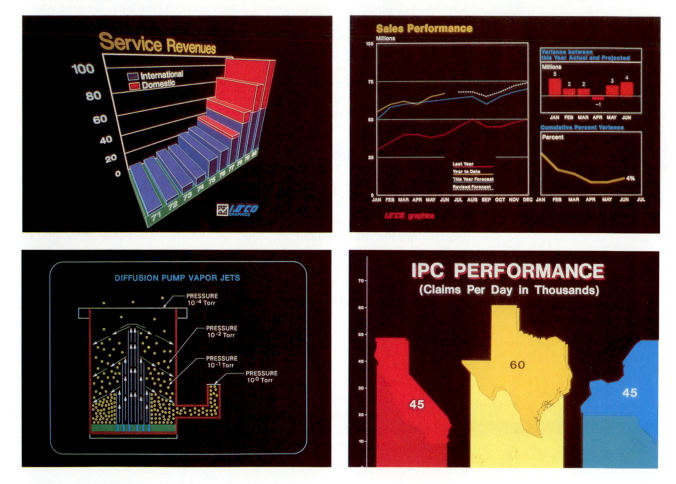

FIGURE 12-7.
Computer-aided design.

Some nonbusiness applications of graphics are in producing weather reports, contour maps, and computer art. **COMPUTER-AIDED DESIGN (CAD)** systems use computers to facilitate design of a product (Figure 12-7). The designer works at a terminal, drawing graphical designs either with a special pad that transfers the data to the computer, or directly on the display screen using a light-sensitive rod known as a light pen. The engineer can manipulate and alter the design at the terminal. The type of display screen and printer or plotter used for a CAD system must be of a higher quality than the level necessary for creating graphics for management use.

It is difficult to write programs yourself that produce high-quality graphics. In fact graphics was one of the first areas historically to employ canned programs. Before the advent of display screen output or of printers that could draw, graphic output was by plotter only. Packaged subroutines were supplied with the plotter; users could call the subroutines, giving quite specific data to the subroutines such as where the pen should be placed on the page in terms of x-y coordinates, and the subroutine would handle the still thornier instructions for getting the pen there.

Today graphics software meets most users at a much higher level. User-friendly graphics packages like the one illustrated in Figure 12-8 guide users quickly and painlessly to elegant output that can easily outdo those thousand words. Typically the user selects the desired output from a menu. After making a selection, one or more screens appear asking the user to specify details about the selected graphical form, such as color and texture, and to give the data values to be displayed along with appropriate labels. The actual graphical display is then produced on the specified device.

INTEGRATED PACKAGES

A number of **INTEGRATED SOFTWARE PACKAGES** contain the features of several of the software packages discussed above. For example, Lotus® 1-2-3® by Lotus Development Corporation combines three areas: electronic spreadsheets, data-base management, and graphics. A successor to Lotus 1-2-3, Symphony®, adds word-processing capabilities. Ashton-Tate's Framework® also combines database, spreadsheet, word-processing, and telecommunications capabilities. These multiple-use packages allow a user to move from one feature to another with great ease—say from word processing to database management. A user might create a spreadsheet drawing data from the company's database, and then switch to the word-processing function and incorporate the spreadsheet into a memorandum.

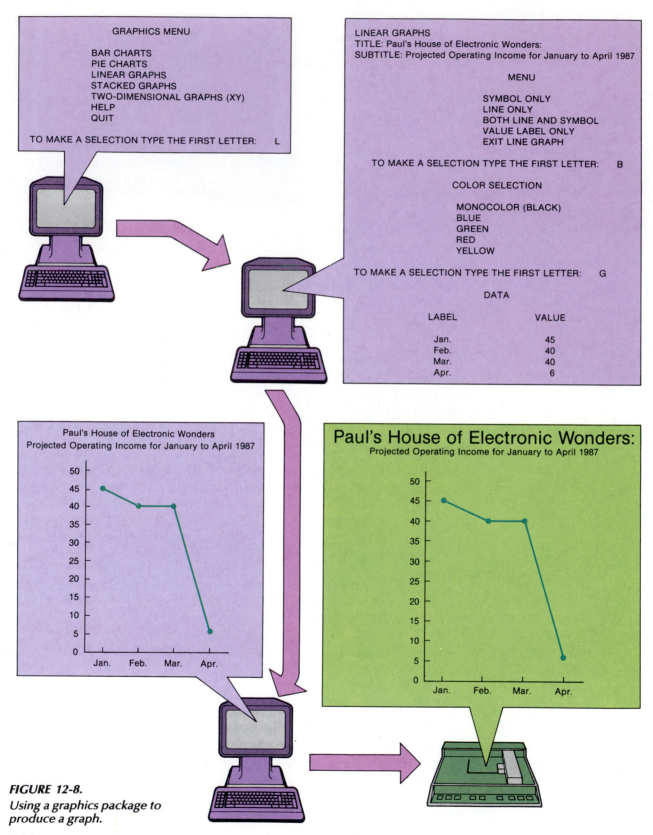

FIGURE 12-8.
Using a graphics package to produce a graph.

Combined packages offer a lot of software for users who require a variety of prepackaged functions. Their price tag is high, however, and users who do not really need all of the functions are probably better served by separately purchasing only those that they do need.

PACKAGES FOR GENERAL BUSINESS

The multipurpose canned software described in the preceding section is useful in many different home and office settings. In this section we will shift our focus to packaged software intended specifically for business functions. These packages come in all sizes, to meet needs ranging from the one-person business or small office with a microcomputer, to major corporations with their powerful mainframes. Even large organizations with extensive in-house staffs of programmers and systems analysts still evaluate and, when appropriate, purchase, packaged software for specific needs; their information systems thus consist of a blend of custom-designed in-house software and packages obtained without the birth pains of development.

ACCOUNTING

There are well over 1000 **ACCOUNTING PACKAGES** available to computer users today. They range from simple bookkeeping and check-register programs for users of home computers, to complex packages costing $100,000 or more for use by corporations.

Some of the advantages of using canned accounting packages can be seen by looking at Freddy Johnson's Travel Agency, with its 71 employees. Success of the company, a sharp drop in hardware prices, plus the need to remain competitive, make it possible for the travel agency to install a computer system to handle accounting and other functions. But the company will not have the resources to develop all of its programs in-house. The cost of developing software is high, and the process difficult and lengthy.

So instead of programming, the agency can purchase a canned payroll system to write the 71 paychecks and maintain records of employee taxes withheld and deductions; purchase an accounts payable system to pay company bills; and buy an accounts receivable system to generate bills to customers and track those that are outstanding until payment. A general ledger program can replace the agency's main bookkeeping records, producing computerized balance sheets and income statements. Another common accounting function to be computerized—inventory—is not required at Freddy Johnson's, since services rather than physical products are sold. The same is true of another popular type of accounting package—tax preparation programs.

When a company switches from a manual to a computer-based information system, it does so first with accounting. Prewritten software—carefully evaluated before purchase to see that it will meet company needs—can deliver the sought-after results in a hurry: more efficient and timely issuance of bills and checks, more up-to-date maintenance of accounting records, lower costs for carrying out the accounting process, and improved cash flow due to measures such as careful tracking of money owed.

MANAGEMENT

As with accounting packages, users can choose from a wide range of **MANAGEMENT-ORIENTED PREWRITTEN SOFTWARE**. Application packages exist in the areas of personnel management, operations management, forecasting, facilities maintenance, and resource management.

In the area of personnel management, for example, software exists to help set up work schedules, create confidential databases for personnel records, and manage the various employee benefit plans. In the area of operations management production control programs assist in scheduling production, in monitoring output, and in quality control. In the area of forecasting the most popular purchased tool is the electronic spreadsheet discussed earlier in the chapter; other packages exist which—based on the input you supply—will project the possible consequences into the future. Facilities maintenance packages control the air-conditioning, heating, lighting, and security systems in offices, warehouses, and factories. Resource management packages assist in determining the optimal levels of production, given an organization's financial, material, and labor resources.

FINANCES FINANCE PACKAGES address such questions as forecasting the company's budget for the next fiscal year, determining the credit-worthiness of clients, or modeling the outcomes of various investment decisions. Often these financial models are included as part of many electronic spreadsheet packages. Nonetheless special prewritten software is available. Such a package might, for example, help Oakriver University decide whether or not to put up a new building for the Foreign Languages Department. A prepackaged capital expenditure analysis program could aid administrators in seeing if the investment made sense in the long run, or whether the university might save money and yet meet expansion needs by postponing construction for now and giving the department two floors of space in another building slated for demolition in ten years.

A user-friendly series of prompts would elicit the relevant data painlessly from a responsible person within the university with access to the financial and other figures needed for modeling. The program would then project the costs and benefits of different options. The program's output might show that erecting the building now, rather than waiting ten years, was the better option. This is based on the assumption that construction costs will continue to escalate: the money saved by not building now, invested in low-risk managed-growth securities, would not grow enough in ten years to match the differential in construction costs.

Naturally the principle that the output of a program can be no better than its input applies. Like management packages, finance packages are meant to be used by those who are experts in their areas of inquiry. The output of such packages is not extensive information, but vital information. Standard accounting packages, on the other hand, are heavy on output, and do not demand the same skill and level of intelligent use since they deal with more routinized operations.

ENGINEERING Another area where packaged software is available to help skilled people make important decisions is in engineering. Engineers can produce three-dimensional graphical designs at a terminal, alter them to their specification, rotate the designs to examine different views, and create a hard copy of the design as well as of the specifications that produced it. This is possible using computer-aided design (discussed earlier in the chapter under "Graphics Packages"). Engineers and their support personnel also can purchase canned software to aid in testing products at various stages of design and production and to carry out quality-assurance procedures.

MANUFACTURING   There are two major applications for prewritten software in the manufacturing process: computer-aided manufacturing and materials management. **COMPUTER-AIDED MANUFACTURING (CAM)** uses a computer to direct the production and assembly process. CAM systems usually direct machine tools and robots, and come in a wide variety of types. With recent packages the user can select the correct sequence of operations from a menu, and can give specifications—for instance, cutting depth—for the operation.

Materials management is concerned with the control of manufacturing inventories. Raw materials on hand can be tallied, reorder points determined, and purchases made in a timely fashion that will neither keep the manufacturing process waiting for want of materials, nor stockpile excessive quantities of those materials. Inventories of the finished product can also be controlled.

MARKETING   In marketing an important goal is to know your customer. Sales call packages help coach salespeople on how to make the right approach. A popular package for salespeople allows the user to develop a "psychological profile" of a potential customer. From this profile the package then generates a suggested sales approach in terms of how to pitch the sales presentation. For example, if the psychological profile shows the client is put off by pushy methods, the salesperson will be advised to use a "soft-sell" approach.

Those involved in marketing have access to a variety of other software tools as well. Specific packages exist for sales analysis and market research, and generalized packages such as database systems can also be helpful for marketing applications. Sales-order software helps speed up the order-processing effort by allowing the salesperson to transmit orders to the information system.

PACKAGES FOR FUN, EDUCATION, AND CONVENIENCE

In addition to multipurpose packaged software and packages for generalized business use, prewritten programs are plentiful strictly for having fun, for education, and for obtaining services in the convenience of your own home.

Computer games
The stock exchange has closed for the day, so it's time to put that spreadsheet away and have some fun. **COMPUTER GAMES**, a microcomputer phenomenon, are played by watching the action or questions on the display screen and responding using the keyboard or joysticks. Joysticks are movable levers like an airplane's control stick, used to control cursor movement or some other facet of a computer game. Today computer games range from those that are a challenge to nothing more than one's reaction time, as in firing missiles at the enemy, to those requiring great patience and mental skill, as in unraveling computerized mystery stories. Games exist that appeal to virtually every type of interest. Figure 12-9 shows some of the games available for purchase.

Computer-assisted instruction
In **COMPUTER-ASSISTED INSTRUCTION (CAI)** a computer is used to teach material to a student or other user, generally on an interactive basis such that the

The "whiz kids" of yesterday have become the "sober kids" of today. Like everything else in the computer industry, it's not as easy as it used to be for young programmers.

"The publisher is demanding a lot more today of the product because of the competition," says Gary Carlston, vice president of Broderbund Software.

"It used to be a publisher was willing to take a risk with a kid and say, 'It's okay if he doesn't go that last 10 percent.' But today, a publisher wants to have confidence that the fellow is willing to go that last 10 percent. You just can't be wild and crazy anymore."

It's the last leg of a software development project that can be the most crucial. It is the time of rewriting the code, polishing it and honing it until the program runs flawlessly. Today's market, saturated with software programs, will tolerate nothing less. . .

The more successful of the teen programmers can go these extra miles. They are a new breed who are more serious, more committed to their work. . . One such teenager is 19-year-old Eric Hammond, who spent nine months—or close to 1,400 hours—writing 8,000 lines of assembler code to complete his popular computer game, "One on One." This game is a simulation of a one-on-one basketball match between two of the best basketball players in the National Basketball Association, Julius Erving and Larry Bird.

Hammond's polished rewriting, plus the novelty of the game concept, helped turn the game into a smashing success.

The uncanny resemblance of the movements of the players on the screen to the actual movements of the two NBA stars has prompted one reviewer to call it "one of the best-executed games in the sports simulation genre."

To learn the intricacies of each movement of these great basketball players, Hammond studied slow-motion films of the 1982 All-Star Game in which Erving and Bird competed.

In addition, since both Bird and Erving promoted the game, Hammond had the opportunity to speak personally with both stars. "I was able to ask Erving what his strategy was in a one-on-one game. (I asked him) what his favorite shots were, his pet shots. . . .

"One on One" has sold more than 35,000 copies at close to $40 a clip. While Hammond doesn't reveal just how much he has made off the program, it's likely that he has earned the typical programmer's share of 7 to 15 percent of the company's profit on the software program. That would make Hammond a wealthy young man.

Source: David Barry, "Coming Down to Earth," *San Jose Mercury News,* Oct. 28, 1984.

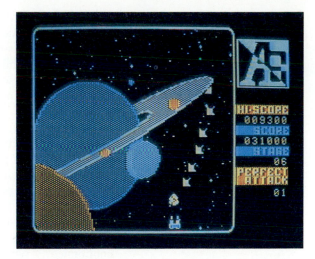

FIGURE 12-9.
A screen from a computer game.

FIGURE 12-10.
Computer-assisted instruction (CAI) allows students to learn at their own pace.

computer corrects incorrect answers immediately after the student gives them. These programs are available for mainframes, minis, and micros, but our focus here will be on micros. CAI packages (see Figure 12-10) run the educational gamut, from flash-card programs for prekindergartners to continuing-education instruction for postgraduate professionals. Packages exist to teach computer languages, prepare students for examinations, teach speed reading, and drill students in Morse code.

CAI is also used in the business world to aid in personnel training. A worker, for example, might be trained to use a new machine or a new process on an old machine with the help of instructional programming. The flight simulators used to train pilots are a particularly sophisticated example of computerized instruction. On a more routine level the tutorial programs that accompany many popular software packages are also examples of CAI.

The trick to a good CAI package is to have features that allow a user to move at his or her own pace. Most CAI packages adopt a format of short

questions to which only one answer is possible; this is amenable to drilling simple mathematical operations, checking a spelling answer, or answering a series of true/false or multiple-choice questions. Unfortunately CAI packages do not do the complete job. Knowing that an answer is wrong is not enough; the person needs to know why. For that a teacher is usually required, as in the past.

Home managers

Tired of the tedium of manually balancing your checkbook? Finding the perfect recipe for that perfect dinner party? Filing the addresses of relatives and friends? Well HOME-MANAGEMENT SOFTWARE—which performs convenience-oriented services as well as some accounting for microcomputer users—is just for you. Or maybe not.

Many home-management packages are available. Figure 12-11 illustrates one such product at work. Whether many of these packages are in fact economically worthwhile is something only you can decide. If you write only 20 checks a month and feel comfortable with rudimentary arithmetic, you may find it cheaper, and perhaps faster, to balance your checkbook with paper and pencil and a small calculator than with a computer.

In addition to packages you can use at home, a variety of information-processing services exist into which you can plug your home computer, for a fee, using telephone lines. These include home banking services to handle such matters as paying bills, at-home ordering service for appliances and consumer goods, services that will provide stock-market and other financial reports, database-search services, and more. Indeed today the computer has come home—even the big computer—as some services will sell you processing time on their powerful minis or mainframes, which you can utilize through your microcomputer over phone lines. Computer services available by teleprocessing were discussed in Chapter 8.

FIGURE 12-11.

Services for the home. This package keeps track of room temperature, lights, and appliances, and lets you write memos to yourself.

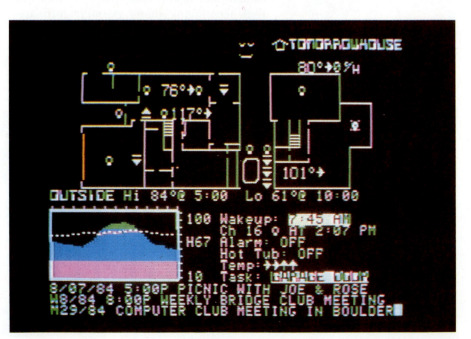

As with selecting a programming language, choosing prewritten software can be quite a challenge. The first step is to identify what your needs are—that is, what problem you wish to solve. You may wish to turn to various sources that regularly evaluate software, such as trade journal reviewers and independent software-testing houses. In addition it helps to know the questions for which you need to find answers. Here we will discuss a few such questions useful for microcomputer and mainframe systems.

What does the program do? This refers to the tasks that the program performs. You must determine what your present and future needs are, and then find the package to satisfy them. For example, one accounting program might handle 200 entries for accounts payable, while another package might handle up to 500.

What machines will it work on? Not every software package will work on all models of the type of computer to which it is geared. For example, some microcomputer packages can be transferred from one microcomputer to another, while others are unique to one system.

Will you need to modify your hardware? A new software package may require more main memory than you have, or a disk-drive system with a larger capacity. Other software may demand output hardware capable of producing high-quality graphics. Always test software on a system like the one you will use it on before you buy it.

What do you do if the software doesn't work? Find out the type of warranty (if any) that accompanies the software. Faults may show up in the actual software, in your equipment, in your installation and use of the software, or because you bought the wrong kind of software to begin with. When the software is defective, your legal recourse varies from state to state. Some suppliers provide support in diagnosing and correcting problems. In the case of packages for mainframes, this support can be extensive.

You should also try to evaluate the financial viability of the software vendor before you buy—less stable companies come and go frequently in this market.

Are there classes or books available to explain to you and any other users how to work with the software? Many classes and books are available for the most popular software systems. For microcomputer software classes may be offered through university extension programs, the store where you purchased the software (sometimes for free), and private classes or tutors.

Does the software come with an accompanying training or tutorial program? A good tutorial will let you progress at your own pace and allow you to skip over material you already know. It should be written in a user-friendly style to avoid intimidating you.

How good does the user documentation look? Ask the salesperson to show you a copy of the documentation supplied with the program. Not only should the documentation be complete, but it should be written in a style you can understand.

How much does the software cost? You should consider not only the initial cost of the software, but also any possible associated costs, such as the cost of buying additional hardware, training people to use the software, changing the data into a usable form, and updating the system as your needs change. As an example of the last point, a good accounts receivable system for a small business should be able to accommodate more customers as the business grows.

How much will it cost to upgrade the software if you need to expand your system? Mentioned in connection with the preceding point, as your needs change you want to continue to be able to use the software. Perhaps there are options or additional parts of the package that can be added as you need them. In any case, if you upgrade your hardware for other reasons, you want the existing software to be able to run on it.

Can you make copies of the software for your own protection? If not, are you given a "backup" copy? If copies can be made, you will need to do so, and to keep them in a different location from the original, so that you can still use the program if the original is damaged. Some software packages are protected against copying. This is to protect the copyright of the vendor and prevent unauthorized copies. For such systems the vendor usually supplies a backup copy with the original. If you can't make your own backup copy and the vendor doesn't supply one, you might find yourself at least temporarily without working software.

WRAP-UP   **THE NEED TO EVALUATE PREWRITTEN SOFTWARE**

Alice Smith, the systems analyst at Oakriver University's Information Processing Center who had set up the demonstration, drew the participants around her for an impromptu meeting before they left.

"I am glad to see nearly everyone has taken literature on the software they're interested in," Alice said.

"And we thank you, Alice, for letting us try it out," said Miguel Abreu, the committee chair.

"The programs will be here for you to use the rest of the week," Alice said. "I would also urge you to read this carefully." She passed out a document produced by the Information Processing Center.

"This memo shows some of the factors you should consider when comparing programs. Things like what machines it actually runs on, how much it costs, and whether it really does what you want it to."

"How will the actual selection procedure work?" Jasper Thomas asked.

Miguel answered. "As representatives of your respective schools, you have to come to a choice, with them, concerning what you need. But two more groups have a say as well. The first group is the committee as a whole. That's because we have to balance our budget at the end and see that we're not creating a hodgepodge of duplicated services and programs. The second group is the Information Processing Center."

"You see," Alice said, "it's our obligation at the Information Processing Center to see that the software you choose is well programmed and decently documented. Also, we like some evidence of vendor support."

"Why are these considerations so important, Alice?" Jasper asked. "You people can always fix up a program if it doesn't run properly, can't you?"

"Yes, Jasper, we can," Alice said. "But we are up to our ears in programming your in-house software. With a solid programming backlog of several months, we want to make sure that any 'packaged' purchases really are packaged. That is, after all, the point of buying them—that neither you nor I need to program them."

Only slightly sobered by Miguel's and Alice's concluding admonitions, the committee members filed past the sparkling animated displays, clutching their piles of brochures.

SUMMARY

- *Prewritten software refers to programs that were written and tested by someone else and are ready to run. The terms "prewritten software," "canned programs," "packaged software," and "off-the-shelf programs" are used interchangeably. Most often prewritten software is purchased. The main advantage of using prewritten software rather than writing it yourself is that it is ready for use right away. The main disadvantage is that you may pay for more program capabilities than you really need or, at the other extreme, may not get a program that exactly fits your needs.*

- *Much of the most popular canned software presents you with a series of choices concerning use of the program that are known as menus.*

- *Some software can be purchased on Read-Only-Memory (ROM) chips called firmware.*

- *Multipurpose packaged software is used in business, at home, and in the schools. The main products are word-processing software, electronic spreadsheets, database management systems (DBMS), electronic mail/message systems (EMMS) (including electronic bulletin boards), graphics packages (including computer-aided design systems), and integrated packages. These are the canned programs that have set the pace for the software industry.*

- *Dedicated word processors are computers designed and used exclusively for word processing.*

- *Packages for general business include those used for accounting, management, finance, engineering, manufacturing, and marketing. Marketing packages can include sales call analysis. Even large organizations with extensive in-house staffs of programmers and systems analysts still use packaged software for specific needs.*

- *Management-oriented prewritten software packages include software for personnel management, operations management, forecasting, facilities maintenance, and resource management. Manufacturing packages include software that directs computer-aided manufacturing (CAM) and software for materials management.*

- *Other popular types of packaged software include computer games, computer-assisted instruction, and home-management packages.*

■ *When choosing prewritten software the first step is to identify your needs. A number of questions can then be asked to determine if the software meets those needs, such as what machines the software runs on, whether it is accompanied by a tutorial or training program, and how much it costs. Carefully selected prewritten software can do what it is supposed to—save users the time, expense, and difficulty of writing the software themselves.*

KEY TERMS

These are the key terms in the order in which they appear in the chapter.

Prewritten software (330)
Canned program (330)
Packaged software (330)
Off-the-shelf program (330)
Menu (332)
Read-only memory chip (ROM) (333)
Word-processing software (333)
Dedicated word processor (333)
Electronic spreadsheet (336)
Database management systems (DBMS) (337)
Electronic mail/message system (EMMS) (339)
Electronic bulletin board (341)

Graphics package (342)
Computer-aided design (CAD) (343)
Integrated software packages (343)
Accounting packages (345)
Management-oriented prewritten software (345)
Finance packages (346)
Computer-aided manufacturing (CAM) (347)
Computer games (347)
Computer-assisted instruction (CAI) (347)
Home-management software (350)

REVIEW QUESTIONS

OBJECTIVE QUESTIONS

_____ 1.
_____ 2.
_____ 3.
_____ 4.

_____ 5.
_____ 6.
_____ 7.
_____ 8.
_____ 9.
_____ 10.

_____ 1.

_____ 2.

TRUE/FALSE: *Put the letter T or F on the line before the question.*

1. A user of a software package needs to know how to write programs in the language the package was written in.
2. Spreadsheet packages are simulated electronic financial worksheets.
3. Software packages are only available for micro- and minicomputers.
4. Computer-aided design (CAD) software does not require graphics hardware support.
5. An otherwise good package might not be used if the user documentation is poor.
6. The availabilty of upgrades is not an important factor in selecting software.
7. The term EMMS means the same thing as electronic bulletin board.
8. A major advantage of off-the-shelf software is its almost immediate availability.
9. Prewritten software always performs as promised.
10. Computer-aided instruction (CAI) is used exclusively in primary and secondary schools.

MULTIPLE CHOICE: *Put the letter of the correct answer on the line before the question.*

1. Which of the following is *not* usually a factor in selecting a software package?
   (a) Price.
   (b) Existing features.
   (c) Documentation.
   (d) Ease of rewriting the program.
2. Spreadsheet packages allow users to
   (a) manipulate data in subparts of the grid.
   (b) manipulate data in columns.
   (c) manipulate data in rows.
   (d) All of the above.

3. The most important advantage of word processing is the
(a) decrease in time required to "type" original documents.
(b) availabilty of spelling checking packages.
(c) decrease in time required to edit text.
(d) capacity to integrate text and other types of data processing.

4. The computerized production of graphical display for engineering is called
(a) computer-aided design.   (c) computer-aided manufacturing.
(b) integrated software.   (d) electronic mail/message systems.

5. Integrated software packages usually do not include
(a) electronic bulletin boards.   (c) file "database" management.
(b) spreadsheets.   (d) graphics.

FILL IN THE BLANK: *Write the correct word or words in the blank to complete the sentence.*

1. Buyers of prewritten software generally pay _____ than purchasers of custom software.

2. Prewritten software often presents you with a _____ listing a series of choices available to you.

3. Prewritten software is generally designed to execute in a _____ fashion.

4. A database management system has three software elements: _____, _____, and _____.

5. A(n) _____ allows people to send memos, messages, and facsimiles electronically.

6. Computers designed exclusively for word processing are called _____.

7. Software _____ is a major problem for creators and marketers of prewritten software.

8. The availability of yearly _____ is a crucial feature in selecting a tax-preparation package.

SHORT ANSWER QUESTIONS

When answering these questions think of concrete examples to illustrate your points.

1. What are two advantages of purchasing prewritten software?
2. What are two disadvantages of purchasing prewritten software?
3. What are the main features of a database management system?
4. What are the desirable features of a word-processing package?
5. How does an electronic bulletin board differ from an electronic mail/message system?
6. Describe some of the features found in integrated software packages.
7. What is an electronic spreadsheet package?
8. What are the uses for electronic mail/message systems?

ESSAY QUESTIONS

1. What are the advantages and disadvantages of prewritten software?
2. What prewritten software might you require for your occupation or your educational training?
3. How does canned software fit into an information system?

SYSTEM SOFTWARE THE MASTER PROGRAMS

After studying this chapter you should understand the following:
■ The two main types of system software, and the functions of each.
■ How an operating system relates to the hardware and to the other software of an information system.
■ The functions of an operating system's four main programs.
■ The differences among batch processing, real-time processing, and time-sharing.
■ Which services are offered by the four main types of processing programs.
■ Some characteristics and examples of operating systems used on microcomputers.

Jasper Thomas and Elizabeth Slater carried their cups of coffee to a table toward the rear of the Oakriver University cafeteria.

"I thought that meeting would last two days instead of just one," Jasper said.

"Me too," Elizabeth said. "Did you understand everything they presented about operating systems?"

"About half of it," Jasper said. "Oh—here comes Ralph."

Ralph Grosse threaded his way toward them, balancing a tray with tea and pastry on it. "Well, here we are all assembled," Ralph said, sitting down across from Jasper and Elizabeth. "To plot."

Elizabeth smiled. "With Ralph here as the representative for Arts and Letters, Jasper for Science, and me for Business, we do have about half the college sewn up. Now we have to figure out our needs. We have until Friday to tell the committee.

"Several departments in Arts and Letters use the computer quite a bit," Ralph said. "We want to avoid having to traipse across campus to do so."

"So you want terminals," Elizabeth said. "You need an operating system that can handle time-sharing. What about you, Jasper?"

"Science isn't worried so much about easy access," Jasper said, "because we know we'll get it. We always have. We want real-time processing to do more sophisticated experiments. And," Jasper lowered his voice, "we want Engineering to get less than they've had in the past."

"For shame," Ralph said.

"Speaking for Business," Elizabeth said, "I'm concerned about our microcomputer operating systems. We use at least five different ones now. I would like to standardize to one system.

"O.K.," Jasper said. "To sum up, Business wants one standard operating system for all its microcomputers. Arts and Letters wants time-sharing. And Science wants real-time capability."

Everyone nodded thoughtfully.

"Do you know what I think?" Ralph said. "I think Science needs its own computer. So if you make your needs sound different from everyone else's, Jasper, you may get it, complete with its real-time operating system."

"Thanks," Jasper said. "I trust you'll vote for that?"

"I will," Ralph said. "I'll be glad that you're not using our machine. Arts and Letters and Business can share the same central mainframe, with a time-sharing operating system. To help Elizabeth, microcomputers *campus-wide* should use the same operating system. So I will point out that this is a concern of Arts and Letters as well, and Jasper, you can do the same."

"So we really didn't plot at all," Elizabeth said. "These ideas will benefit the entire university."

"Except Engineering," Jasper said quietly.

SYSTEM SOFTWARE helps application software (the topic of Chapters 9 through 12) use the computer. System software is prewritten. It does its job with little direction from the user. The most important type of system software, the **OPERATING SYSTEM**, supervises and directs the hardware as well as all other software components of the information system. The main components of the operating system include the job control program, input/output manager, program manager, and memory manager. **PROCESS PROGRAMS**, another type of system software, are subordinate to the operating system and perform specific functions that a user requests, such as translating an application program written in a high-level language into machine language. Process programs consist of language translators, utility programs, and library programs.

As Figure 13-1 suggests, we can imagine the system software as sitting between your application program and the computer hardware. You, the user, occupy the outermost ring. The next ring in is your application program. The application program interacts with the system software components shown in the third ring. The operating system programs are shown in the top half of the system software ring. Dependent on the operating system software are the process programs, shown in the lower half of the ring. These components in turn deal with the hardware, the innermost component, which does the work.

FIGURE 13-1.
The place of system software in the information system.

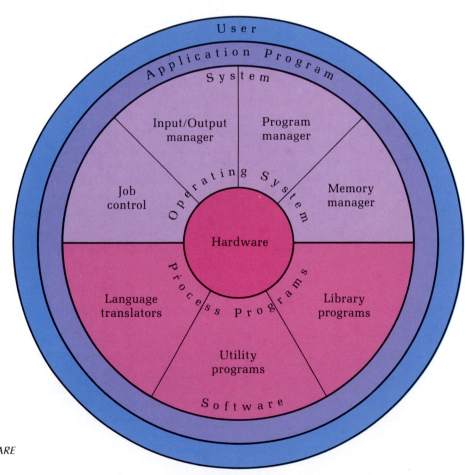

In the truest sense the operating system is in charge of the computer. You may have bought the computer yourself, plugged it in, and turned it on; you may also have selected and installed the operating system. To get any work done, however, you will have to go through the operating system. The operating system performs the formidable job of integrating the components of a computer system into an effective, cohesive unit. It then places this unit at your disposal, and awaits your command.

The first two parts of this chapter will describe the operating systems and process programs used for mainframe computers and minicomputers. As we will see in the third part of the chapter, although the same general concepts apply to microcomputers, the specifics differ somewhat. One difference is that competing brands of microcomputers often use the same operating system, with minor variations. Most mainframe and minicomputer manufacturers, on the other hand, produce an operating system for use on their "family" of machines alone, which will not work on another manufacturer's "family." Microcomputer operating systems will be described in the section "Microcomputer System Software" near the end of the chapter.

Because of their complexity, operating systems and other system software can consume an impressive amount of storage. In fact most computers would not have room for users' programs at all if the computer's main memory had to squeeze in all the system software. Consequently only a fraction of the operating system and process programs are stored in main memory at any one time.

When a computer is turned on, a small memory unit or silicon chip similar to the one inside your calculator or digital watch is activated. This unit transmits a piece of the operating system code to the control unit in the computer, much like a wake-up call. The term for this is **BOOTING** or **BOOTSTRAPPING**. The first piece of code tells the central processing unit where to find the remainder of the operating system. On most computers this will be on a direct-access external storage device such as a magnetic disk. Recently some computer manufacturers have begun to store a computer's operating system directly on silicon chips, giving rise to a new term called firmware, to distinguish it from both software and hardware. (See Chapter 5 for additional information on chips and firmware.)

As the computer needs a particular portion of the operating system or process software, the needed software can be transferred to the computer's main memory. Additional parts of the operating system and process programs can be brought in as required in the same way. Figure 13-2 shows the process graphically. Now we will look more closely at the four parts of an operating system: the job control program, input/output manager, program manager, and memory manager.

JOB CONTROL PROGRAM

The term **JOB** as we will use it is synonymous with "application program and its data." Variations are possible, such as grouping related application programs together as a single job, in which case each program would then be a "job step."

That portion of an operating system known as the **JOB CONTROL PROGRAM** prepares a job to be run. The preparations include checking for valid account numbers and passwords (for the sake of security), assigning input/

FIGURE 13-2.

How the central processing unit loads the operating system into main memory. (1) When power is turned on, the control unit finds the boot program on a ROM (read only memory) chip. (2) The boot program responds with instructions on how to call the rest of the operating system. (3) The control unit can now call the job control program, and (4) order it read into an unused portion of main memory. Additional system software can be called as needed in a similar fashion.

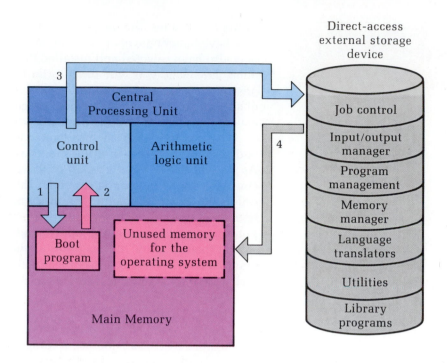

output devices, setting such limits as how long the program should run and how much it should print, monitoring account usage, and determining job execution priorities.

Users give specifications on these matters to the job control program through statements written in a **JOB CONTROL LANGUAGE (JCL).** Job control language conventions vary from one computer manufacturer to another. Through statements written in job control language (known as job control statements), the user can override default values set by the operating system. **DEFAULT VALUES** are those that are assumed when no alternative value is specified by the user. For example, if your operating system normally limits all application programs to 100 pages of printed output, and you know your program will print about 780 pages, then you use the job control language to specify a different limit (say 800) to the job control program.

Job protection

Most users share an information system with others. Users therefore need **ACCOUNT NUMBERS,** identifying who is responsible for a project and its expenses, and individual "secret" **PASSWORDS** to help prevent unauthorized or illegal entry into the system. A password is a code known only to an individual user and the job control program. It should not be given to anyone else.

Special **ACCOUNT NUMBER PROGRAMS** are used to create account numbers and passwords, which under some conditions may be changed every day by users for greater protection. Even legitimate users may be tempted to access restricted materials stored in the information system. Because of this type of abuse, account numbers and passwords may be specially coded to prevent inadvertent (or deliberate) snooping and tampering with data. In a large firm some employees may be allowed to look at data concerning a customer's account, but only certain people with special access codes may alter or destroy the information.

Resource assignment and limit-setting

Another function of the job control program is to designate which actual input/output devices will be used by the application program. For instance, we may have a program that reads input data from magnetic tape and prints output on a printer. The information system will probably have a choice of magnetic tape units, and may have a choice of printers as well. The job control program will assign the devices on its own using default values, unless we specify alternatives.

Knowing that our program is going to print several lengthy reports, we may want to make sure we get the highest-speed printer by overriding the default. In the same way, we can accept or override the job control program's defaults concerning the limit placed on the amount of storage available for the program, how long the program should run, how many pages of printed output it should produce, and other factors.

Job accounting

JOB ACCOUNTING determines the exact usage of resources, such as the central processing unit, peripheral devices, and services such as manual tape handling. In a multiuser environment each account can then be charged for the resources and services used following a predetermined rate schedule. Usually central processing unit time carries the highest charge per hour, peripheral devices carry much lower rates, and manual handling is billed on a per-request basis.

In addition job accounting maintains internal data on computer usage, data access, and other factors. These data are useful for auditing purposes, to tune the information system (such as changing some of those default values) based on how people actually are using it, and to help spot the need for new equipment or point out underutilized hardware that could be phased out.

Job priorities

JOB PRIORITY refers to the ranking of the relative importance of application programs in a multiuser environment. If ten programs—or a thousand—are waiting to be run, the information system needs to know which to tackle first. Organizations need to develop *rules and procedures* to determine which program should have priority over another.

Generally speaking programs that run quickly, use standard input/output devices, and do not require much input/output are given the highest job priorities. At the other extreme are programs that tie up the system for lengthy periods of time (or, in systems that service many users simultaneously, slow it down drastically for the other users). Naturally if one program is vital to an organization and others are clearly secondary, the key program will be given priority even if it is slow.

Sometimes the billing-rate structure can be used as a management tool to encourage or force the use of standard services and low-priority times. Powerful information systems do bog down under some circumstances, as sometimes happens with a college's mainframe computer during student registration processing. QUEUING PROGRAMS order and put on hold the

Among programmers the system programmer comprises a unique breed. Let's see why.

The application programmer (Chapter 10 career box) and the programmer analyst (Chapter 11 career box) deal with designing, coding, testing, and implementing user applications. In contrast the system programmer deals with system software. The system programmer is responsible for keeping the system software humming. In turn the smoothly functioning system software makes it possible for the other programmers to get on with their work.

The main focus of the system programmer is the operating system. No matter how good, all operating systems have errors in them, some of which can bring a computer center to a screeching halt. The system programmer is the emergency-room surgeon who breathes life back into the system. He or she makes emergency repairs by altering code in the operating system. On a non-emergency basis the system programmer helps tailor the operating system to user needs, and monitors the system to see that it is functioning efficiently. When system software is required that is not on hand, the system programmer may adapt other software for the purpose, may write it from scratch, or may participate in its selection and purchase.

The layperson's image of the computer expert as an extremely technical recluse hits closest to home with the system programmer. Any information-system professional must deal with people, but the system programmer must first and foremost know that portion of the operating system for which he or she is responsible. This means extensive experience in programming—particularly in the machine language and assembly language in which the operating system is written. The entry route to this career is therefore through application programming. An application programmer or programmer analyst who enjoys the machine-oriented details more than the user applications, and feels that high-level languages are no fun, may be able to switch to the system programming team at a junior level. As with the other programming positions, different job levels with varying degrees of responsibility and compensation exist within system programming. The way up and out of this career would be to move into information-system management. A died-in-the-wool system programmer, however, will be reluctant to give up contact with complex computer intricacies for administrative chores.

waiting application programs until the system can accommodate them. This does not solve the problem, but—like a line in a bank—at least it is fairer than a free-for-all rush for overloaded facilities.

INPUT/OUTPUT MANAGER

Input and output devices read and write data much more slowly than the computer's central processing unit processes the data. It is not uncommon for a computer to sit inactive while it waits for an input or output operation to be completed. The first commercially available computers sat inactive much of the day, while printers, tape units, and card devices crept along at a relative snail's pace. Today's input/output devices are a lot faster; high-speed printers can produce over 45,000 lines of print per minute. Computers, however, can handle *millions* of operations per *second*.

The **INPUT/OUTPUT MANAGER** is an operating system program that helps overcome the challenges associated with mediating differences between input, output, communication, and processing speeds. An input/output manager supervises the transfer of data from input devices to main memory, and from main memory to output devices.

The input/output manager uses channels and buffers to help deal with the speed difference. **CHANNELS** are paths along which data are sent, together with enough control logic to free the central processing unit from supervising the transfer. The point of placing a level of software (the input/output manager) and of hardware (the channel) between the computer and input/output devices is that once the computer has issued the input/output command, it can go on to other work without waiting for the operation to finish. In this way the computer can read, write, and process all at once.

The second hardware feature that the input/output manager uses to lessen effects of the speed differential is the buffer. A **BUFFER** is a temporary storage area used to accumulate data from the relatively slow input device until enough data are present to justify sending them to the more rapid CPU; likewise a buffer receives a burst of output data from the CPU when it is ready, and parcels the data out at the appropriate speed to the slower output device. Buffers are located within the CPU, input/output devices themselves, and some channels. Figure 13-3 shows the relationship between the input/output manager, buffer, channel, and input/output device.

PROGRAM MANAGER

The **PROGRAM MANAGER** handles the movement of programs (or parts of programs) into main memory so that the computer can execute the program instructions. With early computers program management was not an issue, since the computer ran one program at a time, and all of the program was in main memory at once. Today there are a number of different ways of running programs, most of which entail running more than one program at once. The program manager sorts this out so that the user is not aware that the computer is also being used for other jobs at the same time.

The three major processing modes are batch processing, time-sharing, and real-time processing. A given operating system is designed to handle one or more of these modes. Any mainframe or minicomputer is capable of running a program in any of the modes, provided it has the correct operating system.

In addition to the three different processing modes, we will describe two different execution techniques: multiprogramming and multiprocessing. These techniques are operating-system dependent, and can be used to run programs in any of the three modes (batch, time-sharing, or real-time).

Batch processing

With **BATCH PROCESSING** data are collected over a period of time and processed as a group. In the past, for instance, Oakriver University accumulated all student registration data into one batch. When the registration period was over and the data were complete, the university ran a program to

FIGURE 13-3.
The system software and hard-ware that manage input/out-put.

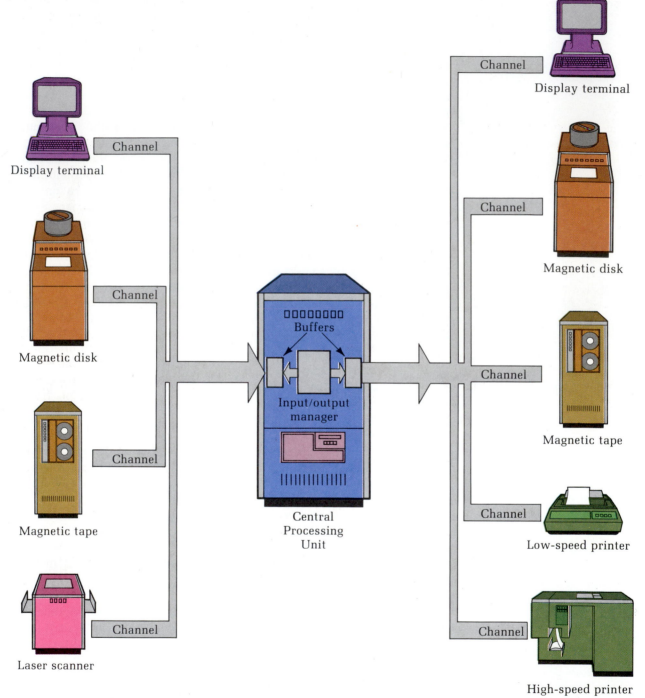

FIGURE 13-4.

Batch processing. A program and all of the data it will process are submitted to the computer all at once.

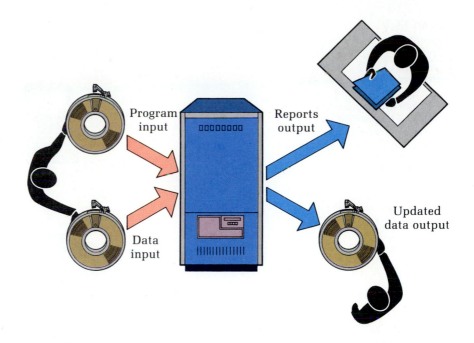

Program input

Reports output

Data input

Updated data output

process the data all at once in one monumental run. Figure 13-4 illustrates the batch-processing concept.

When running any type of program on a computer, one often speaks of the **TURNAROUND TIME**, or **RESPONSE TIME**—the amount of time that elapses between requesting a computer to do something and receiving the results of that request. With batch processing the turnaround time refers to the time between submitting the program to be run and receiving the output from the run.

Sophisticated versions of batch processing are in common use today. Remote job entry stations provide facilities for submitting a program to a computer, and sometimes also for receiving the output from the program run, at a location other than the computer center. Such stations are found, for instance, in different parts of a college campus, or at various points in a factory or across the country.

Time-sharing

TIME-SHARING allows several users to run programs at the same time, by assigning each user a **TIME SLICE** or tiny bit of computer time. During each time slice the computer carries out part of the user's program. When one user's time slice is used up, the system moves on to the next user, and then the next, eventually returning to the first. Because all of this happens so rapidly, users may never be aware of the slicing, but think they have the computer all to themselves. Figure 13-5 shows the time-sharing concept.

Most time-sharing systems are terminal-based and allow for **INTERACTIVE PROCESSING**, with the requests that the user makes, and the responses that the computer gives, taking place as a rapid dialogue. At Paul's House of Electronic Wonders Penny Helmsley can use her terminal to check out a sales rival at the same time that someone in the shipping and receiving

FIGURE 13-5.

A terminal-based time-sharing system. The computer handles each user in turn by cycling repeatedly through a time slice for each. Input/output media other than the display terminals shown will be present, such as direct-access storage for a database and printers for reports.

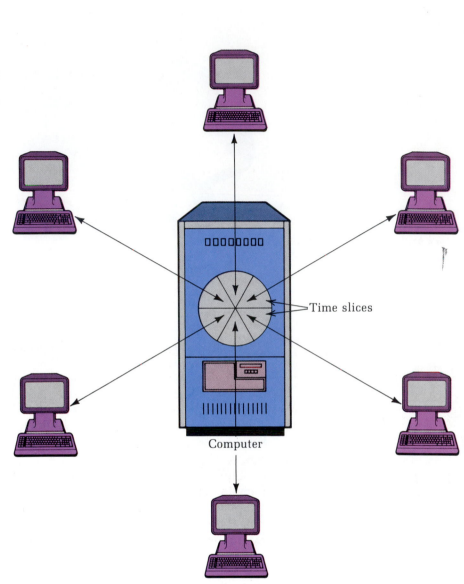

Time slices

Computer

department is making a database query about the best shipper, and at the same time that the accounting department is entering new rules on granting credit. Apart from a lag of a second or two between Penny's request concerning the sales rival and the response, it appears to her that she has exclusive use of the computer. When time-sharing systems have many users, however, response time can slow down considerably (to minutes). Note also that Penny did not actually submit a program to be run from her terminal—she made a request. The operating system brings the appropriate program (or part of it) into main storage, to handle the request. This too is typical of many time-sharing systems.

Real-time processing

With **REAL-TIME PROCESSING**, the computer processes data rapidly enough that the results can be used to influence a process that is still taking place. For example, when travel agent Janis Roberts reserves a seat on a flight for a customer, the airline reservation system updates the records for that flight immediately. Let's say Janis's booking was for the last available seat on the flight. If another travel agent from the next block —or the next continent— tried to book a seat on that flight seconds after Janis did, that agent would be told that the flight was full.

If you think about it for a moment, you can see that this level of service could never be offered with batch processing.

Like time-sharing, real-time processing is generally interactive, and usually involves more than one user of the computer. The principal difference is speed: With a real-time system the response must be immediate. With time-sharing the loss of a few seconds is not so crucial. Real-time processing is more costly and complex than other processing modes, but is often used when the need for speed is vital. Figure 13-6 shows some examples of real-time systems.

FIGURE 13-6.

Real-time processing. (a) In banking. (b) At the New York Stock Exchange. (c) Controlling the space shuttle. (d) In airline reservation systems.

(b)

(d)

The systems used in space navigation are real-time. Banks and credit-card companies often use real-time systems to check customer balances that may well be changing simultaneously because of another transaction. University registration sometimes uses real-time processing.

Multiprogramming

Through some of the techniques we have already described in this chapter, today's computers give the illusion that they perform a number of things at the same time. The fact remains, however, that even the most sophisticated central processing unit only executes one instruction at a time. This is true regardless of the processing mode for the programs (batch, time-sharing, or real-time).

One instruction at a time, however, need not mean one program at a time. The earliest computers did handle only one program at a time. Starting in the early 1960s the concept of multiprogramming was introduced. MULTIPROGRAMMING refers to the concurrent execution of more than one program at a time. Instructions of one program are executed, then instructions of the next program, then instructions of a third program, and so on. Switching between programs occurs when input/output operations are encountered. The operating system's program manager keeps the programs sorted out, directing the CPU as to which to deal with when.

Thus it is possible (and common) for *batch*-processing programs to run several at a time, under control of the operating system, which balances the needs of one program with those of another. In business processing delays often occur during input/output operations (that is, the jobs are I/O bound). While one program is tied up waiting for lengthy input operations to complete, a dozen others might be performing calculations and one or two more producing output. As you have already seen, this same type of logic is used in handling time-sharing programs and multiuser real-time programs.

Multiprocessing

MULTIPROCESSING is not a variant of multiprogramming, but a different concept that is often confused with it. In multiprocessing two or more central processing units execute instructions at the same time. The instructions may be from different programs, or from the same program. *Multiprogramming*, in contrast, handles two or more programs at the same time within a *single* central processing unit.

Multiprocessing configurations vary. Sometimes several computers take on tasks on an egalitarian basis, as if on the principle that "two heads are better than one." Another configuration consists of a larger computer that handles most of the main operations, and subordinate computers that deal with less important tasks, such as editing input, handling the maintenance of files, or supervising the printers.

Both of these configurations (see Figure 13-7) are common for scientific and business applications that require more power than a single computer can deliver. The headquarters of major banks and insurance companies, for example, must do more information processing than a single computer could possibly handle. Some companies find it preferable to use multiple computers linked together in a multiprocessing configuration, rather than to use multiple "stand-alone" computers, because resources can be shared and

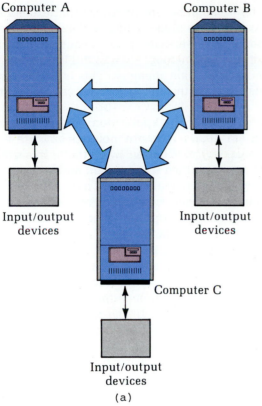

Computer A

Computer B

Input/output
devices

Input/output
devices

Computer C

Input/output
devices

(a)

Computer B   Computer C

Computer A

Input/output
devices

Input/output
devices

Computer D   Computer E

Input/output
devices

Input/output
devices

(b)

FIGURE 13-7.

Two multiprocessing configurations. (a) In this configuration three computers are set up as coprocessors. Each computer will communicate with the others and be able to access the others' main storage. (b) In this configuration one main computer does computations and delegates other tasks to subordinate computers.

conversion problems eliminated. Computers set up for multiprocessing, together with the operating system software necessary to run them as a team, are generally supplied as a convenient package by manufacturers to purchasers.

There are other interesting multiprocessing possibilities. For instance, sometimes computers are linked together to solve and cross-check, independently, the answer to the same problem. An example of this is the five computers onboard each of the U.S. space shuttles, which team up to check calculations for a shuttle's launchings, landings, and navigation.

MEMORY MANAGER   In our discussions of the other parts of the operating system, we have frequently mentioned bringing programs into and out of the computer's main memory. Keeping track of a program's location is the job of the **MEMORY MANAGER.**

You may reasonably ask *why* we must bring programs into and out of main memory rather than just leave them there until they are finished running. That is exactly what early computers did. The problem is that main memory is not that large, and the need arises for programs that exceed it. Even with today's relatively low hardware prices, which make it affordable to pack more main memory into a computer—and even if your program is modest enough to fit entirely within main memory—it will still be necessary to shift some software into and out of main memory. This is so because contemporary operating systems are so big that the major ones cannot fit into the machines that they run.

The memory manager writes parts of the application programs being run and of the operating system—parts that are not needed for the moment—onto a secondary storage device. When software that is in secondary storage is needed in main memory, then it is read in, and something else is kicked out onto secondary storage to make room. The mechanics of how this takes place has always been the concern of the **SYSTEM PROGRAMMER** or operating system designer, and still is. Application programmers—let alone users—need not worry about memory management.

The concept of storing programs partly in and partly outside of main memory is today referred to as **VIRTUAL STORAGE** or **VIRTUAL MEMORY**. What virtual storage or virtual memory does for the programmer is to make main memory appear much larger than it really is (hence the "virtual" in the term—the memory seems to be there, but isn't). The portion of virtual storage that is not actually in main memory is in secondary storage, generally on disk. The memory manager sees that those parts of programs needed at any given time in order to keep the programs running are located in main memory at that time. All the rest is scattered throughout the virtual storage "area," often in a checkerboard-like pattern that—were it not for the coordinating software—would be quite alarming.

The two main techniques that a memory manager uses to implement virtual storage are called paging and segmentation. With **PAGING**, programs are chopped into fixed-length sections (pages). The length of a page is determined by hardware design, and can range from a few hundred to several thousand characters in length. When a portion of a program is needed, the page containing that portion is brought into main memory. The subdivision of a program into pages has nothing to do with program logic.

SEGMENTATION, on the other hand, is related to program logic. With segmentation a program is divided into segments by function or module. One segment of a small program might handle data definition, another calculation, and another output. The aim of segmentation is to avoid the need continually to shuttle pages back and forth, which is not part of the useful work that a computer performs but consumes time anyway. Some memory managers use both paging and segmentation. They divide a program into logical segments, and then further subdivide any segments that exceed the hardware's page size into pages.

PROCESS PROGRAMS

Now that we have completed our look at the operating system, it is time to describe those system software components that the operating system calls upon as required: process programs. We will review the three main types of process programs here—language translators, utility programs, and library programs. All three types of process programs are subordinate to the operating system, and perform specific functions that you, the user, request.

LANGUAGE TRANSLATORS

In Chapter 11 we reviewed machine language, assembly language, and high-level languages such as BASIC, COBOL, and FORTRAN. When you write a program in any of these languages except machine language, it must be translated *into* machine language in order to run on the computer. LANGUAGE TRANSLATORS perform the translation of high-level languages or assembly language into machine language. In addition they check for and identify some types of errors that may be present in the program being translated.

There are three types of language translators: compilers, interpreters, and assemblers. We will describe each in turn.

Compilers

A **COMPILER** translates a complete program written in a high-level language into machine language. Typically you identify, with a job control statement, the language in which your program is written. The job control program of the operating system reads the statement, and calls in the appropriate compiler to translate your program. Compilers are used to translate a number of languages including: COBOL, FORTRAN, Pascal, and some versions of BASIC. The compiling process is shown in Figure 13-8.

Before compiling, your program is known as a **SOURCE PROGRAM**. Using a compiler, your source program goes through three main steps: compile, link-edit, and execution (or go).

During the compile step your source program is treated as if it were data. If any errors in syntax or logic in the source code are encountered, the process stops and a list of error messages is generated. The result of the successful completion of the compile step is an **OBJECT PROGRAM** written in the machine-language-code. The object program can be saved for later recall to permit skipping the compilation step.

During the link-edit process the object program is merged with prewritten object programs—which might include, for example, a routine for calculating square roots. Usually this process passes without any problems. The combined object programs are called the **LOAD PROGRAM**.

The load program is what the CPU actually processes when the program is executed. During the execution step the data to be processed are taken into the CPU. If no data errors are detected, the program will run successfully. You can then save the load program so that you can run it later without having to repeat the translation process.

Interpreters

Like compilers, **INTERPRETERS** translate a program written in a high-level language into machine language. Unlike compilers, interpreters perform the translation one instruction at a time, and then execute the resulting machine-language instructions immediately. On most microcomputers it is an interpreter that translates BASIC into machine language.

With an interpreter, if you make a syntax mistake—such as misspelling a command—the program will stop running. If you have made more than one mistake, you may not discover the second until you fix the first and try running the program again. Since an interpreter does not produce a complete object program, to run the same program a second time you have to save the source program and then translate it again.

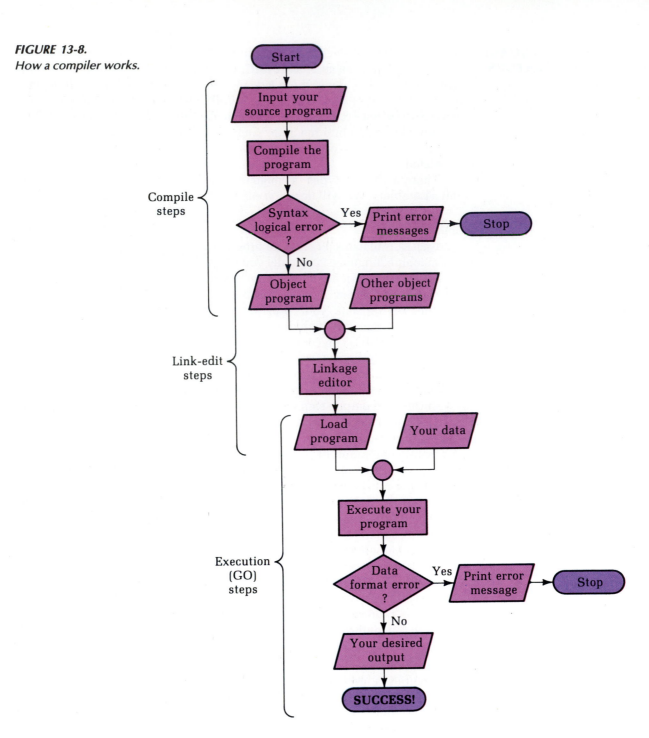

FIGURE 13-8.
How a compiler works.

Compile steps

Start

Input your source program

Compile the program

Syntax logical error ? — Yes → Print error messages → Stop

No

Object program

Other object programs

Link-edit steps

Linkage editor

Load program

Your data

Execution (GO) steps

Execute your program

Data format error ? — Yes → Print error message → Stop

No

Your desired output

SUCCESS!

Interpreters can save a lot of time during program development. With some computers, once the program is running correctly, you can save the source program and have a *compiler* translate it into an object and load program for future runs.

Interpreters and compilers both have certain advantages and disadvantages. Compilers usually require more main memory than interpreters because they translate the source code as a unit. Interpreters require less main memory—which made them popular for microcomputers—because they translate only one line of source code at a time. Compiled programs, however, are faster than interpreted programs because the compiled program is entirely in machine language, whereas the interpreted program must be translated line by line every time it is run.

Assemblers

An **ASSEMBLER** translates a program written in assembly language into machine language. Apart from the fact that it deals with a low-level language rather than a high-level language, and thus has less of a gap to bridge in translation, an assembler operates the same way as a compiler does. It translates your complete source program into an object program, identifying any errors along the way. The assembler will list or display these errors as well as the complete source and object programs. If your program is error-free, the job control program will let you run it immediately, or save the object program so that you can run it later without translating it again.

UTILITY PROGRAMS

Computers must do some types of processing over and over again, such as preparing a disk to receive a file. A **UTILITY PROGRAM** performs such general-purpose processing for the information system. The operating system calls upon utility programs when it needs them, and the user can call upon them too, through job control statements. As with the canned programs described in the last chapter, any prewritten, working code that programmers can utilize without having to write and debug it themselves increases programmer productivity.

Originally utility programs were fairly simple, performing only mundane tasks such as copying data from one storage device to another. Recently there has been an explosion of more complex utility programs that programmers can call upon to do certain operations rather than having to write the code themselves. Some examples of utility programs in use include text-editing programs, diagnostic programs, peripheral interchange programs, and sort/merge programs.

Text-editing programs

A **TEXT-EDITING PROGRAM** can help make alterations in application programs and data. For instance, data can be rearranged, added to, changed, or deleted, before being processed by your program. Lines of your program itself can be altered, deleted, moved, or renumbered. Special format-control programs can even check for the reasonableness of your changes.

Diagnostic programs

DIAGNOSTIC PROGRAMS are used to check for faults in programs or equipment. A good diagnostic program must be able to identify the error, locate it, and explain to the program user what the error means. Some diagnostic programs can be activated by programmers and used to check how well an apparently error-free program is in fact running. Other programs are used by repair personnel. Increasingly, when repair personnel make a service call to fix hardware, they begin work by running such a program to pinpoint the problem.

Peripheral interchange programs

A frequently used type of utility program, **PERIPHERAL INTERCHANGE PROGRAMS** move data from one peripheral device to another. For example, data can be transferred from a magnetic tape to a magnetic disk in preparation for use by an application program that expects its input data on disk. Information can even be shifted between different display terminals and other types of input/output devices.

Sort/merge programs

SORT/MERGE PROGRAMS are used to rearrange, separate, or collate data in alphabetical or numerical order based upon a particular data field that you specify, or upon several such fields. For example, Paul's House of Electronic Wonders may have a list of clients' names and addresses that it uses to send out advertising. The list is in alphabetical order by client name. The post office offers reduced postage rates for mail that has been presorted (that is, sorted by someone other than the post office) by Zip code, carrier route, and street address. A sort utility program could rearrange the customers from the alphabetical list into a list ordered by Zip code (the main sort field that the user specifies). Within a given Zip code customers could be arranged according to carrier route (the second user-specified sort field). Within a given carrier route the customers could be ordered by street address (the third field). This type of rearrangement is extremely useful in everyday business operations, and the beauty of using utility programs to perform it is that—from the user's point of view—it is easy and fast.

LIBRARY PROGRAMS
The prewritten programs (described in the last chapter) that an information system uses are often stored together on a direct-access device. Such centralized programs available for general use are known as **LIBRARY PROGRAMS**. Usually the programs are stored in object-program form, so that translation is not necessary in order to run them. Users can then request the operating system to run a particular prewritten program by means of a job-control statement.

Large information systems often use many prewritten programs. These can be indexed by subject, with lists of available programs circulated throughout the organization. Often a librarian program keeps the program directory up to date, and protects the program library by seeing that users follow the organization's agreed-upon rules to use existing library programs, store new library programs, and delete old ones.

MICROCOMPUTER SYSTEM SOFTWARE
Most of the concepts discussed so far in this chapter apply to the system software used on microcomputers as well. Microcomputers have operating systems that perform the same general functions. Microcomputers can use the virtual storage concept; interleave input/output operations with processing where possible, to avoid tying up the system; use compilers, interpreters, and assemblers to translate programs; rely on utility programs; and so on.

One key difference lies in the fact that many microcomputers are used by only one person at a time. Considerations of sharing resources with others do not apply in this situation. The capabilities of microcomputers are

From the business consumer's point of view, the computer industry is a disaster. The lack of standards has turned every purchase decision into a complicated process of matching available software with acceptable hardware. Most managers don't care about operating systems. Once a manager learns to use a program, he wants to continue using that program, no matter what hardware the company decides to purchase in the future.

As more and more managers face the prospect of retraining their staff if hardware is replaced, software portability is becoming a major issue. Because it can be moved easily from one machine to another, UNIX has a lot to offer to the business world. Software portability, however, is not its only attribute: UNIX is designed to be run in a multi-user environment. In fact, for multi-user applications such as electronic mail, word processing, graphics and a host of multitasking chores, UNIX is clearly the strongest contender among operating systems. . . .

The original UNIX was developed by AT&T's Bell Labs and is available through other vendors licensed by AT&T. Some of the prominent hardware manufacturers that support UNIX are IBM, Digital Equipment Corp., Tandy/Radio Shack, Altos Computer Systems and Convergent Technologies. . . .

Most importantly, UNIX is also available on mini and mainframe computers. This means that a microcomputer supporting UNIX, for example, can be more easily linked to a larger system than one using MS-DOS.

In theory, application software designed under UNIX on one brand or size of computer can, with only minor modifications, run on any other UNIX-based computer. It is possible that a company using the UNIX operating system in-house would never have to replace its application software or retrain employees.

A UNIX system can give a company great flexibility in future system modifications or upgrades. If a company is not happy with its hardware, or more importantly, with the support services offered by a hardware manufacturer, it can simply replace its system with a competing brand without sacrificing their software investment.

Source: From "Setting System Standards" Michael Dutrall, *Business Software,* September 1984.

increasing rapidly, however, and with them the need for operating systems that can handle several users at a time.

A second important distinction is that microcomputer operating systems work with more than one brand of microcomputer. Operating systems for mainframes and minis, however, are usually confined to machines within the same manufacturer's "family," and will not work on another manufacturer's machines. The reason that operating systems work on more than one brand of microcomputer is that most are designed to run on a specific brand of microprocessor chip, and different manufacturers of microcomputers use the same microprocessor chips.

The first popular operating system for microcomputers was **CP/M (CONTROL PROGRAM FOR MICROCOMPUTERS)**. Still widely used today, CP/M consists of a command processor, which interprets the user's instructions and gives the operating system's responses; a basic disk operating system, which handles the user's disk files; and a basic I/O system, which handles all input/output for devices other than disks. Although CP/M is a single-user system, a related operating system—MP/M (Multiuser Program for Microcomputers)—can handle up to five time-sharing users.

The IBM PC (Personal Computer), introduced in 1981, popularized another operating system, **MS/DOS (MICROSOFT DISK OPERATING SYSTEM)**. Due to the popularity of the IBM PC, and the fact that many other computer manufacturers have since designed their hardware and software to be PC compatible, the use of MS/DOS has become widespread today. PC-DOS is a version of MS-DOS specifically for IBM PCs.

In the history of computers (as of nations), serious attempts have surfaced from time to time to make one intelligible to another. The **UNIX** operating system has emerged as such an attempt. Bell Laboratories developed the UNIX operating system for minicomputers that it used for its own research. The operating system became popular on various machines in-house, and soon began to spread outside of Bell Labs. UNIX is now used on microcomputers, minicomputers, and mainframes alike, a unique characteristic that makes it a possible contender for the operating system of the future. A number of UNIX-like operating systems, and systems that add other features to UNIX itself, have also appeared. UNIX can handle multiple users in a time-sharing environment. It employs some interesting software concepts to distance itself from dependence on any particular machine and to encourage program flexibility.

WRAP-UP
OAKRIVER DEFINES ITS OPERATING SYSTEM NEEDS

"I want to thank everyone for their input," Marty Castillo said to the assembled University Computer Users Committee. "The Information Processing Center has collated the data and discussed the matter thoroughly. These are our conclusions."

Marty pulled back the blank first page of his flip charts. "First, microcomputers," he said. "We recommend that all new microcomputers university-wide run on one of two operating systems, MS/DOS or UNIX. That way microcomputer users across campus can share more programs, and we can save money."

"What about the existing microcomputers?" Elizabeth Slater asked.

"Our recommendation is to maintain them with whatever operating system they have now," Marty said. "The most common one is CP/M, which is still well-supported by the vendor."

Marty turned to the next page, labeled "mainframe computer."

"Obviously we cannot pick a specific operating system for the mainframe until we know what hardware we will buy," Marty said.

"However, based on your input, we know what requirements the operating system must meet. It must support time-sharing, with terminals scattered at strategic points around campus. It will also have to run plenty of batch programs."

Marty turned to a new page. "We recognize that some departments have highly specialized needs in an operating system," he said. "Again, we have to wait until we study hardware more closely, but our thinking now is to separate those systems from the mainframe."

"What do you mean?" Jasper Thomas asked.

"I mean that your school, Jasper, will in all likelihood get its own minicomputer, with a real-time operating system to control experiments."

Jasper, Ralph, and Elizabeth exchanged satisfied glances.

"And Engineering will get two," Marty said, "for its own experiments, and to handle its battery of computer-aided design terminals."

Jasper's smile quickly vanished.

SUMMARY

- *System software helps application software use the computer. The most important type of system software, the operating system, supervises and directs the hardware as well as all other software components of an information system. The operating system is made up of four parts: the job control program, input/output manager, program manager, and memory manager. When a computer is turned on, a booting or bootstrapping program tells the computer where to find the rest of the operating system.*
- *The job control program prepares an application program, or job, to be run. Users interact with the job control program through job control language (JCL). Unless the user specifies otherwise with JCL, operations will be governed by default values.*
- *Account number programs are used to create passwords and account numbers for users. Job accounting tracks the exact usage of the system. An organization's rules and procedures determine job priorities and specify the queuing program's decision criteria.*
- *The input/output manager controls the use of channels and buffers to minimize the time the computer spends waiting for the slower input/output devices.*
- *The program manager handles the movement of programs into main memory so that the computer can run them.*
- *Three common modes in which programs are run are batch processing, time-sharing, and real-time. Turnaround, or response, time is the amount of time that elapses between a request for the computer to do something and receipt of the results. With batch processing data are collected over a period of time and processed as a group. Time-sharing allows several users to run programs at the same time by*

assigning each a time slice in quick rotation. With real-time processing the computer processes data rapidly enough for the results of processing to influence a process that is still taking place. Both time-sharing and real-time processing permit interactive processing.

■ *Multiprogramming refers to the concurrent execution of more than one program at a time. In multiprocessing two or more central processing units execute instructions at the same time.*

■ *The memory manager keeps track of a program's location, using virtual storage techniques such as paging and segmentation to shuttle parts of programs and data back and forth between main memory and online storage.*

■ *Process programs are system software components that an operating system calls upon as required, often at a user's request. These include language translators, utility programs, and library programs.*

■ *Language translators include compilers, interpreters, and assemblers. Compilers convert source programs into object programs. Object programs are then linked to other prewritten programs to form load programs for execution. Interpreters translate a program one line at a time. Assemblers translate assembly-language programs.*

■ *Utility programs include text-editing programs, diagnostic programs, peripheral interchange programs, and sort/merge programs.*

■ *Library programs are prewritten programs available for the users of an information system.*

■ *Microcomputer operating systems perform the same general functions as those of mainframes and minicomputers. Differences, however, include the fact that many microcomputers are used by only one person, that microcomputer operating systems work with more than one brand of microcomputer, and that canned software tends to work only on a particular microcomputer operating system. Popular microcomputer operating systems are CP/M, MS/DOS, and UNIX.*

■ *System programmers design and write the system software programs.*

These are the key terms in the order in which they appear in the chapter.

System software (358)
Operating system (358)
Process program (358)
Booting or bootstrapping (359)
Job (359)
Job control program (359)
Job control language (JCL) (360)
Default value (360)
Account number (360)
Password (360)
Account number program (360)
Job accounting (361)
Job priority (361)
Queuing program (361)
Input/output manager (363)
Channel (363)
Buffer (363)
Program manager (363)
Batch processing (363)
Turnaround, or response, time (365)
Time-sharing (365)
Time slice (365)
Interactive processing (365)
Real-time processing (367)

Multiprogramming (368)
Multiprocessing (368)
Memory manager (369)
System programmer (370)
Virtual storage or virtual memory (370)
Paging (370)
Segmentation (370)
Language translator (371)
Compiler (371)
Source program (371)
Object program (371)
Load program (371)
Interpreter (371)
Assembler (373)
Utility program (373)
Text-editing program (373)
Diagnostic program (373)
Peripheral interchange program (374)
Sort/merge program (374)
Library program (374)
CP/M (Control Program for Microcomputers) (375)
MS/DOS (Microsoft Disk Operating System) (376)
UNIX (376)

REVIEW QUESTIONS

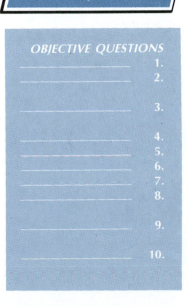

OBJECTIVE QUESTIONS

1. ____
2. ____
3. ____
4. ____
5. ____
6. ____
7. ____
8. ____
9. ____
10. ____

TRUE/FALSE: *Put the letter T or F on the line before the question*

1. Operating systems include language translators and utility programs.
2. An interpreter is a language translator that translates the source program as a single unit.
3. Process programs link users' application programs to the operating system software.
4. An object program is written in machine code.
5. A job consists of a program and its associated data.
6. The program manager is a process program.
7. A password tells the operating system to whom to bill any programming charges.
8. Time-sharing systems require more complex operating systems than batch processing systems.
9. A buffer moderates the speed differential between input and output units and the CPU.
10. Virtual memory requires the user's entire program be present in the CPU during processing.

MULTIPLE CHOICE: *Put the letter of the correct answer on the line before the question.*

_____ 1. A language translator that converts program code written in a high-level language as a unit is a(n)

(a) assembler.   (c) compiler.

(b) interpreter.   (d) None of the above.

_____ 2. Processing modes, such as real-time, are handled by the

(a) input/output manager.   (c) memory manager.

(b) program manager.   (d) language translator.

_____ 3. The portion of the operating system that prepares an application program and its data to be run is the

(a) job control program.   (c) queuing program.

(b) account number program.   (d) source program.

_____ 4. The program that will actually be executed by the CPU is the

(a) job program.   (c) source program.

(b) load program.   (d) object program.

_____ 5. The virtual storage technique in which *arbitrary* parts of a program are moved between the CPU and magnetic disk storage is called

(a) paging.   (c) blocking.

(b) segmentation.   (d) channeling.

FILL IN THE BLANK: *Write the correct word or words in the blank to complete the sentence.*

1. The _____ helps the application software use the computer.

2. The _____ track who is responsible for a project, and _____ protect the project from unauthorized usage.

3. A(n) _____ translates assembly language programs.

4. A(n) _____ is a utility program used to detect for faults in equipment or programs.

5. In the compiling process, the original program, written in a high-level language, is called the _____ program; this program is then translated into a(n) _____ program.

6. A _____ is a pathway for data and programs between the CPU and peripherals.

7. The term _____ refers to the ability for two or more computers linked together to execute simultaneously two or more instructions.

8. The term _____ refers to the ability to process two or more programs concurrently within the same CPU.

9. A peripheral interchange program is an example of a(n) _____.

10. An operating system, _____, is available on both microcomputers and larger CPUs.

SHORT ANSWER QUESTIONS

When answering these questions think of concrete examples to illustrate your points.

1. What are the two main types of system software?

2. What are the four major parts of the operating system?

3. Differentiate between batch, time-sharing, and real-time processing.

4. How does the operating system protect users' data and programs?

5. Is multiprocessing the same as multiprogramming?

6. What are the three major types of processing programs?

7. Differentiate among the different types of language translators.

8. Explain the differences among the operating systems used for microcomputers.

1. How does an operating system relate to other parts of the information system?
2. Describe how a compilable program is processed for execution.
3. Should a user's account number and password be the same? Why or why not?

PART FOUR

We have come a long way in this book, and in a sense have now reached the point of it all. Part One introduced basic information-system concepts, and Parts Two and Three examined in more depth the roles of hardware and software, respectively, in the information system.

Now we turn to information systems themselves. We begin in Chapter 14 by examining management information and decision support systems. Next, Chapter 15 describes how information systems are developed and changed. Design and use of the databases crucial to many information systems are described in Chapter 16, and the important topics of security and privacy are taken up in Chapter 17. Finally Chapter 18 offers some guidelines for buying a computer and setting up your own information system.

CHAPTER 14

INFORMATION SYSTEMS AND COMPUTERS: MANAGEMENT TECHNIQUES

- **THE UNFLAPPABLE IRM**
  MANAGERS: CHARTING A COURSE OVER TROUBLED SEAS
  Making decisions / Management levels / Reports managers need
  MANAGEMENT INFORMATION SYSTEMS
  What an MIS does / Fitting an MIS into a business
  DECISION SUPPORT SYSTEMS
- **CASE IN POINT: The Nucleus of Productivity**
  INFORMATION RESOURCE MANAGEMENT SYSTEMS
  TODAY'S CHANGING ORGANIZATIONS
- **CAREER BOX: Information Resource Manager**
- **WRAP-UP: Upgrading a DSS**

After studying this chapter you should understand the following:
- *Which types of decisions are made at the three management levels.*
- *The characteristics of scheduled listings, and exception, demand, and predictive reports.*
- *How a management information system helps managers to make decisions.*
- *The ways in which a decision support system differs from a management information system.*
- *Which additional functions are offered by an information resource management system.*

Susan Paul, sales manager at Paul's House of Electronic Wonders, returned to her office after having lunch with a group of key clients. She sat down in her chair, and swiveled to face her terminal. Some important decisions had to be made this very afternoon, by her, and the decision support system would come to her aid.

She switched on the terminal. She jumped as the opening bars of Beethoven's Fifth were played by the terminal's audio chip. Simultaneously with the music, a mysterious message appeared on the display screen:

```
HI, I'M SID, YOUR NEW IRM.
```

Susan sat back in her chair and pondered this. She had heard of electronic mail/message systems, but Paul's did not have one. At least not until just now. And the message couldn't have come from a program, because she had not invoked any program yet; she had merely turned on the terminal. Someone, somewhere, must have been fooling around with the system.

"KILL SID," Susan typed, and then cleared the screen. Now she would get to work. She invoked the sales analysis package. A menu appeared on the screen. She selected the options DISPLAY REPORT and TOTAL SALES. The program then displayed the message:

```
WHICH CLIENTS?
```

In response, Susan typed in the names of the six who were of interest to her. All of this information appeared in a listing she had in her office somewhere, but it was buried among other information, and out of date. She wanted the latest information.

"WHICH TIME PERIOD?" the program asked.

Susan typed a starting date of three months ago, and an ending date of today. At lunch she'd heard that one client not present was attempting to corner the market on a certain type of musical chip—perhaps the same kind that had just played Beethoven's Fifth. The client was another wholesaler to whom Paul's often sold. If, however, this other wholesaler were tripling the price of Paul's chip, as Susan was told, she would turn the client into an ex-client today.

Her screen cleared and then the totals for the last three months for the six clients appeared, one line for each client. The customer in question, Honest John's Chipyard, had indeed made massive purchases, but Susan couldn't tell of what.

She requested the menu again, and looked for an option that would tell the specific purchases Honest John's had made. There was no such option on the menu. The interactive part of the decision support system was good, but it could not handle that much detail. Susan would have to turn to the listings after all. The decision support system produced them too, but at scheduled intervals. They gave all the details—enough to drown in.

Susan got up and crossed to the wall of locked cabinets where she kept listings. To get the information she needed for the last three months, she would have to scan 13 listings, one for each week. She decided to call in Gene Tomaselli, a sales trainee, to do the scanning.

As Susan started to explain the assignment to Gene, she was jolted by the opening strain of "Here Comes the Bride." Susan and Gene walked over to the terminal that had played it. Another mysterious message flashed on the screen:

```
SID, YOUR NEW IRM, WILL DROP BY THIS AFTERNOON FOR A
CHAT.
```

Susan was glad Gene had heard and seen it too: She knew she wasn't crazy. She typed in "KILL SID."

The terminal emitted a scream. Susan and Gene stared at the terminal in open-mouthed amazement. Of course it was only a chip that made the sound, but still. . . .

"I wonder if our decision support system has gone absolutely haywire," Susan said.

"Or maybe it's about to hatch something new," Gene suggested.

MANAGERS: CHARTING A COURSE OVER TROUBLED SEAS

Many of you will have already taken a class in management at some point; others have not. In any case we will quickly review some relevant points here.

A *manager* organizes people and other resources to achieve some organizational goal. A manager's activities are known as "management"; sometimes "management" is also used loosely to mean "manager" or "managers."

An *organizational goal* is simply an objective of an organization. To be meaningful goals should be stated in clear terms. Examples might be: "Achieve a 20 percent return on investment" or "Reach number one in beverage sales in northern Oklahoma by 1990." It helps to associate numbers or dates with goals, to have something concrete to measure them against. Unclear or conflicting goals hinder effective management.

A manager's work entails four major activities: planning, organizing, directing, and controlling. *Planning* refers to the process of anticipating opportunities and selecting the best strategy to take advantage of them, in order to meet the organization's goal. Managers at Paul's House of Electronic Wonders, for example, might plan to add a new branch location in anticipation of a growing demand for electronic equipment. Their planning would involve collecting information about possible locations, and estimating the sales that each location might generate.

Organizing concerns the marshaling of resources—people, money, and materials—to achieve a goal. One of the most important parts of organizing is *staffing*, which involves selecting and training the crucial people who can accomplish the goals. *Directing* involves supervising personnel as they work. Organizing and directing are the two management activities that are most evident to nonmanagerial employees.

Controlling is, in effect, a form of feedback. It involves evaluating the organization's progress toward the achievement of its goal and making adjustments as needed. If Paul's House of Electronic Wonders decided to add a new branch, for example, the manager in charge of the expansion would carefully monitor the expense by comparing it against the plan described earlier. Was land purchased on schedule and for the budgeted amount? Is construction proceeding on schedule? And finally, how do sales at the new branch compare with the anticipated figures?

MAKING DECISIONS

To carry out their activities, managers must make decisions. The first step in making a decision is to *define the problem and the decision criteria*. For example, the problem might be whether or not Paul's House of Electronic Wonders' sales analysis system is functioning effectively, and if not, whether it should be replaced with a new one. The criteria for making the decision would involve measurable costs and benefits: How much does the present system cost to operate? Does it produce needed reports in a timely fashion? How much would a new system cost to install and how much would installing it disrupt the organization? What specific benefits would the new system provide?

Once we know what the problem is, we need to *gather data* upon which to base an intelligent decision. We would seek quantitative data, consisting of numerical facts, such as how many sales are made per day. Qualitative data, not expressible as numbers, are also important. An example of qualitative data might be whether people feel excited or intimidated at the idea of having the sales analysis system with which they are already familiar changed.

When the data are in hand, the next step is to *process the data*. We have seen that happen often in this book. Management information systems and decision support systems can help in the processing. We will come in closer contact with these systems later in the chapter. They provide managers with information upon which to base informed decisions.

Even though an up-to-the-nanosecond computer may have provided the information, managers still need to *evaluate the information* themselves. If the information states that orders are being lost due to lack of effective sales analysis, yet nine out of ten employees feel that changing systems would disrupt their work intolerably, the manager has to evaluate how important these factors are. And then comes the point of the whole process: managers must *make the decision*. No respectable computer system relieves managers of this burden, or provides a proven formula to prevent managers from calling some shots dead wrong. Sometimes managers decide to follow the null alternative, which means to do nothing.

Once the decision has been made, the manager's next task is to *implement the decision*. This means to do all of the work necessary to carry it out. If the decision is to install a new sales analysis system, this step involves managing the actual creation and installation of such a system,

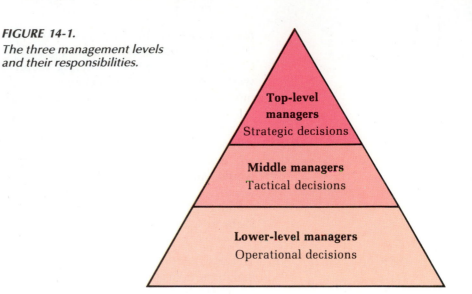

FIGURE 14-1.
The three management levels and their responsibilities.

Top-level managers
Strategic decisions

Middle managers
Tactical decisions

Lower-level managers
Operational decisions

which may take many months. When the decision has been implemented, the manager then needs to *evaluate feedback* on whether or not the solution in fact solved the problem. For example, is Paul's selling more with the new sales analysis system, or less?

MANAGEMENT LEVELS

Now we'll look at the different levels of managers within an organization, because each level needs a different type of information from a management information or decision support system. Managers can be arranged into a three-level hierarchy of top, middle, and low. Figure 14-1 shows the three levels. The figure has a triangular shape to reflect the fact that there are increasingly fewer managers as one moves from the bottom to the top.

Managers at each of the three levels make different types of decisions. *Top-level managers* define organizational goals and make *strategic decisions* involving overall plans (Figure 14-2). Such decisions cover matters that will occur over a time frame stretching from about a year up to ten or more years. Of the four types of management activities outlined earlier, those usually performed by top-level managers are planning and organizing.

Middle managers, such as department heads and plant managers, make short-range *tactical decisions* necessary to carry out the overall plan devised by the top-level managers (Figure 14-3). Carrying out the plan entails developing budgets and acquiring and managing resources over a time frame ranging from about three months to a year. Middle managers spend about an equal amount of time on each of the four management activities— planning, organizing, directing, and controlling.

Lower-level managers, such as project leaders or plant supervisors, have the narrowest scope of all, making operational decisions that put into effect the details of the tactical decisions made by middle managers (Figure 14-4). *Operational decisions* involve the use of existing resources to carry out functions within a budget, and cover events that take place over a time frame ranging from less than a day up to about three months. The primary task for lower-level managers is directing subordinates. Figure 14-5 summarizes the activities carried out by the three levels of managers.

FIGURE 14-2.
Top-level managers determine a company's overall strategy.

FIGURE 14-3.
Middle managers develop the tactics used to bring about the "big picture" envisioned by top-level managers.

FIGURE 14-4.
Lower-level managers supervise the day-to-day operations that get the work done.

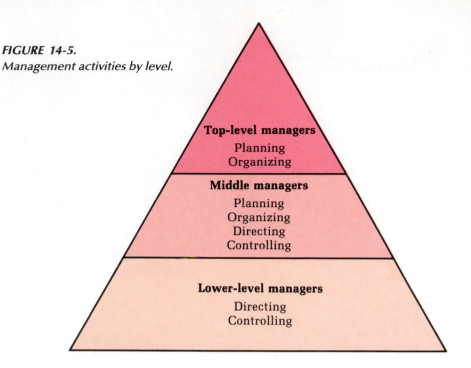

FIGURE 14-5.
Management activities by level.

Top-level managers
Planning
Organizing

Middle managers
Planning
Organizing
Directing
Controlling

Lower-level managers
Directing
Controlling

REPORTS MANAGERS NEED

Management information systems or decision support systems provide information in the form of reports. The reports can be produced in "permanent" form by a printer or graphical output device, or displayed on a screen. Regardless of the medium, the reports differ in terms of how often they are created, the degree of detail they show, and the level of analysis they reflect.

The most common type of report, the **SCHEDULED LISTING**, is created on a regular basis—such as daily, weekly, monthly, or yearly. Scheduled listings tend to show as much detail as possible, and to reflect very little analysis. An example of a scheduled listing is an inventory report that simply lists the quantity of each item in stock.

An **EXCEPTION REPORT** highlights significant changes from whatever conditions are usual. Such a report may be created at regular intervals, or when a special condition arises. Less detail is shown than with a scheduled listing. Since exception reports identify situations that may require action by managers, these reports reflect more analysis than do scheduled listings. An example of an exception report would be a list of inventory items that are out of stock.

A **DEMAND REPORT** is a predefined report that is generated only when requested, and generally concerns a specific topic of interest to a manager. Details shown are confined to the matter of interest, and the information can reflect some analysis. For example, a purchasing manager may be concerned about the out-of-stock inventory items, and request a demand report that ranks late suppliers with the slowest first.

PREDICTIVE REPORTS attempt to identify future trends. These reports are based on specific data, such as those found in scheduled listings, exception reports, and demand reports. Predictive reports go beyond the data at hand, however, to project into the future. They do not show much detail but reflect considerable analysis. Often predictive reports answer "What if?" type of

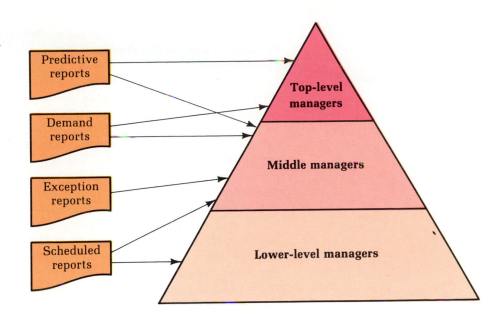

FIGURE 14-6.
*Management report needs by
level.*

questions. A corporate vice-president might request such a report, for
example, by asking what the effect would be on company market share ten
years in the future if the company grew 5 percent in each of those years and
the competitors did not.

Different levels of managers require different reports (see Figure 14-6).
Top-level managers require reports that show little detail and that generally
reflect a fair amount of analysis. Therefore they often use demand reports
and predictive reports to help make planning decisions. In addition top-
level managers may occasionally refer to scheduled listings, as Susan Paul
did in our example at the start of the chapter.

Middle managers rely on scheduled listings supplemented by exception, demand, and predictive reports as necessary. Lower-level managers
tend to work with scheduled listings exclusively.

Naturally we have simplified matters somewhat here, and not all
business organizations have managers categorized this neatly as to level and
reports used. The point is, however, that different levels of managers need
different types of information. It is the job of the management information
system or decision support system to supply that information.

We now look at three ways in which to organize an information system
to provide information to managers: management information systems,
decision support systems, and information resource management systems. Historically each of these systems arose to meet unfilled needs of
management. Each has its strengths and weaknesses. They are not, however, mutually exclusive—elements of all three may coexist within the same
information system.

MANAGEMENT INFORMATION SYSTEMS

A **MANAGEMENT INFORMATION SYSTEM (MIS)** as defined by the American
National Standards Institute (ANSI) is "an information system designed to
aid in the performance of management functions." It processes the transac-

tions of an organization's day-to-day operations, and creates information in the form of reports that support a manager's tasks of planning, organizing, directing, and controlling.

Now that we have defined a management information system, we should also note that many people use the term to mean simply "information system." That is too general for our purposes.

The role of any information system is to provide timely, accurate, and useful information at a reasonable cost and in a secure manner. A good management information system not only should do this, but must also tailor the information to suit the specific level of manager involved. We have already seen that this involves presenting an appropriate amount of detail and processing the data using an appropriate amount of analysis.

Management information systems have their origins in discontent with the type of information that computers produced in the 1960s. Managers got tired of flipping through scheduled listings that presented far too much detail and that reflected little effort to perform the types of analysis that they really needed. Listings tended to stress quantity rather than quality. Printed reports were not unknown that, when folded in the fanlike computer paper, stood taller than the person who requested them. It was very difficult to find the pearls of wisdom in such a printout fast enough to base the right decisions on them.

At the same time that managers were frustrated, computers themselves were getting faster and more powerful, becoming cheaper and easier to use, and demonstrating that they could handle time-sharing and real-time processing as well as the batch processing that produced those listings. Managers wanted to put some of this computing power to work to produce the right information for themselves. Thus management information systems were born.

The concept of the management information system has been shown not to be the end of the line, but the start of a trend. The steps that have followed—decision support systems and information resources management systems—will be described later in the chapter.

WHAT AN MIS DOES   An MIS processes data to create information for managers in the form of scheduled listings, exception reports, demand reports, and predictive reports. Some of these reports can be listings that are produced by batch processing programs. Other managers can request and receive reports almost immediately at terminals serviced by time-sharing or real-time programs.

Like any other information system, a management information system consists of people, rules and procedures, data, software, and hardware. The *people* are, of course, managers and other users, and today at least, if not always in the past, the designers of management information systems strive to make them easy for users to use. The *rules and procedures* concern the types of reports that should be created and who is allowed to see them. Since an MIS can deliver highly distilled, powerful, sensitive data, we want the data in the right hands only. For example, reports generated for top managers that evaluate middle and low-level managers should not be accessible to the people evaluated. Chapter 17 will cover the important topic of security.

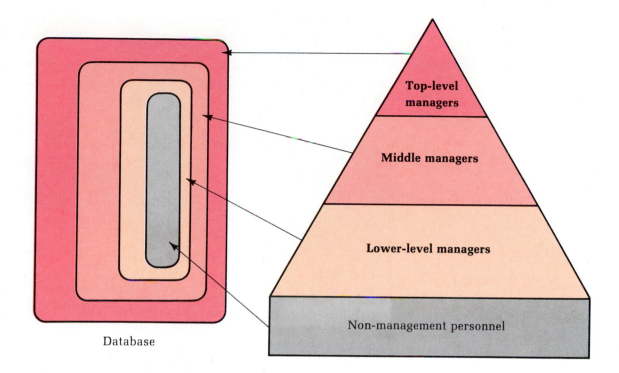

Database

FIGURE 14-7.

Access to the company data-base. Each higher level has access to whatever data are accessible to the lower levels.

Data for an MIS are generally contained in a database. Figure 14-7 shows one approach to using a database for the different levels of manager. Here a single database serves the whole organization, from the president down to nonmanagement personnel. Each level, however, is allowed to work only with the portion of the database that it actually needs. Once again, this is for reasons of security. Bear in mind that security implies not only a mistrust of some scattered individuals, but the concern that someone might unintentionally cause irreparable damage to a database by simply hitting the wrong key. Chapter 16 will explore database design and use in depth.

The *software* for an MIS processes the data, using an appropriate level of analysis for the particular target level of manager, and outputs the right amount of detail. It manages the database and incorporates MIS rules and procedures that, for example, regulate security.

Hardware can be a computer of any size, together with the peripherals necessary to create, promptly and legibly, the desired quantity of output. All but the simplest management information systems require a display termi-nal or microcomputer for the manager(s) served.

With an MIS supplying them with up-to-date and appropriate informa-tion, managers can in fact spend more time planning and less time scouring files and printouts for information or—worse—guessing. Managers can move more quickly, too, in response to the information, making decisions that correct problems or respond to opportunities that might not even have been recognized without an MIS. Graphical output from an MIS (Figure 14-8) can help a manager present his or her case for action to others in the organization, once again saving time (in this case, in preparing or waiting for someone else to prepare charts).

FIGURE 14-8.
Not only do today's systems provide vital information, but they can also express it as graphics that can be used in a presentation or published.

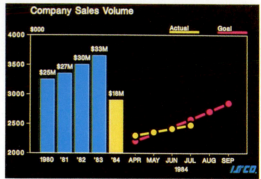

FITTING AN MIS INTO A BUSINESS

Management information systems can be fitted into a corporation in various ways. One method common today is to create a separate department headed by a vice-president for management information systems. This person then oversees all of the operations associated with computers, information systems, and management information systems. Figure 14-9 shows an example of such an organizational structure. Reporting to the vice-president for MIS are the top managers for computer operations, programming, database administration, and systems analysis.

An earlier, less effective approach placed control of all computer systems, including the MIS, in the department that made heaviest use of its services. Usually this was the accounting department. Such an organization made it difficult for people in other areas, such as manufacturing and purchasing, to take advantage of the power of an MIS. The home department, say accounting, would receive quick and efficient service; the rest often had to wait.

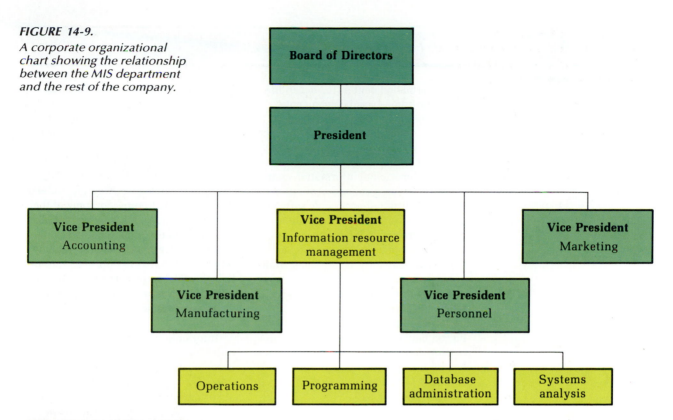

FIGURE 14-9.
A corporate organizational chart showing the relationship between the MIS department and the rest of the company.

Board of Directors

President

Vice President
Accounting

Vice President
Information resource management

Vice President
Marketing

Vice President
Manufacturing

Vice President
Personnel

Operations

Programming

Database administration

Systems analysis

DECISION SUPPORT SYSTEMS

Management information systems can do a lot, but many, at least the oldest of them, tend to be more effective at providing routine information to lower-level and middle managers than nonroutine information to top managers. Thus there has been increasing demand from top management for more sophisticated decision support. One result is the **DECISION SUPPORT SYSTEM (DSS)**, an information system that managers can use easily and that provides highly refined information to help in making nonroutine decisions.

Four major characteristics of a DSS are:

- *The ability to help analyze nonroutine problems*
- *The ability to handle heterogeneous data*
- *Strong analytical capabilities*
- *Ease of use*

Nonroutine problems are often called "semistructured" or "unstructured" problems because there is no agreed-upon "right" way to analyze them. For an executive in an automobile company, for example, an unstructured problem might be to forecast demand for small cars in light of worldwide economic trends and projected changes in the costs of raw materials. A structured problem for the same executive—or at least for another executive in the same company—would be to determine at what level of inventory to reorder dashboard parts from a supplier. An MIS tends to be oriented to structured problems. A DSS, in contrast, is oriented toward unstructured problems.

The information center (IC) began life as a mainframe-based concept conceived by IBM of Canada to deliver more computing power directly into the hands of its users and, not incidentally, to deliver more IBM products to its customers. The original information center was usually just a collection of "user-friendly," terminal-accessible software and hardware. Today's information center users not only have access to these tools, but also a department to which they can turn for products, training and support, on microcomputers as well as mainframes. The centers also typically coordinate and control software and hardware purchases, act as liaison between users and the data processing department, and serve as a catalyst for user interaction. ICs have become the nuclei around which end user computing revolves....

One sometimes reluctant beneficiary of the information center's services is the data processing department, which often misunderstands and resists the development and promotion of the center. Part of this hostility is, of course, based on insecurity—the bulk of new technological developments are aimed towards user independence, which traditional data processing professionals may perceive as threatening.

The resentment also is based on technological progress. As hardware and software tools were touted as more sophisticated, and users became more aware of what computer power could do for their own job productivity, they began to press data processing (DP) with still more development projects. Data processing departments, already overloaded, could not keep up with the demand and users became more and more frustrated with delays. The arrival of microcomputers and new mainframe tools, such as fourth-generation languages, were hailed by users as The Solutions, with those users sometimes naively implying that perhaps their data processing departments and other professional assistance were no longer necessary.

It wasn't long before reality interrupted their euphoria. Most fourth-generation languages, for example, indeed do allow users to program some of their own applications, but they are not always easy to use, making professional training and support vital. Microcomputers almost always improve productivity, but here again, training and continued support are important to enable users to persist and succeed in their efforts.

Information centers provide that training and support that users need. As users become more knowledgeable, they also acquire a greater understanding of the work the DP staff does. This promotes better communication and, thus, a more positive relationship between the two groups. Besides actually improving DP/user relations, the information center tools do enable users to do more and more of their own applications, thus relieving DP departments for more complicated development projects as well as systems and maintenance work....

In a recent survey conducted by Crwth (as in "tooth") Computer Coursewares, Santa Monica, California, 98 percent of the 169 respondents reported that their information centers had significantly improved job productivity. Improved use of information resources was also cited as an important benefit by 98 percent of the respondents, as well as improved computer literacy and an increased understanding of the complexity of system problems....

Source: Reprinted with permission from ICP Business Software Review. Copyright © August 1984, International Computer Programs, Inc., Indianapolis, Indiana.

Heterogeneous data refer to data from a variety of sources. Top-level managers need to analyze data from different sources to make strategic decisions; the sources may include the in-house database as well as external databases. A DSS, unlike the typical MIS, can extract data from different locations.

The analytical capabilities of a DSS are greater than for an MIS. In fact DSS software exists that can handle a whole range of analysis and modeling. Statistical studies can be made of the data, or mathematical models of a business can be built and differing data run through them to see the effects on the outcome.

A good decision support system should be easy to use (user-friendly) in that managers can use it without much training. Skillfully designed display screens and clean documentation help managers determine which program functions they need. As we saw at the start of the chapter, Susan Paul could easily get the decision support system to do what it was able to, by picking commands such as **"DISPLAY REPORT"** from a menu.

Many of today's managers are accustomed to using electronic spreadsheets and interactive financial planning packages on microcomputers to manipulate financial data and make projections into the future (spreadsheets were described in Chapter 12). A DSS, in effect, enables managers to draw on a wide source of data and analyze those data with a variety of such software tools. By using a DSS a manager can retrieve relevant data from the company database or an external database and copy the data to his or her microcomputer system and work with them there.

Decision support systems are usually created using structured design and programming techniques, which gives them considerable flexibility. A module or two can be changed to customize a system or adapt it to new circumstances without throwing the whole thing out and starting from scratch.

MIS and DSS are not mutually exclusive. Both can be combined within the same information system. Although not every business has a DSS, a number of them do. These systems have proved themselves in such areas as budgeting, product planning, analysis of government policy, personnel planning, managing research and development, sales planning, and developing overall corporate plans. Figure 14-10 illustrates the features of one popular decision support system, IFPS (Interactive Financial Planning System).

Another type of decision support system is known as an **EXPERT SYSTEM**. Expert systems are an outgrowth of research into artificial intelligence. They are designed to mimic a human expert in a particular field. Users ask questions in order to tap special "expertise" built into the system in the form of data and rules and procedures. Doctors can pose medical questions of the CADUCEUS and MYCIN expert systems (see Figure 14-11), computer designers can ask help on thorny matters from an expert system known as R1, and geologists in search of oil can pose their questions to PROSPECTOR. Other expert systems help mechanics to repair complicated machinery and teach strategy to military officers. As computers become faster in the future, we can expect expert systems to become more expert, because they will be able to scan more possibilities before finding an answer within an acceptable response time.

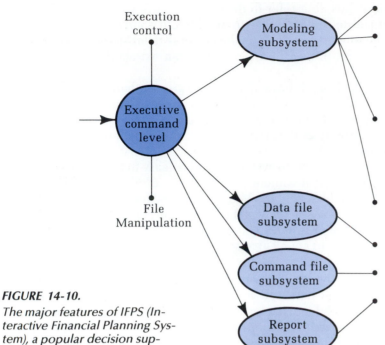

Execution
control

Modeling
subsystem

• Creating and editing models

• Scenario building and model interrogation
    What if analyses
    Backwards solutions (goal-seeking)
    Impact and sensitivity analyses
    Risk analysis

Executive
command
level

• Producing results from model solutions
    Automatic "spreadsheet" printing
    Formal reporting
    Storing results in data files
    Plotting results on graphs

File
Manipulation

Data file
subsystem

• Consolidating and combining models
and solutions

• Creating and editing data files

Command file
subsystem

• Creating and editing command files

FIGURE 14-10.

The major features of IFPS (Interactive Financial Planning System), a popular decision support system package.

Report
subsystem

• Creating and editing formal
report definitions.

From Student Guide to IFPS, by Paul
Gray. Copyright © 1983, McGraw-
Hill Inc.

FIGURE 14-11.
Expert systems can help doctors meet their age-old challenge of diagnosing medical problems correctly.

The director of information systems (described in the Chapter 6 career box) sits at the top of the information systems echelon in many organizations. The recent trend, however, has been to regard information as a company-wide resource that requires an even higher level of management.

This higher level is filled by the information resource manager. The director of information systems reports to the information resource manager, who in turn may report to the chief executive officer of the organization.

The information resource manager is responsible for the total flow and storage of information in an organization. This means that he or she must see that managers get timely, appropriate information when they need it. While this is easily stated, carrying it out involves every possible aspect of information systems. The information must be obtainable by the managers without fuss or undue technical knowledge, must be refined enough to help in making strategic, tactical, or operational decisions, and must be extracted from heterogeneous sources when this is called for. The information systems must hum like a top to achieve this aim.

Carrying out this objective means that the information resource manager is responsible for more than the computer center(s). All of the information-related technical facilities in an organization also come under his or her umbrella: word processing, electronic mail/message systems, and any other area of what has traditionally been thought of as office management that has been automated. In sum the information resource manager is responsible

for designing, implementing, and maintaining an information resource management system so thorough that no scrap of paper or telephone message is too small, and no statistical analysis of disparate data too complex, to merit handling in an expedited manner.

Requirements for filling this job are extensive. As with the position of director of information systems, it is possible to join an organization in a low-level information-processing position and gradually work one's way up. This provides the opportunity to demonstrate technical competence, and ideally a stint as leader of some project—such as developing a system—can give experience in management as well as "exposure" to higher-level managers who can advance one's career.

Once the move to management is made, it is in theory possible to ascend to the top and become information resource manager, with somewhere between dozens and thousands of employees and a highly elaborate pyramid of subordinate managers and specialists. At some point in the ascent, interpersonal and administrative skills become more important than technical knowledge; accordingly, a degree in management or business administration and an extensive, impeccable track record are musts.

Salaries are high and the pressure is intense. Also, heads (yours) tend to roll when things don't work right. Nevertheless, for the aspiring manager who feels a sense of mission in grasping an organization's information needs in all their complexities, and crafting intricate systems to fill them, shooting for this position may be the only possibility.

INFORMATION RESOURCE MANAGEMENT SYSTEMS

In Chapter 4 we discussed the type of hardware and software that fourth-generation computer systems introduced. The main new type of hardware was the microcomputer. Software became more user-friendly, and a host of prepackaged programs appeared to manage databases, analyze data, and perform many other functions. Without this technical progress, the development of information resources management systems would not have been possible.

An **INFORMATION RESOURCE MANAGEMENT SYSTEM (IRMS)** integrates the elements of an information system to optimize the flow and use of information in an organization. IRMS developed as a result of the increasing awareness in business and government that information is a valuable resource that must be managed as efficiently as possible. An IRMS typically includes features of both the MIS and DSS, combining these with newer technologies such as word-processing and electronic mail/message systems in a distributed information-processing environment.

With an IRMS managers or their assistants working at their terminals or microcomputers can use software that retrieves data from a database, analyzes the data, and stores the results of analysis for incorporation into documents produced by a word-processing system. The document can then be output on a laser-xerographic printer in the office, or electronically transmitted to the reprographics department so that multiple copies can be produced and distributed. In addition to documents, the electronic mail/message system can be used to send messages from one person to another in the network.

Exxon Corporation uses a large-scale IRMS run by its Communications and Computer Sciences Department. The network offers managers and other personnel access to decision support systems, office systems such as electronic mail/message systems and word-processing systems, and 16 "client support centers" that provide advice and training as well as the traditional computing power. As you can see, with an IRMS such as this we have come a long way indeed from the way organizations once served up information to their managers almost as an afterthought in those tall, sporadically appearing, unhelpful printouts.

TODAY'S CHANGING ORGANIZATIONS

A major issue facing both managers of information systems and other managers within an organization today is how to survive the pressure brought on by the information-processing age. The source of this tension is in the conflict over how centralized or decentralized an organization should be. The trends seem to point in both directions at once.

On the one hand, the use of widespread teleprocessing promotes centralization by allowing people to tie into a single information-processing center. Vast amounts of data can be entered, transmitted, processed, and retransmitted as output back to distant locations.

In contrast the microcomputer revolution has put undreamed-of processing power into the hands of millions of people. A manager no longer needs to wait days or months to receive a financial analysis. The manager or an assistant can simply use a prepackaged software program, retrieve data from a local or distant database, and quickly perform quite elegant financial modeling—modeling a centralized computer center might be unable or unwilling to provide.

The dilemma for the people who manage information systems is how to cope with these conflicting trends as they evolve. The arena for that evolution is likely to be the distributed data-processing system. As we noted in Chapter 8, distributed data-processing involves tying all computing resources within an organization into a single network. In this chapter we have often spoken of using a DSS or IRMS to retrieve information from an organization's database and process the data locally at a manager's micro-computer, all of which would be impossible without distributed data processing. Thus distributed data processing holds the key to the emergence of ever more powerful management information systems, decision support systems, and information resources management systems.

Distributing information resources throughout an organization—whether within a building or scattered across a continent—may have long-term effects on other managers within an organization, however. Some people have predicted that middle managers will disappear. The top-level managers at headquarters can take over the planning and organizing activities of middle managers—this argument runs—and the lower-level managers at local facilities can handle day-to-day direction of their employees. Other observers have predicted the opposite, that middle managers will thrive as never before because of the availability of the new systems. As with any attempt to see what's coming around the corner, the only thing we can say with certainty is that we don't know what it will be.

WRAP-UP

UPGRADING A DSS

"My name is Sid," the stranger said, stepping into Susan Paul's office. He put down his attaché case on a chair and remained standing. "I'm your new IRM."

"Mine personally?" Susan asked.

"No, the whole company's," Sid said. "As Information Resource Manager, I report straight to Mr. Paul."

Now Susan realized what "IRM" stood for. And she remembered that her brother planned to add a new level above DP manager.

"Sit down, please," she said. "How did you send me the messages?"

"From this," Sid said. "I sent them to all the managers." He opened his attaché case, which turned out to be a portable computer. "You have an electronic mail/message system in place now, Susan. That's really just the beginning."

"Of what?"

"Making your decision support system do more for you," Sid said. "Mr. Paul wants a true information resource management system. Let me just ask you a few questions while I explain. First, what would you like the system to do that it doesn't now?"

"To fill in the gap between the summary reports it displays and the listings that give all the details." Susan described what she'd sought today that the system hadn't been able to give her.

"MORE ANALYSIS," Sid typed on his portable computer. "When we get through," Sid said, "you should be able to request statistical analyses of that client's or any other client's purchases, not just total amounts."

"Wonderful," Susan said.

"Do you ever use external data?" Sid asked.

"I read the papers, trade journals, that sort of thing," Susan said.

Sid frowned. "ACCESS TO EXTERNAL DATABASES," he typed. "With some software that I think we can buy," he said, "you can get at industry-wide financial indicators kept on commercial databases . . ."

Susan interrupted. "Could I run the data on my spreadsheet program?" she asked excitedly.

"I don't see why not," Sid said, at the same time, typing "PREDICTIVE REPORTS."

"I'll be able to do better forecasting," Susan said thoughtfully.

"Yes," Sid said. "I think I've asked you enough for a starter." He shut off his computer and closed it up.

"One more thing," Susan said. "Can you show me how to send the scream?"

"I'd be delighted."

SUMMARY

- A manager organizes people and other resources to achieve some organizational goal. A manager's work entails four activities: planning, organizing, directing, and controlling. To carry out these activities, a manager must make decisions. The steps in making a decision are defining the problem and the decision criteria, gathering data, processing the data, evaluating the information, making the decision, implementing the decision, and evaluating feedback.

- Managers can be arranged into a three-level hierarchy of top-level, middle, and low-level managers. Top-level managers make strategic decisions, middle managers make tactical decisions, and lower-level managers make operational decisions. Top-level managers require reports that show little detail and generally reflect a fair amount of analysis. Therefore they often use demand reports and predictive reports. Middle managers rely on the more detailed scheduled listings supplemented by predictive, demand, and exception reports as necessary. Lower-level managers tend to work with scheduled listings exclusively.

- A management information system (MIS) is an information system designed to aid in the performance of management functions. It processes the transactions of an organization's day-to-day operations, and creates information in the form of reports, in order to support a manager's tasks of planning, organizing, directing, and controlling. Often a separate department within an organization exists for management information systems, headed by a vice-president for MIS.

- *A decision support system (DSS) is an information system that managers can use easily and that provides highly refined information to help in making nonroutine decisions. Four major characteristics of a DSS are the ability to help analyze nonroutine problems, the ability to handle heterogeneous data, strong analytical capabilities, and ease of use. One type of DSS, the expert system, helps specialists in a particular field—such as physicians or geologists—to solve problems.*

- *An information resource management system (IRMS) coordinates the elements of an information system to optimize the flow and use of information in an organization. An IRMS typically includes features of both the MIS and DSS, combining these with word-processing and electronic mail/message systems in a distributed information-processing environment.*

- *Managers of information systems must cope with conflicting trends— on the one hand, toward centralization promoted by widespread teleprocessing, and on the other, toward decentralization promoted by the availability of microcomputers. Resolution of this conflict is likely to take place within the context of distributed data-processing systems. Distributing information resources throughout an organization may have long-term effects on other managers within an organization, however. Whether the effect will be to create more work for middle managers or make them superfluous is not clear.*

KEY TERMS

These are the key terms in the order in which they appear in the chapter.

Scheduled listing (390)
Exception report (390)
Demand report (390)
Predictive report (390)
Management information system (MIS) (391)

Decision support system (DSS) (395)
Expert system (397)
Information resource management system (IRMS) (400)

REVIEW QUESTIONS

OBJECTIVE QUESTIONS

1. _____
2. _____
3. _____
4. _____
5. _____
6. _____

TRUE/FALSE: *Put the letter T or F on the line before the question.*
1. Top managers define organizational roles and overall goals.
2. One of the most important parts of controlling is staffing the organization.
3. Planning is a major function for lower-level managers.
4. Expert systems can only be used in a decision support system (DSS) environment.
5. Lower-level managers are responsible for developing tactical plans.
6. Historically MIS grew out of disatisfaction by managers with the service provided by production-oriented data processing operations.

7. Information resource management systems (IRMS) offer less flexible operations to managers than management information systems (MIS).

8. Decision support systems (DSS) are designed help solve unstructured problems.

9. All trends point toward the demise of the middle manager.

10. The general trend in information system management is away from managing distributed information systems toward managing centralized ones.

MULTIPLE CHOICE: *Put the letter of the correct answer on the line before the question.*

1. The organizational group in need of the narrowest range of data from a corporate database is

(a) top management.   (c) lower-level management.

(b) middle management.   (d) nonmanagement personnel.

2. What is the principal feature of a decision support system (DSS)?

(a) the ability to handle nonroutine types of decisions.

(b) the ability to handle heterogeneous data.

(c) the ability to perform strong analytic modeling in a user friendly environment.

(d) All of the above.

3. The view that information is a valuable organizational asset underlies the development of

(a) decision support systems (DSS).

(b) expert systems.

(c) management information systems (MIS).

(d) information resource management systems (IRMS).

4. The type of information system output least likely to be used by lower-level management for routine decision making is

(a) a scheduled listing.   (c) a demand report.

(b) an exception report.   (d) a predictive report.

5. Expert systems

(a) use methods drawn from the field of artificial intelligence.

(b) should eventually replace MIS departments in most organizations.

(c) are available only for simple applications such as helping people to repair engines.

(d) All of the above.

FILL IN THE BLANK: *Write the correct word or words in the blank to complete the sentence.*

1. The most common type of output for users in information systems is _____.

2. The first step in decision making is to _____.

3. The final step in decision making is to _____.

4. A(n) _____ organizes people and other resources to achieve an organizational goal.

5. Staffing and acquiring money and materials are part of a manager's _____ responsibility.

6. A(n) _____ coordinates the elements of an information system in order to optimize the flow and use of information in an organization.

7. The ability to handle heterogeneous data is a feature of _____.

8. Strategic planning is an activity performed by _____ managers.

9. A(n) _____ report is generated when there is a deviation from normal limits.

10. Lower-level managers commonly make _____ decisions.

When answering these questions think of concrete examples to illustrate your points.

1. What are the activities managers perform?
2. What are the decision-making steps managers follow?
3. What types of reports are used by top managers?
4. Which types of managers have the greatest access to an organization's database?
5. What are the features of a management information system (MIS)?
6. What are the features of a decision support system (DSS)?
7. What are the features of an information resource management system (IRMS)?
8. How do expert systems relate to decision support systems?
9. What are the differences between solving unstructured and structured problems?

1. What are the differences between management information systems (MIS) and decision support systems (DSS)?
2. How do management information systems (MIS) differ from information resource management systems (IRMS)?
3. Which levels of management will benefit from centralized, decentralized, and distributed information systems? Why?

CHAPTER 15

THE SYSTEM DEVELOPMENT PROCESS: A STRUCTURED APPROACH

■ CHILLED MOLASSES
STRUCTURED SYSTEM DEVELOPMENT
PROBLEM RECOGNITION
SYSTEMS ANALYSIS
Preliminary investigation /
■ CAREER BOX: Information-Systems Consultant
Detailed investigation
■ CASE IN POINT: Mercedes Gets a Grip on Inventory Control
SYSTEM DESIGN
Logical design / Physical design / Test design / Design review
SYSTEM DEVELOPMENT
SYSTEM IMPLEMENTATION
Conversion /
■ Changeover Creates Taxing Delay
Training / Acceptance test /
SYSTEM MAINTENANCE
■ WRAP-UP: The Weak Link in the Chain

After studying this chapter you should understand the following:

■ How the traditional and structured approaches to system development differ.
■ Which six steps comprise the system development process.
■ The main tasks of the systems analyst during the detailed investigation.
■ The steps that are followed during the system design stage.
■ The four main techniques for converting from an old to a new system.

Susan Paul entered the executive conference room next to the office of her brother and the firm's owner, Philip Paul. Ed Wieland, a systems analyst at the firm, already sat talking to Mr. Paul.

"Hi Phil, hello Ed," Susan said. "The reason I wanted the three of us to meet is to get to work solving a problem."

Philip turned to Ed. "Susan and I are worried about lost sales."

Ed picked up his pen. "What's causing sales to be lost?" he asked.

"We don't know for sure," Susan said. "That's where you come in."

Ed made a few notes and looked up. "Is there any sort of pattern on the kinds of sales lost?" he asked.

"Low-volume customers," Philip said.

Susan nodded. "Small customers try us a time or two and then go elsewhere."

"Interesting," Ed said. "Any idea why?"

"Shipping and receiving is slower than molasses poured over a polar ice cap," Philip said.

Susan gave her brother a mock punch in the shoulder. "Opinions vary. I think shipping and receiving does just fine. As sales manager I personally keep my eye on them. But purchasing seems to let the warehouse deplete on some items, so that shipping has nothing to ship."

Ed scribbled furiously for a moment longer, and then looked up. "Alright," he said. "The problem is that sales to small customers are being lost, because orders are being shipped too slowly to satisfy the customers. You think the cause for slow shipment might be in shipping and receiving or in purchasing."

"Right," Susan said.

"There's more to the problem," Philip said.

"There usually is more," Ed said with a smile.

"We want to enter the mail-order business," Philip said.

"Mail orders mean more small customers, right?" Ed asked.

"You've got it," Susan said.

"Do I have your O.K. to launch a preliminary investigation of the problem?" Ed asked.

"I'll give it to you in writing today," Phillip said. "And I'll notify the managers of the areas in question that you will be meeting with them soon and conducting investigations with their people."

"Excellent," Ed said.

STRUCTURED SYSTEM DEVELOPMENT

A **SYSTEM** is a set of interrelated elements working together toward a common goal. Within a business the accounting department, personnel department, and sales department are systems—and at a higher level so is the business itself. At Paul's House of Electronic Wonders, the order-fulfillment process can be viewed as a system that crosses departmental lines, involving shipping and receiving, purchasing, and conceivably other departments. (For a refresher on what constitutes a system, turn back to "What is a System?" in Chapter 2.)

Any system goes through a process of birth, growth, maturity, and decline. The **SYSTEM DEVELOPMENT PROCESS** is a method for studying and changing systems as they go through these changes. That is the topic of this chapter. Other terms often used for the same process are "system life cycle" and "system development life cycle."

The system development process has six stages. In chronological order, these are:

1. *Problem recognition*
2. *Systems analysis*
3. *System design*
4. *System development*
5. *System implementation*
6. *System maintenance*

As we saw in the opening example, Paul's House of Electronic Wonders was losing small orders. The problem recognition stage corresponded to Susan Paul and Philip Paul realizing this. By giving Ed Wieland permission to begin studying the problem, Philip Paul launched the second stage of the process, systems analysis. If all goes well, the process will continue through the remaining stages, resulting in a functioning system that solves the problem.

Before we begin our description of each of the six stages, we should note that there are two very different ways to approach the system development process. Let's designate these the "traditional approach" and the "structured approach."

With the traditional approach the user does initiate the system development process, but after that does not figure greatly into the process, and may ultimately get a worthless system. The user comes with his or her problem to the systems analyst. The systems analyst, working with other information system specialists—but in isolation from the user—then proceeds to analyze the problem, design a solution, develop the solution, and present the final product to the user. The user is essentially treated as an outsider whose views and needs would only clutter up the system development process. If the user does not like the delivered system, he or she is free to reject it.

It may seem incredible to you that a real-world business could work this way. When computers were new to businesses, however, nearly all businesses followed this approach. Some still do today. But the trend is toward the structured approach.

In Chapter 9 we described techniques for designing and implementing structured programs. With the structured approach to system development similar techniques are used to help keep costs low, avoid the creation of white elephants, and make systems easier to maintain. These techniques

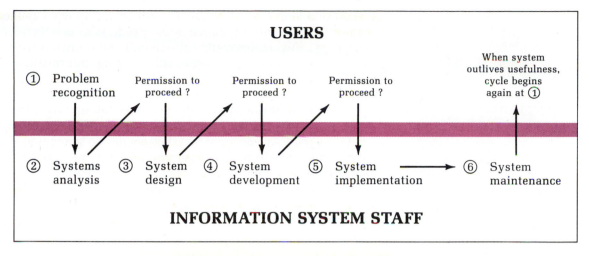

FIGURE 15-1.
The structured approach to system development.

include following a **TOP-DOWN APPROACH** for a system, dividing the system into **MODULES**, and conducting frequent evaluations of the system as it emerges.

With the structured approach the user takes a more active role, and is viewed as the controlling partner in the system development process (see Figure 15-1). The user comes to the systems analyst with the problem, and continues to work with the information system team to analyze the problem and design, develop, and implement the solution. The developing system is constantly checked against user needs, and can have its development stopped at any stage if it deviates too far from them. The active role played by users permits the detection and correction of errors and other misunderstandings early in the system development process. The earlier an error is found and corrected, the lower is the cost of doing so, as we saw back in Figure 9-2 (on page 254). Systems that emerge from the structured approach have a strong likelihood of actually accomplishing what they were supposed to.

PROBLEM RECOGNITION

The first stage of the system development process, **PROBLEM RECOGNITION**, refers to identifying a need or opportunity that a new system could address. "Problem" here does not always mean something wrong; it can also mean a chance to expand or meet new needs. Financial incentives are usually the motivating force behind problem recognition.

In our Paul's House of Electronic Wonders example, the problem actually had two parts, one positive and one negative. The positive problem was that Mr. Paul wanted his firm to expand into the mail-order business. The negative problem was that the firm was losing low-volume sales.

Many other types of problems are possible. For example, a manufacturer might be faced with the problem of disposing of toxic wastes both economically and in accordance with governmental guidelines. Oakriver University might have trouble collecting on loans given to students who later dropped out of school. Problems and opportunities are by no means confined to large organizations. A corner clothing boutique with an inexpensive microcomputer might realize that it could improve its cash flow by more efficient billing procedures.

Most problems are recognized by users and managers. Some, however, are identified by the information system staff, who may be aware of new hardware or software that could better handle some organizational function, or may realize how rusty some still-working information system has become.

SYSTEMS ANALYSIS

Once a problem has been identified in the problem recognition stage just described, managers may feel that the problem is severe enough (or the opportunity attractive enough) that they should do something about it. If so, they can give permission to a systems analyst or systems analysis team to investigate the problem. This does not mean that managers have decided to go ahead and develop a new system; rather, they are interested in "sounding out" what a new system might cost, how it would work, and how long it would take to create it.

The investigation takes the form of systems analysis. **SYSTEMS ANALYSIS** is a method for systematically examining how an existing organization works. In this stage of the system development process, managers or users pass the ball to the systems analysts and in effect say, "O.K., tell me *exactly* what is wrong, and give me some alternatives showing what I might be able to do about it." To see that the analysis remains on target, users are heavily involved in structured systems analysis; for example, if it is performed by a team, a user will be on the team.

Systems analysis is usually divided into two steps: (1) the preliminary investigation and (2) the detailed investigation. Each step ends with a report of the findings to users and managers, providing the opportunity to halt the systems development process if the findings do not look promising, or to proceed to the next stage if they do.

PRELIMINARY INVESTIGATION

The **PRELIMINARY INVESTIGATION** determines the scope of the problem and gives managers data to use in deciding whether or not to perform the next step, detailed analysis. In comparison with the detailed investigation, the preliminary investigation is fast and cheap. The preliminary investigation can be broken down into three steps: (1) evaluating the user's request, (2) determining costs and benefits, and (3) planning detailed analysis.

Evaluating the user's request means pinning down the real problem or opportunity. In perceiving a problem users may not accurately recognize its true scope or nature. For example, Philip Paul thought his firm's problem was due to something amiss in the shipping and receiving department. His sister, however, attributed the problem to the purchasing department. Systems analyst Ed Wieland noted both of these beliefs, and tried to get as many details as he could from both Philip and Susan. His tact and patience here were rewarded not with learning the real cause of the problem, but with acquiring an overview of the existing information system and of managers' feelings about it. Ed would later have to go on to interview other personnel at Paul's and observe how certain activities were actually carried out, to find out the problem's cause.

The next step is determining costs and benefits of proceeding with further development. This cost/benefit analysis involves comparing the

Developing a complete system is an arduous task. This is true even if some or all the components are packaged, for decisions requiring expert judgement are still required to select and combine the right packages.

Many firms place the responsibility for system development in the hands of an information-systems consultant. In the case of smaller organizations or companies that lack employees of their own knowledgeable enough to tackle the job, this may be the only option. Giant firms also hire consultants with some frequency; they may simply have too many projects already in the works to develop another one, they may have begun development but fallen behind with project deadlines, or they too may lack employees with just the right expertise.

Enter the consultant. Ideally this individual is up to the minute in his or her area of expertise, and has impressive experience in exactly the area that the new system will address.

Once selected and placed on the job, the consultant works pretty much like anyone else developing a system. If in charge of the project, the consultant directs systems analysis, system design, system development, and system implementation, and will remain "on call" during system maintenance. For large or complex projects, a number of information-systems consultants may work as a team, each with a particular area of expertise.

Creating a new system from scratch (rather than assembling packages) requires a fair number of noncoms as well as generals. These individuals too can be information-systems consultants, in the guise of systems analysts, programmers, database administrators, training specialists, and other information-systems professionals. Like their manage-rial counterparts, these consultants conduct most of their work on the premises, offering expertise that is lacking, or tied up in-house, at a high price.

How do you find work as a consultant? You have to acquire the knowledge and experience that a consultant sells. The time-honored career path is for someone to begin work as a programmer, move up to a senior-level programmer, systems analyst, or other specialist within an organization, and then quit to become a consultant. There is a great demand for consultants, since businesses are acquiring and expanding their information systems at a breakneck pace, and it is simply not possible always to have just the person needed on the payroll.

Information-systems consultants usually work for consulting firms, which shift consultants on and off of different projects as required. Some independent consultants offer their services directly to employers. Rates of pay range from double to quadruple and more the rates paid to in-house employees performing the same work. Employers are willing to pay these costs because (1) they are desperate and (2) they can let the employee go when the project is done or if they simply do not get along.

This brings up the chief drawback of consulting: you can quickly find yourself between jobs, which tends to flatten out the inflated salary figure. Also, the pressure to produce results on the job is intense enough to eliminate some of the amenities of working life, such as reading the paper in the morning, making friends on the job, or even eating a decent lunch. On the positive side, consultants enjoy the challenge of remaining tops in a particular field, the chance to develop advanced systems at a high level of responsibility, and a certain glamour attached to being a maverick.

benefits (or costs) of the existing system with the possible benefits (or costs) of a new system. It also involves a payback analysis of the new system—an analysis of the costs of the system over a period of years.

Tangible costs and benefits can be measured directly in some fashion—for example, the cost of six programmers working for a year and a half to create a new system. Intangible costs and benefits are important too but cannot be measured directly; for example, once an enlightened paper company satisfactorily worked out the economics of felling a virgin forest, it would still have to reckon with the forest's recreational importance and beauty.

The analyst should attempt to measure tangible and intangible costs of a new system, and compare them with the tangible and intangible benefits. Since preliminary analysis is necessarily rapid and superficial, however, these costs and benefits will only be rough approximations.

The third step of the preliminary investigation is planning the detailed investigation. The approximate time necessary to carry out the detailed investigation should be determined, as well as the resources required—the salaries, office needs, information-processing support, and other day-to-day expenses necessary to support the systems analyst or team.

The systems analyst then prepares a **PRELIMINARY REPORT** for the manager in control of the project. The report states the approximate costs and benefits of developing the new system, and the time and resource needs to carry out detailed analysis.

The manager must examine information in the preliminary report carefully. Even if the cost/benefit analysis appears favorable, there may be reasons not to proceed. For example, other projects awaiting system design and development might have higher priority in that they will ultimately deliver more to the firm.

If the manager decides to proceed, the manager and analyst will together draw up a **PROJECT CHARTER** indicating the nature and scope of the detailed investigation to follow. Top-level management support is vital here, to help ensure that middle and lower-level managers will take the study seriously and allow their people to participate. In addition the charter helps middle and lower-level managers to gauge the extent of disruption the detailed investigation will cause. If, for example, their key employees will be diverted from their duties for countless interviews with analysts, the managers need to alter their own plans to allow for this. The project charter often includes the names of the project members and a timetable for completing interim steps and the entire project.

DETAILED INVESTIGATION

With the preliminary investigation completed and the project charter drawn up, the systems analyst or team can begin the second step of systems analysis, the detailed investigation. The **DETAILED INVESTIGATION** expands upon the preliminary investigation to explain fully the nature of the problem and to offer managers possible solutions; it is more lengthy and more expensive. The detailed investigation can be broken down into five steps:

1   *Define the goal*
2   *Collect facts*
3   *Define system flow*

4 *Define system volume and timing*
5 *Evaluate system performance*

Let's look at each of these steps separately.

Define the goal

In Chapter 14 we said that an organizational goal refers to its purpose or objective, and that the best understood goals are stated in clear terms. The detailed investigation needs such a goal to guide the process. The goal for Paul's House of Electronic Wonders is to reduce the number of small orders lost. Analyst Ed Wieland would be well-advised to have Mr. Paul translate this vague goal into figures—say an increase of $75,000 per year in sales to small customers.

In addition to defining the goal, the analyst needs to set "boundaries" around the problem, to focus the investigation. Ed Wieland will investigate anything that affects the shipment of small orders, which means the shipping and receiving and the purchasing departments. If the data he collects point in a different direction—such as the order-entry process—he will investigate that. But he draws boundaries around the system of interest to exclude unnecessary factors. For example, he is not interested in any problems with the decision support system that Susan Paul uses extensively for sales analysis. Since the concern is small orders, Ed also defines "small order" as an order from a customer for less than $1000.

Collect facts

Collecting facts refers to assembling data on how the existing system works. The existing system is the one with the problem to be corrected, or the opportunity that is not being realized. Collecting facts brings all of an analyst's interpersonal and analytical skills into play, and is one of the more difficult steps of the detailed investigation.

Time and again in this book we have touched on the five information system elements. The analyst needs to collect facts concerning all five elements. Who are the people involved in an organization? What are their tasks? What data are used in the organization? Which rules and procedures are followed? What software and hardware are used?

The analyst can collect facts by (1) assembling documents concerning the organization, (2) conducting interviews, (3) using questionnaires, and (4) observing how the system works. Which combination of techniques is used depends on the problem and the organization. For example, the corner clothing boutique would not design and circulate a questionnaire to its handful of employees, but would simply talk to them (conduct interviews). An automobile factory interested in the opinions of thousands of assembly-line workers, on the other hand, would sidestep the monumental task of interviewing them all by designing and circulating a good questionnaire to a small sample of the employees.

Assembling documents means gathering together any written materials that are related to the way in which the existing system works. Here the analyst is like an archeologist on a dig, happy to find any sort of evidence of the lost civilization suspected of having existed there, from a lowly pottery shard to a complete book of laws. The documents an analyst assembles will provide evidence of how the system works.

FIGURE 15-2.

A grid chart showing the source
documents involved in shipping
and receiving at Paul's House of
Electronic Wonders and the
output reports derived from
those documents.

Input Source Documents	Output Reports			
	Updated Inventory	Accounts Payable	Accounts Receivable	Merchandise Returned
Shipping label, arriving item	X			
Shipping label stub, departing item	X			
Supplier invoice		X		
Customer invoice			X	
Return slip	X	X		X

Documents of interest might be organizational structure charts, procedure manuals, forms, and reports. At Paul's House of Electronic Wonders, every document concerning shipping will interest Ed Wieland. A helpful tool to keep track of these documents and their uses is the grid chart. Figure 15-2 shows an example. This particular chart lists source documents used by the shipping department, and the reports they are used to generate.

Interviews are an important source of information on how the system works. Conducting interviews requires great care. Many people are wary of analysts coming in and studying their jobs, since they feel that these jobs may be taken away or changed. Interviews should be conducted in a tactful and nonthreatening fashion. In reality jobs are rarely taken away, and the interview is the first chance to hint that the new system that may be developed will be positive, helping people to do their jobs better, with less frustration, and more easily.

Questionnaires can survey a greater number of people quickly. Just as conducting interviews is an art, so is designing questionnaires. A question-

FIGURE 15-3.

Two questions from a questionnaire given by Ed Wieland to shipping and receiving and purchasing department employees at Paul's House of Electronic Wonders.

Question 1. What types of orders do you think go out the fastest from your department?

_____ a. Small orders
_____ b. Medium-sized orders
_____ c. Large orders
_____ d. All orders go out equally fast
_____ e. Don't know

Question 2. From your department's point of view do you find that the shipping operation works well or not? Please explain.

_____

_____

_____

naire should ask questions that encourage people to express their opinions; but not lead them down a path preplanned by the analyst. For example, Ed Wieland's questionnaire (Figure 15-3) for people at Paul's does not say that there is a problem, but seeks answers unbiased by Ed's own belief. Findings from the interview may help pinpoint the source of shipping delays to small customers.

All of the other techniques are no substitute for actually seeing what happens. A good systems analyst will observe people at work carrying out their jobs, aware that his or her mere presence will cause people to work differently (most of us tend to speed up when someone is looking over our shoulder). Observation can spot bottlenecks or inefficiencies that documents, interviews, and questionnaires would pass by. Once the analyst or team has collected enough data to work with, the time has come to analyze the data in the next steps of the detailed investigation.

Define system flow

The detailed investigation may reveal that the existing system does not work at all as managers or users thought it did. One way to determine how a system actually operates is to follow the actual flow of work through the system. At Paul's what happens between the time a small order comes in and the time that it goes out? There are two main ways of visually presenting the flow pattern: data-flow diagrams and system flowcharts.

DATA-FLOW DIAGRAMS focus on how data move through the system. Even if our interest concerns the movement of physical goods, we still begin with data. We need to see where data enter the system and at what points data are stored and processed. Figure 15-4 shows the symbols used in a data-flow diagram. Figure 15-5 shows one of the data-flow diagrams Ed Wieland developed at Paul's to trace the process for inventory management. The focus of this diagram is the procedure for ordering replacement supplies. To show the full inventory management system (including procedures for shipping orders) would take several pages of diagrams. As Figure 15-5 shows, Ed found that the inventory file (store) depended on data from marketing, management, accounting, and vendors. In turn data flowed from the inventory file to management and vendors.

FIGURE 15-4.
Symbols used in a data-flow diagram.

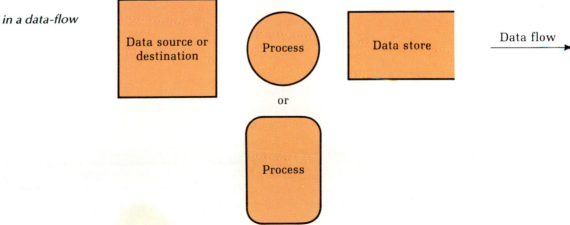

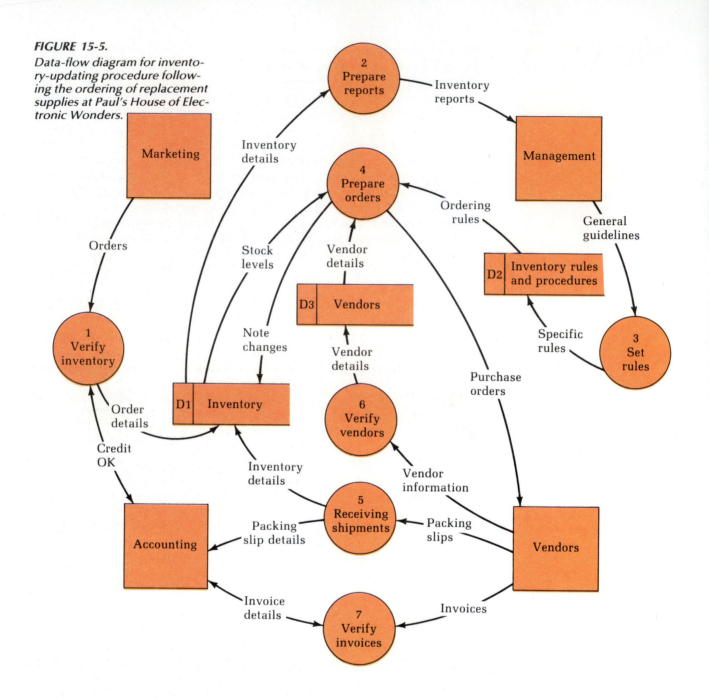

FIGURE 15-5.

Data-flow diagram for inventory-updating procedure following the ordering of replacement supplies at Paul's House of Electronic Wonders.

Marketing

2
Prepare reports

Inventory reports

Management

Inventory details

4
Prepare orders

Ordering rules

General guidelines

Orders

Stock levels

Vendor details

D2 Inventory rules and procedures

D3 Vendors

Specific rules

3
Set rules

1
Verify inventory

Note changes

Order details

D1 Inventory

Vendor details

Purchase orders

Credit OK

6
Verify vendors

Inventory details

5
Receiving shipments

Vendor information

Packing slips

Accounting

Packing slip details

Vendors

Invoice details

7
Verify invoices

Invoices

Clearly inventory data affected a lot of departments at Paul's. For example, purchasing used inventory data to determine when to order items that were getting low in the inventory. The procedure seemed so reasonable that Ed's detective-like suspicions were aroused.

SYSTEM FLOWCHARTS describe the processing effort using symbols that give some details of the hardware used for input and output. In Chapter 10 we saw flowcharts used for describing program logic. Flowcharts employing a different set of symbols are useful for describing the overall way that a

FIGURE 15-6.
Symbols used in a system flow-chart.

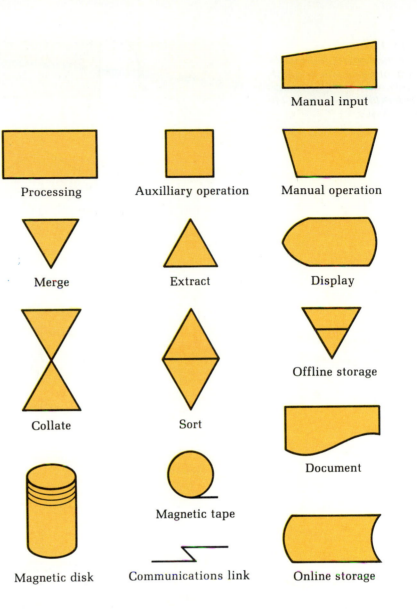

system works. Figure 15-6 shows the symbols that can be used in a system flowchart, and Figure 15-7 shows the way Ed Wieland flowcharted the system for preparing orders for replacement supplies at Paul's. This system flowchart describes what happens in process bubble 4, "Prepare orders," in the data-flow diagram in Figure 15-5.

Regardless of whether system flowcharts, data-flow diagrams, or both, are used, additional tools are available. One is known as the **DECISION-LOGIC TABLE**. In a decision-logic table an analyst can trace complicated logic patterns by following through the possibilities for multiple decisions. At Paul's decision-logic tables are used in the ordering process to state rules for processing back orders.

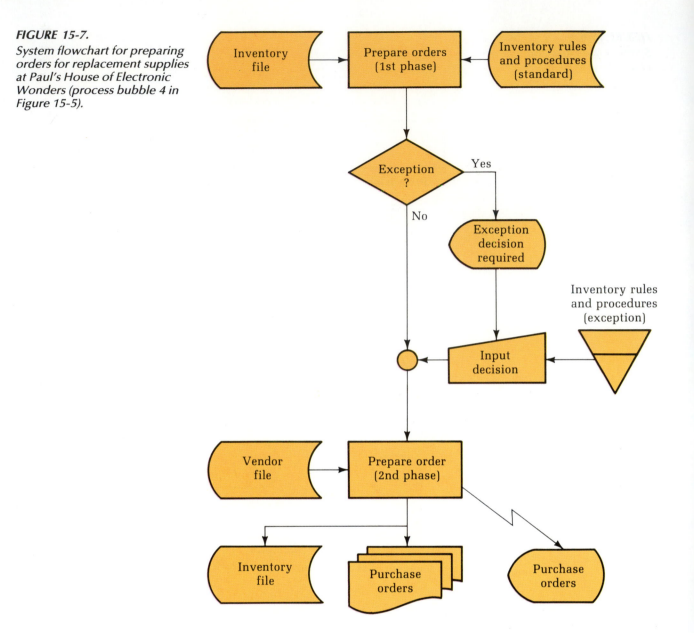

FIGURE 15-7.
System flowchart for preparing orders for replacement supplies at Paul's House of Electronic Wonders (process bubble 4 in Figure 15-5).

Inventory file

Prepare orders (1st phase)

Inventory rules and procedures (standard)

Exception ?

Yes

No

Exception decision required

Inventory rules and procedures (exception)

Input decision

Vendor file

Prepare order (2nd phase)

Inventory file

Purchase orders

Purchase orders

Figure 15-8 shows such a table for deciding whether or not to grant credit to customers. The "conditions" part of the table (known as the condition stub) labels the possible categories into which a customer falls. There is one "rule" column for every possible combination of conditions. For example, following column 3 down, we have an old customer with no outstanding bills owed to Paul's and an acceptable credit rating. Continuing down to the "actions" part of the table (known as the action stub), we see that Paul's would extend this customer credit.

Define system volume and timing
The next step in the detailed investigation is to define system volume and timing. **SYSTEM VOLUME** refers to the number of operations that occur over a

FIGURE 15-8.
The decision-logic table for a credit decision at Paul's House of Electronic Wonders.

		Rules							
		1	2	3	4	5	6	7	8
Conditions	If old customer	Y	Y	Y	N	N	N	Y	N
	And outstanding bills from Paul's	Y	Y	N	Y	N	Y	N	N
	Credit rating acceptable	Y	N	Y	Y	Y	N	N	N
Actions	Extend credit	X		X		X			
	Investigate further				X		X		
	Require prepayment		X					X	X

given period of time. For example, Ed Wieland found through his researches that Paul's House of Electronic Wonders received an average of 68 small orders per day. The average daily total value of small orders was $10,200. As Mr. Paul said when Ed showed him the figure, this was nothing to sneeze at.

SYSTEM TIMING refers to any cycles or time patterns that can be discerned concerning the operations under investigation. For example, Ed noted that small orders picked up substantially in the fall, and dropped off in the summer. He also observed that small orders were given a lower priority than larger ones, and thus were always handled late in the day.

Evaluate system performance

By the time we reach this step in our detailed investigation, we have defined the goal, collected facts, defined the system flow, and defined the system volume and timing. Now we are in a position to evaluate system performance. In other words, we should really be able to figure out how the existing system works, and identify the cause of the problem.

Next the systems analyst or team must also make recommendations on how to solve the problem (or realize the opportunity). The systems analyst prepares a **FEASIBILITY REPORT** containing the complete findings of the detailed investigation. The feasibility report describes how the existing system works, details the nature of the problem with the existing system, and offers alternate solution possibilities. The costs and benefits to the organization should be given for each alternative—including doing nothing.

The cost/benefit figures here should be much more exact and reliable than those supplied at the end of the preliminary investigation, since they result from a much more thorough research process. Appended to the feasibility study are supplementary materials such as data-flow diagrams,

At sticker prices currently ranging from a low of $22,850 for the 190E to $58,100 for the top-of-the-line 500 SEC, the Mercedes automobile has been a status symbol for easily a decade. Owners—or those lucky enough to have a leased car as a corporate perk—have been willing to look the other way when they encountered occasionally slow deliveries and frequently astounding repair costs. The privilege of driving a Mercedes clearly can turn an impatient person into a pussycat. And the privilege of selling those cars to an eager and admiring public can make a dealer equally meek when it comes to "talking back" to executives at headquarters and "the factory."

Yet even the vaunted Mercedes-Benz, probably the most desired company car in the U.S. and Europe, has not been invulnerable to the competitive pressures and changing business climate of the 1980s, particularly in the U.S. market. . . .

In the past few years, however, the company's eyes and ears out in the field—its 400 or so dealers nationwide—have repeatedly complained about the inadequacies of the Mercedes information network. In many instances, it has failed to allocate cars to dealers as expeditiously as they would like. . . .

Responding to dealer prodding—and a tougher marketplace—Mercedes-Benz of North America, the U.S. sales arm of Daimler-Benz, is installing a fully computerized communications network, called MB Net.

What was going wrong? Like sales organizations in any industry, Mercedes-Benz of North America is in the distribution business. It must rely on an allocation system set up by the Daimler-Benz factories at Stuttgart. Unlike dealers of many other makes, a Mercedes dealer cannot simply order a car specifically equipped for one customer and assume that Stuttgart will build that car.

The dealer—and the customer—may or may not get what was ordered. It is often easier to call a nearby dealer and see if that showroom happens to have in stock a model like the one the customer wants. "A large part of this business today is swapping cars with other dealers," a spokesperson explains. . . .

MULLING WHILE MANAGING

"We saw a great need in this area," says George Balinski, manager of data processing. In fact, two top executives at Mercedes-Benz had been mulling over these problems, and in June 1981 they had decided something must be done. As Karl-Heinz Faber, vice president of product compliance and service, and Hans Hinrichs, former vice president of sales and service and now a member of Daimler-Benz's management board, saw the situation, the company had to provide dealers with more support. Brought down to earth, that altruistic notion meant helping dealers get the right car at the right time.

Mercedes' traditional method of doing this was slow, unsure, and irritating. It involved telephone inquiries to the zone office or parts distribution center in the dealership's region. Those queries, in turn, led to telephone searches by the zone or parts office and the inevitable telephone tag between dealers to arrange for the swap or the shipment of parts.

EXECUTIVE DECISIONS

Balinski's data processing people picked up on the Faber and Hinrichs concept and began studying the sales and service operations of other auto manufacturers. "We looked particularly closely at BMW, Volvo, and Volkswagen to see what was going on with their systems," he recalls. "We didn't know if we wanted a home-grown system, such as Volkswagen developed, or if we should buy a package from one of the automotive systems vendors."

By February 1982, Balinski's group had decided and made its project proposal to management: Mercedes should go with Automatic Data Processing Inc., Roseland, N.J. A leading turnkey supplier for the automotive industry, ADP writes the software and puts together hardware from several original equipment manufacturers. The company had sold tailored systems to leading American and foreign automotive manufacturers and was well aware of Mercedes' needs.

Meanwhile, as Balinski's group went about organizing a new system, the dealers were pressing even harder for action. They met regularly with Mercedes' executive management, and put on the pressure all during 1982. . . .

Along with the lobbying that went on at the Executive Committee level, Mercedes management was getting the message from dealers through the zone offices that monitor the dealerships. By early 1982 the MB Net idea that had originated in an executive suite more than a year earlier was gaining sufficient momentum to be treated as top priority by the data processing group. . . .

MAXIMIZING CASH FLOW

Following its analysis of vendors, Bal-

inski's group ran MB Net pilot projects at nine dealerships throughout the U.S. Pilot dealers were chosen from zone office recommendations. "Obviously you want a dealer in this who has his act together," says Balinski. "You don't want one who's negative about computers, or has problems with his dealership as it stands, without computers." Between January and April of [1984] the pilots were "up" and running pretty well, as the Balinski team worked to get the bugs out.

By now, MB Net has finally become a reality. The company already boasts about 50 dealerships equipped with MB Net, and 94% of its dealerships are scheduled to go on-stream by January 1, 1986. . . .

MB Net is supposed to be a more advanced system than networks now in place in the automotive industry. It may be late, says Robert Shawulsky, Mercedes supervisor of dealer systems, "but our system is easier to use and more comprehensive than anything else now running."

Source: From "Computerized Swapping: Mercedes Gets a Grip on Inventory Control," John Hermann, in *Management Technology*, November 1984. Copyright © International Thomson Technology Information.

---

decision-logic tables, sample documents, statistics on questionnaire results, and so on.

The feasibility report is a written document, but is generally accompanied by an oral presentation to users and managers by the systems analyst. Based on the report and presentation, managers can do one of three things:

1   *Decide to study the matter further. This means that additional systems analysis will be performed.*
2   *Decide to proceed with one of the alternatives for improving the system. This means that the systems analyst or systems analysis team can now start on the system design.*
3   *Reject the alternatives and decide to make no changes in the existing system.*

In order to show you the remainder of the system development cycle, we will assume the second decision, so that we can proceed to the system design stage.

SYSTEM DESIGN

We have now completed the problem recognition and systems analysis stages of the system development process. Assuming that managers have approved one of the alternatives to change the system put forth in the feasibility report that resulted from systems analysis, we can proceed with the third stage, system design.

SYSTEM DESIGN is the process of determining, in general and then more detailed terms, the way the new system will be set up. The final details are reserved for the following stage, system development.

System design is a major effort, and at the onset must be planned and scheduled carefully. The same systems analyst or team that performed the systems analysis may continue with the system design; or a new team may be formed that includes specialists in particular design activities. In either case design begins with determining who will perform which tasks, establishing a schedule, and reviewing the feasibility report to refresh oneself on the project.

To assure a satisfactory design, user involvement remains heavy, even if some design considerations are beyond the technical understanding of users. Analysts must regularly touch bases with users, a process greatly simplified if a user is present on the team.

To aid in the system development process, system engineers can create small working models of the system. Called **PROTOTYPING**, this method allows designers and users an opportunity interactively to adjust the model. The design of prototypes involves the same systems development steps as for full-scale systems. Knowledge gained from testing a prototype can then be applied to the full-scale system.

The system design process can be divided into four steps: logical design, physical design, test design, and the design review. We will describe each in turn.

LOGICAL DESIGN

LOGICAL DESIGN refers to creating a conceptual model of the new system. In Chapter 2 we gave a simple model of a system, consisting of input, processing, output, and feedback. In the logical design step we focus on how these four steps will interact within our new information system.

Starting in the logical design step and continuing throughout design, data flow diagrams and system flowcharts are useful tools. Just as they were used to describe the *old* system, here we use the same techniques to design the *new* system.

Logical design begins with the "bottom line" of the new system, the information it is to output. To define the output the analyst must determine what information the users require, how detailed that information must be, and when it is needed. All three points can be best determined by asking the users themselves.

After the general output design is agreed upon, the analyst then works in consultation with the user to determine the input requirements needed to generate the necessary data to support the output. Next the processing steps required to transform the data are worked through. Additionally, system feedback steps are outlined.

Passing through all these steps are data. Analysts often use a data dictionary to keep tabs on the data with which a program will work. A **DATA DICTIONARY** defines each item of data and information handled by a system, giving the item's name, telling what the item is, specifying its format, giving its input source, and specifying its output use.

File or database design is also part of the logical design. The design of the file or database that will store data items, and the relation of one item to another, must be determined. Some output is neither printed nor displayed, but retained on a file or in a database for future use. Chapter 16 will cover file and database design in detail.

PHYSICAL DESIGN

With the logical design complete, we have the data-flow diagram, the system flowchart, general input and output design, and file or database design in hand. We are now ready to settle some "physical" matters about how the new system will work.

In **PHYSICAL DESIGN** we create the physical specifications of the new system. Each element of the information system is examined. The number and types of people required to operate the new system should be outlined. Any new or modified rules and procedures not previously addressed in earlier stages must be proposed. The data configuration—file design or database—must be matched against the other physical elements. The new hardware and software requirements need to be laid out. All of these elements interact, and the system designer must constantly ensure that the *total physical design* is properly constructed.

Again we start with the output stage. Once the basic information needed is agreed upon, the output medium must be chosen. The analyst should then create rough sketches of reports and other output. For example, the analyst fills in a printer layout chart (Figure 15-9) to design the way the headings and data items will physically appear on printed reports. Similar forms are used to design the format of information displayed on a screen (Figure 15-10). The analyst should offer the user alternate designs, and patiently modify the one chosen until the user is satisfied.

With the output settled, the analyst turns to the input from which it will be derived. Working closely with the user, the analyst first determines the medium for input data. Input specifications are then determined, using a record layout form such as that shown in Figure 15-11.

Next in physical design, we also determine the processing mode. Will the new system perform batch processing, time-sharing, real-time processing, or some combination of these? The decision reached here affects the physical design elements.

We can focus on physical design concerning hardware and software requirements. Although systems analysts do not design hardware, they must see that the needed hardware for the new system is in place. The analyst or designer determines the *hardware requirements* of the new system and compares them with the hardware on hand. If new hardware is needed—whether a new optical reader, magnetic disk unit, or a complete computer system—it must be ordered. Now is the time to initiate the ordering process—the lead time between order and delivery can run to many months for some equipment—so that the hardware will be available when we are ready to test and implement the new system.

The first step in ordering equipment involves *requesting equipment proposals* and *price quotations* from vendors, and evaluating the information vendors then provide in order to make the best choice. Factors involved

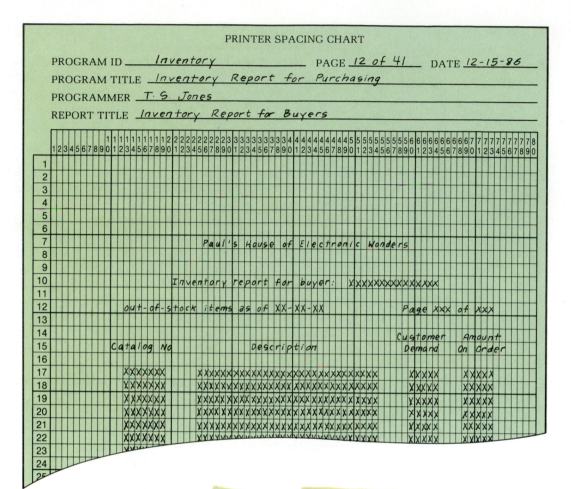

FIGURE 15-9.
A printer layout chart.

in the evaluation include cost, the amount of support and training the vendor provides, and the quality of the documentation. Potential vendors might be required to give a full system test of their equipment. A good vendor will be eager to set up such a test.

Equipment—especially major equipment such as a mainframe computer—need not necessarily be purchased but can be leased. Here again, a comparison of factors such as cost and vendor support and training can provide a basis for deciding whether to lease or buy. Computers have a way of becoming obsolete fast, and leasing does offer users the flexibility of being able to dispose of equipment that suddenly no longer looks as glittering as it once did, without the burden of ownership. Some vendors offer a combined buy-and-lease package, whereby a company may lease the large mainframe computer and perhaps a key peripheral or two, but purchase other peripherals needed to complete the system.

Given the *software requirements*, programs for the system can either be developed in-house or purchased. As Chapter 12 indicated, prepackaged software exists for virtually any function and for use on any size of machine. Prepackaged software has both advantages and drawbacks, as described in Chapter 12. If analysts, user, and managers opt for purchase rather than development of software, the physical design stage is the time to evaluate the available software packages.

FIGURE 15-10.
A screen display form.

SYSTEM _Inventory_   USER APPROVAL _____

PROGRAM _Inventory report for buyers_   DATE _12-17-86_

SCREEN FORM NO. _1 of 6_

```
                    Buyer Follow-up:  Item by catalog number

 3  Enter your name: XXXXXXXXXXXXXXX     Enter your password: XXXXXX

 5  Enter catalog no.: XXXXXX   Description: XXXXXXXXXXXXXXXXXXXXXXXXXXXXXXXXX

 7                             Customer demand: XXXXX    Amount on order: XXXXX

 9  Purchase order no.: XXXXXXX   Vendor: XXXXXXXXXXXXXXXXXXXXXXXXXXXXXXX
10                                Address: XXXXXX XXXXXXXXXXXXXXXXXXXXXXXXXX
11  Delivery date: XX/XX/XX               XXXXXXXXXXXXXXXXX XX XXXXX-XXXX

13  Buyer options -- enter the underlined letter
14        Alter:  create alteration form for purchasing clerk.

16        Purchase order:  view purchase order

18        Next catalog number:  enter the next catalog number

20        Help:  additional instructions

22        Quit:  leave current report module

24  Enter selection: X
```

FIGURE 15-11.
A record layout form.

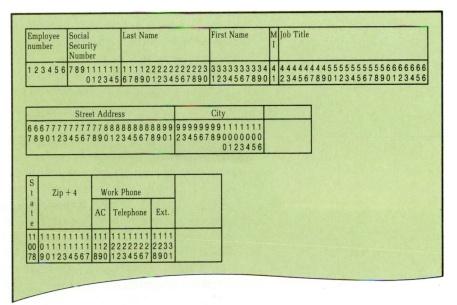

Software that is written entirely in house or modified in house uses structured programming. The analyst designs the program or programs that will make up the new software in modules. A module is a self-contained part of a program, performs a well-defined and simple function, and can be modified or replaced without substantially affecting other modules. This builds considerable flexibility into the system, making it possible to adapt it to future user needs.

The analyst relates the modules of a program to one another following the top-down approach. With this approach the solution is planned starting with the overall design at a general level, and then proceeds to the details. Chapter 9 covers the structured programming concepts that are followed during program development. The output from this design step is a set of HIPO or similar diagrams. Examples are shown in Chapter 9. From such diagrams, together with useful information such as data flow diagrams created earlier in the system design process, programmers can carry out the work of system development.

TEST DESIGN

The analyst must develop a **TEST DESIGN**, a plan for those tests that the new system must pass in order to meet the user's approval. The plans should include tests of all types of normal as well as unusual operating situations. Users can provide analysts with sample transactions to use for both types of tests. Deliberate errors should be included in the test data; later, when the system actually exists and runs the data, users and analysts can then check that it handled both the error and the normal situations properly.

DESIGN REVIEW

Once the logical, physical, and test designs are complete, the analyst assembles the designs to produce a system **DESIGN REPORT**. This report includes the complete output of the system design stage. The responsible analyst first circulates the report to users and managers, and then conducts a formal design review. A **DESIGN REVIEW** is a meeting during which users, managers, and the analyst go over the system design piece by piece to make sure that such a system—if developed—will in fact meet user needs. Many a large system has completed the system design process but failed the design review. If a system fails, the responsible manager can either direct that further efforts on the system be dropped, or that the design be improved to cover the points at issue.

When the responsible manager accepts the system design, then we can move on to the actual development of the new system.

SYSTEM DEVELOPMENT

SYSTEM DEVELOPMENT refers to the creation of the new system based on the results of the design stage. At the start of system development all we have are the various specifications developed during system design; important as these are, they are only a road map to a nonexistent system.

Each element of the information system—people, data, rules and procedures, software and hardware—are addressed during the development process. For example, hardware elements will be selected and assembled for system testing during this phase.

Looking at software, for example, system development means writing and testing programs for the new system. If part or all of the necessary programs have been purchased prepackaged, then design, coding, and documentation of those programs is not necessary, since the vendor will already have done it. Testing, however, is still required, to ensure that the software does what it is supposed to do. Program design, coding, and documentation were described in detail in Chapter 10.

Programming of a large system can take months or even years—longer than the systems analysis or system design stages. As programmers complete and document individual modules, they debug them, using data and techniques they have developed for the purpose. When all of the individual modules or parts of the system appear to be working, then a system test is performed. Here the test design determined in advance during system design (described earlier in the section "Test Design") is followed to the letter, using the error-clogged data that analysts and users have specially developed to trip up the system wherever possible.

Needless to say, passing the system test is a crucial event. Many a good system has failed the first time or two around, been refined, and then passed when given another chance.

Once a system has successfully passed the system test, users and managers have a final opportunity to decide whether or not they want to implement (which means to begin using) the system. Assuming that users were active throughout the systems analysis, design, and development process, and that the test design put the new system through the paces that users believed were necessary, then it is unlikely that users would reject a system at this late stage. Managers, however, might still have a reason to reject the system. For example, organizational priorities might have changed, or the economic picture of the business might have worsened such that additional costs associated with running the new system cannot be borne. Systems are still occasionally killed at this point—or altered substantially to reflect changed conditions—even when millions of dollars have been invested in their design and development. The reason for continual user and manager involvement with the new system is to defuse this possibility in advance.

SYSTEM IMPLEMENTATION

SYSTEM IMPLEMENTATION refers to the changeover from the old system to the new. Each of the information system elements—people, rules and procedures, data, software, and hardware—must be accounted for during system implementation. System implementation can be subdivided into the following tasks: conversion, training, and the acceptance test.

CONVERSION

Conversion entails not only putting the new software and hardware to work successfully, but also changing the data structure as required. For example, an organization's old system may use data files and the new system may require a database. The permanent data on the files must then be transferred to the database, and procedures established so that new data will be entered directly to the database. (Again, we will study databases in Chapter 16.)

As this article indicates, a lot can go wrong during system implementation.

WASHINGTON, D.C.—It's a case of "hurry up and wait." You struggled, fumed and fretted your way through your federal tax return to meet the April 15 deadline, but you may have a long wait for that refund check this year.

The wait is the result of a modernization program that replaced 1960s vintage Honeywell, Inc. 2050A and Control Data Corp. 3500 processors with Sperry Corp. 1184 multiprocessors and that converted 1,500 Internal Revenue Service programs—3.5 million lines of code—from assembly language to structured Cobol.

A wide variety of hardware and software problems have meant that, as of March 29, the IRS had processed 26% fewer individual tax returns than it did at the same time last year, according to IRS spokesman Steven Pyrek. . . .

In a speech last month, IRS Commissioner Roscoe L. Egger Jr. expressed his frustration with the computer problems in the Service Center Replacement System: "With any computer [breaking-in] period, there are software and hardware problems and personnel adjustments. Machines break down. People push wrong buttons. . . . The results are terribly frustrating for taxpayers and us."

The delay in processing returns has not been the only problem caused by the Service Center Replacement System (SCRS). At congressional hearings last month, IRS officials said SCRS problems had caused the backlog of unanswered taxpayer correspondence and adjustments to triple. . . .

Tom Laycock, assistant IRS commissioner for computer services, said the SCRS problems fall into the following three categories:

- *Frequent problems have arisen with the 48 heavily used tape drives, such as creased tapes and tapes that are created on one drive but cannot be read on another.*
- *When hardware problems occur, the IRS frequently must redo hours of input work because the operating software's checkpoint restart feature does not always work. (This feature saves the latest block of input in memory and repositions the tape to begin work again.)*

"Instead of having to redo a half-hour of input, we've had to go back sometimes to redo six or 12 hours [of input]," Laycock explained:

- *IRS programmers are working to correct bugs in the applications software. "[Last year] we recognized that those Cobol programs were not running anywhere near as fast as we needed, so we launched an optimization effort that we had never planned on needing. That caused us not to do as much system acceptability testing as we had wanted to do," Laycock explained.*

The Philadelphia and Brookhaven, N.Y., centers have experienced the most trouble and consequently are about two weeks behind in processing tax returns, Laycock said.

The replacement process began in June 1981 when the IRS awarded a $102.6 million contract to Sperry for new equipment and maintenance—the largest single computer purchase in IRS history.

At the time, the IRS said the hardware change was needed because "the equipment being replaced is up to 16 years old and is no longer manufactured, so it cannot be further upgraded."

Laycock added that it was hard to get spare parts for the old mainframes and virtually impossible to find experienced engineers who would work with the outdated system.

The IRS was ready to make the conversion last November and had to choose between entering the 1985 tax season with old computers unable to handle the load or going ahead with the new system in spite of the impending glitches, officials explained.

"We chose the second option, and, despite the transition problems, we will ultimately increase our capacity and speed dramatically," Egger said recently.

Source: Mitch Bette, *Computerworld,* April 15, 1985. Copyright © 1985 by CW Communications, Inc., Framingham, MA. Reprinted from *Computerworld.*

Four main techniques exist for converting from an old system to a new one:

- *Direct cutover*
- *Parallel*
- *Phased*
- *Pilot*

They differ mainly in how much time each requires and the amount of risk each entails. Figure 15-12 graphically compares the four methods of conversion.

In **DIRECT CUTOVER CONVERSION** (also known as *crash* conversion) the organization stops using the old system and starts using the new all at once. For example, assume that analyst Ed Wieland solved the small-order problem at Paul's House of Electronic Wonders. The new system passed the system test. So Mr. Paul and Ed designate September 1 as the day that the old system will be dropped and the new system used instead. The advantage here is that implementation is swift indeed. On the other hand, once having dismantled the old system in order to install the new, if something goes wrong with the new system, the business has nothing to fall back on. The risk, in other words, is great. Conversion is not often done this way.

With **PARALLEL CONVERSION** the old system and the new run side by side over a period of time. Results of the new system can then be checked against

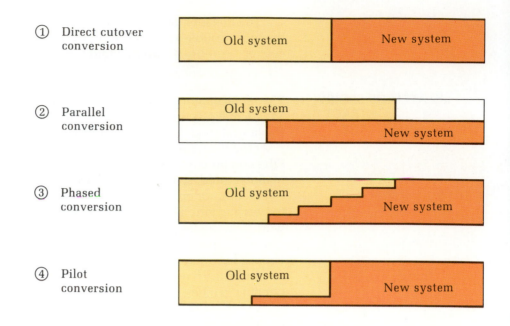

FIGURE 15-12.
The four different types of conversion.

① Direct cutover conversion

Old system | New system

② Parallel conversion

Old system
New system

③ Phased conversion

Old system
New system

④ Pilot conversion

Old system
New system

the results of the old. There are drawbacks to parallel conversion. It can cost quite a lot to run two systems simultaneously. And with the old system still running—the one people are comfortable with—there may be resistance to ever changing to the new system. However, if the new system has problems, parallel conversion minimizes the risks of prematurely depending on it.

PHASED CONVERSION gradually introduces the new system in stages over a period of time. If a given part of the new system fails, the failure can be contained, rather than having it spread throughout the system and halting operations. Phased conversion thus minimizes risk. The disadvantage is that phasing in a new system can take quite a while.

PILOT CONVERSION introduces the new system in its entirety, but only to a small part of the organization. This would not work at Paul's, where only a small part of the organization is concerned to begin with. But in a chain of stores or in a manufacturing company with a number of factories, the new system could be adopted in one and then—once the kinks are ironed out—adopted in the others as well. This minimizes risk to the total organization, but the lengthy experimental period also slows down the implementation.

Finally we should note that a phased or pilot conversion can be performed within the context of a direct cutover or parallel conversion. For example, when introducing the new system to a single factory in a pilot conversion, we can run the new system in parallel with the old, or we could do a direct cutover conversion. With a phased conversion each new phase can be cut over into operation, or can be run in parallel with the old until the results match.

Regardless of the conversion method selected, scheduling and monitoring the conversion process require special consideration. One helpful planning tool is the **GANTT CHART**, which shows how the various steps of a project relate to each other over time. Figure 15-13 shows a Gantt chart for system implementation.

FIGURE 15-13.
Sample Gantt chart for system implementation.

Activity	Month							
	Oct	Nov	Dec	Jan	Feb	Mar	Apr	May
Conversion								
Data		▬▬						
Complete System			▬▬▬▬▬▬▬▬▬					
Training	▬▬▬▬▬▬▬▬▬▬▬▬							
Testing								
Preliminary Tests				▬▬▬▬▬▬▬▬▬				
Acceptance Test							▬▬	

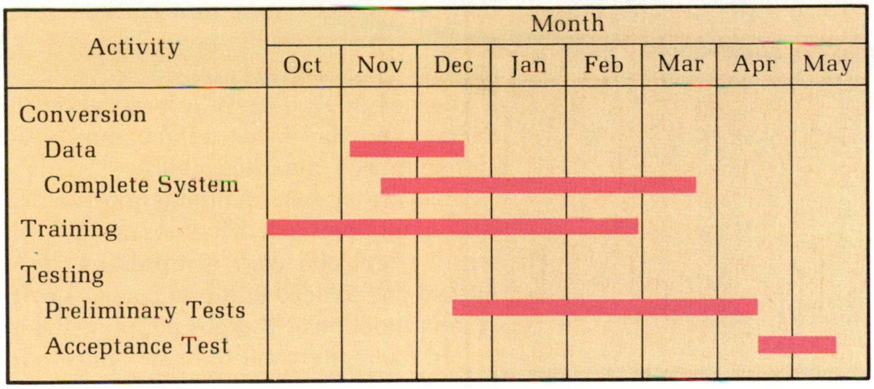

TRAINING   Before users, managers, and operators can work with the new system, they have to know how. Appropriate training courses should be devised for each audience, and conducted in parallel with the end of the system development stage and the start of system conversion. In this way people will be capable of using the new system once it is in place, and work need not grind to a halt. Many different training techniques exist. The goal of the training effort is to reassure employees who feel threatened by a new system, develop competence in using the new system, and guarantee the continued smooth operation of the organization.

Documentation is important to the training effort. Prepared as an ongoing process during the system development phase, documentation exists that is specifically targeted toward (1) users and managers, (2) operators, and (3) programmers. These materials can be used during training and, once training is complete, retained for reference as employees gain confidence and sharpen their skills in using the new system.

ACCEPTANCE TEST   If a parallel, phased, or pilot conversion was performed, a moment arrives when managers must decide whether to go with the new system or continue with the old. (With a direct cutover conversion, managers who suddenly find themselves with a poorly performing new system might wish that they had such an option, but they don't—they are stuck with the new.) We have seen testing at various stages throughout the system development process. The ACCEPTANCE TEST is the last hurdle in system implementation. In this test the new system is evaluated in actual operation, doing real day-to-day work for the organization. Users and managers need to evaluate the test results carefully. The acceptance test provides a final opportunity to decide whether or not the new system solves the problem that it set out to solve. With all the effort taken in its development, it should.

When the responsible manager gives the green light on the new system, the old becomes history, and the new is what an organization will use for the forseeable future. The system development process is not finished yet, however. We still have to keep the system running well, as described in our final section.

SYSTEM MAINTENANCE

SYSTEM MAINTENANCE refers to the continuing process of keeping a system in good working order. Our job is not finished with the successful implementation of a system. Any information system must be properly maintained. Maintenance includes upgrading and extending the system as needed. It also involves solving problems with the system that will inevitably crop up: it is exceedingly rare in a large system to find all the bugs during earlier testing, and those that appear during normal production use of the new system must be handled swiftly.

During system maintenance we reap the rewards of following the structured approach. Modules can be pulled out of the system and tinkered with or replaced without upsetting the whole applecart. Modules can be altered or replaced either to correct errors traced to them, or to permit new system functions—thereby adapting the system to ongoing user needs.

In fact system maintenance must address all elements of our information system. People need continual upgrading or reinforcing of their skills. As the organization's rules and procedures change in response, for example, to new competitive pressures or legal regulations, then the system must be altered accordingly. The data stored in files or databases undergo changes in structure and relationships, and software must be adjusted to changes in the data and in the rules and procedures. Hardware, too, can be altered or replaced to tune the system to greater efficiency.

At the beginning of this chapter, we said that the system development process was a cycle. When we change a module or two of a system, in order to add a new function that a user wants, we need to follow the complete system development process through for those particular modules: problem recognition, systems analysis, system design, system development, system implementation, and system maintenance. With the sort of adaptability that structured system development provides, system maintenance is the longest stage of the system development process—several times longer than any of the preceding stages. Eventually, however, a time will come when our "new" system is truly an old system, despite our fond memories of it, and unable to do things that users demand. It is then that the system development process begins anew for the complete system. We are back, in other words, to the beginning.

WRAP-UP

THE WEAK LINK IN THE CHAIN

At the start of the chapter we saw that Paul's House of Electronic Wonders had a problem filling low-volume orders punctually, and was thereby losing sales to small customers. Mr. Paul also wanted to expand into the mail order business (which meant more small orders). Systems analyst Ed Wieland was given the job of solving the problem.

Ed and an assistant began systems analysis of the problem with a preliminary investigation. They evaluated Mr. Paul's request, calculated the approximate costs and benefits of proceeding with further development, and planned how a detailed investigation would proceed. The complete preliminary investigation took ten days. Ed presented a preliminary report to Mr. Paul and Susan Paul.

In the report Ed recommended that Mr. Paul drop the mail-order idea for the present, until the problem with small orders was solved. "Rather than try to do two things badly," he said, referring to small orders and mail orders, "let's first try to do one thing well" (meaning small orders alone).

Mr. Paul agreed, and gave Ed permission to continue systems analysis.

The next step was the detailed investigation. Here Ed designed a questionnaire (we saw part of it in Figure 15-3), and circulated it to people in the shipping and receiving and the purchasing departments. Using the questionnaire findings to guide him, Ed conducted over a dozen interviews with members of those departments. Both Ed and the assistant observed how the two departments did their work, and wherever Ed found a document that he could photocopy, he did. He enjoyed the private-detective aspect of his work.

Ed defined the data flow and system flow as shown in Figures 15-5 and 15-7. By then he had a fairly complete picture of the order-fulfillment process, and moreover he had put his finger on the problem. Here is how Ed described it in his feasibility report:

The problem, Mr. Paul, is with data flow. When shipping and receiving ships a package, it detaches part of the label on the package. It saves these label stubs until a full day's worth have accumulated. Once the loading docks close, an operator keys in the data on all of the day's label stubs using a key-to-magnetic-tape device. The tape is then taken to the computer room and used for the nightly batch processing run that updates the inventory database. In other words, inventory levels are decreased on the items that were shipped that day.

To the purchasing department, the inventory database is infallible. Purchasing receives exception reports about items that are getting dangerously low, so that it can place timely orders. Purchasing receives regularly scheduled listings summarizing the inventory, and can inquire at terminals at any time about the status of particular items. All of my investigations, Mr. Paul, could find no problem concerning the way in which purchasing used its database or placed orders.

The problem concerns the nightly key-to-tape procedure. This is allowed a limited time between closing of the loading docks and running of the update program. When push comes to shove, some data get left to the next day, or even ignored completely. Consequently the figures that purchasing works with in its database are often inaccurate, and less merchandise is actually in the warehouse than the database indicates.

Our firm has a good record with large orders because of the efficient selection of appropriate shippers, and because of the priority system followed by shipping and receiving: large orders go first. Everyone follows this rule, though I could not find it written down anywhere. If there is not enough merchandise to go around, the small orders simply wait.

Ed recommended either of two courses of action. The first was to change some rules and procedures to require that all data be entered each night. This would mean hiring an additional data-entry operator, and possibly rearranging the computer center's schedule to run the inventory program later at night. But it would not require a new system.

The more expensive option was to use some optical scanners that the shipping and receiving department already had, in order to update the inventory directly. Shipping and receiving used optical scanners to cut down on shipping mistakes; the labels on packages were scanned before shipping, to double-check that the right item was going out. But the scanners were not tied in to the mainframe computer.

If the scanning process that was already being done were used to enter the data on items shipped directly into the database—and a comparable scanning procedure followed for items received—then the nightly key-to-tape procedure could be eliminated. The nightly batch updates of the database could also be eliminated.

Though the second option was far more expensive, and would take nearly a year to design, develop, and implement, Mr. Paul chose this option. Susan Paul provided him with most of the arguments for doing so: all sales—small and large—would benefit through quicker service; the shipping and receiving department would not have to do any additional work, but less; the same database could be retained and used unchanged by the purchasing department; and in all likelihood the new system would pay back its design and development costs in under three years through increased sales.

"And once it's up and running," Mr. Paul said, "I intend to embark on mail orders."

SUMMARY

- A system is a set of interrelated elements working toward a common goal. Any system goes through a process of birth, growth, maturity, and decline. This chain of events, or cycle, is known as the system development process.
- The system development process has six stages: (1) problem recognition, (2) systems analysis, (3) system design, (4) system development, (5) system implementation, and (6) system maintenance. Structured system development employs a top-down approach in which the user plays an active role, and is viewed as the controlling partner. The system is broken down into modules.
- Problem recognition simply means identifying a need or opportunity that a new system could address. Financial incentives, such as making more money or losing less money, are generally the motivating factor behind problem recognition.
- Systems analysis, the next stage, is a method for systematically examining how an existing organization works. It is done in two steps, a preliminary investigation and a detailed investigation.
- The preliminary investigation determines the scope of the problem and gives managers a preliminary report to use in deciding whether

or not to perform the detailed investigation. A project charter defines the scope and duration of the project.

- *In the detailed investigation analysts define the goal, collect facts, define system flow, define system volume and timing, and evaluate system performance. Analysis tools include data-flow diagrams, system flowcharts, decision-logic tables, questionnaires, and interviews. The feasibility report produced at the end of the detailed investigation presents managers with alternative suggestions for new systems that will satisfy the need or act on the opportunity.*

- *If managers give the go-ahead, system design is the next stage. System design is the process of determining, in general and then more detailed terms, the way the new system will be set up. The steps here are logical design, creation of the data dictionary, physical design, test design, the design report, and the design review. Prototyping permits designers to create working models of the new system for testing.*

- *After a system passes the design review, the next stage is system development. Here the new system is created. For software the process consists of program design, coding, documenting, and testing—topics covered in detail in Chapters 9 and 10.*

- *System implementation refers to the changeover from the old system to the new. Conversion from one system to the other must be performed; users, managers, and operators have to be trained; and an acceptance test gives managers a final chance to reject the new system. Assuming that they do not, the new system is up and running. Conversion methods include direct cutover, parallel, phased, and pilot. Gantt charts can be used to schedule implementation, as well as other phases of the system development process.*

- *The final stage of the system development process is system maintenance. This refers to the continuing process of keeping a system in good working order. When errors must be corrected or changes made based on new user needs, the structured approach followed in design and development pays off. Affected parts of a program can be removed and changed without making it necessary to change the whole system.*

- *Eventually, however, systems do reach a point where they are no longer acceptable. The system development process then returns to the beginning of the cycle, to start all over again.*

These are the key terms in the order in which they appear in the chapter.

System (408)
System development process (408)
Top-down approach (409)
Module (409)
Problem recognition (409)
Systems analysis (410)
Preliminary investigation (410)
Preliminary report (412)
Project charter (412)
Detailed investigation (412)
Data-flow diagram (415)
System flowchart (416)
Decision-logic table (417)
System volume (418)
System timing (419)
Feasibility report (419)
System design (422)

Prototyping (422)
Logical design (422)
Data dictionary (422)
Physical design (423)
Test design (426)
Design report (426)
Design review (426)
System development (426)
System implementation (427)
Direct cutover conversion (429)
Parallel conversion (429)
Phased conversion (430)
Pilot conversion (430)
Gantt chart (430)
Acceptance test (431)
System maintenance (432)

REVIEW QUESTIONS

OBJECTIVE QUESTIONS

TRUE/FALSE: *Put the letter T or F on the line before the question.*

1. The system development process works best with a structured bottom-up approach.
2. The first step in the system design stage is physical design.
3. The system implementation stage includes system conversion and acceptance testing.
4. Requests for proposals (or quotations) are part of the logical design process.
5. Questionnaires are a commonly used method to collect facts during the systems analysis phase.
6. Direct cutover is also known as crash conversion.
7. Test design refers to preparing the standards the new system must meet in order to be accepted.
8. The first step of the detailed investigation is to define organizational goals.
9. The role of users in the system development process should be kept at a minimium.
10. System volume and system timing mean the same thing.

MULTIPLE CHOICE: *Put the letter of the correct answer on the line before the question.*

1. Which of the following is not usually used for data collection?
   (a) Questionnaires.   (c) Observation.
   (b) Interviews.   (d) Request for quotation.
2. What is the correct order for these steps in the system design stage?
   (a) Logical design, design review, physical design.
   (b) Physical design, design review, logical design.
   (c) Logical design, physical design, design review.
   (d) Physical design, logical design, design review.

3. What is the correct order for these stages in the system development process?
(a) System design, system development, system implementation, and system maintenance.
(b) System development, system design, system implementation, and system maintenance.
(c) System design, system development, system maintenance, system implementation.
(d) System maintenance, system development, system implementation, and system design.

4. What is not part of the system implementation stage?
(a) Updating the new system.   **(c)** Training.
(b) Acceptance testing.   **(d)** Conversion.

5. The principal outcome of the systems analysis stage is the
(a) project charter.   **(c)** cost/benefit report.
(b) feasibility report.   **(d)** design alternatives report.

FILL IN THE BLANK: *Write the correct word or words in the blank to complete the sentence.*

1. A _____ conversion permits the old and new systems to operate simultaneously for a period of time.

2. The first step in the system development process is _____.

3. A graphic method to trace the flow of data through a system is the _____.

4. Deliberately extreme data should be used in preparing the _____ design.

5. A _____ chart is used to show the sequencing and duration of particular stages in system development process.

6. A _____ is used to illustrate conditions and actions for decision makers.

7. The first step in the logical design step is to determine the _____ requirements.

8. The continuing process of keeping a system in good working order is _____.

9. A _____ visually describes system processes and include some details about the hardware used.

10. A _____ conversion involves converting a small amount of the organization to see if the proposed system should be adopted for the entire organization.

SHORT ANSWER QUESTIONS

When answering these questions think of concrete examples to illustrate your points.

1. What are the six steps in the system development process?
2. Describe the structured approach to system development.
3. What occurs during the problem recognition stage?
4. Describe the main substages of the systems analysis stage.
5. Describe the steps in the system design stage.
6. What steps occur during the system development stage?
7. Describe the tasks found in the system implementation stage.
8. What are the four types of system conversion methods?
9. What is the purpose of system maintenance?

ESSAY QUESTIONS

1. Describe the six major stages of the system development process.
2. Discuss the steps involved in the systems analysis stage.
3. Why does logical design precede physical design?

DATABASES: MANAGING DATA RESOURCES

After studying this chapter you should understand the following:
■ *How fields, records, files, and databases are related in the data hierarchy.*
■ *The main characteristics of the three types of file design.*
■ *What advantages databases offer over files.*
■ *The key steps in creating, using, and maintaining a database.*
■ *How hierarchical, network, and relational databases differ.*

"Good morning, ladies and gentlemen, my name is Vincent Kent." The man stood before a large blackboard with "Databases at Paul's" written at the top.

"I am the database administrator," Vincent said. "A lot of you know me, but I also see new faces here." Users and managers were present from purchasing, sales, accounting, personnel, and other departments. These were all nontechnical people.

"The topic of our course is databases," Vincent said, "but we will have to work our way up to them gradually. 'Data' is a good place to start. Does anyone know what 'data' means?"

Nearly everyone in the room laughed. Vincent was surprised.

"Alright," he said. "You all work with data, of course. You know what I'm talking about. But who can come up with a definition?"

"Facts," Susan Paul said.

"Very good, Susan," Vincent said. "Now, what's the smallest unit that data come in?"

"The record?" Susan asked.

Vincent turned to the board and wrote "record." Above "record" he wrote "file," and above "file" he wrote "database."

"A record is smaller than either a file or a database," Vincent said. "But a field is smaller." He wrote "field" beneath "record." "An example of a field is a social security number, a price, or a purchase order number. This is the level of data that you work with."

"Fields are combined into records," Vincent continued, "and records are combined into files." He drew a big arrow pointing to "file." "Let's hover at the file level for a minute. The files we use here at Paul's for all our databases are direct-access files. They are stored on magnetic disks, which are read by magnetic disk units in the computer room."

Vincent wrote "direct-access" in front of "file." "The 'direct-access' refers to the fact that the disk unit can place its little reader—kind of like the needle or laser reader on your phonograph—right over the spot where the data item is that you are after. The reader doesn't have to digest all of the other data on the way, which would be time consuming. Direct-access is the fastest type of file for that kind of processing."

"Let me ask a question," Susan Paul said. "Why is speed so important with files?"

"Because of the way databases work," Vincent said. "A manager like yourself makes a query at her terminal. Or a programmer asks for data items in a program. The software that handles the database scurries around and locates the data on various files. To answer one minor query of yours, the database software may have to consult data from several files. The software can't spend a lot of time chasing the data. Its job is complicated enough."

BASIC DATA CONCEPTS

Back in Chapter 7 we examined the secondary storage in an information system. Secondary storage supplements main memory by holding data and instructions in machine-readable form outside of the central processing unit but under the central processing unit's control. Although it is a slower operation to store and retrieve data from secondary storage than from main memory, the capacity of secondary storage is much greater, and the cost per unit of data stored is much lower. Without secondary storage today's computers could not hold the system software required to run them, let alone the data that users wish to process. In this chapter we will describe the storage, retrieval, management, and use of data that are stored on secondary storage. Let's take a few moments to brush up on some data concepts, to understand files and databases better.

THE DATA HIERARCHY

Data that an information system works with generally fall into a **DATA HIERARCHY** made up of four categories (Figure 16-1). Moving from the lowest

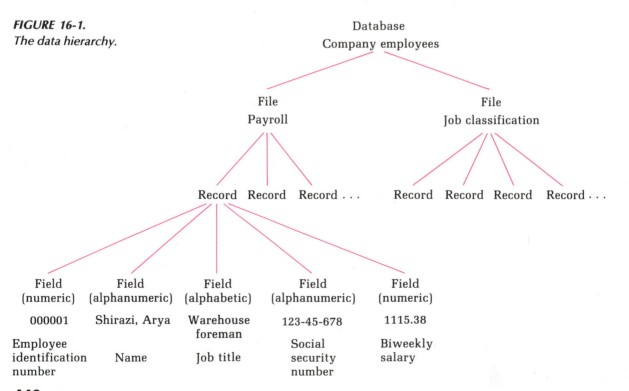

FIGURE 16-1.
The data hierarchy.

level of the hierarchy to the highest, the four categories are the field, record, file, and database.

Fields

At the lowest level data are organized into FIELDS, which represent a single data item. Fields are made up of one or more CHARACTERS, which are individual letters, numbers, or symbols. Once the characters are joined into a field, the field is treated as a unit. A NUMERIC FIELD contains only numbers; an example is the employee identification number in Figure 16-1. An ALPHABETIC FIELD, such as the job title field in Figure 16-1, contains only alphabetic characters. An ALPHANUMERIC FIELD contains any combination of numbers, alphabetic characters, and symbols; an example is the social security number field in Figure 16-1, which has dashes as special characters. Another example is the name field, which contains commas.

Records

A RECORD is made up of a set of related fields. A record can contain from one up to hundreds of fields. Each record contains the field data for a single case. For example, in Figure 16-1 a record contains the employee identification number, name, job title, social security number, and salary fields for a particular employee. Each employee will have his or her own record.

Files

A FILE is a set of related records. Files may contain as few as one or as many as millions of records. In Figure 16-1 one record for each of the company's employees make up the payroll file.

Databases

The highest step in the data hierarchy is the database. A DATABASE is a collection or set of related files. For example, in Figure 16-1 the payroll file and job classification file are combined into a database. Later in the chapter we will see just what this means.

HOW PROGRAMS USE DATA

Programs work with the fields of data within individual records. For example, a program that writes paychecks will, for one employee, read a record such as that shown in Figure 16-1. The program will then use the employee identification number, name, social security number, and bi-weekly salary fields to write that employee's check. Then the program will read another employee's record, and use the corresponding fields for that employee to write his or her check.

In this chapter we will first look at the way in which records are organized into a file, which has a fundamental effect on the way that programs process data from the file. Then, following the data hierarchy up to the highest level, we will learn how databases are constructed and see the advantages of using them.

FILE DESIGN

Historically files came before databases. Although databases represent a step forward from files, they are in fact constructed *from* files. In this section we will examine the different types of files.

FILE DESIGN refers to the technique used by a file to store and retrieve data from storage. There are three main types of file designs: (1) sequential, (2) indexed sequential, and (3) direct-access. Let's look at each type in turn.

SEQUENTIAL FILES

The records in a SEQUENTIAL FILE are arranged in a predetermined order. For example, in Figure 16-2 payroll file records, starting with the record shown in Figure 16-1, are arranged by ascending sequence of employee identification number. The field chosen to order the file is known as a KEY. A key uniquely identifies a record, distinguishing it from all other records. Sometimes a single key is not sufficient uniquely to identify a record. For example, employee name might be used as a key for a file organized in alphabetical sequence. To differentiate employees with the same last name, we would then need an additional key. In such a case the most important key is known as the PRIMARY KEY, and the supplemental key is called the SECONDARY KEY. If you wanted a list of employees within a certain category—for example, a list by job title—you would use a nonunique key—job title. The important point here is that a sequential file is arranged in some sequence, generally in ascending or descending order according to one or more keys contained in the record.

Using sequential files

Sequential files today are contained on magnetic tape or magnetic disk, or on older media such as punch cards. A sequential file can offer programs only one type of access to records: SEQUENTIAL ACCESS. That is, to get to a given record, the program has to read each and every record leading up to it. In a worst case this could amount to reading thousands of records purely to locate one of interest.

As we have seen at earlier points in the book, sequential files are best suited to batch processing programs. The sequential file design and the batch processing technique were the only possibilities for early computer systems. When direct-access storage devices arrived on the scene—and

FIGURE 16-2.

Sequential file organization. Records follow one another in record-key sequence.

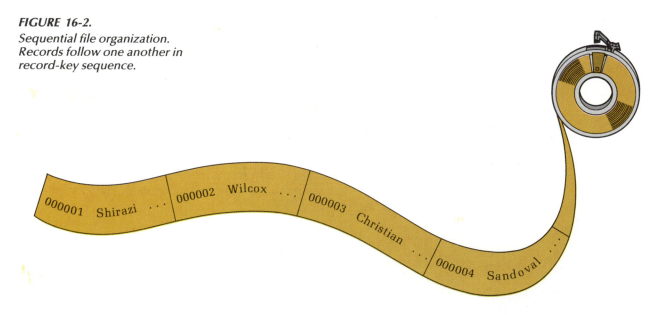

000001 Shirazi . . . 000002 Wilcox . . . 000003 Christian . . . 000004 Sandoval . . .

somewhat later, the use of time-sharing and real-time processing techniques—the picture changed. Time-sharing and real-time systems are less likely to use sequential files.

Most business programs today that use sequential files follow a "model" that we will now describe. The program reads a master file (the old master) in need of updating, and reads a transaction file containing the updates. The program then writes an updated master file (the new master) based on the old master file and the transaction file.

Figure 16-3 shows an example. The program will read transaction record 000004 from the transaction file and then read records from the old master file until it finds a match. When the program doesn't find a match, it simply writes a copy of the unchanged old master file record to the new master file. The program will do this for records 000001, 000002, and 000003. With record 000004 it finds a match with the transaction record. The action code (Delete) for the transaction record specifies a delete; the employee quit or was fired. Accordingly the program does not write 000004 on the new file.

The program then reads transaction record 000006. To find a match it must then read master record 000005 (which it writes unchanged to the new file) and record 000006. The transaction is an update, changing the employee's title and salary; the employee was promoted and got a raise. The program writes the updated version of the record on the new master file.

Next the program reads the last transaction record, number 000008. Then the program reads old master file record 000007, and writes it unchanged to the new master file. Following record 000007 the program adds the new record 000008 from the transaction file, adding a new employee.

Advantages and disadvantages of sequential files

The main advantage of sequential files is that they offer a low-priced means of storing and processing quantities of data. They can use magnetic tape or magnetic disk, and the software that handles sequential files is also less complicated than the software for other file designs. Sequential files are appropriate for batch processing programs that will read and/or write a high proportion of the records in the file. When sequential files are processed as we showed in the example in the last section, the old master and transaction files can be retained for backup; should the new master file be lost or damaged, it can then be regenerated. This automatic creation of backup copies is another advantage.

The prime disadvantage of sequential files is the necessity to read every record on the way to a record of interest, even if thousands of records are involved. This process is simply too slow if only a few records in a file are used. In addition transaction records have to be sorted into the same sequence that the master file follows, which necessitates an extra step. A final disadvantage is that the same data records are present in multiple files, thus wasting storage space.

INDEXED SEQUENTIAL FILES

The records in an **INDEXED SEQUENTIAL FILE** are arranged in a predetermined order as with a sequential file. However, a "road map" to the records also exists, stored as an index. The "indexed" part of the term "indexed

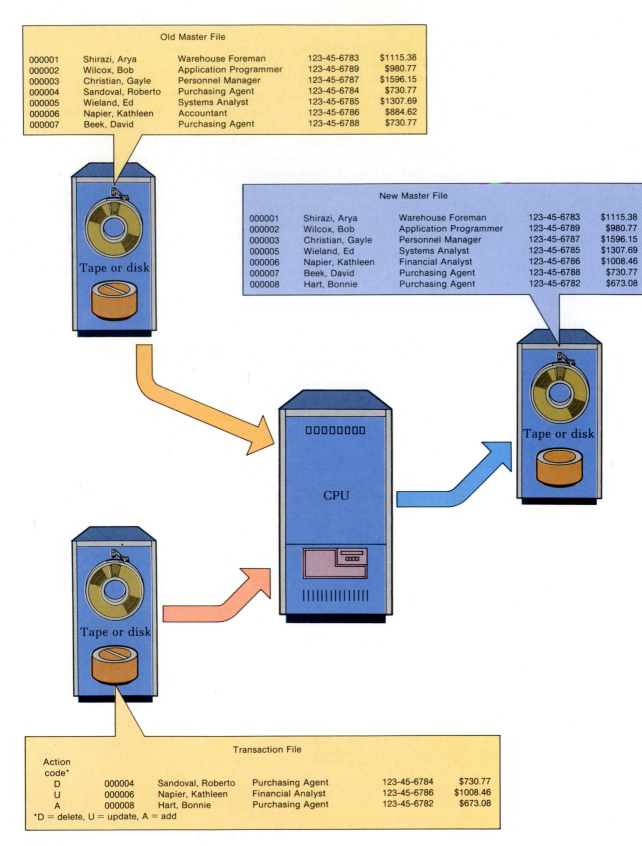

Old Master File

000001	Shirazi, Arya	Warehouse Foreman	123-45-6783	$1115.38
000002	Wilcox, Bob	Application Programmer	123-45-6789	$980.77
000003	Christian, Gayle	Personnel Manager	123-45-6787	$1596.15
000004	Sandoval, Roberto	Purchasing Agent	123-45-6784	$730.77
000005	Wieland, Ed	Systems Analyst	123-45-6785	$1307.69
000006	Napier, Kathleen	Accountant	123-45-6786	$884.62
000007	Beek, David	Purchasing Agent	123-45-6788	$730.77

Tape or disk

New Master File

000001	Shirazi, Arya	Warehouse Foreman	123-45-6783	$1115.38
000002	Wilcox, Bob	Application Programmer	123-45-6789	$980.77
000003	Christian, Gayle	Personnel Manager	123-45-6787	$1596.15
000005	Wieland, Ed	Systems Analyst	123-45-6785	$1307.69
000006	Napier, Kathleen	Financial Analyst	123-45-6786	$1008.46
000007	Beek, David	Purchasing Agent	123-45-6788	$730.77
000008	Hart, Bonnie	Purchasing Agent	123-45-6782	$673.08

Tape or disk

CPU

Tape or disk

Transaction File

Action code*					
D	000004	Sandoval, Roberto	Purchasing Agent	123-45-6784	$730.77
U	000006	Napier, Kathleen	Financial Analyst	123-45-6786	$1008.46
A	000008	Hart, Bonnie	Purchasing Agent	123-45-6782	$673.08

*D = delete, U = update, A = add

sequential file" comes from this index. **The index is in fact a separate file, established** and maintained by system software.

When an application program asks for a record, the system software can use the index to find out approximately where a record is stored. A file is broken up into groups or segments of records. Whereas a typical group might have 25 or 50 records in it, our example in Figure 16-4 has three records per group, to keep matters simple. If a program wants to read record number 000005, it first searches the index, which gives 002 as the address of the group of records that contains record 000005. System software goes straight to the group with the record sought, and then reads each record within the group in sequence, until the record in question is found. We do not, in other words, have to read every record in the file up to the one sought, but only those in the immediate vicinity.

Indexed sequential files can be stored only on direct-access storage devices. Historically indexed sequential files represented an advance over sequential files, because they do offer a kind of direct access. By **DIRECT ACCESS** we mean that a program can go straight to a sought-after data record, rather than having to read all of the records leading up to it first. True direct-access files, which we will cover a bit later in the chapter, offer "more direct" access than do indexed sequential files; nevertheless, **indexed sequential files are a time saver compared with sequential files.**

Using indexed sequential files

Figure 16-5 shows the same master file as the old master file in Figure 16-3. Assuming that this is an indexed sequential file, we can deal with it in two ways. First we can process it sequentially.

FIGURE 16-3.

Processing a sequential file—a sequential update. The update program reads data from both the master file and the transaction file sequentially according to employee identification number. When an ID number in the transaction file matches one in the master file, the record is changed as per the transaction file and the result output to the updated master file.

FIGURE 16-4.

Indexed sequential file organization. Records follow one another in record-key sequence. In addition the starting address of groups of records is kept in an index.

Record Key	Address of Data Segment Containing Record
000001	001
000002	001
000003	001
000004	002
000005	002
000006	002
000007	003

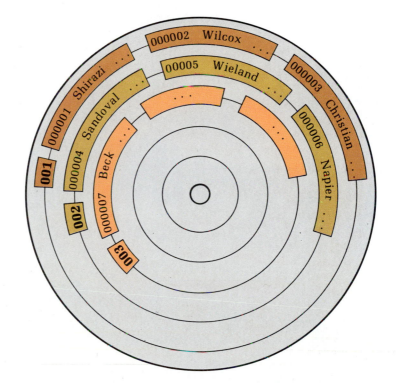

Master File Before Update

Record key (Employee ID)	Address			
000001	001	Shirazi, Arya	Warehouse Foreman	$1115.38
000002	001	Wilcox, Bob	Application Programmer	$980.77
000003	001	Christian, Gayle	Personnel Manager	$1596.15
000004	002	Sandoval, Roberto	Purchasing Agent	$730.77
000005	002	Wieland, Ed	Systems Analyst	$1307.69
000006	002	Napier, Kathleen	Accountant	$884.62
000007	003	Beek, David	Purchasing Agent	$730.77

Update Transactions via Terminal
(Note that transactions are not in sequential order)

Action code*	Record key (Employee ID)			
A	000008	Hart, Bonnie	Purchasing Agent	123-45-6782	$673.08
D	000004	Sandoval, Roberto	Purchasing Agent	123-45-6784	$730.77
U	000006	Napier, Kathleen	Financial Analyst	123-45-6786	$1008.46

*D = delete, U = update, A = add

Display terminal

CPU

disk

Master File After Update Transactions

Record key (Employee ID)	Address			
000001	001	Shirazi, Arya	Warehouse Foreman	$1115.38
000002	001	Wilcox, Bob	Application Programmer	$980.77
000003	001	Christian, Gayle	Personnel Manager	$1596.15
000005	002	Wieland, Ed	Systems Analyst	$1307.69
000006	002	Napier, Kathleen	Financial Analyst	$1008.46
000007	003	Beek, David	Purchasing Agent	$730.77
000008	003	Hart, Bonnie	Purchasing Agent	$673.08

FIGURE 16-5.
Updating an indexed sequential file. An operator enters the updated records on a display terminal. The program then reads the appropriate records from the master file on disk. The two records to be altered, 000004 and 000006, are both stored at address 002 on disk, so the program would read only the records from that address. Record 000008 is a new employee and will be added to the file. The update program makes the appropriate changes and writes the records back onto the master file.

For example, let's say that the personnel manager at Paul's House of Electronic Wonders, wants a list of all current employees in the sequence of their employee numbers. A simple program could read the records of the master file in sequential order and print the contents of each record. This application would not make use of the direct-access potential that the file offers.

The direct-access potential (shown in Figure 16-5) could be used in an update. Let's make the same three changes to the master file that we did in our sequential file example (in Figure 16-3). Someone in the personnel department could make the transactions from a terminal as they occurred, using a time-sharing program, rather than saving them up for an occasional batch run. To get to the record for a particular transaction, the program would not need to read the entire file. Instead, as Figure 16-4 shows, system software would locate the address of the series of records containing the one of interest, and read only those records until the sought-after record could be delivered.

In our example it did not make much difference whether a program had to read all records of the file rather than just a few, since the file only contained seven records. However, real files can contain many thousands of records. Knowing that the record we need to update is contained, say, in group number 900, saves reading all the records in the 899 groups preceding it. Let's say each group contains 25 records. Skipping 899 groups means that there are 22,475 records that we do not need to read. If we have bad luck, perhaps the record we want is the last one in group number 900. In that case we will have to read 24 records first. In a sequential file, however, we would have had to read those 24 *plus* the 22,475 preceding them.

Advantages and disadvantages of indexed sequential files

Indexed sequential files attempt to give the best of two worlds: sequential and direct access. When a program will read and/or write a high proportion of the records in a file, indexed sequential files offer the advantage of sequential access. When only a few records need to be read or written in a file, indexed sequential files offer the advantage of reasonably direct access to those records.

The disadvantages of indexed sequential files are typical of those found in most compromises. Sequential processing goes slower than with a true sequential file. Hardware costs are higher than for those sequential files that are on magnetic tape (rather than magnetic disk). Finally processing most sequential files automatically creates backup copies, a safety plus; processing indexed sequential files does not, so backup procedures must be established and followed to avoid the risk of losing important data. The software that makes indexed sequential processing possible is more expensive than software for sequential processing. However, in today's computer systems this software is usually part of the operating system anyway and so does not really add significantly to costs.

DIRECT-ACCESS FILES

The records in a **DIRECT-ACCESS FILE** are arranged in an order that is *related* to the record key. Exactly how the record location and key are related is determined by program logic. We will explain what that means soon. Another term for direct-access file is **RANDOM-ACCESS FILE**.

Direct-access files offer true direct access. When a program wants to read or write a record, and it knows the key of the record, the reading mechanism of the direct-access storage device can be positioned precisely to the start of the location for that record. There is no need to read other records first. Direct-access files can be stored only on direct-access storage devices.

Using direct-access files

Direct-access files are used in many of today's business applications. They are especially suited to time-sharing and real-time programs, since records can be obtained from large files quickly regardless of where the records are actually stored in those files. Whenever we have given examples in this book of systems that allow users to inquire about the status of data items, and perhaps also to change those items, the files that contain the data are direct-access files.

This is true, for example, of the files containing the inventory data that the purchasing department at Paul's House of Electronic Wonders uses to ascertain when to reorder merchandise. It is true of the decision-support system that Susan Paul used in Chapter 14 to do sales analysis. It is also true of the airlines reservations system used by travel agent Janis Roberts, and by virtually any travel agent who may have reserved a flight or a rental automobile for you.

In the simplest direct-access file, the key field in a record can specify the actual storage address on the direct-access storage device. For example, the key might contain five numbers. The first three could specify the number of the track on the direct-access storage device (tracks were described in Chapter 7), and the last two might specify the number of the record on that track. A key of 21537 would specify a record contained on the 215th track, the 37th record on that track. Given such a precise specification, the storage device would know exactly where to go to find the record.

The problem with this method is that it is very hardware-dependent. If we wanted to move a file to a different type of direct-access storage device, we could not do so without redesigning the file from scratch. Moreover the keys would have to be very carefully designed, and a program reading from (or writing to) the file would have to know these keys. Programs generally seek records based on a key that is an actual field within the record, such as an employee number. How can we keep track of specific disk addresses as well?

The use of relative addressing solves this problem. **RELATIVE ADDRESSING** refers to the use of a key that does not directly refer to the address on the direct-address storage device. Instead the key can be an employee number, airline reservation number, undergraduate course number, or whatever. The number is then converted to an actual storage address through an algorithmic process (see Figure 16-6).

HASHING is a technique that transforms a key into an actual address. With hashing we employ a formula to do the conversion. Many types of formulas can be used. One common technique is to divide the record key by a prime number, and use the remainder that results from the division as the address. A prime number can only be divided evenly by itself and by 1. Any other

FIGURE 16-6.
Direct file organization. Records are generally distributed in
a random pattern across the
storage medium. A formula
converts the key field to the
storage address.

Direct file organization. Records are generally distributed in a random pattern across the storage medium. A formula converts the key field to the storage address.

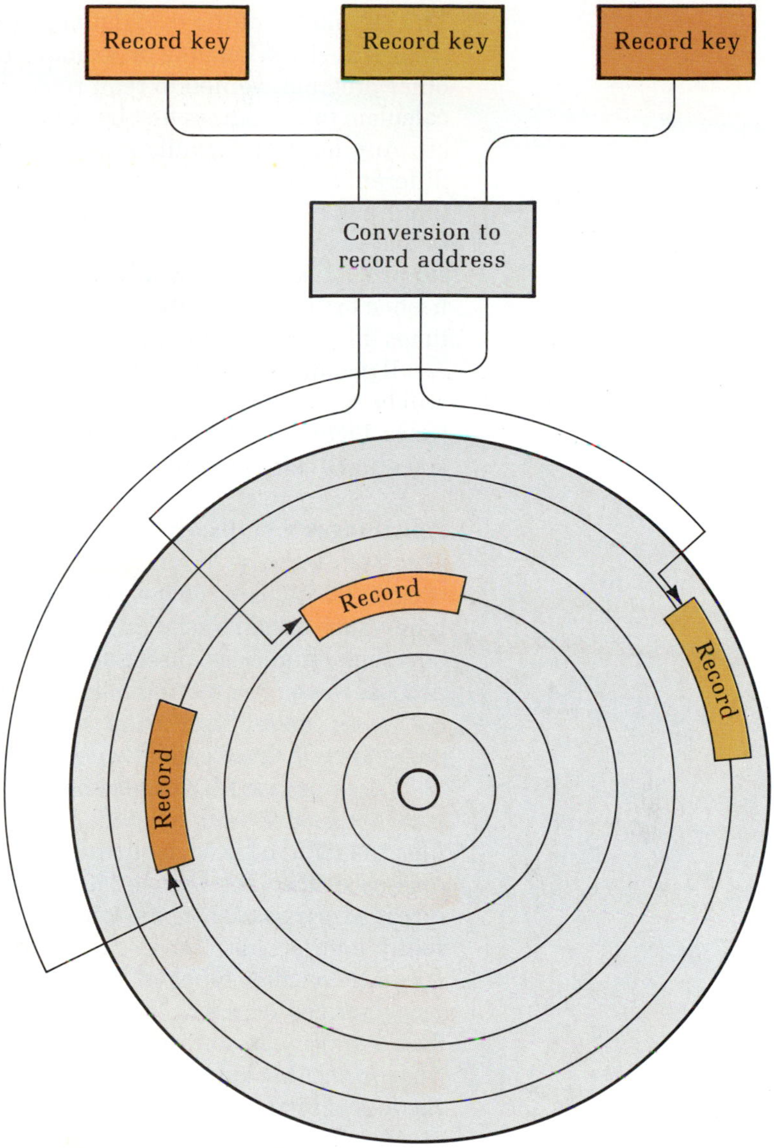

number produces a remainder. For hashing, a prime number near the number of records in a file can be used.

For example, assume that our program is going to write a new file that will contain about 12,000 records. The prime number that is nearest to 12,000 is 12,001. So whenever it is time for our program to write a record to the new file, we can calculate its address by dividing the record key by 12,001. Let's say that our records use social security numbers as their key. A calculation would proceed like this:

Record key 383449709 (a social security number less its dashes)
÷ 12,001 (the prime number we chose)
= 31951 with a remainder of 5758

The remainder of the calculation, 5758, is the address on the direct-access storage device where the program would write the record. Later, when some other program wanted to read records from the same file, it would have to calculate their address first by using the same formula.

Any hashing formula can occasionally produce the same address for different record keys. Then the first record to receive the address is placed there, and a pointer (a file containing the address of another record) is added to that record to direct the search to an overflow area on the direct-access storage device. The overflow area will contain the other record(s) that hashed to the same address. Good hashing formulas minimize the number of times this happens, but it will still happen.

If you think about this procedure for a moment, you can see that records will be scattered about the storage medium in a pattern that appears random (as in Figure 16-6). This type of distribution is why direct-access files are sometimes called random-access files.

Advantages and disadvantages of direct-access files

Direct-access files offer the fastest way to read or write records in a nonsequential order. Since many business transactions are of exactly this type—such as bank-account transactions, airline reservations, or insurance-coverage inquiries—direct-access files offer the most efficient way to process them. Another advantage (shared by indexed sequential files, but not by sequential files) is that there is no need to sort the transactions before using them to update the file.

Direct-access files have to be on direct-access storage devices. These are more expensive than magnetic tape units, which can be used for sequential files. As with indexed sequential access, the software is more complex and expensive than for sequential access, but since the capabilities that make direct access possible come with the operating system in any case, they don't really add to costs. Direct-access files do, however, require more storage space than other types of files. They also tend to be more vulnerable to unauthorized access to the data or to equipment failures. Backup copies of files are usually not automatically produced, as they are with sequential files, so that backup procedures must be established and followed to avoid the loss of vital data.

In effect direct-access files offer a trade-off between speed and cost. A system that is capable of direct-access processing costs more than one that isn't, but the savings in time and efficiency make those costs worthwhile for certain kinds of applications.

INTEGRATED DATABASES

Now that you have an idea of the way that data are physically stored and retrieved in files, we are ready to move on to databases. A database is a collection or set of related files. First in this section, we will see why databases represented a step forward. Then we will describe the management and creation of databases, and differentiate three of the most common types.

WHAT'S WRONG WITH FILES?

Let's assume that you are a programmer at Paul's House of Electronic Wonders and the company has not yet switched to databases. It is your job to write a program that will show where each employee's salary stands in relation to the range of salaries paid for the particular job classification. The salary data you need are contained on the payroll file. The payroll file was created by a program written in the same language (let's say COBOL) in which you will write your program. That means that you should have no basic problem reading the file; but in your program you will still have to go to a lot of trouble describing exactly how the file is set up, so that your program can read it.

To obtain the salary range for a particular job classification, however, you need the job classification file. Once again you need to describe exactly how the file is set up. In addition you find that the field that links the two files—job title—is set up differently in the job classification file than it is in the payroll file, so you must come up with a way to reconcile the two.

When you have completed all this, you will be able to *start* work on writing that part of your program that processes the data contained on the files. Essentially everything you have done up to this point—although it may have taken days—had nothing to do with the job at hand.

This example touches on most of the drawbacks of dealing with files:

- *The data of interest are often contained on different files.*
- *Files may overlap one another or lack integration.*
- *Since files are often program specific, each program tends to keep its own set of files. This means the same data exist in numerous places, which virtually assures that in some places data will be out of date, and which wastes storage space.*
- *Programmers must describe files extensively within their programs before being able to read or write them. Writing and debugging these file descriptions is time consuming.*

For these reasons most programmers, information-system personnel concerned with data resources, and managers prefer databases to files.

THE ADVANTAGES OF DATABASES

With a database data are independent of the application programs that use them. It takes more work to set up a database than to create a file. Once a database is set up, however, it solves each of the problems that we just cited. That is:

- *Data are accessible to any program with a legitimate need for them, regardless of where the data are physically located.*
- *Data are accessible to any program regardless of the language in which the program is written (assuming the database system supports the language used).*
- *Data are not duplicated in different locations.*
- *Programmers need not write and debug extensive file descriptions in order to work with data.*

Because of these characteristics of databases, organizations are willing to pay the considerable costs of creating and maintaining a database. A business that uses a database rather than files can save time and money in developing its application programs, can lower data maintenance costs and storage requirements since the same centralized data are now accessible to all, and can exploit its data more efficiently since they are easier to get at.

The year 1952 saw the initial move toward automation at American [Airlines]—the Reservisor system. . . . Reservisor applied basic computer file technology to the task of keeping track of American's seats and flights.

Soon, however, the automated blackboard bore a shiny, classy new acronym: SABRE, for Semi-Automated Business Reservation Environment. And SABRE's birth marked the beginning of a data base that has grown into the world's largest nonmilitary, realtime computer network as well as the airline industry's most sophisticated travel automation system.

Today SABRE offers an expanding host of conveniences for business travelers in a hurry and passengers seeking relaxing vacation trips. Not only does SABRE issue flight tickets and boarding passes, it can reserve hotel rooms, rental cars and limousines, arrange for special inflight meals, reserve tickets to Broadway plays, issue tickets on Britrail, order bon voyage gifts, and can soon book trips on Amtrak trains and on certain cruise ships. . . .

The system's heart is situated in an American Airlines facility in Tulsa, Oklahoma. From there, SABRE's electronic network reaches throughout the United States and into several foreign countries via 550,000 miles of dedicated data circuits—more than enough wire to reach to the moon and back again or to loop around the earth at the equator at least 20 times.

American Airlines has 15,000 terminals linked to SABRE for its corporate offices, reservation facilities, and ticket counters. And more than 8,200 travel agencies and corporate travel departments subscribe to SABRE. Says [vice-president of marketing automation systems Robert W.] Baker:

"The system now has 65,000 devices hanging off that network, and it runs 365 days a year and about 23 hours a day. We take it down daily for 1 hour for file maintenance."

Inside SABRE's high-security building, the big room full of blinking lights and whirring disk drives looks something like a futuristic launderette "or a big video-game parlor," Baker says.

During a typical business day's peak hours, SABRE handles approximately 900 messages a second. It processes more than 270,000 passenger records daily and keeps track of schedules and seat inventory in 140,000 city pairs, 6.5 million domestic and international airfare combinations and more than 10,000 daily fare changes, and the schedules of about 650 carriers around the world.

If you are in Miami, for instance, and want to fly to Tokyo with stops in Minneapolis/St. Paul, Seattle/Tacoma, and Anchorage, a SABRE-equipped travel agent quickly can book you onto flights best suited for your schedule, even if it means using airlines other than American.

An additional SABRE feature known as SHAARP (SABRE Hotels Automated Availability and Reservations Program) also gives the travel agent instant access to any of more than 9,500 hotel and condominium properties around the world. . . .

SABRE is linked electronically to the telex network of ITT World Communications, Incorporated, and through that hookup any SABRE terminal with access to the network can be used to transmit a message to any hotel, railroad, tour operator, bus company, ground-transportation company, or sightseeing company on the planet. . . .

SABRE will continue to pioneer new conveniences in air travel and unveil new delights, Baker promises. "There is a lot more coming soon that will benefit passengers. But we're also working at least 5 to 10 years ahead. We're working for our children, who will be the keyboard-literate generation."

Source: from "Super Sabre," *American Way,* by Si Dunn, September 1984.

DISADVANTAGES OF DATABASES

There are some disadvantages to databases.

- *With data more readily accessible, they can be more easily abused.*
- *Databases require expensive hardware and software.*
- *Specialized personnel may have to be hired to set up and administer the database, and existing personnel will have to be trained to use it properly.*

In addition people may resist a new system merely because it is new, or because they dislike the idea of giving up control of their "personal" files. Finally, creating a database is a complicated and lengthy process, as we will see later in the chapter.

On balance most organizations seem to find that the advantages outweigh the disadvantages. The trend is toward ever greater use of databases rather than conventional file processing.

Because of the advantages and popularity of databases, prepackaged programs to create and maintain databases are available today for any size of information system, from supercomputers down to microcomputers. Although such programs vary widely, they all offer the advantages we have cited, and share the general features we will now describe.

DATABASE MANAGEMENT SYSTEMS

A **DATABASE MANAGEMENT SYSTEM (DBMS)** is a program that makes it possible to create, use, and maintain a database. When a database management system is used, programmers and users need not be concerned about the way data are organized or retrieved from the direct-access storage device (only rarely are other storage devices used for databases), or about in which particular file the data are contained. A database management system provides *logical* access to data, sheltering users from concern with *physical* placement and handling of the data. Figure 16-7 shows a conceptualized view of the function of a database management system in a modern information system.

Most medium-sized and large businesses with databases have a database administrator. The **DATABASE ADMINISTRATOR** is responsible for setting up databases, maintaining them, and helping programmers and users to utilize them intelligently. (See the Career Box on p. 454).

CREATING A DATABASE

There are several steps in creating a database. These are (1) surveying the data uses, (2) creating the data dictionary, (3) designing the database, and (4) implementing the database.

Surveying the data uses is the first step in creating a database. We need to determine, by asking users, what data they use, when they need them for making decisions, and what operations they perform upon the data. Surveying data uses is generally done during the system development process covered in Chapter 15. Specifically we define the system flow during the detailed investigation stage of systems analysis. The data-flow diagrams prepared at this time show how data enter the system, are stored, and are processed. Later, during the logical design step of system design, additional usage patterns are determined.

A **DATA DICTIONARY** defines each item of data and information handled by a system, giving the item's name, telling what the item is, specifying its format, giving its input source, and specifying its output use. In Chapter 15 we saw that the data dictionary is created during the logical design step of

The database administrator is responsible for creating and maintaining databases. This involves working with systems analysts and programmers to determine the way in which applications will collect and store data, and then creating appropriate databases. Since security is a major concern in administering a database, the database administrator devises protective security measures together with the director of information processing, information resources manager, or information-systems security specialist, and implements these measures on a day-to-day basis. The database administrator also sets up procedures to back up databases at regular intervals.

There is a fair amount of housekeeping to be done to keep a database up and running. The database administrator is responsible for the procedures to add and delete data from the database when valid requests are made.

The best person to educate others concerning databases is the database administrator or a qualified subordinate. It is in the best interests of an organization for programmers to know the structure of the databases and the conventions for retrieving data. Accordingly the good database administrator stresses communication with programmers and users, and must possess good interpersonal skills. Needless to say, the database administrator must also be a detail-oriented administrator. The need for technical competence and creativity comes into play most heavily during database design. The database administrator, in other words, is a well-rounded information-systems professional who has specialized in databases.

Larger firms will maintain a complete staff working for the database administrator. Such a staff is in fact one of the best "ins" to becoming a database administrator in the first place. You can begin as a programmer, or even a clerk, in the database administration group, and more up as your abilities and dedication are recognized.

The other means of entry is in the small organization that may just be discovering its need for a database administrator: this individual will probably be chosen from the ranks of systems analysts.

Career prospects for database administrators are excellent. With file processing reduced in popularity and databases the direction the industry has taken, there is plenty of database administration to be done, and people skilled in the area are in short supply. Particularly useful would be a knowledge of telecommunications and distributed data processing.

---

system design. With the data dictionary in hand, we know the main characteristics of all of the different data elements that a database will contain.

Once we know what data a database should contain, and how the data are used, we are in a position to design the database. We do so with a SCHEMA, a conceptual, or logical, view of the relationships among the data elements in the database. This is crucial, for it is what separates a file from a database. Diverse data items can be defined as related, so that they will be linked by pathways in the database much as if they were contained in the same record of a file. Moreover different users can be presented with their own tailored patterns of data items within the same database. Subschemas are used to describe the particular data items needed for a given application

FIGURE 16-7.

The database in the information system.

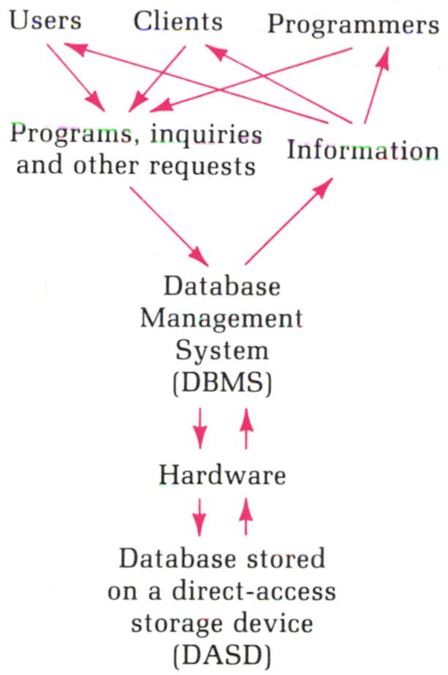

Users   Clients   Programmers

Programs, inquiries   Information
and other requests

Database
Management
System
(DBMS)

Hardware

Database stored
on a direct-access
storage device
(DASD)

or user. We will see how the relationship between data items becomes important in the next sections.

Note that there is a difference between the schema, or logical description of the database, and the physical description of the database—the way data are actually stored. Users don't need to be concerned about the physical description—software in the database management system automatically translates a request for data based on the schema into the physical location of the data on disk.

Schemas and subschemas are written in a **DATA DEFINITION LANGUAGE (DDL)**. Each database management system uses a specific data definition language. Like a programming language, a data definition language has rules and procedures that must be followed if one is to work with it successfully.

With the database design complete, we input the schema and subschemas to the database management system. We also input the physical descriptions of the data needed, such as the volume of data that the database will contain, the key fields to be used for relative addressing, and so on. The actual data can then be input to the database, where the database management system will store the data following the details of the schema and the physical descriptions. Once this demanding process has been completed, the database is ready to use.

USING A DATABASE

As a rule a database can by used in two different ways: (1) through a query language and (2) through a data manipulation language.

A **QUERY LANGUAGE** is offered by a database management system for use by personnel who are not programmers. For example, at Paul's House of Electronic Wonders, purchasing agents who know nothing about computers can sit at their terminals and inquire about the current stock level of an item of interest. The commands that a user needs to type to get the information wanted are fairly simple, and can be learned in a few hours. The beauty of databases really comes into play here, because the user need not have the slightest idea of the storage medium being used for the data item, how the data item's fields are defined, the hashing technique used, the relation of the data item to other data items, and so on. The user need only know what he or she is after. In addition to making inquiries with a query language, authorized users may also make changes in, additions to, and deletions from the database.

Programmers interact with the database differently. They write their application programs in COBOL, BASIC, FORTRAN, or whatever programming language they normally use, provided the database management system can work with that language. In this context the programming language is known as a **HOST LANGUAGE**. When programmers want to work with data from the database, they insert commands from a **DATA MANIPULATION LANGUAGE (DML)** into the program. These make it possible to perform any operation desired on the database. A program that contains DML statements is first run through a precompiler that is part of the database management system. The precompiler translates the DML statements into statements of the programming language. Then the resulting program is compiled and run as usual.

A database must be properly maintained. Often the system itself contains utility programs that help perform such maintenance tasks as adding or deleting fields, creating backup copies of the database, increasing the amount of data that the database can store, and moving the database to a different direct-access storage device. As with any system, however, a time may come when the database can no longer accommodate the volume of change that is needed. Then it is time to go back to the drawing board and design a new database.

TYPES OF DATABASES

In the "Creating a Database" section earlier in the chapter, we said that part of the job was specifying how data items are related to one another. The ability to do this is in fact one of the key differences between a file and a database. In this section we will examine the types of relationships that can be specified.

The three most frequently used structures for relating data items within a database are known as the hierarchical, network, and relational structures.

Hierarchical data bases

In a HIERARCHICAL DATABASE, data elements are related to one another as "parents" and "children" following a treelike structure. A PARENT is merely a data element higher in the hierarchy than the child, and connected to it. A CHILD is a data element subservient to a parent, and connected to it. In a hierarchical database a parent can have more than one child, but each child can have only one parent.

In Figure 16-8 the Item data element is the parent of the Cost, Quantity, Substitute, and Purchase Order data elements. A data element can consist of more than one data item; for example, the Substitute data element consists of the item number and the item name.

Within such a database there will be an entry for each item. For each item we will have the four children shown. Two of the children—Substitute and Purchase Order—can have more than one occurrence per item. When Paul's is out of stock on a particular item, for example, it may ship a replacement. Some items can have more than one possible replacement. Similarly an item may have been ordered from more than one supplier. When each new order was placed, an order data element would have been added to describe the particular order. Hierarchical database systems are available for any size of computer. One of the more popular systems used on mainframes today is IBM's Information Management System (IMS).

Network databases

In a NETWORK DATABASE data elements are related to one another as parents and children as in a hierarchical database, with one difference: a child can have more than one parent.

For example, Figure 16-9 shows the same data as contained in our hierarchical database from Figure 16-8. The difference is that we have added some new data elements on the right of the figure. The Supplier data element is parent to the Purchase Order, Address, and Contact data

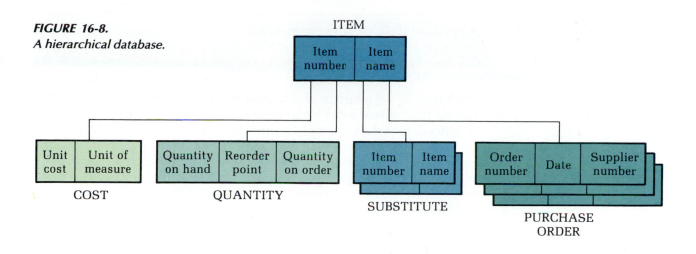

FIGURE 16-8.
A hierarchical database.

elements. In other words, Purchase Order has two parents—Item and Supplier.

In practical terms what this means is that the database management system can deliver data by item (giving the cost, quantity, substitute, and purchase order data) or by supplier (giving the order, address, and contact data). Each view of the data coexists with the other views within the database, and can be quickly utilized. This ability to access data from more than one starting point is the advantage of network databases over hierarchical databases. Network database systems exist for any size of computer. One popular system is IDMS (Integrated Database Management System), produced by Cullinet Software.

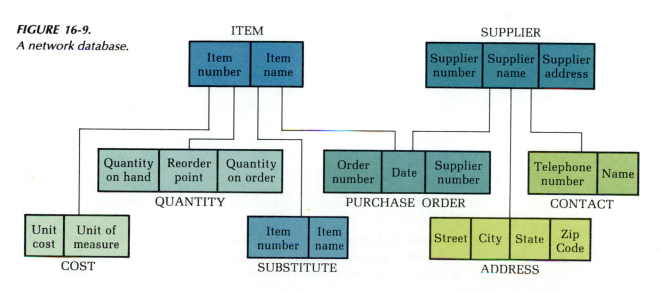

FIGURE 16-9.
A network database.

Ours is an age of information. Paperwork piles up and numbers fly by so fast we hardly have a chance to organize data, never mind make sense of it. Indeed, data management can be a full-time job. Fortunately, it's a job for which your personal computer at work or at home is perfectly suited. Information management systems, alternately called database management systems, can be extremely powerful and flexible tools. At a fairly elementary level, you can create an automated card file for a mailing list or turn your computer into an electronic version of your filing cabinet. At a more sophisticated level, you can track your company's inventory or customize its accounting system. . . .

The number of programs on the market today may seem overwhelming when you first decide to computerize. As with any other purchase, it's wise not to waste your dollars on features you don't want or need. . . .

FILE MANAGEMENT PROGRAMS

The vast majority of file management programs retail for less than $300, making them the least expensive database management programs you can buy. However, although enhanced new versions are continually being introduced, these file managers are also the least sophisticated type of database program. They're designed primarily to manage lists of information and typically address only one file at a time.

These programs perform all the basic data storage, retrieval, manipulation, and limited calculation functions as well as report generation capabilities. But to keep program operation simple, these features are usually severely limited in flexibility, that is, the degree to which they can be modified to meet each user's needs.

File managers are extremely easy to use. Typically, they're menu-driven and require little if any memorization of commands. . . .

Popular programs in this category include PFS:File and PFS:Report from Software Publishing Corporation, Friday from Ashton-Tate, Perfect Filer from Perfect Software, Quickfile from Apple Computer Inc., Qbase from Applied Software Technology, and Visifile from Visicorp. . . .

MID-RANGE DATABASE PROGRAMS

The second group contains the mid-range database management progarms, which usually retail for between $300 and $500. These programs are suitable for developing applications such as general ledgers, sales tracking systems, personnel record systems, and inventory systems. Many can access more than one file of information at a time and sort on multiple key fields. These systems store, sort, manipulate, and retrieve data and create reports with more flexibility than file managers do.

Mid-range programs are generally menu-driven and their menus offer a wider variety of options, which makes them harder to use than file managers. . . Programs in this group include Advanced DB Master from Stoneware Inc., Powerbase from GMS Systems Inc., and Personal Pearl from Pearlsoft.

FULL-FEATURED DATABASE MANAGERS

The third category contains full-featured database management systems, which typically retail for more than $500. In general, these programs use a series of commands to create a variety of applications. So while you may buy a file-management program like PFS:File to use as is, you'd most likely buy a full-featured program like dBASE II to construct custom applications.

Of course, the investment in learning is greater with full-featured command-driven programs, but you reap corresponding increases in the relative sophistication of tasks the programs can perform. Typically, full-featured database managers are designed to process large amounts of data and make independent files of data work together to provide different views of the same information. All these programs allow multiple files to be open simultaneously.

Compared to file managers, full-featured programs, due to their command-driven structure, are relatively difficult to operate for accomplishing simple tasks. However, with the proper programming, these systems can be designed to be even easier to use than file managers. . . .

Packages in this category include dBASE II from Ashton-Tate, R:base Series 4000 from Microrim Inc., Condor 3 from Condor Computer Corporation, T.I.M. IV from Innovative Software, Infostar Plus from Micropro International, and Knowledge Manager from Micro Data Base Systems Inc.

Source: "Making Sense of Database Software," *Popular Computing,* June, 1984. By Michael J. Miller and George F. Goley IV. Reprinted with permission. Copyright © 1984 by McGraw-Hill, Inc. All rights reserved.

Relational databases

A **RELATIONAL DATABASE** views all data items as related to one another in tables. This stands in contrast to the parent/child approach used to describe network and hierarchical database structures. Figure 16-10 shows a relational data structure. This is merely a table that, for a particular original item, gives the substitute item(s) and supplier.

A number of different tables can be used to set up a relational database. For example, we might also set up a table that shows the original item number, original item supplier number, original item supplier name, and quantity on hand. We could go on to devise other tables. The database management system will store the data items in such a way that it can deliver the data from any of the table viewpoints.

Relational database systems are easier to use than hierarchical or network database systems. Relational database systems are available for any size of computer. An example of a relational database system for use by mainframes is IBM's SQL/DS which allows users to make requests for data in the English-like statements of a System Query Language (SQL). The major drawbacks of relational systems are their substantial hardware requirements and their slower speed for complex searches relative to other database structures.

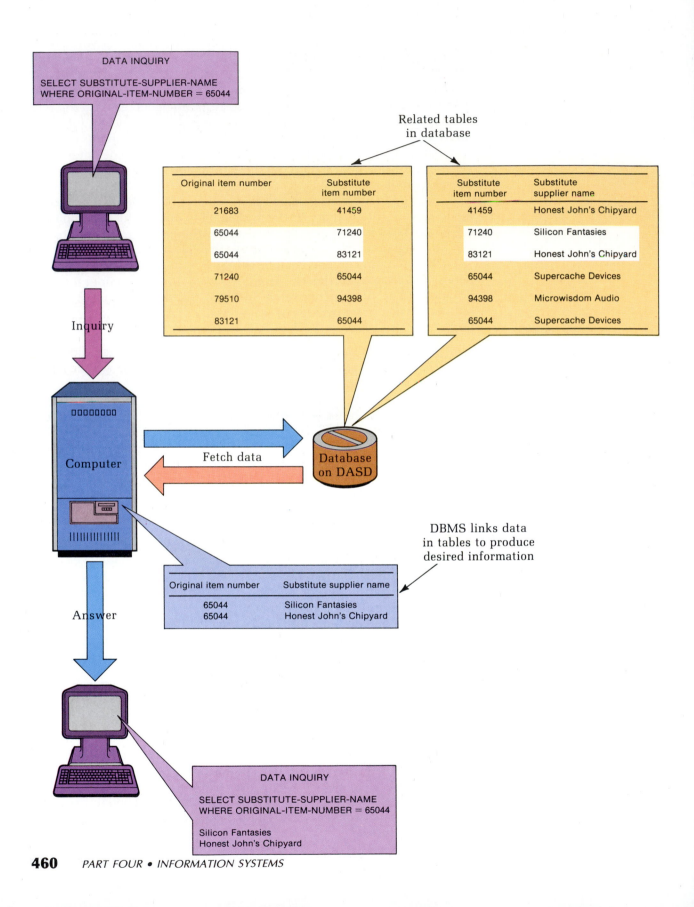

DATA INQUIRY

SELECT SUBSTITUTE-SUPPLIER-NAME
WHERE ORIGINAL-ITEM-NUMBER = 65044

Related tables
in database

Original item number	Substitute item number
21683	41459
65044	71240
65044	83121
71240	65044
79510	94398
83121	65044

Substitute item number	Substitute supplier name
41459	Honest John's Chipyard
71240	Silicon Fantasies
83121	Honest John's Chipyard
65044	Supercache Devices
94398	Microwisdom Audio
65044	Supercache Devices

Inquiry

Computer

Fetch data

Database on DASD

DBMS links data
in tables to produce
desired information

Original item number	Substitute supplier name
65044	Silicon Fantasies
65044	Honest John's Chipyard

Answer

DATA INQUIRY

SELECT SUBSTITUTE-SUPPLIER-NAME
WHERE ORIGINAL-ITEM-NUMBER = 65044

Silicon Fantasies
Honest John's Chipyard

FIGURE 16-10.
Using a relational database.

"Now that you have been exposed to basic database concepts," Vincent Kent said to his class, "it is time to see what we have here at Paul's."

"Is it all one database?" one of the accountants asked.

"No," Vincent said. "We have several different databases. Nearly all of them follow the hierarchical structure. A couple of the newest ones are relational databases."

Since his class seemed to grasp this, Vincent went on. "I would like to describe the structure of some of our databases a little more thoroughly. Let's start with the company employee database. It follows the hierarchical model. The data elements are arranged in this structure."

Vincent walked to the board and sketched the database shown in Figure 16-11, consulting his notes to get all the details right. Then he turned back to the class.

"Gayle Christian," Vincent said, "as personnel manager, did you know you were dealing with this structure when you changed an employee's title?"

"No," Gayle said.

"Of course, there is no reason for you to know how the database is designed in order to use it," Vincent said. "Or to know that the data for one person are spread over different files. But learning the design, as you have in my course, has its advantages. For example, you can see that for any given employee, all seven child data elements exist. That means you can find out any of these things about each employee."

FIGURE 16-11.

The employee database at Paul's House of Electronic Wonders.

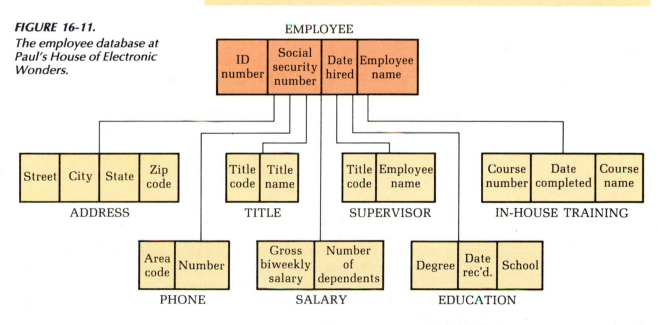

"There is an advantage for database administrators in your knowing the structure, too. You can add as many in-house training elements for employees as you want—each element corresponds to a course that the employee attended—and it doesn't affect my job at all. But when you change the name of a data element, or its size, I'll have to change the database. If you want to add or delete an element, I'll have to change the database."

"In other words," Susan Paul said, "we shouldn't make changes just for fun."

"Right," Vincent said. "Not in the data type, structure, or names. The data *themselves*, however, you can change as often as you want."

"Such as revising a salary," Gayle Christian said.

"That's it," Vincent said. "For example, if you use your query language to call for data on employee Kent, Vincent—and are a user entitled to revise data elements as well as to view them— then go right ahead and add four or five thousand to the figure."

SUMMARY

- Data that an information system works with generally fall into a data hierarchy made up of four categories. Moving from the lowest level of the hierarchy to the highest, these are the field, record, file, and database.

- Fields are composed of characters. A numeric field contains only numbers. An alphabetic field contains only alphabetic characters. An alphanumeric field can contain both numbers and alphabetic characters.

- There are three main types of file design: sequential, indexed sequential, and direct access.

- In a sequential file records are arranged in a predetermined order according to one or more keys contained in the record. Primary keys are unique identifiers for a record; secondary keys are supplemental, nonunique identifiers.

- Sequential files are usually stored on magnetic tape or magnetic disk. A sequential file offers only sequential access to records, and is appropriate for batch processing programs that read and/or write a high proportion of the records in a file. When sequential files are used, backup copies are usually automatically created.

- Disadvantages of sequential files are the necessity to read every record on the way to the record of interest, the need to sort transaction records into the same sequence as the master file, and duplication of data in multiple files.

- Indexed sequential files also arrange records in a predetermined order, but maintain an index giving the location of records. Indexed sequential files must be contained on a direct-access storage device. These files offer either sequential or direct access, but are somewhat more cumbersome with either technique than a true sequential or direct-access file. Hardware and system software costs are higher than for sequential files, and no automatic backup copies are created.

- *In a direct-access file the records are arranged in an order that is related to the record key in a way determined by program logic, most often through relative addressing. Direct-access files must be contained on a direct-access device, and offer direct access to data. Hashing techniques are often used to transform record keys into actual storage addresses.*

- *Direct-access files offer the fastest way to read or write records in nonsequential order. Files may be updated without sorting transactions. Hardware and system software costs are higher than with sequential files, data are somewhat more vulnerable to unauthorized access or equipment failure, and backup copies are not automatically produced.*

- *A database is a collection of related files, and offers users more flexibility than files. With a database data are independent of the application programs that use them; data are accessible to any program regardless of the location of the data or the language in which the program is written; data are not duplicated in different locations; and programmers need not write and debug extensive file descriptions in order to work with data.*

- *Drawbacks of databases include the possibility of data abuse, high hardware and software costs, and the time and effort it takes to create and properly maintain one.*

- *A database management system (DBMS) is a program that makes it possible to create, use, and maintain databases. In most medium-sized and large businesses, a database administrator is responsible for setting up databases and helping users to get the most out of them. Setting up a database involves surveying the data uses, setting up a data dictionary, and designing and implementing the database. Design is done by specifying schemas in a data definition language (DDL).*

- *A database can be used through a query language or a data manipulation language. A query language is geared to managers and users, who can use English-like statements to work with data of interest. Programmers insert statements into their programs in a data manipulation language (DML). Programs must be written in a host language—one the DBMS supports.*

- *One important difference between a file and a database is that a database can specify how data items are related to one another. Three structures are commonly used to relate data items within a database: hierarchical, network, and relational.*

- *In a hierarchical database data elements are related to one another as parents and children in a treelike structure. Parents can have more than one child, but each child can have only one parent.*

- *A network database differs in that children can have more than one parent.*

- *Relational databases view all data items as related to one another in tables, and are easier to use than hierarchical or network databases, although slower for more complex searches.*

- *Database management systems following any of these structures are available for all sizes of computers.*

KEY TERMS

These are the key terms in the order in which they appear in the chapter.

Data hierarchy (440)
Field (441)
Character (441)
Numeric field (441)
Alphabetic field (441)
Alphanumeric field (441)
Record (441)
File (441)
Database (441)
File design (442)
Sequential file (442)
Key (442)
Primary key (442)
Secondary key (442)
Sequential access (442)
Indexed sequential file (443)
Direct access (445)

Direct-access file or random-access
   file (447)
Relative addressing (448)
Hashing (448)
Database management system
   (DBMS) (453)
Database administrator (453)
Data dictionary (453)
Schema (454)
Data definition language (DDL) (455)
Query language (455)
Host language (455)
Data manipulation language
   (DML) (455)
Hierarchical database (456)
Parent (456)
Child (456)
Network database (456)
Relational database (459)

REVIEW QUESTIONS

OBJECTIVE QUESTIONS

TRUE/FALSE: *Put the letter T or F on the line before the question.*

1. In a hierarchical database each "child" data element has only one parent.
2. The data element LASTNAME would make a good primary key field for a list of students.
3. Fields are made up of interrelated records.
4. Sequential files are best to use if the proportion of records to be processed in a file is low.
5. Database security problems can be overcome by using sequential files on magnetic tape to store current data.
6. Indexed sequential files require an index file be read to determine the location of the group of records containing the desired record.
7. A data dictionary contains the schema of the database.
8. A secondary key must be a unique identifier for a record.
9. A database is a set of interrelated files.
10. Network databases are arranged in a treelike structure.

MULTIPLECHOICE: *Put the letter of the correct answer on the line before the question.*

1. Dr D. Carie wants to use a database to keep track of dental patients' visits. Since Dr. Carie already uses a microcomputer for creating patient bills, what type of database is the dentist likely to acquire?
   (a) Hierarchical database.
   (b) Network database.
   (c) Relational database.
   (d) Any of the above would be acceptable.

2. Fly-by-Night Airlines needs to keep track of passenger information. What type of file design would you recommend?

(a) Sequential file.　　　　　　　　**(c)** Direct access file.
(b) Indexed sequential file.　　　　**(d)** Indexed direct file.

3. Database users are concerned with the
(a) Conceptual view of the database.
(b) Physical view of the database.
(c) File design used to store data in the database.
(d) Both the conceptual and physical view of the database.

4. A unique identifier for a record is a
(a) parent.　　　　　　　　　　　**(c)** primary key.
(b) child.　　　　　　　　　　　　**(d)** secondary key.

5. The schema is developed with the _____ of the database management system.
(a) Data-definition language.　　　**(c)** Data-manipulation language.
(b) Host language.　　　　　　　　**(d)** Query language.

FILL IN THE BLANK: *Write the correct word or words in the blank to compute the sentence.*

1. The _____ shows the logical relationships among data elements in the database.

2. A _____ is a software package used to create, use, and maintain the database.

3. A _____ language is offered by a database management system (DBMS) to permit nonprogrammers to access the database.

4. In hierarchical and network databases, _____ data elements are superior to and connected to _____ data elements.

5. The _____ (made up of one or more characters) is the smallest usable part of the data hierarchy.

6. The use of tables to interconnect the data elements is a feature of a _____.

7. With _____ access, to read the last record in a file of 550 records requires reading all 549 preceding records.

8. One child data element can have more than one parent in a _____.

9. The technique used by a file to store and retrieve data from secondary storage is referred to as _____.

10. A _____ defines each item of data handled by a database management system.

When answering these questions think of concrete examples to illustrate your points.

1. What are the three types of file design?
2. How do indexed sequential files differ from direct access files?
3. What does the term "hashing" mean?
4. What is a DBMS?
5. What is a schema?
6. What is the purpose of the data dictionary?
7. What are the differences between hierarchical and network databases?
8. What is a relational database?

1. What are the advantages and disadvantages of using files?
2. What are the steps used in creating a database?
3. What are the advantages and disadvantages of using databases?

CHAPTER 17

SYSTEM CONTROL: DATA INTEGRITY, SECURITY, AND PRIVACY

After studying this chapter you should understand the following:
■ Why control systems are needed for today's information systems.
■ How control techniques can be applied to the five elements of an information system.
■ How accounting and auditing methods are used as information-system controls.
■ Some of the issues and legislation concerning the right to privacy.

"It's a funny thing," Ed Wieland said to Vincent Kent. "I was performing a little audit on the system yesterday. You know, to see what resources were being used. And one person was making heavy use of your inventory database the whole time."

"Why do you find it strange?" asked Vincent, the database administrator at Paul's.

"I thought nothing of it then," Ed said. "But by coincidence, I talked to the purchasing manager right after I'd performed my little audit. So I walked all the way through the purchasing department to get to his office. Well, the whole department was at a meeting. The manager, too. All the terminals were off. So who was using that database?"

Vincent stared at the opposite wall of his office. "A few people in other departments are allowed to look at it," he said, "though they rarely do."

"That's what I thought," Ed said. "Were you folks doing maintenance or something on the database?"

"Yesterday? No, we had other fires to put out."

"Interesting," Ed said.

As a systems analyst, Ed's mind was trained to mistrust appearances and look behind them. He returned to the computer room, sat down at a monitor, and invoked a real-time program to determine which computer resources were presently being used. Over a dozen users were online. Ed made a few queries to the program, and found that two users were retrieving data from the inventory database.

Ed got up and walked briskly to the purchasing department. Once there, he slowed down and tried to note what everyone was doing as he headed toward the purchasing manager's office. Only one terminal was on, and a purchasing agent was working at it. O.K., Ed thought, the other user could be the manager.

Ed knocked on the manager's door. When he got no response, he opened it. The manager was gone. Back in his own office, Ed came to a decision. His gnawing suspicion that someone was eavesdropping into the computer system at Paul's wouldn't go away.

Ed picked up the phone and dialed Mr. Paul. Ed explained his suspicions briefly.

"Who might conceivably be interested in what's stored in our inventory database?" Ed asked.

"Competitors," Mr. Paul said promptly. "We're in the middle of a price war right now. I can name at least four companies that would love to see us go under."

"Interesting," Ed said. "Mr. Paul, I would like your permission to evaluate the controls used on that database. I would like to do so on an emergency basis, and maybe add some equipment that we don't have, so that if somebody's eavesdropping we can catch them at it."

"You're on," Mr. Paul said.

THE NEED FOR SYSTEM CONTROLS

INFORMATION SYSTEM CONTROLS serve to monitor and ensure the proper operation of all five information system elements: people, rules and procedures, data, software, and hardware. Controls help to ensure the integrity of the data, the security of the information system, and the privacy of users and clients of the information system.

DATA INTEGRITY refers to the accuracy of the data. For an information system to output accurate reports, the input to the system and the steps in its processing must be monitored. Sometimes the consequences of inaccurate output can be disastrous. For example, say that a computerized government forecast predicted substantial commodity shortages and other serious economic problems in the near future. Trusting the forecast, various government agencies, private industry, and the governments of other countries could react in panic. Yet the forecast might have resulted from a miskeyed decimal point.

Security is also an important consideration where computers are involved. SECURITY refers to the steps used to protect the five elements of the information system. Let's say that an industrial spy is able to learn how the database of a competitor is structured. Most database management systems do not keep a log of requests for data that do not change the data. So the spy who knew his or her way around the database could make inquiries that would yield valuable trade secrets, even whole files full of them.

PRIVACY refers to the protection of individuals and organizations from unauthorized access to or abuse of data concerning them. Privacy is not always easy to come by in a computerized society. Incidents such as this one have really taken place: A man applies for a life insurance policy, and is turned down when an investigator discovers in a database that the man was once arrested for auto theft. The database does not indicate the outcome of the case, but the investigator rejects the life-insurance application. The truth of the case is that the man was accidentally arrested for stealing his own car. His car was in fact stolen, but by someone else, and the police entered data on the theft into a database. Later the car was recovered in another police jurisdiction, but its recovery was not recorded in the first jurisdiction's database. So when the owner was out driving his recovered car back in his home jurisdiction, he was erroneously arrested for the theft. The arrest report was sent to several other databases run by the state and federal agencies, one of which the insurance investigator consulted. The fact that it was all a mistake, however, was not recorded.

Even the people entrusted with operating an information system can sometimes give in to temptation. A COMPUTER CRIME occurs when a person uses a computer for illegal purposes. In one case a programmer at a bank embezzled money from peoples' accounts by diverting fractions of cents from their accounts into his own. Examples of a range of computer crimes are given in Figure 17-1.

Attitudes toward white-collar crimes of any sort—computer crimes included—used to be rather permissive. Where a street criminal would be jailed, the white-collar criminal was often merely reprimanded or allowed to make restitution. Thus the potential gains were, from the criminal's point of view, worth risking the punishment. Many companies were reluctant to prosecute because publicity surrounding the case would be bad for the company image. Photographs of programmer-embezzlers on the evening

FIGURE 17-1.

Great crimes in computerdom. The photograph shows part of the haul police in the County of Santa Clara California found when they arrested a group of people who had been stealing chips from local manufacturers.

Name	Date	Amount ($M)	1983 Dollars	Comments
Equity Funding	1973	$2,100	$4,851	Computer used to create fictitious policies. Nothing exotic about the computer usage, except manual methods wouldn't have worked for fraud of such magnitude. Pyramid scheme of bilking new investors to pay off old ones. Computer operations people pretty much exonerated.
OPM Leasing	1980	$210	$388	Same computers used as collateral for several loans, fictitious and doctored leases used as collateral. Straightforward bilking, computer involvement relatively little except in provision of returnability in case of technological obsolescence. With OPM gone, computer lessee could lose between $100 million and $250 million on trade-in. Investors defrauded of $210 million.
Boxcars	1971	$110	$280	Two hundred fifty-two Penn Central boxcars worth $11 million were found. DP [Data Processing] system used to divert. Total loss of all railroad's boxcars at time estimated by authorities at 2,800 vehicles. Computerized system must be well understood to effect diversion.
Korean Army	1974	$85	$177	Wholesale defrauding of U.S. military supply system in Korea, estimated in 1977 Congressional testimony to be at least $17 million a year since early 1970s. Use of data processing system to divert materials.
Cenco	1974	$40	$81	Computerized inventory to inflate value of stock.
Chilcott	1977	$45	$77	Bogus computer reports to get investments, inflate assets.
Greenman	1981	$50	$57	Use of computer to razzle-dazzle investors in mutual fund to think Greenman had secret formula for picking stocks. Pyramid scheme.

Name	Date	Amount ($M)	1983 Dollars	Comments
Saxon	1982	$53	$57	Thirteen-year scam of double inventory, kept to inflate revenues. Fortune 500 company goes bankrupt abruptly.
J. Walter Thompson	1981	$31	$35	Ad bookings fabricated and inserted into computerized financial reporting system.
Wells Fargo	1981	$21	$24	Knowledge of the computer system allowed for routine embezzlement to be hidden. Most famous because main beneficiary of the embezzlement was a sports promoter licensing Muhammad Ali's name. Ali not implicated.

Note: Times are approximate or average time of actual perpetration, not date of capture.

Source: Jack B. Rochester, and John Gantz. *The Naked Computer.* New York: Morrow, 1983, pp. 128–129. Reprinted by permission of William Morrow and Company.

news would not fit a bank's image as protector of its customers' hard-earned money.

Today attitudes have changed. Companies are more likely to push for prosecution of such white-collar crimes as embezzlement, tampering with confidential data, and fraud. Additionally, institutions are moving to minimize the risks of losing money from computer-based theft, through some of the security measures we will see in this chapter.

In addition to deliberate abuse of a system, accidental abuse can occur. Personnel can accidentally erase or alter company records, forget to prepare backup copies that turn out to be needed when a system crashes, or commit blunders in operating the hardware.

CONTROLLING AN INFORMATION SYSTEM

In Chapter 14 we saw that managers organize people and other resources to achieve some organizational goal. One goal should be to run an information system that is accurate, secure from internal and external threats, and does not violate privacy. The control techniques that we will now describe are the repertoire of control possibilities available to managers. They should not be added as an afterthought; they should be built into the system as part of the system development process (see Chapter 15).

Which controls are actually used will depend upon the managers and the situation. The same principle applies to running an information system as to running other parts of an organization: the involvement of top-level managers makes the creation and implementation of procedures—in this case control systems—easier.

CONTROLS FOR PEOPLE

Controls for people start with proper training of the user and information-system staff on how to interact with the particular part of the information system that affects them. Two important controls for people are separation of tasks and standardization of work.

Separation of tasks

SEPARATION OF TASKS refers to dividing tasks and responsibilities among a number of different people. There are some good reasons to do so. Almost everyone has heard a story that runs something like this: A trustworthy bookkeeper always helps the boss by doing the accounting and writing the checks. So trustworthy is this individual that he or she is always first in the office, last to leave, and never takes a day off unless the entire office shuts down. One day, however, the boss comes to work and finds the bookkeeper has vanished without a trace, along with funds embezzled gradually over the years.

What went wrong? There was no separation of tasks. Any time that financial or other sensitive matters are processed by an information system, extra care must be taken. No one person should be responsible for handling the data input, the processing, and the output distribution. For instance, the person who writes a payroll program should not also be the operator responsible for feeding blank checks to the printer, or the person who distributes the printed checks. The temptation is great enough that some people will be hard-pressed to resist. In fact some companies contract with an outside service to do payroll checks for the information-processing staff, while allowing the information-processing staff to produce the checks for the rest of the company's employees.

Workers in areas involving an organization's funds should be made to take regularly scheduled vacations and other days off. In addition people should be rotated from task to task—rather than indefinitely assigned to perform the same job. In some companies people are rotated from task to task to minimize the chance of illegal cooperation among several people.

Hiring presumably honest people in the first place can preclude many of these problems. Controls here include careful screening of a potential employee's resume and checking out references.

Rewarding employees for their work through adequate salaries, formal recognition, and plain old praise can forestall many problems. Employee grievances should be given serious attention. A person who feels part of a caring organization will be far less likely to abuse the information system or any other part of the organization.

The penalties for abusing an information system should be made known to users and the information-system staff. These could range from dismissal from a job to civil or criminal legal action. In addition to their existence on the books, the penalties must also be enforced: managers must stand behind them.

For example, computer users at San José State University in California must sign a form that contains this statement:

I certify that the requested account(s) will be used only for related course work, that the proposed use of the SJSU computing services is justified by the program of the California State University and Colleges system. I further understand that the unauthorized use of SJSU computing facilities is a violation of Penal Code 502 and therefore punishable by a fine not exceeding $5,000.00 and/or imprisonment not exceeding three years, and that the account will be cancelled.

Standardization of work

STANDARDIZATION OF WORK means assuring that people have clearly defined tasks. Different employees performing the same type of task should perform it in approximately the same manner. For example, in data-entry operations clerks should follow written conventions as to what data are input, when, and in what format. In program design programmers follow the conventions of structured programming, breaking programs into modules and organizing the modules in a top-down structure. In other words structured programming methods serve as the work standard for programmers. Likewise, rules for structured system development serve as the work standard for those involved in that process.

CONTROLS FOR RULES AND PROCEDURES

The rules and procedures of an organization, and the way in which they are developed, should always reflect a concern for control techniques. Two areas of particular concern are written procedures or standards and exception procedures.

Written procedures or standards

Closely tied to the standardization of work are **WRITTEN PROCEDURES** or **STANDARDS**, which explicitly state the proper steps needed to complete a task. Most people need clear direction in their work. Written standards—that are also enforced—help people understand what their tasks are. These rules and procedures are recorded in a standards manual. Standards should be well thought out and written in a manner that users can understand, to be of any use. To write clearly is not easy, and in larger organizations is the responsibility of writers who specialize in describing standards. Both normal and exceptional operating conditions should be included in the standards. Any changes in procedures are normally worked out in meetings between users and information-system representatives. Users need to feel that their opinions are solicited rather than merely tolerated. The agreed-upon changes should give users enough time to adjust to the new procedures. Of course, occasionally a change in procedure has to be made quickly, say to plug a security breach. There may be no time to meet with users in such a case—especially if one of the users is suspected of being the security problem.

An example of a written standard would be the checkout procedures that a tape librarian follows. When you ask to remove a magnetic tape from the library, the librarian consults the standards manual to determine if that particular tape can be checked out, whether or not you qualify to do so, and whether you can only read the data on the tape or are also allowed to change the data.

Name a tool that has never been used in a crime. You can't. Computers, a modern tool, have been put to the same sorts of uses as shovels, crowbars, and telephones: Here's a look at some.*

Back in the early 1970s, creative employees at Equity Funding put their computer to work to produce insurance policy records for people who didn't exist. These records were then passed on to companies that reinsure policies. When the nonexistent people filed insurance claims—with a little help from their existent friends—the reinsurance companies paid. By the time some former Equity Funding employees blew the whistle, 64,000 out of Equity's 97,000 policyholders were fictitious. The cost of this fraud to stockholders, reinsurers, and creditors was $2.1 billion, making it the largest white-collar crime in history.

Saxon Industries, a now-defunct Fortune 500 company, also found it profitable to juggle its books by computer. For 13 years, employees maintained a fake inventory record. With more goods on hand—according to the computer—than were really in the warehouse, Saxon's financial picture was made to appear rosier than it actually was. This crime was detected only because the company's finances were investigated when it finally went bankrupt, in 1982. The loss was about $53 million.

Until they were jailed in 1983, Myron Goodman and Mordecai Weissman used fake and doctored-up computer leases as collateral to obtain loans for their OPM Leasing company. This was not, of course, the computers' fault. The losses to investors and customers ran into the hundreds of millions of dollars.

None of these crimes used any particularly sophisticated computing techniques. The computer was just another dumb tool, as innocent as the nailfile used to pick the lock of the bank vault.

Since feelings tend to run higher concerning computers than, say, hacksaws, the computer may be the only tool that is itself the *victim* of crimes. Bombs have been planted to destroy computer centers (sometimes successfully), various liquids have been poured on computers' sensitive parts, and data have been destroyed or altered out of sheer cussedness. For example, Keith Noreen sabotaged the Burroughs computer he was supposed to be operating for the benefit of the National Farmers Union, simply because he had an "overpowering urge" to do so. Burroughs picked up the half-million-dollar tab for investigating what it had assumed were defects in its machinery.

Ultimately all of us are the ones who pick up the tab for computer crimes and other crimes. Detecting computer crimes early, or preventing them in the first place, saves us money. Interestingly, computers themselves prove the best tools to catch other computers, tirelessly analyzing years of financial data in order to see where one of their own might have been led astray.

*Cases based on Jack B. Rochester and John Gantz, *The Naked Computer*, 1983.

Exception procedures

EXCEPTION PROCEDURES (also written down) specify what an organization should do when standard operating procedures cannot be followed or do not apply. Exception procedures help organizations by ensuring flexibility. A rigid system that cannot handle unusual situations will not satisfy users or clients.

One useful exception procedure is the one that an organization follows when its computer is not working. Another, familiar to many of you, concerns how to stop the repeated creation of an inaccurate bill for a customer. If the amount of a purchase was entered into the system incorrectly, a customer could be incorrectly billed for ages before the problem was resolved, unless an exception procedure existed for correcting the error. As far as possible, exception procedures should be incorporated into the standards manual. Some organizations require that a log be kept when exception procedures are invoked, to give the organization a record of what was done.

CONTROLS FOR DATA

Data controls affect who is able to view and alter data, and also evaluate the integrity of the data as they move through the system. The purpose of data controls is to ensure that data are neither misused nor subjected to unauthorized alteration or destruction.

Data quality assurance

DATA QUALITY ASSURANCE concerns evaluating data integrity from initial collection through input, processing, storage, and output. Maintaining a high standard of data integrity is one of the most challenging—and most important— tasks of system control.

Just as people have a tendency to believe what they read in books merely because it appears in print, so do people have a tendency to believe computer output because it was produced by such wonderfully complex and futuristic machines. By now, however, you are aware that what computers produce is only as good as what a program that somebody wrote could do with the data that were given to the computer. A classic phrase in information processing is "Garbage in, garbage out" (this phrase even has its own acronym, GIGO). Data quality assurance tries to see that garbage doesn't come out, by checking that the data are accurate at their source and are kept accurate through the different stages of their use.

Various methods for checking the integrity of data exist. VERIFICATION involves checking data by keying them in a second time and, where discrepancies are found, correcting them. The chances are extremely small that a data-entry operator will make the same entry error twice. VALIDATION uses the computer itself, or an intelligent terminal, to see whether or not the data entered lie within reasonable limits or have certain sought-after characteristics. For example, a program could safely reject a social security number that contains a letter, a supplier code that is a negative number, or an order placed in the last century.

CONTROL TOTALS are another technique for finding errors. Typically a clerk compiles a total by hand of monetary amounts (checks, bills, or whatever) in a batch of source documents to be entered. An intelligent terminal or computer compiles its own total during entry, and when all data are in, the two figures should match.

For an example of control totals, let's assume Paul's House of Electronic Wonders carefully controls the printing of payroll checks. Each check run through the printer must be accounted for, including checks damaged by the printer during printing. Various subtotals are accumulated during check printing, and compared against the figures expected by the accounting office. With these controls in place, one type of ploy could not be used at Paul's. Programmers have sometimes shaved pennies off of payroll deductions on employees' checks, accumulated the tiny amounts until they grew large enough, and printed them on blank damaged checks from the trash made out to nonexistent employees. At Paul's both the subtotals and the check control procedure would catch this ruse.

CHECK DIGITS offer another type of control, applying a formula to check the digits of identifiers that follow a specific scheme, such as Universal Product Codes, International Standard Book Numbers, or customer numbers in a well-designed database. Data that do not follow a predetermined pattern—such as names or sums of money—can be checked using other types of formulas.

We saw another type of data check in Chapter 5: the parity bit. PARITY BITS are especially useful in detecting data that are garbled during transmission between computers or between different components of the same computer. Like most of these checks, parity bits cannot tell how to correct the problem, but they can alert users that a problem exists.

Data security measures

DATA SECURITY refers to the protection and care of data. Accidental or deliberate misuse of data can have serious consequences. For example, the rise of distributed data processing has given many people with a microcomputer and an electronic spreadsheet the opportunity to retrieve data from the company database. Sometimes the data are inadvertently changed through the use of incorrect or inappropriate formulas with the spreadsheet. At other times simply nudging an electronic mouse during spreadsheet operations can accidentally change data in the wrong cell. If the altered, incorrect data are stored in the database, they will erase the original, correct data. Some companies have a policy of barring use of electronic mice during spreadsheet operations.

Two data security measures can protect a database: (1) access restriction and (2) backup procedures. These issues were also addressed in Chapter 16. Access restriction can be achieved through carefully thought-out and administered password procedures. Employees can be assigned passwords that restrict them to viewing only the portion of a database that concerns them on a "need-to-know" basis, and that may or may not allow them to alter data there. Figure 17-2 shows how such password-enforced restrictions might work. Passwords can also be used with file systems.

Passwords must be changed frequently to prevent former users of the system, such as disgruntled ex-employees, from reentering the database or file. Also, there is a type of computer enthusiast who delights in cracking passwords purely for the challenge; letting any given password mature to a ripe vintage increases the odds that someone is going to crack the code.

Backup procedures provide a copy of the data as they should be—or the means of reconstructing such a copy—in case the original is damaged or destroyed. Some database management systems will keep a journal of changes to the database. In addition the database in its entirety is copied at prespecified intervals. With a copy on hand of the database in some

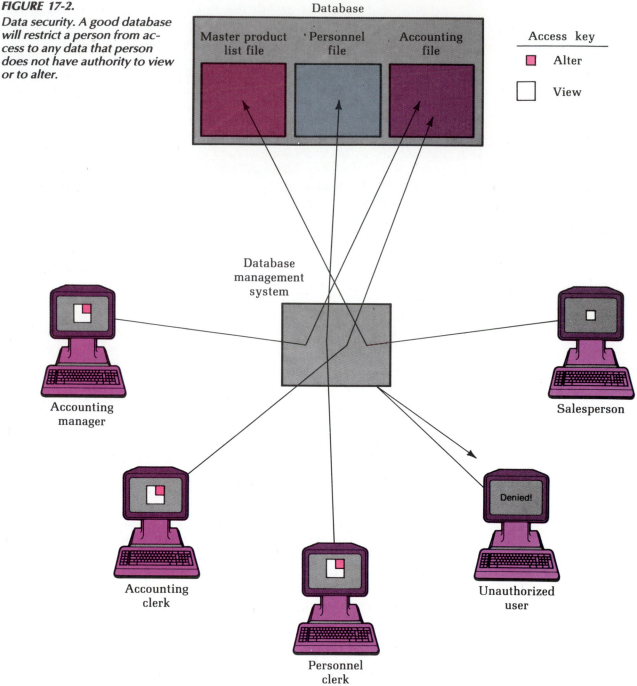

FIGURE 17-2.
Data security. A good database will restrict a person from access to any data that person does not have authority to view or to alter.

Database

Master product list file · Personnel file · Accounting file

Access key

Alter

View

Database management system

Accounting manager

Salesperson

Accounting clerk

Personnel clerk

Denied!

Unauthorized user

previous version, together with a record of all the changes to the database from that version to the present time, an organization can reconstruct its database.

When data are transmitted the possibility of eavesdropping arises. EAVESDROPPING involves tapping into an electronic signal. Data thieves may tap the "line" at any point in the telecommunications link. Microwave signals can be intercepted and read, as can the data traveling via cable. Eavesdroppers can even intercept your log-off signals that indicate that you are finished using your terminal or computer to communicate with a host computer; the eavesdropper can then send back to you the response to a log-off that the host computer normally does—while keeping the line to the host computer wide open and continuing to communicate with it for the eavesdropper's own purposes.

One way to foil eavesdroppers is through encryption. ENCRYPTION refers to the coding or scrambling of data, messages, or programs. Only the sender and receiver know the particular coding technique used, thus locking out any attempts by a third party to decipher a well-designed code. Figure 17-3 shows how a message might be coded for transmission and decoded upon receipt.

CONTROLS FOR SOFTWARE

Software controls are methods that regulate the way that programs are developed, accessed, and maintained. We will explore two major aspects of software control—security and piracy.

Software security measures

Just as data can be altered, so can programs. SOFTWARE SECURITY measures attempt to protect the programs from misuse or tampering. Misuse can occur when a minor maintenance change is sloppily done, thus throwing off the program. Tampering results from people deliberately changing a program to their advantage, such as making the program allow them to get at data that they are not authorized to view.

Concern for security should begin when software development begins. Careful application of structured design and programming techniques can help avoid sloppy programming to begin with. Access to software under development, in use, or being maintained should be governed by log-on procedures, particularly a well-devised scheme of secret passwords that are periodically changed. When passwords are changed and some programmers no longer have a right to one, they don't get a new one.

Copies of software should be kept in both the source program form (before the program is translated) and the object program form (after the program has been translated into machine language).

Once a program is in use—especially if, like a payroll program, it will be heavily used for a long time with occasional maintenance changes—it should be audited periodically to guarantee that it is doing what it is supposed to do. The backup programs and the versions used for daily processing should be compared with one another on a line-by-line basis and evaluated by special test data. If discrepancies appear, they should be carefully evaluated.

Another way to protect programs is to prevent people from getting at them in the first place. The media that contain programs should be kept in a safe place such as a fireproof vault. Backup copies should be stored offsite. Various storage companies will keep both data and program copies in underground sites such as renovated mineshafts. In addition encryption (described under "Data Security Measures") can be used to render software unintelligible to those who don't know the code. Through techniques of this

FIGURE 17-3.

An encrypted message. The encryption code used here is a fairly simple one that involves substituting one character for another. Much more complex, and more difficult to crack codes exist.

Encrypted message:
___RQ___E#G1___Y5G9$GE–9!GI4RC#M

Encryption code:

Original Character:	Coded Character:	Original Character:	Coded Character:
(blank)	G	Q	Z
A	—	R	!
B	1	S	#
C	Y	T	>
D	2	U	9
E	C	V	)
F	I	W	Q
G	U	X	(
H	*	Y	E
I	4	Z	%
J	A	!	M
K	5	#	(blank)
L	R	(	J
M	K	)	X
N	N	,	<
O	–	.	,
P	$		

Decoded message:

ALWAYS BACK UP YOUR FILES!

sort, the integrity of programs can be assessed and reassessed throughout their lives.

Piracy

As we saw in Chapter 12 a large industry exists that is dedicated to creating prepackaged software for all sizes of computers. Substantial investments are made by the producers of prepackaged software, who seek to recover the costs and turn a profit through sales. Frustrating this goal is **SOFTWARE PIRACY**, or the unauthorized duplication of software that can be obtained legally only through purchase. Buyers of prepackaged software often sign contracts stipulating that they will not copy the software or pass it on to someone else.

Nevertheless a lot of prepackaged software exists that—if it was purchased at all—was not purchased from the maker.

For example, considerable trading of software goes on among home computer users. To make it harder to copy a floppy disk and give it to a friend, software manufacturers try many techniques. One method is to scramble the tracks used for the program. A person trying to use standard disk copy methods to copy a floppy disk with scrambled tracks would be foiled. Some microcomputer users, however, have systems capable of exactly duplicating the bit patterns on a disk, one bit at a time, without trying to unscramble the track patterns. This gets past the intended control technique.

A more advanced antipiracy technique is to scatter special bits on the floppy disk with a weak magnetic charge between 0 and 1. These deliberate imperfections are not a problem when the disk is used with the program; however, when the disk is copied, the computer will write the weak bits as either normal-strength 1s or normal-strength 0s. Thus when the operating system of the computer performing the copying operation discovers that the copy and original do not agree, it stops copying.

CONTROLS FOR HARDWARE

Hardware controls ensure that authorized people have access to the equipment needed to perform their jobs, and that unauthorized people do not. All types of hardware need controls: input and output devices, the central processing unit, secondary storage devices, and telecommunications hardware.

Physical security measures

PHYSICAL SECURITY refers to the protection of the hardware and storage media used in information systems from theft, vandalism, and misuse. With the rise of the microcomputer and distributed data processing, physical security has become somewhat more complex than it was a few years ago, when the computer center was guarded like Fort Knox and the problem was thereby largely solved.

Microcomputers can be picked up and carried away. So can their peripheral devices and floppy disks or other removable storage media (Figure 17-4). To prevent theft equipment can be bolted into place and connected to a central alarm system. Identification tags affixed to the equipment can make it easier to recover when stolen. To help prevent

FIGURE 17-4.
Floppy disks can be easily lost or stolen.

FIGURE 17-5.
Physical security measures at a large computer center.

vandalism and misuse, the area containing the equipment can be monitored by closed-circuit cameras during normal operating hours and by special motion detectors outside these hours. Misuse can be thwarted through locks requiring a key to gain access to the microcomputer's on/off switch. Many businesses have electronically controlled entrances for their employees.

Larger computer centers—the classical Fort Knox situation —generally have elaborate physical security procedures. Figure 17-5 shows some of these measures. Access to the computer room is controlled either by a security guard or by a device that reads an employee ID card and decides whether or not the person should be admitted. In either case the person's name and entry date and time can be logged for future reference. After hours motion detectors can be used to sense intruders. To protect against fire, special fire-suppressant (Halon) gas can be released into the computer room at a concentration lethal to the fire but safe for people.

To protect against electrical disturbances, the computer and its peripherals must be properly grounded, and also equipped with devices that protect the hardware from the sudden surges in power that electrical utilities do on occasion deliver. Backup batteries can provide sufficient power to continue running the system at a reduced level of services, or to gain time to store data before shutting down. These protection devices and batteries provide for an uninterruptible power supply (UPS) system.

Fireproof vaults are used to store removable disk packs and magnetic tapes within the computer center. Disks and tapes must then be logged in and logged out by the media librarian.

No matter how thorough our security measures, accidents do still happen. Once an electrician installed a lightning rod at a building under construction and, seeking a ground, found a large metallic object that looked suitable. When the building was completed, the metallic object turned out to be the media vault. Some weeks after the new computer center was opened, a bolt of lightning struck the computer center during a thunderstorm. The lightning rod did its job and passed the massive electrical charge directly to its ground—destroying all of the data contained on the disks and tapes.

Dual processing

There are many organizations that effectively come to a halt when their computer stops working. To prevent the disaster that this can spell, some use the dual processing technique. DUAL PROCESSING uses redundant equipment to provide a means to prevent equipment failures from jeopardizing important projects. When one hardware component fails, the system simply switches to another. Such redundancy in hardware is quite common in the aerospace field. For example, the space shuttle has five onboard computers: four to perform the flight operations and one to monitor the others. Any of the five computers is capable of doing the job unaided, but the redundant computers minimize the chances of the ship being left computerless. For business organizations the same idea can be, and frequently is, used.

Teleprocessing security

Today one rarely has to walk into a computer room to gain access to the computers that are running there. Strong walls and armed security guards have no effect on abuse via telecommunication links. Access can easily be gained using a microcomputer and a modem connected to the central computer via a telecommunications link (Figure 17-6). In an information system we try to balance the needs of legitimate off-site users against the security needs of the system. The system needs to discourage MASQUERADING, which refers to unauthorized users passing themselves off as authorized users. Typically the perpetrator manages to obtain a legitimate user's account number and password. Clever masqueraders can sometimes steal just the account number, and then arrive at the password by mental deduction based on what they know about the person who has the account number—trying out his or her birthdate, the names of family members, and so on, until the right password is hit upon.

A common control method is that most systems permit only two or three attempts at a password before a user is locked out. Then the person must reenter the account number. A log of the attempts may be kept by the system.

Another control technique that can foil such people is the AUTOMATIC CALLBACK. With automatic callback, once a user logs on, the host computer

FIGURE 17-6.

Teleprocessing is a great benefit for many organizations, but it also leaves them vulnerable to the theft of valuable data and information.

attempts to call back the user at his or her regular terminal number, to make sure that this is in fact the terminal that just logged on. A masquerader at a different telephone number will not be connected, as the computer will not have a record of the unauthorized number.

At universities the most common type of masquerading is when illegal users use terminals that have been left logged on by careless students or faculty members. Automatic disconnect devices exist that will turn off such terminals after a given period of time if the user fails to log off.

Masquerading is done by a wide range of people—government spies after national secrets, corporate spies after corporate secrets, nosy people, or individuals interested in cracking a system just for the sake of doing so without any particular malice. Indeed some masqueraders are not out to steal anything beyond the computer's time for carrying out certain processing.

ACCOUNTING AND AUDITING

Both accounting and auditing procedures are utilized by modern information systems for control purposes. We will see some of the ways in which they are used.

ACCOUNTING AND THE INFORMATION SYSTEM

Accounting procedures are applied as control measures to monitor usage of information resources, to control who uses the system, and to bill users for their use of the system.

RESOURCE UTILIZATION PROCEDURES attempt to track and modify patterns of an information system's resources. The operating systems of larger computers maintain statistics on the extent of use of the central processing unit and peripheral devices, and the frequency of data access. On the basis of such information the information-system staff can rearrange peripheral devices to spread the load, phase out old equipment, order new equipment, identify an underutilized database, and so on. By changing the rate structure for computer use, managers can change the pattern of such use. By substantially lowering the evening rates, they might encourage evening use of the computer center by departments unable to afford prime time. In a larger sense an organization's managers can fine-tune and direct the operation of the entire information system using similar techniques. For example, user education, coupled with a high-caliber database administration staff, could encourage users to scrap their proprietary files that are causing an organization so much grief through inconsistent data, high storage costs, and use the company database instead.

The operating system's job control program determines who can use the system in the first place. It checks for valid passwords and account numbers, limits the types of operations that particular users can perform, and often keeps a log of exactly who is using the system and for what purpose. The job control program also keeps the books, recording each user's time spent using the computer and the specific resources used, so that the information-system staff can bill the user on the basis of these records. The operating system does not set policy in such matters, but carries out decisions made by managers of the organization.

Wherever a computer is running today in a large and knowledgeable organization, an information-systems auditor is also at work.

The best place to look for an information-systems auditing position is at places with formally codified rules and procedures, such as a bank. The auditing function will be particularly important at such organizations, and the size of the staff will permit different job levels all the way down to trainee. As with other computer jobs, you can land one most effectively with a four-year computer-related degree and some hands-on experience. Courses in business administration and accounting are also a plus.

Some jobs are not destined to be popular. Like the dentist, the information-systems auditor is someone most computer people respect but would rather forget about if possible; unlike the dentist, the auditor comes to you, unsolicited. Let's listen to a real information-systems auditor describe his job:

I am an edp auditor. It is what I do eight hours a day, five days a week. Edp auditing is my profession, my career, my life. Unfortunately, many of the people I work with . . . have almost no idea what my job entails. . . .

People generally see the EDPA as a computer room busybody, a sort of electronic Mary Worth, who searches diligently for even the most minor infraction. They don't realize that EDPAs must have programming knowledge, an understanding of computer operations, the ability to report uncomfortable truths to upper management, and the ability to provide computerized support and advice to financial auditors. The EDPA has to keep abreast of federal regulations and be aware of innovations in hardware and software technology within the industry. . . .

Since the edp audit function is fairly new, it is rare to find detailed job descriptions for it. But in one form or another, all of the descriptions I have seen usually come down to two items—ver-

ifying controls and identifying exposures. Those two words, exposure and control, seem to cause the greatest misunderstanding. There is, however, a very simple way of remembering what these two words mean to a business: when you think of the word exposure, think about a person standing naked in the snow. If that person were to stand in the snow for long, he could catch a cold. We are not 100% certain that this person will become ill, but it is a reasonable possibility. That is the heart of the word exposure—a reasonable chance that something bad may occur. To the person outside with high-rise gooseflesh, that something is illness or death. To a corporation, losses or bankruptcy are the possibilities.

Now think of the word control and picture layers of clothing on that shivering, blue person. The more layers of clothing you add, the less likely it is that he will catch cold. No amount of clothing can guarantee that this person won't get sick. That risk can only be reduced. If you try to eliminate the risk by piling on the clothes, the person would be unable to move, and might die from suffocation. The effects of exposure and control work the same way with a business.

So what the EDPA does, essentially, is look for the possibility of loss and the degree of risk involved. If the risk is low and the chance of loss is low, odds are that management will elect to accept the risk. Most of the time, the EDPA will find low-loss and low-risk exposures, but will still report them to management. It is up to management to decide what action will be taken. . . .

The EDPA is not the answer to all of management's fears, nor is he an insurance policy against loss or fraud. . . . Management must realize that EDPAs cannot find and solve 100% of their company's problems, but they can help to reduce the possibility of loss.

AUDITING TECHNIQUES

The principal way of monitoring the use and abuse of the information system is through the auditing process. An **AUDIT** is an examination of the information system to test the effectiveness of its various control procedures. Originally limited to going over business accounts to turn up any discrepancies, auditing has expanded to include nonaccounting concerns such as performing detailed reviews of the software used in processing, checking how well the data security measures work, and monitoring user requests to see sensitive data. The job of information-system auditor exists in most larger organizations today, which generally maintain a department of such individuals.

Auditors inspect everything, from the source materials for data input, through the intermediate results, to the final output of a system. Usually auditors do not analyze all of the data that flow through a system, but take a sample and study it intensively. Auditors generally focus on the most valuable parts of an organization: its money, materials, and sensitive data.

A time-honored auditing technique applied to information systems is that of tracing an audit trail. An **AUDIT TRAIL** consists of the physical or visible documentation of the steps that money, documents, or whatever follow through the organization. The principle here is that when a problem is spotted, one should be able to trace it back to its source and correct it there. The particulars of the audit-trail technique have changed over the years. Originally auditors assumed that if what went into a computer system was correct, and what came out of it was correct, the processing must also have been correct. Unfortunately final results can be correct—or look correct—after errors have occurred along the way, or after unscrupulous people have diverted leftover change to their own pockets.

Aware of this problem, auditors moved to auditing *through* the computer. This means that the input and processing steps are closely examined; if they are found to be correct, the output is also assumed to be correct. Test data are created and run through the system to verify the data's accuracy. Unfortunately this approach also has its limits.

The limits crop up with time-sharing or real-time systems. Tracing an audit trail here is almost impossible without the active participation of the computer software itself. Distributed data processing further complicates the picture, with scattered users sharing a database, sending electronic messages hither and yon, and each processing the data in different ways. Fortunately software does exist to perform audits for the complex circumstances under which today's computers operate. Auditing software packages can run simultaneously *with* the programs, user queries, and real-time transactions that are being audited. Indeed, with today's larger and more sophisticated computer systems, auditing is a continuous operation, performed concurrently with other operations.

PROTECTING THE RIGHT TO PRIVACY

In our discussion of control techniques so far in this chapter, we have focused primarily on matters of accuracy and security. Let us now shift our focus to the matter of privacy.

In the dictionary "privacy" means being apart from other people and protected from observation or unauthorized intrusion. With the widespread

FIGURE 17-7.
Some of the major government databases. The number of files retained on people by U.S. federal agencies exceeds 3.5 billion.

FIGURE 17-7.

Some of the major government databases. The number of files retained on people by U.S. federal agencies exceeds 3.5 billion.

Government Agency	Number of Files on People
Departments of Education and Health and Human Services	1,033,999,891
Department of Treasury	780,196,929
Department of Commerce	431,427,589
Department of Defense	333,951,949
Department of Justice	201,474,342
Department of State	110,809,198
Department of Agriculture	33,727,730
Copyright Office	28,408,366
Department of Transportation	24,023,142
Federal Communications Commission	20,870,078
Department of Housing and Urban Development	20,340,642
Department of Labor	16,785,015
Department of Interior	16,708,016
Office of Personnel Management	16,016,799
Department of Energy	8,929,999
Executive Office of the President	30,655
All other federal agencies	452,043,345
Grand total	3,529,743,655

Or 15 files on average for each American

Source: Reprinted from *U.S. News & World Report*, July 12, 1982. Copyright © 1982, U.S. News and World Report, Inc.

presence of information systems that maintain large databases and telecommunications links to other databases, "intrusion" can take on new dimensions. Specifically, the fact that data are collected about us, maintained in databases, traded from one organization to another, and put to various uses, may violate our privacy. In these circumstances protecting our privacy means protecting ourselves from unauthorized access to, or abuse of, data concerning us. Two areas of concern are the gathering of inaccurate or false information, and the abuse of data (whether accurate or inaccurate) once they are gathered. Figure 17-7 suggests the magnitude of the problem.

SELLING YOUR PRIVACY FOR PEANUTS

I was recently asked by a member of the media how long it would take and how much it might cost to compile a dossier on a person. I suggested it would take less than 48 hours and cost less than $100. He then asked what specific kinds of information such a dossier would include. I told him that a "quick and dirty" credit check, which means no confirmation of facts, would produce the following information:

- *The person's name, address and phone number*
- *Date and place of birth*
- *Marital status*
- *Number of dependents*
- *Current employment*
- *Annual income*
- *Assets owned and debts owed*
- *Social security number*
- *Employment history*
- *Prior places of residence*
- *Credit cards*
- *Charge accounts*
- *Open bank loans*
- *Payment history*

For a few hundred dollars more, one could also access the following information.

- *Voting record*
- *Involvement in civil and criminal litigation*
- *Past divorces*
- *Real estate ownership*
- *Mortgages on property*
- *Liens*
- *Accident record*
- *Driving record*
- *Physical handicaps*
- *Political affiliation*
- *Religious preference*
- *Schools and colleges attended*

And again, for a few hundred dollars more, one could access information on a person's:

- *Life-style preferences*
- *Social habits—drinking, drug abuse, sexual preference*
- *Club memberships*

And, if you're willing to go for the "full shot" of a $1,000 fee, you might also be able to determine such other more private data as:

- *Record of arrests*
- *Membership in subversive organizations*

- *Associates, friends and relatives*
- *Military record*
- *Health problems*
- *Psychiatric problems*
- *Mental capacity (IQ)*
- *Personality characteristics*
- *Bank balances*
- *Investments*
- *Media mentions*
- *Academic record*
- *Medical record*
- *Job terminations*
- *Reputation*
- *Encounters with regulatory agencies*
- *Receipt of governmental aid and benefits*
- *Life insurance in force*

The media representative then asked who might undertake the compilation of such a dossier. I said any one of some 10,000 credit and private detective agencies in the country could do so. He seemed shocked by the revelation that for about $1,000 one's personal privacy could be destroyed. "Life has indeed become cheap in America, at least in terms of one's privacy," he said.

The fact is that despite Constitutional guarantees of personal privacy, we live in an open society and an open society is a two-edged sword. We pay a price to maintain an open society. Part of that price is that we trade off one Constitutional guarantee for another, *i.e.,* privacy vs. openness. Freedom of speech, religion and peaceable assembly means that our thoughts, political and religious views are subject to public scrutiny. The Soviets can claim one thing we can't. In Russia, the Communist government does all the dossier compilations and its records are not open to public viewing. There are no privately-owned data banks. In the U.S., privately owned data banks abound and they are growing rapidly. Commercial interests want to know more and more about us—what we believe, value and trust, what we do and why, our attitudes, opinions and feelings about everything from our political choices to the kind of breakfast cereal we most prefer.

Source: Jack Bologna and Timothy A. Schabeck, *ICP Business Software Review,* February/March 1984, p. 48. Copyright © 1984 International Computer Programs, Inc., Indianapolis, Indiana.

How to assure privacy is a major problem facing managers of information systems. Several factors must be taken into account. Managers of an organization need to decide what legitimate rights (if any) government agencies and private organizations have to data that the organization maintains. A company such as Paul's House of Electronic Wonders, for example, would not supply data to outsiders, except to institutions requesting legitimate credit checks and to the government at certain preestablished "exit points" for the data, such as employee withholding tax statements. If audited by the Internal Revenue Service, Paul's would have to supply the information requested. None of these uses need violate the privacy of personnel, but inaccurate information could be proliferated.

Managers also need to address the rights of individuals and organizations to examine the data maintained about them, and to correct data that are legitimately maintained but inaccurate. For example, any employee at Paul's can examine his or her personnel file. If data about the person are found to be wrong—such as specifying the wrong degree obtained, or attributing a prison record to the wrong person—they can be corrected in the personnel file and in the relevant database.

The capacity of some information systems is enormous, and quite a few imposing files and databases are maintained by government agencies and private organizations. Many people are not pleased with this prospect. Figure 17-7 gives some idea of just how much information the federal government alone maintains about its citizens. Add to that the databases maintained by local governments and private organizations, and the total becomes even more impressive.

Many people have been concerned about actual and possible abuses of this data, and proliferation of inaccurate data. The "Big Brother is watching" feeling does not sit well with residents of a democracy; accordingly citizens have pressed for protective legislation, and laws governing the use of databases have been enacted at the national and state levels. National legislation, all stemming originally from the early 1970s, includes the Fair Credit Reporting Act, the Freedom of Information Act, the Education Privacy Act, and the Privacy Act.

The **FAIR CREDIT REPORTING ACT** (1970) gives individuals the right to examine credit records maintained about them by private organizations. If you apply for a charge card, for example, and are denied it on the basis of your credit history, you have the right to inspect the records kept by the agency that denied the credit. The service costs a small fee. You also have the right to inspect your records if granted credit. If you claim the records are wrong, the credit agency is required by this law to investigate the truthfulness of your claim.

The **FREEDOM OF INFORMATION ACT** (1970) gives individuals, as well as organizations, the right to inspect data concerning them that are maintained by agencies of the federal government. In addition the law opens up for your scrutiny some of the files concerning how these agencies run. Information obtained under this act is in the news quite frequently, sometimes indicating that statements made by government officials are inconsistent with data with which they are familiar.

The **EDUCATION PRIVACY ACT** (1974) protects the privacy of students concerning grades and other types of evaluation data maintained by schools. Any public or private school that receives direct or indirect aid from the federal government must abide by this act, which stipulates that students or guardians can view their records and challenge inaccuracies, and that schools may not release the records to others without permission of students or guardians.

Finally, the PRIVACY ACT (1974) offers protection to individuals and organizations from data-gathering abuses by the federal government. The law states that data gathered by a federal agency must have a specific and authorized purpose, and that people can see the data gathered about them, learn how they are used, and have the opportunity to correct any erroneous data. In effect this law expands the Freedom of Information Act described above. In addition to its provisions concerning the government, the act set up the Privacy Protection Study Commission to review privacy questions involving private organizations. This commission has made several recommendations for national legislation regulating the use of data by private organizations.

Since their passage these laws have been modified to take into account the ever-greater pervasiveness of data about individuals in private and governmental databases. Many states and localities have also passed similar legislation. These days, even though "Big Brother" is in fact not only watching, but recording what he sees in databases, at least individuals do have some privacy-protecting weapons with which to fight back, and may even succeed in keeping a certain amount of data all to themselves.

WRAP-UP

SUSPICION CONFIRMED

Suspicious that someone was illegally examining data from the inventory database at Paul's House of Electronic Wonders, Ed Wieland got the go-ahead from Mr. Paul to investigate.

For an entire morning Ed sat in the computer room at a monitor writing down the user identification numbers of people who were using the inventory database. All of the numbers were valid, of course; otherwise the system would not have let the people use the database. Similarly, all of the users clearly knew their passwords.

Passwords were not recorded anywhere, but a list of valid user identification numbers was kept in the computer room. Ed noticed that no one outside of the purchasing department and the shipping and receiving department ever used the database. He made a few quick tours of these areas, and again found one more user logged on than he could actually see using a terminal. The missing person was the manager of the purchasing department.

Ed did not discuss his investigation with the purchasing manager. Instead he advised Mr. Paul to give a directive to the information-processing center ordering that all passwords for all databases be changed the next day. For individual users the loss of a familiar password, and the few moments required to think up a new one, would be only a minor nuisance.

Mr. Paul gave the directive, and the next day Ed again sat at his monitor in the computer room. The person who had been using the manager's I.D. and password to retrieve data from the inventory database had disappeared!

Pleased with his success, Ed went to talk to Mr. Paul.

"Well done, Ed," Mr. Paul said. "I just wish we could have caught them."

"If they'd been in-house, we would have," Ed said. "I'm pretty sure no one who works here was involved. They must have been using a phone line to get in from outside."

"I can see where with a bit of snooping someone from outside could come up with a valid I.D.," Mr. Paul said. "But knowing the password puzzles me."

"A computer thief can often psych it out based on what he or she knows about the particular user. I don't know myself what the password was. But if you try names of kids, schools, hometowns, and dogs long enough, the odds are good of hitting it."

"Ed," Mr. Paul said, "how do we keep this from happening again?"

"First, Mr. Paul, you should ask the database administrator to do a complete audit of the database. We need to see if the thief just looked at data or changed them. After righting that situation, I think we need a regulation that passwords get changed once a month."

"That's all right by me," Mr. Paul said.

"And I would like to install an automatic callback system," Ed said. "That would be a new form of protection that just might shut out intruders. The way it works is that when someone logs on, the computer calls them back immediately at the terminal they're assigned to. If they're not there, then they can't get into the system at all."

"Wonderful," Mr. Paul said. "Let's hope that will be the end of our data theft."

SUMMARY

- *Information system controls serve to monitor and insure the proper operation of all five information system elements. Controls help to assure the integrity of the data, the security of the information system, and the privacy of users and clients of the information system. Controls also help prevent computer crime.*
- *Controls for people include separation of tasks and the standardization of work. Separation of tasks divides tasks and responsibilities among different employees, so that no one person controls financial or other important matters. Standardization of work helps assure a measure of consistency by clearly defining tasks.*
- *Controls for rules and procedures include written procedures or standards and exception procedures. Written procedures or standards codify tasks so that employees can understand them. Exception procedures, which specify what an organization should do when*

standard operating procedures can't be followed, help organizations by ensuring flexibility.

- *Controlling data means assuring the quality of the data and assuring that the data are secure. Data quality assurance concerns evaluating data integrity from initial collection through input, processing, storage, and output. Various means of checking data integrity exist, including verification, validation, control totals, check digits, and parity bits. Data security measures protect data from accidental or deliberate misuse. These measures include restricting access to data through using passwords, making backup copies of important data, and using encryption to foil eavesdropping during data transmission.*

- *Software controls refer to methods that regulate the way that programs are developed, accessed, and maintained. Software security measures include the use of structured design and development techniques throughout the software development process and periodic auditing of programs. Other software security measures are the same as those for data—passwords, backup copies, and encryption. Attempts to control software piracy include various techniques to make it difficult to copy programs.*

- *Hardware controls ensure that authorized people have access to the equipment needed to perform their jobs and that unauthorized people do not. Physical security measures protect the hardware and storage media from theft, vandalism, and misuse. Such protection involves not only physically securing the hardware, but foiling unauthorized users who, by masquerading as authentic users, can enter a system via telecommunications links. One technique for controlling masquerading is the automatic callback. Dual processing provides redundant processing capability in case the primary hardware fails.*

- *Both accounting and auditing procedures are employed by modern information systems for control purposes. Resource utilization procedures monitor the usage of information system resources, control who uses the system, and bill users. Auditing inspects everything from the source materials for data input, through the intermediate results, to the final output. An audit trail consists of the physical or visible documentation of the steps that money, documents, data, or whatever follow through an organization. Auditors employ auditing software packages to help perform their task with today's complex computer systems.*

- *Privacy refers to protection from unauthorized access to, or abuse of, data concerning individuals or organizations. Managers of an organization need to decide what data (if any) should be released to government agencies or private organizations. Managers also need to establish procedures to allow individuals to inspect the data maintained about them, and to correct data that are inaccurate. Legislation that backs up the individual's rights to privacy includes the Fair Credit Reporting Act, the Freedom of Information Act, the Education Privacy Act, and the Privacy Act.*

Information-system control (468)
Data integrity (468)
Security (468)
Privacy (468)
Computer crime (468)
Separation of tasks (471)
Standardization of work (472)
Written procedure or standard (472)
Exception procedure (473)
Data quality assurance (474)
Verification (474)
Validation (474)
Control total (474)
Check digit (475)
Parity bit (475)
Data security (475)

Eavesdropping (476)
Encryption (477)
Software security (477)
Software piracy (478)
Physical security (479)
Dual processing (481)
Masquerading (481)
Automatic callback (481)
Resource utilization procedure (482)
Audit (484)
Audit trail (484)
Fair Credit Reporting Act (488)
Freedom of Information Act (488)
Education Privacy Act (488)
Privacy Act (489)

REVIEW QUESTIONS

OBJECTIVE QUESTIONS

TRUE/FALSE: *Put the letter T or F on the line before the question.*

1. Computer crime occurs when a person uses a computer for illegal purposes.
2. Information system controls only serve to monitor the integrity of data.
3. The check digit in the Universal Product Code is an example of a control total.
4. Integrity refers to the security of the data.
5. Permitting one worker to handle many operations in a sensitive area is a violation of the separation-of-tasks principle.
6. Information systems should not account for exception procedures.
7. Security refers to the steps taken to protect the information system.
8. The Fair Credit Reporting Act (1970) gives people a right to inspect credit reports about them maintained by public agencies.
9. Verification involves checking data by keying them in a second time and correcting any discrepancies found between the two versions.
10. With the rise in the use of microcomputers the privacy issue has become less important.

MULTIPLE CHOICE: *Put the letter of the correct answer on the line before the question.*

1. Access to data concerning individuals and organizations gathered by federal agencies is made possible by the
(a) Fair Credit Reporting Act (1970).
(b) Freedom of Information Act (1970).
(c) Education Privacy Act (1974).
(d) Privacy Act (1974).

2. Dual processing is primarily a _____ control.
(a) people.
(b) rules and procedures.
(c) software.
(d) hardware.

3.
Determining if a data value is within an acceptable range is accomplished by
(a) verification.
(c) check digits.
(b) validation
(d) parity checks.

4.
Illegal users can fool the computer into thinking they are legitimate users through
(a) eavesdropping.
(c) masquerading.
(b) disencryption.
(d) wiretapping.

5.
Protection of individuals and organizations from data-gathering abuses of federal agencies is addressed in the
(a) Fair Credit Reporting Act (1970).
(b) Freedom of Information Act (1970).
(c) Education Privacy Act (1974).
(d) Privacy Act (1974).

FILL IN THE BLANK: *Write the correct word or words in the blank to complete the sentence.*

1. The process of tracing the steps money or items follow through an organization is known as a(n) _____.
2. When auditors check the input and processing steps and assume the output is correct they are _____ the computer.
3. Manuals for users, programmers, and systems analysts are examples of _____.
4. The extra digit on a Universal Product Code is an example of a _____.
5. Maintaining data integrity and restricting unauthorized access to data are issues of _____.
6. _____ procedures monitor and adjust the patterns of information system usage.
7. Listening into transmissions is an example of _____.
8. Data accuracy means the same as _____.
9. Intrusion into your personal records is usually considered a violation of your _____.
10. The coding of data for privacy during transmission is known as _____.

SHORT ANSWER QUESTIONS

When answering these questions think of concrete examples to illustrate your points.

1. What are two examples of controls affecting people in the information system?
2. How can information processing centers reduce the risk of threats to physical security?
3. What means are used to audit online real-time systems?
4. What methods are used for data quality assurance?
5. What are some telecommunications security measures?
6. Why do information systems require exception procedures?
7. Comment on the risks of not separating tasks.
8. What are some examples of software controls?

ESSAY QUESTIONS

1. Discuss the balance between maintaining information security and permitting users opportunities to use the system.
2. What are the major information security controls at your work or school?
3. Discuss whether government agencies should have unrestricted access to data gathered about you and held in private databases.

CHAPTER 18

SELF-ANALYSIS: BUYING YOUR OWN MICROCOMPUTER

■ *THE UNOPENED SEASON*
A PERSONAL INFORMATION SYSTEM
You don't have to do it yourself / Problem recognition / Systems analysis / System design / System development /
■ *CAREER BOX: Microcomputer Specialist*
System implementation / System maintenance
SELECTING YOUR INFORMATION SYSTEM
People / Rules and procedures / Data / Software / Hardware
■ *CASE IN POINT: In-House Computer Stores*
■ *WRAP-UP: A Fall of Leisure*

After studying this chapter you should understand the following:
■ *That not everyone needs a microcomputer.*
■ *The steps of the system development process involved in buying, installing, and using a microcomputer.*
■ *How to consider each of the five information-system elements when selecting a microcomputer.*

Robin Wieland coasted on her bicycle, past the little cottages and shops of Sandy Cove Village, thinking how lucky she was. Life in a resort town, as a year-round resident, suited her just right.

Robin left her bicycle unlocked by the door of her shop, and went in to get ready for business. There wouldn't be much, since this was still the off-season. She rotated the candles in the display window to let today's sun work on the opposite side. She dusted off the vases, bowls, and other ceramic articles in the gallery-like front room. Then she turned the cardboard sign that hung in the door from the "Closed" side to "Open."

Behind the room with her ceramics, the shop had another room that contained greeting cards and postcards. These were for the walk-through tourists on sunny days. On rainy days, when people couldn't go to the beach, they came in and spent more time and bought Robin's ceramics. The candles sold almost any time. Although the candles and cards actually brought in more income than the ceramics, they were not Robin's main concern, as she did not make them. She made the ceramics, with loving care, whenever she could find the time.

The back of the shop contained her workbench, potter's wheel, kiln, and a stack of papers. Whenever her brother, Ed Wieland, a systems analyst, passed through Sandy Cove Village, he pointed to that stack of papers and said that was how she lost her money. It was true enough that Robin was not prompt in sending out reminders for customers who had bought on credit, or in paying her own suppliers even though a discount could often be applied to the bills for early payment. Ed offered to help Robin find ways to manage her paperwork problem. He thought a microcomputer might, perhaps, be useful to her.

Robin stacked a few of the papers and uncovered some cards. Oh no—those were her season openers, and she'd forgotten to send them! Whenever customers made major purchases she noted their home addresses in the guest register. Then about a month before the start of the next season, she sent them a little advertising pamphlet, in the hope that they would stop in again. She felt sure that this little extra touch brought her return business. But this year she hadn't even got the cards off on time!

Yes, things were out of hand. Maybe Ed was right. She didn't know anything about microcomputers, but she decided to look into the matter.

Although this may come as a surprise, you already have a personal information system. You make decisions every day, based upon data that you receive and process into information. If you live with your family or with other people, they too have personal information systems. You do not have to own or have access to a computer to have a workable personal information system.

The same is true, of course, of a business. Long before computers existed, businesses got along just fine. Even today, when major businesses use a computerized information system, smaller ones such as Robin Wieland's shop often do not.

If your personal information system works just fine, then you don't need a computer, regardless of how many of your friends have one or how much advertising you are exposed to. If there is a problem or an unrealized opportunity, however—as there was with Robin's information system—then you might look into buying a computer. It is possible to look and evaluate, step by step, and ultimately decide not to buy if the facts don't seem to justify it.

A useful approach to shopping for a computer is follow the *system development process*, which we described in detail in Chapter 15. In this chapter we'll see how to adapt that process to buying a microcomputer (see Figure 18-1). We will look at each of the steps of the system development process: problem recognition, systems analysis, system design, system development, system implementation, and system maintenance. First, however, a qualifier.

FIGURE 18-1.

If you're thinking about adding a microcomputer to your personal information system, whether for business or home use, the system development process can help you.

YOU DON'T HAVE TO DO IT YOURSELF

With millions of successfully installed microcomputer systems in existence, a fair body of knowledge exists on sizing up the needs of a person or a small business and matching them with an information system. Some of this knowledge is contained in books like this one.

As you will see, many things must be considered in buying a microcomputer. The process of balancing the different factors is time consuming. Although carefully selecting a microcomputer can itself be a beneficial training experience for the person who will use the machine, it is also possible simply to throw the problem in a consultant's lap. The advantage here is that a good consultant knows the alternatives more intimately than you do, and can work more quickly. Ideally—as in hiring a tax accountant or a lawyer—the specialist should more than repay his or her expenses in long-term savings.

A reliable consultant can best be found through the personal recommendation of others who have used the same consultant. Computer user groups, the staff of an information-processing center, or friends, can be a good source of names. Avoid asking vendors for this kind of help. Although computer stores and manufacturers can indeed provide invaluable help, it is usually only within the confines of what they sell.

In this chapter we assume that you are shopping for a microcomputer yourself. If you use a consultant instead, read the chapter anyway. It will help you better understand the factors that a consultant must consider.

PROBLEM RECOGNITION

Problem recognition is the first stage in the system development process. Let's consider a few examples.

- *As an investor in the stock market, you have a need to follow market trends as carefully as possible. You have heard that there are some computerized services that can provide in-depth analysis for a reasonable fee. To obtain such reports, however, you need access to a computer that has a telecommunications link. Your job gives you little time to use the office computer for this purpose.*
- *You are a full-time student at a university. Your major problem is meeting deadlines for term papers. The writing is hard enough, but it is compounded by the fact that you are a poor typist. A word-processing program, you have heard, might help. Besides, the same computer could run video games, which you enjoy playing.*
- *You've had it with your job working 9 to 5 as an underappreciated secretary doing routine typing, filing, and bookkeeping. What you want is a career change so that you can run your own business. You would like to start a secretarial and bookkeeping service in your own home.*

The people involved in each of these situations have different reasons for considering buying a microcomputer and incorporating it into their existing information system. In the example at the start of the chapter, Robin Wieland's reason was to handle her bookkeeping and paperwork more efficiently, in order to have more time to make the ceramics that she sold.

SYSTEMS ANALYSIS

Once we have recognized a problem, the next stage in the system development process is systems analysis. *Systems analysis* refers to examining systematically how an existing system works. In other words, you know that something is wrong with or lacking in your existing, uncomputerized personal information system, but need to pin down *exactly* what is wrong with it, in order to go about righting the situation.

As we saw in Chapter 15 the first step in systems analysis is a preliminary investigation to determine the scope of the problem and to decide whether or not to proceed. Robin Wieland sat down and did some paperwork to determine how many invoices she should send out each month, and how many bills she had to pay herself. Wondering if a computer might also help her do those promotion mailings, she counted up the names on her mailing list. Then she called her brother Ed at Paul's House of Electronic Wonders.

Ed was a trained systems analyst and questioned his sister to determine if she really didn't need a computer to do anything else, such as word processing, inventory, or spreadsheet analysis. Finally she convinced him that all she wanted it for was to take care of bills, and perhaps mailings. Ed told her that her job now was to decide if the cost of a computer system was worth what it would do for her. He mentioned alternatives—she could hire a part-time bookkeeper or use an accounting service. He said that a small microcomputer with a monitor, a single floppy disk drive, a letter-quality printer, and some packaged software to do what she wanted would cost her no more than $2000, and probably quite a bit less. "Is it worth it to you?" he asked.

Where a larger organization would have held meetings to do a formal cost and benefit analysis, Robin simply slept on it for a few nights. Then she calculated how much money she was losing by not paying her suppliers early enough to get the discount: it amounted to several hundred dollars per year. Assuming that a computer would also save her time to turn out more work and to have more time to herself, she decided to take the plunge. In one way or another, she thought, it would pay for itself in a couple of years.

In the formal systems analysis carried out by a larger business, after such a decision a detailed investigation follows. Such an investigation:

1 *Defines the goal.*
2 *Collects facts.*
3 *Defines system flow.*
4 *Defines system volume and timing.*
5 *Evaluates system performance.*

The *goal* refers to the purpose or objective. Robin wants to send out her bills and checks and have enough time left over to do her real work. She has already collected the *facts*, in tallying how many bills she has to pay per average month, how many checks to write herself, and how big her mailing list is. There is no need for her to interview the different users involved, since she is the only one.

The facts collected about a system should address the people, data, rules and procedures, software, and hardware. Figure 18-2 describes all five elements for Robin Wieland's system. *System flow* refers to the actual flow of work through a system. Figure 18-3 shows a data-flow diagram for Robin Wieland's accounts receivable and accounts payable system.

Robin has already estimated *system volume* (number of bills, checks, and people mailed to). As for *timing*, it is useful for her to note that 75 percent of her business occurs in the summer, and that is why she is hopelessly behind then. *Evaluating system performance* refers to stating how the existing system works and identifying the cause of the problem. Robin knew even before she started thinking about getting a computer that she was backlogged in paperwork—in other words, that the system didn't work. Looking at the actual figures, however, made her more clearly aware of how much she had to do during the summer months. The cause of the problem was that she was only one person. She needed a helper. According

FIGURE 18-2.
The elements in Robin Wieland's manual information system.

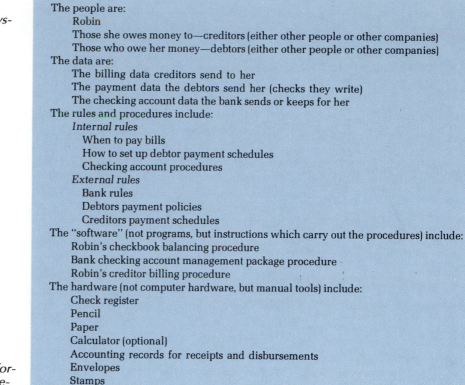

The people are:
    Robin
    Those she owes money to—creditors (either other people or other companies)
    Those who owe her money—debtors (either other people or other companies)
The data are:
    The billing data creditors send to her
    The payment data the debtors send her (checks they write)
    The checking account data the bank sends or keeps for her
The rules and procedures include:
    Internal rules
      When to pay bills
      How to set up debtor payment schedules
      Checking account procedures
    External rules
      Bank rules
      Debtors payment policies
      Creditors payment schedules
The "software" (not programs, but instructions which carry out the procedures) include:
    Robin's checkbook balancing procedure
    Bank checking account management package procedure
    Robin's creditor billing procedure
The hardware (not computer hardware, but manual tools) include:
    Check register
    Pencil
    Paper
    Calculator (optional)
    Accounting records for receipts and disbursements
    Envelopes
    Stamps

FIGURE 18-3.
Robin Wieland's personal information system for accounts receivable and accounts payable. The diagram is simplified to show the general flow of data.

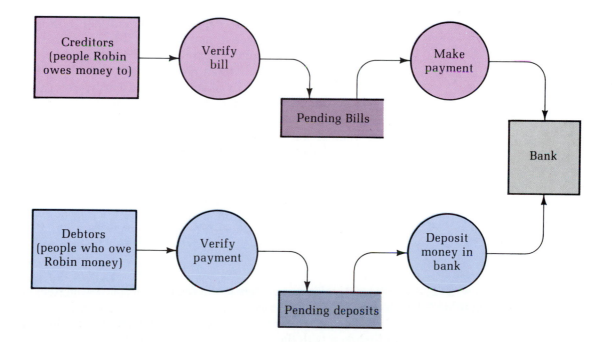

to Ed Wieland's cost estimate—under $2000—a computer would be a lot cheaper than an accounting service or hiring a part-time bookkeeper.

SYSTEM DESIGN

System design determines in general terms the way that a new system should be set up. Here too (as we saw in Chapter 15) there are different steps: logical design, physical design, test design, and the design review.

Logical design refers to creating a nonphysical conceptual design of the input, processing, output and feedback steps for the new system. For Robin's computer system the input data on bills and invoices would be the same as with her manual system, except that she would have to key the data in. Processing would involve simple bookkeeping calculations. Output would be the same invoices and checks as now. The feedback would be how well the new system met her goals. She wasn't sure if she needed a database to help support the system.

Physical design refers to determining what hardware and software are needed. The input and output media would remain the same—with no special designs required. Robin took a morning off to drive to the nearest sizable town and compare prices and systems in several computer stores. Then with price quotations and literature in hand, she returned home to think.

Eventually—after consulting by phone with Ed (who among other things said she didn't need a database)—she worked out her software requirements. Robin couldn't program and was not interested in learning how; her needs would be well served by a small prepackaged accounting program and a simple, inexpensive word-processing program that could produce bills and mailing labels.

Next Robin turned to hardware. She decided on a small microcomputer, floppy disk drive, monitor, and letter-quality printer. She chose a letter-quality printer because both she and Ed agreed that most customers of a handmade-crafts store would not be favorably impressed by bills and mailing labels that were obviously produced by a computer.

Following Ed's advice, Robin next inquired about the reliability of the vendors who made the kinds of software and hardware in which she was interested. Among other things, she wanted to know how much it would cost her, in time as well as money, to maintain her system. And she wanted to know whether she could expand her system later if she wanted to.

Once she had pinpointed the system she wanted, she developed a test design. A *test design* is a plan for the tests that a new system must pass in order to meet the user's approval. Robin decided to use some old accounts receivable, accounts payable, and mailing list data and see if the system could handle it right. In addition she put in some deliberate errors to see what the system would do.

SYSTEM DEVELOPMENT

System development refers to the creation of the new system based on the results of the design stage.

For Robin, developing her system was fairly simple. She drove to town and worked with the test data in the computer store where she planned to

Recently many jobs have sprung up that revolve around microcomputers. Here we interview two people working at such jobs. The first, Mark Shulman, is a microcomputer sales representative. The second, Mark Juliana, is a microcomputer technician. Both are employed by Computerland of Campbell, Calif.

MICROCOMPUTER SALES REPRESENTATIVE

Q: What is your age?
A. 23.
Q. What's your educational background?
A. Four-year degree in business-economics from the University of California at Santa Barbara (UCSB).
Q: How long have you worked in computer sales?
A: Four months, but I also had one year previous experience in sales.
Q: What type of training have you had?
A: I've had training classes through Apple, IBM, and other vendors, training from software vendors, and in-house training concerning software and sales.
Q: Who are your easiest customers?
A: Novices who are open to suggestions and help. I try to be nonintimidating—we hire salespeople who will not scare off customers. I try to support the clients.
Q: Who are your hardest customers?
A: People [programmers] who really know a great deal about computers. They can run circles around me on technical points and make me look silly. Often they need little support, and are simply shopping for the lowest price.
Q: What are the most important qualities for a computer salesperson?
A: 1. Energy. 2. Ability to make quick decisions concerning the product and pricing—often over the phone. 3. Ability to relax customers through the use of humor.
Q: What advice would you give someone considering computer sales?
A: 1. It is an exciting job. 2. You learn something new every day. 3. Unlike

with other jobs, the days seem to go fast. 4. The sales field is more competitive today. 5. There are opportunities for conducting training sessions, consulting, and doing outside sales.

MICROCOMPUTER TECHNICIAN

Q: What is your age?
A: 20.
Q: What's your educational background?
A: I'm currently studying electrical engineering at West Valley Junior College and I plan to complete a four-year degree at California State.
Q: What is your job title?
A: Technician.
Q: How long have you worked as a technician?
A: One year. I started out in shipping and receiving.
Q: What type of training have you had?
A: Vendors' schools—three-day sessions at Apple, IBM, and others. On-the-job training—observing and helping the other technician.
Q: Who are your easiest customers?
A: People in the service industry who understand that the customers are served on a first-come/first-served basis. If the client has a major problem we try to accommodate that client a little faster.
Q: Who are your hardest customers?
A: Customers at both ends of the scale. Novices who are lost in the terminology and need a simple explanation. People [engineers] who think they know everything and insist they tell you how and what component to test.
Q: What are the most important qualities for a computer technician?
A: Tolerance for both people and machines, and an ability to figure out how to repair or modify components on new products without the manufacturer's specifications.
Q: What advice would you give someone considering a career as a computer technician?
A: Get more formal training—digital theory, basic electronics.

place the order. Once she figured out how to use it, the system worked fine with her data, and it caught quite a few of the errors. She decided that her chosen system would meet her needs, and placed her order while she was at the store.

SYSTEM IMPLEMENTATION

When a system has been designed and developed, then it is ready for implementation. *System implementation* refers to the changeover from the old system to the new. Robin decided on parallel conversion, in which the old system (which was her manual one) and the new, computerized system run side by side over a period of time.

First she had to install the hardware in the back room of her shop. Upon unpacking the computer she found the first problem—it had a three-prong plug and the outlet she planned to use was designed for only two prongs. She thought of simply breaking off the third prong—the ground—as she had seen other people do, but phoned her brother Ed first. Ed was upset at the idea of not properly grounding the computer ("because static charges can mess up your data in the machine, and because you can get shocks"). Ed convinced her to hire an electrician to install a properly grounded outlet, and to buy a surge protector to safeguard the microcomputer and its data from the vicissitudes of Sandy Cove Village's power supply. Robin did these things—incurring some unexpected additional costs in the process—and then plugged in the computer.

The peripherals had to be connected to the computer, but she did this herself by following the instructions that came with the machine and gently hooked up the cables to their connections.

As far as security was concerned, she kept her back room locked. That was sufficient in Sandy Cove Village.

With the microcomputer up and running, Robin continued to process her accounts data by hand, but she also keyed them into the computer, and compared the results. All this was painfully frustrating at first—after all, her goal was to reduce the time she spent on paperwork and here she was spending more time at it than ever. Soon, however, the effort paid off. After a couple of weeks of checking every single bit of computer output, and finding that it was correct apart from some mistakes she traced back to her own errors, she switched over to the computer entirely. In the process she had trained herself to use the new system. She was sure she would get better, but she was a proficient beginner.

SYSTEM MAINTENANCE

The final stage of the system development process is system maintenance. *System maintenance* refers to the continuing process of keeping a system in good working order. With Robin's system up and running, she wanted to keep it functioning well. Certain rules had to be followed, such as making periodic backup copies of data and programs as a safeguard in case the originals were accidentally lost. Following her instruction manual, Robin cleaned the microcomputer and peripherals periodically. She also kept the system in a separate room well away from her studio to protect it from dust and the extremes of temperature that her kiln generated.

When she purchased the system, she paid a bit extra for a service contract to cover repairs during the first years of ownership. This particular contract required her to take the computer or faulty peripheral to the store herself. More expensive contracts would have brought a repairperson right to her shop. At the other extreme, having no service contract at all would have left her wondering what to do when the machine broke down. In fact the disk unit broke down several times, and the manufacturer eventually replaced it free of charge.

Having run through the complete system development process, we find Robin Wieland using a different information system at the end than she was at the beginning—and using it effectively. It is possible that this system, too, will eventually change. If her volume of business in Sandy Cove Village quadruples, for example, she might rent a larger shop and hire some employees. The computer system would then have to be modified to accommodate much more data as well as to handle payroll and employee deductions for taxes, social security, insurance, and so on. A good computer system can evolve as needs change. This is as true of a microcomputer as a mainframe. Robin might be able to accommodate new needs by buying new prepackaged software, and by buying new random-access memory (RAM) chips and a second floppy disk drive to expand the system's storage capacity for more data and software.

SELECTING YOUR INFORMATION SYSTEM

Now that we have worked through the system development process for buying, installing, and using a microcomputer, we will address selection criteria in more detail. This section offers a guide for selecting your own microcomputer. A number of checklists are included, to help you choose the right one.

We approach microcomputer selection from the standpoint of the five information-system elements: people, rules and procedures, data, software, and hardware. Naturally there is some overlap among the five categories. Also, you may turn out to have a need that is not covered by the checklists. This guide does not guarantee that you will create the perfect computer system to meet your goals, but it should provide a valuable aid toward creating such a system.

PEOPLE

When you own your own information system you take on three different roles: those of user, client, and information-system staff member. Other people may be involved, however. For example, if you are buying a microcomputer for home use, a number of people will probably use it. If you buy a microcomputer for a small business, you will not be the client, but your customers will.

Figure 18-4 is a checklist you might fill out to describe the user(s) of the information system. It addresses the background, needs, and training requirements of the user(s).

You should carefully explore the cost and quality of the training available. Robin Wieland had no computer experience and would benefit from fairly extensive basic training on how to use her machine. She would want to spend a minimum of time away from her shop going to distant training sessions, however, and would not be able to afford to pay much for training. Her needs would probably be best addressed by taking the basic course offered free by the computer store where she bought the system, and

Characteristics of the Users

Number of users: _____

   Adult/College: _____   Teenage: _____

   Preteen _____   Child _____

Skills of the users (e.g., accounting, clerical, engineering):

   First user: _____

   Second user: _____

   Third user: _____

   Other users: _____

Needs of users: _____

_____

Training Requirements

Type of training:	First User	Second User	Third User	Other User
General:				
Task specific:				
"Hands-on":				
Advanced training:				

Computer Operations

Training: _____

Length of training: _____

Cost of the training sessions: _____

Time of the training sessions: _____

Location of the training sessions: _____

Discounts for several users: _____

Refund conditions: _____

teaching herself the rest back in her shop with the documentation provided.

Someone who already knew something about computers would probably shop around for training that would show how to exploit the computer in more sophisticated ways. It is not necessary to be trained by the same company from which you buy a computer. Local adult education programs are also offered through universities, junior colleges, and high schools.

If other people will use the computer, such as family members or business associates, then they should also be trained on how to use and care for the computer. Once the user(s) have gained basic knowledge of the system, they can upgrade their skills with more advanced courses. In addition various user groups exist in many localities. By attending a meeting or two and making contacts, you can trade experiences with other people who use the same system.

RULES AND PROCEDURES

The application of rules and procedures calls for some diplomacy if you are allowing other people to use your computer. Good rules and procedures should assist users in the proper operation of the information system, and deter improper operation. The rules should be explained to people in a manner that they can understand. For example, instead of telling a small child to respect the integrity of the secondary storage media, it is better to tell the child not to get peanut butter on the floppy disks.

Figure 18-5 gives a checklist for developing rules and procedures. First develop the standard rules, and then work out the exceptions. If a system has more than one user, then the users should work out the rules coopera-

FIGURE 18-5.

A checklist for rules and procedures.

Standard rules regarding who may use the computer and under what conditions:

_____

_____

_____

Exceptional rules: _____

_____

_____

Who makes the rules (primary user? all users?): _____

_____

Backup of data and programs: _____

Storage of data and programs: _____

Privacy of the database, files, or programs: _____

_____

Use of external databases: _____

_____

Protection: _____ Alarm system: _____

Keys to the CPU: _____

Off-site storage of programs and files: _____

tively rather than have one person dictate what the rules will be. The security considerations toward the end of the checklist bear attention. Some systems allow you physically to lock up the computer from unauthorized users, much as you can secure telephones or automobiles.

DATA Figure 18-6 is a checklist to help you determine the data that you require. You begin with the types of output reports, forms, and display screens that

FIGURE 18-6.
A checklist to determine data requirements.

Types of Printed Output

Total number of different documents: _____

	General Features		Special Characteristics	
	Length (range)	Number of copies	Format	Print Style
Document #1:				
Document #2:				
Document #3:				
Document #4:				

Number of forms: _____

	General Features		Special Characteristics	
	Length (range)	Number of copies	Format	Print Style
Form #1:				
Form #2:				
Form #3:				
Form #4:				

Number of labels: _____

	General Features		Special Characteristics	
	Length (range)	Number of copies	Format	Print Style
Label #1:				
Label #2:				
Label #3:				
Label #4:				

Displayed Output

Number of different displays: _____

	General Features	Special Characteristics	
	Size	Graphics Format	Print Style

Display #1: _____

Display #2: _____

Display #3: _____

Display #4: _____

Database or Files Required to Support the Output Documents, Forms, and Display

	Maximum Number of Records	Length of Records	Type of Data (alphabetic, numeric, both)

File #1: _____

File #2: _____

File #3: _____

File #4: _____

Data Sources for the Files

	Entered by User		Received from Data	
	Level of Automation		Communications Link	
	Low	High	Internal	External

File #1: _____

File #2: _____

File #3: _____

File #4: _____

Special data communication requirements (e.g., security): _____

_____

Other data requirements:

_____

you will need from your information system. Then you work back to the data that will be necessary to create the output. You may need more space than this checklist provides.

At several points in this book we have said that data are a valuable resource. Microcomputer users often lose this resource through carelessness. The remedy: regularly make backup copies of your data and your software. Then if something goes wrong, you are not back to square one. Unfortunately most people seem to have to learn this lesson first hand, as when a crucial file on a diskette no longer can be read due to damage to the disk surface.

Creating backup files includes the responsibility of deleting files from time to time that are no longer needed since more recent backup copies have been created. Deleting unneeded files clears space for more data to be stored.

SOFTWARE

Software can represent a considerable expense to someone setting up a personal computer system. You must determine what you want the information system to do, so that you can translate this into the programs that will be needed. And in general you should select your software before you select your hardware.

You may want to read the reviews of competing software packages printed in the various microcomputer magazines. You should also keep a close watch on offers by computer stores to throw in some software packages free with purchase of a computer; if the packages in fact meet your requirements, and the price of the computer is competitive, you may reduce much of the software cost. The main types of packaged software available today are described in Chapter 12.

FIGURE 18-7.
A checklist to assess software needs.

	Operating System	Program Language #1	Program Language #2	Program Language #3	Other System Software
Purpose:					
Hardware:					
Hardware modification:					
Service:					
Classes:					
Tutorial:					
Documentation:					
Cost:					
Upgrades:					
Backup:					

System Software

Business Application Programs

	Business Function #1	Business Function #2	Business Function #3	Business Function #4
Purpose:				
Hardware:				
Hardware modification:				
Service:				
Classes:				
Tutorial:				
Documentation:				
Cost:				
Upgrades:				
Backup:				

Nonbusiness Application Programs

	Word Process.	Communi- cations	Graphics	Educa- tional	Games
Purpose:					
Hardware:					
Hardware modification:					
Service:					
Classes:					
Tutorial:					
Documentation:					
Cost:					
Upgrades:					
Backup:					

Figure 18-7 gives a checklist of factors you should consider in selecting microcomputer software. System software, business application programs, and nonbusiness application programs are each classified according to ten factors. (These are, incidentally, the same ten points given in "Selecting Packaged Software" in Chapter 12.) Let's go over the list.

Purpose refers to what the program does. You should determine what tasks the program performs, and what tasks it does not perform. The program selected should meet your needs. Overkill is a consideration here. You may be impressed by the power of a software package that handles complex databases, electronic spreadsheets, and word processing, when all you need is a program to help you type reports. Buying the all-in-one master package may cost you a lot of money for features that you will never use.

At the same time you should be sure a package does *everything* you have been led to expect it will. For example, if you want to buy a word-processing package to help you write a textbook on, let's say, information systems, and you expect to be working with chapters of about 30 pages, double-spaced, you will be sorely disappointed if you buy a package that can only handle ten-page documents.

Hardware refers to the machine requirements for running the program. Some programs will only run on a computer that uses a particular microprocessor chip; if the computer you are considering buying does not use the right microprocessor, then you can't run the program. Other programs may require more storage than a given machine has, or different peripherals.

Hardware modification may be needed to bring a machine up to the level needed to run a particular program. For example, random access memory (RAM) may have to be added, the board controlling printer options changed, or an additional disk drive purchased.

Service refers to what happens when the software doesn't work. Some software vendors provide a toll-free number to call if the program fails to operate properly. Additionally, the retailer from whom you buy the software may provide a troubleshooting service. To help the troubleshooter, be sure to explain carefully what happened, and be prepared to provide printed output that shows the problem if necessary. In addition to troubleshooting help, a warranty may accompany the software. Depending on the warranty and the state in which you purchased the software, you may be entitled to reimbursement if the package simply doesn't work.

Classes are often available to explain the most popular software packages; these are offered by computer stores, software manufacturers themselves, and some adult education programs. A good class should provide a terminal for each user and stress practical "hands-on" training. Besides classes, books are available that describe the major software packages. Often the same place that sells the software will sell the books that can help people use it. Regular bookstores also maintain an impressive array of books on specific software products; sometimes they sell the software, too.

Tutorial refers to a training or tutorial program that accompanies the software. Most of the better software for business applications comes with a built-in tutorial. Usually this is provided on the same floppy disk, or on the same read-only memory (ROM) chip, as the software itself. With a tutorial you can learn to use the program at your own pace. In addition to finding out if a program has a tutorial, you should ascertain whether or not the program has "help" routines within the main body of the program to assist you if you get stuck.

Documentation is supplied with the program, and can vary in quality. Good documentation can teach you how to use a program and also serve as a reference to answer your questions as you go along. Inadequate documentation, however, will be useless. Ask to see a copy of the documentation that accompanies the program of interest.

Cost is the bottom line. To be considered here is the initial cost of the software as well as associated costs, such as the need for hardware modification and for training users. The cheapest software package is not necessarily the one to purchase: often in the computer field you do get what you pay for. Inexpensive software may have been marked down because of deficiencies as compared with the more expensive competing packages. On the other side of the coin, some software is "free"—thrown in with hardware to attract buyers. Provided the hardware itself is reasonably priced and the software packages are good ones, this can be a real bargain.

Another potential bargain is "public domain" software—software available free to anyone who wants to use it. Public domain software can be found in listings in journals, from user groups and clubs, and from various teleprocessing services. Occasionally you can find high-quality software of this type. It is also possible to get software with little or no documentation that works poorly, if at all.

Upgrades refer to the possibility of changing the program to meet additional or expanded needs. Some vendors allow you to trade in their old software package for upgraded versions. In other instances you will have to pay for an upgraded version, or for options or additional parts that you would like to add to a software package.

Backup copies of the software protect you in case the original copy is damaged or lost. Some software vendors permit you to make copies of the original. Other vendors discourage this, since it leads to piracy of their program; they provide you with an original and a backup copy, and design both to prevent their being easily copied. Software that cannot be copied and is not accompanied by a backup copy should not be purchased.

HARDWARE

The hardware for your microcomputer system consists of the central processing unit and peripheral units for input, output, secondary storage, and telecommunications. Your goal is to select the combination of hardware that best serves your needs. As with software, you may not need the most sophisticated and expensive equipment available. Ask yourself the following questions:

- *Can the hardware process the amount and type of data I require in a reasonable period of time?*
- *Is the hardware within my budget? Consider maintenance expenses as well as the initial cost.*
- *Can the hardware run the software needed to perform my work?*
- *Is the hardware have sufficiently flexibile to meet my expansion needs?*

Microcomputers come in a bewildering variety of types. Trying to gain a picture of which is best for you is complicated by the fact that manufacturers come and go, model lines change, and prices continue to fall. In addition waiting another month or two always holds the promise of new technological developments reaching the marketplace. Nevertheless we offer a checklist (Figure 18-8) to help you keep your bearings. The checklist is divided into sections on the central processing unit, input units, output units, secondary storage units, communications hardware, and physical facilities for the computer system. Let's examine each area in turn.

FIGURE 18-8.

A checklist to assess hardware needs.

Component/Feature	Cost/Description

Central Processing Unit
Type of microprocessor: _____
Random access memory (existing): _____
Random access memory (potential): _____
Types of software on ROM: _____
Size of central processor: _____
Room for expansion of RAM and ROM: _____
Ease of attaching peripherals: _____
Number of peripherals you can attach: _____
Nonportable or portable system? _____
All-weather use? _____
Regular current/batteries? _____
How many people can use the computer at the same time? _____
Type of operating system(s)?: _____
Can it run your programs? _____
Quality of support materials: _____
Maintenance agreement: _____
On-site servicing: _____
Warranty agreement: _____

Input Units
Keyboard: _____
Numeric keypad: _____
Special input needs:
  Optical scanning: _____
  Magnetic scanning: _____
  Graphics: _____
  Mouse: _____
  Voice: _____
  Other: _____

Output Units
Low-quality printer: _____
General-purpose printer: _____
Letter-quality printer: _____
Typeset-quality printer: _____
Graphics printer: _____
Multicolor graphics plotter/printer: _____
Other: _____

Display Terminals
Overall size (diagonal): _____
Monochrome terminal: _____
Screen color (e.g. green on black): _____
Resolution: _____
Graphics: _____
Color terminal: _____
  Number of colors: _____
  Resolution: _____
Capacity for additional monitors: _____

Secondary Storage Units
Cassette tape drive: _____
Reel-to-reel tape drive: _____
Floppy disk system: _____
Single drive: _____
Dual drive: _____

Hard disk system: _____
Number of megabytes required: _____
Optical or video disk: _____
Other: _____

Communications Hardware
Asynchronous: _____
Synchronous: _____
Modem: _____
Telephone line: _____
Local area network: _____

Physical Facilities for the Computer System
Floor space required: _____
Type of desk or table: _____
Proper lighting: _____
Comfortable chair: _____
Type of electrical plugs: _____
Properly grounded?: _____
Space to store supplies: _____
Space to shelve manuals, software, and books: _____
Location for backup disks or tapes: _____
Space to store output: _____
Security alarm system: _____
Uninterruptable power supply: _____
Surge protector: _____
Fire extinguisher: _____
Safe for storing important programs, data and forms: _____

Central processing unit

The microcomputer itself deserves careful consideration from several perspectives. First of all, the microprocessor chip should be one that supports the operating system, other system programs, and application programs that you plan to run.

Another important aspect of the microprocessor is its capacity and speed. Microprocessors today handle 8-, 16-, or 32-bit words. (The earliest microcomputers were 8-bit-word machines, the latest are 32-bit-word machines.) The greater the word size, the more memory the microprocessor can address and the faster it can process data. Under ideal conditions a 16-bit processor will execute instructions two or three times faster than an 8-bit processor. Input/output operations, however, reduce the speed difference to about two times. In addition poorly designed software can eliminate the advantage of the larger-capacity microprocessor almost entirely. Before you run out and buy the latest 32-bit microcomputer, however, consider whether or not you really need the extra speed and capacity.

The amount of *random access memory* (*RAM*) that the computer contains should be adequate to cover your software requirements. Consider too, however, the amount of random access memory that can be added on to the computer to cover future expansion. Also, note the types of software available on *read-only memory* (*ROM*) chips (often called firmware). (For a refresher on the characteristics of these chips, see the sections "Random Access Memory Chips" and "Read-Only Memory Chips" in Chapter 5.)

The steady march of personal computers into the workplace often degenerates into an uncontrollable stampede. Well-laid plans . . . to instill computing harmony within an organization are thrown into chaos by departmental managers who purchase micros that are incompatible with the corporate standard. . . .

Controlling the influx of personal computers into the office requires creative solutions. One such solution being embraced by several organizations is the installation of in-house microcomputer centers. Such centers serve as surrogate retail stores for corporate employees. Employees purchase personal-computer equipment through the centers, billing purchases to their departments.

The personal-computer center offers much more than one-step shopping convenience for an employee in the market for an office micro. Novices can rely on the in-house center's resident experts to configure the right personal-computer system and to provide on-going training and product support. Departments can reduce the costs of their computer purchases because in-house stores offer better prices than outside vendors. Most importantly, an in-house center provides management with a medium for coordinating the flow of micros into the office so that compatibility rather than chaos reigns.

"We view our store as a nice way to help initiate the uninitiated to the computer while promoting certain equipment in a friendly and nondictatorial way," says Ricci Anderson, vice president of technical strategies at Chase Manhattan Bank in New York City. Chase Manhattan has had an in-house micro store since January 1983. . . .

The in-house computer store at American Hoechst Corp., the large chemical and pharmaceutical producer based in Somerville, NJ, is an extension of the corporation's information center. The store contains about a half dozen micro-equipped workstations and is run by a seven-member staff. . . .

The American Hoechst computer store offers a variety of personal computers, including models from IBM, Hewlett-Packard Co., Apple Computer Inc., and Compaq Computer Corp. All offerings in the store have one thing in common—they can communicate with the corporate mainframes. . . .

Another major advantage offered by in-house computer centers, the simplification and streamlining of purchasing procedures, was key to the federal government's decision to set up its own network of computer stores. The prototype Office Technology Plus (OTP) center, located in the General Services Administration (GSA) building in Washington, has been operating since August 1983.

OTP is an in-house store with a twist. The stores are staffed and operated not by government employees, but by an outside retailer. Math Box Inc., a personal-computer retailer based in Rockville, MD, won the contract to operate OTP outlets, bidding against a half dozen other outfits. . . .

In addition to simplifying and streamlining equipment purchases, OTP provides support to users each step of the way. First, OTP provides an educational center for inexperienced users. OTP conducts seminars to introduce new users to applications like word processing, spreadsheets, electronic mail, and database management. Second, OTP gives inexperienced users assistance in selecting the appropriate system and getting it set up. Finally, OTP offers support after purchase.

Source: Timothy Bay, "MIS/DP Takes the Retail Route," *Computer Decisions,* March 12, 1985. Copyright © 1985 Hayden Publishing Company.

The central processing unit should have ports (sockets) capable of connecting the cables for attaching peripherals to the computer. Many microcomputers contain ports for standard peripherals such as a keyboard, display screen, and printer, and expansion slots to accept additional devices of the same or different types. With some microcomputers one or more peripheral devices are already built into the microcomputer cabinet.

You should consider the form of the computer itself. Some are extremely compact and portable, some can run on batteries, and some can even be used outdoors in the rain. Consider your real needs. Do you really intend to program in a rainstorm? If you do not plan to carry the computer about, it probably doesn't matter whether it weighs eight pounds or 40 pounds, and the 40-pounder may sit more stably on a desk. Portability may also mean a display screen too small to be read comfortably for long periods of time.

Although the great bulk of personal computers are used by only one person at a time, some machines can support more than one user simultaneously. If your information system will require more than one user at a time, you should find out if the computer supports this requirement.

The operating system that runs on a particular microcomputer is designed to run on the brand of microprocessor chip that the computer employs. The same tends to be true of application programs. Make sure that the computer you are considering uses the right chip for the programs you are planning to use.

As with software, you will want to look at the quality of the documentation provided by the manufacturer. Most microcomputers provide a tutorial diskette to introduce you to the system. Maintenance agreements should be investigated prior to purchase: they range all the way from the no-maintenance situation, common with home computer users—in which you take any faulty component into a shop and pay to have it fixed yourself—to complete on-site servicing agreements. A key differential between maintenance agreements is price. Warranties generally cover the hardware against manufacturing defects for a limited period of time. Although warranties vary from contract to contract and from one state to another, people generally receive less of a warranty than they think they do. For example, your warranty may indeed cover a defective circuit board in the central processing unit. But you may have to pay the shipping expenses to convey the computer to the shop—possibly the labor costs there as well—and will be without a computer for an indeterminate length of time until yours is fixed.

Input units

The chief input unit on microcomputers is the keyboard. You should make sure that the keyboard for your machine is comfortable to the touch and easy to use. You can determine this by trying out the machine in a computer store. While most keyboards use the sturdy, cubelike keys found on an electronic typewriter, some use "keyboards" consisting of a flat plastic panel or membrane with touch-sensitive areas designated as "keys." Keyboards also differ in the space between keys and the contour of the keys, both of which can affect how well you type. Some machines offer a choice of keyboards. In addition some keyboards are built into the microcomputer, and others can be positioned where the user wishes, up to a certain distance from the microcomputer.

If an otherwise satisfactory computer offers only one keyboard, and you do not find it personally convenient to use, then that may be sufficient reason to reject the computer.

If you will be entering a lot of numeric data, a *numeric keypad* would be handy. This is a closely grouped set of keys used only for entering numbers. Usually a numerical keypad is located at one side of the keyboard. Function keys are also grouped at the side of many keyboards (such as that shown in Figure 6-5). A *function key* enters a program command with a single keystroke, so you don't have to type out the whole command. For example, a function key can return the program to the main menu, advance to the end of a file, or change the format of a document to be output. Not all keyboards contain function keys, and keyboards that do differ in how many they contain.

The other input device frequently used is an *electronic mouse*, which is a palm-sized device that can be rolled on wheels or ball bearings over a surface in order to move a pointer on the display screen, or to input graphical data such as a diagram that the mouse is passed over. Additional devices available include optical scanners, magnetic scanners, graphics tablets or digitizers, light pens, and voice input. These devices, suitable for more specialized applications, are described in Chapter 6.

Output units

The main output devices used by microcomputers are printers and display screens. The basic "starter" system offered by many computer manufacturers does not include a printer, and many home computer users have no printer. You should seriously consider buying one, however, even if your use of a microcomputer—such as running educational programs, doing spreadsheet analysis, or playing games—does not strictly require one. Even for such uses, there are times when it would be handy to print a copy of a display screen, list a program, or create a hard copy of other information.

Printers cost from about $200 on up, and use most of the technologies described in Chapter 6 (in the section "Toward Friendlier Output"). Dot-matrix printers are common for fast output of medium quality; letter-quality printers employing daisy wheels are frequently used for reports that must look typed. On our checklist we have simply listed four quality gradations. Some printers can also handle graphics, in one or more colors. In addition some printers function as plotters.

Like printers, display screens come in a great variety of types and styles. Prices begin at about $100. Display screens employ any of the screen technologies described in Chapter 6 (in the "Screen Technologies" section), and may be either separate or built into the microcomputer unit. Microcomputers can also be connected by means of a small adapter to your television set so you can use it as a display screen. The quality of the display, however, is usually lower than with a display screen designed for the purpose. Because of the poor quality of the image they provide, televison sets are not recommended for word processing or other close work.

You should consider the size of the display. A small screen may be adequate for occasional use, and a larger screen easier on the eyes for frequent use. A basic distinction is between a monocolor screen and a color screen. Monocolor screens display text in a single color such as green or amber. Color screens offer more visual possibilities. "Resolution" refers to the quality of the image: a display screen with good resolution offers a crisp image, and a display screen with poor resolution gives a blurry image. Finally, some display screens can display graphics, and some cannot.

As with other types of hardware, a good way to tell whether or not you like a particular display screen is to go to a computer store or some other location that uses that kind of screen, sit down, and try it out. If after half an hour of typing your eyes are more colorful than the screen, maybe you should choose another.

Secondary storage units

Remember, microcomputers follow the same basic principles as other computers. This means that main memory can hold only the software and data that are currently being processed. Data files, databases, and programs not currently in use must be contained on secondary storage.

Magnetic disk units for either floppy disks or hard disks, magnetic tape units for cassettes or of the reel-to-reel type, and optical disks are all presently available for secondary storage use by microcomputers. Chapter 7 describes these devices in depth.

When you investigate the purchase of a secondary storage device, consider three factors: capacity, price, and speed. All of these factors increase together. The great speed and storage capacity offered by an optical disk system, for example, carries a high price tag that the average microcomputer user of today cannot afford. Hard disk systems, on the other hand, are now becoming commonplace, when only a few years ago they were a luxurious rarity. Magnetic tape as a secondary storage medium for microcomputers is very slow and should, as a rule of thumb, be avoided. In other words, you will probably end up with one or more floppy disk drives and/or a hard disk.

If the amount of secondary storage available on the device(s) you choose is adequate to store the largest program and the largest files that you will use at a given time (plus an expansion factor of say 50 percent), then you will be spared the inconvenience of repeatedly changing disks or tapes to reach different parts of the program or files. A number of software packages are supplied, however, on multiple diskettes. If you have a hard disk system or an optical disk system (and a floppy disk unit to read the program), you can copy the multidisk program onto your single permanent disk.

Communications hardware

In Chapter 8 we discussed teleprocessing. There is good reason to use your microcomputer for teleprocessing. For starters, value-added networks (VANs) such as Tymnet and Telenet exist, which offer you and your microcomputer the ability to send messages and data throughout the network, to read and post items on electronic bulletin boards, to retrieve data from large databases, and to perform processing using host computers that are much larger than your own. The charges for such services are not astronomical. For more information see "Communications, Data, and Computing Power for Sale" in Chapter 8.

Microcomputers used for a small business might also be hooked up to advantage. For example, one computer in each branch of a store might be linked together, in one of the network configurations described in Chapter 8.

To telecommunicate over telephone lines, you need a modem. Some microcomputers have a modem built in; most offer modems as attachments. Considerations here are whether your computer uses asynchronous or synchronous data transmission; this should match the mode used by the other computers or devices with which you want to communicate. Consider, too, the type and cost of the different telephone or communications carriers available. Computers telecommunicating over a short distance might be economically connected using a local area network.

Physical facilities for the computer system

Last but not least, you need to consider where you will put the computer and what facilities—ranging from the chair you sit in to security provisions—will be needed. Don't wait until the packing crates show up—plan first! (See Figure 18-9.)

Figure 18-8 lists a number of considerations worth running through. To begin, you need to consider where you will put the computer, how much space it needs, and the type of lighting and chair needed. The computer and peripherals will require a properly grounded (three-prong) electrical outlet. If your apartment, home, or office does not have one, rewiring may be necessary. If you already have a grounded outlet, buy a plug tester and check the outlet to make certain it is correctly grounded; sometimes they are not. If in doubt, hire an electrician. An antistatic device hooked to the ground wires can reduce the risk of damage to your system.

You should plan for space to store supplies such as computer paper, manuals, and disks or tapes. Although a home computer for family use will probably not require any security arrangements beyond those taken for the other contents of the house or apartment, a microcomputer used for a small business or in the office will. You should find a cabinet or area that can be locked for output and for important blank forms such as checks. The alarm system, locks, or other equipment necessary to provide an appropriate level of security should be priced and compared (security measures are described in the "Physical Security Measures" section of Chapter 17). A surge protector can protect your equipment against fluctuations in voltage and can help safeguard against the loss of data. Finally, even for a home computer, you should have a fire extinguisher (Halon type) for putting out electrical fires.

If you have taken the trouble to consider each of the information-system elements we have described, and filled out all of the checklists, then you are in a position to purchase a microcomputer intelligently. You can shop for computers, and evaluate their respective merits and shortcomings, with confidence.

FIGURE 18-9.
Don't wait until the boxes arrive to decide where to put your new information system. If you don't have a comfortable working environment, you may find you won't be using the system as much as you planned.

WRAP-UP	A FALL OF LEISURE

In the secluded quiet of her potter's workshop/office/computer center, Robin Wieland leaned back and put her feet up. Her computerized information system had been up and running six months now. The busy season was well past: it was midautumn.

Despite the time it had taken to learn how to use the machine properly, and to get the results she wanted with her accounts receivable and accounts payable program, the computer had made the summer much more bearable. It had actually kept her up to date with paperwork—even in the middle of the summer crunch. It had freed her to make more of the ceramics that the summer people were buying, during hours when the shop was closed.

Now in the autumn, she ran accounts receivable once a week, and accounts payable twice a month. Especially with the accounts payable part of the program, she had saved a fair amount of money by paying her suppliers early and qualifying for discounts lost in the past to her poor organization.

It was evening now and Robin was about to leave. She looked around her back room contentedly. In retrospect she supposed she had made some mistakes with her computerization process. She was happy with the machine itself. But she should have taken more formal training instead of running up a big phone bill to her brother. Also, she wished she'd bought a monitor that was easier on the eyes.

And she should have bought a second floppy disk drive, if only to make it easier to prepare backup copies of her files.

As someone fascinated with the properties of materials, she had also learned that floppy disks are very definitely made of plastic. She had placed one on a shelf too near her kiln, without thinking, and came back half an hour later to find a stalactite in a cardboard envelope. Stranger still, after it cooled she painted it with poster paint and sold it for $25 as an information-age sculpture. Unfortunately it had contained some of her files.

She smiled remembering, as she shut off the lights in her shop and locked the front door. She hopped on her bicycle and headed down Main Street to the only other light in sight, Sandy Cove Village's largest art gallery. Due mainly to Robin's experience, the gallery owner had decided to take the plunge and become the second computer user in the village. Robin had promised to stop by for a few minutes to help him prepare a checklist to take along to the computer store. . . .

SUMMARY

- *Using the personal information system that you already have, you make decisions every day, based upon data that you receive and process into information. If this manual personal information system works just fine, then you don't need a computer. If there is a problem or unrealized opportunity, however, then you may. You can either investigate, purchase, and set up a computerized information system yourself, or hire a reliable consultant to do the work for you.*

- *A useful approach to shopping for a computer is to follow the system development process. Problem recognition—recognizing a need or opportunity that a microcomputer could address—is the first stage of this process. Systems analysis, or the systematic examination of how the present system works, comes next. The third stage, system design, determines in general terms the way that a new system should be set up. If the potential user decides to go ahead, system development follows; microcomputer users usually skip this stage, however, by purchasing prepackaged software. System implementation refers to the changeover from the old system to the new. The final stage of the system development process, system maintenance, keeps a system that is up and running in good working order.*

- *Choosing microcomputer hardware and software can be approached from the standpoint of the five information-system elements.*

- *Concerning people, the background, needs, and training requirements of the user(s) should be considered.*

- *Rules and procedures, including security procedures, should be developed diplomatically but responsibly.*

- *Data needs can be determined by beginning with the types of output reports, forms, and display screens that you will need from your information system, and working back to the data necessary to create the output.*

- **Software** *can represent a considerable expense to someone setting up a computer system, and should be evaluated carefully to see that it meets your needs and will perform as expected.*
- **Hardware,** *the most visible part of a computer system, consists of a central processing unit and peripheral units for input, output, secondary storage, and telecommunications. Here, too, among the great variety of devices on the market, your goal is to select the combination of hardware components that best serves your real needs.*

KEY TERMS

Terms in the chapter may be found in the glossary.

OBJECTIVE QUESTIONS

TRUE/FALSE: *Put the letter T or F on the line before the question.*

1. The first step in the system development process is problem recognition.
2. Rules and procedures are not a consideration in selecting a microcomputer for your personal information system.
3. There is no reason to hire a consultant to assist you in selecting a computer.
4. Software is a major expense in creating a microcomputer-based information system.
5. Hardware considerations have an effect on the software you select.
6. Backing up files is not needed with today's microcomputers.
7. System maintenance includes upgrading your system to meet changing needs.
8. System design starts with selecting the personal computer you want.
9. Hardware should be selected independently of the other system components.
10. System development for microcomputers requires writing a large number of application programs.

MULTIPLE CHOICE: *Put the letter of the correct answer on the line before the question.*

1. Liddy Gate has a new law practice specializing in bankruptcy. Her information needs concern monitoring clients cases and performing legal research. She has recently noticed that some clients are not paying their bills on time. In what stage in the system development process is she?
   - **(a)** System development.
   - **(b)** Systems analysis.
   - **(c)** System implementation.
   - **(d)** Problem recognition.

2. Harry Hopeful, president of the local Look-at-the-Bright-Side-Club, is depressed. His organization's files have become hopelessly out of date. What area of his information system should he look at first?
   - **(a)** Hardware.
   - **(b)** Software.
   - **(c)** Rules and procedures.
   - **(d)** Data.

3. The term "RAM" is usually associated with the
   - **(a)** central processing unit.
   - **(b)** input/output units.
   - **(c)** secondary storage units.
   - **(d)** communications units.

4. Perl Woolsey runs a knit shop down at the local shopping mall. She uses a computer program, "Jacquard," to help customers design their own custom color patterns. What peripheral would probably be most important to her for this program?
   - **(a)** Letter-quality printer.
   - **(b)** Color display screen.
   - **(c)** Cassette drive.
   - **(d)** Numeric keypad.

5. Sally and Edward True run a court recording service out of their mother's home. What printer would give the least desirable output for their business?
   - **(a)** Dot-matrix printer.
   - **(b)** Laser printer.
   - **(c)** Ink-jet printer.
   - **(d)** Daisy-wheel printer.

FILL IN THE BLANK: *Write the word or words in the blank to complete the sentence.*

1. A _____ is a training program to help users master a software package or piece of hardware.
2. User _____ tells how to use a particular software package or piece of equipment.
3. Printers, display terminals, and audio units are examples of _____.

4. Software packages can be written onto _____ chips.
5. A microcomputer _____ can help you at various stages of the system development process.
6. The _____ states the conditions under which a vendor will repair or replace a defective hardware or software element.
7. An important rule—often learned by painful experience—is always to _____.
8. Keyboards, joysticks, and numeric keypads are examples of _____.
9. A modem is an example of a _____.
10. Many universities, adult education programs, and computer stores offer _____ to help train users.

SHORT ANSWER QUESTIONS

When answering these questions think of concrete examples to illustrate your points.

1. What is accomplished during the systems analysis stage?
2. At what stage of the system development cycle do you go shopping for the computer?
3. What does this phrase mean? "It has 512K RAM, dual floppies, color graphics card, and built-in modem."
4. What is the difference between ROM and RAM memory?
5. At what point in the system development process do you consider the types of output you need?
6. Can you negotiate over the warranty, sale price, and payment terms for a microcomputer system?
7. Can you think of some information system tasks that do not require a computer?
8. Why is it important to back up your data?

ESSAY QUESTIONS

1. What are your information system needs?
2. Consider the tables displayed in Figures 18-3 to 18-7. Fill them out given your own personal information system needs. (Note: not every topic listed need apply to you).
3. Does everyone need a personal microcomputer? Defend your answer.

PART FIVE

We come to the closing section of this textbook. In Part Four we explored information systems in detail. Where do we go from here? In Chapter 19 we examine the options and prospects for careers in information systems. Chapter 20 presents some of the present and anticipated impacts of computers on our lives.

CAREERS IN INFORMATION SYSTEMS: PROSPECTS AND OPTIONS

After studying this chapter you should understand the following:

■ That a wide range of jobs is available working with information systems.
■ What types of employers offer these jobs.
■ The options available for obtaining education in information systems.
■ The importance of experience.
■ How to prepare a resume and portfolio, and how to be effective in an interview.
■ That information-systems jobs are structured into a career hierarchy.

Ed Wieland unlocked the door to his private office, turned on the lights, and was confronted by the papers strewn across his desk from work he hadn't been able to finish last night. Today was Ed's 28th birthday. He sat down at his desk, but instead of getting right back to work, he asked himself a hard question: Was he where he wanted to be at age 28? A systems analyst at Paul's House of Electronic Wonders?

When Ed first got out of school six years ago, this job would have seemed like a dream come true. Although a graduate of the four-year information systems program at Oakriver University, with top grades and several instructors who would serve as enthusiastic references, Ed found that it wasn't easy to get a job at all. The newspapers were full of want ads for programmers and systems analysts, but they all wanted experience. Fresh out of college, that was the one thing that he didn't have.

Ed sent out about 50 resumes to firms with information systems in his geographical area. The cover letter to each company alluded briefly to his qualifications, and did not mention that he had no experience. The resume made that plain enough by omitting it; the resume described in detail the courses he'd taken at OU, named his degree, and gave the instructor-references.

Ed was pleased to get four positive responses from employers, asking him to come in for an interview. He prepared a portfolio of programs he had written and debugged in school, and took it with him to the interviews. Three of the employers asked him to take a written technical test. Two of the employers offered him a job. Ed took the more interesting.

That first job had been as a programmer-trainee for a small testing-meter manufacturer. The "trainee" part of his title meant that his employment was conditional on his reaching a certain level of proficiency in the first six months. Ed's on-the-job "training" consisted of a foot-high pile of manuals describing the system, and a flowchart for a program that he was supposed to have running in three weeks.

In his first year at the meter company, Ed never wrote anything more exciting than a payroll program. The computer center staff was small. There was only one systems analyst, who, Ed reflected, was not likely to die soon, and Ed felt his chances for advancement were very limited. He got a small raise after the first six months and a larger one after a year. But he turned to the want ads again anyway.

And this time what a difference! He not only had a first-rate college degree, but a year of experience! Many of those jobs that had been closed to him before were open now. Ed had the pick of the field for jobs that required one year of experience as application programmer in COBOL.

Ed chose Paul's House of Electronic Wonders. The staff at Paul's was large enough to include many different types of specialists. Ed wanted to use databases, work on time-sharing rather than batch applications, and be promoted to systems analyst.

Ed was hired by Paul's as an associate analyst, at a substantial increase over his salary at the meter company. The title alone kept Ed pleased for about a year. Soon after he was promoted to systems analyst. And since then he had worked on a variety of different projects. His technical abilities as well as his skills in interacting with people were respected within the information-processing center as well as throughout the firm. Ed had been the group leader of small teams for several system development projects. He and Mr. Paul were friends. Ed earned twice as much now as he had when he left school.

But here he was, 28 years old! He had worked in the computer field for a total of six years, five of them at Paul's. Most of the major projects at Paul's were up and running, and as far as Ed could see, a long maintenance phase was in store. Technically, he didn't see a great deal of challenge in the near future.

Ed liked working with people, and despite the headaches had enjoyed his role as group leader. The management positions at Paul's, however, were all fairly "heavy" in terms of the experience they required—and they were also occupied. Maybe it was time for a move.

Ed dug deep in his bottom desk drawer, to see if he could find an old resume. . . .

INFORMATION-SYSTEMS PERSONNEL

In the Career Boxes throughout this book, we have described various job opportunities in working with information systems. Most of these jobs are available within business and government agencies that use information systems. Nonprofit organizations, such as universities, foundations, and hospitals, also offer the same positions, as do firms within the computer industry itself—hardware manufacturers, software houses, and support and training companies. All in all, there aren't too many larger organizations of any type today that do not use a computer. Major museums, such as the Metropolitan Museum of Art in New York, maintain complete information-processing centers and offer the same types of positions. Ocean-going research ships hire programmers (more likely computer science than information-systems majors—we will see what that means later) to work with information systems while cruising the world. In other words, the possibilities are virtually endless.

Ever since computers sprang onto the scene and many job opportunities with their flashy salaries followed, people have been saying the situation couldn't last. In the 1960s reputable computer journals predicted with confidence that application programmers were a doomed species. Programming languages were getting so easy that anyone could write a program—so the argument ran—and besides, businesses already *had* all those programs. The prediction was dead wrong: far more application programmers are employed today than in the 1960s. Variations of the same prediction have been made repeatedly since then; one day it might come true.

Which job opportunities are the most plentiful at a given time are likely to shift within the information-systems field. No career path, however, has yet to meet its demise. Instead brand-new ones have popped up, such as the small army of people involved in selling, programming, and running microcomputers.

Figure 19-1 lists the different jobs described in the career boxes throughout this book, and the chapter to which you should turn to locate the box again. These jobs are representative of those presently available within the information-systems field. Listed next to each occupation is the element (people, data, and so on) of information systems that is most involved with that career.

In the following sections we describe 34 different types of jobs available working with information systems.* This adds a few to those we covered in the career boxes. We will group the jobs according to which information-system element they work with the most.

Education and experience in using information systems are required for virtually all of these jobs; subsequent sections of the chapter will describe the options for obtaining an education and gaining experience, as well as offer some pointers on how to go about looking for a job.

*This list is based on information in Stephen R. Gray, "1982 DP Salary Survey," *Datamation*, October, 1982, vol. 28, no. 11, p. 128.

FIGURE 19-1.
Career boxes in Chapters 2 through 18.

Chapter	Career Box	Information-System Element
2	Systems analyst	All areas depending on specialization
3	Office manager	All areas
4	Training and education specialist	People
5	Hardware entrepreneur	Hardware
6	Director of information systems	All areas
7	Media librarian	Data
8	Telecommunications manager	Hardware
9	Overview of programming careers	Software
10	Application programmer	Software
11	Programmer analyst	People, software
12	Programmer entrepreneur	Software
13	System programmer	Software
14	Information resource manager	All areas
15	Information systems consultant	All areas
16	Database administrator	Data
17	Information systems auditor	All areas
18	Microcomputer specialist	People, hardware, software

FIGURE 19-2.
Many computer jobs involve working with people of varied backgrounds, like these members of an agricultural cooperative in France. The cooperative uses computers to help its members—farmers and wine producers—manage their businesses.

PEOPLE-ORIENTED JOBS

People-oriented careers (Figure 19-2) involve information-system roles that put you in direct contact with users and clients. The common requirement for each of these careers is the ability to relate well to people. Strong written and oral communication skills are needed, in addition to appropriate information-systems expertise and general business skills. We include top management jobs in the "people" category because these do require a high level of interaction with people, especially with people outside of the computer field.

- *Vice-President of Information Systems.* This person is responsible for all information-systems activities within a firm. With other top-level managers in the company, he or she works out long-range plans and budgets for all computer activities. With subordinates, he or she directs all system development and data-processing activities.
- *Director of Data Processing.* This person is responsible for the operation of information systems, including short and medium-term planning, for setting up budgets, and for supervising personnel.
- *Director of Communications.* This individual manages all telecommunications activities within a company. This includes planning, implementing, and overseeing long-term as well as day-to-day telecommunications activities.
- *Services Coordinator/User Liaison.* Serving as a "bridge" between nontechnical users and technical staff, this person is responsible for communicating user needs to information-system staff, and for representing user interests when problems arise.
- *User Services Staff Member.* Serving as a "bridge" between nontechnical users and technical staff, this individual has a solid background in information systems. He or she offers both general and specific help to users in solving their problems with a system.
- *Systems Analyst.* This person analyzes how existing systems work and designs alternative systems. Responsibilities range from determining the real needs of users through formulating new system requirements in a manner that programmers can work from. Specialties can vary.
- *Technical Writer.* This individual writes manuals and other materials telling users how to use programs, operators how to run them, and programmers how to change them.
- *Librarian.* A librarian organizes and maintains a library of technical documentation for information-system staff members.

- *Training and Education Specialist.* This person designs and teaches courses to users and the information-system staff.

RULES-AND-PROCEDURES-ORIENTED JOBS

Career opportunities in this area are oriented toward helping others to develop and enforce compliance with an organization's rules and procedures. An inquisitive mind is needed for detecting and also preventing violations of institutional rules, particularly those affecting money and privileged data.

- *Information-Systems Security Specialist.* This person is responsible for protecting valuable organizational resources.
- *Information-Systems Auditor.* This person develops and carries out auditing procedures that will uncover possible violations of the rules and procedures that concern organizational resources.

DATA-ORIENTED JOBS

Data-oriented careers involve assisting users in gaining proper access to the data they need. The prerequisite here is the ability to work in a database environment.

- *Manager of Database Administration.* This person guides the overall direction of the database operation. Tasks include assessing corporate database needs, establishing standards, and keeping a data dictionary.
- *Database Administrator.* Responsible for the actual creation and maintenance of a database, the DBA works with systems analysts and programmers to determine the way that applications will collect and store data.

SOFTWARE-ORIENTED JOBS

Software-oriented careers involve, as you might suspect, programming (Figure 19-3). These individuals create and maintain software of different kinds.

FIGURE 19-3.
Programmers are experts in the design and use of software.

- *Application Programmer.* This individual designs, codes, debugs, and maintains application programs.
- *Systems Analyst/Programmer.* The person who holds this job is responsible for the tasks of a systems analyst as well as those of an application programmer or system programmer.
- *System Programmer.* The responsibilities of this individual are to program new system software and to maintain and modify existing system software.

HARDWARE-ORIENTED JOBS

Jobs in this area concentrate on computer equipment (Figure 19-4). By equipment we mean the central processing unit and peripheral devices for input, output, storage, and communication. As a rule the lower-level jobs in this area (such as that of computer operator) are the easiest to obtain in the information-systems field, and the least challenging. You might wonder why, since computer hardware is such a technological marvel. *Designing* computer hardware is complex; *operating* it is less so. The higher-level positions (such as manager of computer operations) differ from the lower-level jobs by the addition of supervisory and planning responsibilities.

- *Manager of Computer Operations.* This person is in charge of keeping the computers and other hardware in an information-processing center running. Responsibilities include scheduling the activities of computer operators and maintenance personnel.
- *Lead Computer Operator.* The responsibilities of this individual are less than those of the manager of computer operations, but more than those of a computer operator. A lead computer operator typically manages the other operators during one shift, or directs the operations of equipment at a remote site.
- *Computer Operator.* This individual assists in running a computer, such as mounting and dismounting storage media. Under supervision a computer operator may operate the main computer console.
- *Production Control Supervisor.* Responsibilities of the production control supervisor are scheduling which job will run when at a large computer center, balancing the full use of resources with the turn-around deadlines for the jobs.
- *Lead Production Control Clerk.* This person is responsible for the activities of production control clerks during one shift, or for directing the scheduling of jobs at a remote site.
- *Production Control Clerk.* The responsibilities of this position are preparing jobs to be processed and collecting the output that the jobs produce.
- *Minicomputer Specialist.* This individual is an expert in a particular model of minicomputer. Responsibilities include installing and sometimes repairing the computer hardware and software, and programming and running the system.
- *Microcomputer Specialist.* This person is an expert in one or more particular models of microcomputer. Responsibilities include installing and sometimes repairing the computer hardware and software, and programming and running the system.

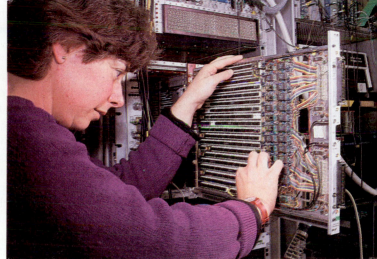

FIGURE 19-4.
A number of jobs focus on computer hardware.

- *Field Service Engineer.* An electronic technician trained by hardware manufacturers, the field service engineer services malfunctioning hardware and also pinpoints software problems.
- *Data-Entry Supervisor.* This individual supervises data-entry operators.
- *Data-Entry Operator.* The job of this person is to enter data into a computer system with one or more different types of data entry device.
- *Word-Processing Supervisor.* This individual is in charge of the flow of work through the word-processing operation, including supervising word-processing operators and hardware.
- *Word-Processing Operator.* This job entails entering, editing, and outputting text on a word-processing system.
- *Magnetic Media Librarian.* The responsibility of this individual is to control the storage and use of removable magnetic storage media.
- *Data Communications/Telecommunications Manager.* This person is responsible for the design and continued operation of teleprocessing and distributed processing networks.
- *Data Communications Analyst.* A specialist within the telecommunications area, this individual designs telecommunications networks and software.
- *Remote Site Administrator.* This person is responsible for managing a site in a distributed processing network. The individual filling this function is often not an information-systems professional but a nontechnical worker who has taken on this function in addition to other duties.
- *Remote Terminal Operator.* This person serves as an operator at a site in a distributed processing network.

We have now reviewed the main information-systems jobs. Let's move on to cover some related job opportunities. Further along in the chapter we will discuss formal and on-the-job training possibilities for obtaining the various types of positions.

The main information-system jobs were described in the preceding section. It is worth remembering that many of these positions exist not only at firms that use computers but also at companies that manufacture or support computer systems. For example, programmers and systems analysts aplenty are used by software manufacturers. Hardware manufacturers (many of whom are also software manufacturers) require not only a variety of different engineers, but also every other information-system career covered above, to support their own operations. Companies exist that train users, which require training and education specialists and technical writers.

You can also sell computer equipment or services. All of the major firms that make computer systems have extensive sales staffs, with positions ranging from sales trainee to vice-president for marketing. A significant feature of selling computer equipment or services is that the best salespeople intimately know what they are selling. They not only can converse more knowledgeably with potential customers that way, but they can get involved with programming and operating the equipment themselves to explore— together with a potential customer—whether or not it meets user needs. Computer stores also require such knowledgeable sales personnel.

Although most positions in information processing are permanent full-time jobs as in any other field, some aren't. Firms often hire consultants to help them through a short-term crunch or to provide expertise that is lacking in-house. For example, major information-system development projects within Fortune 500 companies often employ dozens of personnel and operate with budgets of millions of dollars. Scheduling this type of activity is difficult even today, and often a project that starts out on target will soon fall behind. A common bail-out technique is to hire a drove of consultants. Although the company pays the consultants at least two or three times what an in-house employee costs (benefits included), the firm can release the consultants once the crunch is past.

Most consultants begin in the computer field by working at regular jobs, and then strike out on their own. Some (known as "independents") offer their services directly, perhaps employing a job-locating agent who takes a small percentage of their earnings. Independent consultants have to arrange their own compensation for vacations, sick leave, social security, and medical insurance.

Other consultants work for consulting firms, many of which provide these benefits and find the consulting assignments. Some consulting firms even offer a workplace, resources such as a library, and continuing training. These firms generally take a cut of the earnings equal to that which the consultant receives (the consultant will still earn at least double what the equivalent in-house employee does).

In either the independent or the consulting-firm situation, the drawback is that employment may not be steady. Gaps of a few months may occur between one assignment and another. Some employers are so backlogged today, however, that they will hire "temporary" consultants for periods that turn out to be years at a stretch. Beyond the potential of higher earnings, the advantage of consulting is more freedom: you are free to turn down an assignment if you don't like the work or the people involved. In some situations you also have more freedom concerning work hours.

OTHER FIELDS Shifting your focus from the information industry and information systems does not mean that you have to leave computers behind. Most firms today appreciate at least some minor knowledge of computers and information systems, and some companies require it. Additional training may be offered by the firm. A student hired by an accounting organization, for example, will probably be trained to use the company's income tax preparation, spreadsheet, auditing, and other software. Librarians these days work with terminals and databases rather than card catalogs, and have taken advanced courses in information retrieval. Should you join a law firm, you or someone who works for you is sure to make frequent inquiries at a terminal about legal precedents stored in databases. The list of jobs that involve computers in noncomputer fields is very long, and pretty well covers the entire job spectrum within business, the government, and nonprofit organizations. Figure 19-5, for example, shows an application of computers in forestry.

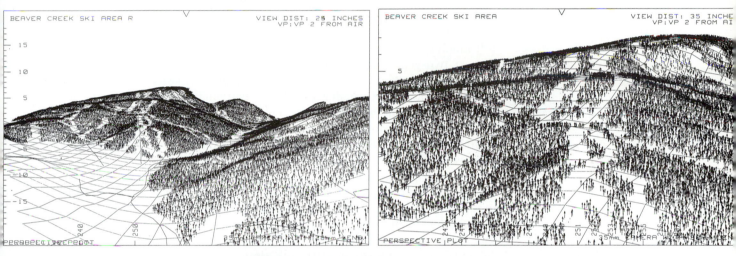

FIGURE 19-5.
More and more, jobs in non-computer fields involve computers. These computer-generated three-dimensional landscape graphics were the result of software developed by the Forest Service of the United States Department of Agriculture. These particular images show various views of a ski area in Colorado. Images such as these are used to assess the impact of various projects on the landscape.

How do you get started in the computer field? The first step is to learn something about computers. There are two ways of doing this: (1) through formal education, and (2) through on-the-job training. Once you have decided on a career in information systems you can—and should—keep up with the field by reading books and magazines on the subject.

FORMAL EDUCATION

Formal education does not guarantee entry into the computer field, but it helps. Almost all new systems analysts are expected to have a bachelor's degree. For programmers a bachelor's degree certainly helps, but more than half of starting programmers have only a high school diploma and some training in a vocational or junior college program. Most computer operators also need only a high school diploma and some vocational or community college training. Starting data-entry operators in general need only a high school diploma.

If your ambitions lie in the direction of jobs that require at least some college education, there are several different routes you can take.

First, you could attend a community or two-year college and take the introductory information-systems courses. If the job you want requires more than a two-year degree, you would want to transfer your credits to a four-year institution and get a bachelor's degree. Credits from a two-year school do not always transfer in full, and you might end up putting in more than a total of four years at college.

You could also take a four-year course of study to begin with, and major in an information-systems program. The names of programs and the degrees they offer vary widely, but they reduce to two main types: information systems and computer science.

An **INFORMATION-SYSTEMS PROGRAM**—which might also be known as data processing, business data processing, management information systems, or information resource management—corresponds to the topics covered in this book, and to the general business-related approach that we have followed. Often coordinated by the university's college of business, an information systems program emphasizes the processing of data to produce information that will be used by a general business or government employer. Courses will include the history and fundamentals of computing, one or more programming languages, the system development process, information resource management systems, and electives covering some of the other areas we have dealt with, such as distributed data processing and database concepts.

The four-year **COMPUTER SCIENCE PROGRAM** (which generally sticks to the one name) follows a slightly different route. Computer science also covers the history and fundamentals of computing, a programming language or two, system development, information resource systems, and other areas discussed in this book. Much more emphasis is given, however, to software design, and sometimes to hardware design as well. The curriculum is more technical than that for information systems, and less oriented toward achieving business-oriented results with computers. Usually the computer science program is administered by its own department or by the college of engineering.

Both programs provide a good foundation in computers and information systems, and offer a degree that will meet the "must be college educated" requirement of a potential employer. Business employers will probably find an information-systems degree more relevant, however. If you wish to design software, the computer science degree is usually preferable.

Another positive component of your education, if you seek a job in business, would be several business courses. An advanced degree, particularly an M.B.A., opens up more business management possibilities. A fair number of people get their B.S., start working, and then pick up their M.B.A. on the side. To teach about computers, an M.S. or Ph.D. in computer science or information systems may be required.

Our comments here have been general; while they probably apply to your school, they may not. Ask your instructor about the programs available at your college or university, and look through the catalog. It would also not hurt to discuss job-seeking and employment experiences with someone who has recently found the kind of job that interests you. If you don't know such a person, try calling up a few corporate personnel departments, or employment agencies that handle computer jobs, and asking their opinions of different degrees. And then, after you have done this type of homework, make up your own mind.

A word of caution—not everyone is cut out for advanced training in information systems. Despite the allure of a "high-technology" field and high salaries, there is a high dropout rate from these programs.

ON-THE-JOB TRAINING

There is another route. Computers exploded onto the scene long before computer science or information-systems courses existed. People learned from others, and taught themselves, on the job. How can you come by on-the-job training today?

First, by getting a bachelor's degree in information systems or computer science, and impressing a potential employer, you may get an entry-level job. This first job is itself viewed by the employer as training—you may even be called a trainee—despite the fact that you have already been trained in school. The training on the job is in applying your general knowledge of information systems to what the employer wants you to do.

Some larger employers have formal in-house training programs that you will be enrolled in; most, however, sit you down and hand you a stack of manuals, let you ask questions, and bring you onboard on a sort of "apprenticeship" basis. In the computer field, we should add, your apprenticeship is done in a year; this does not mean that everyone will regard you as an expert after that time, but that you will no longer be considered a beginner.

Those same employers with the formal in-house training programs may also hire you without a four-year degree, and provide you with on-the-job training. This is the second on-the-job training possibility.

The third type of on-the-job training is that picked up by people who already have a job. If your work entails the use of computers, the opportunity probably exists to learn more about them on the job. It is common for users to become fascinated by the systems that serve them, and cross over into the technical camp and get involved in designing those systems. It is also common for clerical employees without any formal computer training to become proficient enough in their use of a microcomputer or terminal, that they will quit their job and find another on the basis of their computer knowledge.

FIGURE 19-6.
Formal training need not end when you start working. Continuing education courses in information systems are offered at colleges and universities, the training departments of large organizations, and professional organizations.

One more source of on-the-job training is the armed forces. It is possible to get both formal courses and experience in some computer-related fields in the services, and some people begin their careers this way.

Finally, anyone who works can continue to take courses offered by extension programs (Figure 19-6), the training departments of large organizations, professional associations, and so on. Moreover, those of us who work with information systems and computers *have* to take such courses, to remain up to date. Computer professionals who entered the field in the days of vacuum tubes and paper tape would be displayed in glass cases in museums as fossils were it not for such courses, and for other types of on-the-job training. Courses help keep people abreast of new developments, give them the chance to acquire new skills, and positively impress managers with the potential for advancement. Some employers give time off during the day to employees who attend courses not given in-house, and nearly all pay the tuition.

MAGAZINES AND BOOKS

Another way to keep informed while on the job is to read magazines and journals about computers and information systems. General-interest computer magazines include *Infoworld*, *Management Technology*, *Popular Computing*, *Byte*, and *Datamation*. In addition a number of magazines cater to users of particular brands of hardware. The bookstores are also full of books about computers.

EXPERIENCE: WHY YOU NEED IT

The great diversity of organizations that maintain information systems translates into many available jobs. Unfortunately this does not mean that if you do well with your courses and graduate with an information-systems, computer science, or related degree, you will get one of these jobs. Only a relatively small number of positions—about 25,000—are open in the computer field each year to people with no experience. Many more graduates than that are being turned out annually by the numerous colleges and universities offering computer degrees, and so the competition for a small number of positions is fierce.

THE ARTIFICIAL SHORTAGE

There is some irony in this situation. Many firms that use computers, and manufacturers and other companies within the computer industry itself, are short-staffed. Many desperately seek new employees. What they seek, however, are people with a college degree *and also experience* in an area that will be of immediate use to them. Apart from the 25,000 or so avowed entry-level positions, it is as if businesses were unable to take any but the shortest-term perspective toward their employment needs. That is, since there is a shortage of people with experience, why not make it a policy regularly to hire people without experience, and give it to them?

No one knows for sure. Many companies in the Fortune 500 still seem to staff up for what they believe are their personnel needs, find that they fall badly behind on their system development projects, and so—panic stricken—attempt to hire people to help them over the immediate hurdle. Operating in this manner, they simply do not have the six months to teach a beginner what to do, or to help an experienced person transfer his or her skills to their particular system.

GET IT BEFORE GRADUATION

Your task as a new graduate seeking an information-systems job will be to stand out from the pack. One thing you should seriously consider is to work during the summer, or part-time during the school year, before you graduate. Some schools have programs whereby you can meet a portion of your degree requirements by actually working for a business in an information-system position. If your school does not have such a program, then you should check with the college placement office, or with local employers, to see which firms hire summer or part-time employees.

What type of job would you want? Try to find something where you can write programs or use computers, even in a minor way. Pay is not the important thing here. If you can tuck away enough work experience prior to graduation to put on your resume, you will impress potential employers after graduation with your commitment to the field, and will enormously improve your chances of getting a job. Moreover, the experience will probably enable you to start out on a full-time job at a higher earning level, which will more than repay the money "lost" by taking a fairly low paying job to get that experience.

Many colleges and universities have arrangements with local businesses whereby they offer internships and cooperative education programs. If your school has such a program, take advantage of it. Experience in an internship can lead to a job offer.

Once you have acquired your first full-time job and worked with computers for a year, you will *have* experience as far as other employers are concerned. Many jobs will be open to you then, provided your experience is relevant to what the employer is looking for, that you can handle yourself well in an interview, and that your background is otherwise impressive.

FINDING A JOB

Now that we have described the job opportunities, educational options, and need for experience, we would like to suggest how you can put it all together to look for a job. We will suggest where to look, describe the resume and portfolio that you will need, and give pointers for success in job interviews.

WHERE TO LOOK   If your college or university has a placement office, it can help put you in touch with firms seeking information-systems employees. The other prime source of information is employment advertisements. Jobs for computer people are advertised in the want-ad and business sections of all major newspapers, and also in computer magazines such as *Datamation* and *Communications of the ACM*.

When looking for a job don't forget that the most massive employer around is the U.S. government. You can take a civil service examination regardless of whether or not you have a specific job prospect; the results are then circulated to agencies looking for people. You can also first interview with an agency interested in you, and then take the exam. The U.S. government employs every variety of information-systems professional and has well-developed career paths.

State governments offer similar opportunities, as do the governments of larger cities.

A number of reputable employment agencies exist that specialize in placing computer professionals. Their substantial fee is paid by the employer. Although you may receive advice from these agencies, as a new graduate they will generally not be willing to offer you their services, since you have no experience. Once you have worked at your first job for a while and are thinking of a change, they will be very interested.

A technique used successfully by quite a few people with training in information systems but no experience is to "blanket" major employers in their area with their resumes, accompanied in each instance by a well-thought-out cover letter tailored to the particular employer. If you are located in a big city or in a suburban area with extensive industry, it may not be a problem to find 50 names of corporations, government agencies, hospitals, and so on. When you shoot off a whole quiverful of arrows in this manner, naturally most will miss their mark. One or two might not, however.

Last but not least, don't forget personal contacts. Although these, too, will come into play more as you have worked in the field for a while, you may have some already through your college or university or through summer or part-time employment. Don't hesitate to ask people working in the field where they would advise you to look for a job.

THE RESUME   Before starting to look for a job, you should prepare a one-page resume. A **RESUME** is a summary of your educational qualifications and your relevant work experience. There are different formats and approaches, which your college placement office can probably show you. Figure 19-7 gives one example, which we will describe here.

At the top you should place your name, address, and phone number. Do *not* give your age, sex, marital status, or any other personal information; employers are forbidden by law to seek this information, and should not be offered it gratuitously.

If you have work experience related to the job you are seeking, the "experience" section of the resume should come next. Each job rates a brief summarized description, including your job title and responsibilities, and your dates of employment. If the job was part-time, say so.

Following experience—or in place of it if you don't have any—comes

FIGURE 19-7.
A sample resume.

Ed Wieland   (223) 986-3131
1234 Narrowgate Lane
Oakriver, CA 90613

EXPERIENCE

7/81–8/86   Senior Systems Analyst, Paul's House of Electronic
             Wonders, 1500 Commerce Way, Oakriver, CA, 90617.
             Experience in all phases of systems analysis, system de-
             sign, and system maintenance. Supervision of small pro-
             ject teams. Typical projects included development of a
             fully automated inventory update system and design of
             major components of a company-wide decision support
             system. Familiarity with database design and mainte-
             nance, structured programming, distributed processing,
             and control and security techniques.

7/80–6/81   Programmer, Amalgamated Testing Meters, 6124 Sour-
             bush Way, E. Oakriver, CA, 90619. Experience in writ-
             ing, debugging, and maintaining programs in COBOL
             and assembly language for accounting applications. Re-
             sponsibility for a major payroll package.

6/79–9/79   Programming Assistant, Information Processing Center,
   and   Oakriver University. Full-time summer position making
6/78–9/78   updates to production programs in COBOL used by the
             university office of alumni relations.

EDUCATION

9/76–6/80   BS in Information Systems, Oakriver University.
             Courses in accounting, business management, computer
             architecture, software design, systems analysis, struc-
             tured programming, operating systems, COBOL, Pascal,
             database concepts, and telecommunications. As a senior
             project developed an information system for a minicom-
             puter lab.

education. Describe the information-systems program you took, tell what your degree is, and give details of the technical areas covered by the program. Dates would be handy here as well.

Since you may not be able to fill a page even with generous margins, you might want to add two references to the bottom. Instructors impressed with your work may be willing to serve as references. Ask them, however, before you use their names.

You will have to type or word-process more than one draft of your resume before it looks perfect. If you can't produce a perfect copy yourself, pay to have it professionally typed. You should also have it reproduced at a copy or print shop that produces a nice crisp copy, although there is no need to pay for expensive modes of reproduction. Some people believe that the use of a textured, and perhaps discreetly tinted, paper for the resume copies sets theirs apart from the pack.

Whatever, once you have some copies of your resume, you are ready to put them into circulation. There are two ways:

1 *In response to employment advertisements, or to potential employers you are including in your "blanket" survey. Each resume sent should be accompanied by a typed or word-processed letter adapted to that particular employer. If you just send a resume in an envelope, it will probably be made into a paper airplane and flown into the nearest wastebasket.*

2 *To carry with you to interviews. Generally before an interview a firm will ask you to fill out its employment application; provide a copy of your resume as well.*

THE PORTFOLIO

While attending information-systems classes, you will have prepared some programs yourself. Save these! Get a legible printout, together with input and output, and place it in a binder. This collection of good things that you have done is known as your **PORTFOLIO**. Also placed in the binder should be any flowcharts, other diagrams, or documentation (if short) for the program. Separate the different programs or projects by dividers with tabs.

Why go to all this fuss? Because it can help convince an open-minded employer that you do, after all, know how to use the beasts (computers) that you would be hired to use. Some employers will examine the contents of your portfolio carefully. A well-prepared portfolio that gives evidence of skill and depth may spell the difference between someone who gets the job and someone who does not.

THE INTERVIEW

If some of your arrows strike home, you will be asked to come to an **INTERVIEW**. Interviews vary as much as the types of organizations and the individuals within the organizations who give them. Here is a familiar pattern:

1 *You are greeted by a personnel office employee, who asks you to fill out an employment application. You do so.*

2 *The personnel office employee then asks you a few preliminary questions, and sends you on to the head of the part of the organization that is looking for an employee.*

3 *You have a friendly conversation with this person alone. This individual is looking for an employee, and interested in determining—by how you comport yourself and by your answers to questions—whether you might be the one. This interview will probably last between 15 minutes and an hour, and it is the major hurdle that you have to get past.*

4 *The person looking for an employee calls in a colleague or subordinate. This new individual might be the actual project leader under whom you would work. This person may conduct what is known as a "**TECHNICAL INTERVIEW**", which means you are asked very specific questions about computing, such as those concerning particulars of the system that the company uses, to determine how much you know. Sometimes this is done in a question-and-answer manner like an exam, and other times*

informally in what appears to be merely a chat about computers. Some organizations go so far as to administer an actual written and timed test. At the other extreme a genial and well-disposed interviewer may never say a technical word.

5   *The person in charge concludes the interview, thanking you for your time. You should have a good idea how things stand by then, and should know what will happen next.*

Whether your interview follows this pattern or not, and whatever the outcome, merely getting asked to an interview is a mark of favor—it shows that you stand out from the pack. If you do less than perfectly on an interview, or really botch one or two up, chalk it up to experience. A person being interviewed is well on the way to becoming an employee, and eventually things will click.

And when they do, you've started your career.

CASE IN POINT   CHARTING A PATH TO THE TOP

To reach the top of the information-systems organization you not only need skill in a specific area such as programming, but also general knowledge of business and the ability to communicate to both experts and nonexpert managers and users. The typical career path starts at the junior or trainee level, with a position such as programmer trainee or junior programmer-analyst. As you are promoted to more responsible positions up the career ladder, your challenge will be continually to keep up with changes in the field.

Eventually, if you are successful, your task will become more managerial in nature. Within management the higher you go, the more planning oriented your management role will be. Moving up in management may require an advanced degree. The visibility of information-system staff means that your career need not stop at vice-president for information systems, but can continue to climb in the executive ranks of the organization as they relate to many different areas.

If your interest is in experiencing and taking part in the challenges that shape your field, your goal may not lie in advancing up the management job ladder. Nevertheless it is useful to know where the ladder leads. Some organizations have parallel career ladders for management and nonmanagement personnel: for example, it is possible to advance within a given area, such as systems analysis, to a high level of technical expertise without management duties, up to a level roughly comparable in pay and prestige to someone who becomes manager of systems analysis. Still, most companies pay nonmanagers less. The nonmanagement "expert" ladder usually ends at a point like that, however, whereas the other ladder has more rungs above.

Some people are so eager to climb to the top that rather than let an employer decide when and if they advance, over a patient process that can take many years, they simply start at the top—by forming their own company. Thousands of people attempt this every year. Most new businesses fail—approximately 90 percent—but some survive and a few achieve great success.

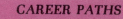
Once you obtain a job in information processing, you may be interested in seeing where it can lead. Let's first consider the career hierarchy and then take a look at professional associations and certification.

THE CAREER HIERARCHY

The organizational hierarchy in the information-system environment is usually divided into functional subareas: hardware operations, systems analysis and design, programming, and database management.

When businesses first began to use computers, information-system functions were handled by the corporate department that used the computer the most, which was usually accounting (see the top half of Figure 19-8). When colleges and universities first began to use computers, usually the engineering department or mathematics department ran the university computer center. Over the years, however, information-system operations have achieved independence from the "home" department the better to

FIGURE 19-8.
How information systems fit into a business organization.

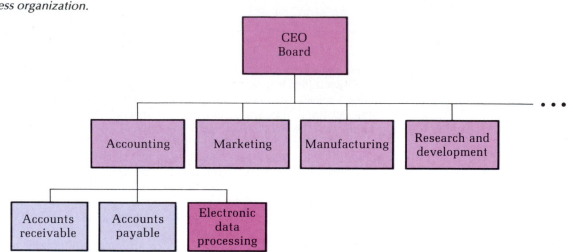

Old Style

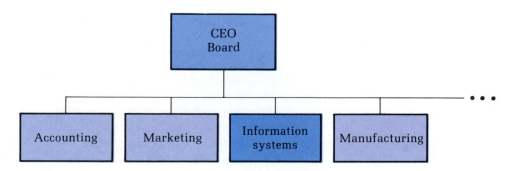

New Style

FIGURE 19-9.

The information-systems career hierarchy. Shown below the job titles are the average 1983 salaries (in thousands of dollars, "K") for people employed by large (right) and small (left) companies.

Source: *Unless otherwise indicated, salaries are based on information from Larry Marion, "The Big Wallet Era,"* Datamation, *September 15, 1984, vol. 30, no. 15, p. 80.* Copyright © Technical Publishing Company, a Dun and Bradstreet Company. All rights reserved.

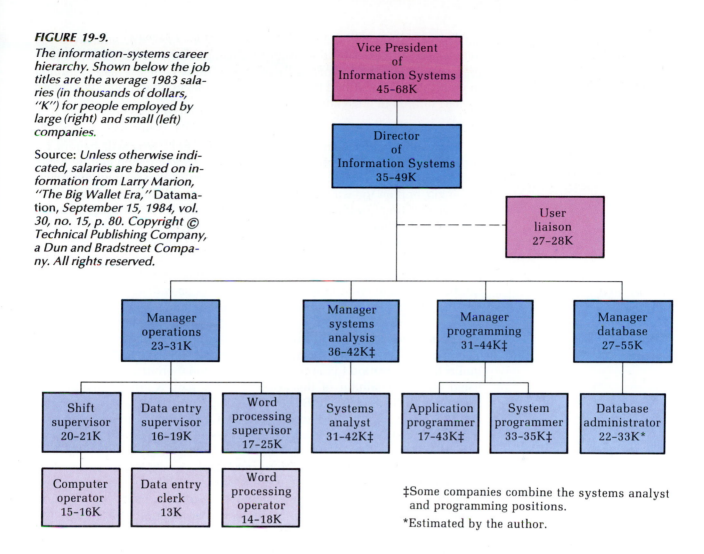

‡Some companies combine the systems analyst and programming positions.

*Estimated by the author.

serve the functions of the entire organization (or college). In part this is true because business information systems now handle a lot more than accounting, and computer centers on campus are used by all disciplines. The bottom half of Figure 19-8 shows the place of information-system functions in most contemporary businesses.

One feature of the change is the elevation of the top-ranking member of the information-system staff from manager to department head, or from director to vice-president. This increase in status allows people who work on the information-system staff access to the highest levels of corporate management. To use corporate jargon, what an information-system staff member does is highly "visible"—to people higher up in the organization, who may remember one's name when promotion time comes around.

The head of the information system staff is often known as the vice-president for information systems or the director of information systems. Below this person come various middle managers, who direct the functional departments such as operations and systems analysis. Figure 19-9 shows the career hierarchy, working from the top down, and gives the average salary figures for the positions. A range is shown for each position: the lower figure is typical of small companies (those with less than $1 million in gross annual sales), and the higher, of larger companies (those with more than $1 million in gross annual sales).

PROFESSIONAL ASSOCIATIONS AND CERTIFICATION

As a participant in the information-processing field, you will benefit by considering yourself a professional rather than someone who merely holds down a particular job. This can have a positive influence on your approach to the job, and on the way that others perceive you. A number of reputable professional organizations exist for computer and information-processing professionals. You can join such groups for a fairly modest annual fee, and be able to participate in meetings with others who share the same interests, receive publications, and make contacts that can help you advance in the profession. Some associations also offer continuing education courses.

In this section we list four such associations, as well as an institute that will test and certify your competence in your field.

American Federation of Information Processing Societies (AFIPS)

The **AMERICAN FEDERATION OF INFORMATION PROCESSING SOCIETIES (AFIPS)** is an umbrella organization for a number of professional groups, including those listed in the remainder of this section. Other AFIPS groups include the Institute of Electrical and Electronics Engineers (IEEE), the American Institute of Certified Public Accountants (AICPA), Women in Data Processing (WDP), and the Black Data Processing Association (BDPA).

Association For Computing Machinery (ACM)

The **ASSOCIATION FOR COMPUTING MACHINERY (ACM)** is the oldest and largest educational and scientific society in the computer industry, with around 70,000 members worldwide. In addition to its national organization the ACM has many local chapters. Student members are welcome. The ACM declares its purpose to be "to advance the sciences and arts of information processing . . .," to encourage the exchange of knowledge concerning information processing among different specialists in the field, and also between specialists and the general public; and "to develop and maintain the integrity and competence of individuals engaged in the practice of information processing."

Toward these ends the ACM sponsors conferences, meetings of special interest groups, and training seminars throughout the world. The ACM publishes *Communications of the ACM* as well as other monthly and quarterly journals, newsletters, and training materials. The ACM has also been active in establishing standards for the teaching of information-system subjects, and publishes an influential curriculum guide for various programs in information systems.

Data Processing Management Association (DPMA)

The **DATA PROCESSING MANAGEMENT ASSOCIATION (DPMA)** is made up mainly of managers and other supervisors of computer centers, as well as educators and vendors in the information-processing industry. The association is organized into several hundred local chapters. Like the ACM, the DPMA has been very active in establishing standards for the teaching of information-systems subjects in colleges and universities, and has developed an influential curriculum guide.

Association of Systems Management (ASM)

The **ASSOCIATION OF SYSTEMS MANAGEMENT (ASM)** is made up of systems analysts and systems managers. Through both its national organization and its local chapters, the ASM offers a wide variety of continuing education courses.

Institute for Certification of Computer Professionals (ICCP)

The **INSTITUTE FOR CERTIFICATION OF COMPUTER PROFESSIONALS (ICCP)** is an umbrella organization responsible for testing the competence of professionals in the computer field. The ICCP offers certification in three major areas: the Certificate in Data Processing (CDP), the Certificate in Computer Programming (CCP), and the Certified System Professional (CSP).

The CDP examination covers five areas: (1) data-processing equipment, (2) computer programming, (3) business management principles, (4) quantitative methods and accounting, and (5) systems analysis and design. The test is currently offered twice a year, to people with five years of experience in the field. Less than half of those who take the exam earn the certificate. The CCP examination tests experienced programmers in COBOL or FORTRAN. The CSP program offers periodic examinations to systems professionals with substantial on-the-job experience.

In the same way that a college degree attests to educational competence in a certain area, passing one of these examinations attests to one's competence in carrying out the actual work.

WRAP-UP	AU REVOIR TO PAUL'S

Ed Wieland, not entirely pleased with what he saw as his future at Paul's, did more than just dust off and update his resume. In spare moments he skimmed the employment ads in the computer magazines circulated through the information-processing center at Paul's. At the next meeting of the local chapter of the professional society to which he belonged, he sounded out a few acquaintances about job prospects at their firms.

"Head-hunters"—the term used for employment agencies that handle computer and other high-level business jobs—routinely called up the computer people at Paul's to see if any were disgruntled and ready for a switch. Wherever you worked with computers, this was a standard feature of the working environment, which Ed initially found somewhat amusing but had grown used to. In the past he'd always told them no. Now, however, he phoned two he had come to know through their calls over the years, and set up lunch appointments.

Ed soon had his hands full with interviews, and had to take several days of "vacation" time off to handle those he couldn't fit into and around lunch hours. Just as it had been when he first got out of school, the interviewing process was useful to Ed. First, it got him out and in touch with employers, computer applications, and people other than those he worked with every day. It reminded him once again how large the computer world was. Second, interviewing made Ed assess himself and his goals.

He decided to go for a senior position in systems analysis, preferably as a manager of a team of systems analysts. He wanted to couple this with an exciting project to develop, and to move to a larger firm where he was certain that his desire to move up the technical management ranks could be realized.

Of the five interviews Ed attended, four of the companies offered him jobs starting immediately. His salary level at Paul's was quite high; two firms only matched it, and two offered substantial increases.

Ed decided to place challenge before money. He accepted a position as lead systems analyst for a large software development house. Although the company only matched his salary at Paul's, it offered him management of a project developing a large software package for mainframes. Ed lived too far away from this company to commute comfortably from his present apartment, and so would have to move, but he felt it was worth it.

Ed decided that once he got settled into the new job he would pursue an advanced degree in the evening. If there was one thing he had learned in his six years of working in the computer field, it was that education never ends.

SUMMARY

- Job opportunities for information-systems personnel can be grouped according to which information-system element they involve the most. People-oriented jobs include vice-president of information systems, director of information systems, director of communications, services coordinator/user liaison, user services staff member, systems analyst, technical writer, librarian, and training and education specialist.
- Rules-and-procedures-oriented jobs are those of information-systems security specialist and information-systems auditor. Data-oriented jobs include manager of database administration and database administrator. Software-oriented jobs are those of application programmer, systems analyst/programmer, and system programmer.
- Hardware-oriented jobs are the most numerous and often the easiest to break into. These include manager of computer operations, lead computer operator, computer operator, production control supervi-

sor, lead production control clerk, production control clerk, minicomputer specialist, microcomputer specialist, field service engineer, data-entry operator, data-entry supervisor, word-processing supervisor, word-processing operator, magnetic media librarian, data communications/telecommunications manager, data communications analyst, remote site administrator, and remote terminal operator.

- All of these positions exist in businesses, government agencies, and nonprofit organizations, as well as at companies that manufacture or support computer systems. In addition many positions exist in the sales of computer equipment and services. Instead of working as a regular employee, it is also possible to work as a consultant.

- Education about computers can be obtained either formally or on the job. Formal education leads to a bachelor's degree in either information systems (the name varies) or computer science. The information-systems program is usually business oriented; the computer science program is usually more technically oriented. Advanced degrees may be necessary for some management positions. On-the-job training is provided by the employer either formally or informally. It is also possible to take courses oneself while employed, and it is always a good idea to keep up with developments in the field by reading magazines and books.

- Experience is required for most information-systems positions. Taking the trouble to work at a summer or part-time job that involves computers before graduation can help to separate you from the large number of people competing for a relatively small number of entry-level jobs.

- Sources to turn to in looking for a job include the college placement office; employment advertisements in newspapers and computer magazines; U.S., state, and local governments; employment agencies; and personal contacts. Some people "blanket" a large number of firms that have not indicated that they are seeking employees, with resumes and cover letters in the hope of awakening interest. Both the resume and portfolio are very important in seeking a job, as is the way that you handle an interview.

- The organizational hierarchy in the information-system environment is usually divided into functional subareas: hardware operations, systems analysis and design, programming, and database management. Information-systems positions can be highly "visible" to top management within an organization. This increases your chances of moving to the top. So do your technical skills, general knowledge of business, and the ability to communicate well to experts as well as to nonexpert managers and users.

- A number of reputable professional organizations serve computer professionals. These include the American Federation of Information Processing Societies (AFIPS), the Association for Computing Machinery (ACM), the Data Processing Management Association (DPMA), and the Association of Systems Management (ASM). The Institute for Certification of Computer Professionals (ICCP) tests the competence of people in the computer field.

These are the key terms in the order in which they appear in the chapter.

Information-systems program (536)
Computer science program (536)
Resume (540)
Portfolio (542)
Interview (542)
Technical interview (542)
American Federation of Information Processing Societies (AFIPS) (546)
Association for Computing Machinery (ACM) (546)
Data Processing Management Association (DPMA) (546)
Association of Systems Management (ASM) (547)
Institute for Certification of Computer Professionals (ICCP) (547)

REVIEW QUESTIONS

OBJECTIVE QUESTIONS

TRUE/FALSE: *Put the letter T or F on the line before the question.*

1. The technical interview is generally the first step in the job-hunting process.
2. Information-systems programs have a more business-oriented thrust than computer science programs.
3. To get a job in the information-systems industry you must have a bachelor's degree.
4. The portfolio can substitute for your resume.
5. In general you don't need experience to gain a good job in the information-system industry.
6. Job seekers should prepare carefully for the interview process.
7. Computer science programs require classes in computer programming.
8. The manager of computer operations has a hardware-oriented position.
9. The resume should be as brief as possible to maintain the interest of the reader, yet cover the relevant topics clearly.
10. The systems analyst job may cover any combination of the information-system elements.

MULTIPLE CHOICE QUESTIONS: *Put the letter of the correct answer on the line before the question.*

1. A student majoring in information systems would probably be required to take classes in
(a) General business.
(b) Systems analysis and design.
(c) Computer programming.
(d) All of the above.

2. A student majoring in computer science would probably not be required to take classes in
(a) Business accounting.
(b) Systems analysis and design.
(c) Computer design.
(d) Computer programming.

3. Technical personnel with the same amount of experience as managers generally earn
(a) More money than managers at most companies.
(b) Less money than managers at most companies.
(c) About the same amount as managers at a few companies.
(d) Both b and c.

4. Eager Hunter has just been turned down for a job after his third interview at Dream-On Corporation. Halfway through the interview he had an informal chat

over coffee with a person who surprisingly turned out to be his potential manager. He hadn't taken the chat very seriously at the time, but when he lost the job, he wondered. What probably happened?

(a) He left his portfolio at home.

(b) He forgot that technical interviews may not even appear to be interviews.

(c) The personnel officer thought he was unqualified.

(d) His resume was too long for the manager to bother with reading.

_____ 5. In writing a resume you should include

(a) Relevant work experience.

(b) Educational background.

(c) Your telephone number.

(d) All of the above.

FILL IN THE BLANK: *Write the correct word or words in the blank to complete the sentence.*

1. The _____ observes how existing systems work and designs alternative systems.

2. The _____ is the oldest and largest professional society in the computer industry.

3. A _____ operator enters text using word-processing equipment.

4. A _____ is a person responsible for writing computer programs.

5. Operating system code would be designed and written by_____.

6. Generally _____ is required for hiring in jobs past the entry level in the information industry.

7. The _____ is the person who might mount and dismount tapes at a computer center.

8. The management of an information-systems database is the reponsibility of the _____.

9. A selected collection of projects you performed in class for use during the job-hunting process is called the _____.

10. The _____ is a professional society focusing on the management issues facing those in the information industry.

SHORT ANSWER QUESTIONS

When answering these questions think of concrete examples to illustrate your points.

1. What are some of the people-oriented jobs in the information-system field?

2. How can you get on-the-job training?

3. What are some of the jobs available in the information industry?

4. What are the major features of a resume?

5. List some hardware-oriented jobs.

6. What is the function of a portfolio?

7. What is the purpose of the technical interview?

8. What are some of the professional organizations in the information field?

ESSAY QUESTIONS

1. Practice writing your resume—you should, of course, pitch it toward a job in information systems.

2. Compare and contrast the training offered by computer science and information-system departments.

3. What occupations in information systems are available to people who choose not to pursue a four-year degree?

COMPUTERS AND THE FUTURE: IMPACTS AND ISSUES

After studying this chapter you should understand the following:
- Some of the major ways that computers and information systems have affected people.
- The characteristics and limitations of robots.
- Some contemporary issues concerning rules and procedures, data, software, and hardware.
- The main possibilities for the evolution of computers and information systems.

The future had entered the Roberts family's life with a bang. In less than a year Janis had gone from being a travel agent who knew nothing about computers, to becoming the mainstay of the information-processing staff at Freddy Johnson's Travel Agency, with several computer courses under her belt.

At the start of Chapter 2 we saw Freddy Johnson's Travel Agency planning its computerization process, and at the end of Chapter 2 we described how the system worked after three months in action. The results were promising. Freddy, the owner, was enthusiastic. Bugs were still being ironed out of the system, however; people were still getting used to it; and all the votes were by no means in. Neither Janis nor Freddy had reason to be pessimistic. Janis had advanced personally at an unprecedented rate, with two promotions within a year and a reputation within the firm as the computer expert. Everything she heard from the branch agency managers and the travel agents themselves suggested that the new system was making it easier for them to work more efficiently, and enabling them to offer clients a new level of service.

George Roberts was also being propelled into the future at Global Electrical Equipment. He was called into his manager's office one morning and told that in two months half of his employees would no longer be human. Seven people were being replaced by robots.

His engineer's mind greeted the new development with enthusiasm. From a managerial vantage point, too, he recognized what Global's directors were doing. The assembly-line operations at Global's different plants were enormous. Robots had been used for years for simple operations such as spot welding. But in his department, right here in Oakriver, the directors wanted him to carry out an experiment that was risky but had great potential impact. In replacing half of his inspectors with robots, George would compare how well they performed against the human inspectors. The results could determine the future of quality-control operations throughout the huge company.

Global's expansion in the use of robots was at the cutting edge of technology. Robots capable of telling whether an appliance such as a toaster worked right were something new. Managing them would be something new as well.

As a manager George was also responsible for the professional, and to a degree the personal, well-being of his employees. His excitement over the robots did not last even a full minute before he felt the same panic that he knew his employees would. Automation phased out jobs! People read it in the paper often enough, and now seven of his employees were going to experience it. It would be

SOCIAL ISSUES AND THE INFORMATION SYSTEM

Each major technological innovation since the dawn of history has had a major effect on society, transforming, or at the least modifying, the way people live. The automobile reshaped the American landscape, creating suburbs, causing cities first to decline and then to regenerate in new form, changing social and leisure patterns, creating unmatched levels of air pollution, and threading concrete ribbons from coast to coast. You can make up a similar list of effects of the telephone, the airplane, electricity, or the atomic bomb. For even more fundamental catalysts of change, turn back in history and consider the taming of fire or the invention of the wheel.

But what about the computer? In its half a century or so of modern existence, it has changed the way that business does business, made space exploration possible, created whole new industries and occupations, and nurtured a vast educational enterprise dedicated to imparting computer proficiency. It has dramatically altered the role that information plays in business and other organizations. Any other technology, profession, or product that you would care to name has probably been computerized: automobiles, home appliances, telephones, medicine, weapons, banking, aeronautics. Chapter 3 outlines a number of such applications, some of them surprising. Little computer chips defrost our refrigerators, run the watches on our wrists, and may soon provide guidance to artificial organs implanted in our bodies.

Yet the computer revolution has only begun. Trying to predict its course is like trying to chart the course of an ocean liner based on its first few movements out of port. We don't really know where the ship is headed. Worse, the computer revolution is like a ship with no captain.

PEOPLE

There are several conflicting views on the impact of computers and information systems on people. Three basic schools of thought exist.

The first view holds that computers have been of great benefit to our society, helping to usher in a new golden age in which people can use computers to lighten their burdens and brighten their lives. Advances in health care, the sciences, and even the arts, have been fostered by the computer, and a computerized business community is better able to turn a profit, benefiting everyone.

The second school of thought is less rosy. According to this view, the addictive use of, and belief in, the power of computers have led us well along the path toward a regimented society. Models of our near future are offered by George Orwell's novel *1984* (though its title refers to a year now past), with its citizens dominated by thought-control police; and by the cold, brutal technocracy depicted in Aldous Huxley's *Brave New World*. Thanks to the computer, millions of jobs have been lost; government databases hold our deepest secrets; and blows have been given to the environment. Worst of all, one of the many errors with which computer systems are rife could lead the United States or the Soviet Union into thinking the other had launched an attack, and so to launch the "counterattack" in earnest that would end life on this planet, plunging it into a nuclear winter.

As you can probably see, neither of these two viewpoints is quite right; yet neither is quite wrong, either. A third school of thought exists. This holds that the net effect of computers upon human society will be essentially neutral. Society has absorbed many profound changes in the past without losing its bearings. With computerization some people will gain, others will lose, but the total effect will not fundamentally change the direction of society. The question for society then becomes one of how to redistribute the "gains" of some members to those other members who lose. Translated into more specific terms, society's problem becomes one of how to retrain people thrown out of their jobs by automation and by the need to use new and unfamiliar technology. Let's look at some of the specifics with which any of these viewpoints works: automation and robotics, job replacement, and job displacement.

Automation and robotics

AUTOMATION refers to the replacement of human control of a process by a machine. Automation may be used to make an existing product more cheaply, rapidly, or safely, or to create a new or refined product to replace an existing one. For example, the use of automation in the production of manufactured goods allows greater control over the quality of a product. In the electronics industry automated testing machines serve to speed up the testing process and to scan incredibly small microcircuit elements that would be difficult or impossible for humans to test.

Most of us work or will have to work to earn a living, and a major fear of some people who work is the loss of their jobs to a robot. A **ROBOT** is a machine capable of coordinating its movements itself by reacting to changes in the system environment. In other words, a robot has sensing devices and a built-in program to direct its movements based on the different input signals or conditions sensed. **ROBOTICS** refers to the study and application of robots.

Their glamorous and threatening public image notwithstanding, the robots of today are capable of handling many dangerous, boring, and dirty jobs (see Figure 20-1). Robots are used in manufacturing for a wide variety of tasks such as welding, lifting, and painting. Some large robots are capable of maneuvering an automobile body while performing welding operations on that body. At the other extreme of size, small, dexterous robots can assemble tiny electric motors.

Some robots are capable of walking and talking to people, and are packaged in a shape with trunk, limbs, and "head," supposedly to make their humanlike qualities more obvious. Kits are available to build your own robot capable of doing routine household chores, such as bringing you a cup of coffee. More significantly, however, robots can do a lot of things hazardous to people. For example, the bomb squad of the New York City Police Department uses a remotely controlled robot to investigate suitcases or packages that may contain a bomb. The robot picks up and places the

FIGURE 20-1.

Robots in our lives. They don't always fit the image presented in fiction. (a) The classic image—Robby the Robot from the 1955 science fiction movie The Forbidden Planet. (b) A walking robot. (c) A large robot used to weld automobiles. (d) A small robot being developed to help severely handicapped people feed themselves. (e) A robot used by the New York City Police Bomb Squad. (f) Robots in health care—a robot used to teach medical students to conduct physical examinations.

(a)

(b)

(c)

(d)

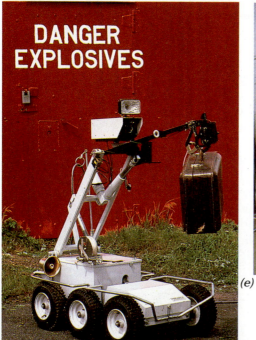

(e)

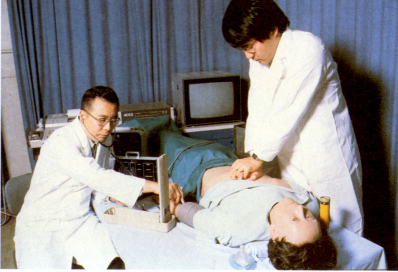

(f)

THE THREE RULES OF ROBOTICS

A honeybee has about a hundred thousand neurons, or circuits, yet can navigate, track, smell, reproduce, and communicate with fellow bees. A robot hooked to the world's largest computer, with many times that number of circuits, would be hard pressed to creep the length of a room without banging into the coffee table.

Once robots get more mobile and more intelligent than honeybees we'll be glad Isaac Asimov gave us the three rules of robotics in his 1940s science-fiction classic, "I, Robot":

- *Rule 1*: A robot must never hurt a human being, or through its actions allow one to come to harm.
- *Rule 2*: Robots must obey human orders, unless they conflict with Rule 1.
- *Rule 3*: A robot must never hurt itself, unless [not] doing so conflicts with Rule 1 or Rule 2.

First Reported Infraction of . . . Rule 1. Kenji Urada, 37, was killed in 1981 [in Japan] by a robot while attempting to repair malfunctioning circuits. The robot—a self-propelled, guided cart—apparently crushed Urada as he probed a circuit that turned out to set the robot in motion. . . .

First Reported Infraction of . . . Rule 2. A robot at American Motors' Jeep plant in Toledo went nuts in November 1982. Instead of spot-welding a piece of sheet metal under a tailgate, the robot grabbed hold of the car and wouldn't let go. Even when one employee hit it with a wooden plank it refused to let go. The assembly line had to be shut down and the robot's plug pulled to rescue the car.

First Reported Infraction of. . . Rule 3. In 1980 a $50,000 experimental arm five feet long went berserk in the University of Florida's Center for Intellectual Machines and Robots, wildly grabbing and smashing at things until it grabbed its own support stand and tore itself in half. Harvey Lipkin, a graduate student working in the lab at the time, observed: "We had a hardware failure."

Source: Jack B. Rochester and John Gantz, *The Naked Computer*, New York: Morrow, 1983, pp. 136–137. Copyright © by Jack B. Rochester and John Gantz. Reprinted by permission of William Morrow and Company.

suspected explosive in a truck with a specially sealed and reinforced cargo area; the truck is then driven outside of the city, and the bomb removed and defused.

Robots are also used in industry to handle radioactive substances while the human beings in charge watch from a safe and sealed-off distance. Their science-fiction billing aside, robots are basically very dumb and do not at all live up to their reputation (see box). For the types of applications we have mentioned, however, robots are being used increasingly, and are subtly transforming manufacturing and other industrial processes.

Job replacement and job displacement

JOB REPLACEMENT occurs when a job held by a person is taken over by a robot or other machine programmed to perform the same task. For example, people trained to weld an automobile chassis on an assembly line may find themselves replaced by robots that can do the job much more rapidly and safely. If their skill cannot be transferred to another operation or to another factory still doing things the old way, the people will have to be trained in a new skill—and quite possibly at a lower salary—to enable them to support themselves and their families.

If no such retraining program is available for them, or if they cannot find another job after attending such a program, then they will join the unemployment rolls. Automation does have its casualties; it would be unrealistic to say otherwise. Society's job is to face rather than ignore the situation, and provide training and employment opportunities for those who lose their jobs.

JOB DISPLACEMENT occurs when the skills necessary to perform a job change. For example, in a typing pool the ability to type accurately was once paramount. Correcting mistakes on hard copy is difficult and time consuming. When word-processing systems entered the picture, accuracy became less important, since correcting mistakes became a lot easier. As a result less capable typists could do the work. While this has displaced some "classical" typists; others have learned to use the new equipment, and continue to thrive in the office environment.

Job replacement and job displacement occur even within the computer field itself. Repair personnel, for example, once worked on large circuits with testing meters and soldering irons; now they run diagnostic programs and replace whole chips or boards rather than tinker with them. Most repair personnel who were used to doing things the old way were also capable of doing them the new way, since it was less demanding. Many voluntarily retrained for other areas of the computer field, however, since they found the new work too repetitive and lacking in challenge.

Some labor-force analysts fear that extensive use of computers will lead to a two-tier society. According to this view, a few skilled managers at the top levels of organizations would direct the work of a vast number of far less skilled people. The middle and lower-level management roles, in other words, would be considerably reduced in scope. The effect would be to reduce drastically chances for upward mobility. Since moving to or toward the top is a prime life goal for many people, this would have far-reaching social consequences.

Even professionals would not be exempt. Engineers, scientists, physicians, attorneys, and teachers all would need to struggle to keep up with changes in their fields. Without constant reeducation (in some cases required by accrediting organizations), professionals would face the risk of becoming technologically outdated in their fields, and would watch their status and earnings fall while more information-proficient colleagues advanced.

Job enhancement

We have presented quite a few negative factors thus far. Fortunately they do no not make up the whole picture. On the positive side, JOB ENHANCEMENT

FIGURE 20-2.
Inside a computer store.

can occur. Some existing jobs can be made far easier, and more enjoyable. New occupations can be created. For example, a vast industry exists now to produce, sell, and support a product that hadn't been invented a dozen years ago, the microcomputer. Besides the vast industrial base that produces the machines and their components, the nation is peppered with computer stores (Figure 20-2), and literally thousands of software companies turn out products for the micros. In addition there is a heavy demand for teachers to train users of these new systems, technical writers to describe them, and repairpersons to fix them.

The main effect of computers on the working world, however, has been that of mainframes and minicomputers. In North America, Western Europe, and Japan virtually every business of any size has been computerized. Considerable resistance was experienced, and the transitional period from doing things without a computer to doing things *well* with a computer sometimes lasted up to a decade, when management might have bargained on six months. With many billions of lines of computer code presently in place in these businesses, and the thralls of conversion for the most part past, management knows that things work better. Most employees will agree.

For example, ask someone who survived the computerization of a bank whether that person would rather check a balance the old way—by consulting outdated ledgers, making phone calls, and guessing —or by using a terminal. Few would want to turn the clock back. Most jobs that entail clerical operations are easier today with computers than they were before computers arrived on the scene, taking some of the drudgery out of work.

The electronic cottage

With the rise of distributed information systems and microcomputers, the age of the electronic cottage has begun, with people able to perform many types of jobs without leaving their homes (Figure 20-3). Working for a distant employer at a home terminal or computer is known as TELECOMMUTING. Although only a fraction of the American work force telecommutes today, the number is growing. Analysts wonder if the effects of the automobile might be undone by telecommuting. The automobile made it possible for people to live at great distances from their jobs—and once many people started to do so, stranded them in traffic each day. Telecommuting places the job right in the home. Just one of the results of this trend is to allow parents more time with their children.

FIGURE 20-3.
Life in the electronic cottage.

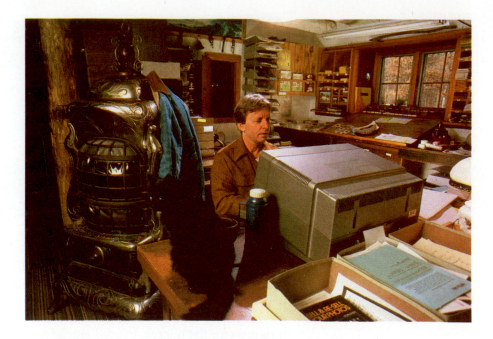

Historically cottage industries flourished just before the start of the industrial revolution, and fostered a piecework orientation that often led to exploitation of workers and an assurance that they could never rise from poverty. Some people wonder if in turning the clock forward with telecommuting, we are really turning it backward. It is not a simple question. Some of the drawbacks and advantages are discussed in the section "Working at Home" in Chapter 3.

RULES AND PROCEDURES

The creation and rapid expansion of communication networks for information systems allow us more quickly to move, analyze, and respond to data. People can make fast decisions—even the wrong ones.

For example, with a manual accounting system, or even a semiautomated system, checks on the people using the system occur over a period of time. If a blunder is committed somewhere along the way, the odds are good that someone will catch it before it reaches the world at large. With an automated system, however, the traditional checks may not operate.

One company went out of business because its automated accounting system was programmed to send out checks against incoming bills, but was not programmed to send out bills to those who owed the company money. Eventually the checks the company wrote bounced, as there was no money to cover them. The company went under.

Early in the days of computerization it was not uncommon for the representatives of a business to blame poor service on the machine. That should never be an excuse now. Most people realize that they, rather than the machines, run businesses. If you are ever told that a request can't be answered because "the computer can't handle it," that means that the company simply doesn't want to deal with your request and give you the proper service. Complain, or at the least ask "Who's in charge here, your managers or your machine?"

FIGURE 20-4.
Electronic banking at home.

The rise of distributed information systems has in fact led to greater responsiveness in handling exceptional conditions. For example, when booking an airline ticket we have come to rely not only on the standardized service that gets us a seat on the right flight, but on attention to exceptional conditions such as our requirement for vegetarian, kosher, or salt-free meals. Individual service is alive and well in the computer age—when the machines are programmed right.

Those of us who do not telecommute can utilize some information services in our home. This is another example of a change in rules and procedures. For example, you can pay your bills or shift money from one account to another (but alas, not make cash withdrawals) using your microcomputer at home (Figure 20-4). You can also query databases, check the latest stock quotations, reserve hotel rooms, and check the weather, without setting one foot out in the rain.

DATA The growth of large, centralized databases and the rise of microcomputers have raised issues of security. Using a modem and a telecommunications link, a determined outsider (or insider) may be able to gain access to confidential data contained in a database, and even to alter or destroy the data. This has in fact occurred.

Another area of concern is the increasing use of home computers to tie into systems to handle banking transactions. In the main, of course, this is a convenient new service. However, dishonest but clever individuals may figure out ways to steal money from the bank or from other people's accounts, all from the convenience of their own home. That is, crooks too may telecommute. It is also possible to sit down at another customer's terminal and, if you know the password, to transfer money from his or her account to yours; could the first user recover the loss here? In addition banks send billions of dollars back and forth via telecommunications links; as we saw in Chapter 17, telecommunications links can be tapped.

With today's reliance on databases, the risk exists of inaccurate data being introduced to a database and then transferred to other databases *ad infinitum* before the error is found. For example, there have been incidents where people have deliberately fabricated false data on others—such as not having paid back loans that they did pay back, or having served prison terms—and placed the data in the records maintained in a database. The false information is usually not detected until the person affected is turned down as a bad credit or insurance risk and realizes something is amiss. As the section "Protecting the Right to Privacy" noted in Chapter 17, legislation exists that enables people to examine and challenge data contained about them in a database.

SOFTWARE　A common complaint about software is that it is oversold by the maker. You can perhaps understand why when you realize that there are over 30,000 different software packages available for microcomputers. From the vendor's point of view, it is difficult to stand out from the pack without promising the moon.

From the user's point of view, it is very difficult to determine which package is right for a particular job. Once you have acquired a given software package, another murky area is entered: If software fails to work properly, or to live up to promises of the moon, who is liable for your business loss? It is not easy to go to court and prove that a program didn't do what it said. To this day most people don't even understand what a program is, let alone the difference between a good one and a bad one.

The software firms themselves do not have easy lives. Suppose you were offered something worth $300 for $3—would you take it? Most people would. That is about how much it costs for the floppy disk needed to copy someone's software package. The loss of sales revenues to the creators and sellers is a major problem, running into tens of millions of dollars per year; this problem tends to stifle interest in creating new products by software developers. One method of countering such program borrowing is to manufacture the software using the more expensive process of "burning" the software onto a read-only memory (ROM) chip; the purchaser pays more for this protection of the vendor.

Factors of buying and selling aside, there is some concern over the power that software has over our lives. All sizable weapons systems today are computerized, as are the satellite surveillance systems that would detect incoming missiles. In other words, these systems are supervised by computer hardware, which is in turn supervised by software, which is, one hopes, supervised by a human being.

The reason for the desirability of the human being in the loop is that software is full of mistakes. Anyone who has ever written a program knows how far from perfect it was. Vendors regularly ship software with an average of two or three lines of incorrect code per 100 lines of code. What if the programs used to run our national defense system are also filled with this level of errors? The fact is that much of the code has never been, and can never be, tested under live conditions. The decision time for the life and death choices to be made by the U.S. or Soviet heads of state before pressing the button has been dramatically shortened, to less than six minutes after the detection of of submarine-launched missiles. That does not leave a whole lot of margin for ironing out software bugs.

HARDWARE

It has been said that computers constitute a clean industry. The once-quiet towns of the Santa Clara Valley of California—which is now informally known throughout the world as Silicon Valley—welcomed the semiconductor firms with their absence of industry's traditional belching smokestacks, their need for workers, and their contributions to the tax rolls. This valley of great wealth, the center of the semiconductor or "chip" industry, has become an industrial disaster area, through the quiet but deadly percolation of chemicals into the groundwater. Ironically these chemicals were not just dumped irresponsibly but were placed in underground tanks, following the best disposal method of the time, in an attempt to avoid the problems that have occurred anyway.

In addition recent studies have shown that a number of the chemicals used in the production of silicon chips have been improperly handled. Some production-line workers have allegedly developed severe health problems due to the chemical processes involved.

There has been little methodical investigation into the health and safety of people who use display screens. As has happened often enough with other inventions or technologies, there is a tendency first to use something extensively, and then, when the damage has been done, to stop and think about whether it was such a good idea. It has become virtually the office norm to work with a terminal, and data-entry operators spend the whole workday looking at them. Visual problems can result, just as they can from watching television for hours on end. The human eye tries to "resolve" what it sees into a crisp image, a process continually frustrated by staring at a blurry image (blurry when compared, say, with print) that cannot be resolved. Display screens also emit a low level of electromagnetic radiation; as yet no one knows whether that will have any long-term effects.

Sitting at a terminal is no bed of roses, either, and can lead to a variety of chronic aches and pains. According to Bernardina Wilcox of the Lauderdale-Wilcox Physical Rehabilitation Center in Anaheim, Calif., "Persons who operate video display terminals have a high rate of back stress and back injury."*

FUTURE TRENDS: THE SHAPE OF TOMORROW

At the 1939 World's Fair in New York City, a number of experts were asked to predict what the most important inventions of the near future would be. They completely missed two of the most significant inventions: the atomic bomb and electronic computers. Making predictions definitely has its limits. Like weather forecasting used to be (before computers), predictions are as often wrong as right. But let's take a chance anyway.

PEOPLE

It is difficult to say who will be the real gainers or losers from the information age. Flexibility seems to be the most important characteristic of

*Walt Murray, Knight-Ridder News Service, taken from *San Jose Mercury-News*, November 18, 1984.

Hackers have been the centerpiece of numerous articles in the popular press expressing grave concern about the dangers of "computer addiction." The nature of this concern varies. There are fears that young people will fall victim to a new kind of addiction with druglike effects: withdrawal from society, narrowing of focus and life purpose, inability to function without a fix. Others fear the spread, via the computer, of characteristics of the "hacker mind." And hackers are almost universally represented as having a very undesirable frame of mind: they prefer machines to sex, they don't care about being productive.

Several years ago *Psychology Today* published an interchange called "The Hacker Papers." It was a warning on the part of some, including some hackers, that hacking was dangerous and depleting, and a defense on the part of others that hacking was a creative outlet like any other. The article prompted a flood of electronic mail debating the question. Artificial intelligence scientist Marvin Minsky presented the strongest defense of the hackers. They are no different from other people seriously devoted to their work, he said. . . .

There are few women hackers. This is a male world. Though hackers would deny that theirs is a macho culture, the preoccupation with winning and of subjecting oneself to increasingly violent tests make their world peculiarly male in spirit, peculiarly unfriendly to women. There is, too, a flight from relationship with people to relationship with the machine—a defensive maneuver more common to men than to women. The computer that is the partner in this relationship offers a particularly seductive refuge to someone who is having trouble dealing with people. It is active, reactive, it talks back. Many hackers first sought out such a refuge during early adolescence, when other people, their feelings, their demands, seemed particularly frightening. They found a refuge in the computer and never moved beyond. Alex is one of these.

Alex spends fifteen hours a day on the computer.

At least fifteen, maybe three for eating, usually a big pancake breakfast with the other guys after a night of hacking. Or sometimes we'll do a dinner in Chinatown at about one in the morning. Six for sleeping. I sleep from about nine in the morning to three, when I go over to the computer center. . . . I would say that I have a perfect interface with the machine . . . perfect for me. I feel totally telepathic with the computer. And it sort of generalizes so that I feel telepathic with the people I am sending mail to. I am glad I don't have to see them face to face. I wouldn't be as personal about myself. And the telepathy with the computer—well, I certainly don't think of it as a person there, but that doesn't mean that I don't feel it as a person there. Particularly since I have personalized my interface with the system to suit myself. So it's like being with another person, but not a strange person. Someone who knows just how I like things done. . . .

Source: Sherry Turkle, *The Second Self: Computers and the Human Spirit*, 1984, pp. 206–211. Copyright © 1984 Sherry Turkle. Reprinted by permission of Simon and Schuster.

Occupation	Percent Growth in Employment 1982–95	Projected Employment in 1995
Computer service technicians	96.8	108,000
Legal assistants	94.3	88,000
Computer system analysts	85.3	471,000
Computer programmers	76.9	471,000
Computer operators	75.8	371,000
Office machine repair persons	71.7	95,000
Physical therapy assistants	67.8	55,000
Electrical engineers	65.3	528,000
Civil engineering technicians	63.9	58,000
Peripheral EDP equipment operators	63.5	80,000

Source: "Employment Projections for 1995," U.S. Department of Labor Bureau of Labor Statistics, March 1984, Bulletin 2197.

people best able to adjust to the changes brought on by computers. Generally speaking people who are well-educated but not overly specialized can adjust easily. Someone who enters the work world today should expect to need retraining every several years, and perhaps even a career change every 10 to 15 years.

Two groups of people will face problems: the less educated, and the educated who cannot or will not adapt to change. For example, some of the major career growth areas today are in fields that didn't even exist 20 years ago. Figure 20-5 projects the ten fastest growing occupations into the future. As you can see, half of these fields are related to information systems. Even some of the other fields not directly related to information systems still involve them; for example, legal assistants help attorneys prepare cases and interview clients, and can benefit from a knowledge of office automation systems and the use of databases to retrieve legal precedents for a case.

Not all information-system-related jobs are expected to grow over the next few years. One category in particular is expected to decline—the number of data-entry operators was 320,000 in 1982; it is projected to be 286,000 in 1995.

The increasing reliance by managers in all industries on computerized decision support systems has led to speculation that these systems might change the role of managers. In a sense, by ceding authority to make certain kinds of routine decisions to computers, some low- and middle-level managers may be putting themselves out of business. The effects are not likely to be so drastic, however. Decision support systems should enhance the quality of information available to managers and their ease of access to it. The systems are not likely, in the near future, to be able to use that information to make decisions. Managers will still be needed for that.

The same may not be true for blue-collar workers. In the future we can expect robots—dubbed the "steel-collar" work force—to have an increasing impact on the human work force. Japan will probably continue to be the major producer as well as user of robots (see Figure 20-6). The United States and Western European countries will also produce tremendous quantities of these machines. Robots now are used primarily in the manufacture of automobiles, trucks, and electronic equipment. The main duties of robots today are simple machining and welding. By 1990 robots are expected to carry out more sophisticated tasks, with their main job being the assembly of machined and welded parts.

Although no one knows for sure, the effect of robots on people employed in manufacturing could be devastating. A study by the Rand Corporation forecasts that the percentage of people employed in manufacturing jobs might decline from about 20 percent of the work force to 2 percent by the year 2000. Naturally someone has to make, control, and repair the robots, which opens up new jobs. But other analysts have predicted that for each job created by the robotics industry, five will be lost. If job loss of this magnitude occurs, severe social and economic problems could result. As we said earlier in the chapter, the issue of providing retraining and new jobs must be faced.

FIGURE 20-6.
Annual robot production estimated for the years 1985 and 1990 for the major Western countries.

Rank	Country	1985 est.	1990 est.
1	Japan	31,000	57,500
2	United States	7,700	31,300
3	West Germany	5,000	12,000
4	United Kingdom	3,000	21,500
5	Sweden	2,300	5,000
6	Italy	1,250	3,500
7	France	1,000	3,000
8	Norway	1,000	2,000
	All other countries	1,750	4,200
	Total worldwide	54,000	140,000

Source: "The Robotics Industry," U.S. Department of Commerce, International Trade Administration, April 1983, p. 20.

RULES AND PROCEDURES

Will rules become more or less rigid in the future? Who will make the rules? Some signs seem to indicate that rules will become less rigid, allowing people greater flexibility over their lives. For example, with telecommuting the rules pertaining to where and when we work have become more relaxed for some people. On the other hand, information systems can now keep track of exactly how you spend your time, and compare your effectiveness with that of other workers using hard data rather than your supervisor's imperfect knowledge. This would seem to point toward less flexibility. As with any crystal-ball gazing, no one really knows for sure.

DATA

Every day more and more data are being compiled about us. Databases keep records on our buying habits, health problems, family life, and other concerns. There has even been talk of setting up a national database to contain all of the information concerning individuals that is presently maintained by different governmental agencies, so that all of the agencies might share it. Using a password and an identifier such as your social security number, many different agencies and people would be able to access confidential data concerning you, whether they needed the data or not. Needless to say, there has been considerable resistance to the idea of a national database.

Issues of centralization aside, data will be managed differently in the future. Database management systems are expected to become cheaper, faster, and easier to use. The systems should be better able to reduce unauthorized access and yet to increase the ease of use by the proper personnel. Database languages will become more powerful yet simpler to use. Inquiries will be made in statements in, or near to, the languages that we speak.

SOFTWARE

Program development will become more automated by the use of computer-assisted programming tools. These design aids will reduce the amount of time programmers need to spend debugging the actual program, and free up time to spend on program design. These methods will force programmers to use structured techniques more consistently in all stages of program development. It is to be hoped that software in the future will contain fewer errors than present-day software, thus offering greater reliability. Programs will be further integrated into hardware through the use of the various types of firmware.

As with database languages, programming languages should continue the trend toward natural languages. Data inquiry languages will permit the user to converse with the hardware in a pattern which the system "learns"—that is, records, analyzes, and retains—to help structure future data-inquiry sessions. Expert systems will become available in a wide variety of fields, and will be addressed to users at different skill levels. For example, in medicine expert systems that use nontechnical terminology may be used to interview patients directly. A physician can then perform an examination or interview and also consult the results of analysis by the expert system, in order better to reach a diagnosis and determine the right course of treatment.

Software is already big business. The emphasis of computer systems has shifted from hardware being virtually the sole focus and investment, to a

FIGURE 20-7.
Projected worldwide sales by U.S. computer companies.

	Sales (in billions of dollars)		
	1981	**1986**	**1990**
Mainframes	17.2	24.8	43.4
Minicomputers	8.8	22.2	38.8
Microcomputers	1.2	3.5	6.1
Peripherals	13.9	18.7	32.7
Software/services	14.9	39.1	68.4
Total	56.0	108.3	189.4

Source: "The Computer Industry," U.S. Department of Commerce, International Trade Administration, April 1983, p. 15 for the 1981 and 1986 data; estimate given for 1990 using the 15 percent compounded annual rate suggested in the report.

point where software is nearly as important (see Figure 20-7). In the future this trend is expected to accelerate. The overall size of the software and computer support industry is expected to grow by 75 percent from 1986 to 1990.

HARDWARE How will we communicate with the computers of the future? In all likelihood it will be differently than we do now. Communication will be based less heavily upon traditional key entry of data and more heavily upon source data automation. Machines capable of reading vast quantities of text or manuscript material will be available to many users. In addition more reliable and flexible voice-recognition systems will be available for the business market.

Figure 20-7 gives projections for computer hardware sales in 1990. Although the breakdown is into the familiar categories of mainframes, minicomputers, and microcomputers, we should expect significant changes. Several new technologies are presently in the works that may give rise to a new breed of machine, or radically transform the existing breeds. Concerning CPU circuitry, the main projects under way are:

■ *Further development of silicon chip semiconductors using* VERY-LARGE-SCALE INTEGRATION (VLSI).

■ *The substitution of* MICROLASERS *for the circuitry in today's computers, possibly leading to the creation of "optical" rather than electronic computers.*

■ *The substitution of* BIOCHIPS, *which utilize molecular structures and processes developed using biotechnology, for the electronic components of today's machines.*

■ *Further development of* JOSEPHSON JUNCTIONS, *which exploit the electrical properties of switches at supercooled temperatures close to absolute zero.*

Regardless of the specific technology that will be used, the central processing units of the future are certain to shrink still more. As we have seen before, smaller means faster when it comes to electrical circuits, since electricity has to traverse a smaller distance with smaller components. At the speed of electricity, shrinking a chip by another fraction of an inch might not seem to matter much; yet it does when electricity must repeatedly traverse the same distance many millions of times. So we can expect to be working with both smaller and faster machines in the future.

One present trend with computers should continue: they will become less visible as they are incorporated into ever more products at home and at work. Computers will be used for process control not only in factories and offices, but at home, monitoring and controlling heating, air-conditioning, and security systems. The electronic components contained in an automobile will continue to increase in sophistication, but will remain essentially invisible to the driver. Microprocessors will record the status of a car's systems, including keeping a record of when the car has been misused. Microprocessors—even smaller, cheaper, and more powerful—will be incorporated into many items that they have not yet reached, including artificial hearts and other organs to replace failed parts of the body.

You may witness the birth of the first computers that really think. ARTIFICIAL INTELLIGENCE, which refers to the study and development of machines that can duplicate some human thought processes, has been a field of lively investigation for years. Today's computers run very fast but only do one thing at a time: their "stunt," in other words, is rapid computation. Everyone knows people can do more without even half trying. People reason, learn, and make decisions based upon partial or ambiguous data. People can do more than one thing at a time, and can deal with unknowns. The long-awaited FIFTH GENERATION of computers being developed both in the United States and Japan may unveil machinery that can more nearly do what we can—that is, think. Perhaps, however, we will still have a few computer generations to go.

WRAP-UP | **THE PLUSES AND THE MINUSES**

At the behemoth Global Electrical Equipment Corporation—where George Roberts found himself heading a pilot application project that used robots as quality-control inspectors—the situation was highly charged. The robots had been on the job for a month. The human situation was George's first concern.

Global's personnel department hired a retraining consultant, to see if something might be done so that inspectors replaced by robots could make lateral moves to acceptable positions. Global offered them quality-control inspection jobs at different plants. Three employees took the jobs, moving away from Oakriver to do so. The remaining employees did not want to leave Oakriver, and George negotiated a promise from management to give them priority for transfers to comparably ranked inspection positions on the assembly line. George well knew, however, that all of the people hated assembly-line work. That was why they had moved to quality control in the first place. However, the offer was the best George could manage; two employees took it, and two left Global in a huff.

In other words, out of George's 15 employees, three had to pull up roots in Oakriver, two had to transfer to jobs they disliked, two had left to seek work elsewhere, and the remaining eight not replaced by robots could read the writing on the wall—if the experiment succeeded, the same fate awaited them. Worse, it awaited most of the quality-control inspectors throughout this plant and at other locations.

On the positive side, George rather liked the machines. He had enrolled in a course at the Automated Intelligence Institute at Oakriver University, and was beginning to understand what made robots tick. These robots had limbs, but there any resemblance to human beings ceased. They were stationary machines, with articulated "arms" able to manipulate and test an appliance once it reached their range of operation on the assembly line. One advantage that even the human co-workers had to concede was that the robots had their test instruments built right into them. That was a hard act to follow. On the other hand, the programs that controlled the robots could not cover all test situations; when a robot encountered an appliance with doubtful but not definitely negative test results, it placed the appliance to the side and called in a human inspector.

All things considered, the experiment dictated by Global's directors probably would pan out. The robots worked about 25 percent faster than people, with lower error rates. George had not seen cost figures, but he was certain that over the long run the robots were substantially cheaper than people, with no expenses for social security, vacations, medical insurance, and so on. Global seemed headed into the future on a track that would increase its profit margin, drop its prices, and help it remain competitive with other highly automated firms both in the United States and abroad.

SUMMARY

- The computer revolution has only begun, and different observers hold conflicting opinions about its impact upon society. People have been affected by automation and robotics, job replacement, and job displacement. Automation refers to the replacement of human control of a process by a machine. Robots today handle many dangerous, boring, and dirty jobs. Job replacement occurs when a job held by a person is taken over by a machine; job displacement takes place when the skills necessary to perform a job change. Computers have been responsible for both.

- On the brighter side computers have also been associated with job enhancement. Some existing jobs have been made far easier, and whole new occupations have been created. In addition some observers claim that with the rise of distributed information systems and microcomputers, the age of the electronic cottage has begun, with people telecommuting to work via a home terminal or microcomputer.
- Computerization has affected the rules and procedures by which businesses operate, speeding up operations and, if anything, making rules more flexible.
- Centralized databases raise issues of the security and accuracy of data maintained about us.
- Social issues involving software include, for the user, questions about the reliability of programs; and for the vendor, loss of revenues to piracy. Another software issue, involving all of us, is the reliance of our national defense system on software that can't be tested under live conditions.
- Social issues involving hardware include possible environmental damage associated with the manufacture of silicon chips and possible health hazards associated with the prolonged use of display screens.
- Some people are expected to gain by the increasing use of computers, and some people to lose. Well-educated but not overly specialized people will probably adjust best. Robots will play an increasing role.
- Some trends—toward telecommuting, for example—suggest that rules and procedures, at least for working patterns, may become more flexible. Other trends—for example, the ability of information systems to keep accurate track of an employee's work patterns—point in the opposite direction.
- Database management systems will be cheaper, faster, and easier to use. The potential concentration of data about individuals in a national database, however, raises concerns about privacy.
- Software design will become more automated through the use of computer-assisted programming tools, and programming languages may continue the trend toward natural languages. Expert systems will become available in a wide variety of fields.
- To communicate with computers of the future we will rely more on source data automation and voice-recognition systems.
- CPUs of the future are certain to shrink still more, and become faster. Current technologies leading in this direction include very-large-scale integration (VLSI) of electronic chips; microlaser-based optical circuitry; biochips; and Josephson junctions.
- We can expect to see increased use of computers in familiar settings such as the home and car.
- Although the gap between the capabilities of computers and human thought is still vast, artificial intelligence has made strides in recent years. Fifth-generation computers may come very close to thinking like humans. And someday we may well witness the birth of such computers.

These are the key terms in the order in which they appear in the chapter.

Automation (555)
Robot (555)
Robotics (555)
Job replacement (558)
Job displacement (558)
Job enhancement (558)
Telecommuting (559)

Very-large-scale integration (VLSI) (568)
Microlaser (568)
Biochip (568)
Josephson junction (568)
Artificial intelligence (569)
Fifth generation (569)

REVIEW QUESTIONS

OBJECTIVE QUESTIONS

TRUE/FALSE: *Put the letter T or F on the line before the question.*

1. Automation refers to the replacement of human control of a process by a robot.
2. Robotics is the study and application of robots.
3. Job replacement occurs when a job held by a person is taken over by a robot or other machine.
4. There are nearly 5000 computer programs available for microcomputers.
5. Artificial intelligence is still 30 to 50 years away.
6. Telecommuting will make it possible to reduce automobile travel needs by office workers.
7. Professionals will be exempt from the impact of computers.
8. Josephson junctions use superheated circuits to speed switching times.
9. The electronic cottage is a form of telecommuting.
10. Very-large-scale integration (VLSI) increases switching speeds on silicion chip circuitry.

MULTIPLE CHOICE QUESTIONS: *Write the letter of the correct answer on the line before the question.*

1. The major producers of robots are
   (a) Japan and the United States.
   (b) Japan and West Germany.
   (c) The Soviet Union and the United States.
   (d) The United States and Western Europe.
2. Which of the following job areas in information processing will grow the least over the next several years?
   (a) Systems analysts.
   (b) Data-entry operators.
   (c) Computer programmers.
   (d) Computer operators.
3. The three rules of robotics
   (a) Are based on a fictional work.
   (b) Are carefully followed.
   (c) Have already been violated.
   (d) Both a and c.
4. Job displacement
   (a) Means the same as job replacement.
   (b) Is not a major concern among workers.
   (c) Occurs when the skills necessary to perform a job change.
   (d) Occurs when a job a person holds is lost to a robot or other machine.

5. Job enhancement means
    (a) Making some existing jobs easier.
    (b) Creating new occupations.
    (c) Creating new industries.
    (d) All of the above.

FILL IN THE BLANK: *Write the correct word or words in the blank to complete the sentence.*

1. The ability to work far from the office environment is known as _____.
2. The study of robots and their applications is _____.
3. A _____ may use organic molecules to store data in future computers.
4. Optical computers may use _____ to replace electronic circuitry.
5. A change in the skills required to perform a job refers to _____.
6. The _____ computers are hoped to be capable of thinking like people.
7. The _____ recalls how people worked at home in the era before the industrial revolution.
8. To pack great numbers of electronic components onto silicon chips, _____ is used.
9. The country of _____ produces the largest number of robots.
10. The term _____ refers to the ability of machines to think like people.

SHORT ANSWER QUESTIONS

When answering these questions think of concrete examples to illustrate your points.

1. What is the difference between job replacement and job displacement?
2. What industries have been created in the information age?
3. Do professionals face threats to their livelihoods from the rise of computers?
4. What is the study of robotics?
5. What impact might the electronic cottage have on society?
6. What hardware advances are expected in the coming years?
7. What is meant by the term "fifth generation"?
8. What impact may future developments have upon rules and procedures?

ESSAY QUESTIONS

1. Who is likely to gain from projected changes in software and hardware?
2. Have computers made jobs you have held easier or more difficult?
3. Have computers had an impact upon your personal life?
4. Comment on the Case in Point, "Hackers—Loving the Machine for Itself."

AN INTRODUCTION TO PROGRAMMING IN BASIC

If you have read at least part of this book, particularly the chapters of Part 3, you are no stranger to programming. The task of this appendix is to bring your knowledge of programming to the hands-on level.

This appendix presents the fundamentals of the BASIC programming language. A major reason for learning a programming language in an introductory course is to gain self-confidence in working with computers. You can achieve some level of competence in programming, as well as a better understanding of the programming process, by designing and writing your own program, testing it, and correcting mistakes. Finally, creating a successfully executing program is a satisfying and rewarding process.

We will use the structured programming methods discussed in Chapters 9 and 10 as an aid in explaining the programming process. Once you have completed this appendix, you should have a solid beginner's knowledge of structured programming, and the ability to write simple working programs that do a variety of things.

After studying this appendix, you should understand the following:

■ How to use structured methods to design a program written in BASIC.
■ How to create problem solutions that combine sequences, decisions, and loops.
■ Some techniques to use to help avoid errors and to diagnose those that do occur in your programs.
■ The ways to document your program design properly using internal program comments, flowcharts, and pseudocode.
■ How to create programs that produce easy-to-read output.

Section One ties together programming concepts to which you have already been introduced in this book. We begin by reviewing the elements of program design and testing. Using the credit-limit problem given in the "Programming and Problem Solving" box of Chapter 2, we then review the program development cycle, the use of flowcharts and pseudocode, and the BASIC language.

THE CREDIT-LIMIT PROBLEM

George and Janis Roberts walk into an appliance store and select a new television set. They decide to pay for it with a bank credit card. Their current credit status at the National Bank of Oakriver is:

```
The Roberts' credit limit       = $1500.00
The Roberts' current balance    = $ 567.53
Price of a new television set   = $ 535.95
```

Presented with these data, most of us would approve the Roberts' new purchase. A computer program can process the same data and come to the same decision.

THE PROGRAM DEVELOPMENT CYCLE

The **PROGRAM DEVELOPMENT CYCLE** (introduced in the "Programming and Problem Solving" section of Chapter 9) gives us some insight into solving this problem. The program development cycle consists of eight steps:

1   **PROBLEM RECOGNITION,** *which means becoming aware that a problem exists.*
2   **PROBLEM DEFINITION,** *which concerns focusing on the problem to find the cause and the solution.*
3   **PROGRAM DESIGN,** *which means specifying the structure of the program in detail.*
4   **PROGRAM CODING,** *which means translating the design into a programming language that will run on a computer.*
5   **PROGRAM TESTING,** *which permits the debugging and correction of flaws in the program.*
6   **PROGRAM IMPLEMENTATION,** *which means using the program.*
7   **PROGRAM MAINTENANCE,** *which involves altering the program to correct previously undetected errors or to meet changes in requirements.*
8   *Beginning the cycle again.*

For the National Bank of Oakriver, the problem of quickly and accurately checking peoples' credit limits was *recognized* by the people involved with the credit-card department. Together with the information-system staff, they *defined the problem.* The next step was *program design.* This set the stage for *program coding,* in which the computer program is actually written. Once the program exists, it will be *tested, implemented,* and *modified* on the basis of feedback from the bank, merchants, and cardholders. Eventually the problem solution cycle will begin again with a new request from the bank.

We will apply the principles of structured programming to the problems presented in this appendix. The programs will be designed using a top-down modular approach, coupled with internal and external documentation to create programs that are easily followed and could be easily modified. Our main focus will be upon using structured programming methods in the area of detailed design—flowcharts and pseudocode.

FLOWCHARTS AND PSEUDOCODE

Designing the details of the program solution can be accomplished by various methods. The two that we will work with are flowcharts and pseudocode. A **FLOWCHART** is a diagram that shows how a program works in terms of sequence, movement of data, and logic. **PSEUDOCODE** is an English-like code that helps the programmer understand the steps needed to execute the program. While less impressive visually than flowcharts, pseudocode is easier to write using a word-processing package. Flowcharts and pseudocode accompany selected programs in this appendix.

Over the years people have come to agree upon which flowchart symbols should represent particular functions. Figure A1-1 illustrates the most commonly used flowchart symbols and the corresponding pseudocode phrases. Moving from left to right in the figure, you can see the desired operation, the flowchart symbol, the corresponding pseudocode phrase, and the meaning of the operation.

FIGURE A1-1.
Flowchart symbols and pseudo-code phrases.

Operation	Flowchart Symbol	Pseudocode Phrase	Meaning
System interrupt [Start, Stop]		START STOP	Notes the beginning or end of a program or subroutine
Input, output		Input, get, read, print, write	All input/output operations
Process		Process, compute, calculate, initialize to a value	Process functions for arithmetic and data manipulation
Decision	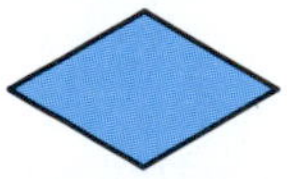	IF ... THEN, or IF ... THEN ... ELSE : : ENDIF	Decision operations for logic tests and comparisons
Preparation		Prepare, initialize	Prepare the program for later stages, set variables to a starting value (used at the beginning of FOR/NEXT loops in BASIC)
Predefined process	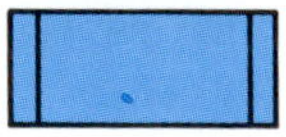	CALL, subroutine	Use of a predefined function: usually a subroutine or library routine
Annotation	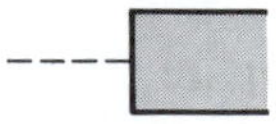	Comment, note, remark, annotate	These comments provide guidance to the reader of the program, but do not affect its operation
Connector	on-page off-page 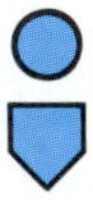	Not used in pseudocode	Connector to other parts of the flowchart on the same or different pages
Flowlines	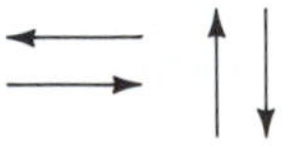	Not used in pseudocode	Shows the direction of the flow, usual flow is from top to bottom and from left to right

As shown in Chapter 10, structured programming employs three basic logic patterns:

- **SEQUENCE**—a set of linear steps to be carried out in the order of their appearance.
- **SELECTION**—comparisons based on decisions or choices to split the program into different paths.
- **LOOP**—repetitive execution of one or a series of steps. There are two types of loops, DOWHILE and DOUNTIL, which vary in the test used to end the loop.

Figure A1-2 expresses the basic logic patterns in both flowcharts and pseudocode. In designing your own programs, be sure to follow carefully any rules of your instructor concerning flowcharting and preparing pseudocode.

FIGURE A1-2.

The logic patterns used in structured programming: sequence, selection, and loop. Both flowchart and pseudocode are shown. (a) Sequence. (b) Selection (IF/THEN/ELSE). (c) Loop.

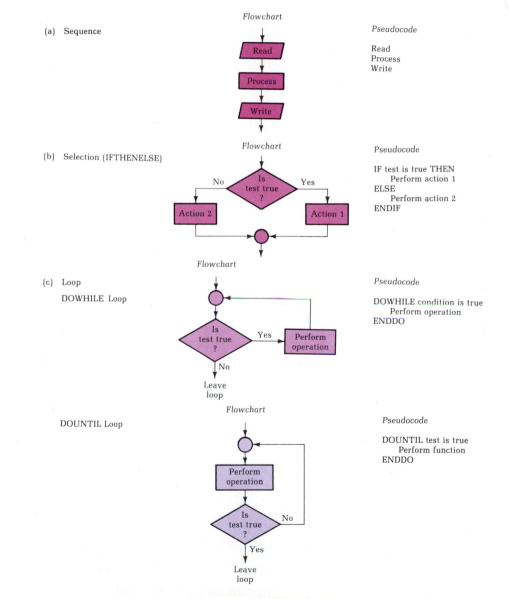

PROGRAM DOCUMENTATION serves to aid the programmer (or supervisor) in understanding the program. Documentation for student-oriented projects can consist of the following components:

1   A description of the problem and its significance. The description can include the variables used and their characteristics. Additionally, a written narrative describing the steps required to solve the problem can be placed in this part.
2   A description of any new or unusual programming procedures.
3   A description of the hardware used. This includes the central processor and the necessary peripheral equipment.
4   A description of the software used. Usually this is just the programming language itself, and any special canned software you may have used.
5   If available, a statement of the run time (actual execution time), and of the total programming time required to solve and write the report for the problem.
6   A statement of the secondary storage requirements of the program.
7   Flowcharts or pseudocode as needed to display accurately the programming steps and patterns of the program.

FIGURE A1-3.
Documentation for the credit-limit problem.

Student name: Michael Franks

Description of the problem and its significance: The problem is to write a program to check a customers's credit-card balance. The program adds the amount to be charged to the customer's current balance and indicates whether the combined charges will exceed the customer's credit limit.

The variables used are:

    B = Current balance
    C = Amount to be charged
    L = Credit limit
    N = The total of the current balance and the amount to be charged.
        N must be less than or equal to the credit limit for the credit
        sale to be approved.

Description of any new or unusual programming procedures: I learned how to write a short interactive program in BASIC. The new commands I used were REM, LET, PRINT, INPUT, IF/THEN/ELSE, and END.

Description of the hardware used: CPU—Hewlett-Packard 3000; peripherals—H-P 125 microcomputer (terminal), H-P line printer, and fixed disk.

Description of the software used: BASIC (H-P version).

Statement of the run time: Not available.

Total programming time: Four hours.

Statement of the secondary storage requirements: three blocks.

Flowchart or pseudocode: Attached.

Program with run: Attached.

Figure A1-3 shows how a student might write parts 1 through 6 of the documentation for our model problem. The flowchart and pseudocode (part 7 of the documentation) appear in Figure A1-4; they show how symbols can be used to diagram the logic of the credit-approval process.

Flowchart

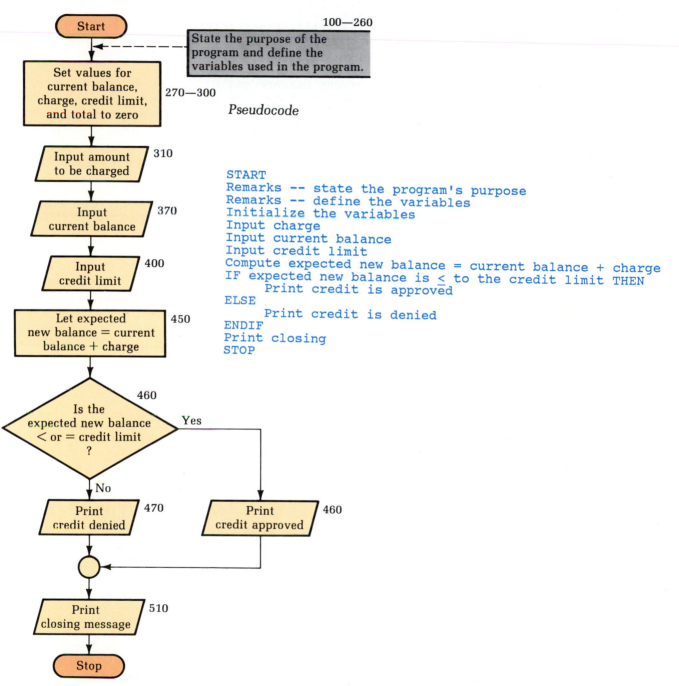

```
START
Remarks -- state the program's purpose
Remarks -- define the variables
Initialize the variables
Input charge
Input current balance
Input credit limit
Compute expected new balance = current balance + charge
IF expected new balance is ≤ to the credit limit THEN
        Print credit is approved
ELSE
        Print credit is denied
ENDIF
Print closing
STOP
```

FIGURE A1-5.

Program for the credit-limit problem.

```
100 REM This program checks a customers's credit balance.
110 REM The program was written by Michael Franks.
120 REM This program adds the amount to be charged to the
130 REM customer's current balance and indicates whether
140 REM the combined amounts will exceed the customer's limit.
150 REM The program is written in the BASIC programming
160 REM language and is run on a Hewlett-Packard 3000 system.
170 REM ****************************************************
180 REM The variables used are:
190 REM           B  =  Current balance
200 REM           C  =  Amount to be charged
210 REM           L  =  Credit limit
220 REM           N  =  The total of the current balance and
230 REM                 the amount to be charged.  N must be
240 REM                 less than or equal to the credit limit
250 REM                 for the credit sale to be approved.
260 REM ****** The following lines execute the program.  ******
270 LET B = 0
280 LET C = 0
290 LET L = 0
300 LET N = 0
310 PRINT "What is the amount to be charged";
320 INPUT C
330 PRINT
340 REM For simplicity we will enter the values for B and L.
350 REM Normally these values are obtained from the bank's credit
360 REM card users database.
370 PRINT "What is the customer's current balance";
380 INPUT B
390 PRINT
400 PRINT "What is the customer's credit limit";
410 INPUT L
420 PRINT
430 PRINT
440 REM  Now we perform the calculation  and  test  our answer.
450 LET N = B + C
460 IF N <= L THEN PRINT "Customer's credit is approved."
470 ELSE PRINT "Customer's credit is not approved!!!"
480 REM The logic test takes two lines using this computer.
490 PRINT
500 PRINT
510 PRINT "End of program -- Have a nice day!"
520 END


RUN
What is the amount to be charged? 535.95

What is the customer's current balance? 567.53

What is the customer's credit limit? 1500.00


Customer's credit is approved.


End of program -- Have a nice day!
```

THE BASIC PROGRAMMING LANGUAGE

Once we have worked out the logic of a problem using a flowchart or pseudocode, we can write and test a program to solve it. The program (Figure A1-5) is written in BASIC (Beginner's All-purpose Symbolic Instruction Code). You might not understand how the entire program works yet. In the following sections, we will use it to help explain the details of BASIC.

Entering the program into the computer, and typing in the system command RUN, lets us execute the program. The actual results appear at the bottom of Figure A1-5. In this appendix we show computer output in color. Note that the numbers in the flowchart (Figure A1-4) correspond to the line numbers in the program. These have been put there to make it easier to follow both the flowchart and the program (later program flowcharts will not include line numbers).

BASIC was developed by John G. Kemeny and Thomas Kurtz, while they were mathematics professors at Dartmouth College. It was designed with the novice programmer in mind. BASIC is used for a wide variety of applications in business, the scientific community, and government. Its merits relative to other languages are discussed in Chapter 11. One note of caution concerns machine independence; with BASIC this is fairly low because there is a lack of standardization among the different dialects. The American National Standards Institute (ANSI) has developed a standard for minimal BASIC or ANSI-BASIC. Places in the readings where the text uses nonANSI-BASIC are identified. *Therefore the code presented in this appendix might need to be modified to work on your computer.* This lack of standardization is most evident in two areas: (1) working with data files and (2) creating sophisticated output displays.

KEY TERMS

These are the key terms in the order in which they appear in the section.

Program development cycle (A-3)
Problem recognition (A-3)
Problem definition (A-3)
Program design (A-3)
Program coding (A-3)
Program testing (A-3)
Program implementation (A-3)
Program maintenance (A-3)
Flowchart (A-4)

Pseudocode (A-4)
Sequence (A-5)
Selection (A-5)
Loop (A-5)
Program documentation (A-6)
BASIC (Beginner's All-purpose Symbolic Instruction Code) (A-9)
ANSI-BASIC (A-9)

In Section Two we run through the characteristics of the BASIC language point by point. We start at the very beginning, with turning on the machine. We then introduce the characters, constants, and variables used in BASIC and describe how to use each of the main BASIC commands. A sample program that demonstrates the concepts is given at the end of the section.

WHERE TO BEGIN

Let us get started. The first step in learning to use BASIC is to learn how to turn on your computer correctly. If you have not already done so, carefully read the computer instruction manual or the instructions posted at your computer lab to find the on/off switch.

Once your machine warms up, you will have to get the attention of the operating system (the programs that supervise the overall operations of the computer). Depending on your computer, the operating system may require you to perform a number of steps before you can actually get down to the business of writing or using programs. This preliminary procedure is often called **LOGGING ON.** Some sample log-on procedures for different computers are shown in Figure A2-1. You tell the operating system what to do through a set of commands called **SYSTEM COMMANDS.** These system commands (also shown in Figure A2-1) communicate important orders to the computer, such as when you want the program you have written to be run. The other system commands help you to save and later recall programs. After you have turned on the machine, you must tell it that you want to use the BASIC programming language. Notice again in Figure A2-1 how the BASIC programming language can be accessed using different computers. The computer will tell you through either a direct message or a change in the format of the display terminal that it is ready to accept instructions you write in the BASIC programming language.

Many systems require you to provide a name for your program. Depending on the system, the program name can be up to six to eight characters long, and must start with an alphabetic character. Check with your instructor.

After you finish with your program, BE SURE TO SAVE IT! The procedure for properly finishing a programming session is called **LOGGING OFF.** When you are keying in your program, it is stored in the CPU. Unless you save your program either on disk or on tape, the program will vanish when you turn off your computer or terminal. Then you will have to retype it all over again.

A LINE OF BASIC

Now we are ready to try our first line of BASIC. We simply want to print out your name. The following line prints what is enclosed within the quotation marks.

```
500 PRINT "My name is Jerry." [carriage return]
```

	Computer System				
	IBM PC/ Microsoft	Hewlett-Packard 3000	Computers Using the CP/M Operating System	Apple II	Digital Equipment
Start-up procedures					
Power switch	Right side	Right rear	Varies	Left rear	Left rear
System response	A>	:	A>	]	Varies by model
Calling BASIC	BASICA	BASIC	MBASIC	No call required, begin typing	BASIC System responds with READY, begin typing
System commands					
Starting a new program called AGE	NEW Now begin typing after the OK appears	NAME AGE Now begin typing after the > appears	NAME "AGE" Now begin typing after the OK appears	NEW	NEW AGE
Listing a program	LIST	LIST	LIST	LIST	LIST
Listing lines 100–140	LIST 100–140	LIST 100–140	LIST 100–140	LIST 100–140	LIST 100–140
Running a program	RUN	RUN	RUN	RUN	RUN
Saving a new program	SAVE "AGE"	SAVE	SAVE "AGE"	SAVE AGE	SAVE
Recalling a saved (old) program	LOAD "AGE"	GET AGE	LOAD "AGE"	LOAD AGE	OLD AGE
Saving a recalled program	SAVE "AGE"	SAVE AGE	SAVE "AGE"	SAVE AGE	SAVE
Deleting a program	KILL "AGE.BAS"	PURGE AGE	KILL "AGE"	DELETE AGE	UNSAVE AGE
Closing a programming session					
You enter	SYSTEM	EXIT	SYSTEM	Nothing	BYE or GOODBYE
System response	A>	:	A>	Nothing	Varies with model
Additional user entry	None	:BYE	None	None	Varies with model
Finished	Turn power off	Turn power off	Turn power off	Turn power off	Turn power off

FIGURE A2-1.

Important system information: start-up procedures, system commands, and closing procedures for selected systems.

To execute the above line, type the system command RUN and press the carriage return. When our sample line is executed by the computer, the output (response) will look like this when displayed:

```
RUN
My name is Jerry.
```

The letter "M" in this phrase will appear in the first column on your display terminal or on the printed output.

Each line of a program begins with a LINE NUMBER (500 will be used throughout as a typical line number). The line number is then followed by a BASIC statement. At the end of each BASIC statement, it is necessary to depress the carriage return or enter key (sometimes indicated by an arrow pointing down and to the left). When we show the formats of BASIC statements, we will omit the carriage return.

The line numbers range from 1 to 9999 on most computers (some accommodate higher numbers). BASIC programs begin executing the program starting with the lowest line number and, unless ordered otherwise, proceed sequentially to the highest number. For clarity depress the space bar to leave a space after the line number. For programming ease many people start their line numbers at 100 and increase them in increments of 10 (100, 110, 120, and so forth). Incrementing by 10 each time allows you to add lines later between the ones you have already written without throwing off the sequence. Most systems will allow you to renumber the lines when you clean up your program before running and listing the final copy.

BASIC has a number of RESERVED WORDS, which have a special meaning to the interpreter or compiler and can only be used as intended—be sure to spell them correctly and use them properly. The BASIC reserved words are listed in Figure A2-2.

If you make a mistake keying in a character, you can always correct it. When just starting out, it might be easier to retype the line completely. Later you will have time to learn how to edit the lines you have written. If you want to erase a complete line of BASIC, simply type the line number and a carriage return and the line will be erased. Depending on your system, to delete a character you can use the backspace key, a delete key, the cursor keys, or the control key and H key simultaneously.

FIGURE A2-2.
Selected reserved words in BASIC.

Reserved words include all BASIC commands, statements, function names, and operator names. Reserved words cannot be used as variable names.

ABS	INPUT	RND
AND	INT	SGN
ATN	LET	SIN
COS	LOG	SQR
DATA	LPRINT	STEP
DEF	MAT	STOP
DIM	MAT PRINT	TAB
ELSE	MAT READ	TAN
END	NEXT	THEN
EXP	OR	TIMER
FNx	PRINT	TO
FOR	RANDOMIZE	USING
GOSUB	READ	WEND
GOTO	REM	WHILE
IF	RESTORE	
IMAGE	RETURN	

Note: Not all reserved words are used on all systems.

CHARACTER SET

In BASIC we use a CHARACTER SET consisting of upper- and lower-case letters, the decimal numbers 0 to 9, and special symbols. We shall explain these symbols as we encounter them.

CONSTANTS

Two types of values are used in BASIC: constants and variables. **CONSTANTS** do not change during execution. There are two types of constants of interest to us: character strings and numeric constants. **CHARACTER STRING CONSTANTS** (also called string constants or literals) are enclosed in quotation marks. Examples include:

```
"a"
"Greetings"
"My name is Jerry"
"67-435-23"
```

Character string constants can contain up to 255 characters.

NUMERIC CONSTANTS can be integers, real numbers with decimal places, or real numbers written in floating-point form. These include:

```
4434              (an integer)
24.455            (a real number in decimal form)
.24455E+2         (the floating-point form for
                   the number 24.455)
```

Most of the problems in this appendix will deal with real numbers in decimal form.

NUMERIC AND CHARACTER VARIABLES

In the foregoing example, to print "My name is Jerry" you simply key in a character string constant. In most problems the items processed involve variables. A **VARIABLE** is a symbol that can take on different values, either numeric or alphabetic. Two major types of variables are used in BASIC:

1 *NUMERIC VARIABLES. These are represented by a single alphabetic character, such as A, Y, or W; by an alphabetic character combined with a number, such as A1, E3, or X7; or (in some systems) by combinations of up to 40 alphabetic characters and a number, such as WEIGHT, TEST1, or FIRSTENCOUNTER.*
2 *CHARACTER STRING VARIABLES. These are represented by combinations of letters, symbols, and numbers ending with a $. The $ tells the computer that the variable is a character string. Examples include H$, X1$, or THISISMYNAME$. They can represent a single character or several words.*

Some systems will not accept variable names that are longer than one letter plus one number and the $ symbol. Check to see if yours is such a system.

The reason we need to identify character strings differently from numbers is that the computer stores each type of value in a different way. If the computer accidentally encounters an alphabetic value where a numeric value is expected, a data format error message is generated—after all, how could you take the square root of your name?

SIMPLE STATEMENTS

We will now look at the most commonly used BASIC statements. Where possible the relevant statements used in the credit-limit problem are displayed (refer to Figure A1-5).

REM STATEMENT

The **REM** statement is a nonexecutable command for writing remarks or comments. The general form of the REM statement is:

```
500 REM remark
```

For example, look over the first lines from the credit-limit program:

```
100 REM This program checks a customers's credit balance.
110 REM The program was written by Michael Franks.
120 REM This program adds the amount to be charged to the
130 REM customer's current balance and indicates whether
140 REM the combined amounts will exceed the customer's limit.
150 REM The program is written in the BASIC programming
160 REM language and is run on a Hewlett-Packard 3000 system.
```

Comment statements help the programmer or other people understand what the program is all about. Sometimes the date on which the program was last modified and the programmers' names are denoted in the REM statements. Often a brief description of the variable names, formulas, and other features of the program will be provided. Additional REM statements are frequently interspersed throughout the program to delineate the various modules for input, processing, and output, as well as to make the program more readable.

PRINT STATEMENT

The **PRINT** statement controls the type and format of output at both the display terminal and the printer. PRINT statements can be used to print character strings, numeric values, literals, or combinations of all three (technically called parameters). The general form of the PRINT statement is:

```
500 PRINT list of parameters
```

On many microcomputer systems, the **LPRINT** statement is used to direct output to the printer. On those types of systems, the PRINT statement affects only the display screen.

Let us look at some examples of PRINT. To print a constant or literal expression, enclose what you want printed in quotation marks ("). The first character, number, or blank after the opening quotation mark is printed in the first column. Here is an example of a BASIC PRINT statement and the resulting output.

```
100 PRINT "This is a literal statement."
```

```
This is a literal statement.
```

To skip a line, simply key in the word PRINT after the line number. This will print or display a blank line, which can help make your output more readable. An example is:

```
200 PRINT
```

To print the value of a single variable, name the variable in your PRINT statement. Here is an example that prints the variable X, which currently has a value of 23.45.

```
300 PRINT X
```

```
23.45
```

Note that the value 23.45 is printed starting in the second column. This is because the first column is reserved for the sign ("+" or "−"), which in this case is "+" and is implied but not printed.

Commas and *semicolons*, separating the variables and literals, can be used to control the placement of the output on a line. Most printers and screens are divided into five zones, although the number varies from system to system. The use of commas activates the default feature (assumptions made by the computer) for single-line placement of output in these zones. Usually the zones are 13 or 14 columns wide with a space after each zone. The examples in this book use 14-column zones with one space between each. Because the zones are only 14 columns wide, long character strings such as peoples' names or street addresses can create unwieldy-looking results using this method of spacing output. With 14 column zones and a one-column separation the zones start in columns 1, 16, 31, 46, and 61. With a 13 column format the zones start in columns 1, 15, 29, 43, and 57.

Let us see how we can print five numeric constants using zones (of course, character string constants and numeric or string variables may be handled in the same way). Here is a statement to print the values 13.5, −67, 46, 487, and 24.3. The output is shown on the line below the PRINT statement.

```
400 PRINT 13.5,  −67,46, 487, 24.3
13.5            −67             46                  487               24.3
```

Let us look at some more examples of zones. Consider a student and several pieces of data concerning her. We want to print out her name, age, major in school, year in school, and place of birth. The actual data are: Cassandra Barker, 25, Business, Senior, Montreal. Because Ms. Barker's name is too long for a 14-column print zone, we must use two print zones to hold it. As a result the output is printed on two lines:

```
500 PRINT "Cassandra Barker", 25, "Business", "Senior", "Montreal"
Cassandra Barker              25               Business       Senior
Montreal
```

If we must get all the data into the first five print zones, we would need to abbreviate her first name:

```
C. Barker       25              Business      Senior          Montreal
```

Semicolons in a PRINT line override the print zone default procedure. In general if you mix literals and variables in the same output line, you can achieve a more readable and attractive display using semicolons rather than commas. This example uses semicolons to display Ms. Barker's data:

```
600 PRINT "Cassandra Barker"; 25; "Business"; "Senior"; "Montreal"
Cassandra Barker  25 Business Senior Montreal
```

Note that with some systems, to achieve properly spaced output using semicolons you have to add a space to the string constant. In other words:

```
700 PRINT "Cassandra Barker "; 25; "Business "; "Senior "; "Montreal"
```

The five numeric constants shown earlier could be printed close together, with a column skipped between each variable, with this statement (not counting the sign):

```
700 PRINT 13.5;  -67; 46; 487; 24.3
    13.5 -67  46  487  24.3
```

Our final example shows a combination of literals and variables. Notice that with this format it is necessary to insert extra spaces (by enclosing spaces within quotation marks) before or after the letters in the literal expression to create the desired attractive output display. In this example the value of N$ is Penny Brown and the value of S is 83.

```
900 PRINT "   "; N$ ;"'s score on the exam is"; S ;"."
```

Prints three blank columns   Puts the apostrophe immediately next to the name   Does not skip a space

The output from this statement is

```
Penny Brown's score on the exam is 83.
```

Later in this appendix we will learn about additional features we can combine with the PRINT command.

READ/DATA STATEMENTS

To perform processing upon data, we must get the data into the program. The data values must be assigned to variables. There are three ways in which a BASIC program accepts data: (1) by using a READ statement, (2) by using an INPUT statement, and (3) by using a LET statement. INPUT and LET statements will be discussed in the following sections.

The **READ** statement tells the computer the data are available and the computer need only search until it finds the first available data (stored on the DATA line). The general form for the READ statement is:

```
500 READ variable(s)
```

When READ statements require DATA statements, they are often linked together as READ/DATA statements. **DATA** statements are nonexecutable—they simply hold data. The general form for the DATA statement is:

```
500 DATA constant(s)
```

Figure A2-3 shows an example of a program using READ/DATA statements. It reads in Ms. Barkers' data and prints them out.

The structure of the DATA line follows certain rules. All data items on a line must be separated by commas. There is no comma after the last data item on the data line. Character strings must be enclosed by quotation marks on most systems. Whenever there are blanks or commas (careful: using commas in this way may generate errors on some systems) in a data item, it must be enclosed in quotation marks; for example:

```
2000 DATA "Lansing Michigan"
```

Let us look at several examples of READ and DATA statements. The first two examples show how to read numeric and character string data. The

FIGURE A2-3.

Program using READ/DATA.

List and run

```
100 REM This is an example of a program using READ/DATA commands.
110 REM The variables are:
120 REM        N$ = Student name
130 REM        A  = Student age
140 REM        M$ = Student major
150 REM        Y$ = Year in school
160 REM        C$ = Home city
170 REM **** Main Program ****
180 REM **** Input Stage ****
190 READ N$, A, M$, Y$, C$
200 REM **** Output Stage ****
210 PRINT "Student Data Report"
220 PRINT
230 PRINT
240 PRINT "Student name  -----  "; N$
250 PRINT "Student age   ------  "; A
260 PRINT "Student major  ----  "; M$
270 PRINT "Year in school  ---  "; Y$
280 PRINT "Home city  --------  "; C$
290 PRINT
300 PRINT
310 PRINT "End of Program"
320 REM **** Data List ****
330 DATA "Cassandra Barker", 25, "Business", "Senior","Montreal"
9999 END
```

```
RUN
Student Data Report


Student name  -----  Cassandra Barker
Student age   ------   25
Student major  ----  Business
Year in school  ---  Senior
Home city  --------  Montreal


End of Program
```

first shows how to read two numeric variables:

```
100 READ A, B
910 DATA 12.3, 23
```

The values 12.3 and 23 are stored in the spots reserved for variables A and B:

```
A         B  Variables
12.3     23  Values
```

The second example reads in a combination of numeric and character strings:

```
200 READ E, G$, S$, T
1000 DATA 45.76, "Tony Andress", "Male", 23
```

The values stored are:

```
E         G$            S$    T  Variables
45.76  Tony Andress   Male   23  Values
```

After a value is stored for a variable using a READ statement, the value can be changed at a later time by executing a second READ statement. The old value is replaced by the new data.

To illustrate, let us read two variables (N$ and A) twice. The first READ line (200) assigns the string Sue and the number 12.4 to the variables. The second READ line (230) then assigns Donna and 56.1 to the respective variables, "erasing" the earlier data in the computer's memory.

```
200 READ N$, A
210 PRINT N$; A
220 PRINT
230 READ N$, A
240 PRINT N$; A
900 DATA "Sue", 12.4
910 DATA "Donna", 56.1
9999 END

RUN
Sue   12.4

Donna   56.1
```

Beginning students often have problems with errors concerning READ/DATA statements. The three most common errors are:

- *Data format errors*
- *Attempting to read nonexistent data*
- *Incorrect ordering of variables and data*

A data format error occurs when the computer cannot match the data with the type specified in the READ statement (as when character string data are read into a real number variable location). Consider the following:

```
350 READ N$, A
900 DATA "John Smith", "Terance Davis"
```

Running a program with these lines would generate a "data format error" message because "A" is a real variable whereas "Terance Davis" is a character string.

The second problem concerns trying to read more data than actually exist in your DATA statements:

```
560 READ B, T, W4
1000 DATA 442.3, 41
```

The attempt to read the third number fails, resulting in an "out of data" message.

Finally, if you enter the wrong data in the DATA statement, you will have the wrong values stored for the variable. (For example if you enter the number 12 instead of 102.) This is the most dangerous because no error message is provided.

INPUT STATEMENT

With the INPUT statement the data will be entered as the program is executed. The general form of the INPUT statement is:

```
500 INPUT variables(s)
```

or

```
500 INPUT "prompt" variable(s)
```

where the prompt is printed directly from the input line.

The input statements used in the credit-limit example are as follows:

```
310 PRINT "What is the amount to be charged";
320 INPUT C
330 PRINT
340 REM For simplicity we will enter the values for B and L.
350 REM Normally these values are obtained from the bank's credit
360 REM card users' database.
370 PRINT "What is the customer's current balance";
380 INPUT B
390 PRINT
400 PRINT "What is the customer's credit limit";
410 INPUT L
```

When the system comes to an INPUT statement, the computer will print a question mark, then pause and wait for your response. The INPUT statement can be used for keying in responses requiring numeric data, alphanumeric data, or a combination of the two. When using INPUT it is a good idea to instruct or prompt the user as to what to do. These prompts should be written to guide the users, not confuse them.

You can use an INPUT statement to input a single variable:

```
150 INPUT F
```

As a response the computer will output:

```
?
```

In response to the question mark, you type in a real number.

You can input both a numeric and a character string variable in this way:

```
250 INPUT K, K$
?
```

In response to the question mark, you type in a real number, then a comma followed by the character string. For example, you might type:

```
? 241.9, "Tobias Hamilton"
```

To let the user know how to respond to the question mark, you should include screen prompts in the program. For example:

```
350 PRINT "In response to the question mark,"
360 PRINT "type in two numbers separated by a comma."
370 INPUT A, B
```

would produce this output:

```
In response to the question mark,
type in two numbers separated by a comma.
? 424.0, 47
```

A prompt can also be incorporated onto a single line. For example:

```
450 INPUT "What is your name"; N$
```

would produce this:

```
What is your name? Tobias Hamilton
```

Input statements using prompts with semicolons permit you to type the data onto the same line as the prompt. The question mark need not be typed into the prompt because the INPUT command automatically places a question mark. Replacing the semicolon with a comma in line 450 suppresses the automatic question mark.

Data format errors in entry are usually detected automatically by the computer. An error message similar to "Redo from start" will appear, for example, when you try to assign a character string value to a numeric variable.

INPUT and READ/DATA statements can be used in the same program. For example, you might use READ/DATA statements to enter raw data into the program. Your responses to INPUT commands might then determine what processing operations to perform upon the data. You could use READ/DATA, for example, to enter a series of numbers, and the INPUT response to indicate whether you want to take an average of the numbers or find and display the highest number read in.

RESTORE STATEMENT

The READ statement has a feature, called a pointer, that keeps track of where the reading process stops. For example, after the following brief program is run, the pointer will be where shown:

```
100 READ A,B
110 PRINT A,B
120 READ A,B
130 PRINT A,B                    ← Pointer is here after execution.
200 DATA 34, 12.45, 45, 51
210 END

RUN
  34              12.45
  45              51
```

The **RESTORE** statement resets the pointer used by the READ statement to the front of the data list. The general format of the RESTORE statement is:

```
500 RESTORE
```

Placing a RESTORE statement at line 115 gives us the following result.

```
100 READ A,B
110 PRINT A,B
115 RESTORE
120 READ A,B                     ← Pointer is here after execution.
130 PRINT A,B
200 DATA 34, 12.45, 45, 51
210 END

RUN
  34              12.45
  34              12.45
```

LET STATEMENT (ASSIGNMENT STATEMENT)

The LET statement is used to assign values to different variables. It is commonly called the ASSIGNMENT STATEMENT. The assignment operator in BASIC is the equal sign (=). The general form of the LET statement is:

```
500 LET variable = expression
```

or without even keying LET:

```
500 variable = expression
```

THE EQUAL SIGN DOES NOT CARRY THE SAME MEANING AS IN ALGEBRA! On the left side of the equal sign is one variable, and on the right of the sign the expression can range from simply another variable or a constant to a complicated mathematical formula. The value of the expression on the right is *assigned* or *placed into* the variable on the left.

In the credit-limit problem, the first LET statements are used to initialize the numeric variables to zero, to make sure no unexpected data are assigned to these variables. At the end of the following excerpt, the LET statement adds the current balance and the new charge to create a new balance.

```
270 LET B = 0
280 LET C = 0
290 LET L = 0
300 LET N = 0
        .
        .
        .
450 LET N = B + C
```

The expression can be either a constant, a variable, or some combination of constants and variables. Both numeric and string constants and variables can be used in LET statements. Some examples of LET statements are as follows:

LET Statement	Meaning
200 LET X = 6	The numeric constant 6 is assigned to the numeric variable X.
400 LET N$ = "Hot"	The character string constant "Hot" is assigned to the character string variable N$.
500 LET H = A + B	The sum of numeric variables A and B is assigned to the numeric variable H.
1000 LET G$ = M$	The value for the character string variable M$ is assigned to the character string variable G$.

Mathematical expressions in LET statements in BASIC follow the same precedence (order of operation) rules you have learned in math classes. Figure A2-4 shows the arithmetic operators used with LET statements. Exponentiation has the highest precedence, and so is performed first if present. The next highest are division and multiplication, followed by addition and subtraction. If two operators of equal precedence are present, they are performed in order from left to right.

Parentheses are used for clarity or to change the precedence. Expressions are solved inside the innermost parentheses first, working outward. Both the left and right parentheses must be used. For example, just as $1 +$

FIGURE A2-4.
*Hierarchy of mathe-
matical operators and
examples in BASIC
from highest to lowest.*

Operation	Algebraic Form	BASIC Form	Example
( ) or [ ]	$((A + B)(A - B))/C$	100 LET X = $((A + B) * (A - B))/C$	$((7 + 2) * (7 - 2))/4 =$ 11.25
Exponentiation	A^X	200 LET Z = A∧X or 200 LET Z = A**X	$3 \wedge 2 = 9$ or $3** = 9$
Multiplication	$(A)(B)$ or $A \times B$	300 N = A*B	$7*2 = 14$
Division (real numbers)	A/B	400 P = A/B	$7/2 = 3.5$
Addition	$A + B$	500 R = A + B	$7 + 2 = 11$
Subtraction	$A - B$	500 Q = A - B	$7 - 2 = 5$

2/3 is not the same as $(1 + 2)/3$, the expression $A + B/C$ will give different results than $(A + B)/C$.

An important rule: A legal LET statement must have *only one variable to the left of the equal sign*. This is a legal statement:

```
200 LET Z = ((A+B)*(A-B))/C
```

These are illegal statements:

```
300 LET 6 = W   Numeric constant on left side
400 LET X∧D = A   Two variables on left side
```

STOP STATEMENT

The **STOP** statement immediately halts the execution of a program. The STOP command looks like this:

```
500 STOP
```

When a STOP statement is encountered, the program flow is diverted to the END statement and the program halts. On some systems there will be a printed message indicating the line where the stop was executed. Figure A2-5 shows an example of a STOP statement.

END STATEMENT

The **END** statement is required for most BASIC programs. An example of an END statement is:

```
9999 END
```

On some systems if you forget an END statement, it will be impossible to save your program for later use. Even though the system used to create the programs given in this appendix does not require this statement, it has been put in, since forgetting it on a different system could be fatal to your program.

The END statement should always have the highest line number of any statement in the program. People commonly assign the END statement a line number of 9999, well above any line number you are likely to use. A

```
100 REM This is an example of a program using READ/DATA commands.
110 REM The variables are:
120 REM          N$ = Student name
130 REM          A  = Student age
140 REM          M$ = Student major
150 REM          Y$ = Year in school
160 REM          C$ = Home city
170 REM **** Main Program ****
180 REM **** Input stage ****
190 READ N$, A, M$, Y$, C$
200 REM **** Output Stage ****
210 PRINT "Student Data Report"
220 PRINT
230 PRINT
240 PRINT "Student name  -----  "; N$
250 PRINT "Student age  ------  "; A
255 STOP
260 PRINT "Student major  ----  "; M$
270 PRINT "Year in school  ---  "; Y$
280 PRINT "Home city  --------  "; C$
290 PRINT
300 PRINT
310 PRINT "End of Program"
320 REM **** Data List ****
330 DATA "Cassandra Barker", 25, "Business", "Senior","Montreal"
9999 END

RUN
Student Data Report


Student name  -----   Cassandra Barker
Student age  ------    25


Stop at line 255
```

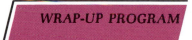

```
Note—this message does not appear on some systems.
```

word of caution: If the line number for your END statement is lower than the numbers of some of the other lines, the higher numbered lines could be permanently lost when you attempt to save your program.

WRAP-UP PROGRAM

This program requires you to use a READ/DATA combination. It calculates the bill for a single customer after reading in the following data:

```
Customer:
     Bits and Bytes Inc.
     67 Main Street
     Last Chance, Nevada 89133
Item Name:
     Microprocessors
Item Quantity:
     1500
Item Price:
     $ 6.85
```

The total cost is calculated as the product of the item quantity and the item cost. Then the output is printed in a clear format.

FIGURE A2-6.

Flowchart, pseudocode, list, and run for Section Two wrap-up program.

Flowchart

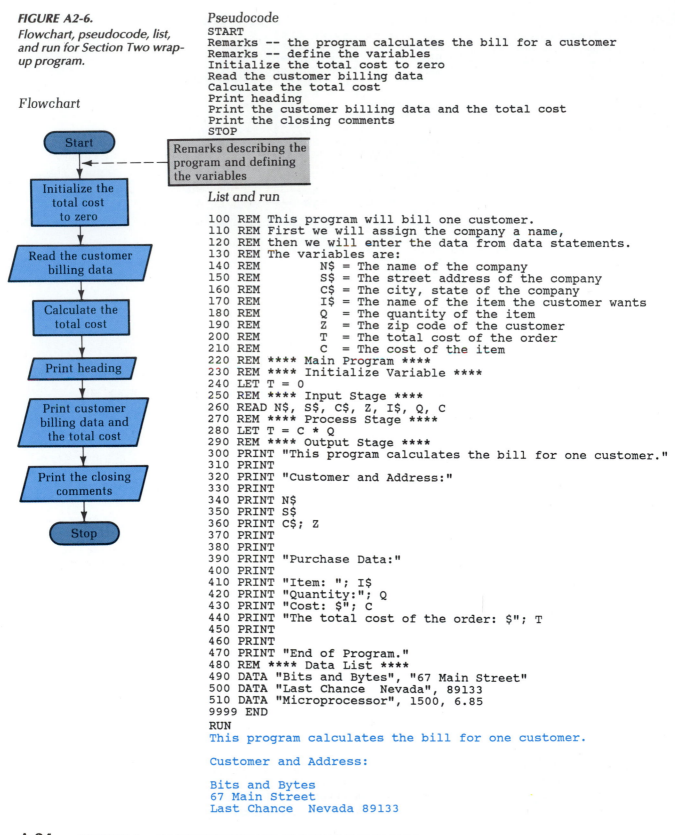

Pseudocode
```
START
Remarks -- the program calculates the bill for a customer
Remarks -- define the variables
Initialize the total cost to zero
Read the customer billing data
Calculate the total cost
Print heading
Print the customer billing data and the total cost
Print the closing comments
STOP
```

Remarks describing the program and defining the variables

List and run

```
100 REM This program will bill one customer.
110 REM First we will assign the company a name,
120 REM then we will enter the data from data statements.
130 REM The variables are:
140 REM          N$ = The name of the company
150 REM          S$ = The street address of the company
160 REM          C$ = The city, state of the company
170 REM          I$ = The name of the item the customer wants
180 REM          Q  = The quantity of the item
190 REM          Z  = The zip code of the customer
200 REM          T  = The total cost of the order
210 REM          C  = The cost of the item
220 REM **** Main Program ****
230 REM **** Initialize Variable ****
240 LET T = 0
250 REM **** Input Stage ****
260 READ N$, S$, C$, Z, I$, Q, C
270 REM **** Process Stage ****
280 LET T = C * Q
290 REM **** Output Stage ****
300 PRINT "This program calculates the bill for one customer."
310 PRINT
320 PRINT "Customer and Address:"
330 PRINT
340 PRINT N$
350 PRINT S$
360 PRINT C$; Z
370 PRINT
380 PRINT
390 PRINT "Purchase Data:"
400 PRINT
410 PRINT "Item: "; I$
420 PRINT "Quantity:"; Q
430 PRINT "Cost: $"; C
440 PRINT "The total cost of the order: $"; T
450 PRINT
460 PRINT
470 PRINT "End of Program."
480 REM **** Data List ****
490 DATA "Bits and Bytes", "67 Main Street"
500 DATA "Last Chance  Nevada", 89133
510 DATA "Microprocessor", 1500, 6.85
9999 END
RUN
This program calculates the bill for one customer.

Customer and Address:

Bits and Bytes
67 Main Street
Last Chance  Nevada 89133
```

```
Purchase Data:

Item: Microprocessor
Quantity: 1500
Cost: $ 6.85
The total cost of the order: $ 10275


End of Program.
```

Figure A2-6 illustrates a possible solution to this problem. Observe how the character strings are read in and then displayed in the output. The cost calculation is shown in line 280 and is blocked off by REM statements.

REVIEW QUESTIONS

MULTIPLE CHOICE

1. For character strings, which of the following is not a valid variable name?
   (a) N$
   (b) NAME$
   (c) N
   (d) N1$

2. Which LET statement is incorrect?
   (a) 100 LET W + 10 = Z
   (b) 200 LET Q = W − 12.4
   (c) 300 N$ = M$
   (d) 400 Z = (10*X)∧2

3. If W = 9, what value will X be assigned in the following?
   `660 LET X = ((3+W)∧2 + (W)∧.5)`
   (a) 28.5
   (b) 87
   (c) 147
   (d) 148.5

4. Which operation will be performed first?
   (a) Exponentiation
   (b) Multiplication
   (c) Addition
   (d) Subtraction

5. The STOP operation:
   (a) Restores the data pointer to the beginning.
   (b) Cancels all preceding commands.
   (c) Diverts the program flow to the END statement.
   (d) Automatically shuts off the computer.

1. What is the reason we might use semicolons in PRINT statements?

2. When would INPUT statements be preferred over READ statements?

3. Write the READ and DATA statements to read the following data.

Name	Weight (kg)	Height (cm)
Tom Herbert	85	190
Linda Jones	50	160
Del Torrez	75	180

4. Write a PRINT statement to print out the data in question 3.

5. Given that 2.2 pounds = 1 kilogram, write a LET statement to convert the weights from kilograms to pounds.

1. Write a program to read and print your name, weight, and age.

2. The Testing Office at Oakriver University has administered 500 advanced-standing tests; 124 students failed the test. Write a program to find out what percentage passed.

3. Write a program to solve the following. Larry Dumas is a passenger on Fly-By–Night Airlines flight 131 from Los Angeles to New York. His ticket costs $150. There is a 6 percent sales tax and a 1.5 percent airport security tax. Both taxes are assessed against the price of the ticket. Write a program to input the ticket price, calculate the separate taxes, and print the subtotals and total bill. Be sure to label your answer.

4. Read in the following data, and convert Ms. Jones' height and weight to inches and pounds respectively.

    Linda Jones   50   160

Remember that 1 kilogram = 2.2 pounds, and 1 centimeter = 0.3937 inch.

Up to this point we have looked at programs that execute in a sequential manner. However, many programming problems require making choices (selection) and repeating steps again and again (looping). In this section we will learn how to create programs using selection and looping procedures. We will cover the IF/THEN/ELSE statements for selection and looping, the GOSUB/RETURN statements for subroutines, and the GOTO statement for looping. A wrap-up program at the end of the section demonstrates selection and looping.

SELECTION PROCEDURES

THE IF/THEN/ELSE STATEMENTS

The IF/THEN/ELSE statements are used for decisions. Often we refer to these statements together as the IF/THEN statement or the IF/THEN/ELSE statement. The IF/THEN/ELSE statement is used for a wide variety of selection procedures as well as loop control operations.

The general form of the IF/THEN/ELSE statement is:

```
500 IF { expression     } THEN { perform one    } ELSE { perform another }
        { is true        }      { operation      }      { operation       }
```

"Performing an operation" can be either a BASIC expression or a line number. If the operation is a BASIC expression, it is executed directly and the program continues at the following line. If a line number is provided, the program branches to that line number and execution of the program continues from there.

The IF/THEN/ELSE statement used in the credit-limit problem extended across two lines as follows:

```
460 IF N <= L THEN PRINT "Customer's credit is approved."
470 ELSE PRINT "Customer's credit is not approved!!!"
```

Depending upon your computer's interpreter or compiler, you can get the same result if the lines are written as:

```
460 IF N <= L THEN PRINT "Customer's credit is approved." ELSE &
    PRINT "Customer's credit is not approved!!!"
```

(The "&" symbol denotes a continuation of a line.) If ELSE is not available on your system, the statement can be rewritten using two IF/THEN statements:

```
460 IF N <= L THEN PRINT "Customer's credit is approved."
470 IF N >  L THEN PRINT "Customer's credit is not approved!!!"
```

following the general form:

```
500 IF { expression     } THEN { perform one }
        { is true        }      { operation   }
```

IF/THEN/ELSE statements can even be nested within one another; that is, an IF/THEN/ELSE statement can be one of the operations to perform.

Within the IF/THEN/ELSE statement, the expression is tested using either relational or logical operators. A **RELATIONAL OPERATOR** compares two values. One numeric value is compared against another numeric value, or a character string value is compared with another character string value. The inequality symbols ($<$, $<=$, $>$, $>=$) and the equality and nonequality symbols ($=$, $<>$) are known as relational operators.

Since numbers can be arranged from smallest to largest, they can be compared with each other. For example, 2 is less than 6 ($2 < 6$) and 21 is greater than 14 ($21 > 14$). Similarly, character strings can be ordered by alphabetizing them. So "ab" is less than "ba" ("ab" $<$ "ba") and "cat" is greater than "bird" ("cat" $>$ "bird").

LOGICAL OPERATORS (AND, OR) test on a true/false basis. Logical operators are called **BOOLEAN OPERATORS** and are often used to combine two or more relational operators into compound relations. Figure A3-1 shows a number of relational and logical operators.

FIGURE A3-1.

Relational and logical operators used with IF/THEN/ELSE statements.

Expression	Symbol	Meaning When the Test Is True
Less than	$<$	The value is less than the test condition.
Less than or equal to	$<=$	The value is less than or equal to the test condition.
Equal to	$=$	The value is exactly equal to the test condition.
Greater than or equal to	$>=$	The value is greater than or equal to the test condition.
Greater than	$>$	The value is greater than the test condition.
Not equal to	$<>$	The value is not equal to the test condition.
Logical OR	OR	At least one condition in the test must be met.
Logical AND	AND	All conditions in the test must be met.

Let us look at several examples using relational and logical operators. In the following statement:

```
100 IF A < B THEN PRINT "Hello" ELSE PRINT "Goodbye"
```

if A is less than B, then "Hello" is printed, while if A is greater than or equal to B, "Goodbye" is printed. Compare this with the example.

```
200 IF C >=450 THEN LET D = K^2 ELSE LET D = K^3
```

If C is greater than or equal to 450, then D = K^2, while if C is less than 450, then D = K^3.

For the example.

```
300 IF N$ = "last name" THEN 1210 ELSE 230
```

N$ must equal "last name" exactly ("Last Name" and "LAST NAME" are not acceptable). So if N$ does equal "last name," then the program continues executing at line 1210; otherwise it continues at 230.

Another example of branching to another line in an IF/THEN/ELSE statement is:

```
400 IF E$ = "END OF DATA" THEN 900
```

This means that if the string variable E$ equals "END OF DATA," then go to line 900. This is useful to end programs in certain situations. For example, line 900 could contain the END statement.

For nonequality, we have:

```
500 IF HOMES <> "APT" THEN PRINT NAME$
```

If a person's home is not an apartment (abbreviated "APT"), then that person's name is printed.

The following examples illustrate compound relational statements. In the statement:

```
600 IF AGE < 21 OR WEIGHT > 160 THEN PRINT STUDENT$
```

A person could either be less than 21 years old or weigh more than 160 pounds, or meet both conditions to be listed. In the example:

```
700 IF AGE > 25 AND SEX$ = "female" THEN LET C = C + 1 ELSE LET N = N + 1
```

we accumulate the number of people in two possible categories: category C records the total number of people who are both over the age of 25 and female, while category N records the total number of people who are not (all males as well as females 25 years old and younger).

Let us create an interactive program that calculates your age given your name and year of birth. We need to use an IF/THEN statement to determine whether or not you had a birthday yet this year. As shown in Figure A3-2, three IF/THEN statements are used. The first (line number 390) determines whether you have correctly answered if you had a birthday yet this year (you literally must type "yes" or "no" in lowercase letters). This compound relational IF statement directs the program to repeat the question if an error occurred. Depending upon your answer, one of the next two IF statements (lines 410 or 420) will calculate your age.

Flowchart

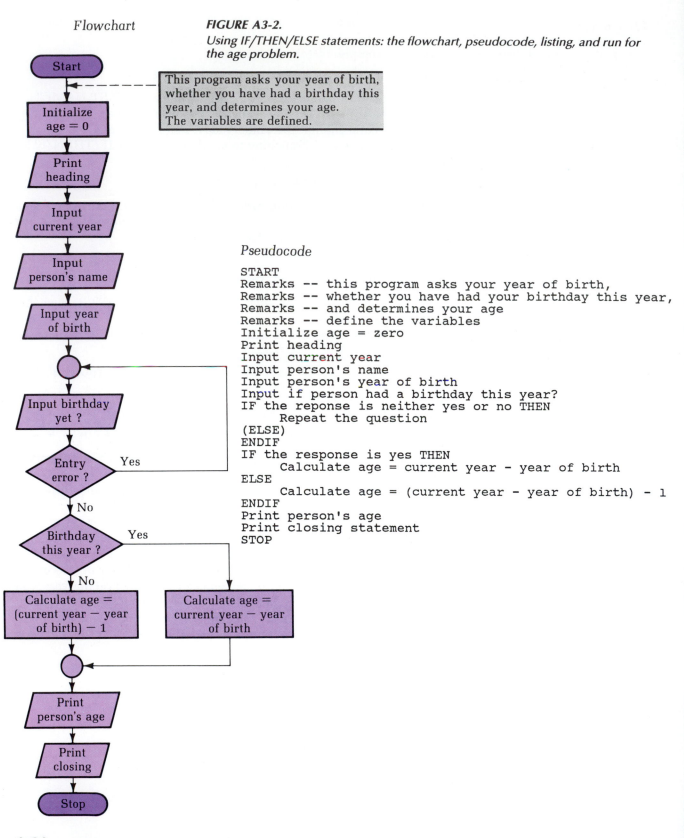

FIGURE A3-2.
Using IF/THEN/ELSE statements: the flowchart, pseudocode, listing, and run for the age problem.

This program asks your year of birth, whether you have had a birthday this year, and determines your age.
The variables are defined.

Pseudocode

```
START
Remarks -- this program asks your year of birth,
Remarks -- whether you have had your birthday this year,
Remarks -- and determines your age
Remarks -- define the variables
Initialize age = zero
Print heading
Input current year
Input person's name
Input person's year of birth
Input if person had a birthday this year?
IF the reponse is neither yes or no THEN
     Repeat the question
(ELSE)
ENDIF
IF the response is yes THEN
     Calculate age = current year - year of birth
ELSE
     Calculate age = (current year - year of birth) - 1
ENDIF
Print person's age
Print closing statement
STOP
```

List and run

```
100 REM This program will ask your name and what year
110 REM you were born in.  Then the program will calculate
120 REM your age.
130 REM The variables are:
140 REM        N$ = Your name
150 REM        A$ = Birthday this year
160 REM        Y  = Your year of birth
170 REM        A  = Your age
180 REM        C  = Current year
190 REM **** Main Program ****
200 REM **** Initialize variable ****
210 LET A = 0
220 REM **** Input Stage ****
230 PRINT
240 PRINT "This  program will ask you your name and year of birth,"
250 PRINT "then it will print your age."
260 PRINT
270 PRINT "What year is it?",
280 INPUT C
290 PRINT
300 INPUT "What is your name?", N$
310 PRINT
320 PRINT "Well, ";N$;", in what year were you born?",
330 INPUT Y
340 PRINT
350 PRINT "Answer yes or no:  Have you had your birthday this year?",
360 INPUT A$
370 REM The next line catches errors in answering the  question,
380 REM and sends the user back to line 350 to reask the question.
390 IF A$ <> "yes" AND A$ <> "no" THEN 350
400 REM **** Process Stage ****
410 IF A$ = "yes" THEN LET A = C - Y
420 IF A$ = "no" THEN LET A = (C - Y) - 1
430 REM **** Output Stage ****
440 PRINT
450 PRINT
460 PRINT "My goodness, ";N$;", you are"; A;" years old!"
470 PRINT
480 PRINT
490 PRINT "End of program."
500 END
```

```
RUN

This program will ask you your name and year of birth,
then it will print your age.

What year is it? 1986

What is your name? Tom

Well, Tom, in what year were you born? 1948

Answer yes or no:  Have you had your birthday this year? Y
Answer yes or no:  Have you had your birthday this year? yes


My goodness, Tom, you are 38 years old!


End of program.
```

Another important control structure is the subroutine. Subroutines are self-contained modules used to perform special functions. They are outside of the main flow of the program. The use of subroutines is an important part of the structured approach to programming. They help organize large programs so that the logic used is easier to follow and modify if necessary.

To call a subroutine in BASIC, the GOSUB statement is used. The RETURN statement is later used to close the subroutine and direct control back to the line following the GOSUB statement. The general form of the GOSUB and RETURN statements are:

```
500 GOSUB line number at start of subroutine
```

and

```
1500 RETURN
```

The structure of a subroutine call is as follows:

```
     .
     .
     .
600 GOSUB 3000
610 REM The main program resumes at this line.
     .
     .
     .
2980 REM Line 2990 halts execution
2990 STOP
3000 REM This is the beginning of the subroutine
     .
     .
     .
3500 REM Line 3510 returns program control to the main program (line 610).
3510 RETURN
     .
     .
     .
9999 END
```

The GOSUB statement (line 600) contains the line number where the subroutine begins. In this case the program flow is directed to line 3000. The computer processes the subroutine until it encounters the RETURN statement (line 3510), which sends control to the line following the GOSUB statement (line 610). The main program then continues to execute until the STOP statement is encountered. The STOP statement prevents accidentally entering the subroutine. Several subroutines can be used in the same program, and they can even be nested. That is, one subroutine can be written inside another.

Let us see how a subroutine can be used to solve the age problem (Figure A3-3). The flowchart uses the predefined function symbol to indicate where the subroutine is called in the process. The flowchart for the subroutine is placed after the main program flowchart. The pseudocode shows the CALL statement to activate the subroutine. As with the flowchart, the pseudocode for the subroutine appears after that for the main program. Observe how the main program flow is sequential in form.

Flowchart

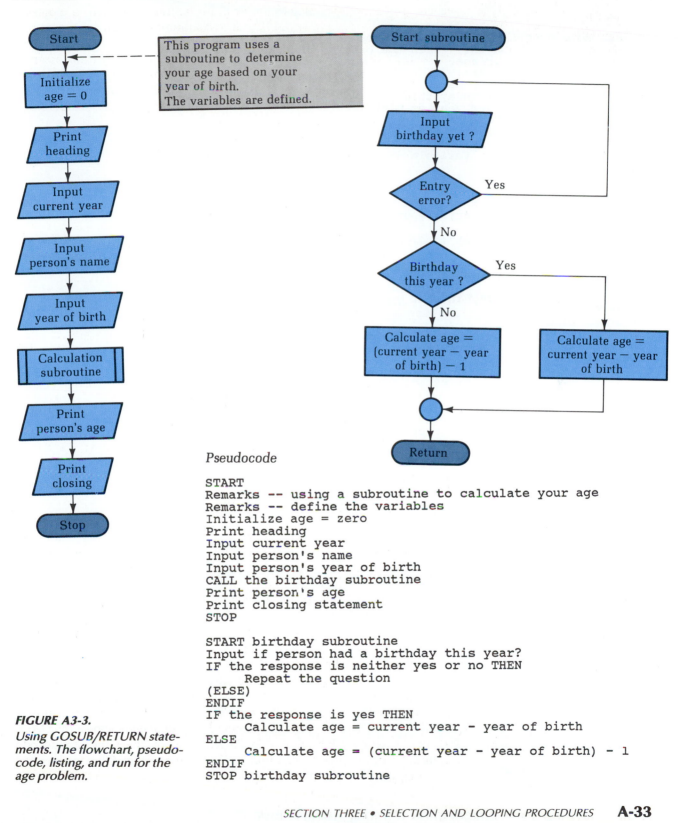

This program uses a subroutine to determine your age based on your year of birth.
The variables are defined.

Pseudocode

```
START
Remarks -- using a subroutine to calculate your age
Remarks -- define the variables
Initialize age = zero
Print heading
Input current year
Input person's name
Input person's year of birth
CALL the birthday subroutine
Print person's age
Print closing statement
STOP

START birthday subroutine
Input if person had a birthday this year?
IF the response is neither yes or no THEN
     Repeat the question
(ELSE)
ENDIF
IF the response is yes THEN
     Calculate age = current year - year of birth
ELSE
     Calculate age = (current year - year of birth) - 1
ENDIF
STOP birthday subroutine
```

FIGURE A3-3.
Using GOSUB/RETURN statements. The flowchart, pseudocode, listing, and run for the age problem.

List and run

```
100 REM This program will ask your name and what year
110 REM you were born in.   Then the program uses a subroutine to
120 REM calculate your age.
130 REM The variables are:
140 REM          N$ = Your name
150 REM          A$ = Birthday this year
160 REM          Y  = Your year of birth
170 REM          A  = Your age
180 REM          C  = Current year
190 REM **** Main Program ****
200 REM **** Initialize Variable ****
210 LET A = 0
220 REM **** Input Stage ****
230 PRINT
240 PRINT "This  program will ask you your name and year of birth,"
250 PRINT "then it will print your age."
260 PRINT
270 PRINT "What year is it";
280 INPUT C
290 PRINT
300 INPUT "What is your name"; N$
310 PRINT
320 PRINT "Well, ";N$;", in what year were you born";
330 INPUT Y
340 GOSUB 1000
350 REM The subroutine returns to this line
360 REM **** Output Stage ****
370 PRINT
380 PRINT
390 PRINT "My goodness, "; N$ ;", you are"; A ;" years old!"
400 PRINT
410 PRINT
420 PRINT "End of program."
430 REM The next line diverts program control to the END statement.
440 STOP
1000 REM **** Birthday Subroutine ****
1010 PRINT
1020 PRINT "Answer yes or no:  Have you had your birthday this year";
1030 INPUT A$
1040 REM The next line catches errors in answering the  question,
1050 REM and sends the user back to line 1020 to reask the question.
1060 IF A$ <> "yes" AND A$ <> "no" THEN 1020
1070 REM **** Process Stage ****
1080 IF A$ = "yes" THEN LET A = C - Y
1090 IF A$ = "no" THEN LET A = (C - Y) - 1
1100 REM The next line returns control to the main program.
1110 RETURN
9999 END
```

```
RUN

This program will ask you your name and year of birth.
then it will print your age.

What year is it? 1986
```

```
What is your name? Tom

Well, Tom, in what year were you born? 1948

Answer yes or no:  Have you had your birthday this year? Y
Answer yes or no:  Have you had your birthday this year? yes


My goodness, Tom, you are 38 years old!


End of program.


Stop at line 440
```

Subroutines could also be used in the billing program from the last section (wrap-up program, Figure A2-6) to process the data selectively. In this case we want to calculate required discounts and sales taxes. Because Paul's House of Electronic Wonders warehouse is located in California and its customer, Bits and Bytes, is located in Nevada, no sales tax should be charged. Additionally, a discount for a volume purchase is available. We need two subroutines to calculate the sales tax and the discount. Both of these subroutines can be called using IF/THEN/ELSE statements containing the GOSUB commands. Figure A3-4 shows the resulting program and subroutines. Notice also how blanks in PRINT statements are used to produce an "attractive" output.

FIGURE A3-4.
Using GOSUB/RETURN statements for the billing problem.

Pseudocode

```
START
Remarks -- describe the billing program
Remarks -- define the variables
Initialize the subtotals, tax owed, and grand total to zero
Read the customer billing data
Calculate the subtotal cost
IF discount  > 0 THEN
    CALL discount calculation subroutine
(ELSE)
ENDIF
IF discount = 0 THEN
    Set subtotals equal to each other
(ELSE)
ENDIF
IF purchaser's state = California THEN
    CALL state sales tax subroutine
(ELSE)
ENDIF
Calculate the grand total
Print heading
Print the customer address and billing data
Print the closing comments
STOP

START discount subroutine
Remarks -- describing the  subroutine
Calculate the discounted total
STOP discount subroutine
```

```
START the sales tax subroutine
Remarks -- the sales tax rate is 6.0 percent
Calculate the sales tax at the appropriate rate
STOP sales tax subroutine
```

List and run

```
100 REM This program will bill one customer.
110 REM We will use subroutines to calculate applicable discounts
120 REM and sales taxes.
130 REM The variables are:
140 REM          N$ = The name of the company
150 REM          A$ = The street address of the company
160 REM          C$ = The city
170 REM          S$ = The state or province
180 REM          Z  = The zip code of the customer
190 REM          I$ = The name of the item the customer wants
200 REM          Q  = The quantity of the item
210 REM          C  = The unit cost of the item
220 REM          D  = The discount for the item
230 REM          S  = The sales tax
240 REM          T1 = The prediscount total cost of the order
260 REM          T2 = The discounted total cost of the order
270 REM          G  = The grand total
280 REM **** Main Program ****
290 REM **** Initialize Variables ****
300 LET T1 = T2 = S = G = 0
310 REM **** Input Stage ****
320 READ N$, A$, C$, S$, Z, I$, Q, C, D
330 REM **** Process Stage ****
340 LET T1 = C * Q
350 REM **** Subroutine Stage ****
360 REM **** The first subroutine calculates the discount. ****
370 IF D <> 0 THEN GOSUB 1000
380 IF D = 0 THEN LET T2 = T1
390 REM **** The second subroutine calculates the sales tax. ****
400 IF S$ = "California" THEN GOSUB 2000
410 LET G = S + T2
420 REM **** Output Stage ****
430 PRINT "This program calculates the bill for one customer."
440 PRINT
450 PRINT "Customer and Address:"
460 PRINT
470 PRINT N$
480 PRINT A$
490 PRINT C$; S$; Z
500 PRINT
510 PRINT "Purchase Data:"
520 PRINT
530 PRINT "                    Item: "; I$
540 PRINT "                Quantity:  "; Q
550 PRINT "                    Cost: $"; C
560 PRINT "                         ---------"
570 PRINT "      The total cost of the order: $"; T1
580 PRINT " The discount percentage: "; D
590 PRINT " The discounted total of the order: $"; T2
600 PRINT "              The sales tax @ 6%: $"; S
610 PRINT "                         ---------"
620 PRINT "             The grand total: $"; G
630 PRINT
640 PRINT
```

```
650 PRINT "                          End of Program"
660 STOP
1000 REM **** Discount Subroutine ****
1010 REM The discounted total is found by multiplying the
1020 REM undiscounted total by 1 minus the discount percentage.
1030 LET T2 = T1 * (1 - (D / 100))
1040 RETURN
2000 REM **** Sales Tax Subroutine ****
2010 REM The sales tax rate is 6 percent.
2020 LET S = T2 * (.06)
2030 RETURN
3000 REM **** Data List ****
3010 DATA "Bits and Bytes", "67 Main Street"
3020 DATA "Last Chance  ", "Nevada", 89133
3040 DATA "Microprocessor", 1500, 6.85, 15
9999 END
```

```
RUN
This program calculates the bill for one customer.

Customer and Address:

Bits and Bytes
67 Main Street
Last Chance  Nevada   89133

Purchase Data:

                Item: Microprocessor
                        Quantity:    1500
                            Cost: $ 6.85
                                  ---------
        The total cost of the order: $ 10275
  The discount percentage:  15
  The discounted total of the order: $ 8733.75
                The sales tax @ 6%: $ 0
                                  ---------
                The grand total: $ 8733.75


                End of Program
```

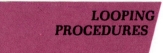

LOOPING PROCEDURES

With many problems we need to perform the same task several times. In the billing problem (Figure A3-4), we only read one company's data into the program for processing, for the sake of simplicity. In typical businesses a large number of customers would be processed in a group during the billing cycle. Procedures are repeated by using loops.

There are two main types of loops: (1) the number of repetitions is known, and (2) the number of repetitions is unknown.

When the number of repetitions is known, we can set the loop by use of a counter. When the number of repetitions is unknown, we must tell the computer when to stop processing the loop by using a trailer value, or sentinel value, at the end of the data to be processed. We will discuss each situation in turn.

USING A COUNTER

The value of a loop **COUNTER** changes by a fixed amount with each iteration (pass through) of the loop. When the counter reaches a predetermined value, the loop is exited. Three steps are involved:

1 Initializing *the counter.*
2 Incrementing *the counter.*
3 Testing *the counter for the end of the loop.*

A sample program is shown in Figure A3-5. Initialization refers to setting the starting value of the counter. Most counters are initialized at 1 or 0. We increment the counter each time we pass through the loop. For example, if a counter is set to 1 and it is incremented by 1 each time through the loop the values will go from 1 to 2 to 3 to 4, and so forth. Each time the loop is executed, the counter value is tested to see whether it is time to exit the loop. Usually we test to see if the counter exceeds a certain value. If the test is false, we stay in the loop for another repetition. If the test is true, we exit the loop and continue the program.

FIGURE A3-5.

How a counter is used in a loop.

List and run

```
100 REM This program uses a counter to read  six  numbers,
120 REM add them, and print out their sum.
130 REM The variables are:
140 REM         A = The counter value
150 REM         X = The number to be added
160 REM         Y = The total of the numbers
170 REM **** Main Program  *****
180 REM **** Initialize Variables ****
190 LET A = 0
200 LET Y = 0
210 REM **** Print Headings ****
220 PRINT "This program reads six numbers,"
230 PRINT "adds them, and prints out the sum."
240 PRINT
250 PRINT
260 PRINT "The numbers are:"
270 PRINT
280 REM **** Begin the Loop ****
290 READ X
300 PRINT X
310 REM The next line accumulates the numbers
320 LET Y = Y + X
330 REM The next line accumulates the counter
340 LET A = A + 1
350 REM The next line tests the counter
360 IF A < 6 THEN.290
370 REM **** Leave the Loop ****
380 REM **** Final Total and Closing ****
390 PRINT
400 PRINT
410 PRINT "The total of the numbers is:"; Y
420 PRINT
430 PRINT
440 PRINT "End of Program"
450 REM **** Data List ****
460 DATA 12.5, 10.27, 7, 15, 170.21, 99
470 END
```

```
RUN
This program reads six numbers,
adds them, and prints out the sum.

The numbers are:

 12.5
 10.27
 7
 15
 170.21
 99


The total of the numbers is: 313.98


End of Program
```

USING A TRAILER VALUE

A loop that tests for a **TRAILER VALUE** is often used during input operations to tell the program when to stop processing input data. We often call this trailer value a sentinel value or test value. Usually a trailer value is not used in the same loop with a counter test. A GOTO statement is used to close the loop when a trailer value is used.

The **GOTO** statement is an unconditional branch that directs the program flow to a specific line number. The general form of the GOTO statement is:

```
500 GOTO another line
```

The line "400 GOTO 300" directs the flow back to line 300. Figure A3-6 shows how to write a simple summation program that reads and adds six numbers by using a loop with a trailer value. The IF/THEN statement in line 270 of the program has an implied or hidden GOTO statement. If you use a trailer value to end a loop containing a read operation, dummy values must be placed in the data statement, otherwise the program will abort with an out-of-data error message. For example, in the program:

```
100 READ X$, A, B
110 IF X$ = "END OF DATA" THEN 300
    .
    .
    .
900 DATA "END OF DATA"
```

the line 900 needs to be rewritten:

```
900 DATA "END OF DATA", 0, 0
```

Sometimes a loop uses a trailer value when the data are first read in. Within this loop an accumulator statement records the number of iterations of the loop. In that way any later counter-controlled loops can use the final accumulated value as the test value for the end of the loop.

List and run

```
100 REM This program uses a loop tested with a trailer value
110 REM to read six numbers, add them, and print out their sum.
120 REM The variables are:
130 REM          X = The number to be added
140 REM          Y = The total of the numbers
150 REM **** Main Program ****
160 REM **** Initialize the Accumulator ****
170 LET Y = 0
180 REM **** Print Headings ****
190 PRINT "This program reads six numbers,"
200 PRINT "adds them, and prints out their sum."
210 PRINT
220 PRINT
230 PRINT "The numbers are:"
240 PRINT
250 REM **** Begin the Loop ****
260 READ X
270 IF X = -9999 THEN 340
280 PRINT X
290 REM The next line accumulates the numbers
300 LET Y = Y + X
310 REM The GOTO command returns the program flow
320 REM to the READ statement in line 260
330 GOTO 260
340 REM **** Leave the Loop ****
350 REM **** Final Total and Closing ****
360 PRINT
370 PRINT
380 PRINT "The total of the numbers is:"; Y
390 PRINT
400 PRINT
410 PRINT "End of Program"
420 REM **** Data List ****
420 DATA 12.5, 10.27, 7, 15, 170.21, 99, -9999
430 END

RUN
This program reads six numbers,
adds them, and prints out their sum.


The numbers are:

 12.5
 10.27
 7
 15
 170.21
 99


The total of the numbers is: 313.98


End of Program
```

We need to distinguish between the functions performed by GOSUB and GOTO statements.

Compare the use of a line number with a GOSUB in an IF/THEN statement. The statement

```
500 IF X = 1 THEN GOTO 700
```

means if X equals 1, then branch to line 700, and the flow of the program continues from line 700 to the end of the program. However, for the statement

```
500 IF X = 1 THEN GOSUB 700
```

the program branches to the subroutine that starts at line 700, but when its RETURN statement is executed, the program continues execution at line 510.

GOTO statements have been rightly criticized by programming professionals because these statements allow the development of sloppy programming habits and work against the principles of structured programming. *GOTO statements are not recommended for any purpose other than closing or exiting a loop.*

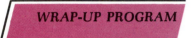

WRAP-UP PROGRAM

Our wrap-up example modifies the Figure A3-4 billing problem to handle additional customers. The object is to use a counter to manage the loop control. A satisfactory program that does this is shown in Figure A3-7. The data for the customers show the units purchased, the unit cost, and the percentage discount respectively.

```
Bits and Bytes
67 Main Street
Last Chance Nevada 89133
Microprocessor, 1500, $6.85, 15

Freddy Johnson's Travel Agency
345 Market Street
Oakriver California 90619
Case of floppy disks, 10, $45, 30

The Terminal Connection
4665 W. 41st Avenue
Oakriver California 90614
Daisy wheel printer, 20, $740, 0
```

Observe how the subroutines are selectively used. Only one customer (Freddy Johnson's Travel Agency) activates both subroutines.

Flowchart

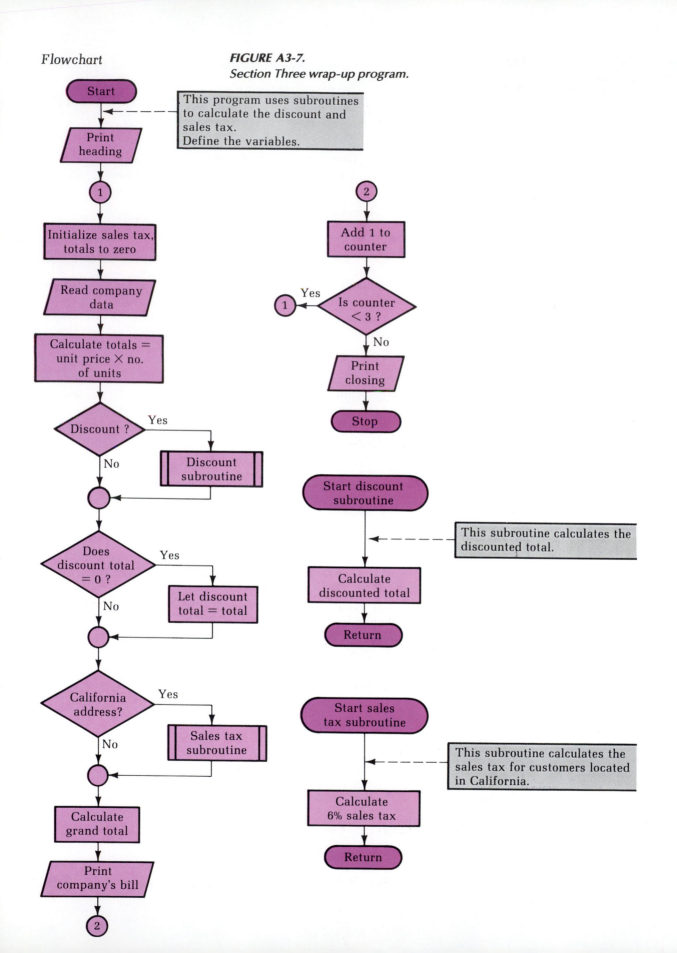

FIGURE A3-7.
Section Three wrap-up program.

Pseudocode

```
START
Remarks -- the program computes the bills for several customers
Remarks -- define the variables
Initialize the counter to zero
Print heading
DOUNTIL counter = number of records
     Initialize the subtotals, tax and grand total to zero
     Read the customer billing data
     Calculate the subtotal cost
     IF discount  > 0 THEN
          CALL discount calculation subroutine
     (ELSE)
     ENDIF
     IF discount = 0 THEN
          Set subtotals equal to each other
     (ELSE)
     ENDIF
     IF purchaser's state = California THEN
          CALL state sales tax subroutine
     (ELSE)
     ENDIF
     Calculate the grand total
     Print the customer address and billing data
     Add one to the counter
ENDDO
Print the closing comments
STOP

START discount subroutine
Remarks -- describing the subroutine
Calculate the discounted total
STOP discount subroutine

START the sales tax subroutine
Remarks -- the sales tax rate is 6.0 percent
Calculate the sales tax at the appropriate rate
STOP sales tax subroutine
```

List and run

```
100 REM This program will use a loop to bill several customers.
110 REM We will use subroutines to calculate applicable discounts
120 REM and sales taxes.
130 REM The variables are:
140 REM       N$ = The name of the company
150 REM       A$ = The street address of the company
160 REM       C$ = The city
170 REM       S$ = The state or province
180 REM       Z  = The zip code of the customer
190 REM       I$ = The name of the item the customer wants
200 REM       Q  = The quantity of the item
210 REM       C  = The unit cost of the item
220 REM       D  = The discount for the item
230 REM       S  = The sales tax
240 REM       T1 = The prediscount total cost of the order
260 REM       T2 = The discounted total cost of the order
270 REM       G  = The grand total
280 REM       A  = The counter
290 REM ****  Main Program ****
300 REM **** Initialize Counter ****
310 LET A = 0
320 REM **** Print Heading ****
```

```
330 PRINT "This program calculates the bills of several customers."
340 PRINT
350 REM **** Begin the Loop ****
360 REM **** Initialize Non-read Variables ****
370 LET T1 = 0
380 LET T2 = 0
390 LET S = 0
400 LET G = 0
410 REM **** Input Stage ****
420 READ N$, A$, C$, S$, Z, I$, Q, C, D
430 REM **** Calculation Stage ****
440 LET T1 = C * Q
450 REM **** Subroutine Stage ****
460 REM **** The first subroutine calculates the discount. ****
470 IF D > 0 THEN GOSUB 1000
480 IF D = 0 THEN LET T2 = T1
490 REM **** The second subroutine calculates the sales tax. ****
500 IF S$ = "California" THEN GOSUB 2000
510 LET G = S + T2
520 REM **** Output Stage ****
530 PRINT "_____"
540 PRINT
550 PRINT "Customer and Address:"
560 PRINT
570 PRINT N$
580 PRINT A$
590 PRINT C$; S$; Z
600 PRINT
610 PRINT "Purchase Data:"
620 PRINT
630 PRINT "                    Item: "; I$
640 PRINT "                        Quantity:  "; Q
650 PRINT "                            Cost: $"; C
660 PRINT "                            ---------"
670 PRINT "      The total cost of the order: $"; T1
680 PRINT " The discount percentage: "; D
690 PRINT " The discounted total of the order: $"; T2
700 PRINT "                The sales tax @ 6%: $"; S
710 PRINT "                            ---------"
720 PRINT "                  The grand total: $"; G
730 PRINT
740 PRINT "_____"
750 LET A = A + 1
760 IF A < 3 THEN 370
770 PRINT
780 PRINT
790 PRINT "                      End of Program"
800 STOP
1000 REM **** Discount Subroutine ****
1010 REM The discounted total is found by multiplying the
1020 REM undiscounted total by 1 minus the discount percentage.
1010 LET T2 = T1 * (1 - (D / 100))
1040 RETURN
2000 REM **** Sales Tax Subroutine ****
2010 REM The sales tax rate is 6 percent.
2020 LET S = T2 * (.06)
2030 RETURN
3000 REM **** Data List ****
```

```
3010 DATA "Bits and Bytes", "67 Main Street"
3020 DATA "Last Chance  ", "Nevada", 89133
3030 DATA "Microprocessor", 1500, 6.85, 15
3040 DATA "Freddy Johnson's Travel Agency", "345 Market Street"
3050 DATA "Oakriver  ","California", 90619
3060 DATA "Case of floppy disks", 10, 45, 30
3070 DATA "The Terminal Connection","4665 W. 41st Avenue"
3080 DATA "Oakriver  ", "California", 90614
3090 DATA "Daisy wheel printers", 20, 740, 0
9999 END
RUN
This program calculates the bill for several customers.
```

Customer and Address:

Bits and Bytes
67 Main Street
Last Chance Nevada 89133

Purchase Data:

```
                 Item: Microprocessor
                        Quantity:   1500
                            Cost: $ 6.85
                                  ---------
            The total cost of the order: $ 10275
      The discount percentage:  15
      The discounted total of the order: $ 8733.75
                  The sales tax @ 6%: $ 0
                                  ---------
                    The grand total: $ 8733.75
```

Customer and Address:

Freddy Johnson's Travel Agency
345 Market Street
Oakriver California 90619

Purchase Data:

```
                 Item: Case of floppy disks
                        Quantity:   10
                            Cost: $ 45
                                  ---------
            The total cost of the order: $ 450
      The discount percentage:  30
      The discounted total of the order: $ 315
                  The sales tax @ 6%: $ 18.9
                                  ---------
                    The grand total: $ 333.9
```

FIGURE A3-7 (cont.)

```
Customer and Address:

The Terminal Connection
4665 W. 41st Avenue
Oakriver   California 90614

Purchase Data:

                  Item: Daisy wheel printer
                          Quantity:   20
                              Cost: $ 740
                                    ---------
         The total cost of the order: $ 14800
      The discount percentage:   0
      The discounted total of the order: $ 14800
                  The sales tax @ 6%: $ 888
                                    ---------
                     The grand total: $ 15688



              End of program


   Stop at line 800
```

KEY TERMS

These are the key terms in the order in which they appear in the section.

IF/THEN/ELSE (A-27)
Relational operator (A-28)
Logical operator or Boolean
 operator (A-28)

GOSUB/RETURN (A-32)
Counter (A-38)
Trailer value (A-39)
GOTO (A-39)

REVIEW QUESTIONS

SHORT ANSWER QUESTIONS

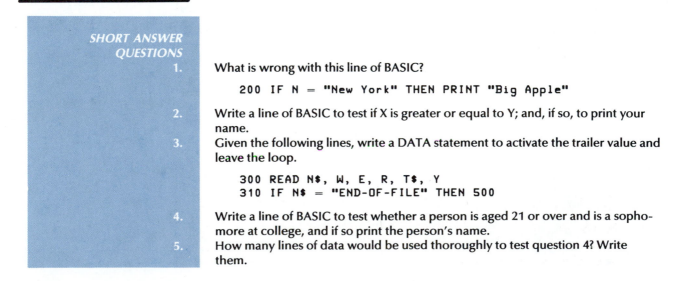

1. What is wrong with this line of BASIC?

   ```
   200 IF N = "New York" THEN PRINT "Big Apple"
   ```

2. Write a line of BASIC to test if X is greater or equal to Y; and, if so, to print your name.

3. Given the following lines, write a DATA statement to activate the trailer value and leave the loop.

   ```
   300 READ N$, W, E, R, T$, Y
   310 IF N$ = "END-OF-FILE" THEN 500
   ```

4. Write a line of BASIC to test whether a person is aged 21 or over and is a sophomore at college, and if so print the person's name.

5. How many lines of data would be used thoroughly to test question 4? Write them.

6. Which of the following are not valid IF/THEN/ELSE statements?

(a) 500 IF N$ = '34' THEN LET Z= N$∧2
  510 ELSE X = X∧2

(b) 600 IF W = "LAST" AND X <> 10 THEN LET X = Z
  610 ELSE X = Y

(c) 700 IF R < 23 OR R < 45 THEN PRINT "OUT OF RANGE"

(d) 800 IF P = 23.45 THEN GOSUB 5000
  810 IF P < 23.45 THEN GOSUB 6000

7. Why is the STOP statement used in programs containing subroutines?

8. To what line does the RETURN statement direct the program flow?

9. How many times will the letter "A" be printed?

```
100 LET X = 0
110 PRINT "A"
120 LET X = X + 1
130 IF X < 7 THEN 110
140 END
```

10. Rewrite the BASIC code in Question 9 to demonstrate using a trailer value.

11. Write the flowchart for the program displayed in Figure A3-4.

12. Write the flowchart and pseudocode for the program displayed in Figure A3-5.

13. Write the flowchart and pseudocode for the program displayed in Figure A3-6.

PROGRAMMING EXERCISES

1. Susan Paul needs to sum up the commissions earned by her salespeople for the past month. Use the data provided to test the solution.

```
Tom Albert        $2234
Harry Jones       $3716
Leon Klaus        $2452
Milt Weiss        $2345
Joe Topaz         $1901
```

2. Dr. Clara Chips wants to give an award to those students who earned A's (90 percent) in her introductory information-systems class. How might she design a program solution to determine who receives an award? She picks five students' grades to test the program

Student Name	Numeric Grade	Letter Grade
Eugene Alton	89	B
John Burton	78	C
Lynne Davis	70	C
Mike Francis	90	A
Cindy Smith	91	A

3. Myrtle, owner of Myrtle's Burgers, needs a program to calculate a 6 percent sales tax on items purchased at her restaurant. Each item and its cost, the subtotal, tax, and grand total must be printed out. Use an INPUT command to ask if the order is "for here or to go?" If it is "for here," use the subroutine to calculate the sales tax. To test the program, use the following order:

1 Superburger @ $1.80
2 Large fries @ $0.80
3 Small shake @ $0.90

To continue the discussion of loops, this section introduces easier loop handling through the use of the FOR/NEXT and WHILE/WEND statements. We then move on to discuss how to set up and process arrays of data. Array processing is done with loops. At the end of the section, the wrap-up program demonstrates array processing to carry out a common operation in business—sorting data.

FOR/NEXT STATEMENTS

Let us take our understanding of counters used in loops one step further. The difficulties with loops using counters are knowing where to place the initialization, incrementation (or decrementation), and testing steps within the program. BASIC provides us with a convenient way to avoid these problems by using the paired **FOR/NEXT** statements to facilitate looping. FOR/NEXT operations reduce the time and energy spent in programming.

The general form of FOR/NEXT statements is:

```
500 FOR I=J TO K    STEP L
    procedure inside the loop
550 NEXT I
```

where

I represents the loop counter
J represents the starting value of the counter
K represents the ending value of the counter
L represents the amount to increment (decrement) each iteration of the counter

The beginning and stopping points for the counter are usually whole numbers. Incrementation loops start with a lower number and stop at a higher one. Decrementation loops follow the opposite approach, from highest to lowest.

Consider a simple example. Figure A4-1 shows the flowchart, pseudo-code, and program using a FOR/NEXT loop to print the word "Greetings" five times. In this example the FOR statement begins counting with the number 1 and goes through the loop five times one digit at a time.

To flowchart a FOR/NEXT loop, we perform five steps (refer to Figure A4-1 and note the location of the explanatory arrows):

1 *At the beginning of the flowchart we use the hexagonal symbol for*

   preparation: ⬡ *Within the beginning symbol, we place the*

   FOR statement and make note of the initial value, increment (or decrement) amount, and test value for the counter.
2 *We flowchart the processing steps within the loop in the usual fashion (see examples earlier in the appendix).*

FIGURE A4-1.

Flowchart, pseudocode, listing, and run for a loop using FOR/NEXT statements.

Flowchart

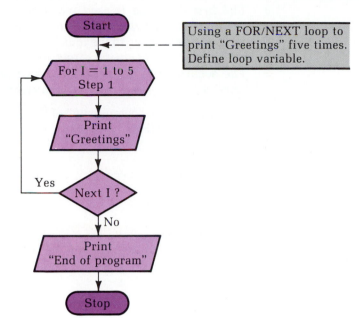

Pseudocode

```
START
Remarks -- concerning the loop and defining the variables
FOR I = 1 TO 5
     Print "Greetings"
NEXT I
Closing statement
STOP
```

List and run

```
100 REM Using the FOR/NEXT procedure
110 REM The variable is:
120 REM          X = The counter in the FOR/NEXT procedure
130 REM **** Main Program ****
140 FOR X = 1 TO 5 STEP 1
150    PRINT "Greetings"
160 NEXT X
170 PRINT
180 PRINT "End of Program."
190 END

RUN
Greetings
Greetings
Greetings
Greetings
Greetings

End of Program.
```

3 At the end of the loop, we use the decision symbol: ◇ Within the decision symbol we write NEXT followed by the loop counter variable and a question mark. Two flow lines exit from this decision symbol.

4 The first flow line is used when there is another loop iteration to perform. It is labeled "Yes" and drawn to the left out of the NEXT symbol, and links up to the middle of the preparation symbol. Be sure to use arrows to indicate the direction of the flow line.

5 The second flow line shows the exit from the loop. This exit line, labeled "No," leads down or to the right from the decision symbol.

In contrast to the "complexity" of the flowcharting method, the pseudo-code for the FOR/NEXT command shows the two command lines flanking the operation you wish to repeat:

```
FOR I = J TO K STEP L
        procedure
NEXT I
```

There are other accepted ways to write flowcharts and pseudocode for FOR/NEXT loops. Your instructor may suggest or require an alternative.

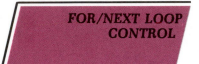

FOR/NEXT LOOP CONTROL

A loop is controlled by a counter variable that determines the number of times the loop is executed. Counter variables can be set to numbers or other variables. Let us look at some examples of loop control. After each set of BASIC code, we see how the results would be printed out.

The first example shows a loop that increases by 1 with each iteration:

```
100 REM A simple loop
110 FOR I = 1 TO 6 STEP 1
120    PRINT "Hello"
140 NEXT I
150 END
```

The output looks like this:

```
Hello
Hello
Hello
Hello
Hello
Hello
```

When the increment is 1, the explicit STEP command can be omitted.

The second FOR/NEXT example demonstrates a loop that begins with a value other than 1 and has a step value other than 1. In this case the initial number and the step value are both set to 3. We use an accumulator to help us trace the flow of this loop.

```
200 REM Any number can be used for the initial value.
210 LET X = 0
220 FOR J = 3 TO 15 STEP 3
230    LET X = X + J
240    PRINT "J ="; J, "X ="; X
250 NEXT J
260 END
```

```
RUN
J = 3          X = 3
J = 6          X = 9
J = 9          X = 18
J = 12         X = 30
J = 15         X = 45
```

The third example illustrates decrementation. We begin with a larger number as our starting value and decrease the value by 4 each time until we reach 0.

```
300 REM Moving backward -- decrementation
310 FOR K = 20 TO 0 STEP -4
320   PRINT "K ="; K
330 NEXT K
340 END

RUN
K = 20
K = 16
K = 12
K = 8
K = 4
K = 0
```

The fourth case shows how to increment by a decimal value. This is useful for accounting programs involving interest payments, depreciation, mortgage problems, and other business applications.

```
400 REM Using fractional steps
410 FOR P = 1 TO 3 STEP .5
420   PRINT "P ="; P
430 NEXT P
440 END

RUN
P = 1
P = 1.5
P = 2
P = 2.5
P = 3
```

The fifth example shows how we can use variables instead of fixed numbers to set the counter, lower value, upper value, and step value. The use of variables allows greater flexibility in setting up frequently used programs. For example, loops used for accepting input data can be altered to accommodate varying numbers of records.

```
500 REM Using variables to define the loop
510 LET I = 3
520 LET J = 10
530 LET K = 2
540 FOR F = I TO J STEP K
550   PRINT "F ="; F
560 NEXT F
570 END

RUN
F = 3
F = 5
F = 7
F = 9
```

Our sixth example shows the proper way to direct the flow when using IF/THEN/ELSE statements within a loop. Depending upon the results of the test, either the number or its squared value is printed out.

```
600 REM Using an IFTHENELSE Statement
610 REM inside a FOR/NEXT loop
620 FOR S = 1 TO 5
630    READ X
640    IF X < 100 THEN PRINT "X ="; X
650    ELSE PRINT "X SQUARED ="; X^2
660 NEXT S
670 DATA 30, 110, 99, 100, 101
680 END

RUN
X = 30
X SQUARED = 12100
X = 99
X SQUARED = 10000
X SQUARED = 10201
```

The program flow is eventually directed to the line containing the NEXT statement. The flow should never be sent to the line with the FOR statement, (an error message would be generated). Because the logical structure used in example 6 is more complex than the previous five, the flowchart and pseudocode steps are shown in Figure A4-2.

FIGURE A4-2.

Flowchart and pseudocode for using an IF/THEN/ELSE statement inside a FOR/NEXT loop.

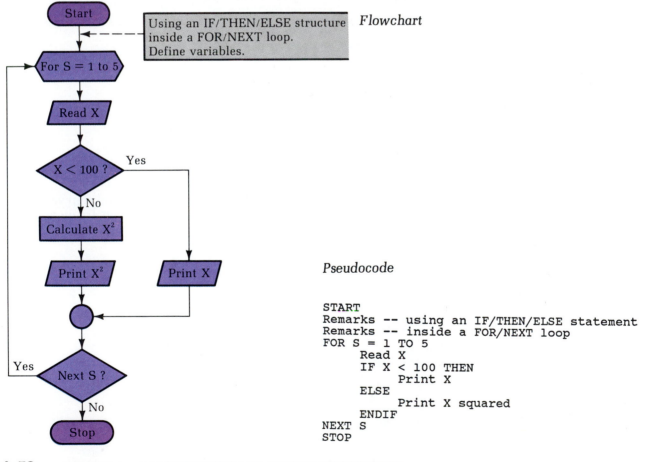

Flowchart

Pseudocode

```
START
Remarks -- using an IF/THEN/ELSE statement
Remarks -- inside a FOR/NEXT loop
FOR S = 1 TO 5
        Read X
        IF X < 100 THEN
                Print X
        ELSE
                Print X squared
        ENDIF
NEXT S
STOP
```

Programs can have more than one FOR/NEXT loop. FOR/NEXT loops can follow each other consecutively through the program. Figure A4-3 illustrates two consecutive loops. Notice that the same variable ("I" in this case) can be used as a counter more than once in the same program. However, the letter chosen as the counter variable for a loop cannot be used for another variable within that loop.

FIGURE A4-3.

Example of two consecutive FOR/NEXT loops in a program.

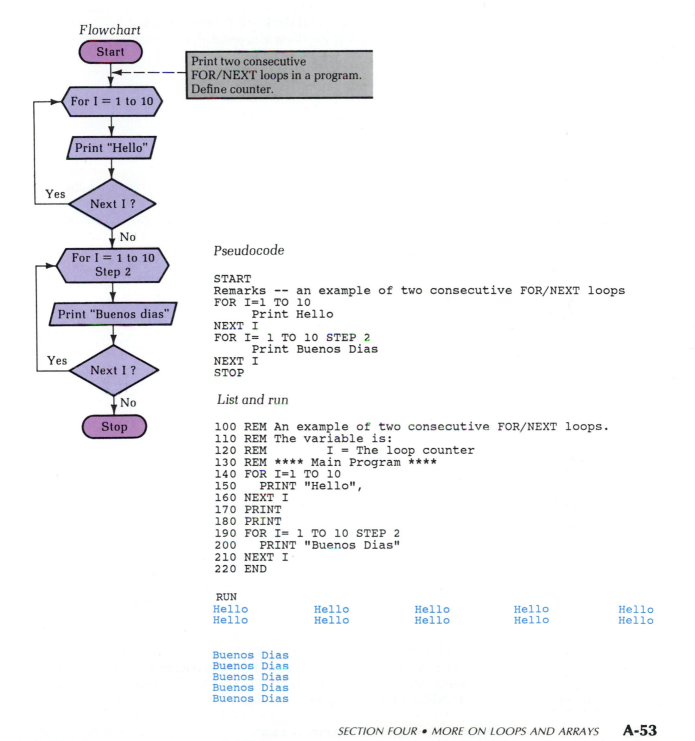

Flowchart

Print two consecutive FOR/NEXT loops in a program. Define counter.

Pseudocode

```
START
Remarks -- an example of two consecutive FOR/NEXT loops
FOR I=1 TO 10
     Print Hello
NEXT I
FOR I= 1 TO 10 STEP 2
     Print Buenos Dias
NEXT I
STOP
```

List and run

```
100 REM An example of two consecutive FOR/NEXT loops.
110 REM The variable is:
120 REM          I = The loop counter
130 REM **** Main Program ****
140 FOR I=1 TO 10
150    PRINT "Hello",
160 NEXT I
170 PRINT
180 PRINT
190 FOR I= 1 TO 10 STEP 2
200    PRINT "Buenos Dias"
210 NEXT I
220 END
```

```
RUN
Hello        Hello        Hello        Hello        Hello
Hello        Hello        Hello        Hello        Hello

Buenos Dias
Buenos Dias
Buenos Dias
Buenos Dias
Buenos Dias
```

NESTED FOR/NEXT LOOPS

FOR/NEXT loops (like any other type of loop) can also be nested one within another. An example of such **NESTED LOOPS** is given in Figure A4-4. Nested loops may even contain three, four, or more embedded loops. Different machines have different maximum levels for nesting. The flowchart and pseudocode show that the inner loop is wholly within the outer loop.

How many times do the inner loops execute? Look at Figure A4-4. The outer loop (FOR I = 1 TO 5) executes five times. For each iteration of the outer loop, the inner loop (FOR J = 2 TO 6) is executed five times: (J = 2, J = 3, J = 4, J = 5, J = 6). For the whole program, the inner loop is executed 25 times (5 × 5).

FIGURE A4-4.

Example of a nested FOR/NEXT loop.

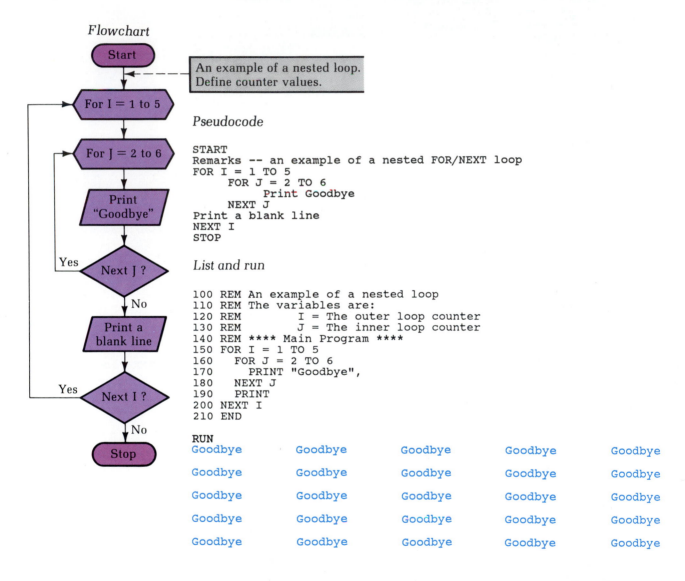

Flowchart

Start

An example of a nested loop. Define counter values.

For I = 1 to 5

For J = 2 to 6

Print "Goodbye"

Next J ? Yes

No

Print a blank line

Next I ? Yes

No

Stop

Pseudocode

```
START
Remarks -- an example of a nested FOR/NEXT loop
FOR I = 1 TO 5
     FOR J = 2 TO 6
          Print Goodbye
     NEXT J
Print a blank line
NEXT I
STOP
```

List and run

```
100 REM An example of a nested loop
110 REM The variables are:
120 REM          I = The outer loop counter
130 REM          J = The inner loop counter
140 REM **** Main Program ****
150 FOR I = 1 TO 5
160    FOR J = 2 TO 6
170      PRINT "Goodbye",
180    NEXT J
190    PRINT
200 NEXT I
210 END
```

```
RUN
Goodbye          Goodbye          Goodbye          Goodbye          Goodbye

Goodbye          Goodbye          Goodbye          Goodbye          Goodbye

Goodbye          Goodbye          Goodbye          Goodbye          Goodbye

Goodbye          Goodbye          Goodbye          Goodbye          Goodbye

Goodbye          Goodbye          Goodbye          Goodbye          Goodbye
```

A NOTE ON DEBUGGING

Each FOR statement requires a NEXT statement at the end of the loop. If you forget the NEXT statement, a "FOR without NEXT" error message will result. Similarly, if you have a NEXT statement but forget a FOR statement, a "NEXT without FOR" error message will result.

Do not overlap nesting loops! The inner loops must be located completely within the outer loop. If you overlap them, the program will fail to run. An example of an improperly created nested loop, and how to correct it, is shown in Figure A4-5. Avoid overlapping any of the looping structures described in this section and IF/THEN/ELSE statements. Properly prepared flowcharts and pseudocode will help prevent such errors.

FIGURE A4-5.
Example of an improperly nested loop and how to correct it.

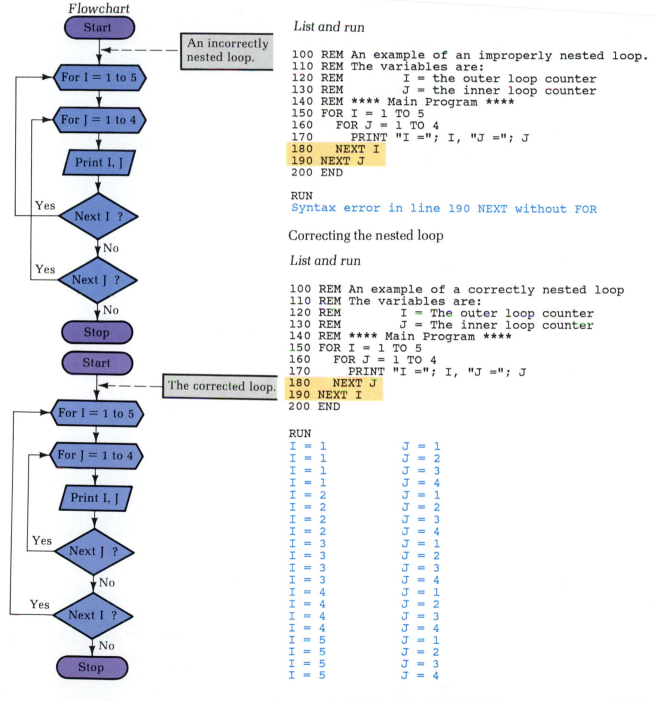

List and run

```
100 REM An example of an improperly nested loop.
110 REM The variables are:
120 REM          I = the outer loop counter
130 REM          J = the inner loop counter
140 REM **** Main Program ****
150 FOR I = 1 TO 5
160    FOR J = 1 TO 4
170       PRINT "I ="; I, "J ="; J
180    NEXT I
190 NEXT J
200 END
```

RUN
Syntax error in line 190 NEXT without FOR

Correcting the nested loop

List and run

```
100 REM An example of a correctly nested loop
110 REM The variables are:
120 REM          I = The outer loop counter
130 REM          J = The inner loop counter
140 REM **** Main Program ****
150 FOR I = 1 TO 5
160    FOR J = 1 TO 4
170       PRINT "I ="; I, "J ="; J
180    NEXT J
190 NEXT I
200 END
```

```
RUN
I = 1          J = 1
I = 1          J = 2
I = 1          J = 3
I = 1          J = 4
I = 2          J = 1
I = 2          J = 2
I = 2          J = 3
I = 2          J = 4
I = 3          J = 1
I = 3          J = 2
I = 3          J = 3
I = 3          J = 4
I = 4          J = 1
I = 4          J = 2
I = 4          J = 3
I = 4          J = 4
I = 5          J = 1
I = 5          J = 2
I = 5          J = 3
I = 5          J = 4
```

A number of microcomputers, notably those using Microsoft BASIC (such as the IBM PC and its compatibles) and Apple computers, permit the use of an extended looping procedure with **WHILE/WEND** statements. The general form is:

```
500 WHILE expression is true
       perform loop operation
550 WEND
```

This loop executes *while* the numeric expression is true. When the program encounters the WEND statement, the loop iteration begins again starting with the test of the numeric expression at the top of the loop. If the test is false, program control is passed to the first executable statement after the WEND statement. WHILE/WEND permits the progammer to make use of the DOWHILE logic directly, which is preferred in structured programming. An example of this loop is shown in the BASIC program:

```
190 REM Demonstrating WHILE/WEND statements
200 Z = 0
210 READ X,Y
220 WHILE X <> Z
230    PRINT Y
240    READ X, Y
250 WEND
260 PRINT
270 PRINT "End of Program."
280 DATA 1, 2
290 DATA 1, 3
300 DATA 1, 4
310 DATA 0, 5
320 DATA 1, 6
330 END

RUN
  2
  3
  4

End of Program.
```

When the 0 in the data is encountered, the loop test in line 220 (the numeric expression $X <> Z$) registers false, and program control is transferred to line 260.

Figure A4-6 illustrates the use of a WHILE/WEND loop to find the sum of six numbers. A sentinel value (test value) of -9999 is used to indicate the end of data, and so end processing. The variable Z is initialized to this value, and when X is set to -9999 in line 330, the test $X <> Z$ in line 300 fails and the loop is exited.

FIGURE A4-6.

*How WHILE/WEND statements
are used in a loop.*

Flowchart

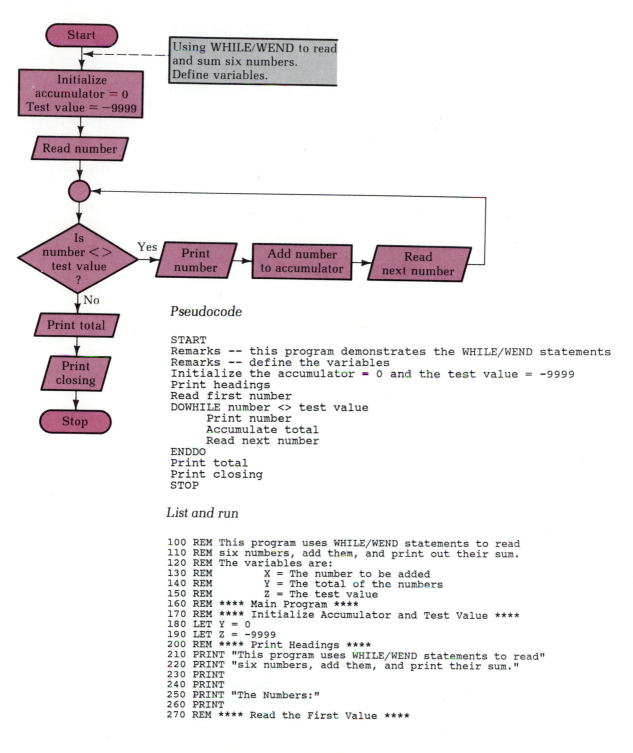

Pseudocode

```
START
Remarks -- this program demonstrates the WHILE/WEND statements
Remarks -- define the variables
Initialize the accumulator = 0 and the test value = -9999
Print headings
Read first number
DOWHILE number <> test value
     Print number
     Accumulate total
     Read next number
ENDDO
Print total
Print closing
STOP
```

List and run

```
100 REM This program uses WHILE/WEND statements to read
110 REM six numbers, add them, and print out their sum.
120 REM The variables are:
130 REM          X = The number to be added
140 REM          Y = The total of the numbers
150 REM          Z = The test value
160 REM **** Main Program ****
170 REM **** Initialize Accumulator and Test Value ****
180 LET Y = 0
190 LET Z = -9999
200 REM **** Print Headings ****
210 PRINT "This program uses WHILE/WEND statements to read"
220 PRINT "six numbers, add them, and print their sum."
230 PRINT
240 PRINT
250 PRINT "The Numbers:"
260 PRINT
270 REM **** Read the First Value ****
```

FIGURE A4-6 *(cont.)*

```
280 READ X
290 REM **** The WHILE/WEND Loop ****
300 WHILE X <> Z
310    PRINT X
320    LET Y = Y + X
330    READ X
340 WEND
350 REM ****  Print the Total and Closing  ****
360 PRINT
380 PRINT
390 PRINT "End of program."
410 DATA 12.5, 10.27, 7, 15, 170.21, 99, -9999
420 END
```

RUN
This program uses WHILE/WEND statements to read
six numbers, add them, and print their sum.

The Numbers:

12.5
10.27
7
15
170.21
99

The total of the numbers is: 313.98

End of program.

ARRAYS AND SUBSCRIPTED VARIABLES

Now that you know about loops, it is time to learn how lists or tables of data can be processed using arrays. The connection here is that arrays are generally processed using loops.

An **ARRAY** is a collection of related data. In an array a single variable name is assigned to hold the data for an entire list or table. For a list the variable name represents a one-dimensional array. Tables are two-dimensional arrays. We shall look at both one- and two-dimensional arrays.

Each location in an array where data are stored is identified by a unique label or subscript. The variable is thus known as a **SUBSCRIPTED VARIABLE**.

The general form for an element in a **ONE-DIMENSIONAL ARRAY** is:

```
variable (location in array)
```

For example, if the array X has 100 numeric elements, they range from X(1) to X(100). If array Y$ has 25 character elements, they range from Y$(1) to Y$(25). Note: some systems will set the initial array location at 0. Thus a 101 element array would range from X(0) to X(100). The subscripted variable X(1) in this case is the second element in the array.

With most systems default procedures permit you to store up to 11 data elements. Thus you must declare your storage requirements using the DIM statement when you have arrays with more than 11 values. In addition, if you create subscripted variables—such as a variable representing the sum of two subscripted variables—be sure to dimension them.

For a **TWO-DIMENSIONAL ARRAY** the general form for a subscripted variable is:

```
variable(row, column)
```

Thus the array element Z(20,12) is in row 20 and column 12. Remember that the rows are declared first and the columns second.

In BASIC we use the **DIM** statement (short for DIMENSION) to declare the data array list or table. The DIM statement reserves storage for array variables. The general form of the DIM statement is:

```
500 DIM variable(maximum subscripts)
```

The values chosen must be integer. They must be large enough to reserve enough storage to hold all of your data elements. Although the values can be larger than the number of data elements, if smaller, the program won't run.

Here are some examples of valid DIM statements.

Line in BASIC	Explanation
100 DIM A(125)	Reserves 125 locations for a one-dimensional array.
200 DIM B(20,15)	Reserves 20 rows and 15 columns for a two-dimensional array.
300 DIM C$(20)	Reserves 20 rows in a one-dimensional array containing string variables. (Depending on the system, a row might store an entire character string element or just a single character.)
400 DIM D$(33,25)	Reserves 33 rows and 25 columns for character strings in a two-dimensional array. (Depending on the system, the column value could refer to characters in a string variable or to the number of string variables in a row.)

To help you to know what to avoid, here are some examples of invalid DIM statements:

500 DIM E(R)	Dimension is not a numeric value.
600 DIM F(12.3)	Dimension is not an integer value.
700 DIM G(10)	Dimension is too low a value.
710 FOR I = 1 TO 20	
720 READ G(I)	
730 NEXT I	

Using arrays permits us to exploit the modular features of structured programming in our BASIC programs. This exploitation is made possible because a value assigned to an array location during the input stage can be recalled for the process and output steps without rereading the data.

To show this point more clearly we will sum a list of twelve numbers and calculate their average. Figure A4-7 shows the program. Notice how the input process and output stages are separated into three loops. The DIM statement is set to 12 to accommodate the number of data values. The average is the sum of all the values divided by the number of values.

FIGURE A4-7.
Using FOR/NEXT statements and a one-dimensional array to calculate the sum and average of 12 numbers.

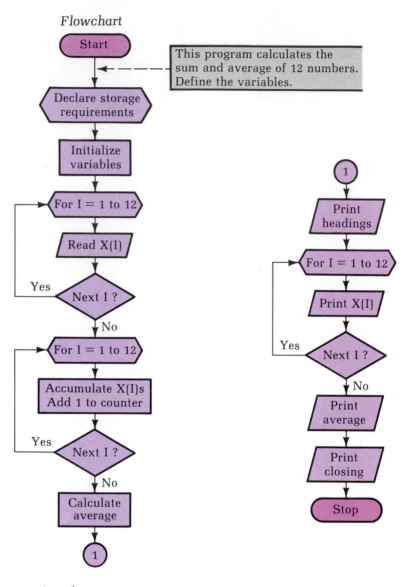

Flowchart

This program calculates the sum and average of 12 numbers. Define the variables.

Pseudocode

```
START
Remarks -- this  program  calculates  the  average of 12 numbers
Remarks -- define the variables
Declare storage for array
Initialize the nonread variables
FOR I = 1 to 12
     Read number
NEXT I
```

```
FOR I = 1 TO 12
     Accumulate total
     Add 1 to the counter
NEXT I
Calculate the average
Print heading
FOR I = 1 TO 12
     Print number
NEXT I
Print the average
Print the closing message
STOP
```

List and run

```
100 REM This program uses arrays and FOR/NEXT statements to
110 REM read twelve numbers, add them, and then calculate their
120 REM average.
130 REM The variables are:
140 REM         A = The average
150 REM         C = The number of values of X
160 REM         X = The array of numbers to be added
170 REM         Y = The total of the numbers
180 REM         I = The loop counter
190 REM **** Main Program ****
200 REM **** Declare Array Storage ****
210 DIM X(12)
220 REM **** Initialize Variables ****
230 LET A = 0
240 LET C = 0
250 LET Y = 0
260 REM **** Input Stage ****
270 FOR I= 1 to 12
280    READ X(I)
290 NEXT I
300 REM **** Process Stage ****
310 FOR I = 1 TO 12
320    LET Y = Y + X(I)
330    LET C = C + 1
340 NEXT I
350 REM **** Calculate Average ****
360 LET A = Y/C
370 REM **** Output Stage ****
380 PRINT "This program uses an array and FOR/NEXT statements to"
390 PRINT "read 12 numbers and calculate their average."
400 PRINT
410 PRINT
420 PRINT "The numbers:"
430 PRINT
440 FOR I = 1 TO 12
450    PRINT X(I)
460 NEXT I
470 PRINT
480 PRINT
490 PRINT "The average of the numbers is:"; A
500 PRINT
510 PRINT
520 PRINT "End of program."
530 REM **** Data List ****
540 DATA 12, 4, 16, 10, 7, 13, 18, 2, 10, 11, 9, 8
550 END
```

```
RUN
This program uses an array and FOR/NEXT statements to
read 12 numbers and calculate their average.

The numbers:

  12
  4
  16
  10
  7
  13
  18
  2
  10
  11
  9
  8


The average of the numbers is: 10


End of program.
```

TWO-DIMENSIONAL ARRAYS

Now let us turn our attention to two-dimensional arrays. Two-dimensional arrays are used to process related data stored in tables. For example, we may want to calculate student grades for school subjects. The row variables could be student names and the column variables could be school subjects. The general form for an m-row by n-column two-dimensional array is:

	Column 1	Column 2		Column n
Row 1	(1,1)	(1,2)	· · ·	(1,n)
Row 2	(2,1)	(2,2)	· · ·	(2,n)
·	·	·		·
·	·	·		·
·	·	·		·
Row m	(m,1)	(m,2)		(m,n)

Figure A4-8 shows a short example of how we can use two-dimensional arrays. We want to store 12 values (34, 31, 86, 47, 91, 23, 72, 85, 84, 92, 61, and 79) in a three-row and four-column array X. We would write the dimension statement as:

```
180 DIM X(3,4)
```

The program prints out the entire array. In addition, to show how we can select one value and print it out, we ask the program to print out the value in X(2,4) separately. Observe in the solution how the nested FOR/NEXT statements are handled.

Flowchart

A program that reads and prints a two-dimensional array.

This program reads and prints a 3 by 4 array.
The value in cell 2, 4 is printed out separately.
Define the variables.

Pseudocode

```
START
Remarks -- this program reads and prints a three by four
Remarks -- two-dimensional array
Define the variable
Declare array storage
FOR I = 1 TO 3
     FOR J = 1 TO 4
          Read X(I,J)
     NEXT J
NEXT I
Print heading
FOR I = 1 TO 3
     FOR J = 1 TO 4
          Print X(I,J)
     NEXT J
NEXT I
Print the value for X(2,4)
STOP
```

List and run

```
100 REM This program reads and prints a three by four
110 REM two-dimensional array.
120 REM The variables are:
130 REM          X = The array variable
140 REM          I = The outer loop counter
150 REM          Y = The inner loop counter
160 REM **** Main Program ****
170 REM **** Declare Array Storage ****
180 DIM X(3,4)
190 REM **** Input Stage ****
200 FOR I = 1 TO 3
210    FOR J = 1 TO 4
220      READ X(I,J)
230    NEXT J
240 NEXT I
250 REM **** Output Stage ****
260 PRINT "This is a three by four array"
270 PRINT
280 FOR I = 1 TO 3
290    FOR J = 1 TO 4
300      PRINT X(I,J);
310    NEXT J
330    PRINT
340 NEXT I
360 PRINT "The value stored in location X(2,4) is:"; X(2,4)
370 REM **** Data List ****
380 DATA 34, 31, 86, 47, 91, 23, 72, 85, 84, 92, 61, 79
390 END
```

FIGURE A4-8 (cont.)

```
RUN
This is a three by four array:

 34   31   86   47

 91   23   72   85

 84   92   61   79

The value stored in location X(2,4) is: 85
```

WRAP-UP PROGRAM

A common problem in business is the sorting of data. Sorting operations are applications of arrays. Our wrap-up program shows how to sort numbers. We use a sorting technique known as a **BUBBLE SORT**. Values that are out of order are switched. Recall that if we read data into a storage location that is already occupied (whether in an array or not), the original value will be replaced by the new value. To avoid losing the original value, a special temporary holding location is used to save a copy of it.

Figure A4-9 shows how the bubble sort works by sorting ten numbers from smallest to largest. The idea behind a bubble sort is to compare pairs of numbers successively, exchanging them if they are in the wrong order. In Figure A4-9 we order the numbers from smallest to largest. The comparisons are made in line 360. For example, if $A(1) <= A(2)$, then the next line executed is line 400, and the inside loop now compares $A(2)$ and $A(3)$. But if $A(1) > A(2)$, the two numbers are out of order and must be switched. A temporary storage location is required. The value stored in $A(1)$ is temporarily stored in T, $A(1)$ is set equal to $A(2)$, and then $A(2)$ is set equal to T. Notice that if we had not used the temporary variable T, the original value of $A(1)$ would have been lost.

At the first completion of the inside loop, the largest number is stored in $A(10)$. The next time through the loop, the next largest number is stored in $A(9)$, and so on until the numbers are sorted from smallest to largest. In the process the smaller numbers appear to "bubble up" the list.

KEY TERMS

These are the key terms in the order in which they appear in the section.

FOR/NEXT (A-48)
Nested loop (A-54)
WHILE/WEND (A-56)
Array (A-58)
Subscripted variable (A-58)

One-dimensional array (A-58)
Two-dimensional array (A-59)
DIM (A-59)
Bubble sort (A-64)

FIGURE A4-9.
Section Four wrap-up program: Sorting numbers.

Flowchart

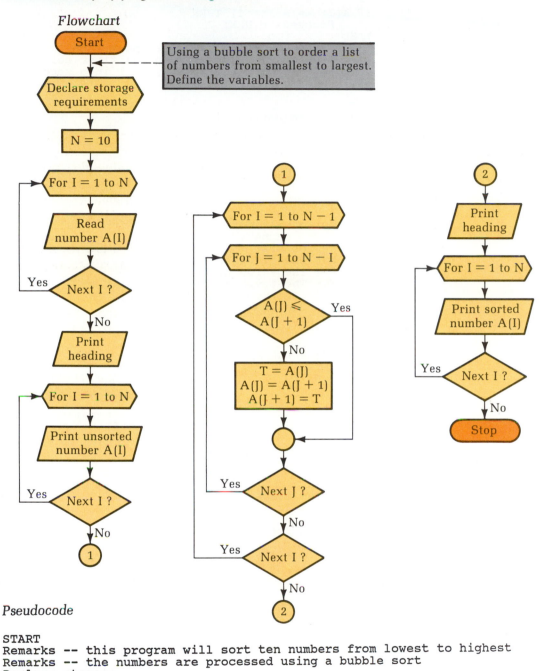

Pseudocode

```
START
Remarks -- this program will sort ten numbers from lowest to highest
Remarks -- the numbers are processed using a bubble sort
Declare storage
Set counter value, N, to 10
FOR I=1 TO N
     Read number
NEXT I
Print heading
FOR I = 1 TO N
     Print unsorted list
NEXT I
```

FIGURE A4-9 (cont.)

```
FOR I = 1 TO N - 1
     FOR J = 1 TO N - I
          IF A(J) <= A(J + 1) THEN
               Proceed to NEXT J
          ELSE
               Store larger number in temporary cell
               Move smaller number into the first cell
               Move number in temporary cell into second cell
          ENDIF
     NEXT J
NEXT I
Print heading for the sorted list
FOR I=1 TO N
     Print number
NEXT I
STOP
```

List and run

```
100 REM This program will sort ten numbers from smallest to
110 REM largest. The numbers are processed using a bubble sort.
120 REM The variables are:
130 REM         N = The dimension of the array
140 REM         A = The value to be sorted
150 REM         T = The temporary holding location
160 REM         I = The outer loop counter
170 REM         J = The inner loop counter
180 REM **** Main Program ****
190 REM **** Declare Array Storage ****
200 DIM A(10)
210 REM **** Input Stage ****
220 LET N = 10
230 FOR I = 1 TO N
240    READ A(I)
250 NEXT I
260 PRINT "The following are the unsorted numbers:"
270 PRINT
280 FOR I = 1 TO N
290    PRINT A(I)
300 NEXT I
310 PRINT
320 PRINT
330 REM **** Process Stage ****
340 FOR I = 1 TO N - 1
350    FOR J = 1 TO N - I
360      IF A(J) <= A(J + 1) THEN 400
370        LET T = A(J)
380        LET A(J) = A(J + 1)
390        LET A(J + 1) = T
400    NEXT J
410 NEXT I
420 REM **** Output Stage ****
430 PRINT "The sorted list:"
440 PRINT
450 FOR I = 1 TO N
460    PRINT A(I)
470 NEXT I
480 REM **** Data List ****
490 DATA 12, 34, 92, 33, 23, 78, 19
500 DATA 54, 21, 49
510 END
```

```
RUN
The following are the unsorted numbers:

   12
   34
   92
   33
   23
   78
   19
   54
   21
   49


The sorted list:

   12
   19
   21
   23
   33
   34
   49
   54
   78
   92
```

REVIEW QUESTIONS

SHORT ANSWER QUESTIONS

1. Determine if there are any errors in the following sets of FOR/NEXT statements.

(a) 100 FOR I = 1 TO 15
    110   READ C
    120   IF C = 100 THEN 100
    130   PRINT C
    140 NEXT I

(b) 200 FOR G = 3 TO 36 STEP 3
    210   READ N$(I)
    230   PRINT N$(I)
    240 NEXT I

(c) 300 FOR K = 2 TO 20 STEP −1
    310   PRINT X(K)
    320 NEXT K

(d) 400 FOR R = 1 TO 10
    410   READ X
    420   PRINT X
    430   LET Z = Z + X
    440   PRINT Z
    450 NEXT R

(e) 500 FOR A = 4 TO 20
    510 FOR Y = 2 TO 30
    520   PRINT A*Y
    530 NEXT A
    540 NEXT Y

2. What are the differences between a FOR/NEXT loop and a WHILE/WEND loop?

3. What is an array? A subscripted variable?

4. Given the following program and data list for a two-dimensional array, what is stored in location X(3,4)?

```
100 DIM X(4,5)
120 FOR I = 1 TO 4
130   FOR E = 1 TO 5
140     READ X(I,E)
160   NEXT E
170 NEXT I
700 DATA 13,  34, 234, 42, 23, 91, 2, 31, 24, 90, 2345
710 DATA 92, 232, 349, 30, 6, 431, 231, 34, 82
```

5. Using the data in question 4, determine the array location for the smallest number. Write a PRINT statement to print out the lowest number.

6. How does using an array affect the structure of your program?

7. What is a bubble sort? How does it work?

8. Write a FOR/NEXT loop to decrement by 4 from 40 to X where X is defined by a LET statement before the loop as 20. In this loop print your name.

1. Paul's House of Electronic Wonders (PHEW) is sending out invoices to three customers. Use either FOR/NEXT or WHILE/WEND statements to process these invoices. Use arrays to separate the input, processing, and output stages within the program. The data include customer name, item purchased, the cost, the quantity purchased, and the discount. For each invoice, calculate both the non-discounted subtotal and the discounted total. Compute the total of all three invoices.

Customer	Item	Cost	Qty	Discount (decimal)
Quick Office	Computer	$400	350	0.20
Handi-chips	Memory chips	$ 1	2000	0.10
The Chipshack	Cables	$ 10	500	0.15

2. Paul's House of Electronic Wonders has hired you to write part of an accounts payable program to determine how much money PHEW owes the following six suppliers. Use FOR/NEXT statements and arrays to process the vendor names and balances. Use the INPUT command to enter the data. Calculate the nondiscount balance, the difference between the current balance and the balance still in the discount period. Print these four fields for each vendor.

Calculate totals for the current discount and nondiscount balances. What percentage of the current balance is nondiscount?

Vendor Name	Current Balance	Discount Balance
Quick Chips	$11,500	$ 8,000
Octopus Cable	$16,500	$14,500
Shanghai Mod.	$ 5,550	$ 3,535
JCN Inc.	$20,160	$18,500
Orient Elec.	$ 3,500	$ 2,850
Applepie Co.	$44,700	$41,340

3. The Oakriver University baseball team has 12 nonpitchers. Use a program with FOR/NEXT or WHILE/WEND statements and arrays to calculate each player's batting average, as well as the team batting average. For any player batting over .325, print the player's name on an all-star list.

Player	At-Bats	Hits
Bill Edwards	123	43
Ronald Trout	131	30
David Freud	85	22
Bobby Dalton	21	6
Reggie Tsang	101	31
Ernie Tobin	119	27
John Young	49	15
Kevin Kline	79	26
Wally Johnson	106	29
Don Lopez	103	29
Gene Kline	52	15
Allan Long	98	25

4. George Roberts supervises 15 quality-control inspectors at Global Electric's Small Appliance Division factory. Certain standards must be met. Inspectors must examine 30 appliances per hour and correctly classify 29 out of the 30, for an error rate of 3.3 percent. From the following sample data, write a program to determine which of the 15 are performing satisfactorily. What is the overall inspection rate? What would you recommend? Use FOR/NEXT statements and arrays in formulating the solution.

Inspector Name	Average Number of Inspections Per Hour	Average Number of Incorrect Choices per Hour
S. Thomas	34	1
R. Baker	35	0
G. Miller	25	3
M. Tanaka	31	2
W. Chou	29	1
I. Halpern	38	1
L. Schwartz	31	0
J. Edwards	30	2
M. Elliot	29	3
E. Gorman	24	1
G. Werton	32	4
H. Warrick	33	1
K. Smith	31	1
W. Hernandez	30	0
O. Parsons	28	0

5. Using the following data list, write a program to sort the people by age from oldest to youngest.

Name	Age in Years
Teri Roberts	34
Jennifer Lee	23
Leon Lawson	19
Sally Feld	43
Ernst Halard	21
Hope Jones	26
Mitch Manor	23
Bobby Carver	24

In this section we cover a variety of topics. First we look at some advanced techniques for creating attractive output—the PRINT TAB and PRINT USING statements. These statements, together with the PRINT operations we covered earlier, give you a great deal of flexibility to produce meaningful user output. A word of caution is in order, however—PRINT TAB and PRINT USING are not standardized. The format for your system may be different from the examples shown here.

Next we describe predefined functions (sometimes called library functions) that provide a quick way to build mathematical functions into your programs. Then we show how you can create your own special functions.

Finally, we will describe how to use matrix operations to simplify programs, especially those that use nested loops. At the end of the section, we will list some additional sources you can turn to if you wish to learn more about BASIC.

THE PRINT TAB STATEMENT

The **PRINT TAB** statement positions output on a line in much the same manner as the tab operation on a typewriter. The general form of the PRINT TAB statement is:

```
500 PRINT TAB (expression); what to print
```

The reserved words PRINT TAB tell the computer that a special output operation is being ordered. The expression within the parentheses indicates the column number where the tabbing function ends. The number can be represented by a constant, as in PRINT TAB(23), or by a variable, as in PRINT TAB(N−1). The next column to the right of the tab number holds the first character of the value to be printed. Always follow the PRINT TAB(expression) in a series by a semicolon. Commas in PRINT TAB statements override the tabbing function. The following line of code illustrates use of the PRINT TAB statement:

```
500 PRINT TAB(14); "Name = "; N$ ; TAB(40); "Age in years ="; A
```

This prints out the following result:

Notice how the line containing the PRINT TAB statement can refer to several different tabbing operations. (Caution: On some systems printing begins in the tabbed column—that is, PRINT TAB(14) may mean begin printing in the 14th column instead of the 15th.)

PRINT TAB statements can be used to create designs for such items as computer greeting cards and pictures. Figure A5-1 shows a program to create a pattern in the shape of an hourglass. The flowchart and pseudocode are left as an exercise in the review questions.

FIGURE A5-1.

Using PRINT TAB statements to create a design of an hourglass.

```
100 REM This program uses PRINT TAB statements to create a
110 REM a picture of an hourglass
120 REM The variable is:
130 REM          G = The loop counter and TAB variable
140 REM **** Main Program ****
150 PRINT
160 PRINT ":=====================:"
170 FOR G = 1 TO 10
180 PRINT " :"; TAB(2 + G); "*"; TAB(23 - G); "*"; TAB(23);":"
190 NEXT G
200 FOR G = 1 TO 9
210 PRINT " :"; TAB(12 - G); "*"; TAB(13 + G); "*"; TAB(23);":"
220 NEXT G
230 PRINT ":=====================:"
240 END
```

RUN

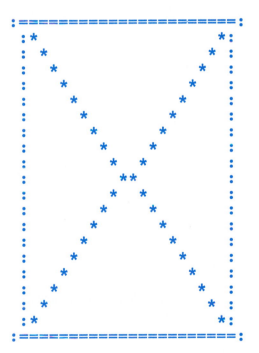

THE PRINT USING STATEMENT

The **PRINT USING** statement formats output, and is one of the most useful methods for creating attractive output. Unfortunately it is not a standard command. Some computer systems have PRINT USING options (Apple Macintosh, IBM, Microsoft, HP, DEC, and several that use CP/M as their operating system) while others do not (most notably early Apple models). The general form of the PRINT USING statement is:

```
500 PRINT USING (line number of IMAGE expressions), what to print
510 Format control symbols
```

IMAGE expressions or format control symbols may be incorporated into the PRINT USING line or located in a separate line elsewhere in the program. Image statements provide a mask or "template" showing how the output will appear. Examples of PRINT USING operations and the IMAGE statements for some of the computer systems you might be using are shown in Figure A5-2. For additional ways of formating output with PRINT USING, or if your computer is not on the list, consult your programming manual or ask your instructor for assistance.

FIGURE A5-2.
PRINT USING operations for several different computer systems. The example requires us to print a person's name and grade-point average in the columns shown. Additional PRINT USING specifications are available for each of these systems—consult your manual.

```
Variable                N$                    A

Example           Thomas Roberts        3.21
Column            00000000011111111111122222222223
number            12345678901234567890123456790


For Hewlett-Packard systems:

200 PRINT USING 210; N$, A
210 IMAGE 5X, 15A, 4X, D.DD


For Digital Equipment Corporation systems:

300 PRINT USING E$; N$, A
310 LET E$ = "         \                \       #.##"


For the Microsoft systems (IBM-PC and others):

400 PRINT USING "         \                \       #.##"; N$; A


For CP/M systems:

500 PRINT USING "         \                \       #.##"; N$; A
```

PREDEFINED FUNCTIONS

There are a number of predefined functions useful for business applications. A **PREDEFINED** or **LIBRARY FUNCTION** is "built into" the BASIC compiler or interpreter. Predefined functions permit you to use a short code word to call up a prewritten subroutine. To find the square root of a variable X, we can use the predefined function **SQR(X)**

```
100 LET A = SQR(X)
```

Several predefined functions are shown in Figure A5-3. Many functions are used in business statistics and operations research. In addition to the square root function just covered, we will take a look at INT(X) and RND.

The **INT(X)** function (integer) returns an integer value for any number X. It returns the largest whole number that is less than or equal to the original number. For positive numbers the INT function truncates (lops off) the fraction or decimal part; so INT(3.98) is 3. With negative numbers the value is the next lower whole number; thus INT(-4.55) is -5. The following program shows how INT works.

FIGURE A5-3.
Representative predefined numeric functions.

Function	Meaning
ABS(X)	The absolute value of X
ATN(X)	The arctangent of X in radians
COS(X)	The cosine of X in radians
EXP(X)	e raised to the X power
INT(X)	The integer value of X
LOG(X)	The natural logrithm of X
RND	A random number between 0 and 1
SIN(X)	The sine of X in radians
SQR(X)	The square root of X
TAN(X)	The tangent of X in radians

```
100 REM An example of how the INT(X) function works.
110 PRINT "Using the INT(X) function."
120 PRINT
130 PRINT "Original      Integer"
140 PRINT " Value         Value"
150 PRINT
160 FOR H = 1 TO 8
170 READ T
180 PRINT T, INT(T)
190 NEXT H
200 DATA 123, -12.05, 224.001, -240.5
210 DATA 544, 2, 23.494, 2923.2

RUN
Using the INT(X) function:

Original   Integer
 Value      Value

 123        123
-12.05     -13
 224.001    224
-240.5     -241
 544        544
 2          2
 23.494     23
 2923.2     2923
```

We can also use INT(X) to round numbers. The general methods for rounding to a whole number and rounding to two decimal places are:

```
500 LET R = INT(X+.5)
510 LET H = INT(100*X+.5)/100
```

For the number 23.494 we get the whole number 23 using line 500 and to two decimal places 23.49 using line 510, since INT(23.494+.5) = 23 and INT(2349.4+.5)/100 = 23.49.

The **RND** function (randomize) can be applied to several business areas such as simulation and sampling that require random numbers. We might also use it to build the element of chance into computer games or to select students randomly for oral presentations. On some systems a variable such as X is required, and it is necessary to write RND(X). The RND function normally is used to generate a series of random numbers between 0 and 1. Since we usually need numbers that cover a far wider range, we can modify these values. Let us take a look at several possibilities:

1   *Unspecified randomization, which creates a random number between the values of 0 and 1. This is accomplished through the use of the function RND.*
2   *Specifying the desired range. The random number needs to be converted into a value in the desired range. The general form N∗RND sets up a range from 0 to N. So 5∗RND will range from 0 to 4.999999. Notice that the value N = 5 is not included (it is an upper bound).*
3   *Creating integer values, which requires that we use the INT function. We can write this as INT(N∗RND). This time INT(5∗RND) returns any one of the integers 0, 1, 2, 3, or 4. Since the function INT is used, the numbers are truncated and 5 is not included. If we wanted integers from 1 to 5, we could have used INT(5∗RND + 1).*

The following programs illustrate each case. In the first example five random numbers are obtained between 0 and 1.

```
100 REM Creating five random numbers between 0 and 1
110 FOR I = 1 TO 5
120 PRINT RND
130 NEXT I
140 END
RUN
 .265294
 .921138
 .621760
 .490045
 .558702
```

The second example shows how we can obtain five random numbers from 0 to 10. The function N∗RND is used with N equal to 10.

```
200 REM Creating five random numbers between 0 and 10
210 FOR I = 1 TO 5
220 PRINT 10*RND
230 NEXT I
240 END
RUN
 1.591769
 8.730564
 2.940274
 5.352216
 .3054085
```

The third example shows how to obtain five random integers from 1 to 5 by converting a random number into an integer. The function used is INT(N∗RND+1), with N equal to 5

```
400 REM Creating five random integers between 1 and 5
410 FOR I = 1 to 5
420 PRINT INT(5*RND + 1)
430 NEXT I
440 END
```

```
RUN
 2
 2
 5
 1
 4
```

Most computer systems will use a standard starting point called a "seed" number to create a set of random numbers. Since the algorithm is known, we really are creating pseudorandom numbers. Each time the RND function is used, the same set of numbers is generated. To overcome this drawback (certainly to relieve boredom in games, if nothing else), you can specify a nonstandard randomization feature. Place on a line before the RND function one of the following RANDOMIZE statements:

```
500 RANDOMIZE
```

or

```
500 RANDOMIZE TIMER
```

Either of these statements will generate fresh numbers, either by permitting you to select a starting number, or by using a value present in the computer's clock as the starting "seed" number.

USER-DEFINED FUNCTIONS

Users can also define functions in BASIC. The general form for creating a USER-DEFINED FUNCTION is:

```
500 DEF function name(dummy variable) = expression
```

One form to call the user-defined function from the main program is:

```
600 LET variable = function name(variable)
```

The function name must begin with FN and be followed by one alphabetic character (or with some systems several characters)—for example, FNx. In line 500, the dummy variable inside the parentheses is used in the mathematical expression to the right of the equal sign. When the function is called from the main program (line 600), the dummy variable is replaced by the variable in the main program and the expression is calculated using that value. For example, consider the lines:

```
180 DEF FNF(D) = (9/5)*D + 32
230 LET F = FNF(C)
```

The function defined in line 180 can be used in a program to convert temperatures from Celsius to Fahrenheit. When the function is called in line 230, whatever is the current value of C (a Celsius temperature) replaces the D in the expression in line 180. Thus F is set to the the equivalent Fahrenheit temperature. A program using this function is shown in Figure A5-4.

Flowchart

FIGURE A5-4.
Temperature conversion with user-defined variables.

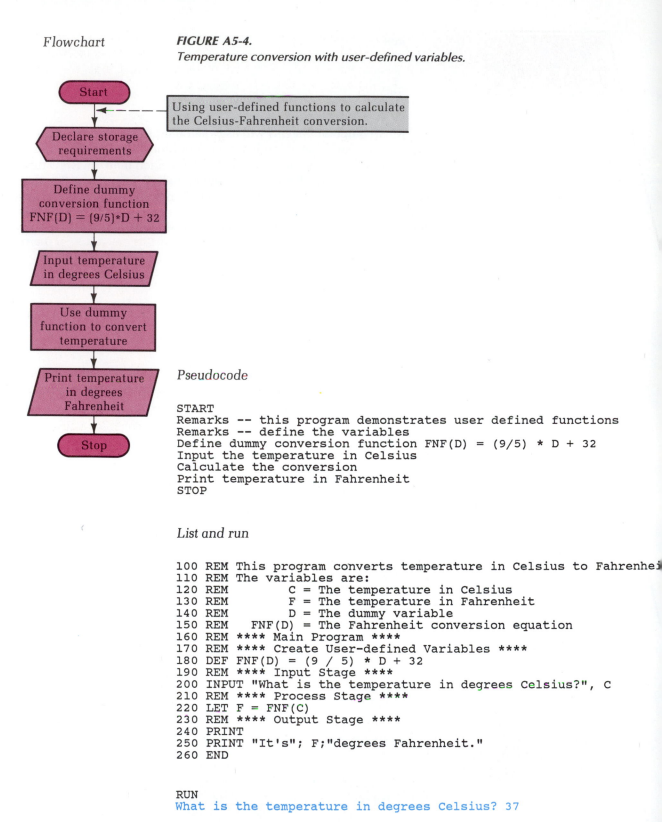

Using user-defined functions to calculate the Celsius-Fahrenheit conversion.

Start

Declare storage requirements

Define dummy conversion function FNF(D) = (9/5)*D + 32

Input temperature in degrees Celsius

Use dummy function to convert temperature

Print temperature in degrees Fahrenheit

Stop

Pseudocode

```
START
Remarks -- this program demonstrates user defined functions
Remarks -- define the variables
Define dummy conversion function FNF(D) = (9/5) * D + 32
Input the temperature in Celsius
Calculate the conversion
Print temperature in Fahrenheit
STOP
```

List and run

```
100 REM This program converts temperature in Celsius to Fahrenhei
110 REM The variables are:
120 REM        C = The temperature in Celsius
130 REM        F = The temperature in Fahrenheit
140 REM        D = The dummy variable
150 REM    FNF(D) = The Fahrenheit conversion equation
160 REM **** Main Program ****
170 REM **** Create User-defined Variables ****
180 DEF FNF(D) = (9 / 5) * D + 32
190 REM **** Input Stage ****
200 INPUT "What is the temperature in degrees Celsius?", C
210 REM **** Process Stage ****
220 LET F = FNF(C)
230 REM **** Output Stage ****
240 PRINT
250 PRINT "It's"; F;"degrees Fahrenheit."
260 END


RUN
What is the temperature in degrees Celsius? 37

It's 98.6 degrees Fahrenheit.
```

A *matrix* is a rectangular array that can be manipulated as a unit. Both one- and two-dimensional arrays are matrices. Some forms of BASIC contain MAT statements, which enable you to operate on matrices.

One general form of the MAT statement is:

```
500 MAT operation matrix
```

where the operation could be READ or PRINT, giving commands such as MAT READ or MAT PRINT. Some examples are:

```
510 MAT READ A
520 MAT PRINT B
```

Line 510 reads in the values for matrix A. If the dimension of A is 5, then five values would be read in. Similarly, line 520 prints the values of matrix B.

The second form of the MAT statement is:

```
600 MAT expression
```

where the expression is a mathematical equation or function involving matrices. Some examples are:

```
610 MAT A = B + C
620 MAT A = B * C
```

The dimensions of the matrices in each expression must be the same. The operations are performed on the individual elements in matrices B and C. The results are stored in matrix A. For example, consider matrices B and C:

$$B = \begin{bmatrix} 1 & 2 \\ 3 & 4 \end{bmatrix}, \qquad C = \begin{bmatrix} 5 & 6 \\ 7 & 8 \end{bmatrix} \quad \text{(elements are added)}$$

Line 610 results in:

$$A = \begin{bmatrix} 1 + 5 & 2 + 6 \\ 3 + 7 & 4 + 8 \end{bmatrix} = \begin{bmatrix} 6 & 8 \\ 10 & 12 \end{bmatrix} \quad \text{(elements are added)}$$

Line 620 results in:

$$A = \begin{bmatrix} 1*5 & 2*6 \\ 3*7 & 4*8 \end{bmatrix} = \begin{bmatrix} 5 & 12 \\ 21 & 32 \end{bmatrix} \quad \text{(elements are multiplied)}$$

Several matrix operations are available. They are used in business, operations research, engineering, and scientific applications.

By now your curiosity about BASIC has been whetted. Many students ask where they can learn more about BASIC. There are several approaches to doing so:

- *Additional classes*
- *Independent programming projects*
- *Further reading*
- *Joining a club*

Most universities and colleges offer advanced classes in BASIC programming. In an advanced class, you would learn about manipulating sequential and direct-access files, and about creating professional-looking output for report forms and graphic displays. You can learn a great deal more about how to use BASIC to solve business programming problems. You may have an opportunity to create a color graphics game.

Occasionally instructors need programming assistants to work on projects. This too can provide you with an opportunity to learn more about BASIC programming. For example, you might help write the code for an interactive inventory update package. Or you might learn how to write a program that retrieves multiple files and extracts data from them.

Additional reading coupled with an independent studies project is another possibility. Here are some books for more advanced BASIC programming projects.

Barron, Jonathan C., *BASIC Programming Using Structured Modules* (New York: Holt, Rinehart and Winston, 1983).

Bui, X. T., *Executive Planning with BASIC* (Berkeley, Calif.: Sybex, 1981).

Finkel, LeRoy, and Jerald R. Brown, *Apple BASIC: Data File Programming—A Self-Teaching Guide* (New York: John Wiley & Sons, 1982).

Johnston, Randolph P., *BASIC Using Micros with an Overview of Software Packages* (Santa Cruz, Calif.: Mitchell, 1983).

Purdum, Jack Jay, *BASIC-80 and CP/M* (New York: Macmillan, 1983).

Silbey, Val, and Alan J. Parker, *BASIC for Business for the VAX and the PDP-11* (Reston, Va.: Reston Publishing, 1983).

Weinman, David, and Barbara L. Kurshan, *VAX-BASIC* (Reston, Va.: Reston Publishing Company, 1983).

Additional sources of help may be found in magazines published by a number of organizations. Usually these magazines are specific to one type of BASIC—say, for the IBM PC. They are available in most college bookstores.

Joining a club provides another opportunity for learning. Users' groups—again specific to a machine—meet to trade advice on programming matters.

WRAP-UP PROGRAM

Our wrap-up program for this section modifies the billing program we have seen earlier (turn back to the version given in Figure A2-6) to use both the PRINT TAB and PRINT USING statements. Figure A5-5 shows this modified program. Notice the state of Nevada has been abbreviated to conform with the style used in most businesses today (NV).

FIGURE A5-5.

Section Five wrap-up program. Modifying the billing program as given in Figure A2-6 to use both the PRINT TAB and PRINT USING statements.

List and run of the billing one customer program.

```
100 REM This program will bill one customer.
110 REM First we will assign the company a name,
120 REM then we will enter the data from a data statement.
130 REM The computer used was the H-P 3000
140 REM The variables are:
150 REM          N$ = The name of the company
```

```
160 REM         A$ = The street address of the company
170 REM         C$ = The city of the company
180 REM         S$ = The state of the company
190 REM         I$ = The name of the item the customer wants
200 REM         Q  = The quantity of the item
210 REM         Z  = The zip code of the customer
220 REM         T  = The total cost of the order
230 REM         C  = The cost of the item
240 REM **** Main Program ****
250 REM ****  Initialize Variable ****
260 LET T = 0
270 REM **** Input Stage ****
280 READ N$, A$, C$, S$, Z, I$, Q, C
290 REM **** Process Stage ****
300 LET T = C * Q
310 REM **** Output Stage ****
320 PRINT TAB(5); "This program computes the bill for one customer."
330 PRINT
340 PRINT TAB(5); "Customer and Address:"
350 PRINT
360 PRINT USING 510; N$
370 PRINT USING 510; A$
380 PRINT USING 520; C$, S$, Z
390 PRINT
400 PRINT
410 PRINT TAB(5); "Purchase Data:"
420 PRINT
430 PRINT USING 530; I$
440 PRINT USING 540; Q
450 PRINT USING 550; C
460 PRINT USING 560; T
470 PRINT
480 PRINT
490 PRINT TAB(10); "End of Program"
500 REM **** Image Statements ****
510 IMAGE 10X, 30A
520 IMAGE 10X, 15A, 2X, 2A, 3X, 5D
530 IMAGE 23X, "Item:", 5X, 25A
540 IMAGE 19X, "Quantity:", 5X, 5D
550 IMAGE 14X, "Cost per item:", 3X, $DDDDDD.DD
560 IMAGE "The total cost of the order:", 3X, $DDDDDD.DD
570 REM **** Data List ****
580 DATA "Bits and Bytes", "67 Main Street"
590 DATA "Last Chance", "NV", 89133
600 DATA "Microprocessor", 1500, 6.85
610 END


RUN
    This program calculates the bill for one customer.

    Customer and Address:

        Bits and Bytes
        67 Main Street
        Last Chance      NV    89133


    Purchase Data:
                        Item:    Microprocessor
                    Quantity:      1500
                Cost per item:   $      6.85
The total cost of the order:   $ 10275.00


        End of Program
```

These are the key terms in the order in which they appear in the section.

PRINT TAB (A-70)
PRINT USING (A-71)
IMAGE (A-72)
Predefined or library function (A-72)
SQR(X) (A-72)
INT(X) (A-72)
RND (A-73)

RANDOMIZE (A-75)
TIMER (A-75)
User-defined function (A-75)
DEF (A-75)
FNx (A-75)
MAT (A-77)
MAT READ (A-77)
MAT PRINT (A-77)

REVIEW QUESTIONS

SHORT ANSWER QUESTIONS

1. Why are semicolons used in PRINT TAB statements rather than commas?
2. What are the advantages of working with PRINT USING?
3. What are the disadvantages of working with PRINT USING?
4. Write the following lines using a PRINT TAB statement.

Name	Job Class	Weekly Salary
Gene Tomaselli	Marketing Trainee	$600.00

5. Reproduce the lines using PRINT USING.
6. Write the pseudocode and flowchart for the hourglass problem in Figure A5-1.
7. Write lines of code to create:
   (a) Random numbers between 1 and 8.
   (b) Random integers between 4 and 15.
8. Write a line of code to round 12.49999 to the nearest 1/1000th.
9. Write a line of code to round the square root of 10 to two decimal places.
10. Write a line of code to take the square root of your age. Use it in a short program.

PROGRAMMING EXERCISES

1. Use PRINT TAB statements to reproduce the following rectangle.

```
*********************************
*                               *
*                               *
*                               *
*                               *
*                               *
*                               *
*                               *
*                               *
*********************************
```

2. Use PRINT TAB statements to reproduce the following picture

```
        *****************
       *  *            *
      *    *            *
     *      *            *
    *        *            *
   *          ***************
    *          *            *
     *        *            *
      *      *            *
       *  *            *
        *****************
```

3. Use PRINT TAB and PRINT USING statements to create a greeting card for a friend.

4. Use MAT statements to read in two 3 by 4 matrices, add them, and print the original matrices and the answer.

5. The graduate business school at Oakriver University has hired you to create a program to select graduates for the MBA program. Admission is based upon a combined total of a student's grade-point average and graduate management aptitude test score. The combined total is found by multiplying the GPA by 200 and adding it to the GMAT score. The minimum combined score is 1150.

   On the final report:

   * First list each student's data, including name, GPA, GMAT, combined score, and admission status.
   * Second list just the names of the people who were admitted.
   * Finally show the number of people who were admitted and their average GPAs and GMATs.

   Use PRINT TAB and PRINT USING statements. Arrays and FOR/NEXT statements are also required.

   Data:

	Name	GPA	GMAT
1	Alice Jones	3.12	345
2	Thomas Robertson	2.56	563
3	Tim Martinez	3.06	583
4	Janis Roberts	3.56	576
5	Orestes Fox	3.01	547
6	Electra Adamson	2.34	463
7	Susan Smith	3.29	492
8	Albert Torrez	3.16	524
9	Tina Osaka	3.45	445
10	Hubert Wong	2.68	522
11	Francis Weiss	3.29	552
12	Barbara Miller	2.98	487
13	Sally O'Brien	3.30	640
14	Lynne Claudette	3.89	714
15	Penny Smith	2.88	453

6. Write a program to toss a coin. Let 1 = a head and 0 = a tail. Print out the results of the first 20 attempts. What percentage was tails? Remember: percentage = (number tails/20) * 100.

7. Let us have some fun; try building your own creature. Consider a real growth industry—genetic technology. Dr. Genie Splitter has a grant to create a new kind of "creature." The double-helix DNA has four components: adenine, cytosine, guanine, and thymine. Adenine only bonds with thymine; and cytosine with guanine. Label the components using the letters A, C, G, and T respectively.

8. The Oakriver University football team has just completed its latest season. The alumni are happy and the coach has not been fired yet. As the team statistician, you still have work to do.

   For each game print out the name of the opponent, the score, whether Oakriver University won or lost, and the absolute difference between the two scores. Next calculate the sum of the points Oakriver University scored and calculate the average. Then do the same for its opponents. Finally calculate the average winning margins and losing margins for Oakriver University for the season. Should the coach keep his job?

Opponents	Score for Oakriver	Score for Opponent
Egmont College	34	28
Big State University	14	24
Even Bigger State University	23	20
Abraham Grant Tech	45	10
College of the Big Spenders	23	44
Semipro State University	3	63
University of Techies	22	22
Oakriver Institute of Technology	10	13
Alpha Omega Classics University	42	17
Seaside Polytechnic University	34	23
MBA University	42	32

9. Both SQR(X) and INT(X) can be used in calculating the economic order quantity (EOQ), a common business application. Paul's House of Electronic Wonders needs to analyze its inventory needs. As the staff inventory analyst, you must determine the economic order quantity for the following items. Use the equation for the EOQ:

$$Q = \sqrt{\frac{2 \times (\text{Annual demand}) \times (\text{Ordering cost})}{(\text{Holding cost}) \times (\text{Unit cost})}}$$

Where

Q = amount of the item to order.
Annual demand = estimated annual demand for the item.
Ordering cost = cost of placing an individual order, including office expenses such as Telex, typing, and personnel costs; usually between $50 and $100 per order.
Holding cost = cost per monetary unit for holding the item in storage, including insurance, borrowing costs, storage space, obsolescence, and other factors; usually between 20 and 40 percent per monetary unit (generally so many cents on the dollar).
Unit cost = price of a single unit of the item, a case, dozen, gross, truckload, or other unit amount.

The data are as follows:

Item Name	Annual Demand	Ordering Cost	Holding Cost	Unit Cost
Memory chip	10,000	70	0.30	2
Printer cable	500	50	0.25	10
Printer	1,200	60	0.30	600
IRM computer	3,000	100	0.30	1,000
Testing switch	100	60	0.25	3
Applebetty computer	4,000	60	0.30	500

The page number of each term is shown in parentheses. An example of each BASIC statement command is shown.

AND   A logical operator used when all conditions must be met in order to perform an operation. (A-12, A-28)

```
600 IF X > 10 AND W < 100 THEN LET R = X*W
```

ANSI-BASIC   A standard for minimal BASIC developed by The American National Standards Institute (ANSI). (A-9)

ARRAY   A collection of related data in list or table form. (A-58)

ASSIGNMENT STATEMENT   Refers to the LET statement in BASIC that assigns values to variables using the equals sign (=). See LET statement. (A-21)

BASIC (BEGINNERS' ALL PURPOSE SYMBOLIC INSTRUCTION CODE)   Interactive programming language developed by John G. Kemeny and Thomas Kurtz with the novice programmer in mind. (A-9)

BOOLEAN OPERATOR   See Logical operator. (A-28)

BUBBLE SORT   A technique for sorting data where pairs of values are tested and the reordered values "bubble-up" the list. (A-64)

CHARACTER SET   Upper- and lowercase alphabetic letters, the decimal numbers 0 to 9, and special symbols, used in BASIC. (A-12)

CHARACTER STRING CONSTANTS   Also called string constants, they are combinations of letters, symbols and numbers enclosed in quotation marks. (A-13)

CHARACTER STRING VARIABLES   Combinations of letters, symbols and numbers represented by a $ at the end of the variable name (F$, MAJOR$). (A-13)

CONSTANT   A symbol that does not change its value during program execution. (A-13)

COUNTER   Variable used to increase or decrease a variable by a fixed amount—often used in loop control. (A-38)

DATA   Nonexecutable statement that stores data in the program. Each data item must be separated by a comma. (A-12, A-16)

```
600 DATA "Tom Smith", 12.3, 45
```

DEF   A reserved word that creates a user-defined function. (A-12, A-75)

```
600 DEF FNX(D) = D*4
```

DIM   A reserved word that declares the number of row and column elements in an array. On some systems DIM declares the maximum number of characters in a string variable. (A-12, A-59)

```
600 DIM X(100, 24), W$(100), Q(1, 24)
```

ELSE   The alternate operation to perform in an IF/THEN/ELSE statement. (A-12, A-27)

```
600 IF S > 23 THEN PRINT "Over limit" ELSE PRINT "Under
limit"
```

END   The last statement in a BASIC program. (A-12, A-22)

```
600 END
```

FLOWCHART Diagram that uses special symbols to aid in communicating the steps needed in writing a program. (A-4)

FNx The function name in a user defined function. The x can be replaced with a numeric or character string variable. (A-12, A-75)

```
600 DEF FNM(D) = D*4
```

FOR/NEXT Paired statements for loop control. (A-48)

```
600 FOR I = 1 TO 10 STEP 2
```

      operation within the loop

```
650 NEXT I
```

GOSUB Statement used in BASIC to access a subroutine. (A-12, A-32)

```
600 GOSUB 3000
```

GOTO Statement used to direct the program to a specific line number. May be used to close a loop but is strongly discouraged in structured programming. (A-12, A-39)

```
600 GOTO 500
```

IF/THEN A conditional statement used for selection and looping operations. (A-27)

```
600 IF Q = 6 THEN LET A = Q*3
```

IF/THEN/ELSE A more advanced conditional statement used for selection and looping operations. (A-27)

```
600 IF Q = 6 THEN LET A = Q*3 ELSE LET A = Q*2
```

IMAGE A statement of some systems used for creating attractive ouput using the computer. Must be called with a PRINT USING statement (A-12, A-72)

```
650 IMAGE"\              \ ####.##"
```

INPUT A statement that ensures that the data entered by the user, as the program is executed, is assigned to a variable. (A-12, A-18)

```
600 INPUT B$, T
```

INT(X) Reserved word that truncates a number to the whole integer less than or equal to the number. (A-12, A-72)

```
600 LET X = INT(R)
```

LET Commonly called an assignment statement, it gives values to different variables. (A-12, A-21)

```
600 LET R = 12 * E
```

LINE NUMBER Appears at the beginning of each line of a program. Unless directed otherwise by your program, these numbers are executed in sequence from lowest to highest. (A-11)

LOGGING OFF Procedure for properly ending a session at the terminal. (A-10)

LOGGING ON Procedure for turning on the computer, getting to the computer operating system, and then activating BASIC. (A-10)

LOGICAL OPERATOR Boolean operator such as OR and AND used in IF/THEN/ELSE statements. (A-28)

LOOP Process whereby the program repetitively executes one or a series of steps. Two major types of loops in BASIC are FOR/NEXT and WHILE/WEND. (A-5)

LPRINT   Statement used on some microcomputers to direct output only to the printer. (A-12, A-14)

```
600 LPRINT "The quick red fox"
```

MAT   A statement that permits various matrix operations. (A-77)

```
600 MAT A = D+C
```

MAT PRINT   Statement for printing a matrix. (A-12, A-77)

```
600 MAT PRINT X
```

MAT READ   Statement for reading a matrix. (A-12, A-77)

```
600 MAT READ Q
```

NESTED LOOP   A loop or several loops completely inside another loop. (A-54)

NEXT   Statement used with a FOR statement for loop control. (A-12, A-48)

```
600 FOR A = 2 TO 7

    operations in loop

650 NEXT A
```

NUMERIC CONSTANTS   Can be integers, real numbers with decimal places, or real numbers written in exponential form. (A-13)

NUMERIC VARIABLES   Real numbers represented by an alphabetic character or an alphabetic character combined with a number. In some systems they may be up to 40 characters (R, TESTSCORE). (A-13)

ONE-DIMENSIONAL ARRAY   Data displayed in a list form. (A-58)

OR   Logical operator that tests true when one or more conditions is true. (A-12, A-28)

```
600 IF X < 1 OR X > 10 THEN PRINT "OUT OF RANGE"
```

PREDEFINED OR LIBRARY FUNCTION   A function that is built into the BASIC compiler or interpreter (INT, SQR, and RND). (A-72)

PRINT   A statement that controls the type and format of output at both the display terminal and printer. (A-12, A-14)

```
600 PRINT "jumped over the lazy brown dog."
```

PRINT TAB   Statement for placing output into certain columns much like the tab operations on a typewriter. (A-70)

```
600 PRINT TAB(23); W$; TAB(35); H
```

PRINT USING   Statement that directs output onto a user-designed format created using an IMAGE statement. (A-71)

```
600 PRINT USING 650; W$, H

650 " \               \    ##.##"
```

PROBLEM DEFINITION   Focusing on the problem to identify exactly what it is and how best to solve it. (A-3)

PROBLEM RECOGNITION   The first and most important step of the system development process. (A-3)

PROGRAM CODING   Translating the program design into a programming language that will run on the computer. (A-3)

PROGRAM DESIGN   Involves specifying the structure of the program in detail. (A-3)

PROGRAM DEVELOPMENT CYCLE Eight steps required to solve a programming problem—recognition, definition, design, coding, testing, implementation, maintenance, and then beginning again. (A-3)

PROGRAM DOCUMENTATION Consists of manuals, display screens, and other materials that tell users how to use the program, operators how to run it, and programmers how to change it. (A-6)

PROGRAM IMPLEMENTATION The actual using of the new program. (A-3)

PROGRAM MAINTENANCE Correcting any previously undetected errors and making any other needed changes. (A-3)

PROGRAM TESTING Checking the program for errors and rewriting parts of the program to correct the mistakes. (A-3)

PSEUDOCODE An English-like code to help the programmer understand the steps needed to execute the program. (A-4)

RANDOMIZE Statement used to tell the computer to generate a fresh list of random numbers. (A-12, A-75)

```
600 RANDOMIZE
```

READ Statement that assigns data from a DATA statement to a particular value. (A-12, A-16)

```
600 READ W, A$, J
```

RELATIONAL OPERATOR Operators $<$, $<=$, $=$, $>=$, $>$, and $<>$ used in IF/THEN/ELSE statements. (A-28)

REM Nonexecutable statement for writing remarks or comments and storing them within the program. (A-12, A-13)

```
600 REM This is a REM statement
```

RESERVED WORD A word that has a precise meaning in BASIC. It must be correctly spelled and used only for its assigned purpose and not as a variable. (A-12)

RESTORE Statement that resets the pointer for the READ statement back to the beginning of the data list. (A-12, A-20)

```
600 RESTORE
```

RETURN A statement in BASIC used to close the subroutine and direct control back to the main program. (A-12, A-32)

```
600 RETURN
```

RND(X) Predefined function for randomizing numbers. (A-74)

```
600 RND(X)
```

SELECTION Logic patterns that use comparisons based on decisions or choices to split a program into different paths. (A-5)

SEQUENCE Set of linear steps to be carried out in the order of their appearance. (A-5)

SQR(X) Predefined function for finding the square root of a number. (A-72)

```
600 SQR(Y)
```

STEP Statement used with FOR/NEXT statements for incrementing and decrementing. (A-12, A-48)

```
600 FOR I = 3 TO 45 STEP 3
```

STOP   Statement that immediately halts the execution of program and sends program control directly to the END statement. (A-12, A-22)

```
600 STOP
```

SUBSCRIPTED VARIABLE   A variable representing an array in which each value is uniquely identified—R(N,Y). (A-58)

```
600 PRINT x(I,J)
```

SYSTEM COMMANDS   The commands we use to communicate with the computer's operating system (RUN, LIST<, and LOAD). (A-10)

THEN   Reserved word used in IF/THEN/ELSE statements to indicate the selection if the test is met. (A-12, A-27)

```
600 IF E < 94 THEN PRINT "Too low!"
```

TIMER   Reserved word when used with RANDOMIZE will generate random numbers using the computer's clock. (A-12, A-75)

```
600 RANDOMIZE TIMER
```

TO   Reserved word indicating a range of numbers such as 1 TO 10. (A-12, A-54)

```
600 FOR I = 2 TO 45
```

TRAILER VALUE   A way to control a loop operation using a test value. (A-39)

TWO-DIMENSIONAL ARRAY   A way of displaying data by locating it in a row and column format. (A-59)

USER-DEFINED FUNCTIONS   Functions created by the user as a "library" function for a specific program. Later the function is called by the part of the program requiring the function. (A-75)

```
600 DEF FNG(D) - D*3
```

```
650 LET R = FNG(6)
```

VARIABLE   A symbol which can take on different values. (A-13)

WHILE/WEND.   Statements used to create a DOWHILE loop structure. (A-56)

```
600 WHILE F <> X
```

operation within the loop

```
650 WEND
```

NUMBER SYSTEMS AND BINARY ARITHMETIC

In this appendix we will describe the number systems most frequently used in connection with computers and the concepts behind them in more detail. The number systems we will discuss are based on the powers of 2, 8, 10, and 16. We will see how whole and fractional values are represented for each type, and we will demonstrate how to convert between the different systems.

The appendix concludes with a presentation of binary arithmetic.

THE DECIMAL NUMBER SYSTEM

The **DECIMAL** or **BASE 10 NUMBER SYSTEM** is our number system of everyday life. The word "decimal" is derived from the Latin word for "ten." The available numerals run from 0 through 9. The base value, in this case 10, determines the number of available numerals in a number system.

As with all number systems, we can represent larger numbers by raising the base to different powers. In looking at powers of 10, we can see how a number can be broken down into both real and fractional or decimal values. For example, take the number 2409.325:

10^3	10^2	10^1	10^0	.	10^{-1}	10^{-2}	10^{-3}	← Powers of 10
1000	100	10	1	.	0.1	0.01	0.001	
2	4	0	9	.	3	2	5	← Decimal number

Under each power its decimal equivalent is written out (for example, $10^3 = 1000$). Thus the decimal number 2409.325 is equal to $(2 \times 1000) + (4 \times 100) + (0 \times 10) + (9 \times 1) + (3 \times 0.1) + (2 \times 0.01) + (5 \times 0.001)$.

Figure B-1 examines the decimal number 179 in detail. The value of each digit in the number is determined by its place value or position. On the top part of Figure B-1 we consider the number 179 in terms of its place

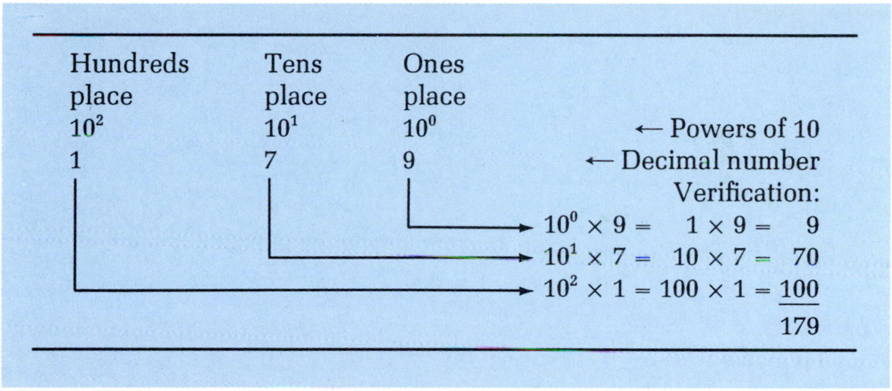

FIGURE B-1.

Place values for a decimal number.

```
Hundreds        Tens       Ones
place           place      place
10²             10¹        10⁰           ← Powers of 10
1               7          9             ← Decimal number
                                         Verification:
                              10⁰ × 9 =   1 × 9 =   9
                              10¹ × 7 =  10 × 7 =  70
                              10² × 1 = 100 × 1 = 100
                                                  179
```

values. The place values, or powers of 10, can be multiplied by any number between 0 and 9, as shown on the bottom part of the figure. (In case you have forgotten, any number raised to the 0 power equals 1; thus 10^0 equals 1.)

THE BINARY NUMBER SYSTEM

The **BINARY (BASE 2) NUMBER SYSTEM** uses only the numerals 0 and 1. "Binary" is derived from the Latin word for "two." Binary is the only number system that your computer understands. It refers to whether switches or electrical currents are "on" (1) or "off" (0).

Here is an example of how the powers of 2 (shown with decimal values for each value of 2) are used to represent the binary number 110110.011:

2^5	2^4	2^3	2^2	2^1	2^0	.	2^{-1}	2^{-2}	2^{-3}	← Powers of 2
32	16	8	4	2	1	.	0.5	0.25	0.125	
1	1	0	1	1	0	.	0	1	1	← Binary number

Thus the decimal equivalent is $(1 \times 32) + (1 \times 16) + (0 \times 8) + (1 \times 4) + (1 \times 2) + (0 \times 1) + (0 \times 0.05) + (1 \times 0.25) + (1 \times 0.125)$ or 54.375.

Figure B-2 compares the first sixteen numbers as represented in decimal, binary, octal, and hexadecimal. Octal (base 8) and hexadecimal (base 16) number systems are also commonly used with computers since they themselves are powers of 2 ($8 = 2^3$ and $16 = 2^4$).

FIGURE B-2.

Comparing the first 16 numbers in the decimal, binary, octal, and hexadecimal number systems.

Decimal		Binary					Octal		Hexa-decimal	
10^1	10^0	2^4	2^3	2^2	2^1	2^0	8^1	8^0	16^1	16^0
	0					0		0		0
	1					1		1		1
	2				1	0		2		2
	3				1	1		3		3
	4			1	0	0		4		4
	5			1	0	1		5		5
	6			1	1	0		6		6
	7			1	1	1		7		7
	8		1	0	0	0	1	0		8
	9		1	0	0	1	1	1		9
1	0		1	0	1	0	1	2		A
1	1		1	0	1	1	1	3		B
1	2		1	1	0	0	1	4		C
1	3		1	1	0	1	1	5		D
1	4		1	1	1	0	1	6		E
1	5		1	1	1	1	1	7		F
1	6	1	0	0	0	0	2	0	1	0

FIGURE B-3.

Place values for a binary number.

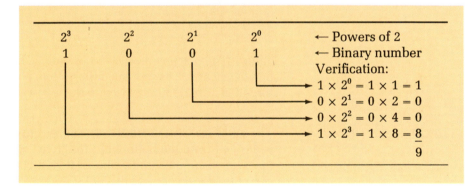

Figure B-3 represents the binary number 1001 in terms of its place values, showing why it is equal to the decimal number 9.

Figure B-4 relates the powers of 2 to the octal and hexadecimal number systems. Observe the patterns. For example, 2^{12}, 8^4, and 16^3 all equal the same decimal value 4096. Since 8 and 16 are powers of 2 and require fewer symbols to represent a number than base 2, the octal and hexadecimal number systems are used to represent values stored inside a computer in less bulky form than binary.

FIGURE B-4.

Comparing place values of the powers of 2, 8, and 16. The equivalent decimal numbers are shown for each.

Binary	Octal	Hexadecimal
$2^0 = 1$	$8^0 = 1$	$16^0 = 1$
$2^1 = 2$		
$2^2 = 4$		
$2^3 = 8$	$8^1 = 8$	
$2^4 = 16$		$16^1 = 16$
$2^5 = 32$		
$2^6 = 64$	$8^2 = 64$	
$2^7 = 128$		
$2^8 = 256$		$16^2 = 256$
$2^9 = 512$	$8^3 = 512$	
$2^{10} = 1024$		
$2^{11} = 2048$		
$2^{12} = 4096$	$8^4 = 4096$	$16^3 = 4096$

It is possible to convert numbers from one number system to their equivalents in another. For example, the binary equivalent for the decimal number 179 is shown in Figure B-5. There are several methods that can be used to convert numbers from one base to another. Figure B-5 uses a process that involves dividing the value written in one number system by the base of the second system—in this case 2. The remainder is placed in a column to the right of the original value. If there is no remainder, a 0 is placed in the column. Next the result of the division excluding the remainder is divided by the base 2. This process is continued until division is no longer possible. Reading the remainders from bottom to top gives us the original value written in base 2.

An alternative method (also shown in Figure B-5) is to refer to a table of values written in different number bases, as in Figure B-4. Using a table is easier to follow in some cases. In Figure B-4 the largest value that is less than or equal to 179 is 2^7 or 128. This is the highest (leftmost) place, and we assign a 1 to it. Next we subtract 128 from 179 and get 51. Since the next place, 2^6 or 64, is greater than 51 the next place value is 0. We continue this process through the lower powers of 2 until there is no further remainder. To verify your answer, you can multiply each binary digit by the appropriate power of 2 and add up the results. You should end up with the same decimal number you started with.

To convert from binary to decimal is a simpler process. Just multiply each place value by the appropriate power of 2 (as you did to check your answer above). For example, the bottom of Figure B-5 shows how binary 10111011010 converts into the decimal number 1498.

BINARY CODED DECIMAL (BCD) NUMBERS

The decimal numbers 0 to 9 can be coded in a scheme known as **BINARY CODED DECIMAL (BCD)**. This is simply a code to represent characters including decimal numbers. Because the binary code in this case is 4 bits wide, it is labeled 4-bit BCD. We can convert the decimal number 179 into three adjacent 4-bit BCD numbers—0001 0111 1001—simply by finding the binary

FIGURE B-5.
Decimal-binary and binary-decimal conversion.

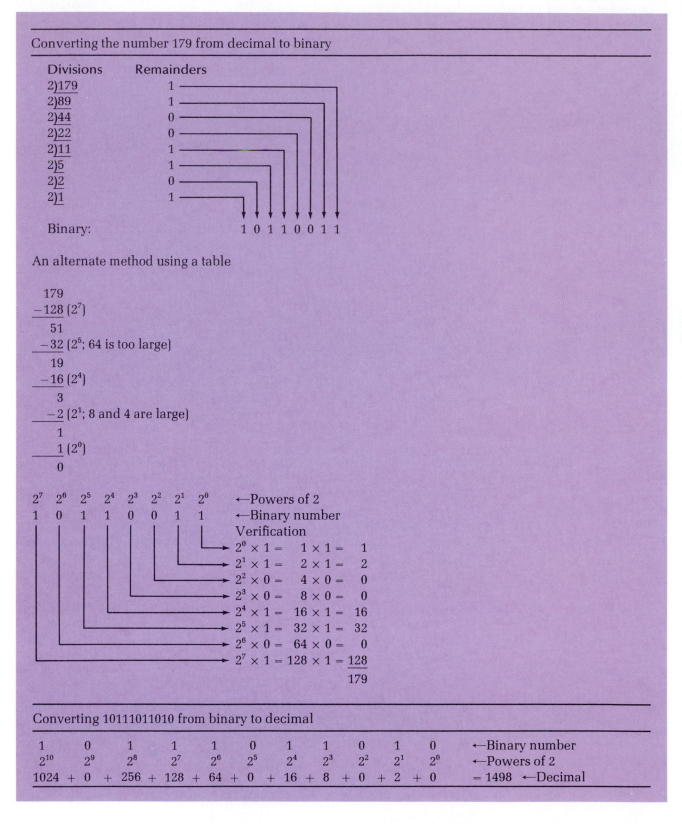

Converting the number 179 from decimal to binary

Divisions	Remainders
2)179	1
2)89	1
2)44	0
2)22	0
2)11	1
2)5	1
2)2	0
2)1	1

Binary: 1 0 1 1 0 0 1 1

An alternate method using a table

$$
\begin{array}{l}
179 \\
-128\ (2^7) \\
\hline
51 \\
-32\ (2^5;\ 64\ \text{is too large}) \\
\hline
19 \\
-16\ (2^4) \\
\hline
3 \\
-2\ (2^1;\ 8\ \text{and}\ 4\ \text{are large}) \\
\hline
1 \\
1\ (2^0) \\
\hline
0
\end{array}
$$

2^7	2^6	2^5	2^4	2^3	2^2	2^1	2^0	←Powers of 2
1	0	1	1	0	0	1	1	←Binary number

Verification

$2^0 \times 1 = 1 \times 1 = 1$
$2^1 \times 1 = 2 \times 1 = 2$
$2^2 \times 0 = 4 \times 0 = 0$
$2^3 \times 0 = 8 \times 0 = 0$
$2^4 \times 1 = 16 \times 1 = 16$
$2^5 \times 1 = 32 \times 1 = 32$
$2^6 \times 0 = 64 \times 0 = 0$
$2^7 \times 1 = 128 \times 1 = \underline{128}$
179

Converting 10111011010 from binary to decimal

1	0	1	1	1	0	1	1	0	1	0	←Binary number
2^{10}	2^9	2^8	2^7	2^6	2^5	2^4	2^3	2^2	2^1	2^0	←Powers of 2
1024 +	0 +	256 +	128 +	64 +	0 +	16 +	8 +	0 +	2 +	0	= 1498 ←Decimal

equivalent for each decimal digit. We can quickly go in the other direction as well, and convert from BCD into decimal. For example, the four adjacent 4-bit BCD values 0001 0100 1001 1000 represent the decimal number 1498. BCD numbers are often used in processing business data, especially calculations involving money. This is so because BCD can process fractional amounts such as 0.1 where there is no exact binary equivalent. Processing is slower, but avoids rounding errors, which might create strange checks for strange amounts, such as $1.099999999999.

THE OCTAL NUMBER SYSTEM

The OCTAL (BASE 8) NUMBER SYSTEM only uses the eight numerals 0 through 7. The term "octal" is derived from the Greek word for "eight." As mentioned earlier, the octal number system is related to binary, since 8 is a power of 2 (2^3). Here is an example of how powers of 8 are used to represent the octal number 4360.234:

8^3	8^2	8^1	8^0	.	8^{-1}	8^{-2}	8^{-3}	← Powers of 8
512	64	8	1	.	0.125	0.016	0.002	
4	3	6	0	.	2	3	4	← Octal number

Thus the decimal equivalent is $(4 \times 512) + (3 \times 64) + (6 \times 8) + (1 \times 0) + (2 \times .125) + (3 \times .016) + (4 \times .002)$ or 2288.306.

The procedures for conversion are essentially the same for octal as for the other numbers. As shown in Figure B-6, we can convert from decimal to octal as well as from octal to decimal.

THE HEXADECIMAL NUMBER SYSTEM

The HEXADECIMAL (BASE 16) NUMBER SYSTEM requires 16 numerals. The term "hexadecimal" is derived by combining the Greek term for "six" with the Latin word for "ten." Hexadecimal values are used to represent binary numbers in human-readable form (16 is equal to 2^4). Hexadecimal numbers reduce the space required for human-readable output of machine instructions or stored data.

The hexadecimal system challenges our creativity, because our decimal system only ranges from 0 to 9 in a place column. The numbers 10 through 15 therefore need special symbols. For convenience the letters A to F are used as these higher numerals. Here is an example of how the powers of 16 are used to represent the hexadecimal number 3A7B.2C5:

16^3	16^2	16^1	16^0	.	16^{-1}	16^{-2}	16^{-3}	← Powers of 16
4096	256	16	1	.	0.0625	0.0039	0.0002	
3	A	7	B	.	2	C	5	← Hexadecimal number

Thus the decimal equivalent is $(3 \times 4096) + (10 \times 256) + (7 \times 16) + (11 \times 1) + (2 \times .0625) + (12 \times .0039) + (5 \times .0002)$ or 14971.1728.

A single hexadecimal numeral can represent four binary place values. For example, binary 1010 is A in hexadecimal. The decimal number equivalent is 10.

The conversion for decimal to base 16 is done in the same way as for binary (Figure B-7, top). To convert from hexadecimal to decimal, we simply multiply each place value by the appropriate power of 16 (Figure B-7, bottom).

Converting the number 179 from decimal to octal

Divisions   Remainders
8)179   3
8)22   6
8)2   2

Octal: 2 6 3

An alternate method using a table

$$179$$
$$-128 \; (2 \times 8^2)$$
$$\overline{51}$$
$$\underline{-48} \; (6 \times 8^1)$$
$$3$$

8^2 8^1 8^0 ←Powers of 8
2   6   3   ←Octal number
                     Verification:
$8^0 \times 3 = 1 \times 3 = 3$
$8^1 \times 6 = 8 \times 6 = 48$
$8^2 \times 2 = 64 \times 2 = \underline{128}$
179

Converting 2732 from octal to decimal

2   7   3   2   ←Octal number
8^3 8^2 8^1 8^0 ←Powers of 8

$1024 + 448 + 24 + 2 \qquad = 1498$ ←Decimal

BINARY ARITHMETIC

In this section we will describe how computers, working solely in binary, perform addition, multiplication, subtraction, and division.

ADDITION

The rules for binary arithmetic are the same as for any other number system; only the number of digits varies. The addition process works like this:

+	0	1
0	0	1
1	1	0 ← (carry 1)

or

$0 + 0 = 0$

$1 + 0 = 1$

$0 + 1 = 1$

$1 + 1 = 0 \leftarrow$ (carry 1 to next column)

Let us look at some examples.

Converting the number 179 from decimal to hexadecimal

Divisions   Remainders
16)179   3
16)11   11 = B

Hexadecimal: B3

An alternative method using a table
   179
-176 (11×16^1)
     3

16^1 16^0 ←Powers of 16
 B   3   ←Hexadecimal number

                    Verification:
                    $16^0 \times 3 = 1 \times 3 = 3$
                    $16^1 \times 11 = 16 \times 11 = \underline{176}$
                                                    179

Converting the hexadecimal number 5DA to decimal

  5   D   A   ←Hexadecimal number (A = 10 and D = 13)
 16^2 16^1 16^0 ←Powers of 16

$1280 + 208 + 10$ = 1498   ←Decimal

		1	11111	1111	→ (carries)
100		1001	10101	101	
+ 11		+ 101	+ 11011	1011	
111		1110	110000	+ 110	
				10110	

$[4 + 3 = 7]\ [9 + 5 = 14]\ [21 + 27 = 48]\ [5 + 11 + 6 = 22]$ ← (verification)

Notice how the carry operation works here.

MULTIPLICATION   Multiplication is very simple using binary numbers. As shown in the following multiplication table, the results are always 0 except when 1 is multiplied by itself.

$\times$	0	1		$0 \times 0 = 0$
0	0	0	or	$1 \times 0 = 0$
1	0	1		$0 \times 1 = 0$
				$1 \times 1 = 1$

Unlike addition there is no carrying with binary multiplication. The following example demonstrates binary multiplication:

```
    1111
×     10
    0000
   1111
  11110
```

Notice that multiplying by 0 gives you a line of 0s. Multiplying by 1 simply copies the original number (with the digits "moved left"). Here are some more examples:

```
   101          110          1000         10101
 ×  10        ×  11        ×   10       ×  1011
   000          110          0000         10101
   101          110          1000         10101
  1010        10010        10000         00000
                                         10101
                                       11100111
```

} partial products

$[5 \times 2 = 10]$ $[6 \times 3 = 18]$ $[8 \times 2 = 16]$ $[21 \times 11 = 231]$ ← (verification)

Since at each stage we are multiplying a number by either 0 or 1, the partial products are either all 0 or copies of the original number.

SUBTRACTION

Subtraction is similar to decimal subtraction. The subtraction table shows the following.

−	0	1
0	0	1 ← (borrow 1 from next column)
1	1	0

or

$0 - 0 = 0$

$1 - 0 = 1$

$0 - 1 = 1$ ← (borrow 1 from next column)

$1 - 1 = 0$

Here are some subtraction examples:

```
                  0                        0
   111          1011         1111         1101
 −  11        −  110        −1010        −1011
   100           101          101           10
```

$[7 - 3 = 4]$ $[11 - 6 = 5]$ $[15 - 10 = 5]$ $[13 - 11 = 2]$ ←(verification)

DIVISION

For division we perform standard operations as shown in the following examples.

$$\begin{array}{r} 011 \\ 11\overline{)\ 1001} \\ \underline{00} \\ 100 \\ \underline{11} \\ 11 \\ \underline{11} \end{array} \qquad \begin{array}{r} 111 \\ 100\overline{)\ 11110} \\ \underline{100} \\ 111 \\ \underline{100} \\ 110 \\ \underline{100} \\ 10 \end{array} \leftarrow \text{(remainder)}$$

$$[9 \div 3 = 3] \quad [30 \div 4 = 7 \text{ with 2 remainder}] \leftarrow \text{(verification)}$$

Since each digit in the quotient can only be a 0 or a 1, binary division involves repeatedly subtracting the divisor until the final remainder is too small.

KEY TERMS

These are the key terms in the order in which they appear in this appendix. The definitions are found in the main glossary.

Decimal (base 10) number
 system (B-3)
Binary (base 2) number
 system (B-3)

Binary coded decimal (BCD) (B-5)
Octal (base 8) number system (B-7)
Hexadecimal (base 16) number
 system (B-7)

REVIEW QUESTIONS

1. Convert the following decimal numbers into binary, 4-bit BCD, octal, and hexadecimal.
   (a) 17   (c) 197
   (b) 56   (d) 1943

2. Convert the following 4-bit BCD into decimal.
   (a) 1001 1000 0110   (c) 0101 0100 0111
   (b) 1000 1001 0001   (d) 0100 0001 0110 0110

3. Convert the following binary numbers into decimal, octal, and hexadecimal.
   (a) 1011   (c) 11011011
   (b) 1110110   (d) 11110101

4. Convert the octal numbers shown into decimal, binary, and hexadecimal.
   (a) 51   (c) 714
   (b) 103   (d) 570

5. Convert the following hexadecimal numbers into decimal, binary, and octal.
   (a) F   (c) A5
   (b) 2B   (d) CBA

6. Perform addition upon these binary numbers.
   (a) 101 + 11   (c) 1010 + 1001 + 1000
   (b) 1011 + 1010   (d) 11011 + 1101 + 111 + 1000

7. Perform multiplication upon the following binary numbers.
   (a) 11 × 11   (c) 1101 × 101
   (b) 101 × 10   (d) 10001 × 110

8. Perform subtraction upon these binary numbers.
   (a) 101 − 11   (c) 1001 − 1001
   (b) 1101 − 10   (d) 10011 − 1010

9. Perform regular division using the following binary numbers.
   (a) 100 ÷ 10   (c) 10000 ÷ 10
   (b) 1111 ÷ 11   (d) 11110 ÷ 110

GLOSSARY OF KEY TERMS

ABACUS An early manual calculating device that dates back thousands of years. (96)

ACCEPTANCE TEST The last test before the new information system is fully implemented. (431)

ACCESS TIME Amount of time necessary to retrieve a data item from secondary storage and place it into main memory. (191)

ACCOUNTING System that maintains organized business and financial records. (66)

ACCOUNTING PACKAGES Prewritten programs ranging from simple bookkeeping and check-register programs to complex packages. (345)

ACCOUNT NUMBER A number or code assigned to users in order to account for who is responsible for a project. (360)

ACCOUNT NUMBER PROGRAM Special system software used to create account numbers and passwords for greater system security. (360)

ACCOUNTS PAYABLE System that keeps track of money that a company owes others. (67)

ACCOUNTS RECEIVABLE System that keeps track of money that is owed to a company. (66)

ACOUSTIC COUPLER Communications hardware that connects a telephone receiver to the computer to perform modulation and demodulation on a temporary basis. (228)

ADA A high-level language named for Lady Ada developed for the U.S. Department of Defense and first released in 1980. It uses software engineering to speed up program design. (318)

ADDRESS Refers to a unique location in main or disk memory. (133)

AIKEN, HOWARD The developer of the Mark I. (101)

ALGORITHM A set of rules that break down the solution to a programming problem into a simple, repetitive procedure. (248)

ALPHABETIC FIELD A field that only contains alphabetic characters. (441)

ALPHANUMERIC FIELD A field that contains both alphabetic characters, numbers, and symbols. (441)

ALU See Arithmetic/logic unit.

AMERICAN FEDERATION OF INFORMATION PROCESSING SOCIETIES (AFIPS) An umbrella organization for a number of professional groups. (546)

ANALOG COMPUTER Computer that processes data by using an analogy to the data—usually a variable level of energy. (130)

ANALYTIC ENGINE Mechanical steam-driven device invented by Charles Babbage that had all the parts of a modern computer but was never successfully completed. (98)

ANNOTATION SYMBOL Represents comments or remarks on the flowchart that do not affect the operation of the program. (275)

APL (A PROGRAMMING LANGUAGE) High-level language designed for engineering and scientific applications, which requires a special keyboard with Greek letters and mathematical symbols. (319)

APPLE I The first commercially successful microcomputer. It was designed by Steven Wozniak and Stephen Jobs. (114)

APPLICATION AREA The types of uses to which a computer can be put: business, government, engineering, and science. (305)

APPLICATION SOFTWARE These programs direct the actual input, processing, and output activities for users. (41)

ARITHMETIC/LOGIC UNIT (ALU) The part of the CPU that performs calculations and logical operations as directed by the control unit. (48, 133)

ARTIFICIAL INTELLIGENCE (AI) The efforts to capture the way humans think and learn applied to computer programs. (118, 569)

ASCII (AMERICAN STANDARD CODE FOR INFORMATION INTERCHANGE) Assigns a specific bit pattern to each of the decimal numbers 0 through 9, lowercase and uppercase alphabet, and commonly used symbols. (141)

ASSEMBLER Part of system software that translates a program written in assembly language into machine language. (373)

ASSEMBLY LANGUAGE A language using mnemonic symbols instead of 1s and 0s which is then translated into machine language. (108, 309)

ASSOCIATION FOR COMPUTING MACHINERY (ACM) The oldest and largest educational and scientific society in the computing industry. (546)

ASSOCIATION FOR SYSTEMS MANAGEMENT (ASM) Professional society for systems analysis and systems managers. (547)

ASYNCHRONOUS TRANSMISSION Sending data one byte at a time. (228)

ATANASOFF-BERRY COMPUTER (ABC) The first electronic computer developed by Dr. John V. Atanasoff and Clifford E. Berry. (102)

ATANASOFF, JOHN V., AND CLIFFORD E. BERRY Developers of the Atanasoff-Berry Computer (ABC). (102)

AUDIO OUTPUT DEVICE A peripheral that allows the user to listen to the computer. (182)

AUDIT An examination of the information system to test the effectiveness of its various control procedures. (484)

AUDIT TRAIL Physical or visible documentation of the steps of data through an organization's information system. (484)

AUTOMATIC CALLBACK Security control technique whereby the computer calls back the user in an attempt to foil masqueraders. (481)

AUTOMATION Refers to the replacement of human control of a process by a machine. (555)

AUXILIARY STORAGE See Secondary storage.

BABBAGE, CHARLES (1792-1871) British mathematician who developed the difference engine and later worked on the analytic engine. (97)

BACKUS, JOHN Developer of the programming language FORTRAN in 1957 while he was at IBM. (110)

BAND PRINTER A line printer that uses an engraved steel band instead of chain to produce a line of print at a time. (177)

BANDWIDTH Refers to the capacity of a communications medium. (224)

BAR CODE READER An optical scanner that reads data coded with the Universal Product Code (UPC). (170)

BASIC. (Beginners' All Purpose Symbolic Instruction Code) Interactive programming language developed by John G. Kemeny and Thomas Kurtz with the novice programmer in mind. (113, 311)

BATCH PROCESSING This stage occurs when data are collected over a period of time and processed as a group. (15, 363)

BILLING Usually part of accounts receivable, it is the preparation of a customer's statement. (68)

BINARY CODED DECIMAL (BCD) A coding scheme to represent decimal numbers and characters in binary. (B-5)

BINARY NUMBER SYSTEM The base 2 number system. The number system that computers use. (108,138,B-3)

BIOCHIP New technology that utilizes molecular structures and processes developed using biotechnology. (568)

BIT Refers to a single binary digit (a 1 or a 0). (138)

BOOTING OR BOOTSTRAPPING Transmitting a piece of the operating system code to the control unit in order to "wake up" the computer. (359)

BUBBLE MEMORY Primary storage using tiny, movable magnetic bubbles implanted in thin film on a garnet wafer. (149, 205)

BUFFER Internal storage area used to balance the transfer of data between hardware components with different transmission speeds. (201, 363) (134)

BYTE A string of adjacent bits that the computer processes as one unit. Usually there are 8 bits per byte. (139)

C A high-level language so named because it was developed from a language called B. (319)

CACHE STORAGE A place in the computer for storing data and instructions not yet ready to be processed. (147)

CAD See Computer-aided design.

CAI See Computer-assisted instruction.

CALCULATING The computer performs mathematical functions on data such as addition, subtraction, multiplication, division, and exponentiation. (16)

CAM See Computer-aided manufacturing.

CANNED PROGRAMS See Prewritten software.

CARD READER A peripheral device that reads holes punched in a paper card. (50)

CASSETTE TAPE A type of secondary storage used on microcomputers, less efficient and slower than floppy disks. (52)

CASSETTE TAPE DEVICE This peripheral is used for reading from and storing data onto cassette-style magnetic tapes. (50)

CENTRALIZED DATA PROCESSING All data processing is done at one central computer center. (216)

CENTRAL PROCESSING UNIT (CPU) See Computer.

CHAIN PRINTER A line printer that uses chains or loops of characters for every print position on a line. (177)

CHANNEL A path along which data are sent, together with enough control logic to free the CPU from supervising the transfer. (363)

CHARACTER PRINTER OR SERIAL PRINTER A peripheral that prints one character at a time. (175)

CHARACTERS The individual letters, numbers, or symbols that go into a field. (40, 441)

CHARGE-COUPLED DEVICE A form of very fast semiconductor storage using tiny storage cells to hold charges. (205)

CHECK BIT See Parity bit.

CHECK DIGITS A type of data integrity control that checks data against predetermined patterns. (475)

CHECKPOINTS Places at which we see if we have successfully completed a step. (248)

CHIEF OR LEAD PROGRAMMER The programmer who manages and reviews the overall activities of the programming project. (255)

CHIEF PROGRAMMER TEAM A group aimed at reducing programming errors through a team effort led by a chief programmer. (255)

CHILD A data element in an hierarchical database that is beneath a "parent" and connected to it. (456)

CLIENT A person who receives the information from the information system. (36)

COAXIAL CABLES One conducting wire surrounded by an insulator which is in turn surrounded by a second conducting wire. (223)

COBOL (Common Business Oriented Language) A high-level language strong in file processing and used extensively today by both businesses and government agencies. (110, 314)

COMMON CARRIER   A company that furnishes communication services for the public. (234)

COMMUNICATING   The act of transmitting data or information from one place to another. (16)

COMMUNICATIONS DEVICES   Consisting of two types of hardware, they link the local user hardware with the host processor and the host processor with the telecommunications media. They also handle the actual transmission of data between local user hardware and the host processor. (52, 215)

COMMUNICATIONS MEDIUM   See Telecommunications medium.

COMMUNICATIONS PROCESSORS   Communications devices that handle the switching and coordination of messages and data and include multiplexors, concentrators, front-end processors, and message switchers. (231)

COMPARING   The computer determines whether two items are the same or different. (16)

COMPILER   A language translator that converts a complete program written in a specific high-level language into machine language. (371)

COMPUTER OR CENTRAL PROCESSING UNIT (CPU)   A very-high-speed electronic device that can accept data and instructions, use the instructions to perform logical and mathematical operations on the data, and report the results of its processing. (8, 130)

COMPUTER-AIDED DESIGN (CAD)   Systems that can create detailed designs in a fraction of the time that conventional methods take. (78, 343)

COMPUTER-AIDED MANUFACTURING (CAM)   Prewritten software that uses a computer to direct the actual production or assembly process. (78, 347)

COMPUTER-ASSISTED INSTRUCTION (CAI)   Prewritten software used to teach material to a student or other user, generally on an interactive basis. (347)

COMPUTER CRIME   The use of a computer for illegal purposes. (468)

COMPUTER GAMES   Games played using a computer with a display screen, and a keyboard or joysticks. (347)

COMPUTERIZED AXIAL TOMOGRAPHY (CAT)   A scanning technique to x-ray the human body from three different directions. (173)

COMPUTER NETWORK   See Network.

COMPUTER-OUTPUT MICROFILM (COM)   System that can produce up to 50,000 lines per minute of output onto microfilm right from the computer using a high-speed camera. (182)

COMPUTER SCIENCE PROGRAM   A technical program of study that covers the history and fundamentals of computing, a programming language or two, system development, information resource systems, and other areas discussed in this book. (536)

COMPUTER SIMULATION   Programs that can model real-world events and attempt to predict possible consequences of those events. (78)

COMPUTER WORD   An expression made up of one or more consecutive bytes. (143)

CONCENTRATOR   A telecommunications device that combines incoming and outgoing messages into a more compact unit and can also be programmed to edit data, compress data, convert between ASCII and EBCDIC, and check for errors. (233)

CONNECTORS   Flowchart symbols of which there are two types: circular and five-sided. (274)

CONTENT CHECK   The second step in debugging process determines if the program solves all the parts of the problem it is supposed to solve. (291)

CONTENTION   Opposite of polling, the peripheral device asks the computer if the medium is free for transmission. (230)

CONTROL MODULE   The module that gives orders to other modules in the program. (259)

CONTROL-AND-PROCESSING MODULE   The element that performs control operations over lower-level modules and carries out processing functions. (259)

CONTROL TOTALS   A technique for checking the integrity of the data. (474)

CONTROL UNIT   The part of the computer that directs the input, processing, and output of data. (48, 131)

COUNTER   A variable that changes by a fixed value each time it is encountered in a program; often used in loop control. (287)

CP/M (CONTROL PROGRAM FOR MICRO-COMPUTERS)   A single-user operating system for microcomputers. (376)

CPU   See Computer.

CRASH CONVERSION   See Direct cutover conversion.

CREDIT ANALYSIS   Methods for determining the credit status of clients. (70)

CRT   See Display terminal.

CURSOR   The movable and sometimes blinking symbol that shows you where you are on the display terminal. (166)

CYLINDERS   A conceptual "slice" of a disk made up of vertical stacks of tracks and a way of storing data on a disk that speeds up seek time. (197)

DAISY-WHEEL PRINTER   Character printer that produces letter-quality output using a print element that spins to the appropriate character. It is slower than most other types of impact printers. (176)

DASD   See Direct Access Storage Device.

DATA   Facts from which information may be drawn. (9)

DATABASE   A set of interrelated files. (41, 441)

DATABASE ADMINISTRATOR   Person responsible for setting up databases, maintaining them, and helping programmers and users to utilize them properly. (453)

DATABASE MANAGEMENT SYSTEMS (DBMS)   Software that allows users with different application needs to create, access, modify, and maintain databases. (117, 338, 453)

DATA CELL   See Magnetic strip cartridge system.

DATA DEFINITION LANGUAGE (DDL) The language used in schemas and sub-schemas for a database. (455)

DATA DICTIONARY Definitions of each item of data and information handled by a system that give format, input source, and output use. (422, 453)

DATA ENTRY The process of getting facts into a form that the computer can interpret. (160)

DATA-FLOW DIAGRAM A visual way to focus on how data move through the system. (415)

DATA HIERARCHY The classification of data from the lowest to highest level: field, record, file, and database. (39, 440)

DATA INTEGRITY The accuracy of the data throughout the system. (468)

DATA MANIPULATION LANGUAGE (DML) The commands programmers use when performing operations on a database. (455)

DATA PROCESSING MANAGEMENT ASSOCIATION (DPMA) Association made up of managers and supervisors of computer centers, educators, and vendors in the information processing industry. (546)

DATA QUALITY ASSURANCE The process of ensuring data integrity throughout the system. (474)

DATA SECURITY The protection and care of data. (475)

DATA-TRANSFER TIME Time it takes to transfer the data from a location either to the computer for reading or from the computer to the disk for writing. (197)

DBMS See Database management system.

DDL See Data definition language.

DEBUGGING The process of finding and correcting errors in programs. (249)

DECENTRALIZED DATA PROCESSING Several computers functioning independently of the others within the same organization. (216)

DECIMAL NUMBER SYSTEM The base 10 number system. (138, B-3)

DECISION-LOGIC TABLE Tool a systems analyst can use to trace complicated logic patterns by following through the possibilities for multiple decisions. (417)

DECISION SUPPORT SYSTEM (DSS) An information system that managers can use easily and that provides highly refined information to help make nonroutine decisions. (395)

DECISION SYMBOL Flowchart symbol that denotes choices based upon comparisons. (278)

DECODER The part of the machine that reads the instruction code and sets circuitry for the operation. (134)

DEDICATED WORD PROCESSOR Mini- or microcomputers especially designed for, and limited to, word-processing. (333)

DEFAULT VALUE A value that is assumed when no alternative value is specified by the user; a maximum number of printed pages might be set for any job as a default value. (360)

DEMAND REPORT A predefined report that is generated only when requested, and generally concerns a specific topic of interest to a manager. (390)

DEMODULATION Process of converting the analog signal back to digital at the receiving modem. (227)

DESIGN REPORT The complete output of the system design stage. (426)

DESIGN REVIEW A meeting at which user, managers, and the systems analyst review the system design. (426)

DESK-CHECKING A debugging technique that can be done before or after running by simply looking at the program. (289)

DESTRUCTIVE WRITE Process of writing new material into a storage location and erasing the old material in the process. (135)

DETAILED HIPO DIAGRAM A schematic that shows in detail the input, processing, and output steps necessary to execute the module. (257)

DETAILED INVESTIGATION The second step of systems analysis. (412)

DIAGNOSTIC PROGRAM Part of system software that checks for faults in programs or equipment. (373)

DIFFERENCE ENGINE A mechanical device invented by Charles Babbage that could generate tables of squares, cubes, and other functions. (98)

DIGITAL COMPUTER The main type of computer in use today and used for many applications. It treats data as discrete values. (130)

DIRECT ACCESS The ability to retrieve or write a given record without first having to process all the records leading up to it. (194, 445)

DIRECT-ACCESS FILE OR RANDOM-ACCESS FILE The file that locates the address of the series of records containing the one required. (447)

DIRECT-ACCESS STORAGE DEVICE (DASD) Another name for magnetic disk units. (194)

DIRECT-CUTOVER CONVERSION Also known as crash conversion, it refers to implementing the new system all at once and dropping the old system at the same time. (429)

DISK OR DISKETTE See Floppy disk.

DISK CARTRIDGE One or two hard disks can be placed into a permanently sealed disk cartridge. (195)

DISK PACK A number of disk platters can be stacked vertically into a disk pack. (195)

DISPLAY TERMINAL OR DISPLAY SCREEN Also known as a CRT (Cathode Ray Tube) or video screen, this peripheral has a television-like screen. It can also have considerable memory depending upon whether it is a "smart" or "dumb" terminal. (50, 164)

DISTRIBUTED DATA-PROCESSING System that shares computing power among several different computers through teleprocessing links into a network. (116, 217)

DML See Data manipulation language.

DOCUMENTATION Materials that explain to users how to use the program, operators how to run it, and programmers how to change it. (255)

DOT-MATRIX PRINTER A common type of character printer that uses tiny pins in a cluster to print a letter, number, or symbol. (175)

DOUNTIL LOOP The process that continues until a specified condition is met. (281)

DOWHILE LOOP The process that continues as long as a condition is true. (281)

DRUM PRINTER A character line printer that uses a rotating cylinder. (178)

DSS See Decision support system.

DUAL PROCESSING Using redundant equipment in case of equipment failures which would jeopardize important projects. (481)

DUMB TERMINAL Display terminal with no information-processing capabilities. (165)

DUMP Debugging technique that prints the storage contents of the central processing unit so the programmer can see where data were actually stored. (289)

DUPLEX TRANSMISSION See Full-duplex transmission.

EARLY PROGRAMMING APPROACH The strategy that stresses getting the initial program for the user done as quickly as possible. (254)

EAVESDROPPING Illegal interception of data being sent via a telecommunications link. (476)

EBCDIC (EXTENDED BINARY CODED DECIMAL INTERCHANGE CODE) Assignment of a bit pattern to each of the decimal numbers 0 through 9, lowercase and uppercase alphabet, and commonly used special symbols. (140)

EDSAC (ELECTRONIC DELAY STORAGE AUTOMATIC COMPUTER) The prototype for today's computers, it uses the stored program concept. (104)

EDUCATION PRIVACY ACT (1974) Protects the privacy of students concerning grades and other types of evaluation data maintained by schools. (488)

"EGOLESS" PROGRAMMING TEAM The most recent approach consists of a closely knit group of people of equal rank who make decisions in a democratic fashion that avoids personal conflict. (257)

ELECTROMECHANICAL ACCOUNTING MACHINE (EAM) This machine used electrical impulses to activate mechanical elements and used punch card technology to process data. (101)

ELECTRONIC BULLETIN BOARD Computer-maintained list of messages that can be posted and read by different computers. (212, 341)

ELECTRONIC COMPUTER Uses only electrical switches and circuitry to carry out processing or computing functions instead of mechanical relays like the Mark I. (102)

ELECTRONIC MAIL See Electronic Mail/Message System.

ELECTRONIC MAIL/MESSAGE SYSTEM (EMMS) Allows people to send memos, messages, facsimiles, illustrations, and so on by electronic means within an office, between branch locations, or across the world. (74, 339)

ELECTRONIC MOUSE Palm-sized device that is rolled across a flat surface with the hand in order to move a pointer or input graphical data. (164)

ELECTRONIC SPREADSHEET A type of software that offers the user a simulated financial worksheet printed with rows and columns on a display screen and an easy way to change figures around within the worksheet. (336)

EMMS See electronic mail/message system.

ENCRYPTION Coding or scrambling of data, messages, or programs in order to foil eavesdroppers. (477)

END-OF-FILE (EOF) FLAG A test value used to mark the end of a program loop. (287)

ENIAC (ELECTRONIC NUMERICAL INTEGRATOR AND CALCULATOR) Built between 1943 and 1946 by John W. Mauchley and J. Presper Eckert, it was used for calculating ballistics tables for the U.S. Army. (102)

ENVIRONMENT The external factors that affect the system. (33)

EPROM (ERASABLE PROGRAMMABLE READ-ONLY MEMORY) PROMs that may be reprogrammed by the user. (149)

ERASABLE PROGRAMMABLE READ-ONLY MEMORY See EPROM.

EXCEPTION PROCEDURES Rules and procedures used when standard operating procedures do not cover a particular situation. (39, 473)

EXCEPTION REPORT A scheduled or special report that highlights significant changes from whatever conditions are usual. (390)

EXECUTION CYCLE The performance of one computer operation. (137)

EXPERT SYSTEM Decision-support-system-based research into artificial intelligence that mimics a human "expert" in a particular field such as medicine. (397)

EXTERNAL STORAGE See Secondary storage.

FAIR CREDIT REPORTING ACT (1970) A law that gives individuals the right to examine credit records maintained about them by private organizations. (488)

FEASIBILITY REPORT The complete findings of the systems analyst's detailed investigation. (419)

FEEDBACK This process allows a system to regulate itself by treating the effect of its output on the environment as new input. (34)

FIBER-OPTIC CABLE Communications medium that uses ultrathin glass filaments that can transmit data with light-beam signals generated by lasers at faster speeds than ordinary cables. (115, 224)

FIELD A single data element such as name, age, or social security number that is treated as a unit. (40, 441)

FIFTH-GENERATION COMPUTER Newest technology in computers now being developed both in the United States and Japan. (569)

FILE A set of related fields such as all the fields for a single customer's travel reservations. (40, 441)

FILE DESIGN Method used by a file to store and retrieve data. Three main types of file design are: sequential, indexed sequential, and direct-access. (442)

FILE-HANDLING ABILITY The facility with which a language can manipulate large input and output data files. (307)

FINANCE The acqustion and use of funds. (69)

FINANCE PACKAGES Prewritten software for forecasting, credit checking, or modeling the outcomes of various investment decisions. (346)

FINANCIAL ANALYSIS Examining and attempting to predict the best way to obtain funds for long- and short-term needs. (69)

FIRMWARE Programs permanently recorded on integrated circuits—a blend of hardware and software. (118, 149)

FIRST-GENERATION COMPUTERS Considerably faster than earlier electro-mechanical devices, these machines used vacuum tubes for internal processing. (104)

FIXED-LENGTH WORDS Words that contain a specific number of bytes. (143)

FLEXIBLE MANUFACTURING SYSTEM (FMS) A system that uses computer-directed machinery throughout the production process. (80)

FLOPPY DISK OR DISKETTE A flexible plastic disk commonly used for storage on all types of computers. Disks come in diameters of 3½", 5¼", and 8". (52, 195)

FLOWCHART Diagram that uses special symbols to aid in communicating the steps needed in writing a program. (42, 259, 274)

FLOWCHART TEMPLATE Plastic guide for drawing flowchart symbols. (274)

FLOWLINES Lines and arrows on a flowchart that link the symbols and help the reader follow the information flow. (274)

FMS See Flexible Manufacturing System.

FORMATTING Organizing of data on a disk surface. The number of bytes that can be stored on a disk depends on its format. (198)

FORTRAN Short for FORmula TRANslator, a high-level scientifi-cally oriented programming language developed at IBM by John Backus and introduced in 1957. (110, 315)

FOURTH-GENERATION COMPUTER This computer is distinguished from the third-generation model by the development of the microprocessor. (113)

FREEDOM OF INFORMATION ACT (1970) A law that gives individuals, as well as organizations, the right to inspect data concerning them that are maintained by agencies of the federal government. (488)

FRONT-END PROCESSOR A minicomputer communications device that oversees input and output operations for a host computer. (233)

FULL-DUPLEX OR DUPLEX TRANSMISSION Simultaneous, bidirectional transmissions. (225)

GANTT CHART A helpful planning tool that shows how various steps of a project relate to one another over time. (430)

GATE An electronic switch used for mathematical or logic operation with several entrances but only one exit. (135)

GENERAL LEDGER Summary of all the accounts in business, used to prepare financial statements and income statements. (67)

GENERAL-PURPOSE COMPUTER The most common digital computer can be used for a variety of large and small business, engineering, and scientific applications. (131)

GRAPHICS PACKAGE Software that allows you to construct and output pictorial information onto display screens, plotters, printers, or transparencies. (342)

GRAPHICS TABLET OR DIGITIZER Electrically wired surfaces upon which a user can draw diagrams for entry as data. (164)

HALF-DUPLEX TRANSMISSION Transmission in one direction at a time, as found, for example, in telegraphs and two-way radios. (225)

HARD COPY Computer printout, usually on paper, but also in the form of punched cards, microfiche, labels, forms, or reprographics machine output. (50)

HARD DISKS OR RIGID DISKS Rigid or metal disks that are part of a peripheral storage device. (50, 194)

HARDWARE Physical equipment used in an information system. (46)

HASHING A technique that transforms a key into an actual address. (448)

HEXADECIMAL NUMBER SYSTEM Base 16 number system. (138, B-7)

HIERARCHICAL DATABASE The arrangement of data elements to one another as "parents" and "children," following a treelike structure. (456)

HIERARCHICAL NETWORK This structure has a main computer at its top with communication links spread downward and outward with the main computer in command. (219)

HIERARCHY PLUS INPUT, PROCESS, OUTPUT (HIPO) A technique of structured programming methods that follows a top-down approach. (257)

HIGH-LEVEL LANGUAGES Computer languages that use English-like statements and mathematical symbols and include: BASIC, Pascal, COBOL, and FORTRAN to name a few. (303)

HIGH-SPEED PRINTER This printer usually is laser-xerographic and can produce a page of output at one time. (179)

HIPO See Hierarchy plus Input, Process, Output.

HOLLERITH, HERMAN (1860-1929) Statistician who developed a tabulating machine using a punch card system. (99)

HOME MANAGEMENT SOFTWARE Prewritten software to help perform convenience-oriented services such as checkbook balancing, recipe recall, and shopping-list generation. (350)

HOPPER, GRACE A major designer of COBOL and considered by many to be the world's second computer programmer (after Lady Ada, Countess of Lovelace.) (110)

HOST LANGUAGE The computer language in which the programmer writes his application program. (455)

HOST PROCESSOR The computer to which the local user hardware is connected and which does the actual processing. (215)

HYBRID COMPUTER   A computer that combines features of both digital and analog computers and is used in a small number of engineering and scientific applications. (130)

IBM 701   Introduced in 1953, it was IBM's first commercial computer. (107)

IBM 650   Produced in 1954, this computer established IBM's dominance in the computer industry. (107)

IBM 360   Most significant computer of third-generation computers, it could serve both scientific and business users. (112)

IC   See Integrated circuit.

ICONS   Pictorial representations of an operation the computer can carry out. (166)

IFTHENELSE   See Selection.

IMPACT PRINTER   Peripheral that physically contacts the paper in order to print output. (175)

INDEXED SEQUENTIAL FILE   Files arranged in a predetermined order but with a separate index file for finding records without reading each in sequence. (443)

INFORMATION   Knowledge communicated in a timely, accurate, and understandable fashion. (10)

INFORMATION RESOURCE MANAGEMENT SYSTEM (IRMS)   This information system coordinates its elements to optimize the flow and use of information as efficiently as possible. (399)

INFORMATION SYSTEM   Timely, accurate, understandable, and relevant information compiled for users. May also be called a data-processing, business-computer, electronic data-processing, or information-processing system. Its five elements are: people, rules and procedures, data, software, and hardware. (11, 35)

INFORMATION SYSTEM CONTROLS   Features that serve to monitor and ensure the proper operation of all five information system elements. (468)

INFORMATION SYSTEM STAFF   The personnel who support the users with assistance in developing and maintaining the system. (36)

INFORMATION SYSTEMS PROGRAM   A business-oriented program of study that might also be known as data processing, business data processing, management information systems, or information resource management. (536)

INITIALIZATION   Setting a counter to a certain value before a program enters a loop. (287)

INK-JET PRINTER   Nonimpact printer that uses electrically charged ink droplets sprayed between two electrically charged plates. (179)

INPUT   The entering of data (from the environment) into an information system (15, 33, 160)

INPUT DEVICE   Hardware that transmits data and software to the CPU for processing. (48)

INPUT/OUTPUT BOUND   Software or programs that strain an information system because of very large input and output requirements. (305)

INPUT/OUTPUT MANAGER   A system program that supervises the transfer of data from input devices to main memory, and from main memory to output devices. (363)

INPUT/OUTPUT SYMBOL   A parallelogram representing any input and output operation. (278)

INPUT STORAGE   Part of main memory that holds data that have been read from an input device. (134)

INSTITUTE FOR CERTIFICATION OF COMPUTER PROFESSIONALS (ICCP)   An umbrella organization responsible for testing the competence of computer professionals in three major areas: the Certificate in Data Processing (CDP); the Certificate in Computer Programming (CCP); and the Certified System Professional (CSP). (547)

INSTRUCTION CYCLE   Time in which the CPU fetches an instruction, selects an op code, and interprets the operand. (137)

INTEGRATED CIRCUIT (IC)   Combining transistors and circuitry into one unit etched onto a silicon chip heralded the third generation of computers. (111)

INTEGRATED SOFTWARE PACKAGES   Prewritten software that contains features such as electronic spreadsheets, database management, and graphics. (343)

INTELLIGENT TERMINAL OR SMART TERMINAL   A display terminal which can perform some processing on its own. (165)

INTERACTIVE PROCESSING   A process whereby the user can make requests to the computer and receive responses as though sharing a dialogue. (307, 365)

INTERACTIVE PROGRAMMING LANGUAGES   Languages that can be written with the computer helping the programmer; BASIC and APL are among them. (308)

INTERBLOCK GAP   Space between "blocks" of records on a magnetic tape allowing the tape to reach operational speed. (201)

INTERPRETER   Language translator that translates an object program one line at a time. (371)

INTERRECORD GAP   Space left between each pair of records on a magnetic tape allowing the tape to reach operational speed. (201)

INTERVIEW   Meeting with a personnel office employee who asks you some preliminary questions and who may send you on to the person or persons who may want to hire you. (542) See also Technical Interview.

INVENTORY MANAGEMENT SYSTEMS   A means of minimizing the cost of ordering and stocking items sold by a company. (68)

IRMS   See Information Resource Management System.

JACQUARD, JOSEPH-MARIE (1752-1834)   Inventor of the Jaquard loom. (97)

JACQUARD LOOM   A machine that used punch cards to weave certain patterns. Forms of this machine are still in use today. Most important, it developed the means of controlling a machine by a variable program. (97)

JOB   An application program and its data. (359)

JOB ACCOUNTING Determining the exact use of resources for a job. (361)

JOB CONTROL LANGUAGE (JCL) The language in which the job control program is written. (360)

JOB CONTROL PROGRAM Part of the operating system that prepares an application program and its data (a job) to be run. (359)

JOB DISPLACEMENT When the skills necessary to perform a job change, this phenomenon results. (558)

JOB ENHANCEMENT Making a job easier and more enjoyable. (558)

JOB PRIORITY Ranking of the relative importance of application programs in a multiuser environment so that programs that run quickly are usually given the highest priority. (361)

JOB REPLACEMENT Occurs when a job held by a person is taken over by a robot or machine programmed to perform the same task. (558)

JOSEPHSON JUNCTIONS Named after Brian Josephson, these circuits use supercooled temperatures and offer extremely fast memory access. (151, 568)

JUNIOR PROGRAMMER Employees used in larger projects to perform the most routine programming tasks. (255)

K (KILO) Storage capacity of 2^{10} or 1024 bits on a chip or 1024 bytes in memory. (148)

KEMENY, JOHN G., AND THOMAS KURTZ Codevelopers of the programming language BASIC. (113)

KEY A field that orders a sequential file and that uniquely identifies a record. (442)

KEYBOARD Typewriter-like sets of keys in tiers used for inputting numeric and alphabetic data. (48, 164)

LAN See Local Area Network.

LANGUAGE TRANSLATORS System software that translates high-level languages or assembly language into machine language. (371)

LARGE-SCALE INTEGRATION (LSI) Process of putting many integrated circuits (ICs) onto a single silicon chip. (113)

LASER-XEROGRAPHIC PRINTER Nonimpact printer that can print an entire page of output of high quality at a very high speed. (179)

LIBRARY PROGRAM Prewritten software usually stored on a direct-access device in object-program form so that translation is not necessary in order to run it. (374)

LIGHT PEN Pencil-like light-sensitive rod that can be pointed at a display screen to perform functions or draw diagrams. (164)

LINE PRINTER Peripheral that prints an entire line at once. (175)

LISP A list-processing language the most important application of which is in the development of artificial intelligence programs. (322)

LIST-PROCESSING LANGUAGE A very-high-level language that processes data in the form of lists. (321)

LOAD PROGRAM The combined object programs the computer actually processes. (371)

LOCAL AREA NETWORK (LAN) Also known as local network, it provides offices with the capability of teleprocessing in a smaller setting. (236)

LOCAL USER HARDWARE One or more peripheral devices (even a computer), having a telecommunications link to the host computer. (215)

LOGICAL DESIGN Determining the logical or conceptual model of input, processing, output, and feedback requirements for the new system. (422)

LOGIC CHECK The fourth and final step in debugging determines if the program produces reasonable results. (291)

LOGIC GATE One of the main components of the ALU, it performs comparisons. (135)

LOGO A very-high-level language derived from LISP during the 1960s and used extensively in schools. (322)

LOOP Process whereby the program repetitively executes one or a series of steps. Two major types of loops are DOWHILE and DOUNTIL. (281)

LOVELACE, LADY ADA AUGUSTA, THE COUNTESS OF (1816-1852) A brilliant mathematician who worked with Charles Babbage on the analytic engine's machine instructions, thus becoming the world's first programmer. (98)

LOW-LEVEL LANGUAGE A language in which each instruction corresponds to an instruction for a particular computer. (302)

LSI See Large-Scale Integration.

MACHINE CYCLE The time required to carry out one operation inside the computer. (137)

MACHINE INDEPENDENCE The ability of a program written to run using one particular make and model of computer to be run on another. (307)

MACHINE LANGUAGE The only language a computer understands and which consists of 1s and 0s. (108, 308)

MACRO INSTRUCTIONS Instructions used in assembly languages to generate several machine-language instructions from a single assembly-language instruction. (310)

MAGNETIC CORE MEMORY Used by second-generation computers, these magnetized "doughnuts" held data in main memory. (108)

MAGNETIC DISK An input, output, and secondary storage medium from the third generation still used today. (112, 192)

MAGNETIC DISK UNIT Peripheral device that can send, receive, and store data at high rates of speed and is sometimes called a direct-access storage device. (50, 194)

MAGNETIC DRUMS Large spinning cylinders with programs and data recorded on them, used by most first-generation computers as main memory media. (105)

MAGNETIC-INK CHARACTER RECOGNITION (MICR) A system of letters, numbers, and symbols imprinted with a special iron-oxide ink used primarily in banking. (171)

MAGNETIC-STRIP CARTRIDGE SYSTEM Also known as data cell, one of the most common types of mass storage. (203)

MAGNETIC TAPE Media that provide rapid, high-capacity secondary storage. (105, 199)

MAGNETIC TAPE CASSETTES Secondary storage devices sometimes used on microcomputers instead of disks. (200)

MAGNETIC TAPE UNIT Also known as a tape drive, this peripheral device can send, receive, and store large amounts of data at high rates of speed. (50, 200)

MAINFRAME COMPUTER A large computer used by business, government, science, engineering, and education in a variety of applications. (22, 152)

MAIN MEMORY OR PRIMARY STORAGE Part of the computer that stores data and instructions that have been input and are waiting to be processed, and stores the results of processing until they are released to output devices or to secondary storage. (48, 133)

MAIN PROGRAM Overall program that directs subroutines. (261)

MANAGEMENT INFORMATION SYSTEM (MIS) An information system that processes the transactions of an organization's day-to-day operations, and creates information in the form of reports that support a manager's tasks of planning, organizing, directing, and controlling. (390)

MANAGEMENT-ORIENTED PREWRITTEN SOFTWARE Programs for the areas of personnel management, operations management, forecasting, facilities maintenance, and resource management. (345)

MARKET ANALYSIS Examination of such issues as sales strategies, market share of competitors, and sales-call strategies. (69)

MARKETING Promotion of goods and services in order to move them from producer to consumer. (69)

MARK I Also known as Automatic Sequence Controlled Calculator, it was an electromechanical computer. (101)

MASQUERADING Unauthorized users passing themselves off as authorized users. (481)

MASS STORAGE Magnetic strip cartridges or data cells, multiple-disk-drive-systems, optical disk systems, and videotape systems on which

enormous quantities of data can be stored. (203)

MATERIALS MANAGEMENT The control of manufacturing inventories. (347)

MATHEMATICAL COMPUTING ABILITY The strengths of a language in expressing calculations and carrying them out efficiently. (307)

MATHEMATICAL GATE One of the three main components of the Arithmetic/Logic Unit, it performs basic calculations. (135)

MAUCHLY, JOHN W., AND J. PRESPER ECKERT Codevelopers of ENIAC. (102)

MEMORY MANAGER Part of the operating system that keeps track of a program's location. (369)

MENU A listing of choices within prewritten software from which to select an operation. (332)

MESSAGE SWITCHER A telecommunications device that helps route messages from many incoming telecommunications media into the front-end processor. (233)

MICROCOMPUTER Smallest type of computer and usually has its CPU upon a single chip. (20, 152)

MICROFICHE Method of storing highly reduced photographs of documents or computer printout on a flat card which may then be viewed on a microfiche machine. (182)

MICROFILM Method of storing highly reduced photographs of documents on reels that can be viewed on a microfilm machine. (182)

MICROLASERS Possible future optical substitute for electronic circuitry in computers. (568)

MICROPROCESSOR A single silicon chip containing the control and arithmetic/logic unit of the computer. First produced commercially by Texas Instruments Corporation in 1971, it paved the way for the development of the microcomputer. (113, 146)

MICROSECONDS Millionths of a second and the speed at which second-generation computers could perform

arithmetic and logical operations. (108)

MICROWAVE SYSTEM A communications medium that uses high-frequency electromagnetic waves to send messages through space to microwave receiving stations. (224)

MILLISECONDS Thousandths of a second—the speed at which first-generation computers could make calculations. (104)

MINICOMPUTER This type is larger, faster, and has more memory capacity than the typical microcomputer. It is frequently used to support scientific and engineering tasks. (20, 152)

MIS See Management Information System.

MIXED NETWORK Also known as an unconstrained network, it uses a combination of the four approaches: star, hierarchical, ring, and multiply-connected. (222)

MNEMONICS Symbolic codes in assembly language that people can remember, for example, as SUB for subtraction. (310)

MODEM Communications hardware that performs the task of modulation and demodulation. (228)

MODULATION Process of converting digital signals by means of a modem into a form that can be carried over analog lines. (226)

MODULE Technique of the structured approach that divides the system or the program into smaller "pieces" that make it easier to understand and maintain. (251, 409)

MS/DOS (MICROSOFT®®/DISC OPERATING SYSTEM) An operating system used for microcomputers. (376)

MULTIDROP LINE A line that links multiple devices on a shared telecommunications line. (231)

MULTIPLE-DISK-DRIVE SYSTEM Type of mass storage that teams up magnetic disk units and is used for large-scale real-time applications such as travel reservation systems and credit card validation systems. (204)

MULTIPLEXERS Sometimes spelled multiplexors, these allow multiple users to share a common telecommunications medium. (232)

MULTIPLY-CONNECTED NETWORK   Computers linked along two or more possible paths. (221)

MULTIPROCESSING   Two or more central processing units executing instructions at the same time from the same or different programs. (368)

MULTIPROGRAMMING   Concurrent execution of more than one program at a time with the program manager directing the CPU. (368)

NANOSECONDS   Billionths of a second and the speed at which third-generation computers can operate. (111)

NARROWBAND OR SUB-VOICE GRADE MEDIUM   This communications medium transmits to and from low-speed data terminals such as teletypewriter and telegraph systems. (224)

NATURAL LANGUAGE   Our speaking languages such as Chinese, English, or Greek. (322)

NETWORK   Group of computers of different sizes linked together with communications devices for teleprocessing. (52, 212)

NETWORK DATABASE   A database similar to a hierarchical database but one in which each "child" can have more than one "parent." (456)

NIBBLE OR NYBBLE   Half of a byte—usually 4 bits. (139)

NONDESTRUCTIVE READ   The ability to look at or copy the data in a storage address without destroying them. (135)

NONIMPACT PRINTER   A peripheral that does not contact the paper in order to print. Thermal, ink-jet, and laser-xerographic are three main nonimpact types of printers. (179)

NUCLEAR MAGNETIC RESONANCE (NMR) Similar to the computerized axial tomography (CAT), this used vibrations emitted by atomic nuclei instead of x-rays. (173)

NUMERIC FIELD   A field that contains only numbers such as an employee number. (441)

OBJECT PROGRAM   What the source program becomes after the compiling step. (371)

OCTAL NUMBER SYSTEM   Base 8 number system. (138, B-7)

OFFLINE STORAGE   Storage not under the direct control of the CPU. (52, 192)

OFF-THE-SHELF PROGRAMS   See Prewritten software.

ONLINE STORAGE   Storage by which the computer can directly access data and software. (52, 192)

OP CODE   See Operation code.

OPERAND   Machine instructions that tell the address of the data that are to be operated on. (133)

OPERATING SYSTEM   A type of system software that supervises and directs all of the other software components plus the computer hardware. The main components of the operating system include the job control program, input/output manager, program manager, and memory manager. (41, 358)

OPERATION CODE OR OP CODE   Machine instructions that tell the computer which operation to perform. (133)

OPERATOR-ORIENTED DOCUMENTATION Paperwork usually consisting of a run manual which describes how to run the program and which peripherals should be online, and so on. (292)

OPTICAL CHARACTER READER   This peripheral can detect printed letters and numbers as well as marks. (170)

OPTICAL DISK SYSTEM   Type of archival mass storage also known as a laser disk system with about 20 times the capacity of a magnetic disk. (204)

OPTICAL MARK READER (OMR)   This peripheral senses marks on special paper forms and converts the marks into binary code. (169)

OPTICAL SCANNER   This peripheral usually uses a laser beam to read product codes or bar codes. (50, 169)

ORDER CHECK   First step in debugging process determines if problem-solving steps are arranged in the right sequence. (289)

ORDER PROCESSING   Entering, processing, and monitoring sales orders in a system. (69)

OUTPUT   The physical form of information in a readable form: permanent copy on paper, temporary form as on a display terminal, or permanent machine-readable storage (magnetic disk or magnetic tape). (18, 34, 160)

OUTPUT DEVICE   Hardware that can produce information in a form that people can read, or it can record it in machine-readable form for secondary storage. (48)

OUTPUT STORAGE   Like input storage, this is also a buffer which transmits information to output devices at a slower speed. (134)

OVERVIEW HIPO DIAGRAM   The general input, process, and output requirements for each programming module. (257)

PACKAGED SOFTWARE   See Prewritten software.

PACKET-SWITCHING   This protocol is used in multiply-connected networks and allows the most efficient use of the network. (230)

PAGING   A virtual storage technique used by the memory manager that chops programs into fixed-length sections. (370)

PAPER TAPE   Along with punch cards, it was the earliest media for input, output, and storage of data. (104)

PARALLEL ARITHMETIC   Performing calculations on all digits of a number (or computer word) simultaneously. (143)

PARALLEL CONVERSION   Implementation of the new system while running the old system side by side over a period of time. (429)

PARENT   A data element in an hierarchical database that is above the "child" and connected to it. (456)

PARITY BIT OR CHECK BIT   A protective measure to spot cases of garbled bytes. (142, 475)

PASCAL   A high-level programming language developed by Niklaus Wirth and named after the French inventor and mathematician Blaise

Pascal. It is a programming language that requires the use of structured programming techniques and is useful in all four application areas. (117, 311)

PASCAL, BLAISE (1623–1662) French mathematician who invented the mechanical calculator, the Pascaline. (96)

PASCALINE The first mechanical calculator, invented by Blaise Pascal, it could add and subtract. (96)

PASSWORD Individual codes assigned or made up by the user to help prevent illegal entry into the information system. (360)

PAYROLL System that keeps track of employee wages, deductions, and benefits, and issues paychecks. (68)

PERIPHERAL EQUIPMENT Input, output, and storage devices. (11)

PERIPHERAL INTERCHANGE PROGRAM Type of utility program that moves data from one peripheral device to another. (374)

PERSONNEL The business operation concerned with recruiting and developing human resources. (70)

PHASED CONVERSION Gradually implementing the new system in stages over a period of time. (430)

PHYSICAL DESIGN Determining the type of operating system plus all the hardware and software requirements of a system. (423)

PHYSICAL SECURITY Protection of the hardware and storage media from theft, vandalism, and misuse. (479)

PICOSECONDS Trillionths of a second and the speed at which some of today's fastest computers can be measured. (115)

PILOT CONVERSION Implementing the new system in its entirety but only to a small part of the organization. (430)

PL/1 (PROGRAMMING LANGUAGE 1) A high-level language developed by Bruce Rosenblatt and George Radin at IBM Corporation to combine the best features of COBOL and FORTRAN. (319)

PLOTTER A peripheral that can output computer graphics. (180)

POINT-OF-ACTIVITY (POA) TERMINAL Input units located where a specific activity occurs, to capture data at their source. (168)

POINT-OF-SALE (POS) TERMINAL Usually combines a cash register with a computer terminal linked to an information system. (88, 169)

POLLING Type of protocols in which the computer checks each device periodically to see if it has a message to send. (230)

PORTFOLIO Collection of good things you have done such as programs, flowcharts, other diagrams, or documentation (if short) for showing a prospective employer. (542)

PREDEFINED FUNCTION SYMBOL A prewritten subprogram or subroutine which is called upon request. (278)

PREDICTIVE REPORT Report that attempts to identify future trends but does not show much detail. (390)

PRELIMINARY INVESTIGATION The first step in systems analysis includes evaluating the user's request, determining costs and benefits, and planning the detailed analysis. (410)

PRELIMINARY REPORT Report prepared by the systems analyst for the client when he completes the preliminary investigation. (412)

PREPARATION SYMBOL A symbol that denotes any steps that involve preliminary or preparatory function such as initializing a variable. (278)

PREWRITTEN SOFTWARE Programs written and tested by someone else and ready to run, also known as canned programs, packaged software, and off-the-shelf programs. (330)

PRIMARY KEY The first key used in a sequential file when a file requires a secondary key. (442)

PRIMARY STORAGE See Main memory.

PRINTER Peripheral device that produces hard or permanent copy. (50)

PRIVACY The protection of individuals and organizations from unauthorized access to or abuse of data concerning them. (468)

PRIVACY ACT (1974) A law that offers protection to individuals and organizations from data-gathering abuses by the federal government. (489)

PROBLEM DEFINITION Focusing on the problem to identify exactly what it is and how best to solve it. (248)

PROBLEM RECOGNITION The first and most important step of the system development process. (55, 248, 409)

PROCESS BOUND A condition in the processing part of the information system created by complex mathematical algorithms in the software or programs overloading the computer. (305)

PROCESS PROGRAM A type of system software subordinate to the operating system that performs specific functions such as translating an application program into machine language. (358)

PROCESSING The stage in which data are transformed into information. (15, 34)

PROCESSING MODULE The lowest level of modules in structured program design which enact the orders required by the higher modules. (259)

PROCESS SYMBOL Flowchart symbol that represents mathematical computations and data manipulation. (278)

PRODUCTION AND OPERATIONS MANAGEMENT Process of organizing people and machinery for converting resources into finished products and services. (78)

PROGRAM See Software.

PROGRAM CODING Translating the program design into a programming language that will run on the computer. (249)

PROGRAM DESIGN Specifying the structure of the program in detail. (248, 423)

PROGRAM DEVELOPMENT CYCLE Eight steps required to solve a programming problem—recognition, definition, design, coding, testing, implementation, maintenance, and then beginning again. (248)

PROGRAM DOCUMENTATION Manuals, display screens, and other materials that tell users how to use the program, operators how to run it, and programmers how to change it. (291)

PROGRAM IMPLEMENTATION The actual using of the new program. (250)

PROGRAM LIBRARY Bank of prewritten algorithms or programming routines. (255)

PROGRAMMABLE READ-ONLY MEMORY See PROM.

PROGRAM MAINTENANCE Correcting any previously undetected errors and making any other needed changes. (250)

PROGRAM MANAGER Part of the operating system that handles the movement of programs (or parts of programs) into main memory so that the computer can execute the program instructions. (363)

PROGRAMMER Person who writes programs or software. (98)

PROGRAMMER-ORIENTED DOCUMENTA-TION Paperwork that focuses on how to maintain and modify the program. (294)

PROGRAMMING Process of creating programs or software. (41, 248)

PROGRAMMING SPECIALIST Person who provides support services to speed and ease a programmer's job. (255)

PROGRAM STORAGE The holding of instructions from both system and application programs which enter the CPU. (134)

PROGRAM TESTING Checking the program for errors and rewriting parts of the program to correct the mistakes. (249)

PROJECT CHARTER Drawn up by the manager of the project and the systems analyst, it outlines the scope of the detailed investigation that is to follow. (412)

PROM (PROGRAMMABLE READ-ONLY MEM-ORY) A chip that can be programmed by the user with commands for later use. (149)

PROTOCOLS Software rules and procedures governing the use of telecommunications media. (229)

PROTOTYPING Refers to a method using small working models of the system to test for flaws. (422)

PSEUDOCODE An English-like code to help the programmer understand the steps needed to execute the program. (259, 274)

PUNCH CARD DEVICES Input and output devices used on the earliest computers and still in use today. (174)

PUNCH CARDS Paper cards that contain data in the form of punched-out holes in designated positions. (97)

QUERY LANGUAGE A way to access the database designed for use by personnel other than programmers. (455)

QUEUEING PROGRAM Part of the operating system that puts the waiting application programs "on hold" until the system can accommodate them. (361)

RAM See Random access memory.

RANDOM-ACCESS FILE See Direct-access file.

RANDOM ACCESS MEMORY (RAM) Memory where accessing a location does not depend upon the last location accessed. (147)

READ ONLY MEMORY (ROM) Chip on which programs have been permanently encoded, sometimes called firmware. (149, 333)

REAL-TIME PROCESSING In real-time processing the computer processes data rapidly enough so that the results can be used to influence a process that is still taking place. (15, 112, 367)

RECALLING The extraction of data from computer storage. (18)

RECORD A set of related fields. (40, 441)

REEL-TO-REEL TAPE One type of secondary storage that records data one byte at a time spreading the bits across the width of the tape. (52, 200)

REGISTER A high-speed temporary storage unit used in several parts of the CPU. (135)

RELATIONAL DATABASE All data items viewed as related to one another, in table form. (459)

RELATIVE ADDRESSING This key uses a field of a record and converts it to an address through an algorithmic process. (448) See also Address.

RPG (REPORT GENERATING LANGUAGE) A very-high-level language developed by the IBM Corporation primarily to service small-business users and primarily a batch-oriented language. (320)

REPROGRAPHICS Computerizing production of graphical and textual output in a variety of media and transmitting it to copiers located elsewhere. (180)

RESOURCE UTILIZATION PROCEDURES Tracking and modifying patterns of an information system's resources and using them in the most effective way. (482)

RESPONSE TIME OR TURNAROUND TIME Amount of time between making an inquiry or request and the start of the response. (191, 365)

RESUME Summary of your educational qualifications and relevant work experience. (540)

RING NETWORK Computers linked in a loop with no central computer in control. (221)

ROBOT A machine capable of coordinating its movements itself by reacting to changes in the environment. (115, 555)

ROBOTICS The study and application of robots. (115, 555)

ROM See Read-only memory.

RULES AND PROCEDURES The written and unwritten guidelines that help govern an organization's operations. (39)

SALES CALL PACKAGE Prewritten software that develops a "psychological profile" of a potential customer and generates a suggested sales approach. (347)

SCHEDULED LISTING The most common type of report created on a regular basis. (390)

SCHEMA A conceptual or logical view of the relationships among the data elements in the database. (454)

SCROLLING The moving of data shown on the screen either forward or backward. (166)

SEARCH TIME Time it takes for the data to spin under the head for writing to or reading from a magnetic disk. (196)

SECONDARY KEY   A supplemental key to distinguish two files that have the same primary key, such as the same last name. (442)

SECONDARY STORAGE, EXTERNAL STORAGE OR AUXILIARY STORAGE   Peripheral device that reads and stores data and programs on a machine-readable medium for later use. (50, 190)

SECOND-GENERATION COMPUTERS   Computers that used transistors instead of vacuum tubes, magnetic cores instead of drums. (108)

SECTORS   Pie-shaped sections of tracks radiating out from the center of the disk. (197)

SECURITY   Steps taken to protect the five elements of the information system. (468)

SEEK TIME   Time required to position the read/write head over the right part of the disk. (196)

SEGMENTATION   A virtual storage technique used by the memory manager in order to reduce transfer time. (370)

SELECTING   Extraction of data with certain characteristics. (18)

SELECTION   Logic patterns that use comparisons based on decisions or choices to split a program into different paths. (279)

SELF-DOCUMENTATION   The extent to which a program can be read and understood by a programmer or supervisor. (307)

SEMICONDUCTOR   Compound that has both conductive and insulative properties such as transistors and integrated circuits. (108)

SENIOR OR BACKUP PROGRAMMER   The employee who carries out assignments under the direction of the chief, or lead, programmer. (255)

SEPARATION OF TASKS   Dividing tasks and responsibilities among a number of different people in the interest of security. (471)

SEQUENCE   Set of linear steps to be carried out in the order of their appearance. (279)

SEQUENTIAL ACCESS   The necessity of reading every record in a file leading up to a desired record. (200, 442)

SEQUENTIAL FILE   Records arranged in a predetermined way and ordered by a field known as a key. (442)

SERIAL ARITHMETIC   The performing of calculations digit by digit rather than on the entire number at once. (143)

SHOCKLEY, WILLIAM, JOHN BARDEEN, AND WALTER H. BRATTAIN   Inventors of the transistor in 1948 at Bell Telephone Laboratories. (108)

SILICON CHIP   A piece of glass etched with integrated circuitry. (111, 144)

SIMPLEX TRANSMISSION   One-way transmission, as found in commercial radio or television. (225)

SIMULATION PROGRAMMING LANGUAGE   A very-high-level language that uses mathematical or logical formulas to model real-world events, and to predict the possible consequences of those events. (321)

SMART TERMINAL   See Intelligent terminal.

SOFT COPY   Temporary information displayed on a terminal. (50)

SOFTWARE OR PROGRAMS   General name for lists of precise instructions written in a language the computer can interpret. (11, 41, 246)

SOFTWARE ENGINEERING   A program-creation method developed over the last decade. (319)

SOFTWARE PIRACY   Unauthorized duplication of software that can be obtained legally only through purchase. (478)

SOFTWARE SECURITY   Attempts to protect programs from misuse or tampering. (477)

SORTING   The act of ordering data into a requested form. (16)

SORT/MERGE PROGRAM   Type of utility program used to rearrange, separate, or collate data into alphabetic or numeric order. (374)

SOURCE DATA AUTOMATION   Refers to the use of machine-readable documents for data entry. (162)

SOURCE DOCUMENT   An original business form such as a sales-order form, time card, or the like. (15)

SOURCE PROGRAM   What a program is called before it goes to the compiler. (371)

SPECIAL-PURPOSE COMPUTER   Digital computer designed for a specific function. (131)

SPEECH RECOGNITION   The ability of an input device to translate the human voice and use it as input media. (173)

STANDARDIZATION OF WORK   Clear definition of tasks so they are performed in approximately the same way each time. (472)

STANDARD OPERATING PROCEDURES (SOP)   Rules and procedures of an organization under normal circumstances. (39)

STAR NETWORK   A central computer connected to remote peripherals or other computers which are not connected to one another. (217)

STORAGE HIERARCHY   Pyramidal view of storage with the fastest and most expensive computer storage at the top of the pyramid and with slower, less expensive, and roomier secondary storage at the bottom. (190)

STORED PROGRAM CONCEPT   Proposed by mathematician John von Neumann, it sped up the time it took to change a program. (103)

STORING   Method of placing data into main memory or secondary storage for later recall. (18)

STRUCTURED PROGRAM   Program that is written using structured program methods and techniques. (251)

STRUCTURED PROGRAMMING   Techniques and methods that produce structured programs by using modular design and discouraging unconditional branches. (251, 308)

STRUCTURED WALKTHROUGH   Review meeting of programming peers to evaluate a programmer's work for errors with no managers present. (257)

SUBROUTINE   A subpart of a program which can be called by another part of a program. (261)

SUBSYSTEMS Systems contained within a larger system. (33)

SUMMARIZING Reducing detailed data into a form that can be more easily understood. (18)

SUPERCOMPUTER Largest and fastest of computers, it executes hundreds of millions of calculations a second. (23, 152)

SUPERSYSTEM System containing two or more smaller systems. (33)

SYNCHRONOUS TRANSMISSION Sending blocks or groups of bytes. (228)

SYNTAX CHECK Third step of debugging process determines if the grammatical style and spelling in the program are correct. (291)

SYSTEM Set of interrelated elements working together to produce a common goal. (11, 408)

SYSTEM DESIGN Stage of systems analysis in which detailed plans or changes are drawn up. (55, 422)

SYSTEM DEVELOPMENT Creation of a new system as drawn up in the system design stage. (55, 426)

SYSTEM DEVELOPMENT PROCESS The method for studying and changing systems. (54, 408)

SYSTEM FLOWCHART Visual representation of the processing effort using symbols that give details of the hardware used for input and output. (416)

SYSTEM IMPLEMENTATION Process of changeover from old to new system including conversion, training, and acceptance testing. (55, 427)

SYSTEM MAINTENANCE Continuing process of keeping a system in good working order. (55, 432)

SYSTEM PROGRAMMER Programmer concerned with the operating system of the computer. (370)

SYSTEMS ANALYSIS A method for examining an existing system in order to determine the cause of the problem. (55, 410)

SYSTEMS ANALYST Person who deals with solving problems in an organization, generally with a computer system. (55)

SYSTEM SOFTWARE Prewritten software that links application software to the computer hardware. (41, 358)

SYSTEM START/TERMINATION SYMBOL Symbol that indicates the beginning or end of a program or a subroutine within a program. (274)

SYSTEM TIMING Any time patterns or cycles that can be discerned concerning the operations under investigation. (419)

SYSTEM VOLUME The number of operations that occur over a given period of time. (418)

TABULATING MACHINE Mechanical device invented by Herman Hollerith in the 1880s that used punch cards. (99)

TAPE DRIVE See Magnetic tape unit.

TECHNICAL INTERVIEW Very specific questions and answers about computing, maybe in the form of a "chat." (542)

TECHNICAL WRITER Person who helps programmers create good documentation of their programs with manuals, easy-to-understand screen displays, and other types of material. (255)

TELECOMMUNICATIONS Transmission of data over distances, usually using a telephone line. (211)

TELECOMMUNICATIONS MEDIUM Also known as communications medium, the physical link by which data are transmitted from one part of the teleprocessing system to another. (223)

TELECOMMUTING An employee works at home through a link between a microcomputer or display terminal and the office. (75, 559)

TELECONFERENCING Using a computer network to link people remotely for a meeting. (75)

TELEPRINTER An early type of terminal still in use, consisting of a keyboard and a printer. (163)

TELEPROCESSING Processing performed by a computer system at a distance from the user. (211)

TERMINAL Input/output device that can send data to, or receive information from, a computer through a telecommunications link. (163)

TEST DESIGN A plan for the tests that the system must pass in order to meet the user's approval. (426)

TEXT-EDITING PROGRAM Part of system software for making changes in application programs, text, and data. (373)

THERMAL PRINTER This nonimpact printer uses treated paper that responds to heat. (179)

THIRD-GENERATION COMPUTER A machine characterized by the use of the integrated circuit and speeding calculations to nanoseconds. (111)

THREE-DIMENSIONAL SCANNER A peripheral that can look at objects in terms of their width, length, and depth. (172)

TIME-SHARING Operating system software that allows many users to share, at the same time, the same computer. (15, 365)

TIME SLICE Tiny amount of computer time during which a computer carries out part of each user's program in turn; it is used by time-sharing systems. (365)

TOKEN PASSING A method used to manage a contention protocol. A token is a set of eight bits (usually 11111111) that permits access to the network and is passed to the next terminal granting each, in turn, access to the network. (230)

TOP-DOWN APPROACH Structured programming method that relates system or programming modules by starting at a general level and proceeding to the details. (251, 409)

TOTAL PROGRAM COST Sum of the cost to write and maintain a program and the cost incurred each time the program is run. (308)

TRACING Debugging technique that uses a special system program to trace the step-by-step flow of your application program. (289)

TRACK Concentric ring of magnetized bits on a hard disk. (197)

TRAILER VALUE A test value placed at the end of a data file used to show when to close a loop. (287)

TRANSISTOR A solid-state semiconductor invented by Shockley, Bardeen, and Brattain in 1948 that replaced the vacuum tube. (108)

TURNAROUND TIME See Response time.

UNIVAC I (UNIVERSAL AUTOMATIC COMPUTER) Available in 1951, it was the first commercially produced computer. (105)

UNIVERSAL PRODUCT CODE (UPC) Data coded as lines (bars) of varying width and found on almost all prepackaged goods. (170)

UNIX An operating system developed by Bell Laboratories that has become popular for many different types of computers. (375)

USERS People who employ the information system for their clients. (36)

USER-FRIENDLY OUTPUT Output which is does not look computerlike, such as a letter or multicolor graphics. (163)

USER-FRIENDLY SOFTWARE Programs that can be used easily, are documented clearly, and describe problems clearly. (320)

USER-ORIENTED DOCUMENTATION Written documents and screen displays that assist the user in exploiting the benefits of the program. (292)

UTILITY PROGRAM Part of system software that performs general-purpose processing for the information system. (373)

VACUUM TUBES Devices used in first-generation computers and considerably faster than electromechanical devices for processing data. (104)

VALIDATION A control either in the computer or an intelligent terminal that checks to see if the data are reasonable. (474)

VALUE-ADDED NETWORK (VAN) Company that leases telecommunications media, databases, and sophisticated computers. (234)

VARIABLE-LENGTH WORD Computer words of varying length. (143)

VERIFICATION Checking data by keying them in a second time. (474)

VERY-HIGH-LEVEL LANGUAGES Computer languages that work very far from the inner workings of the computer and include report generators, simulation languages, and list-processors. (303)

VERY-LARGE-SCALE INTEGRATION (VLSI) Process of placing a great number of IC's on a single silicon chip. (115, 568)

VIDEOTAPE SYSTEM Type of mass storage that uses the videotapes used in home entertainment to record bytes of data. (205)

VIRTUAL STORAGE OR MEMORY Concept of storing programs partly in and partly out of main memory. (370)

VISUAL TABLE OF CONTENTS (VTOC) Shows overall structure of the program and identifies the HIPO diagrams for each module. (257)

VLSI See Very-Large-Scale Integration.

VOICE-GRADE MEDIUM Communications medium that transmits data at a higher speed than narrowband media. (225)

VON NEUMANN, JOHN Mathematician who conceived the stored program concept. (103)

WATSON, THOMAS, SR. The first president of IBM. (102)

WIDEBAND MEDIUM A high volume communications medium that transmits over the widest range of frequencies. (225)

WINDOW The data being worked with that can be seen on the display screen at a given time. (166)

WIRE PAIRS Oldest type of communications medium consists of two copper wires twisted around one another—a telephone line. (233)

WIRTH, NIKLAUS Developer of the Pascal programming language which he named in honor of Blaise Pascal. (118)

WORD PROCESSING SOFTWARE Programs used to create, modify, format, and print text material. (333)

WORD PROCESSING SYSTEM A system that allows people to compose, edit and store text using a computer. (74)

WORKING STORAGE Holds the results of work in progress, such as intermediate answers to mathematical computations the computer is carrying out. (134)

WOZNIAK, STEPHEN, AND STEVEN JOBS Designers of the Apple I, the first commercially successful microcomputer, and founders of Apple Computer Corporation in 1977. (114)

WRITTEN PROCEDURES OR STANDARDS Statements of the proper steps needed to complete a task. (472)

This key contains the answers to the True/False, Multiple Choice, and Fill-In questions from the chapters and the short answers from both appendices. The Instructor's Manual contains the answers to short answer questions, the essay questions, and the programming problems.

CHAPTER 1   True/False: 1. T 2. F 3. F 4. T 5. F 6. F 7. F 8. T 9. F 10. T   **Multiple Choice:** 1. D 2. D 3. B 4. B 5. C   **Fill-In:** 1. information 2. system; common goal 3. program 4. processing; data 5. time-sharing 6. selection; sorting 7. summarizing 8. value; information 9. supercomputer 10. output

CHAPTER 2   True/False: 1. F 2. F 3. T 4. F 5. T 6. F 7. T 8. F 9. F 10. F   **Multiple Choice:** 1. B 2. B 3. C 4. D 5. C 6. C 7. B 8. D 9. D   **Fill-In:** 1. standard; exception 2. information system staff 3. system software 4. Online 5. control; arithmetic/logic; main memory 6. field 7. systems analyst 8. offline 9. people; rules and procedures; data; software; hardware 10. people

CHAPTER 3   True/False: 1. F 2. T 3. F 4. F 5. F 6. T 7. F 8. F 9. F 10. F   **Multiple Choice:** 1. B 2. B 3. B 4. C 5. B   **Fill-In:** 1. production and operations management 2. simulation 3. CAD; CAM; FMS 4. word processing 5. marketing 6. inventory management 7. tele 8. Teleconferencing 9. point-of-sale (POS) 10. electronic mail/message systems (EMMS)

CHAPTER 4   True/False: 1. F 2. F 3. F 4. T 5. F 6. F 7. F 8. F 9. T 10. F   **Multiple Choice:** 1. B 2. B 3. A 4. D 5. D   **Fill-In:** 1. S. Wozniak; S. Jobs 2. FORTRAN; COBOL 3. fourth 4. artificial intelligence 5. third 6. stored program concept 7. BASIC; Kemeny; Kurtz 8. Jacquard 9. abacus 10. Pascal

CHAPTER 5   True/False: 1. F 2. T 3. T 4. F 5. T 6. F 7. F 8. F 9. F   **Multiple Choice:** 1. C 2. C 3. C 4. B 5. C   **Fill-In:** 1. control 2. input; program; working; output 3. read-only memory (ROM) 4. binary 5. analog 6. special-purpose 7. registers 8. general-purpose digital 9. operand

CHAPTER 6   True/False: 1. T 2. F 3. F 4. F 5. F 6. F 7. F 8. F 9. T 10. F   **Multiple Choice:** 1. D 2. A 3. D 4. C 5. C   **Fill-In:** 1. dumb terminal 2. dot-matrix 3. scrolling; windows 4. source data automation 5. character; impact; letter 6. reprographics 7. nonimpact; impact 8. computer-output microfilm 9. CAT; NMR 10. laser-xerographic printer

CHAPTER 7   True/False: 1. F 2. T 3. F 4. F 5. F 6. F 7. F 8. F 9. T 10. F   **Multiple Choice:** 1. C 2. A 3. B 4. D 5. D   **Fill-In:** 1. direct 2. direct access storage device 3. videotape 4. optical disk system 5. access 6. storage hierarchy 7. response 8. formatting 9. sectors 10. seek; search; transfer

CHAPTER 8   True/False: 1. T 2. T 3. T 4. F 5. F 6. F 7. F 8. T 9. T 10. T   **Multiple Choice:** 1. B 2. B 3. C 4. D 5. D   **Fill-In:** 1. modem 2. centralized 3. ring 4. fiber-optic cable; wide 5. Common carriers 6. local area network 7. value added network 8. Synchronous 9. full-duplex or duplex 10. packet switching

CHAPTER 9   True/False: 1. T 2. F 3. T 4. T 5. F 6. T 7. T 8. F 9. F 10. T   **Multiple Choice:** 1. D 2. D 3. C 4. B 5. B   **Fill-In:** 1. main, subroutines. 2. "egoless" 3. structured walkthroughs 4. program coding 5. software or programs 6. program maintenance 7. structured programming 8. chief programmer 9. flowcharts; pseudocode 10. top-down

CHAPTER 10   True/False: 1. F 2. T 3. F 4. F 5. T 6. T 7. F 8. F 9. F   **Multiple Choice:** 1. B 2. D 3. B 4. D 5. B   **Fill-In:** 1. false 2. faster 3. counter; trailer values; end-of-file flags 4. dump 5. ☐   6. logic 7. unconditional branch or GOTO 8. two 9. ENDDO 10. trace

CHAPTER 11   True/False: 1. T 2. F 3. F 4. T 5. F 6. F 7. F 8. T 9. T 10. T   **Multiple Choice:** 1. D 2. B 3. D 4. D 5. C   **Fill-In:** 1. simulation 2. Ada 3. APL 4. input/output bound 5. process bound 6. self-documentation 7. op code or operation code 8. assembly 9. CONFIGURATION

CHAPTER 12   True/False: 1. F 2. T 3. F 4. F 5. T 6. F 7. F 8. F 9. F 10. F   **Multiple Choice:** 1. D 2. D 3. C 4. A 5. A   **Fill-In:** 1. less 2. menu 3. modular 4. data definition; data manipulation; data inquiry 5. electronic mail/message systems (EMMS) 6. dedicated word processors 7. piracy 8. updates

CHAPTER 13   True/False: 1. F 2. F 3. T 4. T 5. F 6. T 7. F 8. F 9. T 10. F   **Multiple Choice:** 1. C 2. B 3. A 4. B 5. A   **Fill-In:** 1. system software 2. account programs; passwords 3. assemblers 4. diagnostic 5. source; object 6. channel 7. multiprocessing 8. multiprogramming 9. utility program 10. UNIX

CHAPTER 14   True/False: 1. T 2. F 3. F 4. F 5. F 6. T 7. F 8. T 9. F 10. F   **Multiple Choice:** 1. D 2. D 3. D 4. D 5. A   **Fill-In:** 1. scheduled listings 2. define the problem and the decision criteria 3. evaluate feedback 4. manager 5. organizing 6. information resource management system (IRMS) 7. decision support system (DSS) 8. top-level 9. exception 10. operational

CHAPTER 15   True/False: 1. F 2. F 3. T 4. F 5. T 6. T 7. T 8. T 9. F 10. F   **Multiple Choice:** 1. D 2. C 3. A 4. A 5. B   **Fill-In:** 1. parallel 2. problem recognition 3. data flow diagram 4. test 5. Gantt 6. decision-logic tables 7. output 8. maintenance 9. system flowchart 10. pilot

CHAPTER 16   True/False: 1. T 2. F 3. T 4. T 5. F 6. T 7. F 8. F 9. T 10. F   **Multiple Choice:** 1. C 2. C 3. A 4. C 5. A   **Fill-In:** 1. schema 2. database management system (DBMS) 3. query 4. parent; child 5. field 6. relational database 7. sequential 8. network database 9. File design 10. data dictionary

CHAPTER 17   True/False: 1. T 2. F 3. F 4. F 5. F 6. T 7. T 8. F 9. T 10. F   **Multiple Choice:** 1. B 2. D 3. B 4. C 5. D   **Fill-In:** 1. audit trail 2. auditing through 3. written procedures or standards 4. check digit 5. data controls 6. Resource utilization 7. eavesdropping 8. data integrity 9. right to privacy 10. encryption

CHAPTER 18   True/False: 1. F 2. F 3. F 4. T 5. F 6. T 7. T 8. F 9. F 10. F   **Multiple Choice:** 1. D 2. D 3. A 4. B 5. A   **Fill-In:** 1. tutorial program 2. documentation 3. peripherals 4. read-only memory (ROM) 5. consultant 6. warranty 7. back-up your files 8. input devices 9. communications unit or peripheral 10. classes

CHAPTER 19   True/False: 1. F 2. T 3. F 4. F 5. F 6. T 7. T 8. T 9. F 10. T   **Multiple Choice:** 1. D 2. A 3. D 4. B 5. D   **Fill-In:** 1. systems analyst **2.** Association for Computing Machinery (ACM) **3.** word processing **4.** programmer **5.** system programmer **6.** Experience **7.** computer operator **8.** database administrator **9.** portfolio **10.** Data Processing Management Association (DPMA)

CHAPTER 20 **True/False: 1.** F **2.** T **3.** T **4.** F **5.** F **6.** T **7.** F **8.** F **9.** T **10.** T   **Multiple Choice: 1.** A **2.** B **3.** D **4.** C **5.** D   **Fill-In: 1.** telecommuting **2.** robotics **3.** biochip **4.** microlasers **5.** job displacement **6.** fifth generation **7.** electronic cottage **8.** very-large-scale-integration (VLSI) **9.** Japan **10.** artificial intelligence

APPENDIX A   **Section 2**   **Multiple Choice: 1.** C **2.** A **3.** C **4.** A **5.** C   **Short Answers: 1.** We use semicolons in a print statement to override the print zones to create better looking output. **2.** INPUT statements are preferred over DATA statements when the exact data are not known at the time of program creation—as in an interactive program run by a user. **3.** 200 READ N$, W, H **4.** 400 PRINT N$, W, H **5.** 500 LET P = W*2.2

Section 3   **1.** N should be N$ **2.** 200 IF X >= Y THEN PRINT "JERRY"   **3.** 900 DATA "END-OF-FILE", 0, 0, 0, "X", 0 **4.** 1000 IF A >=21 AND C$ = "SOPHOMORE" THEN PRINT N$

5. 2000 DATA "TOM", 20, "JUNIOR"
2010 DATA "SUE", 21, "SENIOR"
2020 DATA "RALPH", 20, "SOPHOMORE"
2030 DATA "LINDA", 21, "SOPHOMORE"
2040 DATA "CINDY", 22, "SOPHOMORE"

6. (a) The LET statement is attempting to take the square of a character string and the value 34 is enclosed in single quotes. **(b)** The numeric variable W is set equal to a character string. **(c)** The inequality symbol for R < 45 is incorrect (should be R > 45) or the test R < 23 is redundant. **(d)** This one is correct. **7.** The STOP statement is used to prevent entering accidentally the subroutine. **8.** The RETURN statement directs the program flow back to the line immediately following the GOSUB statement. **9.** 7 times.

10. 100 READ X
110 IF X = 1 THEN 150
120 PRINT "A"
130 GO TO 100
140 DATA 0, 0, 0, 0, 0, 0, 0, 1
150 END

Section 4   **1. (a)** line 120 incorrectly directs the flow to line 100 instead of line 140. **(b)** G should be changed to I. **(c)** the 2 and the 20 in line 300 are in the wrong order for decrementation. **(d)** is correct. **(e)** NEXT A and NEXT Y have been reversed **2.** FOR/NEXT statements use counters for loop control, whereas WHILE/WEND statements use a DOWHILE loop test with dummy value. **3.** An array is an ordered list or table of numbers. A subscripted variable is a data element identified by a unique label. **4.** 349 **5.** 180 PRINT X(2,2) **6.** Arrays permit you to perform input, processing, and output operations in separate modules in a program. **7.** A bubble sort is a procedure for reordering values into a new sequence. It performs the sort procedure by comparing pairs of values and exchanging them if they are in the wrong order.

8. 100 LET X = 20
110 FOR I = 40 TO X STEP − 4
120   PRINT "JERRY"
130 NEXT I

Section 5   **1.** We use semicolons because commas override the tabbing function. **2.** The advantage of working with PRINT USING is the ability to create better looking—less computerlike output. Also we can achieve a greater control over output style. **3.** The disadvantage of working with PRINT USING is the lack of standardization between different computer systems. In addition, some systems do not even have this feature.

4. 200 PRINT TAB(5); N$; TAB(23); J$; TAB(47); "$"; S

5. 300 PRINT USING 310; N$, J$, S
310 "   \   \ \   \ $ ###.##"
Note your answer may be different!

6. (in the instructor's manual)

7. (a) 400 LET X = 8*RND **(b)** 500 LET Z = INT(10*RND + 1)

8. 100 READ X
110 LET V = INT(1000*X + .5)/1000
120 DATA 12.49999

9. 190 INPUT X
200 LET T = INT(100*(SQR(X) + .5)/100

10. 200 INPUT "WHAT IS YOUR AGE", A
210 LET S = SQR(A)
220 PRINT "THE SQUARE ROOT OF YOUR AGE IS:";S
230 END

APPENDIX B   **1. (a)** 10001; 0001 0111; 21; 11 **(b)** 111000; 0101 0110; 70; 38 **(c)** 11000101; 0001 1001 0111; 305; C5 **(d)** 11110010111; 0001 1001 0100 0011; 3627; 797 **2. (a)** 986 **(b)** 891 **(c)** 547 **(d)** 4166 **3. (a)** 11; 13; B **(b)** 118; 166; 76 **(c)** 219; 333; DB **(d)** 245; 365; F5 **4. (a)** 41; 101001; 29 **(b)** 67; 1000011; 43 **(c)** 460; 111001100; 1CC **(d)** 376; 101111000; 178 **5. (a)** 15; 1111; 17 **(b)** 43; 101011; 53 **(c)** 165; 10100101; 245 **(d)** 3258; 110010111010; 6272 **6. (a)** 1000 **(b)** 10101 **(c)** 11011 **(d)** 110111 **7. (a)** 1001 **(b)** 1010 **(c)** 100001 **(d)** 1100110 **8. (a)** 10 **(b)** 1011 **(c)** 0 **(d)** 1001 **9. (a)** 10 **(b)** 101 **(c)** 1000 **(d)** 101

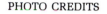

CREDITS

PHOTO CREDITS

Fig. 1-1a: © *Charles Gupton/Stock, Boston/* **b:** *Courtesy General Motors/* **c:** *Reproduced with permission of AT&T/* **d₁:** *Stephen Feldman/Photo Researchers/* **d₂:** *Courtesy Brookhaven National Laboratory and New York University Medical Center/* **e:** © *Jim Cartier/Photo Researchers/* **f₁:** *Digital Scene Simulation (sun) by Digital Productions, Los Angeles, CA* © *1984. All rights reserved./* **f₂:** © *Walt Disney Productions.* **Fig. 1-4:** *Courtesy IBM.* **Fig. 1-11c:** *Courtesy American Airlines.* **Fig. 1-12a,b,c:** *Courtesy Apple Computer, Inc./* **d:** *Courtesy Sperry Corporation.* **Fig. 1-13:** *Courtesy Prime Computer, Inc.* **Fig. 1-14:** *Courtesy Sperry Corporation* **Fig. 1-15:** *Courtesy Cray Research, Inc.*

Fig. 2-10a,b: *Courtesy IBM/* **c:** *Courtesy MSI* **Fig. 2-11a,c:** *Courtesy Sperry Corporation/* **b:** *Courtesy Apple Computer, Inc.* **Fig. 2-12a:** *Courtesy Sperry Corporation/* **b:** *Courtesy Radio Shack, A Division of Tandy Corporation/* **c:** *Courtesy Control Data Corporation/* **d:** *Courtesy Apple Computer, Inc.* **Fig. 2-13a:** *Courtesy Hewlett-Packard Company/* **b:** *Courtesy BASF Systems Corporation/* **c:** *Courtesy IBM* **Fig. 2-14a,c,f:** *Courtesy Sperry Corporation/* **b:** *Courtesy Apple Computer, Inc,/* **d:** *Courtesy NASA/* **e:** *Courtesy Sperry Corporation*

Fig. 3-9: *Courtesy Hewlett-Packard Company* **Fig. 3-10:** *Photo Courtesy Digital Equipment Corporation* **Fig. 3-11:** *Mechanical CAD Application from the WHIZZARD® 3355, Megatek Corporation* **Fig. 3-12:** *Courtesy Chrysler Corporation* **Fig. 3-13:** *Peter Menzel* **Fig. 3-14:** *Courtesy NOAA* **Fig. 3-15:** *Courtesy Mackay School of Mines, University of Nevada Reno and Spot Image* **Fig. 3-16a:** *Courtesy New York Power Pool/* **b:** *Courtesy Site Specifics, Inc./* **c₁,c₁₁:** *Courtesy Southern California Edison/* **d:** *Courtesy Aydin Controls, A Division of Aydin Corporation* **Fig. 3-17a:** *Courtesy Union Pacific Railroad/* **b:** *Courtesy Washington Metropolitan Area Transit Authority* **Fig. 3-18a,b:** *Courtesy U.S. Coast Guard/* **c:** *Courtesy Port Authority of New York & New Jersey* **Fig. 3-19a:** *Courtesy Sperry Corporation/* **b:** *Courtesy NASA* **Fig. 3-20:** *Courtesy Harnischfeger Corporation* **Fig. 3-21:** *Courtesy NCR Corporation*

Fig. 4-1: *Eve Arnold/Magnum* **Fig. 4-2,3:** *Courtesy IBM* **Fig. 4-4:** *The Bettmann Archive* **Fig. 4-5,6,7:** *Courtesy IBM* **Fig. 4-8:** *(right) Courtesy IBM/ (left) Wide World Photos* **Fig. 4-9:** *Courtesy Iowa State University* **Fig. 4-10:** *Courtesy Sperry Corporation* **Fig. 4-11:** *The Bettmann Archive* **Fig. 4-12:** *Courtesy IBM* **Fig. 4-13:** *Courtesy Sperry Corporation* **Fig. 4-14:** *Courtesy IBM* **Fig. 4-16:** *(right) UPI/Bettmann Newsphotos/ (left) Courtesy Bell Laboratories* **Fig. 4-17,18:** *Courtesy IBM* **Fig. 4-19:** *Courtesy U.S. Navy* **Fig. 4-20:** *Courtesy Bell Laboratories* **Fig. 4-21:** *Courtesy IBM* **Fig. 4-22:** *Courtesy True Basic, Inc.* **Fig. 4-23:** *Courtesy Motorola, Inc.* **Fig. 4-24a:** *Courtesy Apple Computer, Inc./* **b:** *Wide World Photos* **Fig. 4-25a:** *Courtesy Sperry Corporation/* **b:** *Courtesy Hewlett-Packard Company/* **c:** *Courtesy IBM* **Fig. 4-26:** *Courtesy Cincinnati Milacron* **Fig. 4-27:** *Courtesy Hewlett-Packard Company*

Fig. 5-8a,f: *Courtesy Sperry Corporation/* **c,g:** *Courtesy Motorola, Inc./* **b,e,d,h:** *National Semiconductor Corporation, a leader in state-of-the-art technology/* **i,j:** *Courtesy Harris Corporation/* **k:** *Courtesy Hewlett-Packard Company* **Fig. 5-9:** *Courtesy Signetics Corporation* **Fig. 5-10,11:** *Courtesy Bell Laboratories*

Fig. 6-2: *Courtesy 3M* **Fig. 6-3a:** *Courtesy Apple Computer, Inc./* **b,c:** *Courtesy Hewlett-Packard Company* **Fig. 6-4a:** *Courtesy Harris Corporation/* **b:** *Courtesy Data General* **Fig. 6-5:** *Courtesy IBM* **Fig. 6-6a:** *Courtesy IBM/* **b:** *Courtesy Radio Shack, A Division of Tandy Corporation/* **c:** *Courtesy Gilbarco, Inc.* **Fig. 6-7:** *Courtesy Hewlett-Packard Company* **Fig. 6-8a:** *Courtesy Citibank/* **b:** *Courtesy of General Electric Company/* **c:** *Courtesy Hewlett-Packard Company* **Fig. 6-10a:** *Courtesy Caere Corporation* **Fig. 6-11:** *Courtesy NCR Corporation* **Fig. 6-12a:** *Courtesy Burroughs Corporation* **Fig. 6-13:** *Courtesy Goddard Space Flight Center & Dr. Robert H. Evans* **Fig. 6-14:** *Courtesy of General Electric Company* **Fig. 6-15:** *Courtesy Texas Instruments* **Fig. 6-17a:** *Courtesy Apple Computer, Inc.* **Fig. 6-18a:** *Courtesy Lanier Business Products, Inc./* **b:** *Courtesy Dataproducts Corporation* **Fig. 6-20:** *Courtesy IBM* **Fig. 6-21:** *Courtesy Radio Shack, A Division of Tandy Corporation* **Fig. 6-22,23a:** *Courtesy IBM* **Fig. 6-23b,c:** *Courtesy Symbolics, Inc.* **Fig. 6-24:** *Courtesy Hewlett-Packard Company* **Fig. 6-25:** *Courtesy Texas Instruments* **Fig. 6-26:** *Courtesy Eastman Kodak Company*

Fig. 7-2: *Courtesy Sperry Corporation* **Fig. 7-3:** *Courtesy Seagate* **Fig. 7-4:** *Courtesy Sperry Corporation* **Fig. 7-5:** *Courtesy BASF Systems Corporation* **Fig. 7-6:** *Courtesy Sperry Corporation* **Fig. 7-7:** *Courtesy Amcodyne* **Fig. 7-8:** *Courtesy 3M* **Fig. 7-9:** *Courtesy Apple Computer, Inc.* **Fig. 7-13a,b:** *Courtesy Sperry Corporation/* **c:** *Courtesy Commodore Business Machines Inc.* **Fig. 7-15:** *Courtesy IBM* **Fig. 7-16:** *Courtesy 3M* **Fig. 7-17:** *Courtesy Bell Laboratories*

Fig. 8-1a: *Courtesy NASD/* **b:** *Courtesy NASA/* **c:** *Courtesy The Source Information Network* **Fig. 8-8a,b,c:** *Courtesy Bell Laboratories/* **d:** *Courtesy Harris Corporation* **Fig. 8-12:** *Courtesy Motorola, Inc.*

Fig. 12-1: *Courtesy Lotus Development Corporation* **Fig. 12-3:** *Courtesy Hewlett-Packard Company* **Fig. 12-6:** *Graphics generated with ISSCO Software* **Fig. 12-7:** *Courtesy Hewlett-Packard Company* **Fig. 12-9:** *Courtesy Coleco Industries, Inc.* **Fig. 12-10a,d:** *Courtesy CBS Software, CBS, Inc./* **b:** *Courtesy Apple Computer, Inc./* **c:** *Courtesy IBM* **Fig. 12-11:** *Rodale's New Shelter* © *1980 Rodale Press, Inc.* **Fig. 13-6a,d:** *Courtesy Sperry Corporation/* **b:** *Catherine Ursillo/Photo Researchers/* **c:** *Courtesy NASA*

Fig. 14-2,4: *Courtesy Sperry Corporation* **Fig. 14-3,8a:** *Courtesy Hewlett-Packard Company* **Fig. 14-8b:** *Graphics generated with ISSCO Software* **Fig. 14-11:** © *Robert I. Sear 1983/Photo Researchers*

Fig. 17-1: *Chuck O'Rear/Woodfin Camp* **Fig. 17-4:** © *1983 Bill Gallery/Stock, Boston* **Fig. 17-5:** *J. P. Laffont/Sygma* **Fig. 17-6:** *Courtesy NASA*

TRADEMARKS

INDEX